ISSUES IN RELIGION

Issues in Religion

A Book of Readings
Second Edition

Allie M. Frazier
Hollins College

Wadsworth Publishing Company
Belmont, California
A Division of Wadsworth, Inc.

ISBN 0-534-21680-3
(Previously ISBN 0-442-21680-7)

14 15—96

Preface

This volume, like its earlier edition, is designed for an introductory course in religion or in philosophy of religion. More resources are presented here than might be required for a one-semester course, but the intention has been to make available a diversity of materials from which to choose.

This Second Edition has changed significantly from the first. Twelve new selections and a new section entitled "Theology and the Contemporary World" have been added to broaden the scope of the book in a variety of ways. There are additional literary selections (Hesse, Goethe, Kafka) and selections from important thinkers missing in the first edition (Marx, Malinowski, Bultmann, Buber). There are further selections concerned with the Eastern religious traditions. Intellectual encounters with Eastern religious perspectives can sensitize the student to universal elements in the religions of the world and can generate provocative questioning regarding divergent approaches to religious problems.

Issues in Religion approaches the study of problems in religious philosophy from an existential point of view. Including literary as well as philosophical texts, it seeks to introduce the reader to the concrete experience of living out of which religious questions arise and to encourage independent inquiry into the nature, the meaning, and the problems of religious life and religious experience. Thus, *Issues in Religion* will, hopefully, illuminate the essential connection between critical thought on religion and the conditions of life in which religious questions and responses originate.

The introductory essays are intended to help the student with the arguments set forth in the selections and to point out the controversies and different ways of dealing with basic questions.

I would like to extend my thanks to my colleague Lawrence Becker for his valuable advice and to my wife, Ruth, for her loyal encouragement and editorial assistance. I am especially grateful to my students at Hollins College: they taught me to appreciate which religious questions are of primary concern to modern students, and they have encouraged the preparation of this volume by demonstrating the tenacity with which this generation attacks the basic issues in religious thought. Finally, I wish to thank my daughters, Rachel and Miriam, for their hard work in the preparation of this second edition. They deserve only the best, but I know they will accept my dedication of this volume to them graciously.

Contents

INTRODUCTION   1
    Suggestions for Further Reading   5

PART I   THE HUMAN CONDITION   7

   1. **Alienation, Guilt, and Suffering**   8
      Dostoevsky: *Underground Man*   9
      Buddhism: *Thirst and Its Consequences*   32
   2. **Aspiration**   35
      Nietzsche: *The Overcoming of Man*   37
      Goethe: *Faust's Wager*   44
   3. **Anxiety and Death**   49
      Tolstoy: *The Death of Iván Ilích*   51
      Rilke: *Chamberlain Brigge's Death*   95
   Suggestions for Further Reading   101

PART II   THE ORIGINS OF RELIGIOUS LIFE   103

   4. **Psychogenic Origins of Religion**   105
      Freud: *Religion as Wish Fulfillment*   107
      Feuerbach: *Religion as Projection of Human Nature*   115
      Marx: *On the Future of Religion*   129
   5. **Sociogenic Origin of Religion**   131
      Durkheim: *Religion's Origin in Society*   133
      Malinowski: *Religion and Primitive Man*   149
   6. **Origin of Religion in Myth**   159
      Campbell: *The Masks of God*   161
      Bultmann: *The Task of Demythologizing*   169
   7. **Transcendental Origin of Religion**   178
      R. Otto: *The Idea of the Holy*   179
      Suzuki: *The Nature of Zen*   189
   Suggestions for Further Reading   201

PART III   MODES OF RELIGIOUS LIFE   203

  8. **Oriental and Occidental Traditions**   205
     Zimmer: *The Meeting of East and West*   206
     Campbell: *The Dialogue in Myth of East and West*   214
  9. **Salvation and Reconciliation**   224
     Upanishads: *Hindu Realization of Brahman*   228
     Zimmer: *Buddhist Nirvana*   233
     Baillie: *Christian Atonement*   241
     Fromm: *Mature Love*   258
 10. **Religious Symbols and Language**   273
     Hesse: *The Adequacy of Religious Language*   276
     Tillich: *Religious Symbols*   278
     Wilson: *Verification and Religious Language*   285
 11. **Religious Knowledge**   294
     Aquinas: *Faith and Reason*   296
     Flew and Others: *Theology and Falsification*   309
     Kierkegaard: *Truth and Subjectivity*   332
  Suggestions for Further Reading   339

PART IV   THE DOCTRINE OF GOD   341

 12. **The Defense of Theism**   343
     Anselm: *The Ontological Argument*   345
     Aquinas: *The Five Ways*   348
     Kant: *The Moral Argument*   351
     Kierkegaard: *The Unchangeableness of God*   363
     Buber: *The I-Thou Relation*   373
 13. **Atheism**   380
     M. Otto: *The Nonexistence of God*   382
     Sartre: *Atheistic Humanism*   388
 14. **The Death of God**   395
     Kafka: *The Imperial Message*   396
     Nietzsche: *Proclamation of God's Death*   397
 15. **Theology and the Contemporary World**   399
     Altizer: *"Death of God" Theology*   400
     Cox: *Theology in a Secular World*   409
     Ruether: *Sexism and the Theology of Liberation*   413
     Enroth, Ericson, Peters: *The Jesus Movement*   422
  Suggestions for Further Reading   429

EDITOR'S POSTSCRIPT   431

INDEX   435

ISSUES IN RELIGION

INTRODUCTION

CRITICAL THOUGHT AND RELIGION

Systematic inquiry into the meaning and truth of religious phenomena appears only after religion has established itself as a viable institution of human life. Such philosophical study of religious phenomena differs sharply from apologetics, "confessional" discourse and theology. The principal aim of religious apologetics is the defense of a particular outlook against its critics. And the purpose of confessional discourse is to witness to the truth of a religion. Both of these forms of discourse lack the distinguishing characteristic of philosophical inquiry into religion which is namely, its fundamental commitment to critical evaluation.

The philosophic examination of religious data ought not to "grind any axes"; it should neither defend nor explain religious data from the viewpoint of a prior commitment to the truth of the data in question. And, insofar as theology can be defined as "faith seeking understanding" it, also, should not be confused with philosophy of religion. The latter, as distinct from theology, seeks a critical understanding of the comprehensive range of religious phenomena both with respect to their function in human life and their possible truth-value.

Religious life, in the forms of emotion, belief, and practice, pervades human culture; it shapes the conduct and experience of men. Because of this fact, the ideal of an unprejudiced examination of religious phenomena is exceptionally difficult to realize. When the perspectives we are examining have such far reaching importance for our lives and destinies, is it reasonable to expect that human beings can be unbiased in studying religion? Religious doctrines and practices involve enormous investments of human emotion and commitment. A religious person feels intensely that he has a fundamental stake in any question relating to the truth of his beliefs. Under such circumstances, can we maintain objectivity and openmindedness as we study religious questions and traditions?

Because of the crucial importance of religion for human life, it is bound to become first an object of man's wonder and then of his reflection. A man's relationship to his own existence and to his world is a natural object of thought. Since religion addresses itself to the most pressing problems of human existence, it is certain to attract our intellectual interest. So, the question is not whether we shall engage in critical thinking about religious phenomena; rather, we need to determine the *way* in which this should be done. To veto the critical examination of religion, in the name of religion, is to deny the rational side of human nature. By the free exercise of human reason mankind has been able to emancipate itself from the blind domination of passion and instinct, from the inhibiting and debilitating effects of irrational superstition and dogma. The continuing expansion of knowledge and the achievement of wisdom requires a fundamental commitment to the enterprise and adventure of critical thinking. There is no *prima facie* evidence that reason and religion must conflict; if evidence is indeed provided by certain religious positions that the conflict is inevitable, then that evidence certainly requires the most careful scrutiny.

RELIGIOUS THOUGHT

Critical thought about religion should be distinguished from religious thought. However, if we assume that the aims of philosophy of religion and religious thought coincide, then we do not credit this distinction. Such a happy coincidence would certainly avert many clashes between the two. Critical thinking, however, is a cantankerous activity. Normally, it refuses to place itself at the service of any vested interest. It persists in finding reasons for doubt in the most embarrassing places. Moreover, critical thought is not pleased to restrict itself to a limited range of experience or evidence. It lives by its pride in having left no assumption unexamined. Can we know prior to thorough examination that the results of critical thought and religious thought coincide? Only at the conclusion of an exploration of religious phenomena may one reasonably judge whether thinking about religion and religious thinking aim at the same goal. The hypothesis that they do so should not be held dogmatically at the beginning of a reflective study of religion.

It would be wise for a person thoughtfully examining religion to consider religious thought *as* a religious phenomenon. Such a provisional hypothesis has the advantage of not settling any fundamental issue prior to investigation. As a matter of fact it conforms to the historical roles generally played by the separate disciplines of philosophy and theology.

Traditionally, religious thought has been an explanation of the meaning of religious consciousness. Doctrines of religion have attempted to formulate in an intelligible and precise manner the communicable truth of religious experience. Religious thinkers usually derive their ideas from frameworks of experience and tradition whose truth they never seriously question. Desiring a precise formulation of received truths, they observe the principles of reasoned thought. Generally speaking, religious thought *has* a truth which it seeks to articulate, whereas critical thought aims at the discovery of truth among the many beliefs claiming to express it.

Religious doctrines formulated in systematic relation to each other, are the terminus of religious thinking. The answers to religious questions are thus religious doctrines. For example, the answer to the question of what is holy, may be Allah, Christ or Buddha. In most religions there are norms by which questions of doctrine are decided—sacred scripture, revelatory events, traditions, religious awareness. But, there *is* a difference between the questions: What is holy? and—Is there anything which is holy? From within religious consciousness and tradition, the first question receives an answer in the form of doctrine. The second question, however, provokes critical inquiry into the meaning of the idea 'holy', and into beliefs which claim to identify the holy according to some norm. Critical inquiry into religion normally concludes in reasoned judgments about the meaning of religious doctrines and their modes of validation. Questioning whether there is something holy may be an expression of idle curiosity, in which case, sustained investigation is unlikely to ensue. However, if the question reflects a genuine interest, then inquiry will, most likely, be initiated. What kind of interests provoke inquiry? Are some interests more compatible with the nature of critical inquiry than others?

We should remember that our interests are not amorphous things. If they were, they would not conflict as violently and painfully as they do in our experience. Human interests frequently reflect the pursuit of values. Whenever we are actively interested in something or someone, something more than idle fascination is at work. Genuine interest ordinarily expresses value judgments whether these judgments are explicit or implicit. When interests are expressed in practical conduct they function as motives which shape our behavior. In order to see how diverse interests variously effect our actions, let us take two hypothetical men intensely interested in the question: Is there anything which is holy?

One thinker hopes to discover a holy something because he believes it will have profound ramifications for his life. As he surveys the various items of experience and the world which bear upon the question, his activity is sustained by the hope that he will discover the object he seeks. The man cares intensely, almost desperately, about how his inquiry will turn out.

Another thinker sets his mind to the same task but his interest is quite different. He seeks to know whether there is anything holy because he wants desperately to know "the truth." He, too, has an intense interest in the outcome of his investigation for in all things, he seeks "the truth." It is not merely idle curiosity which sustains his explorations but rather a passionate desire to extend his knowledge.

Our investigators represent two extremes in a spectrum of interest that is exceptionally broad. Men do initiate searches for these and other reasons. Typically, the motives or interests underlying any inquiry are numerous, and even conflicting. And, after all, the value of undertaking a serious investigation is so that a man may come to know himself more completely in the process. Idle thought is likely to produce only trivial conclusions and precious little self-knowledge. Thought dominated by hope (with only incidental interest in truth) is likely to find what it looks for. Hope begets many children illegitimately and prematurely. Inquiry ruled by a theoretic interest (by love of knowledge for its own sake) may not find what the heart desires. However, it will most often avoid the enticement of shallowness and dogmatism because of its unrelenting commitment to the canons of reason and the evidence of experience.

EXISTENTIAL ANALYSIS AND RELIGIOUS THOUGHT

No one believes that religious questions arise in the mind spontaneously. They have their origin in the limiting situations of human life, e.g. alienation, suffering, guilt, death, and so on. Through an analysis of the conditions of man's life, we gain insight into the way the human predicament is implicated in religious thought. If men did not feel guilty, they would not require divine forgiveness. If men did not experience enslavement to the vicious cycle of desire, pain and death, they probably would not long for the blissful nothingness of Nirvana. In short, religious ideas would elicit little response from man if they were not in some real or imagined sense relevant to the circumstances of his existence. For this reason, religious answers conform in content to the religious questions arising out of the human situation. A man is not likely to respond to answers which have no bearing on his life.

Religious questions need not take conceptual form. Nor must they be explicitly and overtly posed. The verbal formulation of a religious question only makes articulate what is implicit in the conditions under which men live. A vast gulf separates a question which is merely puzzling to human intelligence and a question which expresses man's being. The difference is analogous to a man casually wondering what it would feel like for the dentist to jam his drill into a tooth and a man moaning in the dentist chair with the drill madly whirling in his tooth. It is simply a matter of having a personal stake in the issue of a question that distinguishes idle questioning from questioning expressive of the conditions of man's life. There is no better way of demonstrating to someone the seriousness of his questioning than to show him how his existence is already entangled in both the questioning and the answering.

We begin our study of religion, therefore, with 'existential analysis'. An existential analysis is an effort of critical observation and thought which aims at the discovery of the basic structures or essential characteristics of human existence. Such analysis seeks an accurate description of the fundamental ways in which life is experienced. By proceeding in this way we can bring into clear light the *human* meaning of religious phenomena.

Since religious questions are expressions of man's response to the nature of his existence, the problems of religious life have an unavoidable existential foundation. The bewilderment evident in religious problems—such as: why do the innocent suffer?—why does evil seem to triumph?—is not merely a bewilderment of the human mind, but also, of the human spirit. Vital intellectual concern in religion issues from lived experience, and religious answers should speak to man's predicament.

An existential analysis should introduce one to one's self. It should bring to light the grounds out of which all basic religious questions arise and to which all religious answers are addressed. As such, literature enjoys a grand advantage in providing insight into the nature of human life. In the life situations of fictional characters in great literature, we can encounter our own existence and its dilemmas. Expository prose and philosophic discussions are plagued by a fundamental abstractness, whereas a great literary piece provides existential analysis only indirectly through the action and interior life of its characters, enjoying the advantages of a fully concrete and immediate impact. Literature normally deals with concrete individual experiences; philosophy, on the other hand is frequently too abstract and general. Thus, we begin with literature—with the closest approximation to life that we can find—before proceeding to the more abstract and critical questions that we must consider. This procedure seems entirely justified since no man thinks seriously before experience provides him with specific problems to solve, questions to ask and conflicts of values to resolve.

SUGGESTIONS FOR FURTHER READING

Christian, William A., *Meaning and Truth in Religion.* (Princeton, N.J.: Princeton University Press, 1964). *Careful analysis of the specfic nature of religious questions and of the thought which attempts to resolve them.*

Jaspers, Karl, *The Perennial Scope of Philosophy.* Tr. by Ralph Manheim. (New York: The Philosophical Library, 1949). *Pages 75–112 present an interesting analysis of the relations between philosophy and religion.*

Temple, William, *Nature, Man and God.* (New York: Macmillan & Co., Ltd., 1934). *Part I, Lecture II is a fine. discussion of the tension between philosophy and religion.*

Tillich, Paul, *Systematic Theology, Vol. I.* (Chicago: The University of Chicago Press, 1951). *The Introduction to this volume presents Tillich's theory of the correlation between existential questions and theological answers.*

THE HUMAN CONDITION

A man does not choose to be born. Nor does he elect very many of the conditions under which his life will be lived. He is born to a situation, a world that existed prior to his existence, prior to the entry of his will into the world—a world which does not always bend to his will. Yet his will ineluctably entangles him in complex struggles with the world. To live as a human being is to be subject to structures of experience and existence which lie beyond individual determination—both in practice and in principle. Each person reaches consciousness of himself within certain objective or factual conditions which are neither produced by his will nor necessarily responsive to it. Yet the task confronting him is the appropriation of his life, his very existence, by means of practical activity, deliberative thought, and effort of will.

Each of us has an involvement and thereby an interest in this world; we progressively come to know it as we relate to it and act within it. We discover new facets of our own selves in the process of interacting with the world in which we find ourselves.

A man exists only as he relates within or to situations in the world and so his concern and involvement with the world is also concern and involvement with his own existence. Thus, to speak of a man's concern for his world is to speak of his concern for himself. In all his modes of dealing with the world or his situation, a man is actually dealing with himself, with his own being.

Chapter 1

Alienation, guilt and suffering

Fyodor Dostoevsky's "underground man" symbolizes human alienation from both the self and the world; it presents a clear picture of man in desperate rebellion against his alienation. In narrating this plight, underground man uses the literary form of confession to produce a perpetual flow of self-analysis and self-revelation, and a continuous stream of invectives against both self and society. The confessional tone serves as a natural vehicle of expression for a man living in almost total isolation.

Out of a brutal self-examination, a portrait of a man's existence emerges. Psychic and moral deadlock represent the tragedy of underground man; he is chained to his own consciousness with its perpetual motion and repetitiousness. For all the horror of existence revealed in *Notes*, underground man is a profound analyst of some universal feelings, moods, and motivations. Although the awareness is often morbid, the observation of the subtleties and complexities of experience is astute.

Underground man confronts us with the disabling consequences of human alienation. The dimensions of this alienation are prefigured by his excessive vanity correlated strangely with a total lack of any self-respect. His feeling that "I am one, they are everybody!" reveals both the source of his vanity and the destructive awareness of his isolation; his impotence is the result of his rebellion against a degrading personal and social reality. Excessive self-consciousness has made underground man a victim; although he can rebel against the chaotic forces of his ego and his cultural world, he is incapable of acting in any meaningful fashion in order to overcome his alienation and suffering.

The suffering, alienation, and guilt of underground man are forceful expressions of the "unhappy consciousness." His spirit is poisoned by resentment, pride, ruthless egoism, desperate loneliness, an excessive consciousness, and personal impotence. As an example of certain limiting or circumscribed situations of human life, he points to what is intrinsically nonexceptional: all men as purposive, willing creatures are inevitably drawn into conflict with the forces of their own psyches and the social world, and some degree of alienation is the necessary consequence. Furthermore, all humans, in their attitudes and behavior toward themselves and their fellow men, incur a measure of guilt and suffering, for that reason. The spiritual malaise of underground man gives us a radical or extreme picture of the tragedy of everyman. If, like underground man, we rebel inwardly against isolation, solitude, guilt and suffering, then we should recognize that our destinies can, in some sense, be read in his. Some spiritual

DOSTOEVSKY: UNDERGROUND MAN 9

and physical suffering can be avoided, as can some guilt and alienation. But because we are human and radically finite, we are subject to the "limiting conditions" of our existence. Hence, we cannot completely avoid the alienation resulting from conflict, the guilt incurred by action in the world, or the suffering which is the consequence of internal and external forces over which we have but little control. There are a number of ways in which we seek to evade the consequences imposed by the boundaries of our existence in particular circumstances; but the question remains as to whether a truly meaningful existence can be lived by means of these evasions.

If underground man gives us a painful vision of the *consequences* of human alienation, the Buddhist analysis of thirst provides us with one forceful account of the *cause* of this condition. Underground man's unhappy consciousness is viewed by the Buddhist as the inevitable product of life itself. The will to live, manifested through the passions and drives that pervade our lives, is the architect of human suffering and ensures its perpetuation. The life process is likened to a great fire, a conflagration fed by the fuels of passion, desire, and the more subtle dispositions of our psychic existence. This thirst for life which causes our misery and binds us to the round of birth, decay, old age, and death consists of more than just a persistent search for sensual pleasure. It also entails an almost ineradicable attachment to mistaken beliefs which only hides from us our desperate circumstances. Thus, according to the Buddhists, we do not realize the true imperfection and insubstantiality of our lives, but rather live by evasion and ignorance. Like frantic monkeys, we dance the whirligig of life and suffer the inescapable accompaniment of pain.

Dostoevsky
UNDERGROUND MAN*

[I] I[1] am a sick man . . . I am a spiteful man. I am an unpleasant man. I think my liver is diseased. However, I don't know beans about my disease,

* Fyodor Dostoevsky (1821–1881): Russian novelist and man of letters. *Notes from the Underground* is a devastating critique of the materialism and scientific optimism of the 19th century. This selection is Part I of the two-part work. Part II narrates "underground man's" failure to respond to human love and his inability to establish any meaningful relations with the external world. From the volume NOTES FROM UNDERGROUND *and* THE GRAND INQUISITOR by Fyodor Dostoevsky. Translated by Ralph E. Matlaw. Copyright, ©, 1960 by E. P. Dutton & Co., Inc. Reprinted by permission of the publishers.

[1] The author of these notes and the "Notes" themselves are, of course, imaginary. Nevertheless, such persons as the writer of these notes, not only may, but positively must, exist in our society, considering those circumstances under which our society was in general formed. I wanted to expose to the public more clearly than it is done usually, one of the characters of the recent past. He is one of the representatives of the current generation. In this excerpt, entitled "Underground," this person introduces himself, his views, and, as it were, tries to explain the reasons why he appeared and was bound to appear in our midst. In the following excerpt, the actual notes of this person about several events in his life, will appear. (*Fyodor Dostoevsky*)

and I am not sure what is bothering me. I don't treat it and never have, though I respect medicine and doctors. Besides, I am extremely superstitious, let's say sufficiently so to respect medicine. (I am educated enough not to be superstitious, but I am.) No, I refuse to treat it out of spite. You probably will not understand that. Well, but *I* understand it. Of course, I can't explain to you just whom I am annoying in this case by my spite. I am perfectly well aware that I cannot "get even" with the doctors by not consulting them. I know better than anyone that I thereby injure only myself and no one else. But still, if I don't treat it, it is out of spite. My liver is bad, well then—let it get even worse!

I have been living like that for a long time now—twenty years. I am forty now. I used to be in the civil service, but no longer am. I was a spiteful official. I was rude and took pleasure in being so. After all, I did not accept bribes, so I was bound to find a compensation in that, at least. (A bad joke but I will not cross it out. I wrote it thinking it would sound very witty; but now that I see myself that I only wanted to show off in a despicable way, I will purposely not cross it out!) When petitioners would come to my desk for information I would gnash my teeth at them, and feel intense enjoyment when I succeeded in distressing some one. I was almost always successful. For the most part they were all timid people—of course, they were petitioners. But among the fops there was one officer in particular I could not endure. He simply would not be humble, and clanked his sword in a disgusting way. I carried on a war with him for eighteen months over that sword. At last I got the better of him. He left off clanking it. However, that happened when I was still young. But do you know, gentlemen, what the real point of my spite was? Why, the whole trick, the real vileness of it lay in the fact that continually, even in moments of the worst spleen, I was inwardly conscious with shame that I was not only not spiteful but not even an embittered man, that I was simply frightening sparrows at random and amusing myself by it. I might foam at the mouth, but bring me some kind of toy, give me a cup of tea with sugar, and I would be appeased. My heart might even be touched, though probably I would gnash my teeth at myself afterward and lie awake at night with shame for months after. That is the way I am.

I was lying when I said just now that I was a spiteful official. I was lying out of spite. I was simply indulging myself with the petitioners and with the officer, but I could never really become spiteful. Every moment I was conscious in myself of many, very many elements completely opposite to that. I felt them positively teeming in me, these opposite elements. I knew that they had been teeming in me all my life, begging to be let out, but I would not let them, would not let them, purposely would not let them out. They tormented me till I was ashamed; they drove me to convulsions, and finally, they bored me, how they bored me! Well, are you not imagining, gentlemen, that I am repenting for something now, that I am asking your forgiveness for something? I am sure you are imagining that. However, I assure you it does not matter to me if you are.

Not only could I not become spiteful, I could not even become anything: neither spiteful nor kind, neither a rascal nor an honest man, neither a hero nor an insect. Now, I am living out my life in my corner, taunting myself with the spiteful and useless consolation that an intelligent man cannot seriously become anything and that only a fool can become something. Yes, an intelligent man in the nineteenth century must and morally ought to be pre-eminently a characterless creature; a man of character, an active man, is pre-eminently a limited creature. That is the conviction of my forty years. I am forty years old now, and forty years, after all, is a whole lifetime; after all, that is extreme old age. To live longer than forty years is bad manners; it is vulgar, immoral. Who does live beyond forty? Answer that, sincerely and honestly. I will tell you who do: fools and worthless people do. I tell all old men that to their face, all those respectable old men, all those silver-haired and reverend old men! I tell the whole world that to its face. I have a right to say so, for I'll go on living to sixty myself. I'll live till seventy! Till eighty! Wait, let me catch my breath.

No doubt you think, gentlemen, that I want to amuse you. You are mistaken in that, too. I am not at all such a merry person as you imagine, or as you may imagine; however, if irritated by all this babble (and I can·feel that you are irritated) you decide to ask me just who I am—then my answer is, I am a certain low-ranked civil servant. I was in the service in order to have something to eat (but only for that reason), and when last year a distant relation left me six thousand roubles in his will I immediately retired from the service and settled down in my corner. I used to live in this corner before, but now I have settled down in it. My room is a wretched, horrid one on the outskirts of town. My servant is an old country-woman, spiteful out of stupidity, and, moreover, she always smells bad. I am told that the Petersburg climate is bad for me, and that with my paltry means it is very expensive to live in Petersburg. I know all that better than all these sage and experienced counsellors and monitors. But I am going to stay in Petersburg. I will not leave Petersburg! I will not leave because . . . Bah, after all it does not matter in the least whether I leave or stay.

But incidentally, what can a decent man speak about with the greatest pleasure?

Answer: About himself.

Well, then, I will talk about myself.

[II] Now I want to tell you, gentlemen, whether you care to hear it or not, why I could not even become an insect. I tell you solemnly that I wanted to become an insect many times. But I was not even worthy of that. I swear to you, gentlemen, that to be hyperconscious is a disease, a real positive disease. Ordinary human consciousness would be too much for man's every-day needs, that is, half or a quarter of the amount which falls to the lot of a cultivated man of our unfortunate nineteenth century, especially one who has the particular misfortune to inhabit Petersburg, the most abstract and intentional city in the whole world. (There are intentional and unintentional cities.) It would have been quite enough, for instance, to have the consciousness by which all so-called straightforward persons and men of action live. I'll bet you think I am writing all this to show off, to be witty at the expense of men of action; and what is more, that out of ill-bred showing-off, I am clanking a sword, like my officer. But, gentlemen, whoever can pride himself on his diseases and even show off with them?

However, what am I talking about? Everyone does that. They do pride themselves on their diseases, and I, perhaps, more than any one. There is no doubt about it: my objection was absurd. Yet just the same, I am firmly convinced not only that a great deal of consciousness, but that any consciousness is a disease. I insist on it. Let us drop that, too, for a minute. Tell me this: why did it happen that at the very, yes, at the very moment when I was most capable of recognizing every refinement of "all the sublime and beautiful," as we used to say at one time, I would, as though purposely, not only feel but do such hideous things, such that—well, in short, such as everyone probably does but which, as though purposely, occurred to me at the very time when I was most conscious that they ought not to be done. The more conscious I was of goodness, and of all that "sublime and beautiful," the more deeply I sank into my mire and the more capable I became of sinking into it completely. But the main thing was that all this did not seem to occur in me accidentally, but as though it had to be so. As though it were my most normal condition, and not in the least disease or depravity, so that finally I even lost the desire to struggle against this depravity. It ended by my almost believing (perhaps actually believing) that probably this was really my normal condition. But at first, in the beginning, that is, what agonies I suffered in that struggle! I did not believe that others went through the same things, and therefore I hid this fact about myself as a secret all my life. I was ashamed (perhaps I am even ashamed now). I reached the point of feeling a sort of secret abnormal, despicable enjoyment in returning home to my corner on some disgusting Petersburg night, and being acutely conscious that that day I had again done something loathsome, that what was done could never be undone, and secretly, inwardly gnaw, gnaw at myself for it, nagging and consuming myself till at last the bitterness turned into a sort of shameful accursed sweetness, and finally into real positive enjoyment! Yes, into enjoyment! I insist upon that. And that is why I have started to speak, because I keep wanting to know for a fact whether other people feel such an enjoyment. Let me explain: the enjoyment here consisted precisely in the hyperconsciousness of one's own degradation; it was from feeling oneself that one had reached the last barrier, that it was nasty, but that it could not be otherwise; that you no longer had an escape; that you could never become a different person; that even if there remained enough time and faith for you to change into something else you probably would not want to change; or if you did want to, even then you would do nothing; because perhaps in reality there was nothing for you to change into. And the worst of it, and the root of it all, was that it all proceeded according to the normal and fundamental laws of hyperconsciousness, and with the inertia that was the direct result of those laws, and that consequently one could not only not change but one could do absolutely nothing. Thus it would follow, as the result of hyperconsciousness, that one is not to blame for being a scoundrel, as though that were any consolation to the scoundrel once he himself has come to realize that he actually is a scoundrel. But enough. Bah, I have talked a lot of nonsense, but what have I explained? Can this enjoyment be explained? But I will explain it! I will get to the bottom of it! That is why I have taken up my pen.

To take an instance, I am terribly vain. I am as suspicious and touchy as a hunchback or a dwarf. But to tell the truth, there have been moments when if someone had happened to slap my face I would, perhaps, have even been glad of that. I say, very seriously, that I would probably have been able to discover a peculiar sort of enjoyment even in that—the enjoyment, of course, of despair; but in despair occur the most intense enjoyments, especially when one is very acutely conscious of one's hopeless position. As for the slap in the face—why then the consciousness of being beaten to a pulp would positively overwhelm one. The worst of it is, no matter how I tried, it still turned out that I was always the most to blame in everything, and what is most humiliating of all, to blame for no fault of my own but, so to say, through the laws of nature. In the first place, to blame because I am cleverer than any of the people surrounding me. (I have always considered myself cleverer than any of the people surrounding me, and sometimes, would you believe it, I have even been ashamed of that. At any rate, all my life, I have, as it were, looked away and I could never look people straight in the eye.) To blame, finally, because even if I were magnanimous, I would only have suffered more from the consciousness of all its uselessness. After all, I would probably never have been able to do anything with my magnanimity—neither to forgive, for my assailant may have slapped me because of the laws of nature, and one cannot forgive the laws of nature; nor to forget, for even if it were the laws of nature, it is insulting all the same. Finally, even if I had wanted to be anything but magnanimous, had desired on the contrary to revenge myself on the man who insulted me, I could not have revenged myself on anyone for anything because I would certainly never have made up my mind to do anything, even if I had been able to. Why would I not have made up my mind? I want to say a few words about that in particular.

[III]   After all, people who know how to revenge themselves and to take care of themselves in general, how do they do it? After all, when they are possessed, let us suppose, by the feeling of revenge, then for the time there is nothing else but that feeling left in their whole being. Such a man simply rushes straight toward his object like an infuriated bull with its horns down, and nothing but a wall will stop him. (By the way: facing the wall, such people—that is, the straightforward persons and men of action—are genuinely nonplussed. For them a wall is not an evasion, as for example for us people who think and consequently do nothing; it is not an excuse for turning aside, an excuse for which our kind is always very glad, though we scarcely believe in it ourselves, usually. No, they are nonplussed in all sincerity. The wall has for them something tranquilizing, morally soothing, final—maybe even something mysterious . . . but of the wall later.) Well, such a direct person I regard as the real normal man, as his tender mother nature wished to see him when she graciously brought him into being on the earth. I envy such a man till I am green in the face. He is stupid. I am not disputing that, but perhaps the normal man should be stupid, how do you know? Perhaps it is very beautiful, in fact. And I am all the more convinced of that suspicion, if one can call it so, by the fact that if, for instance, you take the antithesis of the normal man, that is, the hyperconscious man, who has come, of course, not out of the lap of nature but out of a retort (this is almost mysticism, gentlemen, but I suspect this, too), this retort-made man is sometimes so nonplussed in the presence of his antithesis that with all his hyperconsciousness he genuinely thinks of himself as a mouse and not a man. It may be a hyperconscious mouse, yet it is a mouse, while the other is a man, and therefore, etc. And the worst is, he himself, his very own self, looks upon himself as a mouse. No one asks him to do so. And that is an important point. Now let us look at this mouse in action. Let us suppose, for instance, that it feels insulted, too (and it almost always does feel insulted), and wants to revenge itself too. There may even be a greater accumulation of spite in it than in *l'homme de la nature et de la vérité*. The base, nasty desire to repay with spite whoever has offended it, rankles perhaps even more nastily in it than in *l'homme de la nature et de la vérité*, because *l'homme de la nature et de la vérité* through his innate stupidity looks upon his revenge as justice pure and simple; while in consequence of his hyperconsciousness the mouse does not believe in the justice of it. To come at last to the deed itself, to the very act of revenge. Apart from the one fundamental nastiness the unfortunate mouse succeeds in creating around it so many other nastinesses in the form of doubts and questions, adds to the one question so many unsettled questions, that there inevitably works up around it a sort of fatal brew, a stinking mess, made up of its doubts, agitations and lastly of the contempt spat upon it by the straightforward men of action who stand solemnly about it as judges and arbitrators, laughing at it till their healthy sides ache. Of course the only thing left for it is to dismiss all that with a wave of its paw, and, with a smile of assumed contempt in which it does not even believe itself, creep ignominiously into its mouse-hole. There, in its nasty, stinking, underground home our insulted, crushed and ridiculed mouse promptly becomes absorbed in cold, malignant and, above all, everlasting spite. For forty years together it will remember its injury down to the smallest, most shameful detail, and every time will add, of itself, details still more shameful, spitefully teasing and irritating itself with its own imagination. It will be ashamed of its own fancies, but yet it will recall everything, it will go over it again and again, it will invent lies against itself pretending that those things might have happened, and will forgive nothing. Maybe it will begin to revenge itself, too, but, as it were, piecemeal, in trivial ways, from behind the stove, incognito, without believing either in its own right to vengeance, or in the success of its revenge, knowing beforehand that from all its efforts at revenge it will suffer a hundred times more than he on whom it revenges itself, while he, probably will not even feel it. On its deathbed it will recall it all over again, with interest accumulated over all the years. But it is just in that cold, abominable half-despair, half-belief, in that conscious burying oneself alive for grief in the underworld for forty years, in that hyperconsciousness and yet to some extent doubtful hopelessness of one's position, in that hell of unsatisfied desires turned inward, in that fever of oscillations, of resolutions taken for ever and regretted again a minute later—that the savor of that strange enjoyment of which I have spoken lies. It is so subtle, sometimes so difficult to analyze consciously, that somewhat limited people, or simply people with strong nerves, will not understand anything at all in it. "Possibly," you will add on your own account with a grin, "people who have never received a slap in the face will not understand it either," and in that way you will politely hint to me that I, too, perhaps, have been slapped in the face in my life, and so I speak as an expert. I'll bet that you are thinking that. But set your minds at rest, gentlemen, I have not received a slap in the face, though it doesn't matter to me at all what you may think about it. Possibly, I even myself regret that I have given so few slaps in the face during my life. But enough, not another word on the subject of such extreme interest to you.

I will continue calmly about people with strong nerves who do not understand a certain refinement of enjoyment. Though in certain circumstances these gentlemen bellow their loudest like bulls, though this, let us suppose, does them the greatest honor, yet, as I have already said, confronted with the impossible they at once resign themselves. Does the impossible mean the stone wall? What stone wall? Why, of course, the laws of nature, the conclusions of natural science, of mathematics. As soon as they prove to you, for instance, that you are descended from a monkey, then it is no use scowling, accept it as a fact. When they prove to you that in reality one drop of your own fat must be dearer to you than a hundred thousand of your fellow creatures, and that this conclusion is the final solution of all so-called virtues and duties and all such ravings and prejudices, then you might as well accept it, you can't do anything about it, because two times two is a law of mathematics. Just try refuting it

"But really," they will shout at you, "there is no use protesting; it is a case of two times two makes four! Nature does not ask your permission, your wishes, and whether you like or dislike her laws does not concern her. You are bound to accept her as she is, and consequently also all her conclusions. A wall, you see, is a wall—etc. etc." Good God! but what do I care about the laws of nature and arithmetic, when, for some reason, I dislike those laws and the fact that two times two makes four? Of course

I cannot break through a wall by battering my head against it if I really do not have the strength to break through it, but I am not going to resign myself to it simply because it is a stone wall and I am not strong enough.

As though such a stone wall really were a consolation, and really did contain some word of conciliation, if only because it is as true as two times two makes four. Oh, absurdity of absurdities! How much better it is to understand it all, to be conscious of it all, all the impossibilities and the stone walls, not to resign yourself to a single one of those impossibilities and stone walls if it disgusts you to resign yourself; to reach, through the most inevitable, logical combinations, the most revolting conclusions on the everlasting theme that you are yourself somehow to blame even for the stone wall, though again it is as clear as day you are not to blame in the least, and therefore grinding your teeth in silent impotence sensuously to sink into inertia, brooding on the fact that it turns out that there is even no one for you to feel vindictive against, that you have not, and perhaps never will have, an object for your spite, that it is a sleight-of-hand, a bit of juggling, a card-sharper's trick, that it is simply a mess, no knowing what and no knowing who, but in spite of all these uncertainties, and jugglings, still there is an ache in you, and the more you do not know, the worse the ache.

[IV] "Ha, ha, ha! Next you will find enjoyment in a toothache," you cry with a laugh.

"Well? So what? There is enjoyment even in a toothache," I answer. I had a toothache for a whole month and I know there is. In that case, of course, people are not spiteful in silence, they moan; but these are not sincere moans, they are malicious moans, and the maliciousness is the whole point. The sufferer's enjoyment finds expression in those moans; if he did not feel enjoyment in them he would not moan. It is a good example, gentlemen, and I will develop it. The moans express in the first place all the aimlessness of your pain, which is so humiliating to your consciousness; the whole legal system of Nature on which you spit disdainfully, of course, but from which you suffer all the same while she does not. They express the consciousness that you have no enemy, but that you do have a pain; the consciousness that in spite of all the dentists in the world you are in complete slavery to your teeth; that if someone wishes it, your teeth will leave off aching, and if he does not, they will go on aching another three months; and that finally if you still disagree and still protest, all that is left you for your own gratification is to thrash yourself or beat your wall with your fist as hard as you can, and absolutely nothing more. Well then, these mortal insults, these jeers on the part of someone unknown, end at last in an enjoyment which sometimes reaches the highest degree of sensuality. I beg you, gentlemen, to listen sometimes to the moans of an educated man of the nineteenth century who is suffering from a toothache, particularly on the second or third day of the attack, when he has already begun to moan not as he moaned on the first day, that is, not simply because he has a toothache, not just as any coarse peasant might moan, but as a man affected by progress and European civilization, a man who is "divorced from the soil and the national principles," as they call it these days. His moans become nasty, disgustingly spiteful, and go on for whole days and nights. And, after all, he himself knows that he does not benefit at all from his moans; he knows better than anyone that he is only lacerating and irritating himself and others in vain; he knows that even the audience for whom he is exerting himself and his whole family now listen to him with loathing, do not believe him for a second, and that deep down they understand that he could moan differently, more simply, without trills and flourishes, and that he is only indulging himself like that out of spite, out of malice. Well, sensuality exists precisely in all these consciousnesses and infamies. "It seems I am troubling you, I am lacerating your hearts, I am keeping everyone in the house awake. Well, stay awake then, you, too, feel every minute that I have a toothache. I am no longer the hero to you now that I tried to appear before, but simply a nasty person, a scoundrel. Well, let it be that way, then! I am very glad that you see through me. Is it nasty for you to hear my foul moans? Well, let it be nasty. Here I will let you have an even nastier flourish in a minute. . . ." You still do not understand, gentlemen? No, it seems our development and our consciousness must go further to understand all the intricacies of this sensuality. You laugh? I am delighted. My jokes, gentlemen, are of course in bad taste, uneven, involved, lacking self-confidence. But of course that is because I do not respect myself. Can a man with consciousness respect himself at all?

[V] Come, can a man who even attempts to find enjoyment in the very feeling of self-degradation really have any respect for himself at all? I am not saying this now from any insipid kind of remorse. And, indeed, I could never endure to say, "Forgive me, Daddy, I won't do it again," not because I was incapable of saying it, but, on the contrary, perhaps just because I was too capable of it, and in what a way, too! As though on purpose I used to get into trouble on occasions when I was not to blame in the faintest way. That was the nastiest part of it. At the same time I was genuinely touched and repentant, I used to shed tears and, of course, tricked even myself, though it was not acting in the least and there was a sick feeling in my heart at the time. For that one could not even blame the laws of nature, though the laws of nature have offended me continually all my life more than anything. It is loathsome to remember it all, but it was loathsome even then. Of course, in a minute or so I would realize with spite that it was all a lie, a lie, an affected, revolting lie, that is, all this repentance, all these emotions, these vows to reform. And if you ask why I worried and tortured myself that way, the answer is because it was very dull to twiddle one's thumbs, and so one began cutting capers. That is really it. Observe yourselves more carefully, gentlemen, then you will understand that that's right! I invented adventures for myself and made up a life, so as to live at least in some way. How many times it has happened to me—well, for instance, to take offence at nothing, simply on purpose; and one knows oneself, of course, that one is offended at nothing, that one is pretending, but yet one brings oneself, at last, to the point of really being offended. All my life I have had an impulse to play such pranks, so that in the end, I could not control it in myself. Another time, twice, in fact, I tried to force myself to fall in love. I even suffered, gentlemen, I assure you. In the depth of my heart I did not believe in my suffering, there was a stir of mockery, but yet I did suffer, and in the real, regular way I was jealous, I was beside myself, and it was all out of boredom, gentlemen, all out of boredom; inertia overcame me. After all, the direct, legitimate, immediate fruit of consciousness is inertia, that is, conscious thumb twiddling. I have referred to it already, I repeat, I repeat it emphatically: all straightforward persons and men of action are active just because they are stupid and limited. How can that be explained? This way: as a result of their limitation they take immediate and secondary causes for primary ones, and in that way persuade themselves more quickly and easily than other people do that they have found an infallible basis for their activity, and their minds are at ease and that, you know, is the most important thing. To begin to act, you know, you must first have your mind completely at ease and without a trace of doubt left in it. Well, how am I, for example, to set my mind at rest? Where are the primary causes on which I am to build? Where are my bases? Where am I to get them from? I exercise myself in the process of thinking, and consequently with me every primary cause at once draws after itself another still more primary, and so on to infinity. That is precisely the essence of every sort of consciousness and thinking. It must be a case of the laws of nature again. In what does it finally result? Why, just the same. Remember I spoke just now of vengeance. (I am sure you did not grasp that.) I said that a man revenges himself because he finds justice in it. Therefore he has found a primary cause, found a basis, to wit, justice. And so he is completely set at rest, and consequently he carries out his revenge calmly and successfully, as he is convinced that he is doing a just and honest thing. But, after all, I see no justice in it, I find no sort of virtue in it either, and consequently if I attempt to revenge myself, it would only be out of spite. Spite, of course, might overcome everything, all my doubts, and could consequently serve quite successfully in a place of a primary cause, precisely because it is not a cause. But what can be done if I do not even have spite (after all, I began with that just now)? Again, in consequence of those accursed laws of consciousness, my spite is subject to chemical disintegration. You look into it, the object flies off into air, your reasons evaporate, the criminal is not to be found, the insult becomes fate rather than an insult, something like the toothache, for which no one is to blame, and consequently there is only the same outlet left again—that is, to beat the wall as hard as you can. So you give it up as hopeless because you have not found a fundamental cause. And try letting yourself be carried away by your feelings, blindly, without reflection, without a primary cause, repelling consciousness at least for a time; hate or love, if only not to sit and twiddle your thumbs. The day after tomorrow, at the latest, you will begin despising yourself for having knowingly deceived yourself. The result—a soap-bubble and inertia. Oh, gentlemen, after all, perhaps I consider myself an intelligent man only because all my life I have been able neither to begin nor to finish anything. Granted, granted I am a babbler, a harmless annoying babbler, like all of us. But what is to be done if the direct and sole vocation of every intelligent man is babble, that is, the intentional pouring of water through a sieve?

[VI] Oh, if I had done nothing simply out of laziness! Heavens, how I would have respected myself then. I would have respected myself because I would at least have been capable of being lazy; there would at least have been in me one positive quality, as it were, in which I could have believed myself. Question: Who is he? Answer: A loafer. After all, it would have been pleasant to hear that about oneself! It would mean that I was positively defined, it would mean that there was something to be said about me. "Loafer"—why, after all, it is a calling and an appointment, it is a career, gentlemen. Do not joke, it is so. I would then, by rights, be a member of the best club, and would occupy myself only in continually respecting myself. I knew a gentleman who prided himself all his life on being a connoisseur of Lafitte. He considered this as his positive virtue, and never doubted himself. He died, not simply with a tranquil but with a triumphant conscience, and he was completely right. I should have chosen a career for myself then too: I would have been a loafer and a glutton, not a simple one, but, for instance, one in sympathy with everything good and beautiful. How do you like that? I have long had visions of it. That "sublime and beautiful" weighs heavily on my mind at forty. But that is when I am forty, while then—oh, then it would have been different! I would have found myself an appropriate occupation, namely, to drink to the health of everything sublime and beautiful. I would have seized every opportunity to drop a tear into my glass and then to drain it to all that is sublime and beautiful. I would then have turned everything into the sublime and the beautiful; I would have sought out the sublime and the beautiful in the nastiest, most unquestionable trash. I would have become as tearful as a wet sponge. An artist, for instance, paints Ge's picture.[2] At once I drink to the health of the artist who painted Ge's picture, because I love all that is "sublime and beautiful." An author writes "Whatever You Like"[3]; at once I drink to the health of "Whatever You Like" because I love all that is "sublime and beautiful." I would demand respect for doing so, I would persecute anyone who would not show me respect. I would live at ease, I would die triumphantly—why, after all, it is charming, perfectly charming!

[2] N. N. Ge exhibited his "Last Supper" in 1863. Dostoevsky thought it a faulty conception. The sentence makes no grammatical sense and may refer to Shchedrin's article on the painting, wherein its meaning is further distorted so that, in a sense, "a new picture" is created.

[3] An article on improving man written by Shchedrin, in 1863.

And what a belly I would have grown, what a triple chin I would have established, what a red nose I would have produced for myself, so that every passer-by would have said, looking at me: "Here is an asset! Here is something really positive!" And, after all, say what you like, it is very pleasant to hear such remarks about oneself in this negative age, gentlemen.

[VII]   But these are all golden dreams. Oh, tell me, who first declared, who first proclaimed, that man only does nasty things because he does not know his own real interests; and that if he were enlightened, if his eyes were opened to his real normal interests, man would at once cease to do nasty things, would at once become good and noble because, being enlightened and understanding his real advantage, he would see his own advantage in the good and nothing else, and we all know that not a single man can knowingly act to his own disadvantage. Consequently, so to say, he would begin doing good through necessity. Oh, the babe! Oh, the pure, innocent child! Why, in the first place, when in all these thousands of years has there ever been a time when man has acted only for his own advantage? What is to be done with the millions of facts that bear witness that men, *knowingly*, that is, fully understanding their real advantages, have left them in the background and have rushed headlong on another path, to risk, to chance, compelled to this course by nobody and by nothing, but, as it were, precisely because they did not want the beaten track, and stubbornly, wilfully, went off on another difficult, absurd way seeking it almost in the darkness. After all, it means that this stubbornness and willfulness were more pleasant to them than any advantage. Advantage! What is advantage? And will you take it upon yourself to define with perfect accuracy in exactly what the advantage of man consists of? And what if it so happens that a man's advantage *sometimes* not only may, but even must, consist exactly in his desiring under certain conditions what is harmful to himself and not what is advantageous. And if so, if there can be such a condition then the whole principle becomes worthless. What do you think—are there such cases? You laugh; laugh away, gentlemen, so long as you answer me: have man's advantages been calculated with perfect certainty? Are there not some which not only have been included but cannot possibly be included under any classification? After all, you, gentlemen, so far as I know, have taken your whole register of human advantages from the average of statistical figures and scientific-economic formulas. After all, your advantages are prosperity, wealth, freedom, peace—and so on, and so on. So that a man who, for instance, would openly and knowingly oppose that whole list would, to your thinking, and indeed to mine too, of course, be an obscurantist or an absolute madman, would he not? But, after all, here is something amazing: why does it happen that all these statisticians, sages and lovers of humanity, when they calculate human advantages invariably leave one out? They don't even take it into their calculation in the form in which it should be taken, and the whole reckoning depends upon that. There would be no great harm to take it, this advantage, and to add it to the list. But the trouble is, that this strange advantage does not fall under any classification and does not figure in any list. For instance, I have a friend. Bah, gentlemen! But after all he is your friend, too; and indeed there is no one, no one, to whom he is not a friend! When he prepares for any undertaking this gentleman immediately explains to you, pompously and clearly, exactly how he must act in accordance with the laws of reason and truth. What is more, he will talk to you with excitement and passion of the real normal interests of man; with irony he will reproach the short-sighted fools who do not understand their own advantage, for the true significance of virtue; and, within a quarter of an hour, without any sudden outside provocation, but precisely through that something internal which is stronger than all his advantages, he will go off on quite a different tack—that is, act directly opposite to what he has just been saying himself, in opposition to the laws of reason, in opposition to his own advantage—in fact, in opposition to everything. I warn you that my friend is a compound personality, and therefore it is somehow difficult to blame him as an individual. The fact is, gentlemen, it seems that something that is dearer to almost every man than his greatest advantages must really exist, or (not to be illogical) there is one most advantageous advantage (the very one omitted of which we spoke just now) which is more important and more advantageous than all other advantages, for which, if necessary, a man is ready to act in opposition to all laws, that is, in opposition to reason, honor, peace, prosperity—in short, in opposition to all those wonderful and useful things if only he can attain that fundamental, most advantageous advantage which is dearer to him than all.

"Well, but it is still advantage just the same," you will retort. But excuse me, I'll make the point clear, and it is not a case of a play on words, but what really matters is that this advantage is remarkable from the very fact that it breaks down all our classifications, and continually shatters all the systems by lovers of mankind for the happiness of mankind. In short, it interferes with everything. But before I mention this advantage to you, I want to compromise myself personally, and therefore I boldly declare that all these fine systems—all these theories for explaining to mankind its real normal interests, so that inevitably striving to obtain these interests, it may at once become good and noble—are, in my opinion, so far, mere logical exercises! Yes, logical exercises. After all, to maintain even this theory of the regeneration of mankind by means of its own advantage, is, after all, to my mind almost the same thing as—as to claim, for instance, with Buckle, that through civilization mankind becomes softer, and consequently less bloodthirsty, and less fitted for warfare. Logically it does not seem to follow from his arguments. But man is so fond of systems and abstract deductions that he is ready to distort the truth intentionally, he is ready to deny what he can see and hear just to justify his logic. I take this example because it is the most glaring instance of it. Only look about you: blood is being spilled in streams, and in the merriest way, as though it were champagne. Take the whole of the nineteenth century in which Buckle lived. Take Napoleon—both the Great and the present one. Take North America—the eternal union.

Take farcical Schleswig-Holstein. And what is it that civilization softens in us? Civilization only produces a greater variety of sensations in man—and absolutely nothing more. And through the development of this variety, man may even come to find enjoyment in bloodshed. After all, it has already happened to him. Have you noticed that the subtlest slaughterers have almost always been the most civilized gentlemen, to whom the various Attilas and Stenka Razins could never hold a candle, and if they are not so conspicuous as the Attilas and Stenka Razins it is precisely because they are so often met with, are so ordinary and have become so familiar to us. In any case if civilization has not made man more bloodthirsty, it has at least made him more abominably, more loathsomely bloodthirsty than before. Formerly he saw justice in bloodshed and with his conscience at peace exterminated whomever he thought he should. And now while we consider bloodshed an abomination, we nevertheless engage in this abomination and even more than ever before. Which is worse? Decide that for yourselves. It is said that Cleopatra (pardon the example from Roman history) was fond of sticking gold pins into her slave-girls' breasts and derived enjoyment from their screams and writhing. You will say that that occurred in comparatively barbarous times; that these are barbarous times too, because (also comparatively speaking) pins are stuck in even now; that even though man has now learned to see more clearly occasionally than in barbarous times, he is still far from having *accustomed* himself to act as reason and science would dictate. But all the same you are fully convinced that he will inevitably accustom himself to it when he gets completely rid of certain old bad habits, and when common sense and science have completely re-educated human nature and turned it in a normal direction. You are confident that man will then refrain from erring *intentionally*, and will, so to say, willy-nilly, not want to set his will against his normal interests. More than that: then, you say, science itself will teach man (though to my mind that is a luxury) that he does not really have either caprice or will of his own and that he has never had it, and that he himself is something like a piano key or an organ stop, and that, moreover, laws of nature exist in this world, so that everything he does is not done by his will at all, but is done by itself, according to the laws of nature. Consequently we have only to discover these laws of nature, and man will no longer be responsible for his actions and life will become exceedingly easy for him. All human actions will then, of course, be tabulated according to these laws, mathematically, like tables of logarithms up to 108,000, and entered in a table; or, better still, there would be published certain edifying works like the present encyclopedic lexicons, in which everything will be so clearly calculated and designated that there will be no more incidents or adventures in the world.

Then—it is still you speaking—new economic relations will be established, all ready-made and computed with mathematical exactitude, so that every possible question will vanish in a twinkling, simply because every possible answer to it will be provided. Then the crystal palace will be built. Then—well, in short, those will be halcyon days. Of course there is no guaranteeing (this is my comment now) that it will not be, for instance, terribly boring then (for what will one have to do when everything is calculated according to the table?) but on the other hand everything will be extraordinarily rational. Of course boredom may lead you to anything. After all, boredom even sets one to sticking gold pins into people, but all that would not matter. What is bad (this is my comment again) is that for all I know people will be thankful for the gold pins then. After all, man is stupid, phenomenally stupid. Or rather he is not stupid at all, but he is so ungrateful that you could not find another like him in all creation. After all, it would not surprise me in the least, if, for instance, suddenly for no reason at all, general rationalism in the midst of the future, a gentleman with an ignoble, or rather with a reactionary and ironical, countenance were to arise and, putting his arms akimbo, say to us all: "What do you think, gentlemen, hadn't we better kick over all that rationalism at one blow, scatter it to the winds, just to send these logarithms to the devil, and to let us live once more according to our own foolish will!" That again would not matter; but what is annoying is that after all he would be sure to find followers—such is the nature of man. And all that for the most foolish reason, which, one would think, was hardly worth mentioning: that is, that man everywhere and always, whoever he may be, has preferred to act as he wished and not in the least as his reason and advantage dictated. Why, one may choose what is contrary to one's own interests, and sometimes one *positively ought* (that is my idea). One's own free unfettered choice, one's own fancy, however wild it may be, one's own fancy worked up at times to frenzy—why that is that very "most advantageous advantage" which we have overlooked, which comes under no classification and through which all systems and theories are continually being sent to the devil. And how do these sages know that man must necessarily need a rationally advantageous choice? What man needs is simply *independent* choice, whatever that independence may cost and wherever it may lead. Well, choice, after all, the devil only knows . . .

[VIII]   "Ha! ha! ha! But after all, if you like, in reality, there is no such thing as choice," you will interrupt with a laugh. "Science has even now succeeded in analyzing man to such an extent that we know already that choice and what is called freedom of will are nothing other than—"

Wait, gentlemen, I meant to begin with that myself. I admit that I was even frightened. I was just going to shout that after all the devil only knows what choice depends on, and that perhaps that was a very good thing, but I remembered the teaching of science—and pulled myself up. And here you have begun to speak. After all, really, well, if some day they truly discover a formula for all our desires and caprices—that is, an explanation of what they depend upon, by what laws they arise, just how they develop, what they are aiming at in one case or another and so on, and so on, that is, a real mathematical formula—then, after all, man would most likely at once stop to feel desire, indeed, he will be certain to. For who would want to choose by rule? Besides, he will at once be transformed from a human being into an organ stop or something of the sort; for what is a man without desire, without free will and without choice, if not a stop in an organ? What do you think? Let us consider the probability—can such a thing happen or not?

"H'm!" you decide. "Our choice is usually mistaken through a mistaken notion of our advantage. We sometimes choose absolute nonsense because in our stupidity we see in that nonsense the easiest means for attaining an advantage assumed beforehand. But when all that is explained and worked out on paper (which is perfectly possible, for it is contemptible and senseless to assume in advance that man will never understand some laws of nature), then, of course, so-called desires will not exist. After all, if desire should at any time come to terms completely with reason, we shall then, of course, reason and not desire, simply because, after all, it will be impossible to retain reason and *desire* something senseless, and in that way knowingly act against reason and desire to injure ourselves. And as all choice and reasoning can really be calculated, because some day they will discover the laws of our so-called free will—so joking aside, there may one day probably be something like a table of desires so that we really shall choose in accordance with it. After all, if, for instance, some day they calculate and prove to me that I stuck my tongue out at someone because I could not help sticking my tongue out at him and that I had to do it in that particular way, what sort of *freedom* is left me, especially if I am a learned man and have taken my degree somewhere? After all, then I would be able to calculate my whole life for thirty years in advance. In short, if that comes about, then, after all, we could do nothing about it. We would have to accept it just the same. And, in fact, we ought to repeat to ourselves incessantly that at such and such a time and under such and such circumstances, Nature does not ask our leave; that we must accept her as she is and not as we imagine her to be, and if we really aspire to tables and indices and well, even—well, let us say to the chemical retort, then it cannot be helped. We must accept the retort, too, or else it will be accepted without our consent."

Yes, but here I come to a stop! Gentlemen, you must excuse me for philosophizing; it's the result of forty years underground! Allow me to indulge my fancy for a minute. You see, gentlemen, reason, gentlemen, is an excellent thing, there is no disputing that, but reason is only reason and can only satisfy man's rational faculty, while will is a manifestation of all life, that is, of all human life including reason as well as all impulses. And although our life, in this manifestation of it, is often worthless, yet it is life nevertheless and not simply extracting square roots. After all, here I, for instance, quite naturally want to live, in order to satisfy all my faculties for life, and not simply my rational faculty, that is, not simply one-twentieth of all my faculties for life. What does reason know? Reason only knows what it has succeeded in learning (some things it will perhaps never learn; while this is nevertheless no comfort, why not say so frankly?) and human nature acts as a whole, with everything that is in it, consciously or unconsciously, and, even if it goes wrong, it lives. I suspect, gentlemen, that you are looking at me with compassion; you repeat to me that an enlightened and developed man, such, in short, as the future man will be, cannot knowingly desire anything disadvantageous to himself, that this can be proved mathematically. I thoroughly agree, it really can—by mathematics. But I repeat for the hundredth time, there is one case, one only, when man may purposely, consciously, desire what is injurious to himself, what is stupid, very stupid—simply in order *to have the right* to desire for himself even what is very stupid and not to be bound by an obligation to desire only what is rational. After all, this very stupid thing, after all, this caprice of ours, may really be more advantageous for us, gentlemen, than anything else on earth, especially in some cases. And in particular it may be more advantageous than any advantages even when it does us obvious harm, and contradicts the soundest conclusions of our reason about our advantage—because in any case it preserves for us what is most precious and most important—that is, our personality, our individuality. Some, you see, maintain that this really is the most precious thing for man; desire can, of course, if it desires, be in agreement with reason; particularly if it does not abuse this practice but does so in moderation, it is both useful and sometimes even praiseworthy. But very often, and even most often, desire completely and stubbornly opposes reason, and ... and ... and do you know that that, too, is useful and sometimes even praiseworthy? Gentlemen, let us suppose that man is not stupid. (Indeed, after all, one cannot say that about him anyway, if only for the one consideration that, if man is stupid, then, after all, who is wise?) But if he is not stupid, he is just the same monstrously ungrateful! Phenomenally ungrateful. I even believe that the best definition of man is—a creature that walks on two legs and is ungrateful. But that is not all, that is not his worst defect; his worst defect is his perpetual immorality, perpetual—from the days of the Flood to the Schleswig-Holstein period of human destiny. Immorality, and consequently lack of good sense; for it has long been accepted that lack of good sense is due to no other cause than immorality. Try it, and cast a look upon the history of mankind. Well, what will you see? Is it a grand spectacle? All right, grand, if you like. The Colossus of Rhodes, for instance, that is worth something. Mr. Anaevsky may well testify that some say it is the work of human hands, while others maintain that it was created by Nature herself. Is it variegated? Very well, it may be variegated too. If one only took the dress uniforms, military and civilian, of all peoples in all ages—that alone is worth something, and if you take the undress uniforms you will never get to the end of it; no historian could keep up with it. Is it monotonous? Very well. It may be monotonous, too; they fight and fight; they are fighting now, they fought first and they fought last—you will admit that it is almost too monotonous. In short, one may say anything

about the history of the world—anything that might enter the most disordered imagination. The only thing one cannot say is that it is rational.
The very word sticks in one's throat. And, indeed, this is even the kind
of thing that continually happens. After all, there are continually turning
up in life moral and rational people, sages, and lovers of humanity, who
make it their goal for life to live as morally and rationally as possible, to
be, so to speak, a light to their neighbors, simply in order to show them that
it is really possible to live morally and rationally in this world. And so
what? We all know that those very people sooner or later toward the end
of their lives have been false to themselves, playing some trick, often a most
indecent one. Now I ask you: What can one expect from man since he is
a creature endowed with such strange qualities? Shower upon him every
earthly blessing, drown him in bliss so that nothing but bubbles would
dance on the surface of his bliss, as on a sea; give him such economic
prosperity that he would have nothing else to do but sleep, eat cakes and
busy himself with ensuring the continuation of world history and even then
man, out of sheer ingratitude, sheer libel, would play you some loathsome
trick. He would even risk his cakes and would deliberately desire the most
fatal rubbish, the most uneconomical absurdity, simply to introduce into
all this positive rationality his fatal fantastic element. It is just his fantastic
dreams, his vulgar folly, that he will desire to retain, simply in order to
prove to himself (as though that were so necessary) that men still are men
and not piano keys, which even if played by the laws of nature themselves
threaten to be controlled so completely that soon one will be able to desire
nothing but by the calendar. And, after all, that is not all: even if man really
were nothing but a piano key, even if this were proved to him by natural
science and mathematics, even then he would not become reasonable, but
would purposely do something perverse out of sheer ingratitude, simply
to have his own way. And if he does not find any means he will devise
destruction and chaos, will devise sufferings of all sorts, and will thereby
have his own way. He will launch a curse upon the world, and, as only man
can curse (it is his privilege, the primary distinction between him and other
animals) then, after all, perhaps only by his curse will he attain his object,
that is, really convince himself that he is a man and not a piano key! If you
say that all this, too, can be calculated and tabulated, chaos and darkness and
curses, so that the mere possibility of calculating it all beforehand would
stop it all, and reason would reassert itself—then man would purposely
go mad in order to be rid of reason and have his own way! I believe in
that, I vouch for it, because, after all, the whole work of man seems really
to consist in nothing but proving to himself continually that he is a man
and not an organ stop. It may be at the cost of his skin! But he has proved
it; he may become a caveman, but he will have proved it. And after that can
one help sinning, rejoicing that it has not yet come, and that desire still
depends on the devil knows what!

    You will shout at me (that is, if you will still favor me with your shout)
that, after all, no one is depriving me of my will, that all they are concerned

with is that my will should somehow of itself, of its own free will, coincide with my own normal interests, with the laws of nature and arithmetic.

Bah, gentlemen, what sort of free will is left when we come to tables and arithmetic, when it will all be a case of two times two makes four? Two times two makes four even without my will. As if free will meant that!

[IX] Gentlemen, I am joking, of course, and I know myself that I'm joking badly, but after all you know, one can't take everything as a joke. I am, perhaps, joking with a heavy heart. Gentlemen, I am tormented by questions; answer them for me. Now you, for instance, want to cure men of their old habits and reform their will in accordance with science and common sense. But how do you know, not only that it is possible, but also that it is *desirable*, to reform man in that way? And what leads you to the conclusion that it is so *necessary* to reform man's desires? In short, how do you know that such a reformation will really be advantageous to man? And to go to the heart of the matter, why are you *so sure* of your conviction that not to act against his real normal advantages guaranteed by the conclusions of reason and arithmetic is always advantageous for man and must be a law for all mankind? After all, up to now it is only your supposition. Let us assume it to be a law of logic, but perhaps not a law of humanity at all. You gentlemen perhaps think that I am mad? Allow me to defend myself. I agree that man is pre-eminently a creative animal, predestined to strive consciously toward a goal, and to engage in engineering; that is, eternally and incessantly, to build new roads, *wherever they may lead.* But the reason why he sometimes wants to swerve aside may be precisely that he is *forced* to make that road, and perhaps, too, because however stupid the straightforward practical man may be in general, the thought nevertheless will sometimes occur to him that the road, it would seem, almost always does lead *somewhere*, and that the destination it leads to is less important than the process of making it, and that the chief thing is to save the well-behaved child from despising engineering, and so giving way to the fatal idleness, which, as we all know, is the mother of all vices. Man likes to create and build roads, that is beyond dispute. But why does he also have such a passionate love for destruction and chaos? Now tell me that! But on that point I want to say a few special words myself. May it not be that he loves chaos and destruction (after all, he sometimes unquestionably likes it very much, that is surely so) because he is instinctively afraid of attaining his goal and completing the edifice he is constructing? How do you know, perhaps he only likes that edifice from a distance, and not at all at close range, perhaps he only likes to build it and does not want to live in it, but will leave it, when completed, *aux animaux domestiques*—such as the ants, the sheep, and so on, and so on. Now the ants have quite a different taste. They have an amazing edifice of that type, that endures forever—the anthill.

With the anthill, the respectable race of ants began and with the anthill they will probably end, which does the greatest credit to their perseverence and staidness. But man is a frivolous and incongruous creature, and perhaps, like a chessplayer, loves only the process of the game, not the end of it. And who knows (one cannot swear to it), perhaps the only goal on earth to which mankind is striving lies in this incessant process of attaining, or in other words, in life itself, and not particularly in the goal which of course must always be two times two makes four, that is a formula, and after all, two times two makes four is no longer life, gentlemen, but is the beginning of death. Anyway, man has always been somehow afraid of this two times two makes four, and I am afraid of it even now. Granted that man does nothing but seek that two times two makes four, that he sails the oceans, sacrifices his life in the quest, but to succeed, really to find it—he is somehow afraid, I assure you. He feels that as soon as he has found it there will be nothing for him to look for. When workmen have finished their work they at least receive their pay, they go to the tavern, then they wind up at the police station—and there is an occupation for a week. But where can man go? Anyway, one can observe a certain awkwardness about him every time he attains such goals. He likes the process of attaining, but does not quite like to have attained, and that, of course, is terribly funny. In short, man is a comical creature; there seems to be a kind of pun in it all. But two times two makes four is, after all, something insufferable. Two times two makes four seems to me simply a piece of insolence. Two times two makes four is a fop standing with arms akimbo barring your path and spitting. I admit that two times two makes four is an excellent thing, but if we are going to praise everything, two times two makes five is sometimes also a very charming little thing.

And why are you so firmly, so triumphantly convinced that only the normal and the positive—in short, only prosperity—is to the advantage of man? Is not reason mistaken about advantage? After all, perhaps man likes something besides prosperity? Perhaps he likes suffering just as much? Perhaps suffering is just as great an advantage to him as prosperity? Man is sometimes fearfully, passionately in love with suffering and that is a fact. There is no need to appeal to universal history to prove that; only ask yourself, if only you are a man and have lived at all. As far as my own personal opinion is concerned, to care only for prosperity seems to me somehow even ill-bred. Whether it's good or bad, it is sometimes very pleasant to smash things, too. After all, I do not really insist on suffering or on prosperity either. I insist on my caprice, and its being guaranteed to me when necessary. Suffering would be out of place in vaudevilles, for instance; I know that. In the crystal palace it is even unthinkable; suffering means doubt, means negation, and what would be the good of a crystal palace if there could be any doubt about it? And yet I am sure man will never renounce real suffering, that is, destruction and chaos. Why, after all, suffering is the sole origin of consciousness. Though I stated at the beginning that consciousness, in my opinion, is the greatest misfortune for man, yet I know man loves it and would not give it up for any satisfaction. Consciousness, for instance, is infinitely superior to two times two makes four. Once you have two times two makes four, there is nothing left to do or to understand. There will be nothing left but to bottle up your five senses and plunge into contemplation. While if you stick to consciousness, even though you attain the same result, you can at least flog yourself at times, and that will, at any rate, liven you up. It may be reactionary, but corporal punishment is still better than nothing.

[X]   You believe in a crystal edifice that can never be destroyed; that is, an edifice at which one would neither be able to stick out one's tongue nor thumb one's nose on the sly. And perhaps I am afraid of this edifice just because it is of crystal and can never be destroyed and that one could not even put one's tongue out at it even on the sly.

You see, if it were not a palace but a chicken coop and rain started, I might creep into the chicken coop to avoid getting wet, and yet I would not call the chicken coop a palace out of gratitude to it for sheltering me from the rain. You laugh, you even say that in such circumstances a chicken coop is as good as a mansion. Yes, I answer, if one had to live simply to avoid getting wet.

But what is to be done if I have taken it into my head that this is not the only object in life, and that if one must live one may as well live in a mansion. That is my choice, my desire. You will only eradicate it when you have changed my desire. Well, do change it, tempt me with something else, give me another ideal. But in the meantime, I will not take a chicken coop for a palace. Let the crystal edifice even be an idle dream, say it is inconsistent with the laws of nature and that I have invented it only through my own stupidity, through some old-fashioned irrational habits of my generation. But what do I care if it is inconsistent? Does it matter at all, since it exists in my desires, or rather exists as long as my desires exist? Perhaps you are laughing again? Laugh away; I will put up with all your laughter rather than pretend that I am satisfied when I am hungry. I know, anyway, that I will not be appeased with a compromise, with an endlessly recurring zero, simply because it is consistent with the laws of nature and *really* exists. I will not accept as the crown of my desires a block of buildings with apartments for the poor on a lease of a thousand years and, to take care of any contingency, a dentist's shingle hanging out. Destroy my desires, eradicate my ideals, show me something better, and I will follow you. You may say, perhaps, that it is not worth your getting involved in it; but in that case, after all, I can give you the same answer. We are discussing things seriously; but if you won't deign to give me your attention, then, after all, I won't speak to you, I do have my underground.

But while I am still alive and have desires I would rather my hand were withered than to let it bring one brick to such a building! Don't remind me that I have just rejected the crystal edifice for the sole reason that one cannot put out one's tongue at it. I did not say it at all because I am so fond of putting my tongue out. Perhaps the only thing I resented was that of all your edifices up to now, there has not been a single one at which one could not put out one's tongue. On the contrary, I would let my tongue be cut off out of sheer gratitude if things could be so arranged that I myself would lose all desire to put it out. What do I care that things cannot be so arranged, and that one must be satisfied with model apartments? Why then am I made with such desires? Can I have been made simply in order to come to the conclusion that the whole way I am made is a swindle? Can this be my whole purpose? I do not believe it.

But do you know what? I am convinced that we underground folk ought to be kept in tow. Though we may be able to sit underground forty years without speaking, when we do come out into the light of day and break out we talk and talk and talk.

[XI]   The long and the short of it is, gentlemen, that it is better to do nothing! Better conscious inertia! And so hurrah for underground!

Though I have said that I envy the normal man to the point of exasperation, yet I would not care to be in his place as he is now (though I will not stop envying him. No, no; anyway the underground life is more advantageous!) There, at any rate, one can—Bah! But after all, even now I am lying! I am lying because I know myself as surely as two times two makes four, that it is not at all underground that is better, but something different, quite different, for which I long but which I cannot find! Damn underground!

I will tell you another thing that would be better, and that is, if I myself believed even an iota of what I have just written. I swear to you, gentlemen, that I do not really believe one thing, not even one word, of what I have just written. That is, I believe it, perhaps, but at the same time, I feel and suspect that I am lying myself blue in the face.

"Then why have you written all this?" you will say to me.

"I ought to put you underground for forty years without anything to do and then come to you to find out what stage you have reached! How can a man be left alone with nothing to do for forty years?"

"Isn't that shameful, isn't that humiliating?" you will say, perhaps, shaking your heads contemptuously. "You long for life and try to settle the problems of life by a logical tangle. And how tiresome, how insolent your outbursts are, and at the same time, how scared you are! You talk nonsense and are pleased with it; you say impudent things and are constantly afraid of them and apologizing for them. You declare that you are afraid of nothing and at the same time try to ingratiate yourself with us. You declare that you are gnashing your teeth and at the same time you try to be witty so as to amuse us. You know that your witticisms are not witty, but you are evidently well satisfied with their literary value. You may perhaps really have suffered, but you have no respect whatsoever for your own suffering. You may be truthful in what you have said but you have no modesty; out of the pettiest vanity you bring your truth to public exposure, to the market place, to ignominy. You doubtlessly mean to say something, but hide your real meaning for fear, because you lack the resolution to say it, and only have a cowardly impudence. You boast of consciousness, but you are unsure of your ground, for though your mind works, yet your heart is corrupted by depravity, and you cannot have a full, genuine consciousness without a pure heart. And how tiresome you are, how you thrust yourself on people and grimace! Lies, lies, lies!"

Of course I myself have made up just now all the things you say. That, too, is from underground. For forty years I have been listening to your words there through a crack under the floor. I have invented them myself. After all there was nothing else I could invent. It is no wonder that I have learned them by heart and that it has taken a literary form.

But can you really be so credulous as to think that I will print all this and give it to you to read too? And another problem; why do I really call you "gentlemen," why do I address you as though you really were my readers? Such declarations as I intend to make are never printed nor given to other people to read. Anyway, I am not strong-minded enough for that, and I don't see why I should be. But you see a fancy has occurred to me and I want to fulfill it at all costs. Let me explain.

Every man has some reminiscences which he would not tell to everyone, but only to his friends. He has others which he would not reveal even to his friends, but only to himself, and that in secret. But finally there are still others which a man is even afraid to tell himself, and every decent man has a considerable number of such things stored away. That is, one can even say that the more decent he is, the greater the number of such things in his mind. Anyway, I have only lately decided to remember some of my early adventures. Till now I have always avoided them, even with a certain uneasiness. Now, however, when I am not only recalling them, but have actually decided to write them down, I want to try the experiment whether one can be perfectly frank, even with oneself, and not take fright at the whole truth. I will observe, parenthetically, that Heine maintains that a true autobiography is almost an impossibility, and that man is bound to lie about himself. He considers that Rousseau certainly told lies about himself in his confessions, and even intentionally lied, out of vanity. I am convinced that Heine is right; I understand very well that sometimes one may, just out of sheer vanity, attribute regular crimes to oneself, and indeed I can very well conceive that kind of vanity. But Heine judged people who made their confessions to the public. I, however, am writing for myself, and wish to declare once and for all that if I write as though I were addressing readers, that is simply because it is easier for me to write in that way. It is merely a question of form, only an empty form—I shall never have readers. I have made this plain already.

I don't wish to be hampered by any restrictions in compiling my notes. I shall not attempt any system or method. I will jot things down as I remember them.

But here, perhaps, someone will take me at my word and ask me: if you really don't count on readers, why do you make such compacts with yourself—and on paper too—that is, that you won't attempt any system or method, that you will jot things down as you remember them, etc., etc.? Why do you keep explaining? Why do you keep apologizing?

Well, there it is, I answer.

Incidentally, there is a whole psychological system in this. Or, perhaps, I am simply a coward. And perhaps also, that I purposely imagine an audience before me in order to conduct myself in a more dignified manner while I am jotting things down. There are perhaps thousands of reasons.

And here is still something else. What precisely is my object in writing? If it is not for the public, then after all, why should I not simply recall these incidents in my own mind without putting them down on paper?

Quite so; but yet it is somehow more dignified on paper. There is something more impressive in it; I will be able to criticize myself better and improve my style. Besides, perhaps I will really get relief from writing. . . .

Buddhism
THIRST AND ITS CONSEQUENCES*

Chapter XXIV

THIRST

334. The thirst of a thoughtless man grows like a creeper; he runs from life to life, like a monkey seeking fruit in the forest.

335. Whomsoever this fierce thirst overcomes, full of poison, in this world, his sufferings increase like the abounding Bîrana grass.

336. He who overcomes this fierce thirst, difficult to be conquered in this world, sufferings fall off from him, like waterdrops from a lotus leaf.

337. This salutary word I tell you, 'Do ye, as many as are here assembled, dig up the root of thirst, as he who wants the sweetscented Usîra root must dig up the Bîrana grass, that Mâra (the tempter) may not crush you again and again, as the stream crushes the reeds.'

338. As a tree, even though it has been cut down, is firm so long as its root is safe, and grows again, thus, unless the feeders of thirst are destroyed, this pain (of life) will return again and again.

339. He whose thirst running towards pleasure is exceeding strong in

* From the *Dhammapada*, translated by F. Max Müller, and published in *The Sacred Books of the East*, Vol. X (1881).

the thirty-six channels, the waves will carry away that misguided man, viz. his desires which are set on passion.

340. The channels run everywhere, the creeper (of passion) stands sprouting; if you see the creeper springing up, cut its root by means of knowledge.

341. A creature's pleasures are extravagant and luxurious; sunk in lust and looking for pleasure, men undergo (again and again) birth and decay.

342. Men, driven on by thirst, run about like a snared hare; held in fetters and bonds, they undergo pain for a long time, again and again.

343. Men, driven on by thirst, run about like a snared hare; let therefore the mendicant drive out thirst, by striving after passionlessness for himself.

344. He who having got rid of the forest (of lust) (i.e. after having reached Nirvâna) gives himself over to forest-life (i.e. to lust), and who, when removed from the forest (i.e. from lust), runs to the forest (i.e. to lust), look at that man! though free, he runs into bondage.

345. Wise people do not call that a strong fetter which is made of iron, wood, or hemp; far stronger is the care for precious stones and rings for sons and a wife.

346. That fetter wise people call strong which drags down, yields, but is difficult to undo; after having cut this at last, people leave the world, free from cares, and leaving desires and pleasures behind.

347. Those who are slaves to passions, run down with the stream (of desires), as a spider runs down the web which he has made himself; when they have cut this, at last, wise people leave the world, free from cares, leaving all affection behind.

348. Give up what is before, give up what is behind, give up what is in the middle, when thou goest to the other shore of existence; if thy mind is altogether free, thou wilt not again enter into birth and decay.

349. If a man is tossed about by doubts, full of strong passions, and yearning only for what is delightful, his thirst will grow more and more, and he will indeed make his fetters strong.

350. If a man delights in quieting doubts, and, always reflecting, dwells on what is not delightful (the impurity of the body, &c.), he certainly will remove, nay, he will cut the fetter of Mâra.

351. He who has reached the consummation, who does not tremble, who is without thirst and without sin, he has broken all the thorns of life: this will be his last body.

352. He who is without thirst and without affection, who understands the words and their interpretation, who knows the order of letters (those which are before and which are after), he has received his last body, he is called the great sage, the great man.

353. 'I have conquered all, I know all, in all conditions of life I am free from taint; I have left all, and through the destruction of thirst I am free; having learnt myself, whom shall I teach?'

354. The gift of the law exceeds all gifts; the sweetness of the law exceeds

all sweetness; the delight in the law exceeds all delights; the extinction of thirst overcomes all pain.

355. Pleasures destroy the foolish, if they look not for the other shore; the foolish by his thirst for pleasures destroys himself, as if he were his own enemy.

356. The fields are damaged by weeds, mankind is damaged by passion; therefore a gift bestowed on the passionless brings great reward.

357. The fields are damaged by weeds, mankind is damaged by hatred: therefore a gift bestowed on those who do not hate brings great reward.

358. The fields are damaged by weeds, mankind is damaged by vanity: therefore a gift bestowed on those who are free from vanity brings great reward.

359. The fields are damaged by weeds, mankind is damaged by lust: therefore a gift bestowed on those who are free from lust brings great reward.

Chapter 2

Aspiration

If, as underground man claims, all that civilization has done for man is to provide him with an excess of consciousness, man's reaction has not always been to withdraw rebelliously to isolation and impotence. There are other options. Granted, the acute sensitivity and radical honesty of underground man (rare phenomena in actual human existence) tempt one to see his plight as inevitable; these magnifications of ordinary qualities seem bound to produce a schism between a man and his world. The gap between underground man and society as well as the ambiguity of his own unhealthy consciousness produce inertia and spiritual paralysis; they inhibit meaningful action and leave him drowning in the morass of his own isolation and pain. The total thrust of his life seems blocked to such an extent that he can find no center from which to govern his conduct and, hence, cannot aspire to become anything other than what he is.

But, there are other options. If it is true that we cannot escape some degree of alienation, suffering, and guilt because of these given conditions of existence, it is also true that we cannot evade some measure of responsibility for the manner in which we shape our lives and take charge of our existence. For any one of us is also a being who esteems, who values, and who sets goals and ideals for himself which he seeks to realize in his living and by which he hopes to guide his behavior. A man aspires. A man hopes. So long as he lives, he is a process, a coming-to-be, and he is never finished or complete. The demands of the world and his own aspirations and interests continually call him to active engagement in practical life.

The nature of a man's existence remains in some respects an open issue for him, even if, in other respects, it is closed, finished, unalterable. Something, some goal, experience, quality of living, forever remains outstanding in the form of some value unrealized, some aspiration unachieved and, as such, a man is never complete. Were it not for the fact of human self-awareness, this would not be so remarkable, but consciousness of one's existence as incomplete, as partially outstanding, generates an alternative to the static impotence of underground man. A man is a valuing, aspiring creature, who strives to be other than he is in some general or particular respect; as a result of such striving, he finds his existence continually taking on new forms. As goal-seeker and goal-setter, he shows himself to be capable of self-transcendence.

In the western tradition, the philosopher who has most radically and intensely proclaimed the significance of the aspiring nature of man is Friedrich Nietzsche. Under the aegis of the overman (or "higher man"), the ideal man of titanic will and creativity, Nietzsche called humanity to a great crusade against what he termed the "last man," the "human-all-too-human." The "last man" represents for Nietzsche the spiritless mass of humanity which settles for comfort and security, for an existence devoid of tension, devoid of aspiration toward higher values; the last man lacks any vital concern for his own human potentiality for greatness. Nietzsche viewed the Christian ethic as insidious, as weakening the creative force of the human spirit. For the human spirit, he maintained, is dynamic, even chaotic, but it can gain control over its energies by means of its titanic will and determination.

The "last man" has abdicated the sacred duty of persistent self-creation, self-transcendence; he no longer desires or aspires to any goal beyond his present state of self-satisfaction. Wearied of life and its burdens of suffering, guilt, and alienation, the last man becomes a polluted stream, stagnant and unable to move or will beyond himself. Nietzsche urges man to be an "overture," a "bridge," a "dangerous across." These metaphors epitomize the injunction to hold on to the awareness that a man is a process of coming-to-be without any fixed or final nature. Human life is a project, a perpetual act of self-creation and self-transcendence which necessitates the development of a healthy contempt for what humanity has thus far achieved. Notably, Nietzsche's contempt for what *has* been achieved must not be confused with underground man's contempt for, or despair over, what *can* be achieved. The latter produces, as we have seen, as much inertia as does self-satisfaction.

If the inevitable destiny of human life is to suffer, incur guilt, and experience alienation, then the vital question is how a man is to comport himself in relation to these existential conditions which have the capacity to poison his life, weaken his resolve, and undermine all bases for hope and aspiration. Nietzsche's response to this question is unequivocal: a man must achieve spirituality and strength by affirming life even in its most burdensome aspects. Men of great spirit do not cultivate a festering and debilitating resentment against the harsh realities of existence, nor do they harbor feelings of revenge against the radical contingency of their lives. While experiencing the agonies of the human condition, they create a bright new innocence, a new health out of their sickness and despair, by a Promethean effort of will and a tenacious love of life.

Whatever one's final appraisal of Nietzsche's vision, it seems clear that he builds his conception of man upon a legitimate insight into the nature of human life. Aspiration and hope are endemic to human life. Perhaps without them, human existence could not achieve tragic proportions, for the tragic sense of life *is* the consciousness of the limitations of finite human conditions united with an unquenchable thirst to shatter the boundaries that determine our finitude.

Nowhere in dramatic literature are these tragic dimensions of human life portrayed more forcefully than in Goethe's character, Faust. He agrees to wager his very identity on the truth of the principle that life is essentially movement and that no single moment of gratification can be completely fulfilling. Faust literally contracts with Mephistopheles to demonstrate that life's significance is inextricably tied to human aspiration. At the point at which this wager is consummated, Faust appears as the spirit of negation. He has found no answer to the riddle of life; his sweeping denials and doubts embrace love, hope, patience, knowledge, and faith, but they never encompass life itself. He is never brought to the point where he is willing to repudiate the restlessness of the human heart and the endless exertion of will.

Nonetheless, the direction of Faust's striving—to become a whole cosmos in miniature—seems doomed to failure. Is boundless aspiration compatible with finite human life? Yet Faust's impulse to embrace all of experience, to envelop the whole world of life, reflects Goethe's judgment that only by ceaseless, titanic activity can man display the worth of the life that is given him. The Faustian inability to settle for what has been attained has its grounding in the aspiration to bring about the total development of the human personality. Goethe's dictum which best sums up this goal is: "Him who strives incessantly—we can redeem."

Nietzsche
THE OVERCOMING OF MAN*

[3]   When Zarathustra came into the next town, which lies on the edge of the forest, he found many people gathered together in the market place; for it had been promised that there would be a tightrope walker. And Zarathustra spoke thus to the people:

"*I teach you the overman.* Man is something that shall be overcome. What have you done to overcome him?

"All beings so far have created something beyond themselves; and do you want to be the ebb of this great flood and even go back to the beasts rather than overcome man? What is the ape to man? A laughingstock or a painful embarrassment. And man shall be just that for the overman: a

* Friedrich Nietzsche (1844–1900): German philosopher and poet. This selection comprises Sections 3–7 of the "Prologue" of Nietzsche's most important philosophical work, *Thus Spoke Zarathustra*, as well as the first of Zarathustra's "Speeches" entitled "On the Three Metamorphoses." *Zarathustra*, written in a poetic style, is the work in which Nietzsche develops and relates all of the major concepts of his philosophy such as self-overcoming, eternal recurrence, the higher man and the will to power. From THE PORTABLE NIETZSCHE, by Friedrich Nietzsche, edited and translated by Walter Kaufmann. Copyright 1954 by The Viking Press, Inc. Reprinted by permission of The Viking Press, Inc.

laughingstock or a painful embarrassment. You have made your way from worm to man, and much in you is still worm. Once you were apes, and even now, too, man is more ape than any ape.

"Whoever is the wisest among you is also a mere conflict and cross between plant and ghost. But do I bid you become ghosts or plants?

"Behold, I teach you the overman. The overman is the meaning of the earth. Let your will say: the overman *shall be* the meaning of the earth! I beseech you, my brothers, *remain faithful to the earth,* and do not believe those who speak to you of otherworldly hopes! Poison-mixers are they, whether they know it or not. Despisers of life are they, decaying and poisoned themselves, of whom the earth is weary: so let them go.

"Once the sin against God was the greatest sin; but God died, and these sinners died with him. To sin against the earth is now the most dreadful thing, and to esteem the entrails of the unknowable higher than the meaning of the earth.

"Once the soul looked contemptuously upon the body, and then this contempt was the highest: she wanted the body meager, ghastly, and starved. Thus she hoped to escape it and the earth. Oh, this soul herself was still meager, ghastly, and starved: and cruelty was the lust of this soul. But you, too, my brothers, tell me: what does your body proclaim of your soul? Is not your soul poverty and filth and wretched contentment?

"Verily, a polluted stream is man. One must be a sea to be able to receive a polluted stream without becoming unclean. Behold, I teach you the overman: he is this sea; in him your great contempt can go under.

"What is the greatest experience you can have? It is the hour of the great contempt. The hour in which your happiness, too, arouses your disgust, and even your reason and your virtue.

"The hour when you say, 'What matters my happiness? It is poverty and filth and wretched contentment. But my happiness ought to justify existence itself.'

"The hour when you say, 'What matters my reason? Does it crave knowledge as the lion his food? It is poverty and filth and wretched contentment.'

"The hour when you say, 'What matters my virtue? As yet it has not made me rage. How weary I am of my good and my evil! All that is poverty and filth and wretched contentment.'

"The hour when you say, 'What matters my justice? I do not see that I am flames and fuel. But the just are flames and fuel.'

"The hour when you say, 'What matters my pity? Is not pity the cross on which he is nailed who loves man? But my pity is no crucifixion.'

"Have you yet spoken thus? Have you yet cried thus? Oh, that I might have heard you cry thus!

"Not your sin but your thrift cries to heaven; your meanness even in your sin cries to heaven.

"Where is the lightning to lick you with its tongue? Where is the frenzy with which you should be inoculated?

"Behold, I teach you the overman: he is this lightning, he is this frenzy."

When Zarathustra had spoken thus, one of the people cried: "Now we have heard enough about the tightrope walker; now let us see him too!" And all the people laughed at Zarathustra. But the tightrope walker, believing that the word concerned him, began his performance.

[4] Zarathustra, however, beheld the people and was amazed. Then he spoke thus:

"Man is a rope, tied between beast and overman—a rope over an abyss. A dangerous across, a dangerous on-the-way, a dangerous looking-back, a dangerous shuddering and stopping.

"What is great in man is that he is a bridge and not an end: what can be loved in man is that he is an *overture* and a *going under*.

"I love those who do not know how to live, except by going under, for they are those who cross over.

"I love the great despisers because they are the great reverers and arrows of longing for the other shore.

"I love those who do not first seek behind the stars for a reason to go under and be a sacrifice, but who sacrifice themselves for the earth, that the earth may some day become the overman's.

"I love him who lives to know, and who wants to know so that the overman may live some day. And thus he wants to go under.

"I love him who works and invents to build a house for the overman and to prepare earth, animal, and plant for him: for thus he wants to go under.

"I love him who loves his virtue, for virtue is the will to go under and an arrow of longing.

"I love him who does not hold back one drop of spirit for himself, but wants to be entirely the spirit of his virtue: thus he strides over the bridge as spirit.

"I love him who makes his virtue his addiction and his catastrophe: for his virtue's sake he wants to live on and to live no longer.

"I love him who does not want to have too many virtues. One virtue is more virtue than two, because it is more of a noose on which his catastrophe may hang.

"I love him whose soul squanders itself, who wants no thanks and returns none: for he always gives away and does not want to preserve himself.

"I love him who is abashed when the dice fall to make his fortune, and asks, 'Am I then a crooked gambler?' For he wants to perish.

"I love him who casts golden words before his deeds and always does even more than he promises: for he wants to go under.

"I love him who justifies future and redeems past generations: for he wants to perish of the present.

"I love him who chastens his god because he loves his god: for he must perish of the wrath of his god.

"I love him whose soul is deep, even in being wounded, and who can perish of a small experience: thus he goes gladly over the bridge.

"I love him whose soul is overfull so that he forgets himself, and all things are in him: thus all things spell his going under.

"I love him who has a free spirit and a free heart: thus his head is only the entrails of his heart, but his heart drives him to go under.

"I love all those who are as heavy drops, falling one by one out of the dark cloud that hangs over men: they herald the advent of lightning, and, as heralds, they perish.

"Behold, I am a herald of the lightning and a heavy drop from the cloud; but this lightning is called *overman*."

[5]   When Zarathustra had spoken these words he beheld the people again and was silent. "There they stand," he said to his heart; "there they laugh. They do not understand me; I am not the mouth for these ears. Must one smash their ears before they learn to listen with their eyes? Must one clatter like kettledrums and preachers of repentance? Or do they believe only the stammerer?

"They have something of which they are proud. What do they call that which makes them proud? Education they call it; it distinguishes them from goatherds. That is why they do not like to hear the word 'contempt' applied to them. Let me then address their pride. Let me speak to them of what is most contemptible: but that is the *last man*."

And thus spoke Zarathustra to the people: "The time has come for man to set himself a goal. The time has come for man to plant the seed of his highest hope. His soil is still rich enough. But one day this soil will be poor and domesticated, and no tall tree will be able to grow in it. Alas, the time is coming when man will no longer shoot the arrow of his longing beyond man, and the string of his bow will have forgotten how to whir!

"I say unto you: one must still have chaos in oneself to be able to give birth to a dancing star. I say unto you: you still have chaos in yourselves.

"Alas, the time is coming when man will no longer give birth to a star. Alas, the time of the most despicable man is coming, he that is no longer able to despise himself. Behold, I show you the *last man*.

" 'What is love? What is creation? What is longing? What is a star?' thus asks the last man, and he blinks.

"The earth has become small, and on it hops the last man, who makes everything small. His race is as ineradicable as the flea-beetle; the last man lives longest.

" 'We have invented happiness,' say the last men, and they blink. They have left the regions where it was hard to live, for one needs warmth. One still loves one's neighbor and rubs against him, for one needs warmth.

"Becoming sick and harboring suspicion are sinful to them: one proceeds carefully. A fool, whoever still stumbles over stones or human beings! A little poison now and then: that makes for agreeable dreams. And much poison in the end, for an agreeable death.

"One still works, for work is a form of entertainment. But one is careful lest the entertainment be too harrowing. One no longer becomes poor or rich: both require too much exertion. Who still wants to rule? Who obey? Both require too much exertion.

"No shepherd and one herd! Everybody wants the same, everybody is the same: whoever feels different goes voluntarily into a madhouse.

" 'Formerly, all the world was mad,' say the most refined, and they blink.

"One is clever and knows everything that has ever happened: so there is no end of derision. One still quarrels, but one is soon reconciled—else it might spoil the digestion.

"One has one's little pleasure for the day and one's little pleasure for the night: but one has a regard for health.

" 'We have invented happiness,' say the last men, and they blink."

And here ended Zarathustra's first speech, which is also called "the Prologue"; for at this point he was interrupted by the clamor and delight of the crowd. "Give us this last man, O Zarathustra," they shouted. "Turn us into these last men! Then we shall make you a gift of the overman!" And all the people jubilated and clucked with their tongues.

But Zarathustra became sad and said to his heart: "They do not understand me: I am not the mouth for these ears. I seem to have lived too long in the mountains; I listened too much to brooks and trees: now I talk to them as to goatherds. My soul is unmoved and bright as the mountains in the morning. But they think I am cold and I jeer and make dreadful jests. And now they look at me and laugh: and as they laugh they even hate me. There is ice in their laughter."

[6]   Then something happened that made every mouth dumb and every eye rigid. For meanwhile the tightrope walker had begun his performance: he had stepped out of a small door and was walking over the rope, stretched between two towers and suspended over the market place and the people. When he had reached the exact middle of his course the small door opened once more and a fellow in motley clothes, looking like a jester, jumped out and followed the first one with quick steps.

"Forward, lamefoot!" he shouted in an awe-inspiring voice. "Forward, lazybones, smuggler, pale-face, or I shall tickle you with my heel! What are you doing here between towers? The tower is where you belong. You ought to be locked up; you block the way for one better than yourself." And with every word he came closer and closer; but when he was but one step behind, the dreadful thing happened which made every mouth dumb and every eye rigid: he uttered a devilish cry and jumped over the man who stood in his way. This man, however, seeing his rival win, lost his head and the rope, tossed away his pole, and plunged into the depth even faster, a whirlpool of arms and legs. The market place became as the sea when a tempest pierces it: the people rushed apart and over one another, especially at the place where the body must hit the ground.

Zarathustra, however, did not move; and it was right next to him that the body fell, badly maimed and disfigured, but not yet dead. After a while the shattered man recovered consciousness and saw Zarathustra kneeling beside him. "What are you doing here?" he asked at last. "I have long known that the devil would trip me. Now he will drag me to hell. Would you prevent him?"

"By my honor, friend," answered Zarathustra, "all that of which you speak does not exist: there is no devil and no hell. Your soul will be dead even before your body: fear nothing further."

The man looked up suspiciously. "If you speak the truth," he said, "I lose nothing when I lose my life. I am not much more than a beast that has been taught to dance by blows and a few meager morsels."

"By no means," said Zarathustra. "You have made danger your vocation; there is nothing contemptible in that. Now you perish of your vocation: for that I will bury you with my own hands."

When Zarathustra had said this, the dying man answered no more; but he moved his hand as if he sought Zarathustra's hand in thanks.

[7]   Meanwhile the evening came, and the market place hid in darkness. Then the people scattered, for even curiosity and terror grow weary. But Zarathustra sat on the ground near the dead man, and he was lost in thought, forgetting the time. At last night came, and a cold wind blew over the lonely one.

Then Zarathustra rose and said to his heart: "Verily, it is a beautiful catch of fish that Zarathustra has brought in today! Not a man has he caught but a corpse. Human existence is uncanny and still without meaning: a jester can become man's fatality. I will teach men the meaning of their existence—the overman, the lightning out of the dark cloud of man. . . .

*   *   *

"On the Three Metamorphoses"

Of three metamorphoses of the spirit I tell you: how the spirit becomes a camel; and the camel, a lion; and the lion, finally, a child.

There is much that is difficult for the spirit, the strong reverent spirit that would bear much: but the difficult and the most difficult are what its strength demands.

What is difficult? asks the spirit that would bear much, and kneels down like a camel wanting to be well loaded. What is most difficult, O heroes, asks the spirit that would bear much, that I may take it upon myself and exult in my strength? Is it not humbling oneself to wound one's haughtiness? Letting one's folly shine to mock one's wisdom?

Or is it this: parting from our cause when it triumphs? Climbing high mountains to tempt the tempter?

Or is it this: feeding on the acorns and grass of knowledge and, for the sake of the truth, suffering hunger in one's soul?

Or it is this: being sick and sending home the comforters and making friends with the deaf, who never hear what you want?

Or is it this: stepping into filthy waters when they are the waters of truth, and not repulsing cold frogs and hot toads?

Or is it this: loving those who despise us and offering a hand to the ghost that would frighten us?

All these most difficult things the spirit that would bear much takes upon itself: like the camel that, burdened, speeds into the desert, thus the spirit speeds into its desert.

In the loneliest desert, however, the second metamorphosis occurs: here the spirit becomes a lion who would conquer his freedom and be master in his own desert. Here he seeks out his last master: he wants to fight him and his last god; for ultimate victory he wants to fight with the great dragon.

Who is the great dragon whom the spirit will no longer call lord and god? "Thou shalt" is the name of the great dragon. But the spirit of the lion says, "I will." "Thou shalt" lies in his way, sparkling like gold, an animal covered with scales; and on every scale shines a golden "thou shalt."

Values, thousands of years old, shine on these scales; and thus speaks the mightiest of all dragons: "All value of all things shines on me. All value has long been created, and I am all created value. Verily, there shall be no more 'I will.'" Thus speaks the dragon.

My brothers, why is there a need in the spirit for the lion? Why is not the beast of burden, which renounces and is reverent, enough?

To create new values—that even the lion cannot do; but the creation of freedom for oneself for new creation—that is within the power of the lion. The creation of freedom for oneself and a sacred "No" even to duty—for that, my brothers, the lion is needed. To assume the right to new values—that is the most terrifying assumption for a reverent spirit that would bear much. Verily, to him it is preying, and a matter for a beast of prey. He once loved "thou shalt" as most sacred: now he must find illusion and caprice even in the most sacred, that freedom from his love may become his prey: the lion is needed for such prey.

But say, my brothers, what can the child do that even the lion could not do? Why must the preying lion still become a child? The child is innocence and forgetting, a new beginning, a game, a self-propelled wheel, a first movement, a sacred "Yes." For the game of creation, my brothers, a sacred "Yes" is needed: the spirit now wills his own will, and he who had been lost to the world now conquers his own world.

Of three metamorphoses of the spirit I have told you: how the spirit became a camel; and the camel, a lion; and the lion, finally, a child.

Goethe

FAUST'S WAGER*

MEPHISTOPHELES. These all belong to me,
My pretty infantry.
Hear them commending,
Cunning and coy,
Quests never ending,
Action never ending,
Action and joy.
Go from your solitude
Coursing the world, renewed.
There where the sense has bright
Ichor of sweet delight,
There they invite.
   Leave off this traffic with your groping grief,
That like a vulture feeds upon your mind;
No company so vile but brings relief,
And marks you for a man among mankind.
By this I don't suggest
We thrust you in among the common herd.
I'm not the grandest person or the best,
But if you care to take me at my word
And join with me, and make a common quest,
I'm very much at your disposal,
That's my proposal;
I'll make a pact with you,
Without ado,
Find what you crave,
And see you through,
Your comrade and your slave.
FAUST. And what return am I required to make?
MEPHISTOPHELES.
A question time can settle—why insist?
FAUST. Nay, nay, the devil is an egoist,
The help he gives is not for Heaven's sake.
State your conditions clearly, thus and thus:
Such servants in the house are dangerous.

* Johann Wolfgang Goethe (1749–1832): German dramatist, poet, and man of letters. *Faust* generally is considered Goethe's masterpiece. The character of Faust is the paradigm in Western literature of restlessness of spirit and boundless striving. An unrelenting aspiration for a fulfilment beyond mortal reach leads Faust into a compact with the devil; this compact is reproduced in this selection. From *Faust: Part One*, translated by Philip Wayne (Penguin Classics, 1949), pp. 85–91. Copyright © the Estate of Philip Wayne, 1949. Reprinted by permission of Penguin Books Ltd.

MEPHISTOPHELES. Then here below in service I'll abide,
    Fulfilling tirelessly your least decree,
    If when we meet upon the other side
    You undertake to do the same for me.
FAUST. The other side weighs little on my mind;
    Lay first this world in ruins, shattered, blind:
    That done, the new may rise its place to fill.
    From springs of earth my joys and pleasures start,
    Earth's sunlight sees the sorrows of my heart;
    If these are mine no more when I depart,
    The rest concerns me not: let come what will.
    This is a theme to which I close my ears,
    Whether hereafter we shall hate or love,
    Or whether we shall find in distant spheres
    A sense of things below or things above.
MEPHISTOPHELES.
    Now that's the very spirit for the venture.
    I'm with you straight, we'll draw up an indenture;
    I'll show you arts and joys, I'll give you more
    Than any mortal eye has seen before.
FAUST. And what, poor devil, pray, have you to give?
    When was a mortal soul in high endeavour
    Grasped by your kind, as your correlative?
    Yours is the bread that satisfieth never,
    Red gold you have, dissolving without rest,
    Like quicksilver, to mock the gatherer's labour;
    The girl you give will nestle on my breast
    Only to ogle and invite my neighbour;
    Have you the game that only losers play,
    Have you the stars of honour that afflict
    With god-like dreams, only to fade away?
    Then show me fruits that rot before they're picked,
    Or trees that change their foliage every day.
MEPHISTOPHELES.
    A task that gives me little cause to shrink,
    I'll readily oblige you with such treasures.
    But now, my friend, the time is ripe, I think,
    For relishing in peace some tasty pleasures.
FAUST. If I be quieted with a bed of ease,
    Then let that moment be the end of me!
    If ever flattering lies of yours can please
    And soothe my soul to self-sufficiency,
    And make me one of pleasure's devotees,
    Then take my soul, for I desire to die:
    And that's a wager!
MEPHISTOPHELES.   Done!

FAUST.   And done again!
　　If to the fleeting hour I say
　　'Remain, so fair thou art, remain!'
　　Then bind me with your fatal chain,
　　For I will perish in that day.
　　'Tis I for whom the bell shall toll,
　　Then you are free, your service done.
　　For me the clock shall fail, to ruin run,
　　And timeless night descend upon my soul.
MEPHISTOPHELES. This shall be held in memory, beware!
FAUST. And rightly is my offer thus construed!
　　What I propose, I do not lightly dare:
　　While I abide, I live in servitude,
　　And whether yours or whose, why should I care?
MEPHISTOPHELES.
　　I'll wait on you to-night, when you partake
　　Of college gaudy, where the doctors dine;
　　Only—since life, or let's say death's at stake—
　　I'll bring you, please, a couple of lines to sign.
FAUST.
　　So, black and white you want? You've never heard,
　　Good pedant, that a man may keep his word?
　　Is't not enough, a word that I have spoken
　　Threads all my days, for ever to remind me?
　　By changing floods the world itself is broken,
　　Yet you'll invent a little pledge to bind me?
　　And yet the rule—or dream—must be maintained
　　In hearts that cherish honour's edifice.
　　Happy the man who keeps his faith unstained:
　　No sacrifice will come to him amiss.
　　A parchment, notwithstanding, signed and sealed,
　　Is bogey fit to make the bravest yield.
　　The word expires, in passing to the pen,
　　And wax and sheepskin lord it over men.
　　Then, evil spirit, say what is your will:
　　Is't parchment, brass, or marble that you favour?
　　And shall I write with stylus, quill, or graver?
　　See what a choice I offer: take your pick!
MEPHISTOPHELES. No need to overheat your rhetoric.
　　Exaggerating items in your pride,
　　When any scrap of paper's just as good:
　　For signature, we'll use a drop of blood.
FAUST. If this avails to make you satisfied,
　　I'll join you in your little mummer's trick.
MEPHISTOPHELES. Blood is a juice of quality most rare.
FAUST. Pray have no fear that I shall break this bond,

Since all my strength is in the thing I swear,
And its pursuit shall be my only care.
Too high have I aspired, self-pleasing, fond,
When truthfully my rank's no more than yours.
The mighty Spirit spurned my weak despair,
And Nature closed to me her sacred doors.
My thread of thought is severed in despite,
I sicken, long revolted at all learning;
Then let us quench the pain of passion's burning
In the soft depth of sensual delight.
Now let your muffled mysteries emerge,
Breed magic wonders naked to our glance,
Now plunge we headlong in time's racing surge,
Swung on the sliding wave of circumstance.
Bring now the fruits of pain or pleasure forth,
Sweet triumph's lure, or disappointment's wrath,
A man's dynamic needs this restless urge.

MEPHISTOPHELES.

Wealth shall be yours, beyond all fear or favour,
Be pleased to take your pleasures on the wing,
Voluptuous beauty taste in everything,
And may you flourish on the joys you savour.
Fall to, I say; but plunge, and don't be coy.

FAUST. Have you not heard?—I do not ask for joy.
I take the way of turmoil's bitterest gain,
Of love-sick hate, of quickening bought with pain.
My heart, from learning's tyranny set free,
Shall no more shun distress, but takes its toll
Of all the hazards of humanity,
And nourish mortal sadness in my soul.

FAUST. Then say, how best begin?

MEPHISTOPHELES.   Away, Sir, come!
Why hug this learned martyrdom?
We've more exciting plans to launch
Than leading students by the nose;
Leave that to neighbour Doctor Paunch!
Is threshing straw the penance you propose?
The richest items of your knowledge—
And straight I hear one, there outside.

FAUST. No, no, my door is shut to him to-day!

MEPHISTOPHELES. He's waited long, to be denied:
Poor lad, he can't go empty away.
Give me your cap and gown, Sir, quick,
I'll cut a dash in this array;
I'll sound the heights and depths that men can know,
Their very souls shall be with mine entwined,

I'll load my bosom with their weal and woe,
And share with them the shipwreck of mankind.
MEPHISTOPHELES.
　　Listen to me, who have through aeons flown,
　　And chewed this barren food from year to year:
　　No mortal, from the cradle to the bier,
　　Digests the bitter dough; a god alone
　　Can hold this sense of oneness. In a blaze
　　Of lasting light he sees a whole serene,
　　But us he leads in chequered, darkened ways,
　　While yours are broken days
　　With night between.
FAUST. And yet I am resolved.
MEPHISTOPHELES.　　　　　　　Why then, well said!
　　And yet one fear will hardly be denied—
　　For time is short and art is long—I dread
　　Lest you should suffer from a doubtful guide.
　　Choose, Sir, a poet for companionship,
　　And let this gallant range the bounds of thought
　　And every noble branch of knowledge strip,
　　That admirable qualities be brought
　　To crown with glory your illustrious head:
　　The lion-heart,
　　The swiftness of the fleeting hind,
　　The fire of Italy, where passions dart,
　　The northerner's enduring mind.
　　Of secrets that he teaches, first shall be
　　To blend deceit with magnanimity,
　　And with the ardour of a passionate man
　　To fall in love,—according to a plan.
　　Would such a one served me! I'd soon install him,
　　And Mr. Microcosmos I would call him.
FAUST. What then am I, suppose a hostile star
　　Puts such a human crown beyond my reach,
　　And mocks the bliss my senses so beseech?
MEPHISTOPHELES.
　　You are, when all is done—just what you are.
　　Put on the most elaborate curly wig,
　　Mount learned stilts, to make yourself look big,
　　You still will be the creature that you are.
FAUST. I know. In vain I gathered human treasure,
　　And all that mortal spirit could digest:
　　I come at last to recognize my measure,
　　And know the sterile desert in my breast.
　　I have not raised myself one poor degree,
　　Nor stand I nearer to infinity.

Chapter 3

Anxiety and death

According to Nietzsche, the spiritual paralysis and alienation of underground man's life can be transformed by a Protean will which enables men to transcend the burdensome aspects of life and to achieve new health and spirituality. Yet there is a more definitive limit to human alienation and suffering as well as to hope and aspiration, for life lingers but briefly, hurrying toward death. Whether it be a plant, an insect or a man, the grasp which an organism has upon life is tenuous and of short duration. The relentless movement of time reaps the harvest that life has sown and all things die. Time is unwearying, remorseless, and, seemingly, thoughtless. As soon as a man is born, he is at once subject to death. All who share in the movements of life are forfeit to death, but only man, in his self-conscious awareness, can assume an attitude toward his own death.

The ways in which human beings understand and respond to the reality of death unearth fundamental structures of human existence, and to the reflective person unavoidably raises the question of the meaning of human life. That humans have an objective access to the death of others is rendered obvious by such public phenomena as funeral rites, burials, wakes, memorial services, and other conventional responses to death deemed appropriate in a particular culture. Our conventional understanding of the death of others, however, does not give us a genuine access to the death which the dying man "suffers." For all our empathy, for all our solicitude and concern for the dying man, we cannot experience his death. No man can appropriate another's death. In his radical finitude each human being is forfeit to death and must "take on" his own dying according to the assessment of time.

The most persistent manner in which man seeks to understand death is through his encounters with the deaths of others. In Tolstoy's *The Death of Iván Ilích* we see the public and objective understanding of death portrayed with great clarity; what becomes increasingly obvious is that one man's reaction to another's death evades and conceals the truth that each individual person must die alone. Iván Ilích's friends and family experience his death as a social inconvenience, an opportunity for personal advancement, a deliberate effort on Iván's part to make their lifes uncomfortable and complicated, as something which happens to others but surely not to themselves. They expend a considerable lot of time and energy attempting to persuade Iván (and themselves) that he (they) will not die. Their solicitude and concern during the period of Iván's deterioration is designed to mask the fact that he is dying and hence to provide them with some degree of comfort and tranquillity regarding their own deaths.

Iván, at first, is tempted to believe that he is an exception to the inexorability of death, but as his death continues to tighten its hold on him he becomes progressively alienated from the everyday world and its unawareness of the unique and destructive existential certainty of the cognizance of death. Iván's whole existence is opened to his scrutiny as he realizes that he, Iván Ilích, is dying and no one can really comprehend that awesome fact. The confrontation with his own unique death thrusts Iván out of the comfortable, average, conventional existence which he had been living into radical isolation and anxiety about the meaning of his life. Iván comes to realize that his death has been growing within him during all those moments when he had been so preoccupied with establishing himself professionally and building his world according to the rubrics of propriety, decency and success.

The shocking revelation that he is dying is accompanied in Iván's experience by an increasing sense of anxiety or dread. In the face of his imminent demise, Iván comes to view the whole forward thrust of his life toward a conventional career and marriage as trivial and meaningless. As he confronts his radical finitude he becomes anxious about the total meaning of his existence which seems now to have been empty, and without genuine significance. Hence his dying is hedged in by two vast regions of nothingness, the self-deception and paucity of his everyday life on the one hand, and death on the other. These are the objects of Iván's anxiety: a meaningless existence in the world and the nothingness of non-existence.

The melancholy and excrutiating solitude that permeates Rainer Maria Rilke's account of "Chamberlain Brigge's Death" repeats the theme of life-shattering dread that accompanies a personal confrontation with the fact that "I die." Rilke, like Tolstoy, is aware that man lives largely by forgetting that his death is the most awesome and definitive potentiality of existence. He asks, "Is it not just that which is most our own which we know the least?" In the busy concerns of everyday existence with its urgent demands and frequently trivial matters, the possibility which is most definitive for our lives, that which is most our own, is also that which is most frequently placed at the farthest remove from our awareness. As Rilke might put it, the death which grows within our lives, our own deaths, we do not recognize as real but experience only from a distance, camoflaged and masked by numerous other concerns. That which is uniquely and unavoidably our own, our deaths, we place at a distance from us. This most fundamental boundary limits all of our existence from the moment we are born; we fail to recognize it through all the evasive pursuits which our everyday life and conventional thought permit us.

In most cultures it is believed that a preoccupation with death is a symptom of a morbid personality, a diseased life, or paralysis of will. Yet this conventional judgement does not allow us honest access to the truth that our own deaths can be the most potent determinants of our existence. We are often able to sweeten the bitter fruit of other "negative" aspects of life. If we are in pain, if we have professional setbacks, if love fails, then the positive potentialities for existence are damaged, but we can live through and beyond such trials, emerging saddened, perhaps wiser, and certainly with our existence intact. Death is not of the same order; while man has often overcome fever, bankruptcy, sorrow and other disasters, our deaths will not be taken from us and cannot be overcome.

It should not be presumed that the question as to the existence of the human being in some form or other beyond the veil of death is here being prejudged. What is of concern at this particular juncture is the structure of the human condition given concretely in this world. The effort to seek and formulate a description of the conditions under which a man lives his life should be distinguished clearly from any world view or religious interpretation which seeks the full resolution of the problems raised by those conditions. Both Tolstoy and Rilke provide rich insights into the phenomena of death and dying, insofar as these enter the life of each man and help constitute the conditions under which he exists.

Tolstoy
THE DEATH OF IVÁN ILÍCH*

[I] In the large building of the court institutions, during a pause in the case of the Melvínskis, the associates and the prosecuting attorney met in the cabinet of Iván Egórovich Shébek, and started a conversation on the famous Krasóvski case. Fédor Vasílevich grew excited, proving that it was not subject to their jurisdiction. Iván Egórovich stuck to his opinion, while Peter Ivánovich, who had not entered into the discussion from the start, took no part in it, and looked through the *Gazette* which had been handed to him.

"Gentlemen," he said, "Iván Ilích is dead."

"Is it possible?"

"Here, read it," he said to Fédor Vasílevich, giving him the fresh-smelling number of the newspaper.

Within a black border was the following announcement: "Praskóvya Fédorovna Golovín with sincere sorow informs her relatives and acquaintances of the demise of her beloved husband, Iván Ilích Golovín, as-

---

* Leo N. Tolstoy (1828–1910): Russian novelist. *The Death of Iván Ilích*, reproduced in its entirety here, is one of Tolstoy's short novels. From *The Death of Iván Ilích* by Leo N. Tolstoy, translated by Leo Wiener.

sociate member of the court, which took place on February 4th of this year, 1882. The funeral will be on Friday, at one o'clock P.M."

Iván Ilích was an associate of the gentlemen assembled, and they all loved him. He had been ill for several weeks: it was said that his disease was incurable. His post was left open for him, but it was rumoured that in case of his death Aleksyéev would probably be appointed in his place, and that Vínnikov or Shtábel would get Aleksyéev's place. Therefore, upon hearing about Iván Ilích's death, the first thought of every one of the gentlemen collected in the cabinet was as to the significance which this death might have on the changes or promotions of the associates themselves or of their friends.

"Now I shall no doubt get Shtábel's place or Vínnikov's," thought Fédor Vasílevich. "I was promised that long ago, and this promotion will mean for me eight hundred roubles increase, in addition to the chancery."

"I must now ask for the transfer of my brother-in-law from Kalúga," thought Peter Ivánovich. "My wife will be very glad. She will no longer be able to say that I am not doing anything for her relatives."

"I never thought he would get up again," Peter Ivánovich said, aloud. "I am sorry."

"What was the matter with him, anyway?"

"The doctors could not make it out. That is, they did, but each of them differently. When I saw him the last time, I thought he was getting better."

"And here I have not called on him since the holidays. I was meaning to all the time."

"Well, did he have any estate?"

"I think his wife has a little something, but nothing of any consequence."

"Yes, I shall have to go there; but they have been living a terrible distance away."

"That is, from your house. From your house everything is a distance away."

"You really cannot forgive me for living on the other side of the river," Peter Ivánovich said, smiling at Shébek. And they began to talk of the extent of the city distances, and went back to the court session.

In addition to the reflections evoked in each of them by this death about the transpositions and possible changes in the service likely to happen in consequence of it, the very fact of the death of a close friend evoked in all those who heard of it, as it always does, a feeling of joy because it was Iván Ilích who had died and not they.

"How is this? It is he who is dead, and not I," each of them thought or felt.

But the close acquaintances, Iván Ilích's so-called friends, involuntarily thought also of this, that now they would have to perform some very tedious duties of propriety and go to the mass and call on the widow to express their condolence.

His nearest friends were Fédor Vasílevich and Peter Ivánovich.

Peter Ivánovich had been his schoolmate while studying law, and considered himself under obligation to Iván Ilích.

At dinner Peter Ivánovich gave his wife the news of Iván Ilích's death, and his reflections as to the possibility of his brother-in-law's transfer to their circuit, and, without lying down to rest himself, he put on his dress coat and drove to Iván Ilích's house.

At the entrance to Iván Ilích's apartments stood a carriage and two cabs. Down-stairs, in the antechamber, near the hat-rack, and leaning against the wall, stood a tinselled coffin-lid with its tassels and burnished galloons. Two ladies in black were taking off their fur coats. One of them, Iván Ilích's sister, he knew; the other was a stranger to him. Peter Ivánovich's friend, Schwarz, was coming down-stairs, and, seeing the newcomer from the upper step, he stopped and winked to him, as if to say: "Iván Ilích has managed things stupidly; you and I fixed things better."

Schwarz's face with its English side-whiskers and his whole lean figure in the dress coat had, as always, an elegant solemnity about them, and this solemnity, which always contradicted Schwarz's character of playfulness, had here its particular salt. So Peter Ivánovich thought.

Peter Ivánovich allowed the ladies to precede him, and followed them up the staircase. Schwarz did not start to go down, but stopped up-stairs. Peter Ivánovich knew why he did so: he evidently wanted to make an engagement to play a game of vint that day. The ladies went up-stairs to see the widow, and Schwarz, with seriously compressed, strong lips and playful glance, with a motion of his brows showed Peter Ivánovich to the right, to the room where the body lay.

Peter Ivánovich entered, as is always the case, perplexed as to what he would have to do. One thing he knew, and that was that under such circumstances it would never do any harm to make the sign of the cross. But he was not quite sure whether he ought also to make obeisances, and so he chose the middle way: upon entering the room, he began to make the sign of the cross and acted as though he were bowing. At the same time, as much as the motion of his hands and of his head permitted it, he surveyed the room. Two young men, one of them a gymnasiast,—he thought they were nephews,—were leaving the room, making the sign of the cross. An old woman stood motionless and a lady with queerly raised brows was telling her something in a whisper. A sexton, in a Prince Albert, a wide-awake, determined man, was reading something in a loud voice with an expression which excluded every contradiction; Gerásim, a peasant of the buffet-room, was with light steps strewing something on the floor, in front of Peter Ivánovich. As Peter Ivánovich saw this, he at once caught the light odour of the decomposing body.

During his last call on Iván Ilích, Peter Ivánovich had seen this peasant in the cabinet: he had been performing the duty of a nurse, and Iván Ilích was particularly fond of him. Peter Ivánovich kept making the sign of the cross and slightly inclined his head in a central direction between the coffin, the sexton, and the images on the table in the corner of the room. Afterward, when this motion of making the sign of the cross with his hand appeared to him to have lasted long enough, he stopped and began to look at the corpse.

The dead man was lying, as all dead men lie, quite heavily, in corpse-like fashion sinking with the stark members of his body in the bedding of the coffin, with an eternally bent head on a pillow, and displayed, as corpses always do, his yellow, waxen brow with bare spots over his sunken temples, and a towering nose which seemed to be pressing against the upper lip. He was very much changed and much thinner than when Peter Ivánovich had seen him the last time, but, as is the case with all corpses, his face was more beautiful and, above all, more significant than that of a living man. On his face there was an expression of this, that what was necessary to do had been done, and done correctly. Besides, in this expression there was also a rebuke or reminder to the living.

This reminder seemed to Peter Ivánovich out of place, or, at least, having no reference to him. For some reason he felt ill at ease, and so hastened to cross himself again and, as it appeared to him, too precipitously and out of keeping with the proprieties, turned around and walked toward the door.

Schwarz was waiting for him in a middle room, spreading his legs wide, and with both his hands playing behind his back with his silk hat. One glance at Schwarz's playful, natty, and elegant figure refreshed Peter Ivánovich. Peter Ivánovich understood that he, Schwarz, was standing above such things, and did not surrender himself to crushing impressions. His very glance said: the incident of the mass for Iván Ilích can by no means serve as a sufficient reason for declaring the order of the session disturbed, that is, that nothing could keep him that very evening from clicking with the deck of cards after breaking the seal, while the lackey would place four fresh candles on the table; altogether there was no cause for supposing that this incident could keep them from passing an agreeable evening. Indeed, he said so in a whisper to Peter Ivánovich as he passed by, proposing that they meet for the game at the house of Fédor Vasílevich. But it was apparently not Peter Ivánovich's fate to have a game of vint that evening. Praskóvya Fédorovna, an undersized, fat woman, who, in spite of all efforts to the contrary, had been expanding all the time downward from the shoulders, dressed in black, with her head covered with lace, and with the same upturned brows as those of the lady who was standing at the coffin, came out of her apartments with other ladies and, taking them to the door of the room where the dead man lay, said: "The mass will be read at once. Pass in."

Schwarz made an indefinite bow and stopped, evidently neither accepting nor declining the offer. When Praskóvya Fédorovna recognized Peter Ivánovich, she sighed, went up close to him, took his hand, and said: "I know that you were a true friend to Iván Ilích," and looked at him, expecting from him an action which would correspond to these words. Peter Ivánovich knew that, as it was necessary there to make the sign of the cross, so here it was necessary to press her hand, to sigh, and to say: "Believe me!" And so he did. Having done it, he felt that the desired result was achieved: both he and she were touched.

"Come with me: before it begins there, I have to talk with you," said the widow. "Give me your arm."

Peter Ivánovich gave her his arm, and they went to the inner apartments, past Schwarz, who gave Iván Ilích a sad wink.

"There goes the vint! You must not be angry with us if we choose another partner. If you get off, we may play a five-handed game," said his playful glance.

Peter Ivánovich sighed more deeply and more sadly still, and Praskóvya Fédorovna pressed his hand gratefully. Upon entering her drawing-room, which was papered with pink cretonne and was illuminated by a dim lamp, they sat down at the table,—she on a divan, and Peter Ivánovich on a pouffe with crushed springs and unevenly yielding seat. Praskóvya Fédorovna was on the point of cautioning him and asking him to take another seat, but found this cautioning incompatible with her present condition, and so changed her mind.

Seating himself on this pouffe, Peter Ivánovich recalled how Iván Ilích had appointed this room and had consulted him in regard to this very pink cretonne with its green leaves. As the widow, on her way to seat herself, passed by the table (the drawing-room was altogether too full of trifles and of furniture), the black lace of her black mantilla caught on the carving of the table. Peter Ivánovich raised himself in order to disentangle it, and the liberated pouffe began to agitate under him and to push him. The widow began to free her lace herself, and Peter Ivánovich sat down again, choking the riotous pouffe. But the widow did not free the lace entirely, and Peter Ivánovich raised himself again, and again the pouffe became agitated and even clicked. When all this was ended, she took out her clean cambric handkerchief and began to weep. But Peter Ivánovich was cooled off by the episode with the lace and by the struggle with the pouffe, and sat scowling. This awkward situation was interrupted by Sokolóv, Iván Ilích's butler, who came to report that the lot in the cemetery which Praskóvya Fédorovna had chosen would cost two hundred roubles. She stopped weeping and, looking at Peter Ivánovich with the glance of a victim, said in French that it was very hard for her. Peter Ivánovich made a silent sign, which expressed unquestionable assurance that that could not be otherwise.

"Do smoke, if you please," she said, in a magnanimous and at the same time crushed voice, and proceeded to busy herself with Sokolóv concerning the price of the lot. Peter Ivánovich heard, while starting to smoke, how she inquired very circumstantially about the different prices of the land and settled on the lot which she was going to take. Having finished about the lot, she also made her arrangements about the singers. Sokolóv went away.

"I do everything myself," she said to Peter Ivánovich, pushing aside the albums which were lying on the table, and, observing that the ashes were threatening the table, she without delay moved up the ash-tray to Peter

Ivánovich, and said: "I consider it a bit of hypocrisy to assure people that my grief prevents me from attending to practical matters. On the contrary, if there is anything which can, not console, but distract me, it is the cares concerning him." She again drew out her handkerchief, as though getting ready to cry, and suddenly, as though overcoming herself, she shook herself, and began to speak calmly. "But I want to ask you about a certain matter."

Peter Ivánovich made a bow, without permitting the springs of the pouffe, which began to stir under him, to get away.

"The last three days he suffered terribly."

"Suffered terribly?" asked Peter Ivánovich.

"Oh, terribly! The last minutes, nay hours, he never stopped crying. It was unbearable. I cannot understand how I stood it; you could hear him three rooms off. Oh, what I have endured!"

"And was he really in his right mind?" asked Peter Ivánovich.

"Yes," she whispered, "to the last minute. He bade us good-bye within fifteen minutes of his death, and also asked us to take Volódya away."

The thought of the suffering of this man, whom he had known so closely, at first as a merry boy, as his schoolmate, and later, when he was grown, as his partner, suddenly terrified him, in spite of the disagreeable consciousness of his hypocrisy and of that of the woman. He again saw that brow and that nose which pressed against the lip, and he felt terribly for himself.

"Three days of frightful suffering, and death. Why, this may happen to me now, any minute," he thought, and for a moment he felt terribly. But immediately, he did not know himself how, the habitual thought occurred to him that this had happened to Iván Ilích, and not to him, and that this should not and could not happen to him; that if he thought in this manner, he submitted to a gloomy mood, which he ought not to do, as was evident from Schwarz's face. Having reflected thus, Peter Ivánovich calmed himself and interestedly inquired about the details of Iván Ilích's end, as though death was an accident which was peculiar to Iván Ilích but by no means to him.

After many details of the really terrible physical sufferings which Iván Ilích had endured (these details Peter Ivánovich learned only from the way these torments of Iván Ilích affected the nerves of Praskóvya Fédorovna), the widow apparently found it necessary to pass over to business.

"Oh, Peter Ivánovich, it is so hard, so terribly hard, so terribly hard!" and she started weeping again.

Peter Ivánovich sighed and waited for her to clear her nose. When she had done so, he said, "Believe me—" and she became again voluble and made a clear breast of what evidently was her chief business with him. This business consisted in questions as to how to obtain money from the government on the occasion of her husband's death. She made it appear as though she were asking Peter Ivánovich's advice in regard to the pension; but he saw that she knew down to the minutest details, what he did not know, what could be got out of the government in consequence of this death, but that she wanted to find out if it were not possible in some way to get a little more money out of it. Peter Ivánovich tried to discover a means to do so, but, after reflecting a little and out of propriety scolding our government for its stinginess, he said that he thought that nothing more could be got from it. Thereupon she sighed and obviously was trying to find a means for ridding herself of her visitor. He understood this, and so put out his cigarette, pressed her hand, and went into the antechamber.

In the dining-room with a clock, to which Iván Ilích had taken such a fancy that he had purchased it in a bric-à-brac shop, Peter Ivánovich met a priest and a few acquaintances who had come to be present at the mass, and saw Iván Ilích's daughter, a pretty young lady, with whom he was acquainted. She had a gloomy, determined, almost angry look. She bowed to Peter Ivánovich, as though he were guilty of something. Back of the daughter stood, with the same offended look, a wealthy young man, an examining magistrate and an acquaintance of Peter Ivánovich, who, as he had heard, was her fiancé. He bowed dejectedly and was on the point of passing into the room of the dead man, when from under the staircase appeared the small form of a gymnasiast, Iván Ilích's son, who resembled his father terribly. This was little Iván Ilích, such as Peter Ivánovich remembered him in the law school. His eyes were small and such as one generally sees in impure boys of thirteen or fourteen years of age. Upon noticing Peter Ivánovich, the boy began to frown sternly and shamefacedly. Peter Ivánovich nodded to him, and entered the room of the dead man. The mass began, and there were the candles, groans, incense, tears, sobs. Peter Ivánovich stood frowning, looking at his feet in front of him. He did not once cast a glance on the dead man, and did not to the end succumb to the dissolving influences, and was one of the first to leave the room. There was no one in the antechamber. Gerásim, the peasant of the buffet-room, leaped out from the room of the deceased man, and with his powerful hands rummaged among all the fur coats, in order to find the one which belonged to Peter Ivánovich and which he handed to him.

"Well, friend Gerásim?" said Peter Ivánovich, to be saying something. "Are you sorry?"

"It is God's will. We shall all of us be there," said Gerásim, displaying his white, solid peasant teeth; like a man in the heat of intense work, he opened the door in lively fashion, called the coachman, helped Peter Ivánovich in, and jumped back to the porch, as though considering what else he had to do.

It was especially pleasant for Peter Ivánovich to breathe the pure air, after the odour of incense, of the dead body, and of carbolic acid.

"Whither do you command me to drive you?" asked the coachman.

"It is not yet late,—I will make a call on Fédor Vasílevich."

And Peter Ivánovich departed. He indeed found them at the end of the first rubber, so that it was convenient for him to come in as the fifth.

[II] IVÁN ILÍCH's past life was simple and most common, and yet most terrible.

Iván Ilích died at the age of forty-five years, as a member of the court of justice. He was the son of an official who had in various ministries and departments of St. Petersburg made that career which brings people to that state from which, though it becomes evident to them that they are no good for the performance of any essential duty, they none the less cannot be expelled, both on account of their long past service and their ranks, and so receive imaginary, fictitious places, and non-fictitious thousands, from six to ten, with which they live to a good old age.

Such had been the privy councillor, the useless member of all kinds of useless establishments, Ilyá Efímovich Golovín.

He had three sons: Iván Ilích was his second; the eldest had made a similar career to that of his father, only in a different ministry, and was rapidly approaching that official age when one attains that inertia of salary. The third son was a failure. He had continuously ruined himself in various places, and was now serving with the railways, and his father and his brothers, but especially their wives, not only disliked meeting him, but without some extreme need did not even mention his existence. His sister was married to Baron Gref, a St. Petersburg official like his father-in-law.

Iván Ilích was "*le phénix de la famille*," as they said. He was not as cold and as precise as the elder, and not as desperate as the younger. He was intermediate between them,—a clever, lively, agreeable, and decent man. He attended the department of law together with his younger brother. The younger brother did not graduate, and was expelled in his fifth year, while Iván Ilích graduated high in his class. Even while studying law he was what he was later, during his whole life,—a capable, jolly, and affable man, who none the less strictly carried out what he considered to be his duty; and he considered his duty that which was so considered by men in the higher spheres. Neither as a boy nor as a grown man did he curry favour with any one, but from his earliest youth he tended, like a fly to the light, to men who occupied the highest positions in the world, adopted their manner and their views of life, and established friendly relations with them. All the distractions of childhood and youth had passed for him without leaving any great traces; he abandoned himself to sensuality and ambition, and toward the end to the liberalism of the higher classes, but all this within certain limits which his feeling indicated to him correctly.

He had committed acts, while studying law, which had presented themselves to him as great abominations and had inspired him with contempt for himself at the time that he had committed them, but later, when he observed that such acts were also committed by distinguished personages and were not considered to be bad, he, without acknowledging them to be good, completely forgot them and was by no means grieved at the thought of them.

Having graduated from the law school in the tenth class and having received from his father money with which to provide himself with clothes, Iván Ilích ordered them at Charmeur's, attached to his fob a small medal with the inscription, "*Respice finem*," bade good-bye to the prince and to his tutor, dined with his companions at Donon's, and with new trunk, underwear, clothes, shaving and toilet appurtenances, and a plaid, all of them ordered and bought in the best shops, departed from the province to take the place of an official on the governor's special business, which his father had procured for him.

In the province Iván Ilích at once arranged the same easy and pleasant position for himself that he had enjoyed in the law school. He served, made a career for himself, and at the same time passed his time pleasantly and decently; now and then he journeyed to the counties at the command of the authorities, bore himself with dignity both toward those who stood above him and those who stood beneath him, and with precision and incorruptible honesty, which he could not help but be proud of, carried out the business entrusted to him, especially in matters of the dissenters.

In matters of his service he was, in spite of his youth and proneness to light merriment, extremely reserved, official, and even severe; but in matters of society he was often playful and witty, and always good-hearted, decent, and a *"bon enfant,"* as was said of him by his chief and his chief's wife, at whose house he was a close friend.

There was also in the province a liaison with one of the ladies, who obtruded herself on the dandyish jurist; and there was a modiste, and drinking bouts with visiting aids-de-camp, and drives to a distant street after supper; there was also a subserviency to the chief, and even to the wife of the chief, but all this bore upon itself such an elevated tone of decency that it could not be called by any bad words: it all only fitted in with the French saying, *"Il faut que jeunesse se passe."* Everything took place with clean hands, in clean shirts, with French words, and, above all else, in the very highest society, consequently with the approval of most distinguished persons.

Thus Iván Ilích served for five years, and a change was made in the service. There appeared new institutions of law, and new men were needed.

Iván Ilích became such a new man.

Iván Ilích was offered the place of examining magistrate, and accepted it, although this place was in another Government and it became necessary for him to give up the established relations and establish new ones. Iván Ilích was seen off by his friends, a group was formed, a silver cigarette case was presented to him, and he departed for the new place.

Iván Ilích was the same *comme il faut*, decent examining magistrate, who knew how to separate his official duties from his private life and who inspired general respect, that he had been as an official on special business. The post of the examining magistrate itself presented much more interest and attraction to him than the one he had formerly held. In his former office it had been a pleasure to him with an easy gait, and wearing Charmeur's undress uniform, to pass by the trembling petitioners, who were waiting for an audience, and by the official people, who envied him, and to enter directly the chief's private room and sit down with him at tea while smoking a cigarette, but there had been but few people who were directly

dependent on his will. Such people had been chiefs of rural police and dissenters, whenever he was sent out on some special business; and he had
been fond of treating such people, who were dependent on him, politely,
/ almost chummily, and of making them feel that he, who might crush them,
was treating them in a friendly and simple manner. There had been but few
such people.

But now, while he was an examining magistrate, Iván Ilích felt that all,
all without exception,—the most important and most self-satisfied people,
—were in his hands, and that he needed only to write certain words on a
paper with a certain heading, when such an important, self-satisfied man
would be brought to him in the capacity of defendant or witness, who, if
he had no mind to let him sit down, would stand before him and answer
his questions. Iván Ilích never misused this power and, on the contrary, tried
to mitigate its expression; but the consciousness of this power and the
possibility of mitigating it formed for him the chief interest and attraction of
his new service. In the service itself, more especially in his examinations, he
very soon acquired the manner of removing from himself all those circumstances which had nothing to do with the service, and of simplifying every
extremely complicated matter to a form which would permit the matter to
be reflected merely externally on paper, and which completely excluded his
personal view and, above all, made it possible to observe the whole necessary formality. This was a new business, and he was one of the first men
who in practice worked out the application of the statutes of the year 1864.

On arriving in the new city, in the capacity of examining magistrate,
Iván Ilích made new acquaintances and connections, arranged matters for
himself anew, and assumed a somewhat different tone. He placed himself
in a certain dignified aloofness from the provincial authorities, chose the
best circle consisting of members of the legal profession and of the wealthy
gentry who lived in the city, and assumed a tone of slight dissatisfaction
with the government, of moderate liberalism, and of cultured civism. Besides this, Iván Ilích, though making no change in the elegance of his
toilet, in this new office stopped shaving his chin and permitted his beard
to grow as it listed.

In this new city Iván Ilích's life again arranged itself in a most agreeable
manner: the society which found fault with the governor was jolly and
pleasant, the salary was larger, and not a small degree of pleasure was at
that time added by the whist which Iván Ilích began to play, being possessed
of the ability of playing cards merrily, and reflecting rapidly and very
shrewdly, so that on the whole he was always winning.

After two years of service in the new city, Iván Ilích met his future wife.
Praskóvya Fédorovna Míkhel was the most attractive, clever, and brilliant
girl of the circle in which he moved. Among the other amusements and
relaxations from the labours of the examining magistrate, Iván Ilích established playful, light relations with Praskóvya Fédorovna.

Iván Ilích had been in the habit of dancing while he was an official on special business; but being an examining magistrate, he danced only as an exception. He now danced in this sense that, though he was serving in the new institutions and belonged to the fifth class, he could prove, when it came to dancing, that in this line he was better than anybody else. Thus he occasionally danced with Praskóvya Fédorovna toward the end of the evening, and mainly during these dances conquered her. She fell in love with him. He did not have any clear and definite intention of getting married, but when the girl fell in love with him, he put this question to himself: "Indeed, why can't I get married?"

Miss Praskóvya Fédorovna belonged to a good family of the gentry, and she had some little property. Iván Ilích could count on a more brilliant match, but this one was not bad, either. Iván Ilích had his salary, and she, so he hoped, would have as much again. It was a good alliance; she was a sweet, pretty, and absolutely decent woman. To say that Iván Ilích married because he loved his fiancée and found in her a sympathetic relation to his views of life would be as unjust as saying that he married because the people of his society approved of the match. Iván Ilích married for two reasons: he was doing something agreeable for himself in acquiring such a wife, and at the same time did what people in high positions regarded as regular.

And so Iván Ilích got married.

The process of marrying itself and the first period of his marital life, with the conjugal affection, new furniture, new dishes, new linen, passed very well until his wife's pregnancy, so that he began to think that his marriage would not only not impair that character of the easy, agreeable, merry, and always decent life, which was approved of by society and which he regarded as peculiar to life in general, but that it would even intensify it. But beginning with the first month of his wife's pregnancy, there appeared something new, unexpected, disagreeable, oppressive, and indecent, which it had been impossible to expect, and impossible to get rid of.

Without the least provocation, as it seemed to Iván Ilích, "de gaité de cœur," as he said to himself, his wife began to impair the pleasure and decency of life: she was without any cause jealous of him, demanded his attentions, nagged him in everything, and made disagreeable and vulgar scenes with him.

At first Iván Ilích hoped to free himself from the unpleasantness of this situation by means of that same light and decorous relation to life which had helped him out before; he tried to ignore his wife's disposition and continued to live lightly and agreeably, as before: he invited his friends to his house, to have a game, and tried himself to go to the club or to his friends; but his wife one day began with such energy to apply vulgar words to him, and continued so stubbornly to scold him every time that he did not comply with her demands, having apparently determined not to stop until he should submit, that is, should stay at home and experience tedium like herself, that he became frightened. He comprehended that marital life,

at least with his wife, did not always contribute to the pleasures and the
decency of life, but on the contrary frequently violated them, and that,
therefore, it was necessary for him to defend himself against these viola-
tions. Iván Ilích began to look for means for this. His service was the one
thing which impressed Praskóvya Fédorovna, and Iván Ilích began by
means of his service and the duties resulting from it to struggle with his
wife, hedging in his independent world.

With the birth of a child, with the attempts at nursing it and the various
failures in this matter, with the real and imaginary diseases of the child
and of the mother, when Iván Ilích's coöperation was demanded, though he
was unable to comprehend a thing about these matters, the necessity for
hedging in his world outside his family became more imperative for him.

In measure as his wife became more irritable and more exacting, Iván
Ilích more and more transferred the centre of his life into his service. He
began to love his service more and grew to be more ambitious than he had
been before.

Very soon, not more than a year after his marriage, Iván Ilích understood
that marital life, though it presented certain comforts of life, in reality was
a very complex and difficult matter, in relation to which, in order to perform one's duty, that is, to lead a decent life, which is approved by society,
it was necessary to work out a certain relation, just as in the case of the
service.

And Iván Ilích worked out such a relation to the marital life. He demanded from his domestic life nothing but those comforts of a home dinner,
of the hostess, of the bed, which she could give him, and, above all, that
decency of external forms which were determined by public opinion. In
everything else he sought merry enjoyment and decency, and he was thankful when he found them. Whenever he met with opposition and grumbling,
he immediately withdrew to the separate world of his service, in which he
hedged himself in and found his pleasure.

Iván Ilích was esteemed as a good official, and after three years he was
made associate prosecuting attorney. His new duties, their importance, the
possibility of summoning to court and incarcerating any person, the pub-
licity of the speeches, the success which Iván Ilích had in this matter,—all
this attracted him more and more to the service.

There came a succession of children. His wife became more irritable and
grumbled more and more, but his relations to domestic life, as worked out
by him, made him almost impermeable to her irritability.

After seven years of serving in one city, Iván Ilích was transferred to
another Government in the capacity of prosecuting attorney. They moved;
they had little money, and his wife did not like the place to which they
moved. Though his salary was larger than before, the living was more
expensive; besides, two of the children died, and so the domestic life became even more disagreeable for Iván Ilích.

Praskóvya Fédorovna reproached her husband for all mishaps in this their new place of abode. The majority of the subjects of conversation between husband and wife, especially the education of the children, led to questions which recalled former quarrels, and quarrels were ready to burst forth at any moment. There remained only those rare periods of amorousness which came over the two, but did not last long. Those were islets where they anchored for awhile, but they soon set out again into the sea of hidden enmity, which found its expression in their mutual alienation. This alienation might have grieved Iván Ilích, if he had thought that this ought not to be so; but he now recognized this situation not only as normal, but even as the aim of his activity in the family. His aim consisted in freeing himself more and more from these unpleasantnesses and giving them the character of innocuousness and decency; and this he obtained by passing less and less time with his family, and when he was compelled to be with them, he tried to make his position secure by the presence of third parties.

But the chief thing was his service. The whole interest of life centred for him in the official world. This interest absorbed him. The consciousness of his power, of the possibility of ruining any man he wanted to ruin, his importance with his inferiors, even externally, upon entering court or meeting them elsewhere, his success before his superiors and his subordinates, and, above all, the mastery with which he conducted his cases, of which he was conscious,—all this gave him pleasure, and with his conversations with friends, and with dinners and whist, filled his life. Thus, in general, Iván Ilích's life continued to run as he thought that it ought to run,—agreeably and decently.

Thus he lived another seven years. His eldest daughter was now sixteen years old; another child had died, and there was left a boy, a gymnasiast, the subject of their contentions. Iván Ilích wanted to send him to a law school, but Praskóvya Fédorovna, to spite him, sent the boy to a gymnasium. The daughter studied at home and grew well, and the boy, too, studied not badly.

[III]   THUS Iván Ilích's life had run for seventeen years from the time of his marriage. He was now an old prosecuting attorney, who had declined several transfers in the expectation of a more desirable place, when suddenly there happened a disagreeable circumstance which completely upset the calm of his life. Iván Ilích was waiting for the place of presiding judge in a university city; but Góppe somehow got ahead of him, and received that place. Iván Ilích was annoyed at this, began to make reproaches, and quarrelled with him and with the nearer authorities; they grew cold to him, and at the next appointment he was again left out.

That happened in the year 1880. That year was the most difficult one in Iván Ilích's life. In that year it appeared that, on the one hand, the salary was not large enough to live on, and that, on the other, all had forgotten him, and that what in relation to him appeared to him as the greatest and most cruel injustice, to others appeared as an entirely common affair. Even his father did not consider it his duty to help him. He felt that all had abandoned him, considering his situation with thirty-five hundred roubles salary most normal and even fortunate. He alone knew that, with the consciousness of those cases of injustice which had been done him, and with the eternal nagging of his wife, and with the debts which he had begun to make, since he was living beyond his means,—he alone knew that his situation was far from being normal.

To economize, he took that summer a leave of absence and went with his wife to pass the summer in the country with Praskóvya Fédorovna's brother.

In the country without his service, Iván Ilích for the first time experienced not only tedium, but also intolerable despondency, and he decided that it was impossible to live in this manner and that it was necessary to take some decisive measures.

Iván Ilích passed a sleepless night, during which he walked up and down the terrace, and he decided to go to St. Petersburg, to bestir himself, and, in order to punish *them*, who had not appreciated him, to go over to another ministry.

On the next day he went to St. Petersburg, in spite of the dissuasions of his wife and his brother-in-law.

He went there with one thing in view,—to obtain a place which would give him a salary of five thousand a year. He no longer stuck to any ministry, political bias, or manner of activity. All he needed was a place, a place with five thousand, in the administration, in the banks, with the railways, in the institutions of Empress Mary, even in the custom-house,—but it had by all means to be five thousand, and he by all means to leave the ministry, where they did not know how to appreciate him.

This journey of Iván Ilích was crowned by remarkable, unexpected success. In Kursk F. S. Ilín, an acquaintance of his, entered the coach of the first class, and informed him of the contents of the latest despatch received by the governor of Kursk, that shortly a transposition would take place in the ministry: Iván Seménovich was to be appointed in Peter Ivánovich's place.

The proposed transposition had, in addition to its meaning for Russia, a special meaning for Iván Ilích, for, by bringing to the front Peter Petróvich and, apparently, his friend Zákhar Ivánovich, it was extremely favourable for Iván Ilích. Zákhar Ivánovich was Iván Ilích's schoolmate and friend.

In Moscow the news was confirmed. Upon arriving at St. Petersburg, Iván Ilích found Zákhar Ivánovich, from whom he received the promise of a certain place in his former ministry of justice.

A week later he telegraphed to his wife: "Zákhar Míller's place, with first report I receive appointment."

Thanks to this transposition of persons, Iván Ilích suddenly received an appointment in his former ministry, which advanced him two points above his comrades, and gave him a salary of five thousand, and thirty-five hundred for travelling expenses. His whole anger against his former enemies and against the whole ministry was forgotten, and he was quite happy.

Iván Ilích returned to the village merry and satisfied, as he had not been for a long time. Praskóvya Fédorovna herself was merry, and a truce was established between them. Iván Ilích told of how he had been honoured in St. Petersburg, how all those who were his enemies had been put to shame and now were fawning before him, how he was envied his position, and especially how much all loved him in St. Petersburg.

Praskóvya listened to it all, and looked as though she believed it all, and did not contradict him in anything; she only made plans for the new arrangement of life in the city to which they were going to move. Iván Ilích saw with delight that these plans were his plans, that they agreed with one another, and that his arrested life was once more receiving the real character of merry pleasantness and decency which was peculiar to it.

Iván Ilích came back for but a short time. On September the 10th he had to enter upon his new office, and, besides, he needed time to arrange matters in the new place, to transfer everything from the province, to purchase things, to order a lot more,—in short, to arrange matters as they had been determined upon in his mind, and almost in precisely the same manner as had been decided also in Praskóvya Fédorovna's mind.

Now that everything had been arranged so successfully and he and his wife agreed in their aims, and besides lived so little together, they became more friendly with one another than they had been since the first years of their married life. Iván Ilích intended to take his family away at once, but the insistence of his sister and his brother-in-law, who suddenly became unusually amiable and familiarly interested in Iván Ilích and his family, had this effect, that Iván Ilích departed by himself.

Iván Ilích departed, and the happy mood which was produced by his success and the agreement with his wife, one intensifying the other, did not leave him all the time. He found charming quarters, precisely what husband and wife had been dreaming of together. The large, high-studded reception-rooms in the old style, the comfortable, magnificent cabinet, the rooms for his wife and his daughter, the class-room for his son,—everything was as if purposely intended for them; Iván Ilích himself attended to their appointments: he chose the wall-paper, bought more furniture, especially such as was old-fashioned, which gave the aspect of a *comme il faut* style and which he had re-covered, and everything grew and grew, and arrived at the ideal which he had formed for himself. When he had half arranged matters, his arrangement surpassed his expectations. He understood that *comme il faut*, elegant, and non-vulgar character which everything would assume when it was ready.

When he fell asleep, he imagined the parlour as it would be. As he looked at the drawing-room, which was not yet finished, he already saw the fire-place, the screen, the shelves, and those scattered chairs, those dishes and plates along the walls, and the bronzes, when they should all be set up in their proper places. He rejoiced at the thought of how he would surprise Praskóvya and Lízanka, who also had good taste in such things. They were not expecting it at all. He was particularly fortunate in finding and purchasing some old things, which gave it a peculiarly noble aspect. In his letters he purposely represented matters worse than they were, in order to startle them the more. All this interested him so much that even his new service, though he liked it, interested him less than he had expected.

At the sessions he had minutes of absent-mindedness; he was wondering what borders to put on the curtains, whether to have them straight or gathered. He was so busy with this, that he frequently bothered with it himself, transposed the funiture, and himself hung the curtains in different places. One day he climbed a ladder in order to show the paper-hanger how he wanted the drapery hung; he made a misstep and fell, but, as he was a strong and agile man, he caught himself in time, merely striking his side against the window-frame knob. The blow hurt a little, but this soon passed away.

Iván Ilích felt himself particularly happy and well during this time. He wrote: "I feel that fifteen years have jumped off from me." He had intended to be through with it all in September, but it lasted until the middle of October. But it was superb, so not only he said, but also all those who saw it.

In reality it was the same as in the case of all not very wealthy men, who want to be like the rich, and so only resemble one another: there were stuffs, black wood, flowers, rugs, and bronzes, dark and burnished, everything which people of a certain class have in order to resemble all people of a certain class. And everything was so much like it in his house, that it was even impossible to direct one's attention to it, but to him it appeared as something quite special. When he met his family at the railway station and brought them home to his illuminated and fixed-up apartments, and a lackey in a white necktie opened the door into an antechamber which was all adorned with flowers, and they later entered the drawing-room and the cabinet, and went into raptures from pleasure,—he was very happy, led them around everywhere, imbibed their praises and shone with joy. On that evening, when Praskóvya Fédorovna asked him at tea, among other things, how he had fallen, he laughed and impersonated to them how he flew down and frightened the paper-hanger.

"That's what I am a gymnast for. Another man would have been killed, but I barely hit myself right here; when you touch it, it hurts, but it is all going away; it is simply a bump."

And they began to live in their new quarters, in which, as is always the case when people have settled down, there was wanting just one room, and with their new means, to which, as always, only a little, some five hundred roubles, was wanting, and everything was very well. Especially well it was at first, when things were not yet all arranged, and it was necessary still to look after things,—now to buy, now to order, now to transpose, now to fix things. Though there was some disagreement between husband and wife, both were so much satisfied, and they had so much to do, that everything ended without any great quarrels. When there was nothing more to arrange, it became a little tedious and something was wanting, but they made new acquaintances, acquired new habits, and life was filled out.

Iván Ilích passed the morning in the court and returned for dinner, and at first his disposition was good, though it suffered somewhat from the apartments. Every spot on the table-cloth and on the upholstery, a torn cord of the curtain, irritated him. He had put so much labour into the arrangement of things, that every bit of destruction pained him. But, in general, Iván Ilích's life went on as according to his faith it had to run,—lightly, agreeably, and decently. He got up at nine, drank coffe, read the newspaper, then put on his undress uniform, and went to court.

Here he found the collar set in which he had to work: he immediately found his way into it. There were petitioners, inquiries at the chancery, the chancery itself, the sessions,—public and administrative sessions. In all this it was necessary to exclude everything raw and vital, which for ever impairs the regularity of the course of official affairs: it was necessary not to permit any relations with people outside of official ones, and the cause for such relations must be nothing but official, and the relations themselves must be nothing but official. For example, a man comes and wants to find out something. Iván Ilích, as a private citizen, can have no relations with such a man; but if there exists a relation with such a man, as to a member of the court, such a relation as can be expressed on paper with a heading,—within the limits of such relations Iván Ilích does everything, absolutely everything possible, and with this he observes the semblance of human, amicable relations, that is, politeness. The moment the official relation comes to an end, every other relation is also ended. This ability to separate the official side, without mixing it with real life, Iván Ilích possessed in the highest degree, and through long practice and talent he had worked it out to such a degree that at times he permitted himself, like an artist, as though in jest, to mix the human and the official relations. He took this liberty, because he felt himself able always, whenever it should be necessary, again to segregate what was official and reject what was human.

Things went with Iván Ilích not only easily, agreeably, and decently, but even artistically. During pauses he smoked, drank tea, and chatted a bit about politics, a little about general matters, a little about cards, and most of all about appointments. And he returned home tired, but with the feeling of the artist who has finished with precision his part, one of the first violins in the orchestra.

At home the daughter and her mother were either out calling somewhere, or they had guests; the son was in the gymnasium, prepared his lessons with tutors, and studied well such things as are studied in a gymnasium. After dinner, if there were no guests, Iván Ilích at times read a book of which people were talking a great deal, and in the evening sat down to attend to business, that is, he read documents and looked into the laws, comparing depositions and finding corresponding statutes. This neither annoyed him, nor gave him pleasure. He felt ennui when it was possible to play vint; but when there was no vint, this was better than sitting alone or with his wife. His pleasures consisted in small dinners, to which he invited ladies and gentlemen who were distinguished so far as their worldly position was concerned, and in such pastime with them as would resemble the usual pastime of such people, just as his drawing-room resembled all other drawing-rooms.

One time they even had an evening party, and there was some dancing. Iván Ilích felt happy and everything was well, except that he had a great quarrel with his wife on account of the cake and confectionery: Praskóvya Fédorovna had her own plan, but Iván Ilích insisted that everything be purchased from an expensive confectioner, and bought a lot of cake, and the quarrel was due to the fact that the cake was left over, while the confectioner's bill amounted to forty-five roubles. The quarrel was great and disagreeable, so that Praskóvya Fédorovna said to him, "Fool, ninny!" He clutched his head and in his anger made some mention about divorce. But the evening itself was a merry one. The best society was present, and Iván Ilích danced with Princess Trufónov, the sister of the one who was known through the founding of the society of "Carry away my grief."

The official joys were the joys of self-love; the social joys were the joys of vanity; but Iván Ilích's real joys were the joys of the game of vint. He confessed that after everything, after any joyless incidents in his life, it was a joy, which shone like a candle before the rest, to sit down with good players, not bellowing partners, to a game of vint, by all means in a four-handed game ("a five-handed game is annoying, though I pretend that I like it"), and to carry on a clever, serious game (when the cards come your way), then to eat supper and drink a glass of wine. Iván Ilích used to lie down to sleep after a game of vint in a very good frame of mind, especially if his winnings were small (large ones are disagreeable).

Thus they lived. Their society circle consisted of the best, and distinguished and young people called on them.

In their opinions of the circle of their acquaintances, husband, wife, and daughter were in complete agreement. Without having plotted on the subject, they all alike washed their hands clean and freed themselves from all kinds of friends and relatives, slatternly people, who flew at them gushingly in their drawing-room with the Japanese plates along the wall. Soon these slatternly friends stopped flying about, and the Golovíns had nothing but the very best society left. Young men paid court to Lízanka, and Petríshchev, the son of Dmítri Ivánovich Petríshchev, and the only heir to his fortune, as examining magistrate, began to pay attention to Lízanka, so that Iván Ilích even had a talk about this matter with Praskóvya Fédorovna, whether he had not better take them out driving on tróykas, or arrange a performance for them.

Thus they lived, and everything went on thus, without any change, and everything was well.

[IV] ALL were well. It was impossible to call ailment that of which Iván Ilích now and then said that he had a peculiar taste in his mouth and an uncomfortable feeling in the left side of his abdomen.

But it so happened that this discomfort kept growing and passing, not yet into a pain, but into the consciousness of a constant weight in his side and into ill humour. This ill humour, growing and growing all the time, began to spoil the pleasure of the light and decent life which had established itself in the family of the Golovíns. Man and wife began to quarrel more and more often, and soon there disappeared the ease and pleasure, and with difficulty decency alone was maintained. The scenes became more frequent again. Again there were left some islets, but only a few of these, on which husband and wife could meet without any explosion. Praskóvya Fédorovna now said not without reason that her husband was hard to get along with. With her usual habit of exaggerating, she said that he had always had such a terrible character that one had to have her goodness to have stood him for twenty years. It is true, the quarrels now began with him. It was he who began to find fault, always immediately before dinner, and frequently just as he was beginning to eat, during his soup. Now he remarked that some dish was chipped, or the food was not just right, or his son had put his elbow on the table, or there was something wrong with his daughter's hair-dressing. For everything he blamed Praskóvya Fédorovna.

Praskóvya Fédorovna at first retorted and told him disagreeable things, but he once or twice flew into such a rage during the dinner that she understood that this was a morbid condition, which was provoked in him by the partaking of the food, and she curbed herself: she no longer retorted, but only hastened to eat her dinner. Praskóvya Fédorovna regarded her humility as a great desert of hers. Having made up her mind that her husband had a terrible character, and had been the misfortune of her life, she began to pity herself, and the more she pitied herself, the more did she hate her husband. She began to wish that he would die, but she could not wish this, because then there would be no salary. And this irritated her still more against him. She considered herself terribly unfortunate even because his very death could not save her, and she was irritated and concealed her irritation, and this concealed irritation increased her irritation.

After a scene, in which Iván Ilích was particularly unjust, and after which he during the explanation said that he was indeed irritable, but that this was due to his disease, she said to him that if he was ill, he had to undergo a cure, and so demanded of him that he should consult a famous physician.

He went to see him. Everything was as he had expected; everything was done as such things always are. The expectancy, and the assumed importance of the doctor, which was familiar to him and which he knew in himself in the court, and the tapping, and the auscultation, and the questions which demanded previously determined and apparently useless answers, and the significant aspect which seemed to say, "Just submit to us, and we shall arrange everything; we know indubitably how to arrange it all, in the same fashion for any man you please." Everything was precisely as in the court. Just as he assumed a certain mien in respect to the defendants, so the famous doctor assumed the same mien.

The doctor said, "So and so shows that inside of you there is so and so; but if that is not confirmed by the investigation of so and so, we shall have to assume so and so. If we assume so and so, then—". and so forth. Iván Ilích was interested in but one question, and that was, whether his situation was dangerous, or not. But the doctor ignored this irrelevant question. From the doctor's standpoint, this question was idle and not subject to consideration; there existed only a weighing of probabilities,—between a floating kidney, a chronic catarrh, and the disease of the cæcum. This dispute the doctor decided in the presence of Iván Ilích in a brilliant manner in favour of the cæcum, with the proviso that the investigation of the urine might give new symptoms, and then the case would be revised. All that was precisely what Iván Ilích had a thousand times done in just as brilliant a manner in the case of defendants. The doctor made his résumé in just as brilliant a manner, and looked with a triumphant and merry glance over his glasses at the defendant. From the doctor's résumé Iván Ilích drew the conclusion that things were bad, and that it was a matter of indifference to him, the doctor, and, for all that, to all people, but bad for himself. This conclusion morbidly affected Iván Ilích, provoking in him a feeling of great pity for himself and of great anger against this doctor who was indifferent to such an important question.

But he did not say anything; he only got up, put the money down on the table, and said, sighing, "We sick people no doubt frequently put irrelevant questions to you. Is this, in general, a dangerous disease, or not?"

The doctor cast a stern glance at him with one eye, above his glasses, as though saying, "Defendant, if you do not remain within the limits of the questions put to you, I shall be obliged to order your removal from the court-room."

"I have already told you what I consider necessary and proper," said the doctor. "Further things will be disclosed in the invesitgation."

And the doctor made a bow.

Iván Ilích went out slowly, gloomily seated himself in the sleigh, and drove home. All the way he continued analyzing everything which the doctor had said, trying to translate all those mixed, obscure scientific terms into simple language, and to read in them an answer to the question, "Am I in bad shape, in very bad shape, or is it still all right?" And it seemed to him that the meaning of everything said by the doctor was that he was in bad shape. Everything in the streets appeared sad to Iván Ilích. The drivers were sad, the houses were sad, the passers-by, the shops were sad. But this pain, this dull, grinding pain, which did not leave him for a minute, seemed, in connection with the doctor's obscure words, to receive another, a more serious meaning. Iván Ilích now watched it with another, a heavy feeling.

He came home and began to tell his wife about it. His wife listened to him, but in the middle of the conversation his daughter entered, with a hat on her head; she was getting ready to drive out with her mother. She made an effort to sit down and listen to all that tiresome talk, but did not hold out, and her mother, too, did not stop to hear the end of it.

"Well, I am very glad," said his wife. "So now, be sure and take the medicine regularly. Give me the recipe,—I will send Gerásim to the apothecary's."

And she went out to get dressed.

He did not dare to draw breath while she was in the room, but when she left, he heaved a deep sigh.

"Well," he said, "maybe it is, indeed, all right yet."

He began to take medicine, to carry out the doctor's prescriptions, which were changed in consequence of the urine investigation. But here it somehow happened that in this investigation and in what was to follow after it things became mixed up. It was impossible for him to make his way to the doctor himself, and it turned out that things were done differently from what the doctor had ordered. Either the doctor had forgotten something or told an untruth, or was hiding something from him.

But Iván Ilích none the less began punctually to carry out the doctor's instructions, and at first found some consolation in performing this duty.

Iván Ilích's chief occupation, since his visit to the doctor, became a punctual execution of the doctor's instructions as regards hygiene and the taking of medicine and the watching of his disease and of all the functions of his organism. People's diseases and health became his chief interest. When they spoke in his presence of sick people, of such as had died or were recuperating, especially of a disease which resembled his own, he, trying to conceal his agitation, listened, inquired, and made deductions as to his own disease.

The pain did not subside; but Iván Ilích made efforts over himself, in order to make himself believe that he was feeling better. He was able to deceive himself so long as nothing agitated him. But the moment he had some unpleasantness with his wife, some failure in his service, bad cards in vint, he immediately felt the full force of his disease. Formerly he had borne these failures, hoping that he would mend what was bad, would struggle and gain some success, would get a full hand; but now every failure sapped his strength, and cast him into despair. He said to himself: "I had just begun to mend, and the medicine had begun to act, when this accursed misfortune or unpleasantness befell me—" And he was furious at the misfortune or at the people who caused him an unpleasantness and were killing him, and he felt that this anger was killing him, but was unable to keep from it. It would seem that it must have become clear to him that this embitterment against circumstances and people only intensified his disease, and that, therefore, he ought to pay no attention to unpleasant incidents; but he made the very contrary reflection: he said that he needed calm, and watched everything which impaired his calm, and became irritable with every least impairment. What made his condition worse was his reading books on medicine and consulting doctors. His health declined so evenly that he was able to deceive himself when he compared one day with another, —there was little difference. But when he consulted doctors, it seemed to him that he was growing worse, and very rapidly at that; but, in spite of that, he constantly consulted doctors.

This month he called on another celebrity: the other celebrity told him almost the same as the first celebrity, but put the questions differently. The consultation with this celebrity only increased Iván Ilích's doubt and fear. The friend of a friend of his, a very good doctor, determined the disease in a still different manner, and, although he promised a cure, he with his questions and assumptions still more confused Iván Ilích and intensified his doubts. A homœopathist determined the disease in a still different way and gave him some medicine, and he took it for a week, secretly from all. But at the end of the week he felt no relief and lost his confidence in all former treatments and in the present one, too, and so became still more dejected. At one time a lady acquaintance told him of a cure by means of holy images. Iván Ilích caught himself listening attentively and believing the actuality of the fact. This incident frightened him.

"Is it possible I have mentally grown so feeble?" he said to himself. "Nonsense! It's all bosh! I must not submit to my small faith, but, selecting one physician, must strictly adhere to his treatment. I shall do so. It's all over with that. I will not think, and will stick to the one treatment until summer. We shall know what to do after that. Now there is an end to wavering!"

It was easy to say all that, but impossible to execute it. The pain in his side was still annoying and seemed to be increasing and growing more constant; the taste in his mouth grew more and more queer,—he thought a disgusting smell came from his mouth,—and his appetite and his strength grew weaker and weaker. It was impossible for him to deceive himself: something terrible, new, and more significant than anything that had ever taken place in his life was now going on in him. He alone knew of it, and all those who surrounded him did not understand it, or did not wish to understand it, and thought that everything in the world was going on as before. That tormented him more than anything. His home folk, especially his wife and his daughter, who were in the very heat of calls, he saw, did not understand a thing about it and were annoyed because he was so cheerless and so exacting, as though it were his fault. Though they tried to conceal this, he saw that he was an obstacle to them, but that his wife had worked out for herself a certain relation to his disease and held on to it independently of what he said and did. This relation was like this:

"You know," she would say to her friends, "Iván Ilích, like all good people, is unable strictly to take the prescribed cure. To-day he will take the drops and eat what he is ordered to eat, and will go to bed early; to-morrow, if I do not watch him, he will forget to take the medicine, will eat some sturgeon (and he is not allowed to eat that), and will sit up playing vint until one o'clock.

" 'When did I do it?' Iván Ilích will say in anger. 'Just this once at Peter Ivánovich's.'

" 'And yesterday at Shébek's.'

" 'It makes no difference, I cannot sleep from pain anyway.'

" 'Whether from pain or from anything else, you will never get well this way, and you only torment us.' "

Praskóvya Fédorovna's external relation to her husband's ailment, which she expressed to him as much as to others, was this, that Iván Ilích had himself to blame for this ailment, and that this whole ailment was a new annoyance which he was causing his wife. Iván Ilích felt that that came involuntarily from her, but that did not make it any easier for him.

In the court Iván Ilích observed, or thought that he observed, the same strange relation to himself: now it seemed to him that people peeped at him as at a man who was soon to make a place vacant; now his friends began in a jesting manner to tease him on account of his suspiciousness, as though the fact that something terrible and horrible, something unheard-of, which was taking place in him and gnawing at him and drawing him somewhere, were a most agreeable subject for jests. He was particularly irritated by Schwarz, who with his playfulness, vivacity, and *comme il faut* ways reminded him of what he had been ten years before.

Friends come to have a game, and they sit down at the table. The cards are dealt; the new cards are separated, and the diamonds are placed with the diamonds,—seven of them. The partner says, "Without trumps," and supports two diamonds. What else should one wish? It ought to be jolly and lively,—a clean sweep. And suddenly Iván Ilích feels such a gnawing pain, such a bad taste in his mouth, and it feels so queer to him to be able with all that to find any pleasure in a clean sweep.

He looks at Mikhaíl Mikháylovich, his partner, as he with the hand of a sanguine man strikes the table and politely and condescendingly refrains from sweeping in the stakes and moves them up to Iván Ilích, in order to give him the pleasure of taking them in, without going to much trouble or stretching his hand far.

"Does he really think that I am so feeble that I cannot stretch out my hand?" thinks Iván Ilích, and he forgets what is trumps, and unnecessarily trumps his own cards, and loses the clean sweep by three points, and, what is more terrible still, he sees Mikhaíl Mikháylovich suffering, and that makes no difference to him. And it is terrible for him to think that it makes no difference to him.

All see that it is hard for him, and they say to him: "We can stop, if you are tired. You had better rest."

Rest? No, he is not in the least tired,—he will finish the rubber. All are sad and silent. Iván Ilích feels that it is he who has cast this gloom over them, and he cannot dispel it. They eat supper and leave, and Iván Ilích is left alone with the consciousness that his life is poisoned for him and poisons others, and that this poison does not weaken him, but more and more penetrates all his being.

And it was with this consciousness, in addition to the physical pain, and with terror, that he had to lie down in his bed, and often be unable from pain to sleep the greater part of the night. In the morning he had to get up again, go to the court, or, if not in court, stay at home all the twenty-four hours of the day, each of which was a torment. And he had to live by himself on the edge of perdition, without a single man to understand or pity him.

[V] THUS passed a month, and two months. Before New Year his brother-in-law arrived in the city, and stopped at their house. Iván Ilích was at court. Praskóvya Fédorovna was out shopping. Upon entering his cabinet, Iván Ilích found there his brother-in-law, a healthy sanguine man, who was himself unpacking his satchel. Upon hearing Iván Ilích's steps, he raised his head and for a second looked at him in silence. This glance disclosed everything to Iván Ilích. The brother-in-law opened his mouth to exclaim something in amazement, but held himself back. This motion confirmed everything.

"Well, have I changed?"

"Yes—there is a change."

And no matter how much Iván Ilích afterward led his brother-in-law up to talk about his appearance, his brother-in-law kept quiet about it. Praskóvya Fédorovna came home, and the brother-in-law went to see her. Iván Ilích locked the door and began to look at himself in the mirror, at first straight, and then from one side. He took the photograph of himself and his wife and compared it with what he saw in the mirror. The change was tremendous. Then he bared his arms as high as the elbow; he looked at them, pulled down the sleeves, sat down on an ottoman, and grew darker than night.

"I must not, I must not," he said to himself. He went up to the table, picked up a law case, and began to read it, but was unable to do so. He opened the door and went into the parlour. The door to the drawing-room was closed. He went up to it on tiptoe, and began to listen.

"No, you exaggerate it," said Praskóvya Fédorovna.

"Exaggerate? No. You do not see it, he is a dead man,—look into his eyes. There is no light in them. What is the matter with him?"

"Nobody knows. Nikoláev" (that was the second doctor) "said something, but I do not know what. Leshchetítski" (that was the famous doctor) "said, on the contrary—"

Iván Ilích walked away and went to his room; he lay down and began to think: "The kidney, a floating kidney." He recalled everything which the doctors had told him about how it had torn itself away and was floating around. He tried with an effort of the imagination to catch this kidney, and to arrest and fasten it. So little was needed for that, he thought. "No, I will call on Peter Ivánovich before I do anything else." (This was that friend whose friend was a doctor.) He rang the bell, ordered the horse to be hitched up, and got himself ready to go.

"Whither are you going, *Jean?*" asked his wife, with a peculiarly sad and strangely kind expression.

This strangely kind expression made him furious. He cast a gloomy glance at her.

"I have some business with Peter Ivánovich."

He drove to the house of his friend, who had a friend who was a doctor. With him he drove to the doctor. He found him at home, and conversed with him for a long time.

By analyzing anatomically and physiologically the details of what, according to the doctor's opinion, was going on in him, he understood it all.

There was a thing, just a little thing, in his blind gut. All this might change for the better. Strengthen the energy of one organ, weaken the activity of another, there will take place a suction, and all will be well. He was a little too late for dinner. He dined and conversed merrily, but could not for a long time go back to his room to attend to his business. Finally he went to his cabinet, and immediately sat down to work. He read some cases and worked, but the consciousness of the fact that he had a reserved, important, confidential matter, with which he would busy himself after he was through, did not leave him. When he was through with work he recalled that this confidential matter was his thoughts about the blind gut. But he did not abandon himself to them: he went to the drawing-room for tea.

There were guests there, and they talked, and played the piano, and sang; there was also the investigating magistrate, his daughter's intended. Iván Ilích, according to Praskóvya Fédorovna's remark, passed a jollier evening than ever; but he did not for a moment forget the fact that he had some reserved, important thoughts about the blind gut.

At eleven o'clock he excused himself, and went to his room. Ever since the beginning of his disease he had slept by himself, in a small room near his cabinet. He went there, undressed himself, and took up a novel by Zola, but did not read it,—he was thinking. In his imagination took place the desired improvement in his blind gut. There was a suction and a secretion, and the regular activity was reëstablished.

"Yes, that is all correct," he said to himself. "All one has to do is to come to Nature's aid."

He thought of his medicine. He raised himself up, took the medicine, and lay down on his back, watching the beneficial effect of the medicine and the destruction of his pain by it.

"Take it regularly and avoid deleterious influences, that is all; I am beginning to feel a little better, much better."

He began to feel his side, but it did not pain to the touch.

"Yes, I do not feel it,—really it is much better now."

He put out the light, and lay down on his side. The blind gut is improving, and being sucked in. Suddenly he experienced his old, dull, gnawing pain,—it was stubborn, calm, and serious. In the mouth was the same familiar, abominable taste. His heart was pinched, his head was dizzy.

"My God, my God!" he muttered, "again and again, and it will never stop."

Suddenly the matter presented itself to him from an entirely different side.

"The blind gut, the kidney!" he said to himself. "It is not a question of the blind gut, nor of the kidney, but of life and—death. Yes, there was life, and it is going away and away, and I cannot retain it. Yes. Why should I deceive myself? Is it not evident to all outside of me that I am dying? The question is only in the number of weeks and days—perhaps now. There was light, but now it is darkness. I was here until now, but now I am going thither. Whither?"

He was chilled, and his breath stopped. He heard only the beats of his heart.

"I shall be no longer, so what will there be? There will be nothing. But where shall I be, when I am no longer? Can it be death? No, I will not die."

He leaped up and wanted to light a candle; he groped about with trembling hands, dropped the candle with the candlestick on the floor, and again fell back on the pillow.

"What's the use? It makes no difference," he said to himself, looking with open eyes into the darkness. "Death, yes, death. And not one of them knows, or wants to know, and they have no pity. They are playing." (He was hearing beyond the door the peal of voices and of a ritornelle.) "It makes no difference to them, but they, too, will die. Foolishness! First I, and they after me; they will come to the same. And they are making merry. Beasts!"

Malice was choking him. He felt painfully and intolerably oppressed. It could not be that all should be fated to experience this terrible fear. He got up.

"Something is not quite right; I must calm myself, I must consider everything from the beginning."

And he began to consider.

"Yes, the beginning of the disease. I struck my side, and I was all the time the same, to-day and to-morrow,—I had a little pain, then more, then the doctors, then a gnawing pain, then despair, again the doctors; and I kept coming nearer and nearer to the abyss. There is less strength. Nearer and nearer. And I wore myself out,—I have no light in my eyes. And there is death, and I am thinking all the time of the blind gut. I am thinking of mending the gut, but this is death. Is it really death?"

Again he was assailed by terror: he breathed heavily, and bent over, trying to find a match, and pressed with his elbow against the foot-rest. The foot-rest was in his way and caused him pain, so he grew angry at it and in his anger pressed harder against it and threw it down. In his despair he lost his breath and threw himself down on his back, expecting death to come at once.

At this time the guests were departing. Praskóvya Fédorovna was seeing them off. She heard something fall, and entered the room.

"What is the matter with you?"

"Nothing. I dropped it accidentally."

She went out and brought a candle. He was lying down, breathing heavily and fast, like a man who had run a verst, and looked at her with an arrested glance.

"What is the matter with you, Jean?"

"Noth—ing. I—dropped—it."

"What is the use of telling her? She will not understand it," he thought. She did not understand it indeed. She lifted the foot-rest, lighted a candle for him, and hurried away. She had to see a guest off.

When she came back he was still lying on his back, looking at the ceiling.

"How are you? Are you feeling worse?"

"Yes."

She shook her head, and sat awhile.

"Do you know, Jean? I think it would be well to send for Leshchetítski."

This meant that she wanted to send for the famous doctor, and not to spare any expense. He smiled a sarcastic smile, and said, "No." She sat awhile, and then went up to him and kissed his brow.

He hated her with all the strength of his soul just as she was kissing him, and he made an effort over himself not to push her back.

"Good night. God will grant you to fall asleep."

"Yes."

[VI] Iván Ilích saw that he was dying, but he was not only not used to this, but simply did not understand and was absolutely unable to understand it.

That example of a syllogism which he had learned from Kiesewetter's logic, "Caius is a man, men are mortal, consequently Caius is mortal," had all his life seemed true to him only in regard to Caius, but by no means to him. That was Caius the man, man in general, and that was quite true; but he was not Caius, and not man in general; he had always been an entirely, entirely different being from all the rest; he had been Ványa with his mother, with his father, Mítya; and Volódya, with his toys, the coachman, and the nurse; then Kátenka, with all the joys, sorrows, and delights of childhood, boyhood, youth. Had there ever existed for Caius that odour of the striped leather ball, which Ványa had been so fond of? Had Caius kissed his mother's hand in the same way, and had the silk of the folds of his mother's dress rustled in the same way for Ciaus? Had he been as riotous about patties at the Law School? Had Caius been in love like him? Had Caius been able to conduct a session like him?

"Caius is indeed mortal, and it is proper for him to die, but for me, Ványa, Iván Ilích, with all my feelings and thoughts, for me it is an entirely different matter. It cannot be proper for me to die. That would be too terrible."

That was the way he felt about it.

"If I were to die like Caius, I should know it, and an inner voice would tell me so, but nothing similar has been the case with me, and I and all my friends understood that it is not all the same as with Caius. But now it is like this!" he said to himself. "It is impossible! It cannot be, but it is so. How is this? How is this to be comprehended?"

And he was unable to understand, and tried to dispel this thought as being false, irregular, and morbid, and to substitute for it other, regular, healthy thoughts. But this thought,—not merely thought, but, as it were, reality,—came back and stood before him.

And he invoked in the place of this thought other thoughts in rotation, in the hope of finding a support in them. He tried to return to former trains of thought, which heretofore had veiled the thought of death from him. But, strange to say, what formerly had veiled, concealed, and destroyed the consciousness of death, now could no longer produce this effect. Of late Iván Ilích passed the greater part of his time in these endeavours to reëstablish his former trains of feeling, which had veiled death from him.

He said to himself, "I will busy myself with my service, for have I not lived by it heretofore?" and he went to court, dispelling all doubts from himself; he entered into conversations with his associates, and seated himself in his customary manner, casting a distracted, pensive glance upon the crowd, and leaning with both his emaciated hands on the rests of the oak chair, leaning over to an associate, as on former occasions, moving up the case, and whispering, and then, suddenly casting an upward glance and seating himself straight, he pronounced the customary words and began the case. But suddenly, in the middle, the pain in his side, paying no attention to the period of the development of the case, began its own gnawing work. Iván Ilích listened to it and dispelled the thought of it, but it continued its work and came and stationed itself right in front of him and looked at him, and he was dazed, and the fire went out in his eyes, and he began to ask himself again, "Is it possible *it* alone is true?" And his associates and his men under him saw in surprise and sorrow that he, such a brilliant and shrewd judge, was getting mixed and making blunders. He shook himself, tried to come back to his senses, and somehow managed to bring the session to a close, and returned home with the sad consciousness that his judicial work could not, as it had done of old, conceal from him what he wished to be concealed, and that by means of his judicial work he could not be freed from *it*. And, what was worst of all, was this, that *it* drew him toward itself, not that he might be able to do something, but only that he might look at it,

straight into its eyes,—that he might look at it and, without doing anything,
might suffer unutterably.

And, while trying to escape this state, Iván Ilích sought consolation and
other shields, and the other shields appeared and for a short time seemed to
save him, but very soon they were again, not destroyed, but made transparent, as though *it* penetrated through everything, and nothing could
shroud *it*.

During this last period he entered the drawing-room which he himself
had furnished,—that drawing-room where he had fallen, for which he,—as
he thought with sarcasm and ridicule,—for the arrangement of which he had
sacrificed his life, for he knew that his disease had begun with that hurt; he
entered and saw that there was a nick in the table. He looked for the cause
of it, and found it in the bronze adornment of the album which was bent
at the edge. He took the album, an expensive one,—he had made it himself
with love,—and was annoyed at the carelessness of his daughter and her
friends,—here there was a tear, and there the photographs were turned
bottom side up. He brought it all carefully back into shape and bent the
adornment back again.

Then occurred to him the thought of transplanting all this *établissement*
with the albums to another corner, near the flowers. He called up a lackey;
either his daughter or his wife came to his rescue: they did not agree and
contradicted him,—he quarrelled and grew angry; but everything was good,
for he did not think of it,—*it* was not to be seen.

But just then his wife said, as he moved the things, "Let the servants do
it, you will only hurt yourself," and suddenly *it* flashed above the screen,
and he saw *it*. *It* flashed by, and he still hopes that *it* will pass, but he involuntarily listens to one side,—*it* is still seated there and still causing him
the same gnawing pain, and he can no longer forget, and *it* looks at him
quite clearly from behind the flowers. What is this all for?

"And it is true that I lost my life on this curtain, as though in the storm-
ing of a fortress. Is it really so? How terrible and how stupid! It cannot be!
It cannot be, but it is so."

He went into his cabinet, and lay down there, and was again left all
alone with *it*,—face to face with *it*,—and there was nothing he could do
with *it*. All he had to do was to look at it and grow cold.

[VII] How it all happened in the third month of Iván Ilích's disease is
hard to tell, because it all happened imperceptibly step by step, but what
happened was that his wife, and his son, and the servants, and his acquaintances, and the doctors, and, above all else, he himself knew that the
whole interest in him consisted for others in nothing but the question how
soon he would vacate the place, would free the living from the embarrassment produced by his presence, and would himself be freed from his
sufferings.

He slept less and less: he was given opium, and they began to inject morphine into him. But this did not make it easier for him. The dull dejection which he experienced in his half-sleeping state at first gave him relief as something new, but later it grew to be the same, and even more agonizing, than the sharp pain.

They prepared particular kinds of food for him according to the doctor's prescriptions; but these dishes tasted to him more and more insipid, and more and more abominable.

Special appliances, too, were used for his evacuations, and every time this was a torture to him,—a torture on account of the impurity, the indecency, and the smell, and from the consciousness that another person had to take part in it.

But in this most disagreeable matter Iván Ilích found his consolation. The peasant of the buffet, Gerásim, always came to carry out his vessel. Now Gerásim was a clean, fresh young peasant, who had improved much on his city food. He was always merry and precise. At first the sign of this cleanly man, who was dressed in Russian fashion and did this detestable work, embarrassed Iván Ilích.

One time, upon getting up from the vessel, and being unable to lift up his trousers, he dropped down into a soft chair and looked in terror at his bared, impotent thighs with their sharply defined muscles.

Gerásim, in heavy boots, spreading about him the agreeable odour of tar from his boots and of the freshness of the winter air, stepped into the room with heavy tread. He wore a clean hempen apron and a clean chintz shirt, the sleeves of which were rolled up on his bare, strong, youthful arms, and without looking at Iván Ilích, and apparently repressing the joy of life which shone upon his face, in order not to offend the patient, he walked over to the vessel.

"Gerásim," Iván Ilích said, in a feeble voice.

Gerásim trembled, apparently in fear of having done something wrong, and with a rapid motion turned to the patient his fresh, kindly, simple, youthful face, which was just beginning to be covered with a beard.

"What do you wish?"

"I suppose this is unpleasant for you. Excuse me. I cannot help it."

"Not at all, sir." And Gerásim flashed his eyes and displayed his youthful, white teeth. "Why should you trouble yourself? You are sick."

And with his strong, agile hands he did his usual work, and walked out, stepping lightly. Five minutes later he returned, stepping as lightly as before.

Iván Ilích was sitting in the chair in the same posture.

"Gerásim," he said, when Gerásim had put down the vessel, which had been washed clean, "please, come here and help me."

Gerásim went up to him.

"Lift me up. It is hard for me to do it all alone, and I have sent Dmítri away."

Gerásim went up to him: with his strong arms he embraced him as lightly as he stepped, raised him skilfully and softly, held him up, with one hand pulled up his trousers, and wanted to put him down again in the chair. But Iván Ilích asked to be taken to the divan. Gerásim without an effort, and as though without pressing against him, took him, almost carried him, to the divan, and seated him on it.

"Thank you. How skilfully and well you do everything."

Gerásim smiled again, and was on the point of leaving. But Iván Ilích felt so well with him that he did not want to dismiss him.

"Be so kind as to push that chair up to me. No, that,—under my feet. I feel more at ease when my legs are raised."

Gerásim brought him the chair, which he put down evenly on the floor without making a noise with it, and raised Iván Ilích's feet on the chair. It seemed to Iván Ilích that he felt more at ease while Gerásim was raising up his legs.

"I feel more at ease when my legs are higher," said Iván Ilích. "Put that pillow under me."

Garásim did so. He raised the legs and put the pillow down. Again Iván Ilích felt better while Gerásim was holding his legs. When Gerásim put them down, he thought he felt worse.

"Gerásim," he said to him, "are you busy now?"

"Not at all, sir," said Gerásim, who had learned from city folk how to talk to gentlemen.

"What else have you to do?"

"What else have I to do? I have done everything, and have only to chop some wood for to-morrow."

"If so, hold up my legs a little higher,—can you do it?"

"Why not? I can."

Gerásim raised his legs higher. And it seemed to Iván Ilích that in this position he did not feel any pain at all.

"And how about the wood?"

"Do not trouble yourself. We shall get time for it."

Iván Ilích ordered Gerásim to sit down and hold his legs, and entered into a conversation with him. And, strange to say, it seemed to him that he felt better so long as Gerásim was holding his legs.

From that time on Iván Ilích began to call in Gerásim, and made Gerásim keep his legs on his shoulders, and was fond of talking with him. Gerásim did this lightly, gladly, simply, and with a goodness which affected Iván Ilích. Health, strength, vivacity in all other people offended Iván Ilích; but Gerásim's strength and vivacity did not sadden him,—it soothed him.

Iván Ilích's chief suffering was from a lie. This lie, for some reason accepted by all, was this, that he was only sick and not dying, and that he needed but to be calm and be cured, and then all would go well. He knew full well that, no matter what they might do, nothing would come of it but still more agonizing suffering and death. And he was tormented by this lie and by this, that they would not confess what all, and he, too, knew, but insisted on lying about him in this terrible situation, and wanted and compelled him to take part in this lie. The lie, the lie, this lie which was perpetrated on him on the day previous to his death and which was to reduce this terrible, solemn act of his death to the level of all their visits, curtains, sturgeon at dinner, was dreadfully painful for Iván Ilích. And, strange to say, often, while they were perpetrating their jests on him, he was within a hair's breadth of shouting out to them, "Stop lying! You know, and I, too, know that I am dying,—so stop at least your lying." But he had never the courage to do it.

The horrible, terrible act of his dying, he saw, was by all those who surrounded him reduced to the level of an accidental unpleasantness and partly to that of an indecency (something the way they treat a man who, upon entering a drawing-room, spreads a bad odour), through that very "decency" which he had been serving all his life; he saw that no one would pity him, because no one wanted even to understand his position. Gerásim was the only one who understood this position and pitied him. And so Iván Ilích never felt happy except when he was with Gerásim. He felt well when Gerásim, frequently whole nights at a stretch, held his legs and would not go to bed, saying, "Please not to trouble yourself, Iván Ilích, I shall get enough sleep yet;" or when he, passing over to "thou," suddenly added, "If thou wert not a sick man it would be different, but as it is, why should I not serve thee?"

Gerásim was the only one who did not lie; everything proved that he alone understood what the matter was, and did not consider it necessary to conceal it, but simply pitied his emaciated, feeble master. Once, when Iván Ilích sent him away, he went so far as to say:

"We shall all of us die. Why should we not trouble ourselves?" with which he meant to say that he did not find his labour annoying, for the reason that he was doing it for a dying man, and that he hoped that in the proper time some one would do the same for him.

Besides this lie, or in consequence of it, Iván Ilích was most annoyed by this, that no one pitied him the way he wanted to be pitied; at certain moments, after long sufferings, Iván Ilích wanted most of all, however much he was ashamed to acknowledge the fact, that some one should pity him like a sick child. He wanted to be petted, kissed, and fondled, as they pet and console children. He knew that he was an important member of the court and that his beard was streaked gray, and that, therefore, that was impossible; but he none the less desired it. In his relations with Gerásim there was something resembling it, and so his relations with Gerásim gave him consolation.

Iván Ilích feels like crying, and wants to be petted and cried over; and there comes his associate, member Shébek, and, instead of crying and being petted, Iván Ilích assumes a serious, stern, pensive aspect, and from inertia expresses his opinion on the decree of the court of cassation, and stubbornly sticks to his view. This lie all around him and in himself more than anything else poisoned the last days of Iván Ilích's life.

[VIII]   It was morning. It was morning, because Gerásim went away, and Peter the lackey came in his place: he put out the candles, drew aside one curtain, and began softly to fix up the room. Whether it was morning or evening, Friday or Sunday, did not make the slightest difference,—it was all the same: the gnawing, agonizing pain, which did not subside for a minute; the consciousness of the hopelessly receding, but not yet receded life; the same impending, terrible, hateful death, which alone was reality, and still the same lie. Where could there be here days, weeks, and hours of the day?

"Do you command me to bring you tea?"

"His order demands that gentlemen should drink tea in the morning," he thought, but he said only:

"No."

"Do you not wish to go over to the divan?"

"He has to tidy up the room, and I am in his way,— I am an impurity, a nuisance," he thought, and all he said was:

"No, leave me."

The lackey bustled a little while. Iván Ilích extended his hand. Peter came up, ready to serve him.

"What do you wish?"

"The watch."

Peter got the watch which was lying under Iván Ilích's hand, and gave it to him.

"Half-past eight. Have they not got up yet?"

"Not yet, sir. Vasíli Ivánovich" (that was his son) "has gone to the gymnasium, and Praskóvya Fédorovna has commanded that she be wakened, if you should ask for her. Do you command me?"

"No, don't."

"Maybe I had better try some tea?" he thought.

"Yes, tea. Bring me tea."

Peter started to go out. Iván Ilích felt terribly at being alone.

"How can I keep him? Yes, the medicine."

"Peter, give me the medicine."

"Why not? Maybe the medicine will help me yet."

He took a spoonful and swallowed it.

"No, it will not help me. It is all nonsense and a deception," he decided, the moment he had the familiar, detestable, hopeless taste in his mouth. "No, I can no longer believe. But the pain, the pain, what is it for? If it would only stop for just a minute."

And he sobbed. Peter came back.

"No, go. Bring me some tea."

Peter went away. When Iván Ilích was left alone, he groaned, not so much from pain, no matter how terrible it was, as from despondency. "Always the same and the same, all these endless days and nights. If it would only come at once. What at once? Death, darkness. No, no. Anything is better than death!"

When Peter came back with the tea on a tray, Iván Ilích for a long time looked distractedly at him, being unable to make out who he was, or what he wanted. Peter was confounded by this look. When Peter looked confounded, Iván Ilích came to his senses.

"Yes," he said, "the tea; all right, put it down. Only help me to get washed, and let me have a clean shirt."

And Iván Ilích got up to wash himself. Stopping occasionally, he washed his hands and face, cleaned his teeth, began to comb his hair, and looked into the mirror. He felt terribly, especially so, because his hair lay flat over his pale brow.

As his shirt was being changed, he knew that he would feel more terribly still if he looked at his body, and so he did not look at himself. But all was ended. He put on his morning-gown, covered himself with a shawl, and sat down in a chair to his tea. For a minute he felt himself refreshed, but the moment he began to drink the tea there was again the same taste, and the same pain. He with difficulty finished his glass and lay down, stretching his legs. He lay down, and dismissed Peter.

Again the same. Now a drop of hope would sparkle, and now a sea of despair would be agitated, and all the time the pain, and the pain, and the despondency, and again the same and the same. He felt terribly despondent by himself and wanted to call some one in, but he knew in advance that in the presence of others it would be worse still.

"If I just had some morphine again,—I should forget. I will tell him, the doctor, to think out something else. It cannot go on this way, it cannot."

Thus an hour, two hours pass. But now there is the bell in the antechamber. Perhaps the doctor. Indeed, it is the doctor, fresh, vivacious, fat, jolly, with an expression which seems to say, "Now there you are all frightened, but we will fix it all in a minute." The doctor knows that this expression is of no use here, but he has put it on once for all and cannot take it off, like a man who in the morning puts on his dress coat and goes out calling.

The doctor rubs his hands briskly and in a consoling manner.

"I am cold. It is a cutting frost. Just let me get warmed up," he says with an expression which says that all that is necessary is for him to get warmed up, and as soon as he is warm he will fix it all.

"Well, how is it?"

Iván Ilích feels that the doctor wants to say, "How are our affairs?" but that he himself feels that it would not do to speak in this manner, and so he says, "How did you pass the night?"

Iván Ilích looks at the doctor with a questioning expression:

"Will you never feel ashamed of lying?"

But the doctor does not want to understand the expression, and Iván Ilích says:

"Just as terribly as ever. The pain does not pass away, does not subside. If it would stop just a little!"

"You patients are always like that. Well, sir, now, it seems, I am all warmed up, and even most exact Praskóvya Fédorovna would not be able to object to my temperature. Well, sir, good morning," and the doctor presses his hand.

Throwing aside his former playfulness, the doctor begins with a serious glance to investigate the patient, his pulse, his temperature, and there begin tappings and auscultations.

Iván Ilích knows full well and indubitably that all this is nonsense and mere deception, but when the doctor, getting down on his knees, stretches out over him, leaning his ear now higher up, and now lower down, and with a significant expression on his face makes over him all kinds of gymnastic evolutions, Iván Ilích submits to it, as he submitted to the speeches of the lawyers, though he knew well that they were ranting all the time, and why they were ranting.

The doctor was still kneeling on the divan, tapping at something, when Praskóvya Fédorovna's silk dress rustled at the door, and there was heard her reproach to Peter for not having announced to her the doctor's arrival.

She comes in, kisses her husband, and immediately proceeds to prove that she got up long ago, and that only by a misunderstanding did she fail to be present when the doctor came.

Iván Ilích looks at her, examines her whole figure, and finds fault with the whiteness, chubbiness, and cleanliness of her hands and neck, the gloss of her hair, and the sparkle of her vivacious eyes. He hates her with the whole strength of his soul. Her touch makes him suffer from an access of hatred toward her.

Her relation to him and his sickness is still the same. As the doctor had worked out for himself a relation to his patients, which he was unable to divest himself of, so she had worked out a certain relation to him,—that he was somehow not doing what he ought to do, and was himself to blame for it, and she lovingly reproached him for it,—and was unable to divest herself of this relation to him.

"Well, he pays no attention. He does not take the medicine on time. Above all else, he lies down in a position which, no doubt, is injurious to him,—with his legs up."

She told the doctor how he made Gerásim hold up his legs.

The doctor smiled a contemptuously kind smile:

"Well, what is to be done? These patients at times invent such foolish things,—but we can forgive them."

When the examination was ended, the doctor looked at his watch, and Praskóvya Fédorovna announced to Iván Ilích that she did not care what he would do, but she had sent for a famous doctor, who in company with Mikhaíl Danílovich (so the ordinary doctor was called) would make an examination and have a consultation.

"Don't object to this, if you please. I am doing this for my own sake," she said ironically, giving him to understand that she was doing everything for his sake, and in this way did not give him the right to refuse her. He was silent, and frowned. He felt that this lie which surrounded him was becoming so entangled that it was getting hard to make out anything.

She was doing everything about him for her own sake, and she told him that she was doing for herself everything that she really was doing for herself, as though it were such an incredible thing that he ought to understand it as the exact opposite.

Indeed, at half-past eleven the famous doctor arrived. Again there were auscultations and significant conversations in his presence and in another room about the kidney and the blind gut, and questions and answers with such significant looks that instead of the real question about life and death, which alone now stood before him, there again came forward the question about the kidney and the blind gut, which were not acting as they ought to, and which Mikhaíl Danílovich and the celebrity will for this reason attack and compel to get better.

The famous doctor departed with a serious, but not with a hopeless, look. In reply to the timid question, which Iván Ilích directed to him with eyes raised to him and shining with terror and hope, as to whether there was any possibility of recovery, he replied that he could not guarantee it, but that it was possible. The glance of hope with which Iván Ilích saw the doctor off was so pitiful that, seeing it, Praskóvya Fédorovna even burst out into tears as she went out of the cabinet, in order to give the famous doctor his fee.

The elation of spirit, produced by the doctor's encouragement, did not last long. There were again the same room, the same pictures, curtains, wallpaper, bottles, and the same paining, suffering body. Iván Ilích began to groan; they gave him an injection, and he forgot himself.

When he came to, it was growing dark; they brought him his dinner. He took with difficulty some soup, and again it was the same, and again nightfall.

After dinner, at seven o'clock, the room was entered by Praskóvya Fédorovna, who was dressed as for an evening entertainment, with swelling, raised up breasts, and traces of powder on her face. She had talked to him in the morning of going to the theatre. Sarah Bernhardt was in the city, and they had a box which he had insisted that they should take. Now he forgot about it, and her attire offended him. But he concealed his offence when he recalled that he himself had insisted on their taking a box and going, because this was for the children an educational, æsthetic enjoyment.

Praskóvya Fédorovna came in satisfied with herself, but seemingly guilty. She sat down for awhile, asked him about his health, as he saw, merely to ask, but not to find out, knowing that there was nothing to find out, and began to speak of what she wanted to speak of, that she would not go at all if the box had not been engaged, and that with her were going Hélène, and their daughter, and Petríshchev (their daughter's fiancé), and that it was impossible to let them go by themselves. It really would give her more pleasure to stay at home; but he must be sure and do in her absence according to the doctor's prescription.

"Yes, Fédor Petróvich" (the fiancé) "wanted to come in. May he? And Líza."

"Let them come in."

The daughter came in. She was all dressed up, with a bared youthful body, that body which caused him to suffer so much; but she exposed it. She was strong, healthy, apparently in love, and vexed at the disease, suffering, and death, which interfered with her happiness.

There entered also Fédor Petróvich, in dress coat, with his hair fixed à la Capoul, with a long sinewy neck, tightly surrounded by a white collar, with an enormous white chest and close-fitting trousers over powerful thighs, with a white handkerchief drawn over his hand, and with an opera hat.

After him imperceptibly crawled in the little gymnasiast, in a brand-new uniform,—poor fellow,—and with terrible blue marks under his eyes, the meaning of which Iván Ilích knew.

His son always looked pitiful to him, and terrible was his frightened and compassionate glance. Besides Gerásim, it seemed to Iván Ilích, Vásya was the only one who understood and pitied him.

All sat down, and again asked about his health. There ensued a silence. Líza asked her mother about the opera-glass. Mother and daughter exchanged words about who was at fault for having mislaid it. It was an unpleasant incident.

Fédor Petróvich asked Iván Ilích whether he had seen Sarah Bernhardt. At first Iván Ilích did not understand what it was they were asking him, but later he said:

"No, and have you seen her already?"

"Yes, in Adrienne Lecouvreur."

Praskóvya Fédorovna said that she was particularly good in this or that. Her daughter objected. There ensued a conversation about the art and the realism of her play, that very conversation which is always one and the same.

In the middle of the conversation Fédor Petróvich looked at Iván Ilích, and grew silent. The others looked at him, too, and grew silent. Iván Ilích was looking with glistening eyes ahead of him, apparently vexed at them. It was necessary to mend all this, but it was impossible to do so. It was necessary to interrupt the silence. Nobody could make up his mind to do so, and all felt terribly at the thought that now the decent lie would somehow be broken, and every one would see clearly how it all was. Líza was the first to make up her mind. She interrupted the silence. She wanted to conceal what all were experiencing, but she gave herself away:

"If we are to go at all, it is time we started," she said, looking at her watch, a present from her father, and she smiled at the young man a faint, significant smile about something which they alone knew, and got up, causing her dress to rustle.

All arose, said good-bye, and departed.

When they went out, it seemed to Iván Ilích that he was feeling easier: there was no lie,—it departed with them,—but the pain was still left. The old pain, the old terror made him feel neither harder, nor easier. It was all worse.

Again minute after minute elapsed, and hour after hour, and again the same, and again no end, and more and more terrible the inevitable end.

"Yes, call Gerásim," he answered to Peter's question.

[IX] HIS wife returned late in the night. She entered on tiptoe, but he heard her. He opened his eyes and hastened to shut them again. She wanted to send Gerásim away and to sit up with him. He opened his eyes, and said:

"No, go."

"Do you suffer very much?"

"It makes no difference."

"Take some opium."

He consented, and took some. She went away.

Until about three o'clock he was in agonizing oblivion. It seemed to him that he with his pain was being shoved somewhere into a narrow, black, and deep bag, and shoved farther and farther, without coming out of it. And this terrible act was accompanied by suffering. And he was afraid, and wanted to go through the bag, and fought, and helped along. And suddenly he tore away, and fell, and woke up. The same Gerásim was sitting at his feet on the bed, drowsing calmly and patiently. But Iván Ilích was lying, his emaciated, stockinged feet resting on Gerásim's shoulders, and there was the same candle with the shade, and the same uninterrupted pain.

"Go away, Gerásim," he whispered.

"Never mind, sir, I will sit up."

"No, go."

He took off his feet, and lay down sidewise on his arm and began to feel pity for himself. He just waited for Gerásim to go to the adjoining room, and no longer restrained himself, but burst out into tears, like a child. He wept on account of his helplessness, his terrible loneliness, the cruelty of men, the cruelty of God, the absence of God.

"Why hast Thou done all this? Why didst Thou bring me to this? Why, why dost Thou torment me so terribly?"

He did not expect any answer, and was weeping because there was no answer and could be none. The pain rose again, but he did not stir, did not call. He said to himself:

"Go on, strike me! But for what? What have I done to Thee? For what?"

Then he grew silent and stopped not only weeping, but also breathing, and became all attention: it was as though he listened, not to the voice which spoke with sounds, but to the voice of his soul, to the train of thoughts which rose in him.

"What do you want?" was the first clear expression, capable of being uttered in words, which he heard.

"What do you want? What do you want?" he repeated to himself. "What? Not to suffer. To live!" he answered.

And again he abandoned himself wholly to attention, to such tense listening, that his pain even did not distract him.

"To live? To live how?" asked the voice of his soul.

"To live as I used to live before,—well, pleasantly."

"As you lived before, well and pleasantly?" asked a voice. And he began in imagination to pass in review the best minutes of his pleasant life. But, strange to say, all these best minutes of his pleasant life now seemed to him to be different from what they had seemed to be before,—all of them, except the first recollections of childhood. There, in childhood, there had been something really agreeable, with which it would be possible to live if life should return; but the man who had experienced those pleasant sensations was no more; it was like a recollection of somebody else.

As soon as there began that which resulted in the present man, in Iván Ilích, everything which then had appeared as joys now melted in his sight and changed into something insignificant and even abominable.

And the farther away from childhood and nearer to the present, the more insignificant and doubtful were the joys. This began with the law school. There had been there something truly good; there had been there merriment, friendship, hopes. But in the upper classes these good minutes had happened more rarely; those were the recollections of the love of woman. Then all got mixed, and there was still less of what was good. Farther on there was still less of what was good, and the farther, the less.

"The marriage—so sudden, and the disenchantment, and the odour from my wife's mouth, and sensuality, and hypocrisy! And this dead service, and these cares about the money, and thus passed a year, and two, and ten, and twenty,—all the time the same. The farther, the deader. It was as though I were going evenly down-hill, imagining that I was going up-hill. And so it was. In public opinion I went up-hill,—and just in that proportion did my life vanish under me.—And now it is all done,—go and die!

"So what is this? Why? Impossible. It cannot be that life should be so senseless and so abominable! And if it has indeed been so abominable and meaningless, what sense is there in dying, and in dying with suffering? Something is wrong.

"Perhaps I did not live the proper way," it suddenly occurred to him. "But how can that be, since I did everything that was demanded of me?" he said to himself, and immediately he repelled from himself this only solution of the whole enigma of life and of death, as something totally impossible.

"What do you want now? To live? To live how? To live as you live in the court, when the bailiff proclaims, 'The court is coming!' The court is coming, the court is coming!" he repeated to himself. "Here is the court! But I am not guilty!" he shouted in anger. "For what?" And he stopped weeping and, turning his face to the wall, began to think of nothing but this one thing: "Why, for what is all this terror?"

But, no matter how much he thought, he found no answer. And when the thought occurred to him, and it occurred to him often, that all this was due to the fact that he had not lived in the proper way, he immediately recalled all the regularity of his life, and dispelled this strange thought.

[X]   Two more weeks passed. Iván Ilích no longer rose from his divan. He did not want to lie in his bed, and lay on the divan. Lying nearly all the time with his face to the wall, he suffered in loneliness the same insoluble sufferings, and in loneliness thought the same insoluble thought. "What is this? Is this really death?" And an inner voice answered him: "Yes, it is." "What are these torments for?" and the voice answered: "For no special reason." After that and outside of that there was nothing.

From the very beginning of his sickness, from the first time that he went to see the doctor, his life was divided into two opposite moods which gave way to one another: now it was despair and the expectancy of incredible and terrible death, and now hope and an absorbing observation of the activity of his body. Now there was before his eyes nothing but his kidney or gut, which had for the time being deflected from the fulfilment of its obligations, and now it was the one incomprehensible, terrible death, from which it was impossible to be freed in any way whatever.

These two moods alternated from the very beginning of his sickness; but the farther his disease proceeded, the more doubtful and fantastic did his imagination grow in respect to the kidney, and the more real came to be the consciousness of impending death.

He needed but to recall what he had been three months before and what he now was, to recall how evenly he had been going down-hill, in order that every possibility of hope should be destroyed.

During the last stage of the loneliness in which he was, lying with his face turned to the back of the divan, of that loneliness amidst a populous city and his numerous acquaintances and his family,—a loneliness fuller than which can nowhere be found,—neither at the bottom of the sea, nor in the earth,—during the last stages of this terrible loneliness Iván Ilích lived in his imagination only in the past. One after another there arose before him pictures of his past. They always began with what was nearest in time and ran back to what was most remote, to childhood, and there they stopped. If Iván Ilích thought of the stewed prunes which he was offered to-day to eat, he recalled the raw, wrinkled French prunes of his childhood, their particular taste, and the abundance of saliva when he reached the stone, and side by side with this recollection of the taste there arose a whole series of recollections from that time,—the nurse, the brother, the toys.

"I must not think of this,—it is too painful," Iván Ilích said to himself, and again transferred himself to the present. A button on the back of the divan and wrinkles in the morocco. "The morocco is expensive,—not durable,—there was a quarrel on account of it. It was a different kind of morocco, and a different quarrel, when we tore father's portfolio, and were punished, and mother brought us patties." And again his thoughts stopped at his childhood, and again he felt a pain, and tried to dispel it and to think of something else.

And again, together with this train of his recollections, another train of recollections passed through his soul as to how his disease increased and grew. Again it was the same: the farther back, the more there was of life. There was more good in life and more of life itself. Both blended.

"Just as my suffering is growing worse and worse, so my whole life has been getting worse and worse," he thought. There was one bright point there behind, in the beginning of life, and then everything grows blacker and blacker, and goes faster and faster. "In inverse proportion to the square of the distance from death," thought Iván Ilích. And this representation of a stone flying downward with increasing rapidity fell into his soul. Life, a series of increasing sufferings, flew more and more rapidly toward its end, a most terrible suffering. "I fly—" He trembled, and shook, and wanted to resist; but he knew that it was useless to resist, and again he looked at the back of the divan with eyes weary from looking, which could not help but look at what was in front of him, and he waited and waited for that terrible fall, push, and destruction.

"It is impossible to resist," he said to himself. "But if I only understood what it is all for. And this is impossible. One might be able to explain it, if it could be said that I had not lived properly. But that can by no means be asserted," he said to himself, as he recalled all the lawfulness, regularity, and decency of his life. "It is impossible to admit this," he said to himself, smiling with his lips, as though some one could see this smile of his and be deceived by it. "There is no explanation! Torment, death—Why?"

[XI] THUS passed two weeks. During these weeks there took place an event which had been desired by Iván Ilích and his wife. Petríshchev made a formal proposal. This happened in the evening. On the following day Praskóvya Fédorovna entered her husband's room, wondering how she should announce Fédor Petróvich's proposal to Iván Ilích, but that very night Iván Ilích had taken a turn for the worst. Praskóvya Fédorovna found him on the same divan, but in a new position. He was lying on his back and groaning and looking in front of him with an arrested glance.

She began to speak of the medicines. He transferred his look to her. She did not finish saying what she had begun,—such malice, especially to her, was expressed in this glance.

"For Christ's sake, let me die in peace," he said.

She wanted to go away, but just then her daughter entered, and she went up to him to greet him. He looked at his daughter in the same way as at his wife, and in reply to her questions about his health he said dryly to her that he would soon free them all from himself. Both grew silent and, after sitting awhile, went out.

"In what way is it our fault?" Líza said to her mother. "It is as though we had done something. I am sorry for papa, but why does he torment us?"

The doctor arrived at the usual hour. Iván Ilích answered him, "Yes, no," without taking his glance of fury from him, and finally said:

"You know yourself that nothing will help me, so let it go."

"We can alleviate your suffering," said the doctor.

"You cannot do that, either,—let it go."

The doctor went into the drawing-room and informed Praskóvya Fédorovna that he was in a very bad state, and that there was one means,— opium,—in order to alleviate the sufferings, which must be terrible.

The doctor said that his physical suffering was terrible, and that was true; but more terrible than his physical suffering was his moral suffering, and in this lay his chief agony.

His moral suffering consisted in this, that on that night, as he looked upon Gerásim's sleepy, good-natured face with its prominent cheek-bones, it suddenly occurred to him, "What if indeed my whole life, my conscious life, was not the right thing?"

It occurred to him that what before had presented itself to him as an utter impossibility, namely, that he had passed all his life improperly, might after all be the truth. It occurred to him that those faint endeavours at struggling against that which was regarded as good by persons in superior positions, faint endeavours which he had immediately repelled from himself, might be real, while everything else might be the wrong thing. He tried to defend all this to himself. And suddenly he felt the weakness of everything which he was defending, and there was nothing to defend.

"And if this is so," he said to himself, "and I go away from life with the consciousness of having ruined everything which was given me, and that it is impossible to mend it, what then?"

He lay down on his back and began to pass his life in review in an entirely new fashion. When, in the morning, he saw the lackey, then his wife, then his daughter, then the doctor, every one of their motions, every word of theirs confirmed for him the terrible truth which had been revealed to him the night before. In them he saw himself, all that he had been living by, and saw clearly that all that was not the right thing, that it was all a terrible, huge deception, which concealed both life and death. This consciousness increased, multiplied tenfold his physical sufferings. He groaned and tossed about and picked at his clothes. It seemed to him that his clothes choked and suffocated him. And for this he hated them.

He was given a big dose of opium and he fell into oblivion, but at dinner the same began once more. He drove all away from himself, and tossed from one place to another.

His wife came to him, and said:

"Jean, my darling, do this for me." ("For me?") "It cannot hurt, and frequently it helps. Healthy people frequently do it."

He opened his eyes wide.

"What? Communion? What for? It is not necessary! Still—"

She burst out weeping.

"Yes, my dear? I will send for our priest,—he is such a nice man."

"All right, very well," he muttered.

When the priest came and took his confession, he softened, seemed to feel a relief from his doubts, and so from his suffering, and for a moment was assailed by hope. He began once more to think of his blind gut and the possibility of mending it. He took his communion with tears in his eyes.

When, after the communion, he was put down on the bed, he for a moment felt easier, and again there appeared hope of life. He began to think of the operation which had been proposed to him. "I want to live, to live," he said to himself. His wife came back to congratulate him; she said the customary words, and added:

"Truly, are you not feeling better?"

Without looking at her, he said, "Yes."

Her attire, her figure, the expression of her face, the sound of her voice, —everything told him one and the same thing: "It is not the right thing. Everything which you have lived by is a lie, a deception, which conceals from you life and death." The moment he thought so, there arose his hatred, and with his hatred came physical, agonizing sufferings, and with the sufferings the consciousness of inevitable, near perdition. Something new had taken place: something began to screw up and shoot, and to choke him.

The expression of his face, when he uttered, "Yes," was terrible. Having said this "Yes," he looked straight into her face and with unusual rapidity for his weakness turned his face downward, and called out:

"Go away, go away, leave me alone!"

[XII] FROM this moment there began that cry which lasted for three days and was so terrible that it was not possible to hear it without horror through two doors. At the moment when he answered his wife, he understood that he was lost, that there was no return, that the end had come, the real end, and yet his doubt was not solved,—it remained the doubt it had been.

"Oo! Oo! Oo!" he cried, in various intonations. He had begun to cry, "I do not want to!" and continued to cry the sound "oo."

During the three days, in the course of which time did not exist for him, he fluttered about in that black bag whither an invisible, invincible force was shoving him. He struggled as a prisoner condemned to death struggles in the hands of the hangman, knowing that he cannot be saved; and with every minute he felt that, in spite of all the efforts of the struggle, he was coming nearer and nearer to what terrified him. He felt that his suffering consisted in his being shoved into that black hole, and still more in his not being able to get through it. What hindered him from crawling through was the consciousness of this, that his life was good. This justification of his life grappled him and did not allow him to get on and tormented him more than anything.

Suddenly a certain force pushed him in the chest and in the side, and still more compressed his throat, and he fell into the hole, and there, at the end of the hole, there was some light. What happened to him was what happens in a railway car, when a man thinks that he is riding forward, while he is riding backward, and suddenly discovers the real direction.

"Yes, it was all the wrong thing," he said to himself, "but that is nothing. It is possible, it is possible to do the right thing. What is the right thing?" he asked himself, and suddenly grew quiet.

This happened at the end of the third day, two hours before his death. At just this time the little gymnasiast stole quietly up to his father, and walked over to his bed. The dying man was crying pitifully and tossing about his hands. His hand fell on the head of the little gymnasiast. The little gymnasiast caught it and pressed it to his lips, and burst out weeping.

Just then Iván Ilích tumbled in and saw the light, and it was revealed to him that his life had not been what it ought to have been, but that it was still possible to mend it. He asked himself: "What is the right thing?" and he grew silent, and listened. Here he felt that some one was kissing his hand. He opened his eyes and glanced at his son. He was sorry for him. His wife came up to him. He glanced at her. She looked at him with a desperate expression, her mouth being wide open and the tears remaining unwiped on her nose. He was sorry for her.

"Yes, I am tormenting them," he thought. "They are sorry, but they will be better off when I am dead." That was what he meant to say, but he did not have the strength to utter it. "However, what is the use of talking? I must do," he thought. He indicated his son to his wife with his glance, and said:

"Take him away—am sorry—and you, too—"

He wanted to add, "Forgive," but said, "Forgigive," and being unable to correct himself, he waved his hand, knowing that who needed would understand.

Suddenly it became clear to him that what had been vexing him and could not come out, now was coming out all at once, from two sides, from ten sides, from all sides. They were to be pitied; it was necessary to do something to save them pain, to free them and free himself from these sufferings.

"How good and how simple!" he thought. "And the pain?" he asked himself. "What of it? Well, pain, where are you?"

He began to listen.

"Yes, here it is. Well, let it pain."

"And death? Where is it?"

And he sought his former customary fear of death, and could not find it.
"Where is it? What death?"
There was no fear, because there was also no death.
Instead of death there was a light.
"So this it is!" he suddenly spoke out in a loud voice "What joy!"
For him all this took place in one moment, and the significance of this moment no longer changed. But for those who were present the agony lasted two hours longer. Something palpitated in his heart, and his emaciated body jerked. Then the palpitation and the râle grew rarer and rarer.
"It is ended!" some one said over him.
He heard these words and repeated them in his soul.
"Death is ended," he said to himself. "It is no more."
He inhaled the air, stopped in the middle of his breath, stretched himself, and died.
March 22, 1886.

Rilke

CHAMBERLAIN BRIGGE'S DEATH*

[I]   This excellent hôtel is very ancient. Even in King Clovis' time people died in it in a number of beds. Now they are dying there in 559 beds. Factory-like, of course. Where production is so enormous an individual death is not so nicely carried out; but then that doesn't matter. It is quantity that counts. Who cares anything today for a finely-finished death? No one. Even the rich, who could after all afford this luxury of dying in full detail, are beginning to be careless and indifferent; the wish to have a death of one's own is growing ever rarer. A while yet, and it will be just as rare as a life of one's own. Heavens, it's all there. One arrives, one finds a life, ready made, one has only to put it on. One wants to leave or one is compelled to: anyway, no effort: Voilà votre mort, monsieur. One dies just as it comes; one dies the death that belongs to the disease one has (for since one has come to know all diseases, one knows, too, that the different lethal terminations belong to the diseases and not to the people; and the sick person has so to speak nothing to do).

* Rainer Maria Rilke (1875–1926): German poet. *The Notebooks of Malte Laurids Brigge* is Rilke's major prose work. The narrator of *Notebooks*, a young man examining the meaning of his life, vividly describes his inner feelings and thoughts while remembering his childhood and relating powerful scenes that have influenced his life. Portions of Books I and II are reproduced here. From THE NOTEBOOKS OF MALTE LAURIDS BRIGGE by Rainer Maria Rilke. Translated by M. D. Herter Norton. By permission of W. W. Norton & Company, Inc., New York and The Hogarth Press Ltd., London. Copyright 1949 by W. W. Norton & Company, Inc.

In sanatoria, where people die so willingly and with so much gratitude to doctors and nurses, they die from one of the deaths attached to the institution; that is favorably regarded. But when one dies at home, it is natural to choose that polite death of genteel circles, with which a first-class funeral is so to say inaugurated, with the whole sequence of its delightful formalities. The poor then stand outside such a house and gaze their fill. Their death is, of course, banal, without any fuss. They are glad when they find one that fits approximately. Too large it may be: one always keeps growing a little. Only when it does not meet round the chest or when it strangles, then there is difficulty.

When I think back to my home, where there is nobody left now, I imagine that formerly this must have been otherwise. Formerly one knew (or perhaps one guessed it) that one had one's death within one, as a fruit its kernel. The children had a little death within them and the grown-ups a big one. The women had it in their womb and the men in their breast. One *had* it, and that gave one a singular dignity and a quiet pride.

My grandfather, old Chamberlain Brigge, still looked as if he carried a death within him. And what a death it was: two months long and so loud that it could be heard as far off as the manor farm.

The long, old manor house was too small for this death; it seemed as if wings would have to be added, for the chamberlain's body grew larger and larger, and he wanted continually to be carried out of one room into another, falling into a terrible rage when, though the day had not yet come to an end, there was no room left in which he had not already lain. Then the whole troop of men-servants, maids and dogs, that he always had about him, had to go upstairs with him, under the usherance of the major-domo, into the room in which his saintly mother had died, which had been kept exactly as she had left it twenty-three years before and in which no one else had ever been allowed to set foot. Now the whole pack burst in. The curtains were drawn back, and the robust light of a summer afternoon inspected all the shy, frightened objects and turned clumsily around in the suddenly opened-up mirrors. And the people did likewise. There were chamber-maids who, in their curiosity, did not know where their hands were loitering, young men-servants who gaped at everything, and older retainers who went about trying to recollect all that had been told them about this close-locked room in which they now found themselves at last.

But the dogs especially seemed to find their sojourn in a room where everything had a smell uncommonly exciting. The tall, lean Russian wolf-hounds ran busily back and forth behind the armchairs, crossed the apartment in long dance-steps with a swinging movement, reared like heraldic animals, and looked, resting their slender paws on the white-and-gold window-sill, with tense pointed faces and backdrawn foreheads, to right and left out into the courtyard. Small glove-yellow dachshunds sat in the large silk-upholstered easy-chair near the window, looking as though everything were quite in order, and a sullen-looking rubican setter rubbed his back along the edge of a gilt-legged table, causing the Sèvres cups on its painted tray to tremble.

Yes, for these absent-minded, drowsy things it was a terrible time. From books that some hasty hand had clumsily opened rose-leaves would tumble, to be trampled underfoot; small fragile objects were seized, and, when they were immediately broken, quickly put back again; many hidden things, too, were thrust beneath curtains, or even flung behind the gilt net-work of the fire-screen and from time to time something fell, fell muffled on carpeting, fell clear on the hard parquetry, but here and there it smashed, shattering sharply or cracking apart almost inaudibly, for these things, pampered as they were, could not survive any sort of fall.

And had it occurred to anyone to ask what caused all this, what had called down upon this anxiously guarded room the full measure of destruction,—there would have been but one answer: Death.

The death of Chamberlain Christoph Detlev Brigge at Ulsgaard. For he lay, welling large out of his dark blue uniform, in the middle of the floor and never stirred. In his big, stranger's face, no longer familiar to anyone, the eyes had fallen shut: he did not see what was happening. They had tried at first to lay him on the bed, but this he had resisted, for he detested beds since those first nights in which his illness had grown. Besides, the bed up there had proved too small, so nothing else remained but to lay him thus upon the carpet; for downstairs again he had refused to go.

So now he lay there, and one might think that he had died. The dogs, as it slowly began to grow dark, had one after the other squeezed through the crack in the door. Only the rubican setter with the sullen face sat beside his master, and one of his broad, tufted forepaws lay on Christoph Detlev's big, grey hand. Most of the servants, too, were now standing outside in the white corridor, which was brighter than the room; those, however, who still remained within glanced furtively now and then at the great darkening heap in the middle, and they wished that it were nothing more than a large garment over some rotten thing.

But it was something more. It was a voice, that voice which seven weeks before no one had known yet: for it was not the voice of the chamberlain. It was not Christoph Detlev to whom this voice belonged, but Christoph Detlev's death.

Christoph Detlev's death had been living at Ulsgaard for many, many days now and had spoken to everyone and demanded: demanded to be carried, demanded the blue room, demanded the little salon, demanded the large hall. Demanded the dogs, demanded that people should laugh, talk, play and be quiet and all at the same time. Demanded to see friends, women, and people who were dead, and demanded to die itself: demanded. Demanded and shouted.

For when night had fallen and those of the overwearied domestics who were not on watch tried to go to sleep, then Christoph Detlev's death would shout, shout and groan, roar so long and so constantly that the dogs, at first howling along with him, were silent and did not dare lie down, but stood on their long, slender, trembling legs, and were afraid. And when they heard it in the village roaring through the spacious, silvery, Danish summer night, they rose from their beds as if there were a thunderstorm, put on their clothes and remained sitting round the lamp without a word until it was over. And women near their time were laid in the most remote rooms and in the most impenetrable closets; but they heard it, they heard it, as if it were in their own bodies, and they pled to be allowed to get up too, and came, white and wide, and sat among the others with their blurred faces. And the cows that were calving at that time were helpless and bound, and from the body of one they tore the dead fruit with all the entrails, as it would not come at all. And everyone did their daily work badly and forgot to bring in the hay, because they spent the day dreading the night and because they were so fagged out by all their continuous watchings and terrified arisings, that they could not remember anything. And when they went on Sundays to the white, peaceful church, they prayed that there might no longer be a master at Ulsgaard: for this was a dreadful master. And what they all thought and prayed the pastor said aloud from the height of his pulpit; for he also had no nights any more and could not understand God. And the bell said it, having found a terrible rival that boomed the whole night through, and against which, even though it took to sounding with all its metal, it could do nothing. Indeed, they all said it; and there was one among the young men who dreamed that he had gone to the manor-house and killed the master with his pitch-fork; and they were so exasperated, so done, so overwrought, that they all listened as he told his dream, and, quite unconsciously, looked at him to see if he were really equal to such a deed. Thus did they feel and speak throughout the whole district where, only a few weeks before, the chamberlain had been loved and pitied. But though they talked thus, nothing changed. Christoph Detlev's death, which dwelt at Ulsgaard, was not to be hurried. It had come to stay for ten weeks, and for ten weeks it stayed. And during that time it was more master than ever Christoph Detlev Brigge had been; it was like a king who, afterward and forever, is called the Terrible.

That was not the death of just any dropsical person; it was the wicked, princely death which the chamberlain had carried within him and nourished on himself his whole life long. All excess of pride, will and lordly vigor that he himself had not been able to consume in his quiet days, had passed into his death, that death which now sat, dissipating, at Ulsgaard.

How the chamberlain would have looked at anyone who asked of him that he should die any other death than this. He was dying his own hard death.

And when I think of the others whom I have seen or about whom I have heard: it is always the same. They all have had a death of their own. Those men who carried theirs inside their armor, within, like a prisoner; those women who grew very old and small, and then on a huge bed, as on a stage, before the whole family, the household and the dogs, passed away in discreet and seignorial dignity. Even the children, and the very little ones at that, did not die just any child's death; they pulled themselves together and died that which they already were, and that which they would have become.

And what a melancholy beauty it gave to women when they were pregnant and stood there, and in their big bodies, upon which their slender hands instinctively rested, were *two* fruits: a child and a death. Did not the dense, almost nourishing smile on their quite vacant faces come from their sometimes thinking that both were growing? . . .

[II]   Since then I have reflected a good deal on the fear of death, not without taking into consideration certain personal experiences of my own. I believe I may well say that I have felt it. It has overtaken me in the busy town, in the midst of people, often without any reason. Often, indeed, there have been abundant reasons; when for example a person on a bench fainted and everybody stood around and looked at him, and he was already far beyond fear: then I had his fear. Or that time in Naples: that young creature sat there opposite me in the street car and died. At first it looked like a fainting spell; we even drove on for a while. But then there was no doubt that we had to stop. And behind us vehicles halted and piled up, as though there would never be any more moving in that direction. The pale, stout girl might have quietly died like that, leaning against the woman beside her. But her mother would not allow this. She contrived all possible difficulties for her. She disordered her clothes and poured something into her mouth which could no longer retain anything. She rubbed her forehead with a liquid someone had brought, and when the eyes, at that, rolled back a little, she began to shake her to make her gaze come forward again. She shouted into those eyes that heard nothing, she pushed and pulled the whole thing to and fro like a doll, and finally she raised her arm and struck the puffy face with all her might, so that it should not die. That time I was afraid.

But I had already been afraid before. For example, when my dog died. The one who laid the blame on me once and for all. He was very sick. I had been kneeling beside him the whole day, when he suddenly gave a bark, jerky and short, as he used to do when a stranger entered. A bark like that had been agreed on between us for such cases, and I glanced involuntarily at the door. But it was already in him. I anxiously sought his eyes, and he too sought mine; but not to bid me farewell. His look was hard and surprised. He reproached me with having allowed it to enter. He was convinced I could have prevented it. It was now clear that he had always overrated me. And there was no time left to explain to him. He continued to gaze at me surprised and solitary, until it was over.

Or I was afraid when in autumn, after the first night frosts, the flies came into the rooms and revived once again in the warmth. They were singularly dried up and took fright at their own buzzing; one could see they didn't quite know what they were doing. They sat there for hours and let themselves be, until it occurred to them that they were still alive; then they flung themselves blindly in every direction and didn't know what to do when they got there, and one could hear them falling down again here and there and elsewhere. And finally they crawled about everywhere and slowly strewed death all over the room.

But even when I was alone I could be afraid. Why should I pretend that those nights had never been, when in fear of death I sat up, clinging to the fact that sitting at least was still something alive: that the dead did not sit. This always happened in one of those chance rooms which promptly left me in the lurch when things went badly with me, as if they feared to be cross-examined and become involved in my troubles. There I sat, probably looking so dreadful that nothing had the courage to stand by me; not even the candle, which I had just done the service of lighting it, would have anything to do with me. It burned away there by itself, as in an empty room. My last hope then was always the window. I imagined that outside there, there still might be something that belonged to me, even now, even in this sudden poverty of dying. But scarcely had I looked thither when I wished the window had been barricaded, blocked up, like the wall. For now I knew that things were going on out there in the same indifferent way, that out there, too, there was nothing but my loneliness. The loneliness I had brought upon myself and to the greatness of which my heart no longer stood in any sort of proportion. People came to my mind whom I had once left, and I did not understand how one could forsake people.

My God, my God, if any such nights await me in the future, leave me at least one of those thoughts that I have sometimes been able to pursue! It is not unreasonable, this that I ask; for I know that they were born of my very fear, because my fear was so great. When I was a boy, they struck me in the face and told me I was a coward. That was because I was still bad at being afraid. Since then, however, I have learned to be afraid with real fear, fear that increases only when the force that engenders it increases. We have no idea of this force, except in our fear. For it is so utterly inconceivable, so totally opposed to us, that our brain disintegrates at the point where we strain ourselves to think it. And yet, for some time now I have believed that it is *our own* force, all our own force that is still too great for us. It is true we do not know it; but is it not just that which is most our own of which we know the least? Sometimes I reflect on how heaven came to be and death: through our having distanced what is most precious to us, because there was still so much else to do beforehand and because it was not secure with us busy people. Now times have elapsed over this, and we have become accustomed to lesser things. We no longer recognize that which is our own and are terrified by its extreme greatness. May that not be?

SUGGESTIONS FOR FURTHER READING

Barrett, William, *Irrational Man, A Study in Existentialist Philosophy*. (Garden City, N.Y.: Doubleday & Co., 1958). *Excellent introduction to the main themes of existential thought for the beginning student. The early chapters present an interesting analysis of the cultural crisis that gave rise to existentialism.*

Brown, Norman O., *Life Against Death: The Psychoanalytical Meaning of History*. (New York: Vintage Books, 1959). *Part III is a presentation of a psychoanalytic exploration of the meaning of death.*

Groff, William Laurens, *Rainer Maria Rilke; Creative Anguish of a Modern Poet*. (Princeton, N.J.: Princeton University Press, 1956). *Part VII has an excellent account of Rilke's understanding of death and of the theme of death in Rilke's poetry.*

Harper, Ralph, *The Seventh Solitude: Man's Isolation in Kierkegaard, Dostoevsky, and Nietzsche*. (Baltimore: Johns Hopkins Press, 1965). *Focuses upon the themes of alienation, guilt, anxiety, and loneliness in the thought of three men who have contributed substantially to the existentialist tradition.*

Hubben, William, *Four Prophets of Our Destiny: Kierkegaard, Dostoevsky, Nietzsche, Kafka*. (New York: Macmillan Co., 1952). *Good presentation of how these four thinkers contributed to modern man's understanding of his predicament.*

Jackson, Robert Louis, *Dostoevsky's Underground Man in Russian Literature*. (Gravenhage: Mouton & Co., 1958). *The Introduction and first three chapters of this work contain a systematic analysis of Notes From Underground.*

Rilke, Rainer Maria, *Duino Elegies*. Tr. by J. B. Leishman and Stephen Spender. (New York: W. W. Norton & Co., 1939). *Rilke's greatest poetic work.*

PART 2

THE ORIGINS OF RELIGIOUS LIFE

Religious doctrines purport to answer questions arising out of the human situation and to interpret the structures of existence. Many other kinds of doctrines are set to the same task (e.g., psychotherapeutic theory), so this function of religious doctrine alone may not be used as a means of identifying which doctrines are in fact religious doctrines. Indeed, the critical mind will not want to prejudge the issue of what can count as a religious doctrine. The fact that an idea has its origin in "sacred" literature or tradition is insufficient for judging the idea religious, for the religiosity of the idea is then made to rest upon the religious character of the literature or tradition from which it is derived. How, then, does one decide that the literature or tradition is religious? Nor is the claim that an idea originates in religious consciousness any better, for once more, some warrant is needed to support such claims that the "consciousness" referred to is, indeed, "religious." The demand for such a warrant might be dispensed with provided there are no other interpretations of the consciousness in question and no other descriptions claimed for it. This is unlikely, especially in the context of a thoroughly empirical psychology. So the task of distinguishing religious experience and doctrines from other kinds of experience and doctrines remains a difficult one.

The task of uncovering the origins of the religious life is further complicated by the fact that religion is not reducible to a set of doctrinal concepts. The religious life also embraces a complex of human patterns of behavior, emotional sets, and social functions. Indeed, some interpreters of religion would want religion reduced to merely one of these.

Major problems do arise when we seek to understand such questions as: What is the origin of what we call religious life, including religious ideas, religious experience, the function of religion in human society, and the peculiar dispositional set of religion? Is it conceivable that religious ideas occur in the mind as the result of experiences which carry within them their own self-validating credentials? Are religious ideas the consequence of the fertility of the human imagination joined with the relative insecurity of human life? Is the complex that we call religious life reducible, in its entirety, to its social or psychological function?

The question of the meaning of religious living inevitably involves the question of how religion arises in human experience, with the problem of the origin of religious consciousness and religious behavior. What, then, are some of the different interpretations of the origins of religious life?

Chapter 4

Psychogenic origins of religion

The view that religion, in both its practical and theoretical aspects, has an anthropocentric origin and meaning probably has its roots in the earliest dawn of speculative concern with phenomena. The thesis, defended by both Sigmund Freud and Ludwig Feuerbach, that religions originate in man is not unique wtih them, but they developed such a consistent analysis of the meaning of religion, and their understandings of religion were so thoroughly integrated with their views of the human and cultural realities, that their statements of this particular position seem authoritative.

Freud's concern with religious beliefs and practices was part of his total effort to understand the dynamics of the human psyche and its complex relations with the physical and cultural world. Hence, he was not concerned with the theoretical abstractions of speculative religious philosophy or theology. The speculative content of religious thought, he believed, only served to conceal the hidden, but concrete nature of religion, which was emotional. He wished to remove masks in order to examine the human experience itself.

Freud approached the external, objective manifestations of religious belief much as he would approach, in therapy, the manifest content of a dream or the overt behavior of a troubled personality—as symptomatic of some psychic disorientation acting as defense mechanisms masking the real areas of trouble. The principle governing his prognosis of the human illness caused by religion paralleled his central therapeutic principle: where the *id* is, there shall the *ego* be. Where the reality principle is lacking, there it shall be brought into dynamic play in order to harmonize or adjust the forces of the psyche in their restless struggle and tension.

Freud's preoccupation with the genesis and growth of personality structures and with the dynamics attending that growth, is closely related to his critique and understanding of religion. Religious beliefs and practices are the consequence of emotional needs for authority and protection. In the adult personality's need for religion Freud sees childish needs for security reborn. Religion is a way in which man, by using intricately disguised childhood psychic models and mechanisms, seeks to remedy the threatening situations he encounters in everyday life. The holy powers of religious traditions are merely objects of wish fulfillment, and differ from private fantasies only to the extent that religious illusions are shared publicly. They are social phenomena, but that fact does not mitigate against their true natures; namely, that they are manifested dreams of the insecure and childlike psyche which has developed neither enough knowledge nor courage to live in an alien and indifferent environment.

The easy reconciliation to a hostile or indifferent world afforded the personality through religious beliefs and practices is purchased at too high a cost. Such apparent reconciliation is merely an evasion of what Freud sees as a permanent, unavoidable conflict between the self and others and the self and nature. Freud would have us exercise rational self-control, based upon increasing knowledge of the dynamics of the human psyche, its structures, and its relations with other selves and the world. Religious faith is no solution to real problems. Finding the source of religious ideas embedded in the human psyche, Freud concludes that religious beliefs are *entirely* human. If we seek answers to basic problems which arise out of the human predicament and situation, then shouldn't we realize that the answers which religious doctrine provides are inadequate and meaningless to the fundamental problems issuing from man's condition?

Ludwig Feuerbach also defends the thesis that the essence of religion is anthropological. Religion is an "objectification" of the most primitive needs of man, having no content that is not grounded in human nature. Historically, men achieve their first, indirect, knowledge of themselves through religious beliefs and practices. Feuerbach's claim is that a man knows himself first, in his essence, as projected outside of himself into a religious reality; only after encountering his own objectification as that religious reality can he discover and know his inner human nature.

Feuerbach's insistence that Divine Essence is man's objectification of his own nature might seem to be a rather thorough-going atheism, but an unqualified charge of atheism could only be founded on an inadequate comprehension of his thought. While denying the existence of a transcendental subject of divine predicates, Feuerbach does insist that the predicates or descriptive properties, when interpreted in terms of their human significance, have a profound religious meaning. It is this unusual distinction in his thought which has led certain thinkers to brand his perspective a "devout" atheism.

Freud and Feuerbach both insist upon the anthropocentric character of religion, although they do it for different reasons and within different interpretive frameworks. Both insist that the prototype for the divine being is the human being. Freud discovers the prototype in the father figure and finds the grounds for the projection of the earthly father upon a cosmic scale in infantile feelings of insecurity, helplessness, and alienation. Feuerbach, on the other hand, discovers the model for the divine essence in universal humanity, idealized and projected beyond the actual limitations of finitude. In confronting God, man confronts himself and his own humanity as well as experiencing the power of his primitive feelings and sensuality through this projected being. He meets himself in the divine other; in the history of religion we may discern man's continuous uncovering of himself through the mediation of the holy other.

Are the conflicts and questions that arise out of the human condition to be resolved within either of these frameworks? Has Freud or Feuerbach shown that the ground for the fundamental questions regarding human life is also the soil out of which the tree of knowledge and reconciliation grows?

Marx would object violently to the reduction of religion to anthropology made by Freud and Feuerbach. Such a reduction of the meaning of religion to either the dynamics of the human psyche or to the "essence" of humanity does not go nearly far enough. What is required, urges Marx, is a further criticism of the concrete circumstances of human life itself, and this in terms of its material (social and economic) conditions. Marx would agree with Freud that religious ideas are illusions and function narcotically; indeed, they reverse the actual conditions in which men live. However, the source of this deceptiveness is not to be found in the dynamics of the personality in its developing phases, but rather in the contradictory structures and interactions of social and economic life. While Feuerbach's principal aim was to expose and analyze the human essence of religion, Marx seeks to examine the historical conditions of human life in order to find within the secular world the need for the invention of a sacred world.

Moreover, contends Marx, the very existence of a perfected world beyond the earth points to the desperate circumstances of our historical life such that it requires the invention of a more heavenly state. In Marx's analysis, the constructive element is not limited to the discovery of the human origin of religion, but rather the additional revolutionary demand that the conditions requiring the existence of such a sacred world be abolished. In Marx, theological criticism becomes criticism of the secular world and, hence, a movement toward political reform.

Freud
RELIGION AS WISH FULFILLMENT*

[III] In what does the peculiar value of religious ideas lie?

We have spoken of the hostility to civilization which is produced by the pressure that civilization exercises, the renunciations of instinct which it

* Sigmund Freud (1856–1939): Austrian pioneer of the psychoanalytic movement. This selection is from The Future of An Illusion. This book marks a movement in Freud's thought away from clinical concerns to an interest in the problems of civilization. It is an investigation into the origin and meaning of religious ideas. Thanks to Sigmund Freud Copyrights Ltd., Mr. James Strachey and The Hogarth Press Ltd. for permission to quote from The Future of An Illusion (1927), vol. 21 of the Standard Edition of The Complete Psychological Works of Sigmund Freud. Reprinted here also by permission of LIVE-RIGHT Publishers, N.Y.

demands. If one imagines its prohibitions lifted—if, then, one may take any woman one pleases as a sexual object, if one may without hesitation kill one's rival for her love or anyone else who stands in one's way, if, too, one can carry off any of the other man's belongings without asking leave—how splendid, what a string of satisfactions one's life would be! True, one soon comes across the first difficulty: everyone else has exactly the same wishes as I have and will treat me with no more consideration than I treat him. And so in reality only one person could be made unrestrictedly happy by such a removal of the restrictions of civilization, and he would be a tyrant, a dictator, who had seized all the means to power. And even he would have every reason to wish that the others would observe at least one cultural commandment: 'thou shalt not kill'.

But how ungrateful, how short-sighted after all, to strive for the abolition of civilization! What would then remain would be a state of nature, and that would be far harder to bear. It is true that nature would not demand any restrictions of instinct from us, she would let us do as we liked; but she has her own particularly effective method of restricting us. She destroys us—coldly, cruelly, relentlessly, as it seems to us, and possibly through the very things that occasioned our satisfaction. It was precisely because of these dangers with which nature threatens us that we came together and created civilization, which is also, among other things, intended to make our communal life possible. For the principal task of civilization, its actual *raison d'être*, is to defend us against nature.

We all know that in many ways civilization does this fairly well already, and clearly as time goes on it will do it much better. But no one is under the illusion that nature has already been vanquished; and few dare hope that she will ever be entirely subjected to man. There are the elements, which seem to mock at all human control: the earth, which quakes and is torn apart and buries all human life and its works; water, which deluges and drowns everything in a turmoil; storms, which blow everything before them; there are diseases, which we have only recently recognized as attacks by other organisms; and finally there is the painful riddle of death, against which no medicine has yet been found, nor probably will be. With these forces nature rises up against us, majestic, cruel and inexorable; she brings to our mind once more our weakness and helplessness, which we thought to escape through the work of civilization. One of the few gratifying and exalting impressions which mankind can offer is when, in the face of an elemental catastrophe, it forgets the discordancies of its civilization and all its internal difficulties and animosities, and recalls the great common task of preserving itself against the superior power of nature.

For the individual, too, life is hard to bear, just as it is for mankind in general. The civilization in which he participates imposes some amount of privation on him, and other men bring him a measure of suffering, either in spite of the precepts of his civilization or because of its imperfections. To this are added the injuries which untamed nature—he calls it Fate—inflicts on him. One might suppose that this condition of things would result in a permanent state of anxious expectation in him and a severe injury to his natural narcissism. We know already how the individual reacts to the injuries which civilization and other men inflict on him: he develops a corresponding degree of resistance to the regulations of civilization and of hostility to it. But how does he defend himself against the superior powers of nature, of Fate, which threaten him as they threaten all the rest?

Civilization relieves him of this task; it performs it in the same way for all alike; and it is noteworthy that in this almost all civilizations act alike. Civilization does not call a halt in the task of defending man against nature, it merely pursues it by other means. The task is a manifold one. Man's self-regard, seriously menaced, calls for consolation; life and the universe must be robbed of their terrors; moreover his curiosity, moved, it is true, by the strongest practical interest, demands an answer.

A great deal is already gained with the first step: the humanization of nature. Impersonal forces and destinies cannot be approached; they remain eternally remote. But if the elements have passions that rage as they do in our own souls, if death itself is not something spontaneous but the violent act of an evil Will, if everywhere in nature there are Beings around us of a kind that we know in our own society, then we can breathe freely, can feel at home in the uncanny and can deal by psychical means with our senseless anxiety. We are still defenseless, perhaps, but we are no longer helplessly paralysed; we can at least react. Perhaps, indeed, we are not even defenseless. We can apply the same methods against these violent supermen outside that we employ in our own society; we can try to adjure them, to appease them, to bribe them, and, by so influencing them, we may rob them of a part of their power. A replacement like this of natural science by psychology not only provides immediate relief, but also points the way to a further mastering of the situation.

For this situation is nothing new. It has an infantile prototype, of which it is in fact only the continuation. For once before one has found oneself in a similar state of helplessness: as a small child, in relation to one's parents. One had reason to fear them, and especially one's father; and yet one was sure of his protection against the dangers one knew. Thus it was natural to assimilate the two situations. Here, too, wishing played its part, as it does in dream-life. The sleeper may be seized with a presentiment of death, which threatens to place him in the grave. But the dream-work knows how to select a condition that will turn even that dreaded event into a wish-fulfilment: the dreamer sees himself in an ancient Etruscan grave which he has climbed down into, happy to find his archaeological interests satisfied.[1] In the same way, a man makes the forces of nature not simply into persons with whom he can associate as he would with his equals—that would not do justice to the overpowering impression which those forces make on him—but he gives them the character of a father. He turns them into gods, following

---

[1] [This was an actual dream of Freud's, reported in Chapter VI (G) of *The Interpretation of Dreams* (1900a), *Standard Ed.*, 5, 454-5.]

in this, as I have tried to show,[2] not only an infantile prototype but a phylogenetic one.

In the course of time the first observations were made of regularity and conformity to law in natural phenomena, and with this the forces of nature lost their human traits. But man's helplessness remains and along with it his longing for his father, and the gods. The gods retain their threefold task: they must exorcize the terrors of nature, they must reconcile men to the cruelty of Fate, particularly as it is shown in death, and they must compensate them for the sufferings and privations which a civilized life in common has imposed on them.

But within these functions there is a gradual displacement of accent. It was observed that the phenomena of nature developed automatically according to internal necessities. Without doubt the gods were the lords of nature; they had arranged it to be as it was and now they could leave it to itself. Only occasionally, in what are known as miracles, did they intervene in its course, as though to make it plain that they had relinquished nothing of their original sphere of power. As regards the apportioning of destinies, an unpleasant suspicion persisted that the perplexity and helplessness of the human race could not be remedied. It was here that the gods were most apt to fail. If they themselves created Fate, then their counsels must be deemed inscrutable. The notion dawned on the most gifted people of antiquity that Moira [Fate] stood above the gods and that the gods themselves had their own destinies. And the more autonomous nature became and the more the gods withdrew from it, the more earnestly were all expectations directed to the third function of the gods—the more did morality become their true domain. It now became the task of the gods to even out the defects and evils of civilization, to attend to the sufferings which men inflict on one another in their life together and to watch over the fulfilment of the precepts of civilization, which men obey so imperfectly. Those precepts themselves were credited with a divine origin; they were elevated beyond human society and were extended to nature and the universe.

And thus a store of ideas is created, born from man's need to make his helplessness tolerable and built up from the material of memories of the helplessness of his own childhood and the childhood of the human race. It can clearly be seen that the possession of these ideas protects him in two directions—against the dangers of nature and Fate, and against the injuries that threaten him from human society itself. Here is the gist of the matter. Life in this world serves a higher purpose; no doubt it is not easy to guess what that purpose is, but it certainly signifies a perfecting of man's nature. It is probably the spiritual part of man, the soul, which in the course of time has so slowly and unwillingly detached itself from the body, that is the object of this elevation and exaltation. Everything that happens in this world is an expression of the intentions of an intelligence superior to us,

[2] [See Section 6 of the fourth essay in *Totem and Taboo* (1912–13), *Standard Ed.*, 13, 146 ff.]

which in the end, though its ways and byways are difficult to follow, orders everything for the best—that is, to make it enjoyable for us. Over each one of us there watches a benevolent Providence which is only seemingly stern and which will not suffer us to become a plaything of the over-mighty and pitiless forces of nature. Death itself is not extinction, is not a return to inorganic lifelessness, but the beginning of a new kind of existence which lies on the path of development to something higher. And, looking in the other direction, this view announces that the same moral laws which our civilizations have set up govern the whole universe as well, except that they are maintained by a supreme court of justice with incomparably more power and consistency. In the end all good is rewarded and all evil punished, if not actually in this form of life then in the later existences that begin after death. In this way all the terrors, the sufferings and the hardships of life are destined to be obliterated. Life after death, which continues life on earth just as the invisible part of the spectrum joins on to the visible part, brings us all the perfection that we may perhaps have missed here. And the superior wisdom which directs this course of things, the infinite goodness that expresses itself in it, the justice that achieves its aim in it—these are the attributes of the divine beings who also created us and the world as a whole, or rather, of the one divine being into which, in our civilization, all the gods of antiquity have been condensed. The people which first succeeded in thus concentrating the divine attributes was not a little proud of the advance. It had laid open to view the father who had all along been hidden behind every divine figure as its nucleus. Fundamentally this was a return to the historical beginnings of the idea of God . . .

Let us now take up the thread of our enquiry. What, then, is the psychological significance of religious ideas and under what heading are we to classify them? The question is not at all easy to answer immediately. After rejecting a number of formulations, we will take our stand on the following one. Religious ideas are teachings and assertions about facts and conditions of external (or internal) reality which tell one something one has not discovered for oneself and which lay claim to one's belief. Since they give us information about what is most important and interesting to us in life, they are particularly highly prized. Anyone who knows nothing of them is very ignorant; and anyone who has added them to his knowledge may consider himself much the richer . . .

We must ask where the inner force of those doctrines lies and to what it is that they owe their efficacy, independent as it is of recognition by reason. I think we have prepared the way sufficiently for an answer to both these questions. It will be found if we turn our attention to the psychical origin of religious ideas. These, which are given out as teachings, are not precipitates of experience or end-results of thinking: they are illusions, fulfilments of the oldest, strongest and most urgent wishes of mankind. The secret of their strength lies in the strength of those wishes. As we already know, the terrifying impression of helplessness in childhood aroused the need for protection—for protection through love—which was provided by the father; and the recognition that this helplessness lasts throughout life made it necessary to cling to the existence of a father, but this time a more powerful one. Thus the benevolent rule of a divine Providence allays our fear of the dangers of life; the establishment of a moral world-order ensures the fulfilment of the demands of justice, which have so often remained unfulfilled irt human civilization; and the prolongation of earthly existence in a future life provides the local and temporal framework in which these wish-fulfilments shall take place. Answers to the riddles that tempt the curiosity of man, such as how the universe began or what the relation is between body and mind, are developed in conformity with the underlying assumptions of this system. It is an enormous relief to the individual psyche if the conflicts of its childhood arising from the father-complex—conflicts which it has never wholly overcome—are removed from it and brought to a solution which is universally accepted.

When I say that these things are all illusions, I must define the meaning of the word. An illusion is not the same thing as an error; nor is it necessarily an error. Aristotle's belief that vermin are developed out of dung (a belief to which ignorant people still cling) was an error; so was the belief of a former generation of doctors that *tabes dorsalis* is the result of sexual excess. It would be incorrect to call these errors illusions. On the other hand, it was an illusion of Columbus's that he had discovered a new sea-route to the Indies. The part played by his wish in this error is very clear. One may describe as an illusion the assertion made by certain nationalists that the Indo-Germanic race is the only one capable of civilization; or the belief, which was only destroyed by psycho-analysis, that children are creatures without sexuality. What is characteristic of illusions is that they are derived from human wishes. In this respect they come near to psychiatric delusions. But they differ from them, too, apart from the more complicated structure of delusions. In the case of delusions, we emphasize as essential their being in contradiction with reality. Illusions need not necessarily be false—that is to say, unrealizable or in contradiction to reality. For instance, a middle-class girl may have the illusion that a prince will come and marry her. This is possible; and a few such cases have occurred. That the Messiah will come and found a golden age is much less likely. Whether one classifies this belief as an illusion or as something analogous to a delusion will depend on one's personal attitude. Examples of illusions which have proved true are not easy to find, but the illusion of the alchemists that all metals can be turned into gold might be one of them. The wish to have a great deal of gold, as much gold as possible, has, it is true, been a good deal damped by our present-day knowledge of the determinants of wealth, but chemistry no longer regards the transmutation of metals into gold as impossible. Thus we call a belief an illusion when a wish-fulfilment is a prominent factor in its motivation, and in doing so we disregard its relations to reality, just as the illusion itself sets no store by verification.

Having thus taken our bearings, let us return once more to the question of religious doctrines. We can now repeat that all of them are illusions and insusceptible of proof. No one can be compelled to think them true, to believe in them. Some of them are so improbable, so incompatible with everything we have laboriously discovered about the reality of the world, that we may compare them—if we pay proper regard to the psychological differences—to delusions. Of the reality value of most of them we cannot judge; just as they cannot be proved, so they cannot be refuted. We still know too little to make a critical approach to them. The riddles of the universe reveal themselves only slowly to our investigation; there are many questions to which science to-day can give no answer. But scientific work is the only road which can lead us to a knowledge of reality outside ourselves. It is once again merely an illusion to expect anything from intuition and introspection; they can give us nothing but particulars about our own mental life, which are hard to interpret, never any information about the questions which religious doctrine finds it so easy to answer. . . .

We now observe that the store of religious ideas includes not only wish-fulfilments but important historical recollections. This concurrent influence of past and present must give religion a truly incomparable wealth of power. But perhaps with the help of an analogy yet another discovery may begin to dawn on us. Though it is not a good plan to transplant ideas far from the soil in which they grew up, yet here is a conformity which we cannot avoid pointing out. We know that a human child cannot succesfully complete its development to the civilized stage without passing through a phase of neurosis sometimes of greater and sometimes of less distinctness. This is because so many instinctual demands which will later be unserviceable cannot be suppressed by the rational operation of the child's intellect but have to be tamed by acts of repression, behind which, as a rule, lies the motive of anxiety. Most of these infantile neuroses are overcome spontaneously in the course of growing up, and this is especially true of the obsessional neuroses of childhood. The remainder can be cleared up later still by psycho-analytic treatment. In just the same way, one might assume, humanity as a whole, in its development through the ages, fell into states analogous to the neuroses, and for the same reasons—namely because in the times of its ignorance and intellectual weakness the instinctual renunciations indispensable for man's communal existence had only been achieved by it by means of purely affective forces. The precipitates of these processes resembling repression which took place in prehistoric times, still remained attached to civilization for long periods. Religion would thus be the universal obsessional neurosis of humanity; like the obsessional neurosis of children, it arose out of the Oedipus complex, out of the relation to the father. If this view is right, it is to be supposed that a turning-away from religion is bound to occur with the fatal inevitability of a process of growth, and that we find ourselves at this very juncture in the middle of that phase of development. . . .

Thus I must contradict you when you go on to argue that men are completely unable to do without the consolation of the religious illusion, that without it they could not bear the troubles of life and the cruelties of reality. That is true, certainly, of the men into whom you have instilled the sweet—or bitter-sweet—poison from childhood onwards. But what of the other men, who have been sensibly brought up? Perhaps those who do not suffer from the neurosis will need no intoxicant to deaden it. They will, it is true, find themselves in a difficult situation. They will have to admit to themselves the full extent of their helplessness and their insignificance in the machinery of the universe; they can no longer be the centre of creation, no longer the object of tender care on the part of a beneficent Providence. They will be in the same position as a child who has left the parental house where he was so warm and comfortable. But surely infantilism is destined to be surmounted. Men cannot remain children for ever; they must in the end go out into 'hostile life'. We may call this *'education to reality'*. Need I confess to you that the sole purpose of my book is to point out the necessity for this forward step?

You are afraid, probably, that they will not stand up to the hard test? Well, let us at least hope they will. It is something, at any rate, to know that one is thrown upon one's own resources. One learns then to make a proper use of them. And men are not entirely without assistance. Their scientific knowledge has taught them much since the days of the Deluge, and it will increase their power still further. And, as for the great necessities of Fate, against which there is no help, they will learn to endure them with resignation. Of what use to them is the mirage of wide acres in the moon, whose harvest no one has ever yet seen? As honest smallholders on this earth they will know how to cultivate their plot in such a way that it supports them. By withdrawing their expectations from the other world and concentrating all their liberated energies into their life on earth, they will probably succeed in achieving a state of things in which life will become tolerable for everyone and civilization no longer oppressive to anyone. Then, with one of our fellow-unbelievers, they will be able to say without regret:

> Den Himmel überlassen wir
> Den Engeln und den Spatzen.[1]

---

[1] ['We leave Heaven to the angels and the sparrows.' From Heine's poem *Deutschland* (Caput I). The word which is here translated 'fellow-unbelievers'—in German *'Unglaubensgenossen'*—was applied by Heine himself to Spinoza. It had been quoted by Freud as an example of a particular kind of joke-technique in his book on jokes (1905c), *Standard Ed.*, 8, 77.]

Feuerbach
RELIGION AS PROJECTION OF HUMAN NATURE*

What we have hitherto been maintaining generally, even with regard to sensational impressions, of the relation between subject and object, applies especially to the relation between the subject and the religious object.

In the perceptions of the senses consciousness of the object is distinguishable from consciousness of self; but in religion, consciousness of the object and self-consciousness coincide. The object of the senses is out of man, the religious object is within him, and therefore as little forsakes him as his self-consciousness or his conscience; it is the intimate, the closest object. "God," says Augustine, for example, "is nearer, more related to us, and therefore more easily known by us, than sensible, corporeal things." The object of the senses is in itself indifferent—independent of the disposition or of the judgment; but the object of religion is a selected object; the most excellent, the first the supreme being; it essentially presupposes a critical judgment, a discrimination between the divine and the nondivine, between that which is worthy of adoration and that which is not worthy. And here may be applied, without any limitation, the proposition: the object of any subject is nothing else than the subject's own nature taken objectively. Such as are a man's thoughts and dispositions, such is his God; so much worth as a man has, so much and no more has his God. Consciousness of God is self-consciousness, knowledge of God is self-knowledge. By his God thou knowest the man, and by the man his God; the two are identical. Whatever is God to a man, that is his heart and soul; and conversely, God is the manifest inward nature, the expressed self of a man,—religion the solemn unveiling of a man's hidden treasures, the revelation of his intimate thoughts, the open confession of his love-secrets.

But when religion—consciousness of God—is designated as the self-consciousness of man, this is not to be understood as affirming that the religious man is directly aware of this identity; for, on the contrary, ignorance of it is fundamental to the peculiar nature of religion. To preclude this misconception, it is better to say, religion is man's earliest and also indirect form of self-knowledge. Hence, religion everywhere precedes philosophy, as in the history of the race, so also in that of the individual. Man first of all sees his nature as if *out of* himself, before he finds it in himself. His own nature is in the first instance contemplated by him as that of another being. Religion is the childlike condition of humanity; but the child

* Ludwig Feuerbach (1804–1872): German philosopher. The selection comprises the essay, "The Essence of Religion Considered Generally," from the first chapter of his book, *The Essence of Christianity*. This work is an investigation into the meaning of religious phenomena. By means of a thorough analysis of the doctrines and ceremonies of Christianity, Feuerbach hopes to establish the thesis that the substance of all religion is to be found in human nature. From *The Essence of Christianity* by Ludwig Feuerbach, translated by George Eliot. Gloucester, Mass.: Peter Smith Publishers, 1854.

sees his nature—man—out of himself; in childhood a man is an object to himself, under the form of another man. Hence the historical progress of religion consists in this: that what by an earlier religion was regarded as objective, is now recognised as subjective; that is, what was formerly contemplated and worshipped as God is now perceived to be something *human*. What was at first religion becomes at a later period idolatry; man is seen to have adored his own nature. Man has given objectivity to himself, but has not recognised the object as his own nature: a later religion takes this forward step; every advance in religion is therefore a deeper self-knowledge. But every particular religion, while it pronounces its predecessors idolatrous, excepts itself—and necessarily so, otherwise it would no longer be religion —from the fate, the common nature of all religions: it imputes only to other religions what is the fault, if fault it be, of religion in general. Because it has a different object, a different tenor, because it has transcended the ideas of preceding religions, it erroneously supposes itself exalted above the necessary external laws which constitute the essence of religion—it fancies its object, its ideas, to be superhuman. But the essence of religion, thus hidden from the religious, is evident to the thinker, by whom religion is viewed objectively, which it cannot be by its votaries. And it is our task to show that the antithesis of divine and human is altogether illusory, that it is nothing else than the antithesis between the human nature in general and the human individual; that, consequently, the object and contents of the Christian religion are altogether human.

Religion, at least the Christian, is the relation of man to himself, or more correctly to his own nature (*i.e.*, his subjective nature); but a relation to it, viewed as a nature apart from his own. The divine being is nothing. else than the human being, or, rather, the human nature purified, freed from the limits of the individual man, made objective—*i.e.*, contemplated and revered as another, a distinct being. All the attributes of the divine nature are, therefore, attributes of the human nature.

In relation to the attributes, the predicates, of the Divine Being, this is admitted without hesitation, but by no means in relation to the subject of these predicates. The negation of the subject is held to be irreligion, nay, atheism; though not so the negation of the predicates. But that which has no predicates or qualities, has no effect upon me; that which has no effect upon me has no existence for me. To deny all the qualities of a being is equivalent to denying the being himself. A being without qualities is one which cannot become an object to the mind, and such a being is virtually non-existent. Where man deprives God of all qualities, God is no longer anything more to him than a negative being. To the truly religious man, God is not a being without qualities, because to him he is a positive, real being. The theory that God cannot be defined, and consequently cannot be known by man, is therefore the offspring of recent times, a product of modern unbelief.

As reason is and can be pronounced finite only where man regards sensual enjoyment, or religious emotion, or æsthetic contemplation, or moral sentiment, as the absolute, the true; so the proposition that God is unknowable or undefinable, can only be enunciated and become fixed as a dogma, where this object has no longer any interest for the intellect; where the real, the positive, alone has any hold on man, where the real alone has for him the significance of the essential, of the absolute, divine object, but where at the same time, in contradiction with this purely wordly tendency, there yet exist some old remains of religiousness. On the ground that God is unknowable, man excuses himself to what is yet remaining of his religious conscience for his forgetfulness of God, his absorption in the world: he denies God practically by his conduct,—the world has possession of all his thoughts and inclinations,—but he does not deny him theoretically, he does not attack his existence; he lets that rest. But this existence does not affect or incommode him; it is a merely negative existence, an existence without existence, a self-contradictory existence—a state of being which, as to its effects, is not distinguishable from non-being. The denial of determinate, positive predicates concerning the divine nature is nothing else than a denial of religion, with, however, an appearance of religion in its favour, so that it is not recognised as a denial; it is simply a subtle, disguised atheism. The alleged religious horror of limiting God by positive predicates is only the irreligious wish to know nothing more of God, to banish God from the mind. Dread of limitation is dread of existence. All real existince, i.e., all existence which is truly such, is qualitative, determinative existence. He who earnestly believes in the Divine existence is not shocked at the attributing even of gross sensuous qualities to God. He who dreads an existence that may give offence, who shrinks from the grossness of a positive predicate, may as well renounce existence altogether. A God who is injured by determinate qualities has not the courage and the strength to exist. Qualities are the fire, the vital breath, the oxygen, the salt of existence. An existence in general, an existence without qualities, is an insipidity, an absurdity. But there can be no more in God than is supplied by religion. Only where man loses his taste for religion, and thus religion itself becomes insipid, does the existence of God become an insipid existence—an existence without qualities.

There is, however, a still milder way of denying the divine predicates than the direct one just described. It is admitted that the predicates of the divine nature are finite, and, more particularly, human qualities, but their rejection is rejected; they are even taken under protection, because it is necessary to man to have a definite conception of God, and since he is man he can form no other than a human conception of him. In relation to God, it is said, these predicates are certainly without any objective validity; but to me, if he is to exist for me, he cannot appear otherwise than as he does appear to me, namely, as a being with attributes analogous to the human. But this distinction between what God is in himself, and what he is for me destroys the peace of religion, and is besides in itself an unfounded and untenable distinction. I cannot know whether God is something else in himself or for himself than he is for me; what he is to me is to me all that he is. For me, there lies in these predicates under which he exists for me, what he is in himself, his very nature; he is for me what he can alone ever be for me. The religious man finds perfect satisfaction in that which God is in relation to himself; of any other relation he knows nothing, for God is to him what he can alone be to man. In the distinction above stated, man takes a point of view above himself, *i.e.*, above his nature, the absolute measure of his being; but this transcendentalism is only an illusion; for I can make the distinction between the object as it is in itself, and the object as it is for me, only where an object can really appear otherwise to me, not where it appears to me such as the absolute measure of my nature determines it to appear—such as it must appear to me. It is true that I may have a merely subjective conception, *i.e.*, one which does not arise out of the general constitution of my species; but if my conception is determined by the constitution of my species, the distinction between what an object is in itself, and what it is for me ceases; for this conception is itself an absolute one. The measure of the species is the absolute measure, law, and criterion of man. And, indeed, religion has the conviction that its conceptions, its predicates of God, are such as every man ought to have, and must have, if he would have the true ones—that they are the conceptions necessary to human nature; nay, further, that they are objectively true, representing God as he is. To every religion the gods of *other* religions are only notions concerning God, but its own conception of God is to it God himself, the true God—God such as he is in himself. Religion is satisfied only with a complete Deity, a God without reservation; it will not have a mere phantasm of God; it demands God himself. Religion gives up its own existence when it gives up the nature of God; it is no longer a truth when it renounces the possession of the true God. Scepticism is the arch-enemy of religion; but the distinction between object and conception—between God as he is in himself, and God as he is for me—is a sceptical distinction, and therefore an irreligious one.

That which is to man the self-existent, the highest being, to which he can conceive nothing higher—that is to him the Divine Being. How then should he inquire concerning this being, what he is in himself? If God were an object to the bird, he would be a winged being: the bird knows nothing higher, nothing more blissful, than the winged condition. How ludicrous would it be if this bird pronounced: To me God appears as a bird, but what he is in himself I know not. To the bird the highest nature is the bird-nature; take from him the conception of this, and you take from him the conception of the highest being. How, then, could he ask whether God in himself were winged? To ask whether God is in himself what he is for me, is to ask whether God is God, is to lift oneself above one's God, to rise up against him.

Wherever, therefore, this idea, that the religious predicates are only anthropomorphisms, has taken possession of a man, there has doubt, has unbelief, obtained the mastery of faith. And it is only the inconsequence of faint-heartedness and intellectual imbecility which does not proceed from this idea to the formal negation of the predicates, and from thence to the negation of the subject to which they relate. If thou doubtest the objective truth of the predicates, thou must also doubt the objective truth of the subject whose predicates they are. If thy predicates are anthropomorphisms, the subject of them is an anthropomorphism too. If love, goodness, personality, &c., are human attributes, so also is the subject which thou presupposest, the existence of God, the belief that there is a God, an anthropomorphism—a presupposition purely human. Whence knowest thou that the belief in a God at all is not a limitation of man's mode of conception? Higher beings —and thou supposest such—are perhaps so blest in themselves, so at unity with themselves, that they are not hung in suspense between themselves and a yet higher being. To know God and not oneself to be God, to know blessedness and not oneself to enjoy it, is a state of disunity, of unhappiness. Higher beings know nothing of this unhappiness; they have no conception of that which they are not.

Thou believest in love as a divine attribute because thou thyself lovest; thou believest that God is a wise, benevolent being because thou knowest nothing better in thyself than benevolence and wisdom; and thou believest that God exists, that therefore he is a subject—whatever exists is a subject, whether it be defined as substance, person, essence, or otherwise—because thou thyself existest, are thyself a subject. Thou knowest no higher human good than to love, than to be good and wise; and even so thou knowest no higher happiness than to exist, to be a subject; for the consciousness of all reality, of all bliss, is for thee bound up in the consciousness of being a subject, of existing. God is an existence, a subject to thee, for the same reason that he is to thee a wise, a blessed, a personal being. The distinction between the divine predicates and the divine subject is only this, that to thee the subject, the existence, does not appear an anthropomorphism, because the conception of it is necessarily involved in thy own existence as a subject, whereas the predicates do appear anthropomorphisms, because their necessity—the necessity that God should be conscious, wise, good, &c.,—is not an immediate necessity, identical with the being of man, but is evolved by his self-consciousness, by the activity of his thought. I am a subject, I exist, whether I be wise or unwise, good or bad. To exist is to man the first datum; it constitutes the very idea of the subject; it is presupposed by the predicates. Hence man relinquishes the predicates, but the existence of God is to him a settled, irrefragable, absolutely certain, objective truth. But, nevertheless, this distinction is merely an apparent one. The necessity of the subject lies only in the necessity of the predicate. Thou art a subject only in so far as thou art a human subject; the certainty and reality of thy existence lie only in the certainty and reality of thy human attributes. What the subject is lies only in the predicate; the predicate is the *truth* of the subject—the subject only the personified, existing predicate, the predicate conceived as existing. Subject and predicate are distinguished only as existence and essence. The negation of the predicates is therefore the negation of the subject. What remains of the human subject when abstracted from the human attributes? Even in the language of common life the divine predicates —Providence, Omniscience, Omnipotence—are put for the divine subject.

The certainty of the existence of God, of which it has been said that it is as certain, nay, more certain to man than his own existence, depends only on the certainty of the qualities of God—it is in itself no immediate certainty. To the Christian the existence of the Christian God only is a certainty; to the heathen that of the heathen God only. The heathen did not doubt the existence of Jupiter, because he took no offence at the nature of Jupiter, because he could conceive of God under no other qualities, because to him these qualities were a certainty, a divine reality. The reality of the predicate is the sole guarantee of existence.

Whatever man conceives to be true, he immediately conceives to be real (that is, to have an objective existence), because, originally, only the real is true to him—true in opposition to what is merely conceived, dreamed, imagined. The idea of being, of existence, is the original idea of truth; or, originally, man makes truth dependent on existence, subsequently, existence dependent on truth. Now God is the nature of man regarded as absolute truth,—the truth of man; but God, or, what is the same thing, religion, is as various as are the conditions under which man conceives this his nature, regards it as the highest being. These conditions, then, under which man conceives God, are to him the truth, and for that reason they are also the highest existence, or rather they are existence itself; for only the emphatic, the highest existence, is existence, and deserves this name. Therefore, God is an existent, real being, on the very same ground that he is a particular, definite being; for the qualities of God are nothing else than the essential qualities of man himself, and a particular man is what he is, has his existence, his reality, only in his particular conditions. Take away from the Greek the quality of being Greek, and you take away his existence. On this ground it is true that for a definite positive religion—that is, relatively—the certainty of the existence of God is *immediate;* for just as involuntarily, as necessarily, as the Greek was a Greek, so necessarily were his gods Greek beings, so necessarily were they real, existent beings. Religion is that conception of the nature of the world and of man which is essential to, *i.e.,* identical with, a man's nature. But man does not stand above this his necessary conception; on the contrary, it stands above him; it animates, determines, governs him. The necessity of a proof, of a middle term to unite qualities with existence, the possibility of a doubt, is abolished. Only that which is apart from my own being is capable of being doubted by me. How then can I doubt of God, who is my being? To doubt of God is to doubt of myself. Only when God is thought of abstractly, when his predicates are the result of philosophic abstraction, arises the distinction or separation between subject and predicate, existence and nature—arises the fiction that the existence or the subject is something else than the predicate, something immediate, indubitable, in distinction from the predicate, which is held to be doubtful. But this is only a fiction. A God who has abstract predicates has also an abstract existence. Existence, being, varies with vary-ing qualities.

The identity of the subject and predicate is clearly evidenced by the progressive development of religion, which is identical with the progressive development of human culture. So long as man is in a mere state of nature, so long is his god a mere nature-god—a personification of some natural force. Where man inhabits houses, he also encloses his gods in temples. The temple is only a manifestation of the value which man attaches to beautiful buildings. Temples in honour of religion are in truth temples in honour of architecture. With the emerging of man from a state of savagery and wildness to one of culture, with the distinction between what is fitting for man and what is not fitting, arises simultaneously the distinction be-tween that which is fitting and that which is not fitting for God. God is the idea of majesty, of the highest dignity: the religious sentiment is the senti-ment of supreme fitness. The later more cultured artists of Greece were the first to embody in the statues of the gods the ideas of dignity, of spiritual grandeur, of imperturbable repose and serenity. But why were these qualities in their view attributes, predicates of God? Because they were in themselves regarded by the Greeks as divinities. Why did those artists exclude all disgusting and low passions? Because they perceived them to be unbecoming, unworthy, unhuman, and consequently ungodlike. The Homeric gods eat and drink;—that implies eating and drinking is a divine pleasure. Physical strength is an attribute of the Homeric gods: Zeus is the strongest of the gods. Why? Because physical strength, in and by itself, was regarded as something glorious, divine. To the ancient Germans the highest virtues were those of the warrior; therefore their supreme god was the god of war, Odin,—war, "the original or oldest law." Not the attribute of the divinity, but the divineness or deity of the attribute, is the first true Divine Being. Thus what theology and philosophy have held to be God, the Absolute, the Infinite, is not God; but that which they have held not to be God is God: namely, the attribute, the quality, whatever has reality. Hence he alone is the true atheist to whom the predicates of the Divine Being,—for example, love, wisdom, justice,—are nothing; not he to whom merely the subject of these predicates is nothing. And in no wise is the ne-gation of the subject necessarily also a negation of the predicates considered in themselves. These have an intrinsic, independent reality; they force their recognition upon man by their very nature; they are self-evident truths to him; they prove, they attest themselves. It does not follow that goodness, justice, wisdom, are chimæras because the existence of God is a chimæra, nor truths because this is a truth. The idea of God is dependent on the idea of justice, of benevolence; a God who is not benevolent, not just, not wise, is no God; but the converse does not hold. The fact is not that a quality is divine because God has it, but that God has it because it is in itself divine: because without it God would be a defective being. Justice, wisdom, in general every quality which constitutes the divinity of God, is determined and known by itself independently, but the idea of God is determined by the qualities which have thus been previously judged to be worthy of the divine nature; only in the case in which I identify God and justice, in which I think of God immediately as the reality of the idea of justice, is the idea of God self-determined. But if God as a subject is the determined, while the quality, the predicate, is the determining, then in truth the rank of the godhead is due not to the subject, but to the predicate.

Not until several, and those contradictory, attributes are united in one being, and this being is conceived as personal—the personality being thus brought into especial prominence—not until then is the origin of religion lost sight of, is it forgotten that what the activity of the reflective power has converted into a predicate distinguishable or separable from the subject, was originally the true subject. Thus the Greeks and Romans deified accidents as substances; virtues, states of mind, passions, as independent beings. Man, especially the religious man, is to himself the measure of all things, of all reality. Whatever strongly impresses a man, whatever produces an unusual effect on his mind, if it be only a peculiar, inexplicable sound or note, he personifies as a divine being. Religion embraces all the objects of the world: everything existing has been an object of religious reverence; in the nature and consciousness of religion there is nothing else than what lies in the nature of man and in his consciousness of himself and of the world. Religion has no material exclusively its own. In Rome even the passions of fear and terror had their temples. The Christians also made mental phenomena into independent beings, their own feelings into qualities of things, the passions which governed them into powers which governed the world, in short predicates of their own nature, whether recognised as such or not, into independent subjective existences. Devils, cobolds, witches, ghosts, angels, were sacred truths as long as the religious spirit held undivided sway over mankind.

In order to banish from the mind the identity of the divine and human predicates, and the consequent identity of the divine and human nature, recourse is had to the idea that God, as the absolute, real Being, has an infinite fulness of various predicates, of which we here know only a part, and those such as are analogous to our own; while the rest, by virtue of which God must thus have quite a different nature from the human or that which is analogous to the human, we shall only know in the future—that is, after death. But an infinite plenitude or multitude of predicates which are really different, so different that the one does not immediately involve the other, is realised only in an infinite plenitude or multitude of different beings or individuals. Thus the human nature presents an infinite abundance of different predicates, and for that very reason it presents an infinite abundance of different individuals. Each new man is a new predicate, a new phasis of humanity. As many as are the men, so many are the powers, the properties of humanity. It is true that there are the same elements in every individual, but under such various conditions and modifications that they appear new and peculiar. The mystery of the inexhaustible fulness of the divine predicates is therefore nothing else than the mystery of human nature considered as an infinitely varied, infinitely modifiable, but, consequently, phenomenal being. Only in the realm of the senses, only in space and time, does there exist a being of really infinite qualities or predicates. Where there are really different predicates there are different times. One man is a distinguished musician, a distinguished author, a distinguished physician; but he cannot compose music, write books, and perform cures in the same moment of time. Time, and not the Hegelian dialectic, is the medium of uniting opposites, contradictories, in one and the same subject. But distinguished and detached from the nature of man, and combined with the idea of God, the infinite fulness of various predicates is a conception without reality, a mere phantasy, a conception derived from the sensible world, but without the essential conditions, without the truth of sensible existence, a conception which stands in direct contradiction with the Divine Being considered as a spiritual, i.e., an abstract, simple, single being; for the predicates of God are precisely of this character, that one involves all the others, because there is no real difference between them. If, therefore, in the present predicates I have not the future, in the present God not the future God, then the future God is not the present, but they are two distinct beings. But this distinction is in contradiction with the unity and simplicity of the theological God. Why is a given predicate a predicate of God? Because it is divine in its nature, i.e., because it expresses no limitation, no defect. Why are other predicates applied to him? Because, however various in themselves, they agree in this, that they all alike express perfection, unlimitedness. Hence I can conceive innumerable predicates of God, because they must all agree with the abstract idea of the Godhead, and must have in common that which constitutes every single predicate a divine attribute. Thus it is in the system of Spinoza. He speaks of an infinite number of attributes of the divine substance, but he specifies none except Thought and Extension. Why? Because it is a matter of indifference to know them; nay, Because they are in themselves indifferent, superfluous; for with all these innumerable predicates, I yet always mean to say the same thing as when I speak of Thought and Extension. Why is Thought an attribute of substance? Because, according to Spinoza, it is capable of being conceived by itself, because it expresses something indivisible, perfect, infinite. Why Extension or Matter? For the same reason. Thus, substance can have an indefinite number of predicates, because it is not their specific definition, their difference, but their identity, their equivalence, which makes them attributes of substance. Or rather, substance has innumerable predicates only because (how strange!) it has properly no predicate; that is, no definite, real predicate. The indefinite unity which is the product of thought, completes itself by the indefinite multiplicity which is the product of the imagination. Because the predicate is not *multum*, it is *multa*. In truth, the positive predicates are Thought and Extension. In these two infinitely more is said than in the nameless innumerable predicates; for they express something definite—in them I have something. But substance is too indifferent, too apathetic to be *something*; that is, to have qualities and passions; that it may not be something, it is rather nothing.

Now, when it is shown that what the subject is lies entirely in the attributes of the subject; that is, that the predicate is the true subject; it is also proved that if the divine predicates are attributes of the human nature, the subject of those predicates is also of the human nature. But the divine predicates are partly general, partly personal. The general predicates are the metaphysical, but these serve only as external points of support to religion; they are not the characteristic definitions of religion. It is the personal predicates alone which constitute the essence of religion—in which the Divine Being is the object of religion. Such are, for example, that God is a Person, that he is the moral Lawgiver, the Father of mankind, the Holy One, the Just, the Good, the Merciful. It is, however, at once clear, or it will at least be clear in the sequel, with regard to these and other definitions, that, especially as applied to a personality, they are purely human definitions, and that consequently man in religion—in his relation to God—is in relation to his own nature; for to the religious sentiment these predicates are not mere conceptions, mere images, which man forms of God, to be distinguished from that which God is in himself, but truths, facts, realities. Religion knows nothing of anthropomorphisms; to it they are not anthropomorphisms. It is the very essence of religion, that to it these definitions express the nature of God. They are pronounced to be images only by the understanding, which reflects on religion, and which while defending them yet before its own tribunal denies them. But to the religious sentiment God is a real Father, real Love and Mercy; for to it he is a real, living, personal being, and therefore his attributes are also living and personal. Nay, the definitions which are the most sufficing to the religious sentiment are precisely those which give the most offence to the understanding, and which in the process of reflection on religion it denies. Religion is essentially emotion; hence, objectively also, emotion is to it necessarily of a divine nature. Even anger appears to it an emotion not unworthy of God, provided only there be a religious motive at the foundation of this anger.

But here it is also essential to observe, and this phenomenon is an extremely remarkable one, characterising the very core of religion, that in proportion as the divine subject is in reality human, the greater is the apparent difference between God and man; that is, the more, by reflection on religion, by theology, is the identity of the divine and human denied, and the human, considered as such, is depreciated. The reason of this is, that as what is positive in the conception of the divine being can only be human, the conception of man, as an object of consciousness, can only be negative. To enrich God, man must become poor; that God may be all, man must be nothing. But he desires to be nothing in himself, because what he takes from himself is not lost to him, since it is preserved in God. Man has his being in God; why then should he have it in himself? Where is the necessity of positing the same thing twice, of having it twice? What man withdraws from himself, what he renounces in himself, he only enjoys in an incomparably higher and fuller measure in God.

The monks made a vow of chastity to God; they mortified the sexual passion in themselves, but therefore they had in heaven, in the Virgin Mary, the image of woman—an image of love. They could the more easily dispense with real woman in proportion as an ideal woman was an object of love to them. The greater the importance they attached to the denial of sensuality, the greater the importance of the heavenly virgin for them: she was to them in the place of Christ, in the stead of God. The more the sensual tendencies are renounced, the more sensual is the God to whom they are sacrificed. For whatever is made an offering to God has an especial value attached to it; in it God is supposed to have especial pleasure. That which is the highest in the estimation of man is naturally the highest in the estimation of his God; what pleases man pleases God also. The Hebrews did not offer to Jehovah unclean, ill-conditioned animals; on the contrary, those which they most highly prized, which they themselves ate, were also the food of God.

Wherever, therefore, the denial of the sensual delights is made a special offering, a sacrifice well-pleasing to God, there the highest value is attached to the senses, and the sensuality which has been renounced is unconsciously restored, in the fact that God takes the place of the material delights which have been renounced. The nun weds herself to God; she has a heavenly bridegroom, the monk a heavenly bride. But the heavenly virgin is only a sensible presentation of a general truth, having relation to the essence of religion. Man denies as to himself only what he attributes to God. Religion abstracts from man, from the world; but it can only abstract from the limitations, from the phenomena; in short, from the negative, not from the essence, the positive, of the world and humanity: hence, in the very abstraction and negation it must recover that from which it abstracts or believes itself to abstract. And thus, in reality, whatever religion consciously denies—always supposing that what is denied by it is something essential, true, and consequently incapable of being ultimately denied—it unconsciously restores in God. Thus, in religion man denies his reason; of himself he knows nothing of God, his thoughts are only worldly, earthly; he can only believe what God reveals to him. But on this account the thoughts of God are human, earthly thoughts: like man, he has plans in his mind, he accommodates himself to circumstances and grades of intelligence, like a tutor with his pupils; he calculates closely the effect of his gifts and revelations; he observes man in all his doings; he knows all things, even the most earthly, the commonest, the most trivial. In brief, man in relation to God denies his own knowledge, his own thoughts, that he may place them in God. Man gives up his personality; but in return, God, the Almighty, infinite, unlimited being, is a person; he denies human dignity, the human *ego*; but in return God is to him a selfish, egoistical being, who in all things seeks only himself, his own honour, his own ends; he represents God as simply seeking the satisfaction of his own selfishness, while yet he frowns on that of every other being; his God is the very luxury of egoism. Religion further denies goodness as a quality of human nature; man is wicked, corrupt, incapable of good; but, on the other hand, God is only good—the Good Being. Man's nature demands as an object goodness, personified as God; but is it not hereby declared that goodness is an essential tendency of man? If my heart is wicked, my understanding perverted, how can I perceive and feel the holy to be holy, the good to be good? Could I perceive the beauty of a fine picture if my mind were æsthetically an absolute piece of perversion? Though I may not be a painter, though I may not have the power of producing what is beautiful myself, I must yet have æsthetic feeling, æsthetic comprehension, since I perceive the beauty that is presented to me externally. Either goodness does not exist at all for man, or, if it does exist, therein is revealed to the individual man the holiness and goodness of human nature. That which is absolutely opposed to my nature, to which I am united by no bond of sympathy, is not even conceivable or perceptible by me. The holy is in opposition to me only as regards the modifications of my personality, but as regards my fundamental nature it is in unity with me. The holy is a reproach to my sinfulness; in it I recognise myself as a sinner; but in so doing, while I blame myself, I acknowledge what I am not, but ought to be, and what, for that very reason, I, according to my destination, can be; for an "ought" which has no coresponding capability does not affect me, is a ludicrous chimæra without any true relation to my mental constitution. But when I acknowledge goodness as my destination, as my law, I acknowledge it, whether consciously or unconsciously, as my own nature. Another nature than my own, one different in quality, cannot touch me. I can perceive sin as sin, only when I perceive it to be a contradiction of myself with myself—that is, of my personality with my fundamental nature. As a contradiction of the absolute, considered as another being, the feeling of sin is inexplicable, unmeaning.

The distinction between Augustinianism and Pelagianism consists only in this, that the former expresses after the manner of religion what the latter expresses after the manner of Rationalism. Both say the same thing, both vindicate the goodness of man; but Pelagianism does it directly, in a rationalistic and moral form; Augustinianism indirectly, in a mystical, that is, a religious form. For that which is given to man's God is in truth given to man himself; what a man declares concerning God, he in truth declares concerning himself. Augustinianism would be a truth, and a truth opposed to Pelagianism, only if man had the devil for his God, and, with the consciousness that he was the devil, honoured, reverenced, and worshipped him as the highest being. But so long as man adores a good being as his God, so long does he contemplate in God the goodness of his own nature.

As with the doctrine of the radical corruption of human nature, so is it with the identical doctrine, that man can do nothing good, i.e., in truth, nothing of himself—by his own strength. For the denial of human strength and spontaneous moral activity to be true, the moral activity of God must also be denied; and we must say, with the Oriental nihilist or pantheist:

the Divine being is absolutely without will or action, indifferent, knowing nothing of the discrimination between evil and good. But he who defines God as an active being, and not only so, but as morally active and morally critical,—as a being who loves, works, and rewards good, punishes, rejects, and condemns evil,—he who thus defines God only in appearance denies human activity, in fact, making it the highest, the most real activity. He who makes God act humanly, declares human activity to be divine; he says: A god who is not active, and not morally or humanly active, is no god; and thus he makes the idea of the Godhead dependent on the idea of activity, that is, of human activity, for a higher he knows not.

Man—this is the mystery of religion—projects his being into objectivity,[1] and then again makes himself an object to this projected image of himself thus converted into a subject; he thinks of himself as an object to himself, but as the object of an object, of another being than himself. Thus here. Man is an object to God. That man is good or evil is not indifferent to God; no! He has a lively, profound interest in man's being good; he wills that man should be good, happy—for without goodness there is no happiness. Thus the religious man virtually retracts the nothingness of human activity, by making his dispositions and actions an object to God, by making man the end of God—for that which is an object to the mind is an end in action; by making the divine activity a means of human salvation. God acts, that man may be good and happy. Thus man, while he is apparently humiliated to the lowest degree, is in truth exalted to the highest. Thus, in and through God, man has in view himself alone. It is true that man places the aim of his action in God, but God has no other aim of action than the moral and eternal salvation of man: thus man has in fact no other aim than himself. The divine activity is not distinct from the human.

How could the divine activity work on me as its object, nay, work in me, if it were essentially different from me; how could it have a human aim, the aim of ameliorating and blessing man, if it were not itself human? Does not the purpose determine the nature of the act? When man makes his moral improvement an aim to himself, he has divine resolutions, divine projects; but also, when God seeks the salvation of man, he has human ends and a human mode of activity corresponding to these ends. Thus in God man has only his own activity as an object. But for the very reason that he regards his own activity as objective, goodness only as an object, he necessarily receives the impulse, the motive not from himself, but from this object. He contemplates his nature as external to himself, and this nature as goodness; thus it is self-evident, it is mere tautology to say that the impulse to good comes only from thence where he places the good.

---

[1] The religious, the original mode in which man becomes objective to himself, is (as is clearly enough explained in this work) to be distinguished from the mode in which this occurs in reflection and speculation; the latter is voluntary, the former involuntary, necessary—as necessary as art, as speech. With the progress of time, it is true, theology coincides with religion.

God is the highest subjectivity of man abstracted from himself; hence man can do nothing of himself, all goodness comes from God. The more subjective God is, the more completely does man divest himself of his subjectivity, because God is, *per se*, his relinquished self, the possession of which he however again vindicates to himself. As the action of the arteries drives the blood into the extremities, and the action of the veins brings it back again, as life in general consists in a perpetual systole and diastole; so is it in religion. In the religious systole man propels his own nature from himself, he throws himself outward; in the religious diastole he receives the rejected nature into his heart again. God alone is the being who acts of himself, —this is the force of repulsion in religion; God is the being who acts in me, with me, through me, upon me, for me, is the principle of my salvation, of my good dispositions and actions, consequently my own principle and nature,—this is the force of attraction in religion.

The course of religious development which has been generally indicated consists specifically in this, that man abstracts more and more from God, and attributes more and more to himself. This is especially apparent in the belief in revelation. That which to a later age or a cultured people is given by nature or reason, is to an earlier age, or to a yet uncultured people, given by God. Every tendency of man, however natural—even the impulse to cleanliness, was conceived by the Israelites as a positive divine ordinance. From this example we again see that God is lowered, is conceived more entirely on the type of ordinary humanity, in proportion as man detracts from himself. How can the self-humiliation of man go further than when he disclaims the capability of fulfilling spontaneously the requirements of common decency? The Christian religion, on the other hand, distinguished the impulses and passions of man according to their quality, their character; it represented only good emotions, good dispositions, good thoughts, as revelations, operations—that is, as dispositions, feelings, thoughts,—of God; for what God reveals is a quality of God himself: that of which the heart is full overflows the lips; as is the effect such is the cause; as the revelation, such the being who reveals himself. A God who reveals himself in good dispositions is a God whose essential attribute is only moral perfection. The Christian religion distinguishes inward moral purity from external physical purity; the Israelites identified the two. In relation to the Israelitish religion, the Christian religion is one of criticism and freedom. The Israelite trusted himself to do nothing except what was commanded by God; he was without will even in external things; the authority of religion extended itself even to his food. The Christian religion, on the other hand, in all these external things made man dependent on himself, *i.e.*, placed in man what the Israelite placed out of himself in God. Israel is the most complete presentation of Positivism in religion. In relation to the Israelite, the Christian is an *esprit fort*, a free-thinker. Thus do things change. What yesterday was still religion is no longer such to-day; and what to-day is atheism, to-morrow will be religion.

Marx
ON THE FUTURE OF RELIGION*

For Germany the *criticism of religion* is in the main complete, and criticism of religion is the premise of all criticism.

The *profane* existence of error is discredited after its *heavenly oratio pro aris et focis*[1] has been rejected. Man, who looked for a superman in the fantastic reality of heaven and found nothing there but the *reflection* of himself, will no longer be disposed to find but the *semblance* of himself, the non-human [*Unmensch*] where he seeks and must seek his true reality.

The basis of irreligious criticism is: *Man makes religion*, religion does not make man. In other words, religion is the self-consciousness and self-feeling of man who has either not yet found himself or has already lost himself again. But *man* is no abstract being squatting outside the world. Man is *the world of man*, the state, society. This state, this society, produce religion, *a reversed world-consciousness*, because they are a *reversed world*. Religion is the general theory of that world, its encyclopedic compendium, its logic in a popular form, its spiritualistic *point d'honneur*, its enthusiasm, its moral sanction, its solemn completion, its universal- ground for consolation and justification. It is *the fantastic realization* of the human essence because the *human essence* has no true reality. The struggle against religion is therefore mediately the fight against *the other world*, of which religion is the spiritual *aroma*.

Religious distress is at the same time the *expression* of real distress and the *protest* against real distress. Religion is the sigh of the oppressed creature, the heart of a heartless world, just as it is the spirit of a spiritless situation. It is the *opium* of the people.

The abolition of religion as the *illusory* happiness of the people is required for their *real* happiness. The demand to give up the illusions about its condition is the *demand to give up a condition which needs illusions*. The criticism of religion is therefore *in embryo the criticism of the vale of woe*, the *halo* of which is religion.

Criticism has plucked the imaginary flowers from the chain not so that man will wear the chain without any fantasy or consolation but so that he will shake off the chain and cull the living flower. The criticism of religion

---

* Karl Marx (1818–1883): German political philosopher and economist. This selection is taken from an essay written by Marx in 1844 entitled "Contribution to the Critique of Hegel's Philosophy of Right." It reflects his view that religion is the opiate of the people and that the revolutionary communist movement will bring about a revaluation of religion. From Karl Marx and Friedrich Engels, *On Religion*, Moscow Foreign Languages Publishing House, 1955, pp. 41–42.

1 Speech for the altars and hearths.—ED.

disillusions man to make him think and act and shape his reality like a man who has been disillusioned and has come to reason, so that he will revolve round himself and therefore round his true sun. Religion is only the illusory sun which revolves round man as long as he does not revolve round himself.

The task of history, therefore, once the *world beyond the truth* has disappeared, is to establish the *truth of this world.* The immediate *task of philosophy,* which is at the service of history, once the *saintly form* of human self-alienation has been unmasked, is to unmask self-alienation in its *unholy forms.* Thus the criticism of heaven turns into the criticism of the earth, the *criticism of religion* into the *criticism of right* and the *criticism of theology* into the *criticism of politics.*

Chapter 5

Sociogenic origins of religion

Man is a social being. Social relations constitute and determine much of his life. Human existence is shared existence, and the daily dependence upon others is fundamental to living. Social relationships and institutions are the soil out of which human life grows and is nurtured. Therefore, the impact of the social reality upon the maturation of the human spirit cannot be ignored in the study of the origins of religious beliefs and practices.

Freud emphasized the psychogenic source of religion, but realized the social function of such beliefs. He viewed civilization and culture mainly as a repressive system of coercions operating on the human psyche, restraining it from certain actions while sanctioning others by means of social mores. Religion is simply one more form of repression in the cultural system. The rituals and divine figures of religion constitute an externalization of moral authority, reinforcing cultural restraints by providing them with a sacred, holy basis.

By no means, however, did Freud fail to realize the necessity for a systematic, operative system of restraints in society. Culture is an organization of social relations in which man's destructive and aggressive tendencies may be checked while providing, simultaneously, the means for cooperative human endeavors in the struggle for survival, for reasonable gratification of basic urges, and for protection from the hostile forces of nature, both physical and human. For these important reasons, some measure of restraint is essential; but excessive repression is not productive of healthy growth and human development. Religion, according to Freud, tends to support and nourish restraints that are not based on a rational understanding of human nature or of man's social relationships.

Emile Durkheim shares Freud's conviction that religious beliefs cannot be mere illusions, but in his search for the underlying reality he is not led, as was Freud, to the dynamics of the human psyche and its inevitable tensions. Rather, Durkheim believes that the causal grounds for religious belief and ritual are social forces. Since society is encountered in human life as the dominant, formative force, Durkheim maintains that it alone is capable of engendering the feeling of the sacred and the divine in its members. Moreover society enables persons to transcend their individual limitations and thereby enhances human existence. Since these are typical fruits of religious beliefs, and religion originates in society, why not recognize that what we take to be divine providence is nothing more than society, viewed as sacred? Durkheim argues that men do not always perceive the reality behind the sacred; they do not realize that the power and strength of the divine come from society.

Furthermore, in contrast to Freud, Durkheim defends the thesis that the rites and rituals of religion increase social cohesiveness and give sustenance and courage to its participants. Through religious ceremony and observance, the moral fibre of the whole community is renewed, and the continued existence of society depends on such renewals. Religious traditions and practices are the foundations for a continuing society as one generation perishes in giving birth to another.

While Freud envisions the displacement of religious illusions by a scientific system of knowledge, Durkheim views science merely as a perfected form of religious thought. Freud sees a vast chasm between the illusions of religious thinking and the rationality of scientific thought. Durkheim insists that religious and scientific thought both develop out of the same source—society; thus defining religion and science as representing merely two different stages in society's developing understanding of itself.

Malinowski's studies of primitive society convinced him that Durkheim was essentially correct in urging that religion is a profoundly social affair. However, he could not agree with the reductionist character of Durkheim's theory: that is, his tendency to reduce the sacred to social forces. Malinowski's observations led him to conclude that the sacred and the profane are clearly distinguishable in primitive societies and, hence, that there are dimensions of a society's life which are purely secular in nature and which have no tendency to produce religious phenomena.

The focus of his attention tended, therefore, to settle upon the practical consequences of religious activity in the primitive world. Religion, for primitive man, is a quite distinctive mode of behavior, a pragmatic disposition composed largely of reason, feeling, and will. Indeed, religious beliefs function for primitive man as a means of establishing and confirming those mental attitudes which are crucial to his survival. Because of their survival values, these mental sets are highly prized in the primitive's life. Among such valued attitudes are an abiding confidence in and reverence for traditional ways of doing things, a persistent urge to maintain harmony with the natural environment, and courage in the face of the vicissitudes of life. Malinowski discovered that these dispositions are embodied in and maintained by the cultic practices and ceremonies of primitive religion. Truths of profound importance for survival are expressed in the myths of the sacred tradition, and these myths both explain and support the cultic practice of primitive society.

In the final analysis, Malinowski seems to feel that the function of religion in the primitive world is to render sacred certain dimensions of the social world. He found this work of translation in such religious activities as initiation ceremonies, totem mysteries, and funeral rites. This view brings him into sharp disagreement with Durkheim who believes that religion *derives* its sanctity *from* society.

Durkheim

RELIGION'S ORIGIN IN SOCIETY*

In a general way, it is unquestionable that a society has all that is necessary to arouse the sensation of the divine in minds, merely by the power
that it has over them; for to its members it is what a god is to his wor-
shippers. In fact, a god is, first of all, a being whom men think of as superior
to themselves, and upon whom they feel that they depend. Whether it be a
conscious personality, such as Zeus or Jahveh, or merely abstract forces
such as those in play in totemism, the worshipper, in the one case as in the
other, believes himself held to certain manners of acting which are imposed
upon him by the nature of the sacred principle with which he feels that he
is in communion. Now society also gives us the sensation of a perpetual dependence. Since it has a nature which is peculiar to itself and different from
our individual nature, it pursues ends which are likewise special to it; but,
as it cannot attain them except through our intermediacy, it imperiously
demands our aid. It requires that, forgetful of our own interests, we make
ourselves its servitors, and it submits us to every sort of inconvenience,
privation and sacrifice, without which social life would be impossible. It is
because of this that at every instant we are obliged to submit ourselves to
rules of conduct and of thought which we have neither made nor desired,
and which are sometimes even contrary to our most fundamental inclinations and instincts.

Even if society were unable to obtain these concessions and sacrifices
from us except by a material constraint, it might awaken in us only the idea
of a physical force to which we must give way of necessity, instead of
that of a moral power such as religions adore. But as a matter of fact, the
empire which it holds over consciences is due much less to the physical
supremacy of which it has the privilege than to the moral authority with
which it is invested. If we yield to its orders, it is not merely because it is
strong enough to triumph over our resistance; it is primarily because it is
the object of a venerable respect.

We say that an object, whether individual or collective, inspires respect
when the representation expressing it in the mind is gifted with such a force
that it automatically causes or inhibits actions, *without regard for any con-*

* Emile Durkheim (1858–1917): French sociologist particularly interested in the
sociology of religion. The selection is drawn from Chapter VII and the Conclusion of
Elementary Forms of Religious Life. The thesis of this book, based on evidence from
religious belief and practice in primitive society, is that religion has a social basis.
Reprinted with permission of the Macmillan Company, New York, from *The Elementary
Forms of the Religious Life* by Emile Durkheim. Translated by Joseph Ward Swain.
Copyright 1915 by George Allen & Unwin, Ltd., London. First Free Press paperback
edition 1963.

sideration relative to their useful or injurious effects. When we obey somebody because of the moral authority which we recognize in him, we follow out his opinions, not because they seem wise, but because a certain sort of physical energy is imminent in the idea that we form of this person, which conquers our will and inclines it in the indicated direction. Respect is the emotion which we experience when we feel this interior and wholly spiritual pressure operating upon us. Then we are not determined by the advantages or inconveniences of the attitude which is prescribed or recommended to us; it is by the way in which we represent to ourselves the person recommending or prescribing it. This is why commands generally take a short, peremptory form leaving no place for hesitation; it is because, in so far as it is a command and goes by its own force, it excludes all idea of deliberation or calculation; it gets its efficacy from the intensity of the mental state in which it is placed. It is this intensity which creates what is called a moral ascendancy. . . .

Since it is in spiritual ways that social pressure exercises itself, it could not fail to give men the idea that outside themselves there exist one or several powers, both moral and, at the same time, efficacious, upon which they depend. They must think of these powers, at least in part, as outside themselves, for these address them in a tone of command and sometimes even order them to do violence to their most natural inclinations. It is undoubtedly true that if they were able to see that these influences which they feel emanate from society, then the mythological system of interpretations would never be born. But social action follows ways that are too circuitous and obscure, and employs psychical mechanisms that are too complex to allow the ordinary observer to see whence it comes. As long as scientific analysis does not come to teach it to them, men know well that they are acted upon, but they do not know by whom. So they must invent by themselves the idea of these powers with which they feel themselves in connection, and from that, we are able to catch a glimpse of the way by which they were led to represent them under forms that are really foreign to their nature and to transfigure them by thought.

But a god is not merely an authority upon whom we depend; it is a force upon which our strength relies. The man who has obeyed his god and who, for this reason, believes the god is with him, approaches the world with confidence and with the feeling of an increased energy. Likewise, social action does not confine itself to demanding sacrifices, privations and efforts from us. For the collective force is not entirely outside of us; it does not act upon us wholly from without; but rather, since society cannot exist except in and through individual consciousness, this force must also penetrate us and organize itself within us; it thus becomes an integral part of our being and by that very fact this is elevated and magnified.

There are occasions when this strengthening and vivifying action of society is especially apparent. In the midst of an assembly animated by a common passion, we become susceptible of acts and sentiments of which we are incapable when reduced to our own forces; and when the assembly is dissolved and when, finding ourselves alone again, we fall back to our ordinary level, we are then able to measure the height to which we have been raised above ourselves. History abounds in examples of this sort. It is enough to think of the night of the Fourth of August, 1789, when an assembly was suddenly led to an act of sacrifice and abnegation which each of its members had refused the day before, and at which they were all surprised the day after. This is why all parties, political, economic or confessional, are careful to have periodical reunions where their members may revivify their common faith by manifesting it in common. To strengthen those sentiments which, if left to themselves, would soon weaken, it is sufficient to bring those who hold them together and to put them into closer and more active relations with one another. This is the explanation of the particular attitude of a man speaking to a crowd, at least if he has succeeded in entering into communion with it. His language has a grandiloquence that would be ridiculous in ordinary circumstances; his gestures show a certain domination; his very thought is impatient of all rules, and easily falls into all sorts of excesses. It is because he feels within him an abnormal over-supply of force which overflows and tries to burst out from him; sometimes he even has the feeling that he is dominated by a moral force which is greater than he and of which he is only the interpreter. It is by this trait that we are able to recognize what has often been called the demon of oratorical inspiration. Now this exceptional increase of force is something very real; it comes to him from the very group which he addresses. The sentiments provoked by his words come back to him, but enlarged and amplified, and to this degree they strengthen his own sentiment. The passionate energies he arouses re-echo within him and quicken his vital tone. It is no longer a simple individual who speaks; it is a group incarnate and personified.

Beside these passing and intermittent states, there are other more durable ones, where this strengthening influence of society makes itself felt with greater consequences and frequently even with greater brilliancy. There are periods in history when, under the influence of some great collective shock, social interactions have become much more frequent and active. Men look for each other and assemble together more than ever. That general effervescence results which is characteristic of revolutionary or creative epochs. Now this greater activity results in a general stimulation of individual forces. Men see more and differently now than in normal times. Changes are not merely of shades and degrees; men become different. The passions moving them are of such an intensity that they cannot be satisfied except by violent and unrestrained actions, actions of super-human heroism or of bloody barbarism. This is what explains the Crusades, for example, or many of the scenes, either sublime or savage, of the French Revolution. Under the influence of the general exaltation, we see the most mediocre and inoffensive bourgeois become either a hero or a butcher. And so clearly are all these mental processes the ones that are also at the root of religion that the individuals themselves have often pictured the pressure before which they thus gave way in a distinctly religious form. The Crusaders believed that they felt God present in the midst of them, enjoining them to go to the conquest of the Holy Land; Joan of Arc believed that she obeyed celestial voices.

But it is not only in exceptional circumstances that this stimulating action of society makes itself felt; there is not, so to speak, a moment in our lives when some current of energy does not come to us from without. The man who has done his duty finds, in the manifestations of every sort expressing the sympathy, esteem or affection which his fellows have for him, a feeling of comfort, of which he does not ordinarily take account, but which sustains him, none the less. The sentiments which society has for him raise the sentiments which he has for himself. Because he is in moral harmony with his comrades, he has more confidence, courage and boldness in action, just like the believer who thinks that he feels the regard of his god turned graciously towards him. It thus produces, as it were, a perpetual sustenance for our moral nature. Since this varies with a multitude of external circumstances, as our relations with the groups about us are more or less active and as these groups themselves vary, we cannot fail to feel that this moral support depends upon an external cause; but we do not perceive where this cause is nor what it is. So we ordinarily think of it under the form of a moral power which, though immanent in us, represents within us something not ourselves: this is the moral conscience, of which, by the way, men have never made even a slightly distinct representation except by the aid of religious symbols.

In addition to these free forces which are constantly coming to renew our own, there are others, which are fixed in the methods and traditions which we employ. We speak a language that we did not make; we use instruments that we did not invent; we invoke rights that we did not found; a treasury of knowledge is transmitted to each generation that it did not gather itself, etc. It is to society that we owe these varied benefits of civilization, and if we do not ordinarily see the source from which we get them, we at least know that they are not our own work. Now it is these things that give man his own place among things; a man is a man only because he is civilized. So he could not escape the feeling that outside of him there are active causes from which he gets the characteristic attributes of his nature and which, as benevolent powers, assist him, protect him and assure him of a privileged fate. And of course he must attribute to these powers a dignity corresponding to the great value of the good things he attributes to them.

Thus the environment in which we live seems to us to be peopled with forces that are at once imperious and helpful, august and gracious, and with which we have relations. Since they exercise over us a pressure of which we are conscious, we are forced to localize them outside ourselves, just as we do for the objective causes of our sensations. But the sentiments which they inspire in us differ in nature from those which we have for simple visible objects. As long as these latter are reduced to their empirical characteristics as shown in ordinary experience, and as long as the religious imagination has not metamorphosed them, we entertain for them no feeling which resembles respect, and they contain within them nothing that is able to raise us outside ourselves. Therefore, the representations which express them appear to us to be very different from those aroused in us by collective influences. The two form two distinct and separate mental states in our consciousness, just as do the two forms of life to which they correspond. Consequently, we get the impression that we are in relations with two distinct sorts of reality and that a sharply drawn line of demarcation separates them from each other: on the one hand is the world of profane things, on the other, that of sacred things.

Also, in the present day just as much as in the past, we see society constantly creating sacred things out of ordinary ones. If it happens to fall in love with a man and if it thinks it has found in him the principal aspirations that move it, as well as the means of satisfying them, this man will be raised above the others and, as it were, deified. Opinion will invest him with a majesty exactly analogous to that protecting the gods. This is what has happened to so many sovereigns in whom their age had faith: if they were not made gods, they were at least regarded as direct representatives of the deity. And the fact that it is society alone which is the author of these varieties of apotheosis, is evident since it frequently chances to consecrate men thus who have no right to it from their own merit. The simple deference inspired by men invested with high social functions is not different in nature from religious respect. It is expressed by the same movements: a man keeps at a distance from a high personage; he approaches him only with precautions; in conversing with him, he uses other gestures and language than those used with ordinary mortals. The sentiment felt on these occasions is so closely related to the religious sentiment that many peoples have confounded the two. In order to explain the consideration accorded to princes, nobles and political chiefs, a sacred character has been attributed to them. In Melanesia and Polynesia, for example, it is said that an influential man has *mana,* and that his influence is due to this *mana.* However, it is evident that his situation is due solely to the importance attributed to him by public opinion. Thus the moral power conferred by opinion and that with which sacred beings are invested are at bottom of a single origin and made up of the same elements. That is why a single word is able to designate the two.

In addition to men, society also consecrates things, especially ideas. If a belief is unanimously shared by a people, then, for the reason which we pointed out above, it is forbidden to touch it, that is to say, to deny it or to contest it. Now the prohibition of criticism is an interdiction like the others and proves the presence of something sacred. Even to-day, howsoever great may be the liberty which we accord to others, a man who should totally deny progress or ridicule the human ideal to which modern societies are attached, would produce the effect of a sacrilege. There is at least one principle which those the most devoted to the free examination of everything tend to place above discussion and to regard as untouchable, that is to say, as sacred: this is the very principle of free examination.

This aptitude of society for setting itself up as a god or for creating gods was never more apparent than during the first years of the French Revolution. At this time, in fact, under the influence of the general enthusiasm, things purely laical by nature were transformed by public opinion into sacred things: these were the Fatherland, Liberty, Reason. A religion tended to become established which had its dogmas, symbols, altars and feasts. It was to these spontaneous aspirations that the cult of Reason and the Supreme Being attempted to give a sort of official satisfaction. It is true that this religious renovation had only an ephemeral duration. But that was because the patriotic enthusiasm which at first transported the masses soon relaxed. The cause being gone, the effect could not remain. But this experiment, though short-lived, keeps all its sociological interest. It remains true that in one determined case we have seen society and its essential ideas become, directly and with no transfiguration of any sort, the object of a veritable cult.

All these facts allow us to catch glimpses of how the clan was able to awaken within its members the idea that outside of them there exist forces which dominate them and at the same time sustain them, that is to say in fine, religious forces: it is because there is no society with which the primitive is more directly and closely connected. The bonds uniting him to the tribe are much more lax and more feebly felt. Although this is not at all strange or foreign to him, it is with the people of his own clan that he has the greatest number of things in common; it is the action of this group that he feels the most directly; so it is this also which, in preference to all others, should express itself in religious symbols. . . .

Our entire study rests upon this postulate that the unanimous sentiment of the believers of all times cannot be purely illusory. We admit that these religious beliefs rest upon a specific experience whose demonstrative value is, in one sense, not one bit inferior to that of scientific experiments, though different from them. We, too, think that "a tree is known by its fruits," and that fertility is the best proof of what the roots are worth. But from the fact that a "religious experience," if we choose to call it this, does exist and that it has a certain foundation—and, by the way, is there any experience which has none?—it does not follow that the reality which is its foundation conforms objectively to the idea which believers have of it. The very fact that the fashion in which it has been conceived has varied infinitely in different times is enough to prove that none of these conceptions express it adequately. If a scientist states it as an axiom that the sensations of heat and light which we feel correspond to some objective cause, he does not conclude that this is what it appears to the senses to be. Likewise, even if the impressions which the faithful feel are not imaginary, still they are in no way privileged intuitions; there is no reason for believing that they inform us better upon the nature of their object than do ordinary sensations upon the nature of bodies and their properties. In order to discover what this object consists of, we must submit them to an examination and elaboration analogous to that which has substituted for the sensuous idea of the world another which is scientific and conceptual.

This is precisely what we have tried to do, and we have seen that this reality, which mythologies have represented under so many different forms, but which is the universal and eternal objective cause of these sensations *sui generis* out of which religious experience is made, is society. We have shown what moral forces it develops and how it awakens this sentiment of a refuge, of a shield and of a guardian support which attaches the believer to his cult. It is that which raises him outside himself; it is even that which made him. For that which makes a man is the totality of the intellectual property which constitutes civilization, and civilization is the work of society. Thus is explained the preponderating rôle of the cult in all religions, whichever they may be. This is because society cannot make its influence felt unless it is in action, and it is not in action unless the individuals who compose it are assembled together and act in common. It is by common action that it takes consciousness of itself and realizes its position; it is before all else an active co-operation. The collective ideas and sentiments are even possible only owing to these exterior movements which symbolize them, as we have established. Then it is action which dominates the religious life, because of the mere fact that it is society which is its source.

In addition to all the reasons which have been given to justify this conception, a final one may be added here, which is the result of our whole work. As we have progressed, we have established the fact that the fundamental categories of thought, and consequently of science, are of religious origin. We have seen that the same is true for magic and consequently for the different processes which have issued from it. On the other hand, it has long been known that up until a relatively advanced moment of evolution, moral and legal rules have been indistinguishable from ritual prescriptions. In summing up, then, it may be said that nearly all the great social institutions have been born in religion. Now in order that these principal aspects of the collective life may have commenced by being only varied aspects of the religious life, it is obviously necessary that the religious life be the eminent form and, as it were, the concentrated expression of the whole collective life. If religion has given birth to all that is essential in society, it is because the idea of society is the soul of religion.

Religious forces are therefore human forces, moral forces. It is true that since collective sentiments can become conscious of themselves only by fixing themselves upon external objects, they have not been able to take form without adopting some of their characteristics from other things: they have thus acquired a sort of physical nature; in this way they have come to mix themselves with the life of the material world, and then have considered themselves capable of explaining what passes there. But when they are considered only from this point of view and in this rôle, only their most superficial aspect is seen. In reality, the essential elements of which these collective sentiments are made have been borrowed by the understanding. It ordinarily seems that they should have a human character only when they are conceived under human forms; but even the most impersonal and the most anonymous are nothing else than objectified sentiments.

It is only by regarding religion from this angle that it is possible to see its real significance. If we stick closely to appearances, rites often give the effect of purely manual operations: they are anointings, washings, meals. To consecrate something, it is put in contact with a source of religious energy, just as to-day a body is put in contact with a source of heat or electricity to warm or electrize it; the two processes employed are not essentially different. Thus understood, religious technique seems to be a sort of mystic mechanics. But these material manœuvres are only the external envelope under which the mental operations are hidden. Finally, there is no question of exercising a physical constraint upon blind and, incidentally, imaginary forces, but rather of reaching individual consciousnesses, of giving them a direction and of disciplining them. It is sometimes said that inferior religions are materialistic. Such an expression is inexact. All religions, even the crudest, are in a sense spiritualistic: for the powers they put in play are before all spiritual, and also their principal object is to act upon the moral life. Thus it is seen that whatever has been done in the name of religion cannot have been done in vain: for it is necessarily the society that did it, and it is humanity that has reaped the fruits.

But, it is said, what society is it that has thus made the basis of religion? Is it the real society, such as it is and acts before our very eyes, with the legal and moral organization which it has laboriously fashioned during the course of history? This is full of defects and imperfections. In it, evil goes beside the good, injustice often reigns supreme, and the truth is often obscured by error. How could anything so crudely organized inspire the sentiments of love, the ardent enthusiasm and the spirit of abnegation which all religions claim of their followers? These perfect beings which are gods could not have taken their traits from so mediocre, and sometimes even so base a reality.

But, on the other hand, does someone think of a perfect society, where justice and truth would be sovereign, and from which evil in all its forms would be banished for ever? No one would deny that this is in close relations with the religious sentiment; for, they would say, it is towards the realization of this that all religions strive. But that society is not an empirical fact, definite and observable; it is a fancy, a dream with which men have lightened their sufferings, but in which they have never really lived. It is merely an idea which comes to express our more or less obscure aspirations towards the good, the beautiful and the ideal. Now these aspirations have their roots in us; they come from the very depths of our being; then there is nothing outside of us which can account for them. Moreover, they are already religious in themselves; thus it would seem that the ideal society presupposes religion, far from being able to explain it.

But, in the first place, things are arbitrarily simplified when religion is seen only on its idealistic side: in its way, it is realistic. There is no physical or moral ugliness, there are no vices or evils which do not have a special divinity. There are gods of theft and trickery, of lust and war, of sickness and of death. Christianity itself, howsoever high the idea which it has made of the divinity may be, has been obliged to give the spirit of evil a place in its mythology. Satan is an essential piece of the Christian system; even if he is an impure being, he is not a profane one. The anti-god is a god, inferior and subordinated, it is true, but nevertheless endowed with extended powers; he is even the object of rites, at least of negative ones. Thus religion, far from ignoring the real society and making abstraction of it, is in its image; it reflects all its aspects, even the most vulgar and the most repulsive. All is to be found there, and if in the majority of cases we see the good victorious over evil, life over death, the powers of light over the powers of darkness, it is because reality is not otherwise. If the relation between these two contrary forces were reversed, life would be impossible; but, as a matter of fact, it maintains itself and even tends to develop.

But if, in the midst of these mythologies and theologies we see reality clearly appearing, it is none the less true that it is found there only in an enlarged, transformed and idealized form. In this respect, the most primitive religions do not differ from the most recent and the most refined. For example, we have seen how the Arunta place at the beginning of time a mythical society whose organization exactly reproduces that which still exists to-day; it includes the same clans and phratries, it is under the same matrimonial rules and it practises the same rites. But the personages who compose it are ideal beings, gifted with powers and virtues to which common mortals cannot pretend. Their nature is not only higher, but it is different, since it is at once animal and human. The evil powers there undergo a similar metamorphosis: evil itself is, as it were, made sublime and idealized. The question now raises itself of whence this idealization comes.

Some reply that men have a natural faculty for idealizing, that is to say, of substituting for the real world another different one, to which they transport themselves by thought. But that is merely changing the terms of the problem; it is not resolving it or even advancing it. This systematic idealization is an essential characteristic of religions. Explaining them by an innate power of idealization is simply replacing one word by another which is the equivalent of the first; it is as if they said that men have made religions because they have a religious nature. Animals know only one world, the one which they perceive by experience, internal as well as external. Men alone have the faculty of conceiving the ideal, of adding something to the real. Now where does this singular privilege come from? Before making it an initial fact or a mysterious virtue which escapes science, we must be sure that it does not depend upon empirically determinable conditions.

The explanation of religion which we have proposed has precisely this advantage, that it gives an answer to this question. For our definition of the sacred is that it is something added to and above the real: now the ideal answers to this same definition; we cannot explain one without explaining the other. In fact, we have seen that if collective life awakens religious thought on reaching a certain degree of intensity, it is because it brings about a state of effervescence which changes the conditions of psychic activity. Vital energies are over-excited, passions more active, sensations stronger; there are even some which are produced only at this moment. A man does not recognize himself; he feels himself transformed and consequently he transforms the environment which surrounds him. In order to account for the very particular impressions which he receives, he attributes to the things with which he is in most direct contact properties which they have not, exceptional powers and virtues which the objects of every-day experience do not possess. In a word, above the real world where his profane life passes he has placed another which, in one sense, does not exist except in thought, but to which he attributes a higher sort of dignity than to the first. Thus, from a double point of view it is an ideal world.

The formation of the ideal world is therefore not an irreducible fact which escapes science; it depends upon conditions which observation can touch; it is a natural product of social life. For a society to become conscious of itself and maintain at the necessary degree of intensity the sentiments which it thus attains, it must assemble and concentrate itself. Now this concentration brings about an exaltation of the mental life which takes form in a group of ideal conceptions where is portrayed the new life thus awakened; they correspond to this new set of psychical forces which is added to those which we have at our disposition for the daily tasks of existence. A society can neither create itself nor recreate itself without at the same time creating an ideal. This creation is not a sort of work of supererogation for it, by which it would complete itself, being already formed; it is the act by which it is periodically made and remade. Therefore when some oppose the ideal society to the real society, like two antagonists which would lead us in opposite directions, they materialize and oppose abstractions. The ideal society is not outside of the real society; it is a part of it. Far from being divided between them as between two poles which mutually repel each other, we cannot hold to one without holding to the other. For a society is not made up merely of the mass of individuals who compose it, the ground which they occupy, the things which they use and the movements which they perform, but above all is the idea which it forms of itself. It is undoubtedly true that it hesitates over the manner in which it ought to conceive itself; it feels itself drawn in divergent directions. But these conflicts which break forth are not between the ideal and reality, but between two different ideals, that of yesterday and that of to-day, that which has the authority of tradition and that which has the hope of the future. There is surely a place for investigating whence these ideals evolve; but whatever solution may be given to this problem, it still remains that all passes in the world of the ideal.

Thus the collective ideal which religion expresses is far from being due to a vague innate power of the individual, but it is rather at the school of collective life that the individual has learned to idealize. It is in assimilating the ideals elaborated by society that he has become capable of conceiving the ideal. It is society which, by leading him within its sphere of action, has made him acquire the need of raising himself above the world of experience and has at the same time furnished him with the means of conceiving another. For society has constructed this new world in constructing itself, since it is society which this expresses. Thus both with the individual and in the group, the faculty of idealizing has nothing mysterious about it. It is not a sort of luxury which a man could get along without, but a condition of his very existence. He could not be a social being, that is to say, he could not be a man, if he had not acquired it. It is true that in incarnating themselves in individuals, collective ideals tend to individualize themselves. Each understands them after his own fashion and marks them with his own stamp; he suppresses certain elements and adds others. Thus the personal ideal disengages itself from the social ideal in proportion as the individual personality develops itself and becomes an autonomous source of action. But if we wish to understand this aptitude, so singular in appearance, of living outside of reality, it is enough to connect it with the social conditions upon which it depends.

I'herefore it is necessary to avoid seeing in this theory of religion a simple restatement of historical materialism: that would be misunderstanding our thought to an extreme degree. In showing that religion is something essentially social, we do not mean to say that it confines itself to translating into another language the material forms of society and its immediate vital necessities. It is true that we take it as evident that social life depends upon its material foundation and bears its mark, just as the mental life of an individual depends upon his nervous system and in fact his whole organism. But collective consciousness is something more than a mere epiphenomenon of its morphological basis, just as individual consciousness is something more than a simple efflorescence of the nervous system. In order that the former may appear, a synthesis *sui generis* of particular consciousnesses is required. Now this synthesis has the effect of disengaging a whole world of sentiments, ideas and images which, once born, obey laws all their own. They attract each other, repel each other, unite, divide themselves, and multiply, though these combinations are not commanded and necessitated by the condition of the underlying reality. The life thus brought into being even enjoys so great an independence that it sometimes indulges in manifestations with no purpose or utility of any sort, for the mere pleasure of affirming itself. We have shown that this is often precisely the case with ritual activity and mythological thought.

But if religion is the product of social causes, how can we explain the individual cult and the universalistic character of certain religions? If it is born *in foro externo*, how has it been able to pass into the inner conscience of the individual and penetrate there ever more and more profoundly? If it is the work of definite and individualized societies, how has it been able to detach itself from them, even to the point of being conceived as something common to all humanity?

In the course of our studies, we have met with the germs of individual religion and of religious cosmopolitanism, and we have seen how they were formed; thus we possess the more general elements of the reply which is to be given to this double question.

We have shown how the religious force which animates the clan particularizes itself, by incarnating itself in particular consciousnesses. Thus secondary sacred beings are formed; each individual has his own, made in his own image, associated to his own intimate life, bound up with his own destiny, it is the soul, the individual totem, the protecting ancestor, etc. These beings are the object of rites which the individual can celebrate by himself, outside of any group; this is the first form of the individual cult. To be sure, it is only a very rudimentary cult; but since the personality of the individual is still only slightly marked, and but little value is attributed to it, the cult which expresses it could hardly be expected to be very highly developed as yet. But as individuals have differentiated themselves more and more and the value of an individual has increased, the corresponding cult has taken a relatively greater place in the totality of the religious life and at the same time it is more fully closed to outside influences.

Thus the existence of individual cults implies nothing which contradicts or embarrasses the sociological interpretation of religion; for the religious forces to which it addresses itself are only the individualized forms of collective forces. Therefore, even when religion seems to be entirely within the individual conscience, it is still in society that it finds the living source from which it is nourished. We are now able to appreciate the value of the radical individualism which would make religion something purely individual: it misunderstands the fundamental conditions of the religious life. If up to the present it has remained in the stage of theoretical aspirations which have never been realized, it is because it is unrealizable. A philosophy may well be elaborated in the silence of the interior imagination, but not so a faith. For before all else, a faith is warmth, life, enthusiasm, the exaltation of the whole mental life, the raising of the individual above himself. Now how could he add to the energies which he possesses without going outside himself? How could he surpass himself merely by his own forces? The only source of life at which we can morally reanimate ourselves is that formed by the society of our fellow beings; the only moral forces with which we can sustain and increase our own are those which we get from others. Let us even admit that there really are beings more or less analogous to those which the mythologies represent. In order that they may exercise over souls the useful direction which is their reason for existence, it is necessary that men believe in them. Now these beliefs are active only when they are partaken by many. A man cannot retain them any length of time by a purely personal effort; it is not thus that they are born or that they are acquired; it is even doubtful if they can be kept under these conditions. In fact, a man who has a veritable faith feels an invincible need of spreading it: therefore he leaves his isolation, approaches others and seeks to convince them, and it is the ardour of the convictions which he arouses that strengthens his own. It would quickly weaken if it remained alone.

It is the same with religious universalism as with this individualism. Far from being an exclusive attribute of certain very great religions, we have found it, not at the base, it is true, but at the summit of the Australian system. Bunjil, Daramulun or Baiame are not simple tribal gods; each of them is recognized by a number of different tribes. In a sense, their cult is international. This conception is therefore very near to that found in the most recent theologies. So certain writers have felt it their duty to deny its authenticity, howsoever incontestable this may be.

And we have been able to show how this has been formed.

Neighbouring tribes of a similar civilization cannot fail to be in constant relations with each other. All sorts of circumstances give an occasion for it: besides commerce, which is still rudimentary, there are marriages; these international marriages are very common in Australia. In the course of these meetings, men naturally become conscious of the moral relationship which united them. They have the same social organization, the same division into phratries, clans and matrimonial classes; they practise the same rites of initiation, or wholly similar ones. Mutual loans and treaties result in re-inforcing these spontaneous resemblances. The gods to which these mani-festly identical institutions were attached could hardly have remained distinct in their minds. Everything tended to bring them together and con-sequently, even supposing that each tribe elaborated the notion independ-ently, they must necessarily have tended to confound themselves with each other. Also, it is probable that it was in inter-tribal assemblies that they were first conceived. For they are chiefly the gods of initiation, and in the initiation ceremonies, the different tribes are usually represented. So if sacred beings are formed which are connected with no geographically de-termined society, that is not because they have an extra-social origin. It is because there are other groups above these geographically determined ones, whose contours are less clearly marked: they have no fixed frontiers, but include all sorts of more or less neighbouring and related tribes. The par-ticular social life thus created tends to spread itself over an area with no definite limits. Naturally the mythological personages who correspond to it have the same character; their sphere of influence is not limited; they go beyond the particular tribes and their territory. They are the great inter-national gods.

Now there is nothing in this situation which is peculiar to Australian societies. There is no people and no state which is not a part of another society, more or less unlimited, which embraces all the peoples and all the States with which the first comes in contact, either directly or indirectly; there is no national life which is not dominated by a collective life of an international nature. In proportion as we advance in history, these inter-national groups acquire a greater importance and extent. Thus we see how, in certain cases, this universalistic tendency has been able to develop itself to the point of affecting not only the higher ideas of the religious system, but even the principles upon which it rests.

Thus there is something eternal in religion which is destined to survive all the particular symbols in which religious thought has successively enveloped itself. There can be no society which does not feel the need of upholding and reaffirming at regular intervals the collective sentiments and the collective ideas which make its unity and its personality. Now this moral remaking cannot be achieved except by the means of reunions, assemblies and meetings where the individuals, being closely united to one another, reaffirm in common their common sentiments; hence come ceremonies which do not differ from regular religious ceremonies, either in their object, the results which they produce, or the processes employed to attain these results. What essential difference is there between an assembly of Christians celebrating the principal dates of the life of Christ, or of Jews remembering the exodus from Egypt or the promulgation of the decalogue, and a reunion of citizens commemorating the promulgation of a new moral or legal system or some great event in the national life? . . .

In summing up, then, we must say that society is not at all the illogical or a-logical, incoherent and fantastic being which it has too often been considered. Quite on the contrary, the collective consciousness is the highest form of the psychic life, since it is the consciousness of the consciousnesses. Being placed outside of and above individual and local contingencies, it sees things only in their permanent and essential aspects, which it crystallizes into communicable ideas. At the same time that it sees from above, it sees farther; at every moment of time, it embraces all known reality; that is why it alone can furnish the mind with the moulds which are applicable to the totality of things and which make it possible to think of them. It does not create these moulds artificially; it finds them within itself; it does nothing but become conscious of them. They translate the ways of being which are found in all the stages of reality but which appear in their full clarity only at the summit, because the extreme complexity of the psychic life which passes there necessitates a greater development of consciousness. Attributing social origins to logical thought is not debasing it or diminishing its value or reducing it to nothing more than a system of artificial combinations; on the contrary, it is relating it to a cause which implies it naturally. But this is not saying that the ideas elaborated in this way are at once adequate for their object. If society is something universal in relation to the individual, it is none the less an individuality itself, which has its own personal physiognomy and its idiosyncrasies; it is a particular subject and consequently particularizes whatever it thinks of. Therefore collective representations also contain subjective elements, and these must be progressively rooted out, if we are to approach reality more closely. But howsoever crude these may have been at the beginning, the fact remains that with them the germ of a new mentality was given, to which the individual could never have raised himself by his own efforts: by them the way was opened to a stable, impersonal and organized thought which then had nothing to do except to develop its nature.

Also, the causes which have determined this development do not seem to be specifically different from those which gave it its initial impulse. If logical thought tends to rid itself more and more of the subjective and personal elements which it still retains from its origin, it is not because extra-social factors have intervened; it is much rather because a social life of a new sort is developing. It is this international life which has already resulted in universalizing religious beliefs. As it extends, the collective horizon enlarges; the society ceases to appear as the only whole, to become a part of a much vaster one, with indetermined frontiers, which is susceptible of advancing indefinitely. Consequently things can no longer be contained in the social moulds according to which they were primitively classified; they must be organized according to principles which are their own, so logical organization differentiates itself from the social organization and becomes autonomous. Really and truly human thought is not a primitive fact; it is the product of history; it is the ideal limit towards which we are constantly approaching, but which in all probability we shall never succeed in reaching.

Thus it is not at all true that between science on the one hand, and morals and religion on the other, there exists that sort of antinomy which has so frequently been admitted, for the two forms of human activity really come from one and the same source. Kant understood this very well, and therefore he made the speculative reason and the practical reason two different aspects of the same faculty. According to him, what makes their unity is the fact that the two are directed towards the universal. Rational thinking is thinking according to the laws which are imposed upon all reasonable beings; acting morally is conducting one's self according to those maxims which can be extended without contradiction to all wills. In other words, science and morals imply that the individual is capable of raising himself above his own peculiar point of view and of living an impersonal life. In fact, it cannot be doubted that this is a trait common to all the higher forms of thought and action. What Kant's system does not explain, however, is the origin of this sort of contradiction which is realized in man. Why is he forced to do violence to himself by leaving his individuality, and, inversely, why is the impersonal law obliged to be dissipated by incarnating itself in individuals? Is it answered that there are two antagonistic worlds in which we participate equally, the world of matter and sense on the one hand, and the world of pure and impersonal reason on the other? That is merely repeating the question in slightly different terms, for what we are trying to find out is why we must lead these two existences at the same time. Why do these two worlds, which seem to contradict each other, not remain outside of each other, and why must they mutually penetrate one another in spite of their antagonism? The only explanation which has ever been given of this singular necessity is the hypothesis of the Fall, with all the difficulties which it implies, and which need not be repeated here. On the other hand, all mystery disappears the moment that it is recognized that impersonal reason is only another name given to collective thought. For this is possible only through a group of individuals; it supposes them, and in their turn, they suppose it, for they can continue to exist only by grouping themselves together. The kingdom of ends and impersonal truths can realize itself only by the co-operation of particular wills, and the reasons for which these participate in it are the same as those for which they co-operate. In a word, there is something impersonal in us because there is something social in all of us, and since social life embraces at once both representations and practices, this impersonality naturally extends to ideas as well as to acts.

Perhaps some will be surprised to see us connect the most elevated forms of thought with society: the cause appears quite humble, in consideration of the value which we attribute to the effect. Between the world of the senses and appetites on the one hand, and that of reason and morals on the other, the distance is so considerable that the second would seem to have been able to add itself to the first only by a creative act. But attributing to society this preponderating rôle in the genesis of our nature is not denying this creation; for society has a creative power which no other observable being can equal. In fact, all creation, if not a mystical operation which escapes science and knowledge, is the product of a synthesis. Now if the synthesis of particular conceptions which take place in each individual consciousness are already and of themselves productive of novelties, how much more efficacious these vast syntheses of complete consciousnesses which make society must be! A society is the most powerful combination of physical and moral forces of which nature offers us an example. Nowhere else is an equal richness of different materials, carried to such a degree of concentration, to be found. Then it is not surprising that a higher life disengages itself which, by reacting upon the elements of which it is the product, raises them to a higher plane of existence and transforms them.

Thus sociology appears destined to open a new way to the science of man. Up to the present, thinkers were placed before this double alternative: either explain the superior and specific faculties of men by connecting them to the inferior forms of his being, the reason to the senses, or the mind to matter, which is equivalent to denying their uniqueness; or else attach them to some super-experimental reality which was postulated, but whose existence could be established by no observation. What put them in this difficulty was the fact that the individual passed as being the *finis naturæ*—the ultimate creation of nature; it seemed that there was nothing beyond him, or at least nothing that science could touch. But from the moment when it is recognized that above the individual there is society, and that this is not a nominal being created by reason, but a system of active forces, a new manner of explaining men becomes possible. To conserve his distinctive traits it is no longer necessary to put them outside experience. At least, before going to this last extremity, it would be well to see if that which surpasses the individual, though it is within him, does not come from this super-individual reality which we experience in society. To be sure, it cannot be said at present to what point these explanations may be able to reach, and whether or not they are of a nature to resolve all the problems. But it is equally impossible to mark in advance a limit beyond which they cannot go. What must be done is to try the hypothesis and submit it as methodically as possible to the control of facts. This is what we have tried to do.

Malinowski
RELIGION AND PRIMITIVE MAN*

1. *The Creative Acts of Religion.* It will be best to face the facts first and, in order not to narrow down the scope of the survey, to take as our watchword the vaguest and most general of indices: "Life." As a matter of fact, even a slight acquaintance with ethnological literature is enough to convince anyone that in reality the physiological phases of human life, and, above all, its crises, such as conception, pregnancy, birth, puberty, marriage, and death, form the nuclei of numerous rites and beliefs. Thus beliefs about conception, such as that in reincarnation, spirit-entry, magical impregnation, exist in one form or another in almost every tribe, and they are often associated with rites and observances. During pregnancy the expectant mother has to keep certain taboos and undergo ceremonies, and her husband shares at times in both. At birth, before and after, there are various magical rites to prevent dangers and undo sorcery, ceremonies of purification, communal rejoicings and acts of presentation of the newborn to higher powers or to the community. Later on in life the boys and, much less frequently, the girls have to undergo the often protracted rites of initiation, as a rule shrouded in mystery and marred by cruel and obscene ordeals.

Without going any further, we can see that even the very beginnings of human life are surrounded by an inextricably mixed-up medley of beliefs and rites. They seem to be strongly attracted by any important event in life, to crystallize around it, surround it with a rigid crust of formalism and ritualism—but to what purpose? Since we cannot define cult and creed by their objects, perhaps it will be possible to perceive their function.

* Bronislaw Malinowski (1884–1942): Polish anthropologist. This selection comes from Malinowski's famous essay "Magic, Science and Religion." His observations of primitive societies led him to some striking theses regarding the origin of religious rites and their meaning for primitive man. This selection is reprinted from *Science, Religion and Reality*, edited by Joseph Needham (1925), pp. 37–43, 45–52. Reprinted by permission of The Society for Promoting Christian Knowledge.

A closer scrutiny of the facts allows us to make from the outset a prelim-inary classification into two main groups. Compare a rite carried out to prevent death in childbed with another typical custom, a ceremony in cele-bration of a birth. The first rite is carried out as a means to an end, it has a definite practical purpose which is known to all who practice it and can be easily elicited from any native informant. The post-natal ceremony, say a presentation of a newborn or a feast of rejoicing in the event, has no purpose: it is not a means to an end but an end in itself. It expresses the feelings of the mother, the father, the relatives, the whole community, but there is no future event which this ceremony foreshadows, which it is meant to bring about or to prevent. This difference will serve us as a *prima facie* distinction between magic and religion. While in the magical act the under-lying idea and aim is always clear, straightforward, and definite, in the re-ligious ceremony there is no purpose directed toward a subsequent event. It is only possible for the sociologist to establish the function, the sociological *raison d'être* of the act. The native can always state the end of the magical rite, but he will say of a religious ceremony that it is done because such is the usage, or because it has been ordained, or he will narrate an explana-tory myth.

In order to grasp better the nature of primitive religious ceremonies and their function, let us analyze the ceremonies of initiation. They present right through the vast range of their occurrence certain striking similarities. Thus the novices have to undergo a more or less protracted period of seclusion and preparation. Then comes initiation proper, in which the youth, passing through a series of ordeals, is finally submitted to an act of bodily mutilation: at the mildest, a slight incision or the knocking out of a tooth; or, more severe, circumcision; or, really cruel and dangerous, an operation such as the subincision practiced in some Australian tribes. The ordeal is usually as-sociated with the idea of the death and rebirth of the initiated one, which is sometimes enacted in a mimetic performance. But besides the ordeal, less conspicuous and dramatic, but in reality more important, is the second main aspect of initiation: the systematic instruction of the youth in sacred myth and tradition, the gradual unveiling of tribal mysteries and the exhibition of sacred objects.

The ordeal and the unveiling of tribal mysteries are usually believed to have been instituted by one or more legendary ancestors or culture heroes, or by a Superior Being of superhuman character. Sometimes he is said to swallow the youths, or to kill them, and then to restore them again as fully initiated men. His voice is imitated by the hum of the bull-roarer to inspire awe in the uninitiated women and children. Through these ideas initiation brings the novice into relationship with higher powers and personalities, such as the Guardian Spirits and Tutelary Divinities of the North American Indians, the Tribal All-Father of some Australian Aborigines, the Mythologi-cal Heroes of Melanesia and other parts of the world. This is the third fundamental element, besides ordeal and the teaching of tradition, in the rites of passing into manhood.

Now what is the sociological function of these customs, what part do they play in the maintenance and development of civilization? As we have seen, the youth is taught in them the sacred traditions under the most impressive conditions of preparation and ordeal and under the sanction of Supernatural Beings—the light of tribal revelation bursts upon him from out of the shadows of fear, privation, and bodily pain.

Let us realize that in primitive conditions tradition is of supreme value for the community and nothing matters as much as the conformity and conservatism of its members. Order and civilization can be maintained only by strict adhesion to the lore and knowledge received from previous generations. Any laxity in this weakens the cohesion of the group and imperils its cultural outfit to the point of threatening its very existence. Man has not yet devised the extremely complex apparatus of modern science which enables him nowadays to fix the results of experience into imperishable molds, to test it ever anew, gradually to shape it into more adequate forms and enrich it constantly by new additions. The primitive man's share of knowledge, his social fabric, his customs and beliefs, are the invaluable yield of devious experience of his forefathers, bought at an extravagant price and to be maintained at any cost. Thus, of all his qualities, truth to tradition is the most important, and a society which makes its tradition sacred has gained by it an inestimable advantage of power and performance. Such beliefs and practices, therefore, which put a halo of sanctity round tradition and a supernatural stamp upon it, will have a "survival value" for the type of civilization in which they have been evolved.

We may, therefore, lay down the main function of initiation ceremonies: they are a ritual and dramatic expression of the supreme power and value of tradition in primitive societies; they also serve to impress this power and value upon the minds of each generation, and they are at the same time an extremely efficient means of transmitting tribal lore, of insuring continuity in tradition and of maintaining tribal cohesion.

We still have to ask: What is the relation between the purely physiological fact of bodily maturity which these ceremonies mark, and their social and religious aspect? We see at once that religion does something more, infinitely more, than the mere "sacralizing of a crisis of life." From a natural event it makes a social transition, to the fact of bodily maturity it adds the vast conception of entry into manhood with its duties, privileges, responsibilities, above all with its knowledge of tradition and the communion with sacred things and beings. There is thus a creative element in the rites of religious nature. The act establishes not only a social event in the life of the individual but also a spiritual metamorphosis, both associated with the biological event but transcending it in importance and significance.

Initiation is a typically religious act, and we can see clearly here how the ceremony and its purpose are one, how the end is realized in the very consummation of the act. At the same time we can see the function of such acts in society in that they create mental habits and social usages of inestimable value to the group and its civilization. . . .

When we pass to nutrition, the first thing to be noted is that eating is for primitive man an act surrounded by etiquette, special prescriptions and prohibitions, and a general emotional tension to a degree unknown to us. Besides the magic of food, designed to make it go a long way, or to prevent its scarcity in general—and we do not speak here at all of the innumerable forms of magic associated with the procuring of food—food has also a conspicuous role in ceremonies of a distinctly religious character. First-fruit offerings of a ritual nature, harvest ceremonies, big seasonal feasts in which crops are accumulated, displayed, and, in one way or another, sacralized, play an important part among agricultural people. Hunters, again, or fishers celebrate a big catch or the opening of the season of their pursuit by feasts and ceremonies at which food is ritually handled, the animals propitiated or worshipped. All such acts express the joy of the community, their sense of the great value of food, and religion through them consecrates the reverent attitude of man towards his daily bread.

To primitive man, never, even under the best conditions, quite free from the threat of starvation, abundance of food is a primary condition of normal life. It means the possibility of looking beyond the daily worries, of paying more attention to the remoter, spiritual aspects of civilization. If we thus consider that food is the main link between man and his surroundings, that by receiving it he feels the forces of destiny and providence, we can see the cultural, nay, biological importance of primitive religion in the sacralization of food. We can see in it the germs of what in higher types of religion will develop into the feeling of dependence upon Providence, of gratitude, and of confidence in it.

Sacrifice and communion, the main forms in which food is ritually ministered, can now be held in a new light against the background of man's early attitude of religious reverence towards the providential abundance of food. That the idea of giving, the importance of the exchange of gifts in all phases of social contact, plays a great role in sacrifice seems—in spite of the unpopularity of this theory nowadays—unquestionable in view of the new knowledge of primitive economic psychology. Since the giving of gifts is the normal accompaniment of all social intercourse among primitives, the spirits who visit the village or the demons who haunt some hallowed spot, or divinities when approached are given their due, their share sacrificed from the general plenty, as any other visitors or persons visited would be. But underlying this custom there is a still deeper religious element. Since food is to the savage the token of the beneficence of the world, since plenty gives him the first, the most elementary, inkling of Providence, by sharing in food sacrificially with his spirits or divinities the savage shares with them in the beneficial powers of his Providence already felt by him but not yet comprehended. Thus in primitive societies the roots of sacrificial offerings are to be found in the psychology of gift, which is to the communion in beneficent abundance. . . .

3. *Man's Selective Interest in Nature.* This brings us to the subject of totemism, briefly defined in the first section. As may have been seen, the following questions have to be asked about totemism. First, why does a primitive tribe select for its totems a limited number of species, primarily animals and plants; and on what principles is this selection made? Secondly, why is this selective attitude expressed in beliefs of affinity, in cults of multiplication, above all in the negative injunctions of totemic taboos, and again in injunctions of ritual eating, as in the Australian "totemic sacrament"? Thirdly and finally, why with the subdivision of nature into a limited number of selected species does there run parallel a subdivision of the tribe into clans correlated with the species?

The above outlined psychology of the primitive attitude towards food and its abundance and our principle of man's practical and pragmatic outlook lead us directly to an answer. We have seen that food is the primary link between the primitive and providence. And the need of it and the desire for its abundance have led man to economic pursuits, collecting, hunting, fishing, and they endow these pursuits with varied and tense emotions. A number of animal and vegetable species, those which form the staple food of the tribe, dominate the interests of the tribesmen. To primitive man nature is his living larder, to which—especially at the lowest stages of culture—he has to repair directly in order to gather, cook, and eat when hungry. The road from the wilderness to the savage's belly and consequently to his mind is very short, and for him the world is an indiscriminate background against which there stand out the useful, primarily the edible, species of animals or plants. Those who have lived in the jungle with savages, taking part in collecting or hunting expeditions, or who have sailed with them over the lagoons, or spent moonlit nights on sandbanks waiting for the shoals of fish or for the appearance of turtle, know how keen and selective is the savage's interests, how it clings to the indications, trails, and to the habits and peculiarities of his quarry, while it yet remains quite indifferent to any other stimuli. Every such species which is habitually pursued forms a nucleus round which all the interests, the impulses, the emotions of a tribe tend to crystallize. A sentiment of social nature is built round each species, a sentiment which naturally finds its expression in folklore, belief, and ritual.

It must also be remembered that the same type of impulse which makes small children delight in birds, take a keen interest in animals, and shrink from reptiles, places animals in the front rank of nature for primitive man. By their general affinity with man—they move, utter sounds, manifest emotions, have bodies and faces like him—and by their superior powers—the birds fly in the open, the fishes swim under water, reptiles renew their skins and their life and can disappear in the earth—by all this the animal, the intermediate link between man and nature, often his superior in strength, agility, and cunning, usually his indispensable quarry, assumes an exceptional place in the savage's view of the world.

The primitive is deeply interested in the appearance and properties of beasts; he desires to have them and, therefore, to control them as useful and edible things; sometimes he admires and fears them. All these interests meet and, strengthening each other, produce the same effect: the selection, in man's principal preoccupations, of a limited number of species, animal first, vegetable in the second place, while inanimate or man-made things are unquestionably but a secondary formation, an introduction by analogy, of objects which have nothing to do with the substance of totemism.

The nature of man's interest in the totemic species indicates also clearly the type of belief and cult to be there expected. Since it is the desire to control the species, dangerous, useful, or edible, this desire must lead to a belief in special power over the species, affinity with it, a common essence between man and beast or plant. Such a belief implies, on the one hand, certain considerations and restraints—the most obvious being a prohibition to kill and to eat; on the other hand, it endows man with the supernatural faculty of contributing ritually to the abundance of the species, to its increase and vitality . . .

Totemism appears thus as a blessing bestowed by religion on primitive man's efforts in dealing with his useful surroundings, upon his "struggle for existence." At the same time it develops his reverence for those animals and plants on which he depends, to which he feels in a way grateful, and yet the destruction of which is a necessity to him. And all this springs from the belief of man's affinity with those forces of nature upon which he mainly depends. Thus we find a moral value and a biological significance in totemism, in a system of beliefs, practices, and social arrangements which at first sight appears but a childish, irrevelent, and degrading fancy of the savage.

4. *Death and the Reintegration of the Group.* Of all sources of religion, the supreme and final crisis of life—death—is of the greatest importance. Death is the gateway to the other world in more than the literal sense. According to most theories of early religion, a great deal, if not all, of religious inspiration has been derived from it—and in this orthodox views are on the whole correct. Man has to live his life in the shadow of death, and he who clings to life and enjoys its fullness must dread the menace of its end. And he who is faced by death turns to the promise of life. Death and its denial—Immortality—have always formed, as they form today, the most poignant theme of man's forebodings. The extreme complexity of man's emotional reactions to life finds necessarily its counterpart in his attitude to death. Only what in life has been spread over a long space and manifested in a succession of experiences and events is here at its end condensed into one crisis which provokes a violent and complex outburst of religious manifestations.

Even among the most primitive peoples, the attitude towards death is infinitely more complex and, I may add, more akin to our own, than is usually assumed. It is often stated by anthropologists that the dominant feeling of the survivors is that of horror at the corpse and of fear of the ghost. This twin attitude is even made by no less an authority than Wilhelm Wundt the very nucleus of all religious belief and practice. Yet this assertion is only a half-truth, which means no truth at all. The emotions are extremely complex and even contradictory; the dominant elements, love of the dead and loathing of the corpse, passionate attachment to the personality still lingering about the body and a shattering fear of the gruesome thing that has been left over, these two elements seem to mingle and play into each other. This is reflected in the spontaneous behavior and in the ritual proceedings at death. In the tending of the corpse, in the modes of its disposal, in the post-funerary and commemorative ceremonies, the nearest relatives, the mother mourning for her son, the widow for her husband, the child for the parent, always show some horror and fear mingled with pious love, but never do the negative elements appear alone or even dominant.

The mortuary proceedings show a striking similarity throughout the world. As death approaches, the nearest relatives in any case, sometimes the whole community, forgather by the dying man, and dying, the most private act which a man can perform, is transformed into a public, tribal event. As a rule, a certain differentiation takes place at once, some of the relatives watching near the corpse, others making preparations for the pending end and its consequences, others again performing perhaps some religious acts at a sacred spot. Thus in certain parts of Melanesia the real kinsmen must keep at a distance and only relatives by marriage perform the mortuary services, while in some tribes of Australia the reverse order is observed.

As soon as death has occurred, the body is washed, anointed and adorned, sometimes the bodily apertures are filled, the arms and legs tied together. Then it is exposed to the view of all, and the most important phase, the immediate mourning begins. Those who have witnessed death and its sequel among savages and who can compare these events with their counterpart among other uncivilized peoples must be struck by the fundamental similarity of the proceedings. There is always a more or less conventionalized and dramatized outburst of grief and wailing in sorrow, which often passes among savages into bodily lacerations and the tearing of hair. This is always done in a public display and is associated with visible signs of mourning, such as black or white daubs on the body, shaven or disheveled hair, strange or torn garments.

The immediate mourning goes on round the corpse. This, far from being shunned or dreaded, is usually the center of pious attention. Often there are ritual forms of fondling or attestations of reverence. The body is sometimes kept on the knees of seated persons, stroked and embraced. At the same time these acts are usually considered both dangerous and repugnant, duties to be fulfilled at some cost to the performer. After a time the corpse has to be disposed of. Inhumation with an open or closed grave; exposure in caves or on platforms, in hollow trees or on the ground in some wild desert place, burning or setting adrift in canoes—these are the usual forms of disposal.

This brings us to perhaps the most important point, the two-fold contradictory tendency, on the one hand to preserve the body, to keep its form intact, or to retain parts of it; on the other hand the desire to be done with it, to put it out of the way, to annihilate it completely. Mummification and burning are the two extreme expressions of this two-fold tendency. It is impossible to regard mummification or burning or any intermediate form as determined by mere accident of belief, as a historical feature of some culture or other which has gained its universality by the mechanism of spread and contact only. For in these customs is clearly expressed the fundamental attitude of mind of the surviving relative, friend or lover, the longing for all that remains of the dead person and the disgust and fear of the dreadful transformation wrought by death.

One extreme and interesting variety in which this double-edged attitude is expressed in a gruesome manner is sarcocannibalism, a custom of partaking in piety of the flesh of the dead person. It is done with extreme repugnance and dread and usually followed by a violent vomiting fit. At the same time it is felt to be a supreme act of reverence, love, and devotion. In fact it is considered such a sacred duty that among the Melanesians of New Guinea, where I have studied and witnessed it, it is still performed in secret, although severely penalized by the white Government. The smearing of the body with the fat of the dead, prevalent in Australia and Papuasia is, perhaps, but a variety of this custom.

In all such rites, there is a desire to maintain the tie and the parallel tendency to break the bond. Thus the funerary rites are considered as unclean and soiling, the contact with the corpse as defiling and dangerous, and the performers have to wash, cleanse their body, remove all traces of contact, and perform ritual lustrations. Yet the mortuary ritual compels man to overcome the repugnance, to conquer his fear, to make piety and attachment triumphant, and with it the belief in a future life, in the survival of the spirit.

And here we touch on one of the most important functions of religious cult. In the foregoing analysis I have laid stress on the direct emotional forces created by contact with death and with the corpse, for they primarily and most powerfully determine the behavior of the survivors. But connected with these emotions and born out of them, there is the idea of the spirit, the belief in the new life into which the departed has entered. And here we return to the problem of animism with which we began our survey of primitive religious facts. What is the substance of a spirit, and what is the psychological origin of this belief?

The savage is intensely afraid of death, probably as the result of some deep-seated instincts common to man and animals. He does not want to realize it as an end, he cannot face the idea of complete cessation, of annihilation. The idea of spirit and of spiritual existence is near at hand, furnished by such experiences as are discovered and described by Tylor. Grasping at it, man reaches the comforting belief in spiritual continuity and in the life after death. Yet this belief does not remain unchallenged in the complex, double-edged play of hope and fear which sets in always in the face of death. To the comforting voice of hope, to the intense desire of immortality, to the difficulty, in one's own case, almost the impossibility, of facing annihilation there are opposed powerful and terrible forebodings. The testimony of the senses, the gruesome decomposition of the corpse, the visible disappearance of the personality—certain apparently instinctive suggestions of fear and horror seem to threaten man at all stages of culture with some idea of annihilation, with some hidden fears and forebodings. And here into this play of emotional forces, into this supreme dilemma of life and final death, religion steps in, selecting the positive creed, the comforting view, the culturally valuable belief in immortality, in the spirit independent of the body, and in the continuance of life after death. In the various ceremonies at death, in commemoration and communion with the departed, and worship of ancestral ghosts, religion gives the body and form to the saving beliefs.

Thus the belief in immortality is the result of a deep emotional revelation, standardized by religion, rather than a primitive philosophic doctrine. Man's conviction of continued life is one of the supreme gifts of religion, which judges and selects the better of the two alternatives suggested by self-preservation—the hope of continued life and the fear of annihilation. The belief in spirits is the result of the belief in immortality. The substance of which the spirits are made is the full-blooded passion and desire for life, rather than the shadowy stuff which haunts his dreams and illusions. Religion saves man from a surrender to death and destruction, and in doing this it merely makes use of the observations of dreams, shadows, and visions. The real nucleus of animism lies in the deepest emotional fact of human nature, the desire for life.

Thus the rites of mourning, the ritual behavior immediately after death, can be taken as pattern of the religious act, while the belief in immortality, in the continuity of life and in the nether world, can be taken as the prototype of an act of faith. Here, as in the religious ceremonies previously described, we find self-contained acts, the aim of which is achieved in their very performance. The ritual despair, the obsequies, the acts of mourning, express the emotion of the bereaved and the loss of the whole group. They endorse and they duplicate the natural feelings of the survivors; they create a social event out of a natural fact. Yet, though in the acts of mourning, in the mimic despair of wailing, in the treatment of the corpse and in its disposal, nothing ulterior is achieved, these acts fulfill an important function and possess a considerable value for primitive culture.

What is this function? The initiation ceremonies we have found fulfill theirs in sacralizing tradition; the food cult, sacrament and sacrifice bring man into communion with providence, with the beneficent forces of plenty; totemism standardizes man's practical, useful attitude of selective interest towards his surroundings. If the view here taken of the biological function of religion is true, some such similar role must also be played by the whole mortuary ritual.

The death of a man or woman in a primitive group, consisting of a limited

number of individuals, is an event of no mean importance. The nearest relatives and friends are disturbed to the depth of their emotional life. A small
community bereft of a member, especially if he be important, is severely
mutilated. The whole event breaks the normal course of life and shakes the
moral foundations of society. The strong tendency on which we have insisted in the above description: to give way to fear and horror, to abandon
the corpse, to run away from the village, to destroy all the belongings of the
dead one—all these impulses exist, and if given way to would be extremely
dangerous, disintegrating the group, destroying the material foundations of
primitive culture. Death in a primitive society is, therefore, much more than
the removal of a member. By setting in motion one part of the deep forces
of the instinct of self-preservation, it threatens the very cohesion and solidarity of the group, and upon this depends the organization of that society,
its tradition, and finally the whole culture. For if primitive man yielded always to the disintegrating impulses of his reaction to death, the continuity
of tradition and the existence of material civilization would be made
impossible.

We have seen already how religion, by sacralizing and thus standardizing
the other set of impulses, bestows on man the gift of mental integrity.
Exactly the same function it fulfills also with regard to the whole group.
The ceremonial of death which ties the survivors to the body and rivets them
to the place of death, the beliefs in the existence of the spirit, in its beneficent influences or malevolent intentions, in the duties of a series of commemorative or sacrificial ceremonies—in all this religion counteracts the
centrifugal forces of fear, dismay, demoralization, and provides the most
powerful means of reintegration of the group's shaken solidarity and of the
re-establishment of its morale.

In short, religion here assures the victory of tradition and culture over
the mere negative response of thwarted instinct.

Chapter 6

Origin of religion in myth

The mythological background of both primitive and modern religious traditions has long been recognized. Religious historians have made remarkable discoveries of universal mythic figures and events that appear in the most ancient religions as well as the most modern. The recurrence of mythological motifs and their pervasiveness in religious consciousness and in ritual practices makes necessary an understanding of the relationship between mythic thought and religious beliefs and practices.

The content of a myth is conveyed by symbols arranged and articulated so as to narrate the actions of a divine figure, a cosmic process, or an event of great significance for man. Not all symbols employed in myths are, however, contingent. For example, the symbolism of sexual generation in the Judeo-Christian myth of the Fall is not arbitrary or contingent, because sexual generation does participate in the process of becoming. Yet symbols are also human creations. A natural event, like birth only becomes a symbol when human beings respond to it as such. Symbols presuppose symbolic response, and such response is always dependent upon circumstances and environment. We express the dependence of most symbols upon community understanding and participation by saying that men make symbols. However, we should not ignore the equally fundamental fact that symbols, and their vehicle, the myth, make men.

Mythic consciousness and symbolic response partly define man, but while symbols and myths are *pervasive* human facts, are they necessary? We have already seen that Freud thought we should eliminate the symbols and myths of religion and replace them with the signs of science. Clearly the most pressing issue with regard to myths and their symbols is the question of their truthfulness. If the pervasive myths of mankind are subjective modes of experience, completely lacking in objective reference, then these myths have interest and value only as psychological and cultural phenomena reflecting the uncritical emotional life and fertile imagination. If, on the other hand, myths make some reality manifest to us, if they uncover real structures and modes of being that are inaccessible to scientific probing, then their significance and cognitive value for life is immense. The psychological and social functions of myths have never been denied, but in dealing with their function, as that of revealing ontological and religious truths inaccessible to rational inquiry, it is wise to proceed with caution.

It is undeniable that religious consciousness and practice has always been deeply rooted in mythological thought and response to myth. The problem of how this involvement is to be interpreted is a central concern for the reflective student of religious phenomena. Myths and their symbols are necessary if, and only if, the signs of science prove to be inadequate. The problem of universality is severe for mythic "truth" in a way that it is not for scientific truth. The statements of science are cross-culturally intelligible in a way that myths may not be. What, then, does it mean to say that a myth is true, that a Greek can understand something of reality that a Hindu cannot? Nonetheless, the suspicion that myths are somehow necessary for full comprehension of certain aspects of reality remains. The language of signs is exceptionally powerful, but can words, in their abstractness, ever exhaust the concrete movements of the spirit? Can we avoid, in religion, turning to myths which point to and participate in the structures of reality?

Issues such as these lie at the center of Joseph Campbell's essay entitled "The Masks of God" which is an exploration of the nature and function of mythology and of its significance for religion. Campbell argues that a literal interpretation of mythic thought and response perverts its meaning, while a flat rejection of mythological constructs actually prevents us from discovering meaningful truths. In fact, Campbell maintains that mythic beliefs do reveal aspects of reality, otherwise hidden from the rational, pragmatic intellect, through man's participation in a dimension of life which is accessible only in mythic response.

A rather different approach to the mythic content of religious tradition is presented in Bultmann's essay on the necessity of demythologizing the teaching (kerygma) of the New Testament. Bultmann insists that New Testament mythology cannot be accepted by modern man, for it entails a cosmology which is prescientific and addresses itself to the consciousness of a preurban, preindustrial man. The imperative task of theology becomes, therefore, the serious work of stripping away the mythic framework of New Testament teaching in order to preserve the truth of that teaching freed from its obsolete trappings. Agreeing with Campbell that myths point beyond themselves to significant realities, he warns against the translation of the imagery of myth into objective truth. What is required to preserve the genuine validity of mythic perspectives is to expose that understanding of human existence embodied in the myth which has a continuing and universal meaning for man.

Campbell
THE MASKS OF GOD*

[1.]   The artist eye, as Thomas Mann has said, has a mythical slant upon life; therefore, the mythological realm—the world of the gods and demons, the carnival of their masks and the curious game of "as if" in which the festival of the lived myth abrogates all the laws of time, letting the dead swim back to life, and the "once upon a time" become the very present— we must approach and first regard with the artist's eye. For, indeed, in the primitive world, where most of the clues to the origin of mythology must be sought, the gods and demons are not conceived in the way of hard and fast, positive realities. A god can be simultaneously in two or more places— like a melody, or like the form of a traditional mask. And wherever he comes, the impact of his presence is the same: it is not reduced through multiplication. Moreover, the mask in a primitive festival is revered and experienced as a veritable apparition of the mythical being that it represents —even though everyone knows that a man made the mask and that a man is wearing it The one wearing it, furthermore, is identified with the god during the time of the ritual of which the mask is a part. He does not merely represent the god; he *is* the god. The literal fact that the apparition is com- posed of A, a mask, B, its reference to a mythical being, and C, a man, is dismissed from the mind, and the presentation is allowed to work without correction upon the sentiments of both the beholder and the actor. In other words, there has been a shift of view from the logic of the normal secular sphere, where things are understood to be distinct from one another, to a theatrical or play sphere, where they are accepted for what they are *experi- enced* as being and the logic is that of "make believe"—"as if."
   We all know the convention, surely! It is a primary, spontaneous device of childhood, a magical device, by which the world can be transformed from banality to magic in a trice. And its inevitability in childhood is one of those universal characteristics of man that unite us in one family. It is a primary datum, consequently, of the science of myth, which is concerned precisely with the phenomenon of self-induced belief.

* Joseph Campbell (1904–   ): American mythologist. The selections are taken from Campbell's three volume work, *The Masks of God*. The first selection is from the essay entitled, "The Lesson of the Mask" in the introduction to the volume "Primitive Mythology." The second selection is from the "Conclusion" of the volume "Occidental Mythology." In his three volumes, Campbell examines the roots of the mythologies of the world and draws upon insights from archaeology, anthropology, psychology and other disciplines in doing so. From *The Masks of God: Primitive Mythology* by Joseph Campbell. Copyright © 1959 by Joseph Campbell; from *The Masks of God: Occidental Mythology* by Joseph Campbell. Copyright © 1964 by Joseph Campbell. All Rights Reserved. Both excerpts reprinted by permission of The Viking Press, Inc., New York and Martin Secker & Warburg Limited, London.

"A professor," wrote Leo Frobenius in a celebrated paper on the force of the daemonic world of childhood, "is writing at his desk and his four-year-old little daughter is running about the room. She has nothing to do and is disturbing him. So he gives her three burnt matches, saying, 'Here! Play!' and, sitting on the rug, she begins to play with the matches, Hansel, Gretel, and the witch. A considerable time elapses, during which the professor concentrates upon his task, undisturbed. But then, suddenly, the child shrieks in terror. The father jumps. 'What is it? What has happened?' The little girl comes running to him, showing every sign of great fright. 'Daddy, Daddy,' she cries, 'take the witch away! I can't touch the witch any more!' " . . .

This vivid, convincing example of a child's seizure by a witch while in the act of play may be taken to represent an intense degree of the daemonic mythological experience. However, the attitude of mind represented by the game itself, before the seizure supervened, also belongs within the sphere of our subject. For, as J. Huizinga has pointed out in his brilliant study of the play element in culture, the whole point, at the beginning, is the *fun* of play, not the rapture of seizure. "In all the wild imaginings of mythology a fanciful spirit is playing," he writes, "on the border-line between jest and earnest." "As far as I know, ethnologists and anthropologists concur in the opinion that the mental attitude in which the great religious feasts of savages are celebrated and witnessed is not one of complete illusion. There is an underlying consciousness of things 'not being real.' " And he quotes, among others, R. R. Marett, who, in his chapter on "Primitive Credulity" in *The Threshold of Religion*, develops the idea that a certain element of "make-believe" is operative in all primitive religions. "The savage," wrote Marett, "is a good actor who can be quite absorbed in his role, like a child at play; and also, like a child, a good spectator who can be frightened to death by the roaring of something he knows perfectly well to be no 'real' lion."

"By considering the whole sphere of so-called primitive culture as a play-sphere," Huizinga then suggests in conclusion, "we pave the way to a more direct and more general understanding of its peculiarities than any meticulous psychological or sociological analysis would allow." And I would concur wholeheartedly with this judgment, only adding that we should extend the consideration to the entire field of our present subject.

In the Roman Catholic mass, for example, when the priest, quoting the words of Christ at the Last Supper, pronounces the formula of consecration —with utmost solemnity—first over the wafer of the host (*Hoc est enim Corpus meum:* "for this is My Body"), then over the chalice of the wine (*Hic est enim Calix Sanguinis mei, novi et aeterni Testamenti: Mysterium fidei: qui pro vobis et pro multis effundetur in remissionem peccatorum:* "For this is the Chalice of My Blood, of the new and eternal testament: the mystery of faith: which shall be shed for you and for many unto the remission of sins"), it is to be supposed that the bread and wine become the body and blood of Christ, that every fragment of the host and every drop of the wine is the actual living Savior of the world. The sacrament, that is to say, is not conceived to be a *reference,* a mere sign or symbol to arouse in us a train of thought, but is God himself, the Creator, Judge, and Savior of the Universe, here come to work upon us directly, to free our souls (created in His image) from the effects of the Fall of Adam and Eve in the Garden of Eden (which we are to suppose existed as a geographical fact).

Comparably, in India it is believed that, in response to consecrating formulae, deities will descend graciously to infuse their divine substance into the temple images, which are then called their throne or seat (*pītha*). It is also possible—and in some Indian sects even expected—that the individual himself should become a seat of deity. In the *Gandharva Tantra* it is written, for example, "No one who is not himself divine can successfully worship a divinity"; and again, "Having become the divinity, one should offer it sacrifice."

Furthermore, it is even possible for a really gifted player to discover that everything—absolutely everything—has become the body of a god, or reveals the omnipresence of God as the ground of all being. There is a passage, for example, among the conversations of the nineteenth-century Bengalese spiritual master Ramakrishna, in which he described such an experience. "One day," he is said to have reported, "it was suddenly revealed to me that everything is Pure Spirit. The utensils of worship, the altar, the door frame—all Pure Spirit. Men, animals, and other living beings—all Pure Spirit. Then like a madman I began to shower flowers in all directions. Whatever I saw I worshiped."

Belief—or at least a game of belief—is the first step toward such a divine seizure. The chronicles of the saints abound in accounts of their long ordeals of difficult practice, which preceded their moments of being carried away; and we have also the more spontaneous religious games and exercises of the folk (the amateurs) to illustrate for us the principle involved. The spirit of the festival, the holiday, the holy day of the religious ceremonial, requires that the normal attitude toward the cares of the world should have been temporarily set aside in favor of a particular mood of dressing up. The world is hung with banners. Or in the permanent religious sanctuaries— the temples and cathedrals, where an atmosphere of holiness hangs permanently in the air—the logic of cold, hard fact must not be allowed to intrude and spoil the spell. The gentile, the "spoil sport," the positivist, who cannot or will not play, must be kept aloof. Hence the guardian figures that stand at either side of the entrances to hold places: lions, bulls, or fearsome warriors with uplifted weapons. They are there to keep out the "spoil sports," the advocates of Aristotelean logic, for whom A can never be B; for whom the actor is never to be lost in the part; for whom the mask, the image, the consecrated host, tree, or animal cannot become God, but only a reference. Such heavy thinkers are to remain without. For the whole purpose of entering a sanctuary or participating in a festival is that one should be overtaken by the state known in India as "the other mind" (Sanskrit, *anya-manas:* absent-mindedness, possession by a spirit), where one is "beside oneself," spellbound, set apart from one's logic of self-possession and overpowered by the force of a logic of "indissociation"—wherein A is B, and C also is B.

"One day," said Ramakrishna, "while worshiping Shiva, I was about to offer a bel-leaf on the head of the image, when it was revealed to me that this universe itself is Shiva. Another day, I had been plucking flowers when it was revealed to me that each plant was a bouquet adorning the universal form of God. That was the end of my plucking flowers. I look on man in just the same way. When I see a man, I see that it is God Himself, who walks on earth, rocking to and fro, as it were, like a pillow floating on the waves."

From such a point of view the universe is the seat (*pīṭha*) of a divinity from whose vision our usual state of consciousness excludes us. But in the playing of the game of the gods we take a step toward that reality—which is ultimately the reality of ourselves. Hence the rapture, the feelings of delight, and the sense of refreshment, harmony, and re-creation! In the case of a saint, the game leads to seizure—as in the case of the little girl, to whom the match revealed itself to be a witch. Contact with the orientation of the world may then be lost, the mind remaining rapt in that other state. For such it is impossible to return to this other game, the game of life in the world. They are possessed of God; that is all they know on earth and all they need to know. And they can even infect whole societies, so that these, inspired by their seizures, may likewise break contact with the world and spurn it as delusory, or as evil. Secular life then may be read as a fall— a fall from Grace, Grace being the rapture of the festival of God.

But there is another attitude, more comprehensive, which has given beauty and love to the *two* worlds: that, namely, of the *līlā*, "the play," as it has been termed in the Orient. The world is not condemned and shunned as a fall, but voluntarily entered as a game or dance, wherein the spirit plays.

Ramakrishna closed his eyes. "Is it only this?" he said. "Does God exist only when the eyes are closed, and disappear when the eyes are opened?" He opened his eyes. "The Play belongs to Him to whom Eternity belongs, and Eternity to Him to whom the Play belongs. . . . Some people climb the seven floors of a building and cannot get down; but some climb up and then, at will, visit the lower floors."

The question then becomes only: How far down or up the ladder can one go without losing the sense of a game? Professor Huizinga, in his work already referred to, points out that in Japanese the verb *asobu*, which refers to play in general—recreation, relaxation, amusement, trip or jaunt, dissipation, gambling, lying idle, or being unemployed—also means to study at a university or under a teacher; likewise, to engage in a sham fight; and finally, to participate in the very strict formalities of the tea ceremony. He continues:

The extraordinary earnestness and profound gravity of the Japanese ideal of life is masked by the fashionable fiction that everything is only play. Like the *chevalerie* of the Christian Middle Ages, Japanese *bushido* took shape almost entirely in the play-sphere and was enacted in play-forms. The language still preserves this conception in the *asobase-kotoba* (literally play-language) or polite speech, the mode of address used in conversation with persons of higher rank. The convention is that the higher classes are merely playing at all they do. The polite form for "you arrive in Tokyo" is, literally, "you play arrival in Tokyo"; and for "I hear that your father is dead," "I hear that your father has played dying." In other words, the revered person is imagined as living in an elevated sphere where only pleasure or condescension moves to action.

From this supremely aristocratic point of view, any state of seizure, whether by life or by the gods, must represent a fall or drop of spiritual *niveau*, a vulgarization of the play. Nobility of spirit is the grace—or ability —to play, whether in heaven or on earth. And this, I take it, this *noblesse oblige*, which has always been the quality of aristocracy, was precisely the virtue (ἀρετή) of the Greek poets, artists, and philosophers, for whom the gods were true as poetry is true. We may take it also to be the primitive (and proper) mythological point of view, as contrasted with the heavier positivistic; which latter is represented, on the one hand, by religious experiences of the literal sort, where the impact of a daemon, rising to the plane of consciousness from its place of birth on the level of the sentiments, is taken to be objectively real, and, on the other, by science and political economy, for which only measurable facts are objectively real. For if it is true, as the Greek philosopher Antisthenes (born c. 444 B.C.) has said, that "God is not like anything: hence no one can understand him by means of an image," or, as we read in the Indian Upanishad,

> It is other, indeed, than the known
> And, moreover, above the unknown!

then it must be conceded, as a basic principle of our natural history of the gods and heroes, that whenever a myth has been taken literally its sense has been perverted; but also, reciprocally, that whenever it has been dismissed as a mere priestly fraud or sign of inferior intelligence, truth has slipped out the other door.

And so what, then, is the sense that we are to seek, if it be neither here nor there?

Kant, in his *Prolegomena to Every Future System of Metaphysics*, states very carefully that all our thinking about final things can be only by way of *analogy*. "The proper expression for our fallible mode of conception," he declares, "would be: that we imagine the world *as if* its being and inner character were derived from a supreme mind" (italics mine).

Such a highly played game of "as if" frees our mind and spirit, on the one hand, from the presumption of theology, which pretends to know the laws of God, and, on the other, from the bondage of reason, whose laws do not apply beyond the horizon of human experience.

I am willing to accept the word of Kant, as representing the view of a considerable metaphysician. And applying it to the range of festival games and attitudes just reviewed—from the mask to the consecrated host and temple image, transubstantiated worshiper and transubstantiated world—I can see, or believe I can see, that a principle of release operates throughout the series by way of the alchemy of an "as if"; and that, through this, the impact of all so-called "reality" upon the psyche is transubstantiated. The play state and the rapturous seizures sometimes deriving from it represent, therefore, a step rather *toward* than away from the ineluctable truth; and belief—acquiescence in a belief that is not quite belief—is the first step toward the deepened participation that the festival affords in that general will to life which, in its metaphysical aspect, is antecedent to, and the creator of, all life's laws.

The opaque weight of the world—both of life on earth and of death, heaven, and hell—is dissolved, and the spirit freed, not *from* anything, for there was nothing from which to be freed except a myth too solidly believed, but *for* something, something fresh and new, a spontaneous act.

From the position of secular man (Homo sapiens), that is to say, we are to enter the play sphere of the festival, acquiescing in a game of belief, where fun, joy, and rapture rule in ascending series. The laws of life in time and space—economics, politics, and even morality—will thereupon dissolve. Whereafter, re-created by that return to paradise before the Fall, before the knowledge of good and evil, right and wrong, true and false, belief and disbelief, we are to carry the point of view and spirit of man the player (Homo ludens) back into life; as in the play of children, where, undaunted by the banal actualities of life's meager possibilities, the spontaneous impulse of the spirit to identify itself with something other than itself for the sheer delight of play, transubstantiates the world—in which, actually, after all, things are not quite as real or permanent, terrible, important, or logical as they seem. . . .

[2.]   In the long view of the history of mankind, four essential functions of mythology can be discerned. The first and most distinctive—vitalizing all—is that of eliciting and supporting a sense of awe before the mystery of being. Professor Rudolf Otto has termed this recognition of the *numinous* the characteristic mental state of all religions properly so called. It antecedes and defies definition. It is, on the primitive level, demonic dread; on the highest, mystical rapture; and between there are many grades. Defined, it may be talked about and taught; but talk and teaching cannot produce it. Nor can authority enforce it. Only the accident of experience and the sign symbols of a living myth can elicit and support it; but such signs cannot be invented. They are found. Whereupon they function of themselves. And those who find them are the sensitized, creative, living minds that once were known as seers, but now as poets and creative artists. More important, more effective for the future of a culture than its statesmen or its armies are these masters of the spiritual breath by which the clay of man wakes to life.

The second function of mythology is to render a cosmology, an image of the universe that will support and be supported by this sense of awe before the mystery of a presence and the presence of a mystery. The cosmology has to correspond, however, to the actual experience, knowledge, and mentality of the culture folk involved. So we note that when the priestly watchers of the skies in ancient Sumer, c. 3500 B.C., learned of the order of the planets, the entire mythic system of the nuclear Near East stepped away from the simple primitive themes of the hunting and planting tribes. The grandiose vision of a mathematically impersonal temporal and spatial order came into being, of which the world vision of the Middle Ages—no less than that of ancient India, that of China, and that of Yucatan—was but a late variant. Today that vision has dissolved. And here we touch upon a crucial problem of the religions of our time; for the clergies, generally, still are preaching themes from the first to fourth millenniums B.C.

No one of adult mind today would turn to the Book of Genesis to learn of the origins of the earth, the plants, the beasts, and man. There was no flood, no tower of Babel, no first couple in paradise, and between the first known appearance of men on earth and the first buildings of cities, not one generation (Adam to Cain) but a good two million must have come into this world and passed along. Today we turn to science for our imagery of the past and of the structure of the world, and what the spinning demons of the atom and the galaxies of the telescope's eye reveal is a wonder that makes the babel of the Bible seem a toyland dream of the dear childhood of our brain.

A third function of mythology is to support the current social order, to integrate the individual organically with his group; and here again, in the long view, we see that a gradual amplification of the scope and content of the group has been the characteristic sign of man's advance from the early tribal cluster to the modern post-Alexandrian concept of a single world-society. Against the amplitude of this challenging larger concept numerous provinces still stand out, as, for example, those of the various national, racial, religious, or class mythologies, which may once have had their reason but today are out of date.

The social function of a mythology and of the rites by which it is rendered is to establish in every member of the group concerned a "system of sentiments" that can be depended upon to link him spontaneously to its ends. The "system of sentiments" proper to a hunting tribe would be improper to an agricultural one; that proper to a matriarchy is improper to a patriarchy; and that of any tribal group is improper to this day of developed individuals crossing paths from east to west and from north to south.

The older mythic orders gave authority to their symbols by attributing them to gods, to culture heroes, or to some such high impersonal force as the order of the universe; and the image of society itself, thus linked to the greater image of nature, became a vessel of religious awe. Today we know, for the most part, that our laws are not from God or from the uni-

verse, but from ourselves; are conventional, not absolute; and that in breaking them we offend not God but man. Neither animals nor plants, not the
zodiac or its supposed maker, but our fellows have now become the masters
of our fate and we of theirs. In the recent past it may have been possible
for intelligent men of good will honestly to believe that their own society
(whatever it happened to be) was the only good, that beyond its bounds
were the enemies of God, and that they were called upon, consequently, to
project the principle of hatred outward upon the world, while cultivating
love within, toward those whose "system of sentiments" was of God.
Today, however, there is no such outward. Enclaves of national, racial,
religious, and class provincialism persist, but the physical facts have made
closed horizons illusory. The old god is dead, with his little world and his
little, closed society. The new focal center of belief and trust is mankind.
And if the principle of love cannot be wakened actually within each—as it
was mythologically in God—to master the principle of hate, the Waste
Land alone can be our destiny and the masters of the world its fiends.

The fourth function of mythology is to initiate the individual into the
order of realities of his own psyche, guiding him toward his own spiritual
enrichment and realization. Formerly—but in archaic cultures still—the
way was to subordinate all individual judgment, will, and capacities absolutely to the social order: the principle of ego (as we have seen in *Oriental
Mythology*) was to be suppressed and, if possible, even erased; while the
archetypes, the ideal roles, of the social order were impressed upon all
inexorably, according to their social stations. In a world of static forms,
such a massacre of the creative personality was acceptable, and where the
archaic mind prevails today such patterning still goes on. One may take it
as a point in evidence of the advanced position of Europe in the way of
respect for the individual that, whereas Hitler's massacre of some 5,000,000
Jews evokes (and properly so) horror from all sides, Stalin's of 25,000,000
Russians passes almost without notice, and the present Chinese orgy is
entirely overlooked. Both by the Orient and by the Occident such inhumanity is recognized as normal for the great East, whereas better things
are expected of ourselves—and rightly so. For it was in Europe alone that
the principle of individual judgment and responsibility was developed in
relation not to a fixed order of supposed divine laws, but to a changing
context of human actualities, rationally governed. The fostering in Europe,
first among the Greeks, then the Romans, of the principle of ego—not as
the mere "I will," "I want," of the nursery (Freud's "Pleasure Principle"),
but as the informed, rational faculty of responsible judgment ("Reality
Principle")—has endowed us and our particular world with an order of
spirituality and psychological problematic that is different in every way from
that of the archaic Oriental mind. And this humanistic individualism has
released powers of creativity that have brought about in a mere two centuries changes in the weal and woe of man such as no two millenniums
before had ever worked. The result being that where the old patterns of

morality are retained they no longer match the actualities even of the local, let alone the world, scene. The adventure of the Grail—the quest within for those creative values by which the Waste Land is redeemed—has become today for each the unavoidable task; for, as there is no more any fixed horizon, there is no more any fixed center, any Mecca, Rome, or Jerusalem. Our circle today is that announced, c. 1450, by Nicolaus Cusanus (1401–1464): whose circumference is nowhere and whose center is everywhere; the circle of infinite radius, which is also a straight line. . . .

Some, perhaps, will desire to bow still to a mask, out of fear of nature. But if there is no divinity in nature, the nature that God created, how should there be in the idea of God, which the nature of man created?

"By my love and hope, I conjure thee," called Nietzsche's Zarathustra: "cast not away the hero in thy soul!"

Bultmann
THE TASK OF DEMYTHOLOGIZING*

A. The Problem

1. THE MYTHICAL VIEW OF THE WORLD AND THE MYTHICAL EVENT OF REDEMPTION

The cosmology of the New Testament is essentially mythical in character. The world is viewed as a three-storied structure, with the earth in the centre, the heaven above, and the underworld beneath. Heaven is the abode of God and of celestial beings—the angels. The underworld is hell, the place of torment. Even the earth is more than the scene of natural, everyday events, of the trivial round and common task. It is the scene of the supernatural activity of God and his angels on the one hand, and of Satan and his daemons on the other. These supernatural forces intervene in the course of nature and in all that men think and will and do. Miracles are by no means rare. Man is not in control of his own life. Evil spirits may take possession of him. Satan may inspire him with evil thoughts. Alternatively, God may inspire his thought and guide his purposes. He may grant him heavenly visions. He may allow him to hear his word of succour or demand. He may give him the supernatural power of his Spirit. History does not follow a

* Rudolf Bultmann (1884–   ): German theologian. Bultmann's primary concern has been the study of Christian scripture from the point of view of existential philosophy. This selection is part of a dialogue on the true meaning of the biblical message and how we might have access to that meaning. From Rudolf Bultmann, "The Task of Demythologizing," in *Kerygma and Myth*, edited by Hans Bartsch (1953), pp. 1–12, 15–16. Reprinted by permission of the Society for Promoting Christian Knowledge, London.

smooth unbroken course; it is set in motion and controlled by these supernatural powers. This aeon is held in bondage by Satan, sin, and death (for
"powers" is precisely what they are), and hastens towards its end. That end
will come very soon, and will take the form of a cosmic catastrophe. It will
be inaugurated by the "woes" of the last time. Then the Judge will come
from heaven, the dead will rise, the last judgment will take place, and men
will enter into eternal salvation or damnation.

*This then is the mythical view of the world which the New Testament
presupposes when it presents the event of redemption which is the subject
of its preaching.* It proclaims in the language of mythology that the last time
has now come. "In the fulness of time" God sent forth his Son, a pre-
existent divine Being, who appears on earth as a man. He dies the death
of a sinner on the cross and makes atonement for the sins of men. His
resurrection marks the beginning of the cosmic catastrophe. Death, the
consequence of Adam's sin, is abolished, and the daemonic forces are
deprived of their power. The risen Christ is exalted to the right hand of
God in heaven and made "Lord" and "King." He will come again on the
clouds of heaven to complete the work of redemption, and the resurrection
and judgement of men will follow. Sin, suffering and death will then be
finally abolished. All this is to happen very soon; indeed, St. Paul thinks
that he himself will live to see it.

All who belong to Christ's Church and are joined to the Lord by Baptism
and the Eucharist are certain of resurrection to salvation, unless they forfeit
it by unworthy behaviour. Christian believers already enjoy the first instal-
ment of salvation, for the Spirit is at work within them, bearing witness
to their adoption as sons of God, and guaranteeing their final resurrection.

2. THE MYTHOLOGICAL VIEW OF THE WORLD OBSOLETE

All this is the language of mythology, and the origin of the various themes
can be easily traced in the contemporary mythology of Jewish Apocalyptic
and in the redemption myths of Gnosticism. To this extent *the kerygma is
incredible to modern man, for he is convinced that the mythical view of the
world is obsolete.* We are therefore bound to ask whether, when we preach
the Gospel to-day, we expect our converts to accept not only the Gospel
message, but also the mythical view of the world in which it is set. If not,
does the New Testament embody a truth which is quite independent of its
mythical setting? If it does, theology must undertake the task of stripping
the Kerygma from its mythical framework, of "demythologizing" it.

Can Christian preaching expect modern man *to accept the mythical view
of the world as true?* To do so would be both senseless and impossible. It
would be senseless, because there is nothing specifically Christian in the
mythical view of the world as such. It is simply the cosmology of a pre-
scientific age. Again, it would be impossible, because no man can adopt a
view of the world by his own volition—it is already determined for him by

his place in history. Of course such a view is not absolutely unalterable, and the individual may even contribute to its change. But he can do so only when he is faced by a new set of facts so compelling as to make his previous view of the world untenable. He has then no alternative but to modify his view of the world or produce a new one. The discoveries of Copernicus and the atomic theory are instances of this, and so was romanticism, with its discovery that the human subject is richer and more complex than enlightenment or realism had allowed, and nationalism, with its new realization of the importance of history and the tradition of peoples.

It may equally well happen that truths which a shallow enlightenment had failed to perceive are later rediscovered in ancient myths. Theologians are perfectly justified in asking whether this is not exactly what has happened with the New Testament. At the same time it is impossible to revive an obsolete view of the world by a mere fiat, and certainly not a mythical view. For all our thinking to-day is shaped for good or ill by modern science. A blind acceptance of the New Testament mythology would be irrational, and to press for its acceptance as an article of faith would be to reduce Christian faith to the level of a human achievement. Wilhelm Herrmann pointed this out many years ago, and one would have thought that his demonstration was conclusive. It would involve a sacrifice of the intellect which could have only one result—a curious form of schizophrenia and insincerity. It would mean accepting a view of the world in our faith and religion which we should deny in our everyday life. Modern thought as we have inherited it provides us with *a motive for criticizing the New Testament view of the world.*

Man's knowledge and mastery of the world have advanced to such an extent through science and technology that it is no longer possible for anyone seriously to hold the New Testament view of the world—in fact, there is hardly anyone who does. What meaning, for instance, can we attach to such phrases in the creed as "descended into hell" or "ascended into heaven?" We no longer believe in the three-storied universe which the creeds take for granted. The only honest way of reciting the creeds is to strip the mythological framework from the truth they enshrine—that is, assuming that they contain any truth at all, which is just the question that theology has to ask. No one who is old enough to think for himself supposes that God lives in a local heaven. There is no longer any heaven in the traditional sense of the word. The same applies to hell in the sense of a mythical underworld beneath our feet. And if this is so, we can no longer accept the story of Christ's descent into hell or his Ascension into heaven as literally true. We can no longer look for the return of the Son of Man on the clouds of heaven or hope that the faithful will meet him in the air (I Thess. 4.15ff).

Now that the forces and the laws of nature have been discovered, we can no longer believe *in spirits, whether good or evil.* We know that the stars are physical bodies whose motions are controlled by the laws of the universe, and not daemonic beings which enslave mankind to their service. Any influence they may have over human life must be explicable in terms of the ordinary laws of nature; it cannot in any way be attributed to their malevolence. Sickness and the cure of disease are likewise attributable to natural causation; they are not the result of daemonic activity or of evil spells. *The miracles of the New Testament* have ceased to be miraculous, and to defend their historicity by recourse to nervous disorders or hypnotic effects only serves to underline the fact. And if we are still left with certain physiological and psychological phenomena which we can only assign to mysterious and enigmatic causes, we are still assigning them to causes, and thus far are trying to make them scientifically intelligible. Even occultism pretends to be a science.

It is impossible to use electric light and the wireless and to avail ourselves of modern medical and surgical discoveries, and at the same time to believe in the New Testament world of daemons and spirits. We may think we can manage it in our own lives, but to expect others to do so is to make the Christian faith unintelligible and unacceptable to the modern world.

The mythical eschatology is untenable for the simple reason that the parousia of Christ never took place as the New Testament expected. History did not come to an end, and, as every schoolboy knows, it will continue to run its course. Even if we believe that the world as we know it will come to an end in time, we expect the end to take the form of a natural catastrophe, not of a mythical event such as the New Testament expects. And if we explain the parousia in terms of modern scientific theory, we are applying criticism to the New Testament, albeit unconsciously.

But natural science is not the only challenge which the mythology of the New Testament has to face. There is the still more serious challenge presented by *modern man's understanding of himself*.

Modern man is confronted by a curious dilemma. He may regard himself as pure nature, or as pure spirit. In the latter case he distinguishes the essential part of his being from nature. In either case, however, *man is essentially a unity*. He bears the sole responsibility for his own feeling, thinking, and willing. He is not, as the New Testament regards him, the victim of a strange dichotomy which exposes him to the interference of powers outside himself. If his exterior behaviour and his interior condition are in perfect harmony, it is something he has achieved himself, and if other people think their interior unity is torn asunder by daemonic or divine interference, he calls it schizophrenia.

Although biology and psychology recognize that man is a highly dependent being, that does not mean that he has been handed over to powers outside of and distinct from himself. This dependence is inseparable from human nature, and he needs only to understand it in order to recover his self-mastery and organize his life on a rational basis. If he regards himself as spirit, he knows that he is permanently conditioned by the physical, bodily part of his being, but he distinguishes his true self from it, and knows that he is independent and responsible for his mastery over nature.

In either case he finds *what the New Testament has to say about the "Spirit"* (πνεῦμα) and the sacraments utterly strange and incomprehensible. Biological man cannot see how a supernatural entity like the πνεῦμα can penetrate within the close texture of his natural powers and set to work within him. Nor can the idealist understand how a πνεῦμα working like a natural power can touch him and influence his mind and spirit. Conscious as he is of his own moral responsibility, he cannot conceive how baptism in water can convey a mysterious something which is henceforth the agent of all his decisions and actions. He cannot see how physical food can convey spiritual strength, and how the unworthy receiving of the Eucharist can result in physical sickness and death (I Cor. 11.30). The only possible explanation is that it is due to suggestion. He cannot understand how anyone can be baptized for the dead (I Cor. 15.29).

We need not examine in detail the various forms of modern *Weltanschauung*, whether idealist or naturalist. For the only criticism of the New Testament which is theologically relevant is that which arises *necessarily* out of the situation of modern man. The biological *Weltanschauung* does not, for instance, arise necessarily out of the contemporary situation. We are still free to adopt it or not as we choose. The only relevant question for the theologian is the basic assumption on which the adoption of a biological as of every other *Weltanschauung* rests, and that assumption is the view of the world which has been moulded by modern science and the modern conception of human nature as a self-subsistent unity immune from the interference of supernatural powers.

Again, the biblical doctrine that *death is the punishment of sin* is equally abhorrent to naturalism and idealism, since they both regard death as a simple and necessary process of nature. To the naturalist death is no problem at all, and to the idealist it is a problem for that very reason, for so far from arising out of man's essential spiritual being it actually destroys it. The idealist is faced with a paradox. On the one hand is a spiritual being, and therefore essentially different from plants and animals, and on the other hand he is the prisoner of nature, whose birth, life, and death are just the same as those of the animals. Death may present him with a problem, but he cannot see how it can be a punishment for sin. Human beings are subject to death even before they have committed any sin. And to attribute human mortality to the fall of Adam is sheer nonsense, for guilt implies personal responsibility, and the idea of original sin as an inherited infection is sub-ethical, irrational, and absurd.

The same objections apply to *the doctrine of the atonement.* How can the guilt of one man be expiated by the death of another who is sinless— if indeed one may speak of a sinless man at all? What primitive notions of guilt and righteousness does this imply? And what primitive idea of God? The rationale of sacrifice in general may of course throw some light on the theory of the atonement, but even so, what a primitive mythology it is, that a divine Being should become incarnate, and atone for the sins of men through his own blood! or again, one might adopt an analogy from the law courts, and explain the death of Christ as a transaction between God and man through which God's claims on man were satisfied. But that would make sin a juridicial matter; it would be no more than an external transgression of a commandment, and it would make nonsense of all our ethical standards. Moreover, if the Christ who died such a death was the preexistent Son of God, what could death mean for him? Obviously very little, if he knew that he would rise again in three days!

The *resurrection of Jesus* is just as difficult, if it means an event whereby a supernatural power is released which can henceforth be appropriated through the sacraments. To the biologist such language is meaningless, for he does not regard death as a problem at all. The idealist would not object to the idea of a life immune from death, but he could not believe that such a life is made available by the resuscitation of a corpse. If that is the way God makes life available for man, his action is inextricably involved in a nature miracle. Such a notion he finds intolerable, for he can see God at work only in the life of the spirit (which is for him the only real life) and in the transformation of his personality. But, quite apart from the incredibility of such a miracle, he cannot see how an event like this could be the act of God, or how it could affect his own life.

Gnostic influence suggests that this Christ, who died and rose again, was not a mere human being but a God-man. His death and resurrection were not isolated facts which concerned him alone, but a cosmic event in which we are all involved. It is only with effort that modern man can think himself back into such an intellectual atmosphere, and even then he could never accept it himself, because it regards man's essential being as nature and redemption as a process of nature. And as for the pre-existence of Christ, with its corollary of man's translation into a celestial realm of light, and the clothing of the human personality in heavenly robes and a spiritual body— all this is not only irrational but utterly meaningless. Why should salvation take this particular form? Why should this be the fulfilment of human life and the realization of man's true being?

B. The Task before Us

1. NOT SELECTION OR SUBTRACTION

Does this drastic criticism of the New Testament mythology mean the complete elimination of the kerygma?

Whatever else may be true, we cannot save the kerygma by selecting some of its features and subtracting others, and thus reduce the amount of mythology in it. For instance, it is impossible to dismiss St. Paul's teaching about the unworthy reception of Holy Communion or about baptism for the dead, and yet cling to the belief that physical eating and drinking can have a spiritual effect. If we accept one idea, we must accept everything which the New Testament has to say about Baptism and Holy Communion, and it is just this one idea which we cannot accept.

It may of course be argued that some features of the New Testament mythology are given greater prominence than others: not all of them appear with the same regularity in the various books. There is for example only one occurrence of the legends of the Virgin birth and the Ascension; St. Paul and St. John appear to be totally unaware of them. But, even if we take them to be later accretions, it does not affect the mythical character of the event of redemption as a whole. And if we once start subtracting from the kerygma, where are we to draw the line? The mythical view of the world must be accepted or rejected in its entirety.

At this point absolute clarity and ruthless honesty are essential both for the academic theologian and for the parish priest. It is a duty they owe to themselves, to the Church they serve, and to those whom they seek to win for the Church. They must make it quite clear what their hearers are expected to accept and what they are not. At all costs the preacher must not leave his people in the dark about what he secretly eliminates, nor must he be in the dark about it himself. In Karl Barth's book *The Resurrection of the Dead* the cosmic eschatology in the sense of "chronologically final history" is eliminated in favour of what he intends to be a nonmythical "ultimate history." He is able to delude himself into thinking that this is exegesis of St. Paul and of the New Testament generally only because he gets rid of everything mythological in I Corinthians by subjecting it to an interpretation which does violence to its meaning. But that is an impossible procedure.

If the truth of the New Testament proclamation is to be preserved, the only way is to demythologize it. But our motive in so doing must not be to make the New Testament relevant to the modern world at all costs. The question is simply whether the New Testament message consists exclusively of mythology, or whether it actually demands the elimination of myth if it is to be understood as it is meant to be. This question is forced upon us from two sides. First there is the nature of myth in general, and then there is the New Testament itself.

2. THE NATURE OF MYTH

The real purpose of myth is not to present an objective picture of the world as it is, but to express man's understanding of himself in the world in which he lives. Myth should be interpreted not cosmologically, but anthropologically, or better still, existentially. Myth speaks of the power or the powers which man supposes he experiences as the ground and limit of his world and of his own activity and suffering. He describes these powers in terms derived from the visible world, with its tangible objects and forces, and from human life, with its feelings, motives, and potentialities. He may, for instance, explain the origin of the world by speaking of a world egg or a world tree. Similarly he may account for the present state and order of the world by speaking of a primeval war between the gods. He speaks of the other world in terms of this world, and of the gods in terms derived from human life.

Myth is an expression of man's conviction that the origin and purpose of the world in which he lives are to be sought not within it but beyond it—that is, beyond the realm of known and tangible reality—and that this realm is perpetually dominated and menaced by those mysterious powers which are its source and limit. Myth is also an expression of man's awareness that he is not lord of his own being. It expresses his sense of dependence not only within the visible world, but more especially on those forces which hold sway beyond the confines of the known. Finally, myth expresses man's belief that in this state of dependence he can be delivered from the forces within the visible world.

Thus myth contains elements which demand its own criticism—namely, its imagery with its apparent claim to objective validity. The real purpose of myth is to speak of a transcendent power which controls the world and man, but that purpose is impeded and obscured by the terms in which it is expressed.

Hence the importance of the New Testament mythology lies not in its imagery but in the understanding of existence which it enshrines. The real question is whether this understanding of existence is true. Faith claims that it is, and faith ought not to be tied down to the imagery of New Testament mythology. . . .

5. AN EXISTENTIALIST INTERPRETATION THE ONLY SOLUTION

The theological work which such an interpretation involves can be sketched only in the broadest outline and with only a few examples. We must avoid the impression that this is a light and easy task, as if all we have to do is to discover the right formula and finish the job on the spot. It is much more formidable than that. It cannot be done single-handed. It will tax the time and strength of a whole theological generation.

The mythology of the New Testament is in essence that of Jewish apocalyptic and the Gnostic redemption myths. A common feature of them both is their basic dualism, according to which the present world and its human inhabitants are under the control of daemonic, satanic powers, and stand in need of redemption. Man cannot achieve this redemption by his own efforts; it must come as a gift through a divine intervention. Both types of mythology speak of such an intervention: Jewish apocalyptic of an imminent world crisis in which this present aeon will be brought to an end and the new aeon ushered in by the coming of the Messiah, and Gnosticism of a Son of God sent down from the realm of light, entering into this world in the guise of a man, and by his fate and teaching delivering the elect and opening up the way for their return to their heavenly home.

The meaning of these two types of mythology lies once more not in their imagery within its apparent objectivity but in the understanding of human existence which both are trying to express. In other words, they need to be interpreted existentially. A good example of such treatment is to be found in Hans Jonas's book on Gnosticism.

Our task is to produce an existentialist interpretation of the dualistic mythology of the New Testament along similar lines. When, for instance, we read of daemonic powers ruling the world and holding mankind in bondage, does the understanding of human existence which underlies such language offer a solution to the riddle of human life which will be acceptable even to the nonmythological mind of to-day? Of course we must not take this to imply that the New Testament presents us with an anthropology like that which modern science can give us. It cannot be proved by logic or demonstrated by an appeal to factual evidence. Scientific anthropologies always take for granted a definite understanding of existence, which is invariably the consequence of a deliberate decision of the scientist, whether he makes it consciously or not. And that is why we have to discover whether the New Testament offers man an understanding of himself which will challenge him to a genuine existential decision.

Chapter 7

Transcendental origin of religion

In considering the psychogenic, sociogenic and mythological sources of religion, the focus has been restricted primarily to what might be termed 'immanent' interpretations of religious beliefs and practices. In other words, those interpretations which are compatible with the hypothesis that answers to religious questions originate totally within the human condition. The truths of religious life, from this perspective, may be viewed as *human* truths even though they derive from a variety of sources, such as the dynamics of the human psyche, social forces, the myth-making faculty.

But, perhaps, religious truths are given or revealed to man. According to this view, the structures of finitude, of the human situation, could not possibly give rise to basic religious truths even though human life may contain the potential for response to a transcendent being. Religious truths break in upon man's life and reveal to him its inadequacies and inescapable limits while simultaneously manifesting a wholly transcendent religious reality. The manifestation of divine reality is not to be derived from an analysis of the human situation.

Rudolf Otto insists upon the centrality of transcendence in his conception of the origin and character of religious experience. Religious consciousness is defined by a unique quality of awareness which Otto calls "numinous." In giving a descriptive account of numinous consciousness, Otto wishes to establish the hypothesis that religious consciousness points beyond itself to a transcendental holy power. This supernatural power, toward which religious experience points and to which it responds, breaks in upon human reality shattering its normal rational categories of communication and cognition, persuading it of its own radical creaturehood. Shaken to the foundations of his existence by a confrontation with the Holy Other in numinous consciousness, man responds in worship and awe, and experiences a renewal of his existence.

The nature of transcendence in religious experience is also emphasized in Eastern religious thought. In Zen Buddhism, for example, the attainment of satori or enlightenment involves the radical "going beyond" the boundaries of the normal life of the self and its experienced world. Satori, says D. T. Suzuki, is at the heart of Zen Buddhism and indicates the achievement of a vision of reality denied to ordinary empirical consciousness. The "sense of the beyond" is a characteristic mark of the experience of enlightenment and is accompanied by the rending of the veil of illusion and ignorance that constitute the ego's ordinary experiences of self and nature. The "opening of the third eye," as the achievement of satori is often called, results in a radically new perspective upon human existence. Previously experienced tensions and alienation are now perceived to be aspects of a most perfect spiritual harmony. The attainment of enlightenment is revolutionary for the human being, analogous to the spiritual enhancement of life called conversion. The whole of human existence is renewed in the heat and fire of the religious vision. While the potential for satori lies within mankind's categories. New life and new light break in upon the human condition as well as by man's intellect and perceptual apparatus which creates dualistic categories. New life and new light break in upon the human condition as though from an external reality, while in fact that reality, although hidden in egotism and ignorance, is always present.

R. Otto

THE IDEA OF THE HOLY*

[II.] 'HOLINESS'—'the holy'—is a category of interpretation and valuation peculiar to the sphere of religion. It is, indeed, applied by transference to another sphere—that of Ethics—but it is not itself derived from this. While it is complex, it contains a quite specific element or 'moment', which sets it apart from 'the Rational' in the meaning we gave to that word above, and which remains inexpressible—an ἄρρητον or *ineffabile*—in the sense that it completely eludes apprehension in terms of concepts. The same thing is true (to take a quite different region of experience) of the category of the beautiful.

Now these statements would be untrue from the outset if 'the holy' were merely what is meant by the word, not only in common parlance, but in philosophical, and generally even in theological usage. The fact is we have come to use the words *holy, sacred* (heilig) in an entirely derivative sense, quite different from that which they originally bore. We generally take 'holy' as meaning 'completely good'; it is the absolute moral attribute, denoting the consummation of moral goodness. In this sense Kant calls the will which remains unwaveringly obedient to the moral law from the motive of duty a 'holy' will; here clearly we have simply the *perfectly moral* will.

---

* Rudolf Otto (1869–1937): German religious philosopher. Otto's *Idea of the Holy* is a classic in the field of religious thought. The selection reproduces Chapters II and V, and part of Chapter IV. This book is basically an inquiry into the non-rational facets in the idea of God and their relation to the problems of religious knowledge. From *The Idea of the Holy* by Rudolf Otto, translated by J. W. Harvey. Second Edition, 1950. Reprinted by permission of Oxford University Press, New York.

In the same way we may speak of the holiness or sanctity of Duty or Law, meaning merely that they are imperative upon conduct and universally obligatory.

But this common usage of the term is inaccurate. It is true that all this moral significance is contained in the word 'holy', but it concludes in addition—as even we cannot but feel—a clear overplus of meaning, and this it is now our task to isolate. Nor is this merely a later or acquired meaning; rather, 'holy', or at least the equivalent words in Latin and Greek, in Semitic and other ancient languages, denoted first and foremost *only* this overplus: if the ethical element was present at all, at any rate it was not original and never constituted the whole meaning of the word. Any one who uses it to-day does undoubtedly always feel 'the morally good' to be implied in 'holy'; and accordingly in our inquiry into that element which is separate and peculiar to the idea of the holy it will be useful, at least for the temporary purpose of the investigation, to invent a special term to stand for 'the holy' *minus* its moral factor or 'moment', and, as we can now add, minus its 'rational' aspect altogether.

It will be our endeavour to suggest this unnamed Something to the reader as far as we may, so that he may himself feel it. There is no religion in which it does not live as the real innermost core, and without it no religion would be worthy of the name. It is pre-eminently a living force in the Semitic religions, and of these again in none has it such vigour as in that of the Bible. Here, too, it has a name of its own, viz. the Hebrew *qādôsh*, to which the Greek ἅγιος and the Latin *sanctus*, and, more accurately still, *sacer*, are the corresponding terms. It is not, of course, disputed, that these terms in all three languages connote, as part of their meaning, *good, absolute goodness*, when, that is, the notion has ripened and reached the highest stage in its development. And we then use the word 'holy' to translate them. But this 'holy' then represents the gradual shaping and filling in with ethical meaning, or what we shall call the 'schematization', of what was a unique original feeling-response, which can be in itself ethically neutral and claims consideration in its own right. And when this moment or element first emerges and begins its long development, all those expressions (*qādôsh*, ἅγιος, *sacer*, &c.) mean beyond all question something quite other than 'the good'. This is universally agreed by contemporary criticism, which rightly explains the rendering of *qādôsh* by 'good' as a mistranslation and unwarranted 'rationalization' or 'moralization' of the term.

Accordingly, it is worth while, as we have said, to find a word to stand for this element in isolation, this 'extra' in the meaning of 'holy' above and beyond the meaning of goodness. By means of a special term we shall the better be able, first, to keep the meaning clearly apart and distinct, and second, to apprehend and classify connectedly whatever subordinate forms or stages of development it may show. For this purpose I adopt a word coined from the Latin *numen*. *Omen* has given us *ominous*, and there is no reason why from *numen* we should not similarly form a word 'numinous'. I shall speak then of a unique 'numinous' category of value and of a definitely 'numinous' state of mind, which is always found wherever the category is applied. This mental state is perfectly *sui generis* and irreducible to any other; and therefore, like every absolutely primary and elementary datum, while it admits of being discussed, it cannot be strictly defined. There is only one way to help another to an understanding of it. He must be guided and led on by consideration and discussion of the matter through the ways of his own mind, until he reach the point at which 'the numinous' in him perforce begins to stir, to start into life and into consciousness. We can co-operate in this process by bringing before his notice all that can be found in other regions of the mind, already known and familiar, to resemble, or again to afford some special contrast to, the particular experience we wish to elucidate. Then we must add: 'This X of ours is not precisely *this* experience, but akin to this one and the opposite of that other. Cannot you now realize for yourself what it is?' In other words our X cannot, strictly speaking, be taught, it can only be evoked, awakened in the mind; as everything that comes 'of the spirit' must be awakened.

[IV.]   *The Analysis of 'Tremendum'*. We said above that the nature of the numinous can only be suggested by means of the special way in which it is reflected in the mind in terms of feeling. 'Its nature is such that it grips or stirs the human mind with this and that determinate affective state.' We have now to attempt to give a further indication of these determinate states. We must once again endeavour, by adducing feelings akin to them for the purpose of analogy or contrast, and by the use of metaphor and symbolic expressions, to make the states of mind we are investigating ring out, as it were, of themselves.

Let us consider the deepest and most fundamental element in all strong and sincerely felt religious emotion. Faith unto Salvation, Trust, Love—all these are there. But over and above these is an element which may also on occasion, quite apart from them, profoundly affect us and occupy the mind with a wellnigh bewildering strength. Let us follow it up with every effort of sympathy and imaginative intuition wherever it is to be found, in the lives of those around us, in sudden, strong ebullitions of personal piety and the frames of mind such ebullitions evince, in the fixed and ordered solemnities of rites and liturgies, and again in the atmosphere that clings to old religious monuments and buildings, to temples and to churches. If we do so we shall find we are dealing with something for which there is only one appropriate expression, *mysterium tremendum*. The feeling of it may at times come sweeping like a gentle tide, pervading the mind with a tranquil mood of deepest worship. It may pass over into a more set and lasting attitude of the soul, continuing, as it were, thrillingly vibrant and resonant, until at last it dies away and the soul resumes its 'profane', non-religious mood of everyday experience. It may burst in sudden eruption up from the depths of the soul with spasms and convulsions, or lead to the strangest excitements, to intoxicated frenzy, to transport, and to ecstasy. It has its wild and demonic forms and can sink to an almost grisly horror and shuddering. It has its crude, barbaric antecedents and early manifestations, and again it may be developed into something beautiful and pure and glorious. It may become the hushed, trembling, and speechless humility of the creature in the presence of—whom or what? In the presence of that which is a *Mystery* inexpressible and above all creatures.

It is again evident at once that here too our attempted formulation by means of a concept is once more a merely negative one. Conceptually 'mysterium' denotes merely that which is hidden and esoteric, that which is beyond conception or understanding, extraordinary and unfamiliar. The term does not define the object more positively in its qualitative character. But though what is enunciated in the word is negative, what is meant is something absolutely and intensely positive. This pure positive we can experience in feelings, feelings which our discussion can help to make clear to us, in so far as it arouses them actually in our hearts.

To get light upon the positive 'quale' of the object of these feelings, we must analyse more closely our phrase *mysterium tremendum*, and we will begin first with the adjective.

'Tremor' is in itself merely the perfectly familiar and 'natural' emotion of *fear*. But here the term is taken, aptly enough but still only by analogy, to denote a quite specific kind of emotional response, wholly distinct from that of being afraid, though it so far resembles it that the analogy of fear may be used to throw light upon its nature. There are in some languages special expressions which denote, either exclusively or in the first instance, this 'fear' that is more than fear proper. The Hebrew *hiqdīsh* (hallow) is an example. To 'keep a thing holy in the heart' means to mark it off by a feeling of peculiar dread, not to be mistaken for any ordinary dread, that is, to appraise it by the category of the numinous. But the Old Testament throughout is rich in parallel expressions for this feeling. Specially noticeable is the *emāt* of Yahweh ('fear of God'), which Yahweh can pour forth, dispatching almost like a daemon, and which seizes upon a man with paralysing effect. It is closely related to the δεῖμα πανικόν of the Greeks. Compare Exodus xxiii. 27: 'I will send my fear before thee and will destroy all the people to whom thou shalt come . . .'; also Job ix. 34; xiii. 21 ('Let not his fear terrify me'; 'Let not thy dread make me afraid'). Here we have a terror fraught with an inward shuddering such as not even the most menacing and overpowering created thing can instil. It has something spectral in it. . . .

Not only is the saying of Luther, that the natural man cannot fear God perfectly, correct from the standpoint of psychology, but we ought to go further and add that the natural man is quite unable even to shudder (*grauen*) or feel horror in the real sense of the word. For 'shuddering' is something more than 'natural', ordinary fear. It implies that the mysterious is already beginning to loom before the mind, to touch the feelings. It implies the first application of a category of valuation which has no place in the everyday natural world of ordinary experience, and is only possible to a being in whom has been awakened a mental predisposition, unique in kind and different in a definite way from any 'natural' faculty. And this newly-revealed capacity, even in the crude and violent manifestations which are all it at first evinces, bears witness to a completely new function of experience and standard of valuation, only belonging to the spirit of man.

Before going on to consider the elements which unfold as the 'tremendum' develops, let us give a little further consideration to the first crude, primitive forms in which this 'numinous dread' or *awe* shows itself. It is the mark which really characterizes the so-called 'Religion of Primitive Man', and there it appears as 'daemonic dread'. This crudely naïve and primordial emotional disturbance, and the fantastic images to which it gives rise, are later overborne and ousted by more highly-developed forms of the numinous emotion, with all its mysteriously impelling power. But even when this has long attained its higher and purer mode of expression it is possible for the primitive types of excitation that were formerly a part of it to break out in the soul in all their original naïveté and so to be experienced afresh. That this is so is shown by the potent attraction again and again exercised by the element of horror and 'shudder' in ghost stories, even among persons of high all-round education. It is a remarkable fact that the physical reaction to which this unique 'dread' of the uncanny gives rise is also unique, and is not found in the case of any 'natural' fear or terror. We say: 'my blood ran icy cold', and 'my flesh crept'. The 'cold blood' feeling may be a symptom of ordinary, natural fear, but there is something non-natural or supernatural about the symptom of 'creeping flesh'. And any one who is capable of more precise introspection must recognize that the distinction between such a 'dread' and natural fear is not simply one of degree and intensity. The awe or 'dread' *may* indeed be so overwhelmingly great that it seems to penetrate to the very marrow, making the man's hair bristle and his limbs quake. But it may also steal upon him almost unobserved as the gentlest of agitations, a mere fleeting shadow passing across his mood. It has therefore nothing to do with intensity, and no natural fear passes over into it merely by being intensified. . . .

We have been attempting to unfold the implications of that aspect of the 'mysterium tremendum' indicated by the adjective, and the result so far may be summarized in two words, constituting, as before, what may be called an 'ideogram', rather than a concept proper, viz. 'absolute unapproachability'.

It will be felt at once that there is yet a further element which must be added, that, namely, of 'might', 'power', 'absolute overpoweringness'. We will take to represent this the term 'majestas', majestly—the more readily because any one with a feeling for language must detect a last faint trace of the numinous still clinging to the word. The 'tremendum' may then be rendered more adequately 'tremenda majestas', or 'aweful majesty'. This second element of majesty may continue to be vividly preserved, where the first, that of unapproachability, recedes and dies away, as may be seen, for example, in Mysticism. It is especially in relation to this element of majesty or absolute overpoweringness that the creature-consciousness, of which we have already spoken, comes upon the scene, as a sort of shadow or subjective reflection of it. Thus, in contrast to 'the overpowering' of which we are conscious as an object over against the self, there is the feeling of one's own abasement, of being but 'dust and ashes' and nothingness. . . .

Here we must revert once again to Schleiermacher's expression for what we call 'creature-feeling', viz. the 'feeling of dependence'. We found fault with this phrase before on the ground that Schleiermacher thereby takes as basis and point of departure what is merely a secondary effect; that he sets out to teach a consciousness of the religious *object* only by way of an inference from the shadow it casts upon *self*-consciousness. We have now a further criticism to bring against it, and it is this. By 'feeling of dependence' Schleiermacher means consciousness of *being conditioned* (as effect by cause), and so he develops the implications of this logically enough in his sections upon Creation and Preservation. On the side of the deity the correlate to 'dependence' would thus be 'causality', i.e. God's character as all-causing and all-conditioning. But a sense of this does not enter at all into that immediate and first-hand religious emotion which we have in the moment of worship, and which we can recover in a measure for analysis; it belongs on the contrary decidedly to the *rational* side of the idea of God; its implications admit of precise conceptual determination; and it springs from quite a distinct source. The difference between the 'feeling of dependence' of Schleiermacher and that which finds typical utterance in the words of Abraham already cited might be expressed as that between the consciousness of *createdness* (Geschaffenheit) and the consciousness of *creaturehood* (Geschöpflichkeit). In the one case you have the creature as the work of the divine creative act; in the other, impotence and general nothingness as against overpowering might, dust and ashes as against 'majesty'. In the one case you have the fact of having been created; in the other, the status of the creature. And as soon as speculative thought has come to concern itself with this latter type of consciousness—as soon as it has come to analyse this 'majesty'—we are introduced to a set of ideas quite different from those of creation or preservation. We come upon the ideas, first, of the annihilation of self, and then, as its complement, of the transcendent as the sole and entire reality. These are the characteristic notes of Mysticism in all its forms, however otherwise various in content. For one of the chiefest and most general features of Mysticism is just this *self-depreciation* (so plainly parallel to the case of Abraham), the estimation of the self, of the personal 'I', as something not perfectly or essentially real, or even as mere nullity, a self-depreciation which comes to demand its own fulfillment in practice in rejecting the delusion of selfhood, and so makes for the annihilation of the self. And on the other hand Mysticism leads to a valuation of the transcendent object of its reference as that which through plenitude of being stands supreme and absolute, so that the finite self contrasted with it becomes conscious even in its nullity that 'I am nought, Thou art all'. There is no thought in this of any causal relation between God, the creator, and the self, the creature. The point from which speculation starts is not a 'consciousness of absolute dependence'—of myself as result and of a divine cause—for that would in point of fact lead to insistence upon the reality of the self; it starts from a consciousness of the absolute superiority or supremacy of a power other than myself, and it is only as it falls back upon ontological terms to achieve its end—terms generally borrowed from natural science—that that element of the 'tremendum', originally apprehended as 'plenitude of power', becomes transmuted into 'plenitude of being'.

This leads again to the mention of Mysticism. No mere inquiry into the genesis of a thing can throw any light upon its essential nature, and it is hence immaterial to us how Mysticism historically arose. But essentially Mysticism is the stressing to a very high degree, indeed the overstressing, of the non-rational or supra-rational elements in religion; and it is only intelligible when so understood. The various phases and factors of the non-rational may receive varying emphasis, and the type of Mysticism will differ according as some or others fall into the background. What we have been analysing, however, is a feature that recurs in all forms of Mysticism everywhere, and it is nothing but the 'creature-consciousness' stressed to the utmost and to excess, the expression meaning, if we may repeat the contrast already made, not 'feeling of our createdness' but 'feeling of our creaturehood', that is, the consciousness of the littleness of every creature in face of that which is above all creatures. . . .

There is, finally, a third element comprised in those of 'tremendum' and 'majestas', awefulness and majesty, and this I venture to call the *urgency* or *energy* of the numinous object. It is particularly vividly perceptible in the 'ὀργή' or 'Wrath'; and it everywhere clothes itself in symbolical expressions—vitality, passion, emotional temper, will, force, movement, excitement, activity, impetus. These features are typical and recur again and again from the daemonic level up to the idea of the 'living' God. We have here the factor that has everywhere more than any other prompted the fiercest opposition to 'philosophic' God of mere rational speculation, who can be put into a definition. And for their part the philosophers have condemned these expressions of the energy of the numen, whenever they are brought on to the scene, as sheer anthropomorphism. In so far as their opponents have for the most part themselves failed to recognize that the terms they have borrowed from the sphere of human conative and affective life have merely value as analogies, the philosophers are right to condemn them. But they are wrong, in so far as, this error notwithstanding, these terms stood for a genuine aspect of the divine nature—its non-rational aspect—a due consciousness of which served to protect religion itself from being 'rationalized' away.

For wherever men have been contending for the 'living' God and for voluntarism, there, we may be sure, have been non-rationalists fighting rationalists and rationalism. It was so with Luther in his controversy with Erasmus; and Luther's 'omnipotentia Dei' in his *De Servo Arbitrio* is nothing but the union of 'majesty'—in the sense of absolute supremacy—with this 'energy', in the sense of a force that knows not stint nor stay, which is urgent, active, compelling, and alive. In Mysticism, too, this element of 'energy' is a very living and vigorous factor, at any rate in the 'voluntaristic' Mysticism, the Mysticism of love, where it is very forcibly seen in that 'consuming fire' of love whose burning strength the mystic can hardly bear, but begs that the heat that has scorched him may be mitigated, lest he be himself destroyed by it. And in this urgency and pressure the mystic's 'love' claims a perceptible kinship with the ὀργή itself, the scorching and consuming wrath of God; it is the same 'energy', only differently directed. 'Love', says one of the mystics, 'is nothing else than quenched Wrath'. . . .

[V.] We gave to the object to which the numinous consciousness is directed the name 'mysterium tremendum', and we then set ourselves first to determine the meaning of the adjective 'tremendum'—which we found to be itself only justified by analogy—because it is more easily analysed than the substantive idea 'mysterium'. . . .

It might be thought that the adjective itself gives an explanation of the substantive; but this is not so. It is not merely analytical; it is a synthetic attribute to it; i.e. 'tremendum' adds something not necessarily inherent in 'mysterium'. It is true that the reactions in consciousness that correspond to the one readily and spontaneously overflow into those that correspond to the other; in fact, any one sensitive to the use of words would commonly feel that the idea of 'mystery' (*mysterium*) is so closely bound up with its synthetic qualifying attribute 'aweful' (*tremendum*) that one can hardly say the former without catching an echo of the latter, 'mystery' almost of itself becoming 'aweful mystery' to us. But the passage from the one idea to the other need not by any means be always so easy. The elements of meaning implied in 'awefulness' and 'mysteriousness' are in themselves definitely different. The latter may so far preponderate in the religious consciousness, may stand out so vividly, that in comparison with it the former almost sinks out of sight; a case which again could be clearly exemplified from some forms of Mysticism. Occasionally, on the other hand, the reverse happens, and the 'tremendum' may in turn occupy the mind without the 'mysterium'.

This latter, then, needs special consideration on its own account. We need an expression for the mental reaction peculiar to it; and here, too, only one word seems appropriate though, as it is strictly applicable only to a 'natural' state of mind, it has here meaning only by analogy: it is the word 'stupor'. *Stupor* is plainly a different thing from *tremor*; it signifies blank wonder, an astonishment that strikes us dumb, amazement absolute. Taken, indeed, in its purely natural sense, 'mysterium' would first mean merely a secret or a mystery in the sense of that which is alien to us, uncomprehended and unexplained; and so far 'mysterium' is itself merely an ideogram, an analogical notion taken from the natural sphere, illustrating, but incapable of exhaustively rendering, our real meaning. Taken in the religious sense, that which is 'mysterious' is—so give it perhaps the most striking expression—the 'wholly other' (. . .) that which is quite beyond the sphere of the usual, the intelligible, and the familiar, which therefore falls quite outside the limits of the 'canny', and is contrasted with it, filling the mind with blank wonder and astonishment. . . .

In accordance with laws of which we shall have to speak again later, this feeling or consciousness of the 'wholly other' will attach itself to, or sometimes be indirectly aroused by means of, objects which are already puzzling upon the 'natural' plane, or are of a surprising or astounding character; such as extraordinary phenomena or astonishing occurrences or things in inanimate nature, in the animal world, or among men. But here once more we are dealing with a case of association between things specifically different—the 'numinous' and the 'natural' moment of consciousness—and not merely with the gradual enhancement of one of them—the 'natural'—till it becomes the other. As in the case of 'natural fear' and 'daemonic dread' already considered, so here the transition from natural to daemonic amazement is not a mere matter of degree. But it is only with the latter that the complementary expression 'mysterium' perfectly harmonizes, as will be felt perhaps more clearly in the case of the adjectival form 'mysterious'. No one says, strictly and in earnest, of a piece of clockwork that is beyond his grasp, or of a science that he cannot understand: 'That is "mysterious" to me.'

It might be objected that the mysterious is something which is and remains absolutely and invariably beyond our understanding, whereas that which merely eludes our understanding for a time but is perfectly intelligible in principle should be called, not a 'mystery', but merely a 'problem'. But this is by no means an adequate account of the matter. The truly 'mysterious' object is beyond our apprehension and comprehension, not only because our knowledge has certain irremovable limits, but because in it we come upon something inherently 'wholly other', whose kind and character are incommensurable with our own, and before which we therefore recoil in a wonder that strikes us chill and numb.

This may be made still clearer by a consideration of that degraded offshoot and travesty of the genuine 'numinous' dread or awe, the fear of ghosts. Let us try to analyse this experience. We have already specified the peculiar feeling-element of 'dread' aroused by the ghost as that of 'grue', grisly horror (*gruseln, gräsen*). Now this 'grue' obviously contributes something to the attraction which ghost-stories exercise, in so far, namely, as the relaxation of tension ensuing upon our release from it relieves the mind in a pleasant and agreeable way. So far, however, it is not really the ghost itself that gives us pleasure, but the fact that we are rid of it. But obviously this is quite insufficient to explain the ensnaring attraction of the ghost-story. The ghost's real attraction rather consists in this, that of itself and in an uncommon degree it entices the imagination, awakening strong interest and curiosity; it is the weird thing itself that allures the fancy. But it does this, not because it is 'something long and white' (as some one once defined a ghost), nor yet through any of the positive and conceptual attributes which fancies about ghosts have invented, but because it is a thing that 'doesn't really exist at all', the 'wholly other', something which has no place in our scheme of reality but belongs to an absolutely different one, and which at the same time arouses an irrepressible interest in the mind.

But that which is perceptibly true in the fear of ghosts, which is, after all, only a caricature of the genuine thing, is in a far stronger sense true of the 'daemonic' experience itself, of which the fear of ghosts is a mere off-shoot. And while, following this main line of development, this element in the numinous consciousness, the feeling of the 'wholly other,' is heightened and clarified, its higher modes of manifestation come into being, which set the numinous object in contrast not only to everything wonted and familiar (i.e., in the end, to nature in general), thereby turning it into the 'supernatural', but finally to the world itself, and thereby exalt it to the 'supramundane', that which is above the whole world-order.

In Mysticism we have in the 'Beyond' (ἐπέκεινα) again the strongest stressing and over-stressing of those non-rational elements which are already inherent in all religion. Mysticism continues to its extreme point this contrasting of the numinous object (the numen), as the 'wholly other', with ordinary experience. Not content with contrasting it with all that is of nature or this world, Mysticism concludes by contrasting it with Being itself and all that 'is', and finally actually calls it 'that which is nothing'. By this 'nothing' is meant not only that of which nothing can be predicated, but that which is absolutely and intrinsically other than and opposite of everything that is and can be thought. But while exaggerating to the point of paradox this *negation* and contrast—the only means open to conceptual thought to apprehend the 'mysterium'—Mysticism at the same time retains the *positive quality* of the 'wholly other' as a very living factor in its over-brimming religious emotion.

But what is true of the strange 'nothingness' of our mystics holds good equally of the 'sūnyam' and the 'sūnyatā', the 'void' and 'emptiness' of the Buddhist mystics. This aspiration for the 'void' and for becoming void, no less than the aspiration of our western mystics for 'nothing' and for becoming nothing, must seem a kind of lunacy to any one who has no inner sympathy for the esoteric language and ideograms of Mysticism, and lacks the matrix from which these come necessarily to birth. To such an one Buddhism itself will be simply a morbid sort of pessimism. But in fact the 'void' of the eastern, like the 'nothing' of the western, mystic is a numinous ideogram of the 'wholly other'.

These terms, 'supernatural' and 'transcendent' (literally, supramundane: *überweltlich*), give the appearance of positive attributes, and, as applied to the mysterious, they appear to divest the 'mysterium' of its originally negative meaning and to turn it into affirmation. On the side of conceptual thought this is nothing more than appearance, for it is obvious that the two terms in question are merely negative and exclusive attributes with reference to 'nature' and the 'world' or cosmos respectively. But on the side of the feeling-content it is otherwise; that *is* in very truth positive in the highest degree, though here too, as before, it cannot be rendered explicit in conceptual terms. It is through this positive feeling-content that the concepts of the 'transcendent' and 'supernatural' become forthwith designations for a unique 'wholly other' reality and quality, something of whose special character we can *feel*, without being able to give it clear conceptual expression.

Suzuki
THE NATURE OF ZEN*

The Sense of Zen

Zen in its essence is the art of seeing into the nature of one's own being, and it points the way from bondage to freedom. By making us drink right from the fountain of life, it liberates us from all the yokes under which we finite beings are usually suffering in this world. We can say that Zen liberates all the energies properly and naturally stored in each of us, which are in ordinary circumstances cramped and distorted so that they find no adequate channel for activity.

This body of ours is something like an electric battery in which a mysterious power latently lies. When this power is not properly brought into operation, it either grows mouldy and withers away or is warped and expresses itself abnormally. It is the object of Zen, therefore, to save us from going crazy or being crippled. This is what I mean by freedom, giving free play to all the creative and benevolent impulses inherently lying in our hearts. Generally, we are blind to this fact, that we are in possession of all the necessary faculties that will make us happy and loving towards one another. All the struggles that we see around us come from this ignorance. Zen, there-

* D. T. Suzuki (1870–1966): Japanese philosopher and interpreter of Zen Buddhism to the West. The selections presented here include part of Chapter I, "The Sense of Zen," and part of Chapter IV, "Satori, or Enlightenment," in a collection of Suzuki's essays entitled, *Zen Buddhism—Selected Writings of D. T. Suzuki*. From *Zen Buddhism— Selected Writings of D. T. Suzuki*, edited by William Barrett (New York: Doubleday & Co., 1956). Reprinted by permission of Hutchinson Publishing Group Ltd., London.

fore, wants to open a "third eye," as Buddhists call it, to the hitherto undreamed-of region shut away from us through our own ignorance. When the cloud of ignorance disappears, the infinity of the heavens is manifested, where we see for the first time into the nature of our own being. We now know the signification of life, we know that it is not blind striving, nor is it a mere display of brutal forces, but that while we know not definitely what the ultimate purport of life is, there is something in it that makes us feel infinitely blessed in the living of it and remain quite contented with it in all its evolution, without raising questions or entertaining pessimistic doubts.

When we are full of vitality and not yet awakened to the knowledge of life, we cannot comprehend the seriousness of all the conflicts involved in it which are apparently for the moment in a state of quiescence. But sooner or later the time will come when we have to face life squarely and solve its most perplexing and most pressing riddles. Says Confucius, "At fifteen my mind was directed toward study, and at thirty I knew where to stand." This is one of the wisest sayings of the Chinese sage. Psychologists will all agree to this statement of his; for, generally speaking, fifteen is about the age youth begins to look around seriously and inquire into the meaning of life. All the spiritual powers until now securely hidden in the subconscious part of the mind break out almost simultaneously. And when this breaking out is too precipitous and violent, the mind may lose its balance more or less permanently; in fact, so many cases of nervous prostration reported during adolescence are chiefly due to this loss of the mental equilibrium. In most cases the effect is not very grave and the crisis may pass without leaving deep marks. But in some characters, either through their inherent tendencies or on account of the influence of environment upon their plastic constitution, the spiritual awakening stirs them up to the very depths of their personality. This is the time you will be asked to choose between the "Everlasting No" and the "Everlasting Yea." This choosing is what Confucius means by "study"; it is not studying the classics, but deeply delving into the mysteries of life.

Normally, the outcome of the struggle is the "Everlasting Yea", or "Let thy will be done"; for life is after all a form of affirmation, however negatively it might be conceived by the pessimists. But we cannot deny the fact that there are many things in this world which will turn our too sensitive minds towards the other direction and make us exclaim with Andreyev in "The Life of Man": "I curse everything that you have given. I curse the day on which I was born. I curse the day on which I shall die. I curse the whole of my life. I fling everything back at your cruel face, senseless Fate! Be accursed, be forever accursed! With my curses I conquer you. What else can you do to me? . . . With my last thought I will shout into your asinine ears: Be accursed, be accursed!" This is a terrible indictment of life, it is a complete negation of life, it is a most dismal picture of the destiny of man on earth. "Leaving no trace" is quite true, for we know nothing of our future except that we all pass away, including the very earth from which we have come. There are certainly things justifying pessimism.

Life, as most of us live it, is suffering. There is no denying the fact. As long as life is a form of struggle, it cannot be anything but pain. Does not a struggle mean the impact of two conflicting forces, each trying to get the upper hand of the other? If the battle is lost, the outcome is death, and death is the fearsomest thing in the world. Even when death is conquered, one is left alone, and the loneliness is sometimes more unbearable than the struggle itself. One may not be conscious of all this, and may go on indulging in those momentary pleasures that are afforded by the senses. But this being unconscious does not in the least alter the facts of life. However insistently the blind may deny the existence of the sun, they cannot annihilate it. The tropical heat will mercilessly scorch them, and if they do not take proper care they will all be wiped away from the surface of the earth.

The Buddha was perfectly right when he propounded his "Fourfold Noble Truth", the first of which is that life is pain. Did not everyone of us come to this world screaming and in a way protesting? To come out into cold and prohibitive surroundings after a soft, warm motherly womb was surely a painful incident, to say the least. Growth is always attended with pain. Teething is more or less a painful process. Puberty is usually accompanied by a mental as well as a physical disturbance. The growth of the organism called society is also marked with painful cataclysms, and we are at present witnessing one of its birth-throes. We may calmly reason and say that this is all inevitable, that inasmuch as every reconstruction means the destruction of the old regime, we cannot help going through a painful operation. But the cold intellectual analysis does not alleviate whatever harrowing feelings we have to undergo. The pain heartlessly inflicted on our nerves is ineradicable. Life is, after all arguing, a painful struggle.

This, however, is providential. For the more you suffer the deeper grows your character, and with the deepening of your character you read the more penetratingly into the secrets of life. All great artists, all great religious leaders, and all great social reformers have come out of the intensest struggles which they fought bravely, quite frequently in tears and with bleeding hearts. Unless you eat your bread in sorrow, you cannot taste of real life. Mencius is right when he says that when Heaven wants to perfect a great man it tries him in every possible way until he comes out triumphantly from all his painful experiences.

To me Oscar Wilde seems always posing or striving for an effect; he may be a great artist, but there is something in him that turns me away from him. Yet he exclaims in his De Profundis: "During the last few months I have, after terrible difficulties and struggles, been able to comprehend some of the lessons hidden in the heart of pain. Clergymen and people who use phrases without wisdom sometimes talk of suffering as a mystery. It is really a revelation. One discerns things one never descerned before. One approaches the whole of history from a different standpoint." You will observe here what sanctifying effects his prison life produced on his character. If he had had to go through a similar trial in the beginning of his career, he might have been able to produce far greater works than those we have of him at present.

We are too ego-centered. The ego-shell in which we live is the hardest thing to outgrow. We seem to carry it all the time from childhood up to the time we finally pass away. We are, however, given many chances to break through this shell, and the first and greatest of them is when we reach adolescence. This is the first time the ego really comes to recognize the "other". I mean the awakening of sexual love. An ego, entire and undivided, now begins to feel a sort of split in itself. Love hitherto dormant deep in his heart lifts its head and causes a great commotion in it. For the love now stirred demands at once the assertion of the ego and its annihilation. Love makes the ego lose itself in the object it loves, and yet at the same time it wants to have the object as its own. This is a contradiction, and a great tragedy of life. This elemental feeling must be one of the divine agencies whereby man is urged to advance in his upward walk. God gives tragedies to perfect man. The greatest bulk of literature ever produced in this world is but the harping on the same string of love, and we never seem to grow weary of it. But this is not the topic we are concerned with here. What I want to emphasize in this connection is this: that through the awakening of love we get a glimpse into the infinity of things, and that this glimpse urges youth to Romanticism or to Rationalism according to his temperament and environment and education.

When the ego-shell is broken and the "other" is taken into its own body, we can say that the ego has denied itself or that the ego has taken its first steps towards the infinite. Religiously, here ensues an intense struggle between the finite and the infinite, between the intellect and a higher power, or, more plainly, between the flesh and the spirit. This is the problem of problems that has driven many a youth into the hands of Satan. When a grown-up man looks back to these youthful days he cannot but feel a sort of shudder going through his entire frame. The struggle to be fought in sincerity may go on up to the age of thirty, when Confucius states that he knew where to stand. The religious consciousness is now fully awakened, and all the possible ways of escaping from the struggle or bringing it to an end are most earnestly sought in every direction. Books are read, lectures are attended, sermons are greedily taken in, and various religious exercises or disciplines are tried. And naturally Zen too comes to be inquired into.

How does Zen solve the problem of problems?

In the first place, Zen proposes its solution by directly appealing to facts of personal experience and not to book-knowledge. The nature of one's own being where apparently rages the struggle between the finite and the infinite is to be grasped by a higher faculty than the intellect. For Zen says it is the latter that first made us raise the question which it could not answer by itself, and that therefore it is to be put aside to make room for something higher and more enlightening. For the intellect has a peculiarly disquieting quality in it. Though it raises questions enough to disturb the serenity of the mind, it is too frequently unable to give satisfactory answers to them. It upsets the blissful peace of ignorance and yet it does not restore the former state of things by offering something else. Because it points out ignorance, it is often considered illuminating, whereas the fact is that it disturbs, not necessarily always bringing light on its path. It is not final, it waits for something higher than itself for the solution of all the questions it will raise regardless of consequences. If it were able to bring a new order into the disturbance and settle it once for all, there would have been no need for philosophy after it had been first systemized by a great thinker, by an Aristotle or by a Hegel. But the history of thought proves that each new structure raised by a man of extraordinary intellect is sure to be pulled down by the succeeding ones. This constant pulling down and building up is all right as far as philosophy itself is concerned; for the inherent nature of the intellect, as I take it, demands it and we cannot put a stop to the progress of philosophical inquiries any more than to our breathing. But when it comes to the question of life itself we cannot wait for the ultimate solution to be offered by the intellect, even if it could do so. We cannot suspend even for a moment our life-activity for philosophy to unravel its mysteries. Let the mysteries remain as they are, but live we must. The hungry cannot wait until a complete analysis of food is obtained and the nourishing value of each element is determined. For the dead the scientific knowledge of food will be of no use whatever. Zen therefore does not rely on the intellect for the solution of its deepest problems.

By personal experience it is meant to get at the fact at first hand and not through any intermediary, whatever this may be. Its favourite analogy is: to point at the moon a finger is needed, but woe to those who take the finger for the moon; a basket is welcome to carry our fish home, but when the fish are safely on the table why should we eternally bother ourselves with the basket? Here stands the fact, and let us grasp it with the naked hands lest it should slip away—this is what Zen proposes to do. As nature abhors a vacuum, Zen abhors anything coming between the fact and ourselves. According to Zen there is no struggle in the fact itself such as between the finite and the infinite, between the flesh and the spirit. These are idle distinctions fictitiously designed by the intellect for its own interest. Those who take them too seriously or those who try to read them into the very fact of life are those who take the finger for the moon. When we are hungry we eat; when we are sleepy we lay ourselves down; and where does the infinite or the finite come in here? Are not we complete in ourselves and each in himself? Life as it is lived suffices. It is only when the disquieting intellect steps in and tries to murder it that we stop to live and imagine ourselves to be short of or in something. Let the intellect alone, it has its usefulness in its proper sphere, but let it not interfere with the flowing of the life-stream. If you are at all tempted to look into it, do so while letting it flow. The fact of flowing must under no circumstances be arrested or med-dled with; for the moment your hands are dipped into it, its transparency is disturbed, it ceases to reflect your image which you have had from the very beginning and will continue to have to the end of time.

Almost corresponding to the "Four Maxims" of the Nichiren Sect, Zen has its own four statements:

"A special transmission outside the Scriptures;
No dependence upon words and letters;
Direct pointing to the soul of man;
Seeing into one's nature and the attainment of
　　　　　　　　　　　　　　　　Buddhahood."

This sums up all that is claimed by Zen as religion. Of course we must not forget that there is a historical background to this bold pronunciamento. At the time of the introduction of Zen into China, most of the Buddhists were addicted to the discussion of highly metaphysical questions, or satisfied with the merely observing of the ethical precepts laid down by the Buddha or with the leading of a lethargic life entirely absorbed in the contemplation of the evanescence of things worldly. They all missed apprehending the great fact of life itself, which flows altogether outside of these vain exercises of the intellect or of the imagination. Bodhi-Dharma and his successors recog-nized this pitiful state of affairs. Hence their proclamation of "The Four Great Statements" of Zen as above cited. In a word, they mean that Zen has its own way of pointing to the nature of one's own being, and that when this is done one attains to Buddahood, in which all the contradictions and disturbances caused by the intellect are entirely harmonized in a unity of higher order.

For this reason Zen never explains but indicates, it does not appeal to circumlocution, nor does it generalize. It always deals with facts, concrete and tangible. Logically considered, Zen may be full of contradictions and repetitions. But as it stands above all things, it goes serenely on its own way. As a Zen master aptly puts it, "carrying his home-made cane on the shoulder, he goes right on among the mountains one rising above another". It does not challenge logic, it simply walks its path of facts, leaving all the rest to their own fates. It is only when logic neglecting its proper functions tries to step into the track of Zen that it loudly proclaims its principles and forcibly drives out the intruder. Zen is not an enemy of anything. There is no reason why it should antagonize the intellect which may sometimes be utilized for the cause of Zen itself. . . .

Satori, or Enlightenment

[1] The essence of Zen Buddhism consists in acquiring a new viewpoint on life and things generally. By this I mean that if we want to get into the inmost life of Zen, we must forgo all our ordinary habits of thinking which

control our everyday life, we must try to see if there is any other way of judging things, or rather if our ordinary way is always sufficient to give us the ultimate satisfaction of our spiritual needs. If we feel dissatisfied somehow with this life, if there is something in our ordinary way of living that deprives us of freedom in its most sanctified sense, we must endeavor to find a way somewhere which gives us a sense of finality and contentment. Zen proposes to do this for us and assures us of the acquirement of a new point of view in which life assumes a fresher, deeper, and more satisfying aspect. This acquirement, however, is really and naturally the greatest mental cataclysm one can go through with in life. It is no easy task, it is a kind of fiery baptism, and one has to go through the storm, the earthquake, the overthrowing of the mountains, and the breaking in pieces of the rocks.

This acquiring of a new point of view in our dealings with life and the world is popularly called by Japanese Zen students "satori" (*wu* in Chinese). It is really another name for Enlightenment (*anuttara-samyak-sambodhi*), which is the word used by the Buddha and his Indian followers ever since his realization under the Bodhi-tree by the River Nairanjana. There are several other phrases in Chinese designating this spiritual experience, each of which has a special connotation, showing tentatively how this phenomenon is interpreted. At all events there is no Zen without satori, which is indeed the Alpha and Omega of Zen Buddhism. Zen devoid of satori is like a sun without its light and heat. Zen may lose all its literature, all its monasteries, and all its paraphernalia; but as long as there is satori in it it will survive to eternity. I want to emphasize this most fundamental fact concerning the very life of Zen; for there are some even among the students of Zen themselves who are blind to this central fact and are apt to think when Zen has been explained away logically or psychologically, or as one of the Buddhist philosophies which can be summed up by using highly technical and conceptual Buddhist phrases, Zen is exhausted, and there remains nothing in it that makes it what it is. But my contention is, the life of Zen begins with the opening of satori (*kai wu* in Chinese).

Satori may be defined as an intuitive looking into the nature of things in contradistinction to the analytical or logical understanding of it. Practically, it means the unfolding of a new world hitherto unperceived in the confusion of a dualistically-trained mind. Or we may say that with satori our entire surroundings are viewed from quite an unexpected angle of perception. Whatever this is, the world for those who have gained a satori is no more the old world as it used to be; even with all its flowing streams and burning fires, it is never the same one again. Logically stated, all its opposites and contradictions are united and harmonized into a consistent organic whole. This is a mystery and a miracle, but according to the Zen masters such is being performed every day. Satori can thus be had only through our once personally experiencing it.

Its semblance or analogy in a more or less feeble and fragmentary way is gained when a difficult mathematical problem is solved, or when a great discovery is made, or when a sudden means of escape is realized in the midst of most desperate complications; in short, when one exclaims "Eureka! Eureka!" But this refers only to the intellectual aspect of satori, which is therefore necessarily partial and incomplete and does not touch the very foundations of life considered one indivisible whole. Satori as the Zen experience must be concerned with the entirety of life. For what Zen proposes to do is the revolution, and the revaluation as well, of oneself as a spiritual unity. The solving of a mathematical problem ends with the solution, it does not affect one's whole life. So with all other particular questions, practical or scientific, they do not enter the basic life-tone of the individual concerned. But the opening of satori is the remaking of life itself. When it is genuine—for there are many simulacra of it—its effects on one's moral and spiritual life are revolutionary, and they are so enhancing, purifying, as well as exacting. When a master was asked what constituted Buddhahood, he answered, "The bottom of a pail is broken through." From this we can see what a complete revolution is produced by this spiritual experience. The birth of a new man is really cataclysmic.

In the psychology of religion this spiritual enhancement of one's whole life is called "conversion". But as the term is generally used by Christian converts, it cannot be applied in its strict sense to the Buddhist experience, especially to that of the Zen followers; the term has too affective or emotional a shade to take the place of satori, which is above all noetic. The general tendency of Buddhism is, as we know, more intellectual than emotional, and its doctrine of Enlightenment distinguishes it sharply from the Christian view of salvation; Zen as one of the Mahayana schools naturally shares a large amount of what we may call transcendental intellectualism, which does not issue in logical dualism. When poetically or figuratively expressed, satori is "the opening of the mind-flower", or "the removing of the bar", or "the brightening up of the mind-works". . . .

V. CHIEF CHARACTERISTICS OF SATORI

1. *Irrationality.* By this I mean that satori is not a conclusion to be reached by reasoning, and defies all intellectual determination. Those who have experienced it are always at a loss to explain it coherently or logically. When it is explained at all, either in words or gestures, its content more or less undergoes a mutilation. The uninitiated are thus unable to grasp it by what is outwardly visible, while those who have had the experience discern what is genuine from what is not. The satori experience is thus always characterized by irrationality, inexplicability, and incommunicability.

Listen to Tai-hui once more: "This matter [i.e. Zen] is like a great mass of fire; when you approach it your face is sure to be scorched. It is again like a sword about to be drawn; when it is once out of the scabbard, someone is sure to lose his life. But if you neither fling away the scabbard nor approach the fire, you are no better than a piece of rock or of wood. Coming to this pass, one has to be quite a resolute character full of spirit." There is nothing here suggestive of cool reasoning and quiet metaphysical or epistemological analysis, but of a certain desperate will to break through an insurmountable barrier, of the will impelled by some irrational or unconscious power behind it. Therefore, the outcome also defies intellection or conceptualization.

2. *Intuitive insight*. That there is noetic quality in mystic experiences has been pointed out by James in his *Varieties of Religious Experience,* and this applies also to the Zen experience known as satori. Another name for satori is "ken-sho" (*chien-hsing* in Chinese) meaning "to see essence or nature", which apparently proves that there is "seeing" or "perceiving" in satori. That this seeing is of quite a different quality from what is ordinarily designated as knowledge need not be specifically noticed. Hui-k'e is reported to have made this statement concerning his satori which was confirmed by Bodhidharma himself: "[As to my satori], it is not a total annihilation; it is knowledge of the most adequate kind; only it cannot be expressed in words." In this respect Shen-hui was more explicit, for he says that "the one character *chih* (knowledge) is the source of all mysteries".

Without this noetic quality satori will lose all its pungency, for it is really the reason of satori itself. It is noteworthy that the knowledge contained in satori is concerned with something universal and at the same time with the individual aspect of existence. When a finger is lifted, the lifting means, from the viewpoint of satori, far more than the act of lifting. Some may call it symbolic, but satori does not point to anything beyond itself, being final as it is. Satori is the knowledge of an individual object and also that of Reality which is, if I may say so, at the back of it.

3. *Authoritativeness*. By this I mean that the knowledge realized by satori is final, that no amount of logical argument can refute it. Being direct and personal it is sufficient unto itself. All that logic can do here is to explain it, to interpret it in connection with other kinds of knowledge with which our minds are filled. Satori is thus a form of perception, an inner perception, which takes its place in the most interior part of consciousness. Hence the sense of authoritativeness, which means finality. So, it is generally said that Zen is like drinking water, for it is by one's self that one knows whether it is warm or cold. The Zen perception being the last term of experience, it cannot be denied by outsiders who have no such experience.

4. *Affirmation*. What is authoritative and final can never be negative. For negation has no value for our life, it leads us nowhere; it is not a power that urges, nor does it give one a place to rest. Though the satori experience is sometimes expressed in negative terms, it is essentially an affirmative attitude towards all things that exist; it accepts them as they come along regardless of their moral values. Buddhists call this *kshanti*, "patience", or more properly "acceptance", that is, acceptance of things in their supra-relative or transcendental aspect where no dualism of whatever sort avails.

Some may say that this is pantheistic. The term, however, has a definite philosophic meaning and I would not see it used in this connection. When so interpreted the Zen experience exposes itself to endless misunderstand-ings and "defilements". Tai-hui says in his letter to Miao-tsung: "An ancient sage says that the Tao itself does not require special disciplining, only let it not be defiled. I would say: To talk about mind or nature is defiling; to talk about the unfathomable or the mysterious is defiling; to practice medi-tation or tranquillization is defiling; to direct one's attention to it, to think about it is defiling; to be writing about it thus on paper with a brush is especially defiling. What then shall we have to do in order to get ourselves oriented, and properly apply ourselves to it? The precious vajra sword is right here and its purpose is to cut off the head. Do not be concerned with human questions of right and wrong. All is Zen just as it is, and right here you are to apply yourself." Zen is Suchness—a grand affirmation.

5. *Sense of the Beyond.* Terminology may differ in different religions, and in satori there is always what we may call a sense of the Beyond; the ex-perience indeed is my own but I feel it to be rooted elsewhere. The indi-vidual shell in which my personality is so solidly encased explodes at the moment of satori. Not, necessarily, that I get unified with a being greater than myself or absorbed in it, but that my individuality, which I found rigidly held together and definitely kept separate from other individual ex-istences, becomes loosened somehow from its tightening grip and melts away into something indescribable, something which is of quite a different order from what I am accustomed to. The feeling that follows is that of a complete release or a complete rest—the feeling that one has arrived finally at the destination. "Coming home and quietly resting" is the expression generally used by Zen followers. The story of the prodigal son in the *Saddharmapun-darika*, in the *Vajra-samadhi*, and also in the New Testament points to the same feeling one has at the moment of a satori experience.

As far as the psychology of satori is considered, a sense of the Beyond is all we can say about it; to call this the Beyond, the Absolute, or God, or a Person is to go further than the experience itself and to plunge into a theol-ogy or metaphysics. Even the "Beyond" is saying a little too much. When a Zen master says, "There is not a fragment of a tile above my head, there is not an inch of earth beneath my feet," the expression seems to be an appro-priate one. I have called it elsewhere the Unconscious, though this has a psychological taint.

6. *Impersonal Tone.* Perhaps the most remarkable aspect of the Zen ex-perience is that it has no personal note in it as is observable in Christian mystic experiences. There is no reference whatever in Buddhist satori to such personal and frequently sexual feelings and relationships as are to be gleaned from these terms: flame of love, a wonderful love shed in the heart, embrace, the beloved, bride, bridegroom, spiritual matrimony, Father, God, the Son of God, God's child, etc. We may say that all these terms are interpretations based on a definite system of thought and really have noth-ing to do with the experience itself. At any rate, alike in India, China, and Japan, satori has remained thoroughly impersonal, or rather highly in-tellectual.

Is this owing to the peculiar character of Buddhist philosophy? Does the experience itself take its colours from the philosophy or theology? Whatever this is, there is no doubt that in spite of its having some points of similitude to the Christian mystic experience, the Zen experience is singularly devoid of personal or human colourings. Chao-pien, a great government officer of the Sung dynasty, was a lay-disciple of Fach'uan of Chiang-shan. One day after his official duties were over, he found himself leisurely sitting in his office, when all of a sudden a clash of thunder burst on his ear, and he realized a state of satori. The poem he then composed depicts one aspect of the Zen experience:

> "Devoid of thought, I sat quietly by the desk in my official room,
> With my fountain-mind undisturbed, as serene as water;
> A sudden clash of thunder, the mind-doors burst open,
> And lo, there sitteth the old man in all his homeliness."

This is perhaps all the personal tone one can find in the Zen experience, and what a distance between "the old man in his homeliness" and "God in all his glory," not to say anything about such feelings as "the heavenly sweetness of Christ's excellent love," etc.! How barren, how unromantic satori is when compared with the Christian mystic experiences!

Not only satori itself is such a prosaic and non-glorious event, but the occasion that inspires it also seems to be unromantic and altogether lacking in supersensuality. Satori is experienced in connection with any ordinary occurrence in one's daily life. It does not appear to be an extraordinary phenomenon as is recorded in Christian books of mysticism. Someone takes hold of you, or slaps you, or brings you a cup of tea, or makes some most commonplace remark, or recites some passage from a sutra or from a book of poetry, and when your mind is ripe for its outburst, you come at once to satori. There is no romance of love-making, no voice of the Holy Ghost, no plenitude of Divine Grace, no glorification of any sort. Here is nothing painted in high colours, all is grey and extremely unobtrusive and unattractive.

7. *Feeling of Exaltation.* That this feeling inevitably accompanies satori is due to the fact that it is the breaking-up of the restriction imposed on one as an individual being, and this breaking up is not a mere negative incident but quite a positive one fraught with signification because it means an infinite expansion of the individual. The general feeling, though we are not always conscious of it, which characterizes all our functions of consciousness, is that of restriction and dependence, because consciousness itself is the outcome of two forces conditioning or restricting each other. Satori, on the contrary, essentially consists in doing away with the opposition of two terms in whatsoever sense—and this opposition is the principle of consciousness as before mentioned, while satori is to realize the Unconscious which goes beyond the opposition.

To be released of this, therefore, must make one feel above all things intensely exalted. A wandering outcast maltreated everywhere not only by others but by himself finds that he is the possessor of all the wealth and power that is ever attainable in this world by a mortal being—if this does not give him a high feeling of self-glorification, what could? Says a Zen master, "When you have satori you are able to reveal a palatial mansion made of precious stones on a single blade of grass; but when you have no satori, a palatial mansion itself is concealed behind a simple blade of grass."

Another Zen master, evidently alluding to the *Avatamsaka*, declares: "O monks, lo and behold! A most auspicious light is shining with the utmost brilliancy all over the great chiliocosm, simultaneously revealing all the countries, all the oceans, all the Sumerus, all the suns and moons, all the heavens, all the lands—each of which number as many as hundreds of thousands of kotis. O monks, do you not see the light?" But the Zen feeling of exaltation is rather a quiet feeling of self-contentment; it is not at all demonstrative, when the first glow of it passes away. The Unconscious does not proclaim itself so boisterously in the Zen consciousness.

8. *Momentariness.* Satori comes upon one abruptly and is a momentary experience. In fact, if it is not abrupt and momentary, it is not satori. This abruptness (*tun*) is what characterizes the Hui-neng school of Zen ever since its proclamation late in the seventh century. His opponent Shen-hsiu was insistent on a gradual unfoldment of Zen consciousness. Hui-neng's followers were thus distinguished as strong upholders of the doctrine of abruptness. This abrupt experience of satori, then, opens up in one moment (*ekamuhurtena*) an altogether new vista, and the whole existence is appraised from quite a new angle of observation.

SUGGESTIONS FOR FURTHER READING

Cornforth, Maurice, *Dialectical Materialism: An Introductory Course, Vol. III: The Theory of Knowledge.* (London: Lawrence and Wishart, Ltd., 1954). *Chapter 7 presents a good account of the Marxist position on the origin and status of religious ideology.*

Fromm, Erich, *Psychoanalysis and Religion.* (London: Victor Gollancz, 1951). *Examination of the nature and function of religion from a psychological point of view.*

Hook, Sidney, ed., *Religious Experience and Truth.* (New York: New York University Press, 1961). *A collection of essays on problems in philosophy of religion. Excellent essays on Tillich's conception of religious symbolism. Also, excellent general investigations into the problems of truth, myth, knowledge, and language in religion.*

Jaspers, Karl and Bultmann, Rudolf, *Myth and Christianity*. (New York: Noonday Press, 1958). *A dialogue on the problem of the possibility of religion without myth.*

Lee, R. S., *Freud and Christianity*. (New York: Wyn, 1949). *Fine treatment of Freud's critique of religion.*

Marx, Karl and Engels, Friedrich, *On Religion*. (London: Lawrence and Wishart, Ltd., 1958). *A collection of Marxist writing critical of religion.*

Mascall, E. L., *Existence and Analogy* (London: Longman's, Green & Co., Ltd., 1949). *Chapter 5 contains a good exploration of the doctrine of analogy as it relates to religious epistemology.*

PART 3

MODES OF RELIGIOUS LIFE

The diversity of religious responses to life, both theoretical and practical, is a consequence of many factors. Although religious perspectives may originate in commonly shared human situations, such perspectives have all undergone historical development—development caused by specific social, geographical, political, and economic conditions. Although at a very abstract level, we may say that forms of human experience are universal—all men, whether oriental or occidental, peasant or aristocrat, primitive or modern, share in the forms of cognitive, conative, and affective experience —the peculiarities of experience are principally determined by the circumstances in which men live. Historical circumstances set frameworks in which men strive, appropriate, and order their experiences; where human circumstances differ, we may expect not only differences in the interpretation of religious consciousness but also differences in its qualities and content.

Our purpose here is to explore some of the modes of the religious response to life. The comprehensive forms of religious life are belief, practice, and dispositional structures. Religious belief is manifested in doctrines, creeds, theological and apologetic tracts. The range of religious practice is immense, including such phenomena as ritual, ceremony, art, righteous conduct, and so on. By "dispositional structures" is meant the prevailing tendencies in the human personality to respond in predetermined ways to the diversity of experience. These dispositions constitute a complex of attitudes or proclivities which condition both conduct and belief. The essays we are about to consider bring to view distinct modes of belief and practice; they help us to discover the effects that different traditions of religious thought have upon our thinking about basic religious questions. They also help to clarify the ways in which alternative interpretations of the nature and function of religious life pose fundamental problems for the study of religious questions.

The forms of religious life selected for scrutiny here could be viewed as horizons along which we can discover the various latitudes and altitudes of human religious experience. As our position varies, so will what is seen along the horizon. In fact, what is seen along these different horizons will vary so greatly that at times we shall find it difficult to say that we are always looking at the "same thing." But such a judgment presupposes that we already *know* what religious experience is like. Actually, the exploration of these horizons, like the controlled observations of the experimental scientist, uncovers for us the basic data which are the subject matter of a critical study of religion.

Chapter 8

Oriental and occidental traditions

Comprehending an Eastern religious tradition requires immense discipline of mind and a considerable capacity for openmindedness. Westerners can amass information about Eastern religious life simply by cataloging the facts in an encyclopedic fashion. Such "factual" knowledge, however, reveals only the husks of oriental thought and ritual; it is not equivalent to comprehending either its significance or meaning. An adequate understanding of the religious traditions of the East requires that its human significance be appropriated. The examination of non-Western religions involves an inquiry into the hopes, aspirations, value-commitments, and world views of religious persons in the East. The "externals" of the various Eastern religions—their myths, beliefs, rituals—must be approached with a view to discovering what these "externals" *mean* to the persons who produce them, participate in them, and respond to them.

To discern the human importance of another religious tradition is not a simple task. After all, it is only by sustained effort and persistent thought that a man can manage to isolate and define the basic categories and myths by which his *own* experience is organized and made intelligible. But the reward for serious examination of other religious traditions is a considerable enrichment of one's personal consciousness. One's own religious life is clarified in the course of such a comparative study; one also sees old religious problems, and indeed the whole human predicament, in new perspectives. Regardless of the particular attitude a Westerner takes toward religion, an introduction to the very different spirit of Eastern religious thought can have a liberating effect. Such a study can free him from a naïve acceptance of doctrines as established facts, allow him the opportunity to understand his own religious beliefs and experiences more completely and in juxtaposition to radically different beliefs, practices, and dispositional structures.

Heinrich Zimmer's brief essay touches upon some of the dominant themes of Eastern religious thought as they contrast with religious wisdom in the West. Zimmer points to the radical intertwining of life and thought in the Eastern tradition; he contrasts this to the outlook of the West which is more devoted to a kind of "controlling knowledge" where the knower separates what is known from the conduct of his life. Western thought is exoteric, objective and oriented towards verification according to established procedures, whereas Eastern thought is oriented toward religious intuition and the realization of spiritual unity. According to Zimmer, the status of the self and its orientation to religious insights are crucial differences between the two religious traditions.

Joseph Campbell examines the mythological foundations of Eastern and Western religious thought. The basic myth of the East is what he describes as 'eternal return'; in contrast, the fundamental myth of the West is what he terms 'cosmic restoration'. In the differences between these two myths, Campbell sees the chasm which separates the religious vision and practice of the East from that of the West. Each myth carries with it an interpretation of man's place in the cosmos and of his resultant predicament. The fundamental difference between the two myths seems to be most apparent in their diverse conceptions of time. The myth of "eternal return" makes the process of change and becoming a purely phenomenal reality and hence, illusory. Thus, in the East the great aim of the religious man is to find that overall cosmic unity that is hidden behind the veil of temporal succession and cosmic change. Time ought not to be and man, caught up in the endless process of repetitive cycles, is necessarily conditioned by time. Hence, there grows up in Eastern religious thought an aversion to time and a sustained effort to escape the cycle of birth, decay, death, and suffering, a cycle that is regarded as illusory. In the West, the dominant myth of "cosmic restoration" has the effect of drawing mankind to an engagement in time for the purpose of restoring a fallen cosmos. Man is summoned to an historical commitment and to labor in the hope of restoring himself and his world to a proper relationship with the Divine Creator. According to Campbell, the key concepts of most Western religious thought, since all are variations of one primal myth, is revelation, relationship, and community. In the East, the key concepts of religious thought are recognition, realization, release, and reunion.

Zimmer

THE MEETING OF EAST AND WEST*

[1.] We of the Occident are about to arrive at a crossroads that was reached by the thinkers of India some seven hundred years before Christ. This is the real reason why we become both vexed and stimulated, uneasy

* Heinrich Zimmer (1890–1943): German Indologist. The selection here is taken from the chapter entitled, "The Meeting of East and West," in Zimmer's *Philosophies of India*. This book is a survey and intensive analysis of the fundamental concepts, practices, and art of the Indian religious traditions. It covers such diverse religious traditions as Buddhism, Brahmanism, Jainism, Sankhya-Yoga and others. From *Philosophies of India* by Heinrich Zimmer, edited by Joseph Campbell. Bollingen Series XXVI. Copyright 1951 by Bollingen Foundation, New York. Distributed by Pantheon Books. Pp. 1–8, 12–14, 56–57, 63, 65–66. Reprinted by permission of the Bollingen Foundation, New York and Routledge & Kegan Paul Ltd., London.

yet interested, when confronted with the concepts and images of Oriental wisdom. This crossing is one to which the people of all civilizations come in the typical course of the development of their capacity and requirement for religious experience, and India's teachings force us to realize what its problems are. But we cannot take over the Indian solutions. We must enter the new period our own way and solve its questions for ourselves, because though truth, the radiance of reality, is universally one and the same, it is mirrored variously according to the mediums in which it is reflected. Truth appears differently in different lands and ages according to the living materials out of which its symbols are hewn.

Concepts and words are symbols, just as visions, rituals, and images are; so too are the manners and customs of daily life. Through all of these a transcendent reality is mirrored. They are so many metaphors reflecting and implying something which, though thus variously expressed, is ineffable, though thus rendered multiform, remains inscrutable. Symbols hold the mind to truth but are not themselves the truth, hence it is delusory to borrow them. Each civilization, every age, must bring forth its own.

We shall therefore have to follow the difficult way of our own experiences, produce our own reactions, and assimilate our sufferings and realizations. Only then will the truth that we bring to manifestation be as much our own flesh and blood as is the child its mother's; and the mother, in love with the Father, will then justly delight in her offspring as His duplication. The ineffable seed must be conceived, gestated, and brought forth from our own substance, fed by our blood, if it is to be the true child through which its mother is reborn: and the Father, the divine Transcendent Principle, will then also be reborn—delivered, that is to say, from the state of non-manifestation, non-action, apparent non-existence. We cannot borrow God. We must effect His new incarnation from within ourselves. Divinity must descend, somehow, into the matter of our own existence and participate in this peculiar life-process.

According to the mythologies of India, this is a miracle that will undoubtedly come to pass. For in the ancient Hindu tales one reads that whenever the creator and sustainer of the world, Visnu, is implored to appear in a new incarnation, the beseeching forces leave him no peace until he condescends. Nevertheless, the moment he comes down, taking flesh in a blessed womb, to be again made manifest in the world which itself is a reflex of his own ineffable being, self-willed demonic forces set themselves against him; for there are those who hate and despise the god and have no room for him in their systems of expansive egoism and domineering rule. These do everything within their power to hamper his career. Their violence, however, is not as destructive as it seems; it is no more than a necessary force in the historic process. Resistance is a standard part in the recurrent cosmic comedy that is enacted whenever a spark of supernal truth, drawn down by the misery of creatures and the imminence of chaos, is made manifest on the phenomenal plane.

"It is the same with our spirit," states Paul Valéry, "as with our flesh:

both hide in mystery what they feel to be most important. They conceal it from themselves. They single it out and protect it by this profundity in which they ensconce it. Everything that really counts is well veiled; testimony and documents only render it the more obscure; deeds and works are designed expressly to misrepresent it."

The chief aim of Indian thought is to unveil and integrate into consciousness what has been thus resisted and hidden by the forces of life—not to explore and describe the visible world. The supreme and characteristic achievement of the Brāhman mind (and this has been decisive, not only for the course of Indian philosophy, but also for the history of Indian civilization) was its discovery of the Self (ātman) as an independent, imperishable entity, underlying the conscious personality and bodily frame. Everything that we normally know and express about ourselves belongs to the sphere of change, the sphere of time and space, but this Self (ātman) is forever changeless, beyond time, beyond space and the veiling net of causality, beyond measure, beyond the dominion of the eye. The effort of Indian philosophy has been, for millenniums, to know this adamantine Self and make the knowledge effective in human life. And this enduring concern is what has been responsible for the supreme morning calm that pervades the terrible histories of the Oriental world—histories no less tremendous, no less horrifying, than our own. Through the vicissitudes of physical change a spiritual footing is maintained in the peaceful-blissful ground of Ātman; eternal, timeless, and imperishable Being.

Indian, like Occidental, philosophy imparts information concerning the measurable structure and powers of the psyche, analyzes man's intellectual faculties and the operations of his mind, evaluates various theories of human understanding, establishes the methods and laws of logic, classifies the senses, and studies the processes by which experiences are apprehended and assimilated, interpreted and comprehended. Hindu philosophers, like those of the West, pronounce on ethical values and moral standards. They study also the visible traits of phenomenal existence, criticizing the data of external experience and drawing deductions with respect to the supporting principles. India, that is to say, has had, and still has, its own disciplines of psychology, ethics, physics, and metaphysical theory. But the primary concern—in striking contrast to the interests of the modern philosophers of the West—has always been, not information, but transformation: a radical changing of man's nature and, therewith, a renovation of his understanding both of the outer world and of his own existence; a transformation as complete as possible, such as will amount when successful to a total conversion or rebirth.

In this respect Indian philosophy sides with religion to a far greater extent than does the critical, secularized thinking of the modern West. It is on the side of such ancient philosophers as Pythagoras, Empedocles, Plato, the Stoics, Epicurus and his followers, Plotinus, and the Neoplatonic thinkers. We recognize the point of view again in St. Augustine, the medieval mystics such as Meister Eckhart, and such later mystics as Jakob Böhme of Silesia. Among the Romantic philosophers it reappears in Schopenhauer.

The attitudes toward each other of the Hindu teacher and the pupil bowing at his feet are determined by the exigencies of this supreme task of transformation. Their problem is to effect a kind of alchemical transmutation of the soul. Through the means, not of a merely intellectual understanding, but of a change of heart (a transformation that shall touch the core of his existence), the pupil is to pass out of bondage, beyond the limits of human imperfection and ignorance, and transcend the earthly plane of being.

There is an amusing popular fable which illustrates this pedagogical idea. It is recorded among the teachings of the celebrated Hindu saint of the nineteenth century, Śrī Rāmakrishna. Anecdotes of this childlike kind occur continually in the discourses of the Oriental sages; they circulate in the common lore of the folk and are known to everyone from infancy. They carry the lessons of India's timeless wisdom to the homes and hearts of the people, coming down through the millenniums as everybody's property. Indeed India is one of the great homelands of the popular fable; during the Middle Ages many of her tales were carried into Europe. The vividness and simple aptness of the images drive home the points of the teaching; they are like pegs to which can be attached no end of abstract reasoning. The beast fable is but one of the many Oriental devices to make lessons catch hold and remain in the mind.

The present example is of a tiger cub that had been brought up among goats, but through the enlightening guidance of a spiritual teacher was made to realize its own unsuspected nature. Its mother had died in giving it birth. Big with young, she had been prowling for many days without discovering prey, when she came upon this herd of ranging wild goats. The tigress was ravenous at the time, and this fact may account for the violence of her spring; but in any case, the strain of the leap brought on the birth throes, and from sheer exhaustion she expired. Then the goats, who had scattered, returned to the grazing ground and found the little tiger whimpering at its mother's side. They adopted the feeble creature out of maternal compassion, suckled it together with their own offspring, and watched over it fondly. The cub grew and their care was rewarded; for the little fellow learned the language of the goats, adapted his voice to their gentle way of bleating, and displayed as much devotion as any kid of the flock. At first he experienced some difficulty when he tried to nibble thin blades of grass with his pointed teeth, but somehow he managed. The vegetarian diet kept him very slim and imparted to his temperament a remarkable meekness.

One night, when this young tiger among the goats had reached the age of reason, the herd was attacked again, this time by a fierce old male tiger, and again they scattered; but the cub remained where he stood, devoid of fear. He was of course surprised. Discovering himself face to face with the terrible jungle being, he gazed at the apparition in amazement. The first moment passed; then he began to feel self-conscious. Uttering a forlorn bleat, he plucked a thin leaf of grass and chewed it, while the other stared.

Suddenly the mighty intruder demanded: "What are you doing here among these goats? What are you chewing there?" The funny little creature bleated. The old one became really terrifying. He roared, "Why do you make this silly sound?" and before the other could respond, seized him roughly by the scruff and shook him, as though to knock him back to his senses. The jungle tiger then carried the frightened cub to a nearby pond, where he set him down, compelling him to look into the mirror surface, which was illuminated by the moon. "Now look at those two faces. Are they not alike? You have the pot-face of a tiger; it is like mine. Why do you fancy yourself to be a goat? Why do you bleat? Why do you nibble grass?"

The little one was unable to reply, but continued to stare, comparing the two reflections. Then it became uneasy, shifted its weight from paw to paw, and emitted another troubled, quavering cry. The fierce old beast seized it again and carried it off to his den, where he presented it with a bleeding piece of raw meat remaining from an earlier meal. The cub shuddered with disgust. The jungle tiger, ignoring the weak bleat of protest, gruffly ordered: "Take it! Eat it! Swallow it!" The cub resisted, but the frightening meat was forced between his teeth, and the tiger sternly supervised while he tried to chew and prepared to swallow. The toughness of the morsel was unfamiliar and was causing some difficulty, and he was just about to make his little noise again, when he began to get the taste of the blood. He was amazed; he reached with eagerness for the rest. He began to feel an unfamiliar gratification as the new food went down his gullet, and the meaty substance came into his stomach. A strange, glowing strength, starting from there, went out through his whole organism, and he commenced to feel elated, intoxicated. His lips smacked; he licked his jowls. He arose and opened his mouth with a mighty yawn, just as though he were waking from a night of sleep—a night that had held him long under its spell, for years and years. Stretching his form, he arched his back, extending and spreading his paws. The tail lashed the ground, and suddenly from his throat there burst the terrifying, triumphant roar of a tiger.

The grim teacher, meanwhile, had been watching closely and with increasing satisfaction. The transformation had actually taken place. When the roar was finished he demanded gruffly: "Now do you know what you really are?" and to complete the initiation of his young disciple into the secret lore of his own true nature, added: "Come, we shall go now for a hunt together in the jungle." . . .

According to the thinking and experience of India, the knowledge of changing things does not conduce to a realistic attitude; for such things lack substantiality, they perish. Neither does it conduce to an idealistic outlook; for the inconsistencies of things in flux continually contradict and refute each other. Phenomenal forms are by nature delusory and fallacious. The one who rests on them will be disturbed. They are merely the particles of a vast universal illusion which is wrought by the magic of Self-forgetfulness, supported by ignorance, and carried forward by the deceived passions. Naïve unawareness of the hidden truth of the Self is the primary cause of all the misplaced emphases, inappropriate attitudes, and consequent self-torments of this auto-intoxicated world.

There is obviously implicit in such an insight the basis for a transfer of all interest not only from the normal ends and means of people of the world, but also from the rites and dogmas of the religion of such deluded beings. The mythological creator, the Lord of the Universe, is no longer of interest. Only introverted awareness bent and driven to the depth of the subject's own nature reaches that borderline where the transitory super-impositions meet their unchanging source. And such awareness can finally succeed even in bringing consciousness across the border, to merge—perish and become therewith imperishable—in the omnipresent substratum of all substance. That is the Self (*ātman*), the ultimate, enduring, supporting source of being. That is the giver of all these specialized manifestations, changes of form, and deviations from the true state, these so-called *vikāras*: transformations and evolutions of the cosmic display. Nor is it through praise of and submission to the gods, but through knowledge, knowledge of the Self, that the sage passes from involvement in what is here displayed to a discovery of its cause.

And such knowledge is achieved through either of two techniques: 1. a systematic disparagement of the whole world as illusion, or 2. an equally thoroughgoing realization of the sheer materiality of it all.

This we recognize as precisely the non-theistic, anthropocentric position that we ourselves are on the point of reaching today in the West, if indeed we are not already there. For where dwell the gods to whom we can uplift our hands, send forth our prayers, and make oblation? Beyond the Milky Way are only island universes, galaxy beyond galaxy in the infinitudes of space—no realm of angels, no heavenly mansions, no choirs of the blessed surrounding a divine throne of the Father, revolving in beatific consciousness about the axial mystery of the Trinity. Is there any region left in all these great reaches where the soul on its quest might expect to arrive at the feet of God, having become divested of its own material coil? Or must we not now turn rather inward, seek the divine internally, in the deepest vault, beneath the floor; hearken within for the secret voice that is both com-manding and consoling; draw from inside the grace which passeth all understanding?

We of the modern Occident are at last prepared to seek and hear the voice that India has heard. But like the tiger cub we must hear it not from the teacher but from within ourselves. Just as in the period of the deflation of the revealed gods of the Vedic pantheon, so today revealed Christianity has been devaluated. The Christian, as Nietzsche says, is a man who behaves like everybody else. Our professions of faith have no longer any discernible bearing either on our public conduct or on our private state of hope. The sacraments do not work on many of us their spiritual transformation; we are bereft and at a loss where to turn. Meanwhile, our academic secular philosophies are concerned rather with information than with that redemptive transformation which our souls require. And this is the reason why a glance at the face of India may assist us to discover and recover something of ourselves.

The basic aim of any serious study of Oriental thought should be, not merely the gathering and ordering of as much detailed inside information as possible, but the reception of some significant influence. And in order that this may come to pass—in line with the parable of the goat-fosterling who discovered he was a tiger—we should swallow the meat of the teaching as red and rare as we can stand it, not too much cooked in the heat of our ingrained Occidental intellect (and, by no means, from any philological pickle jar), but not raw either, because then it would prove unpalatable and perhaps indigestible. We must take it rare, with lots of the red juices gushing, so that we may really taste it, with a certain sense of surprise. Then we will join, from our transoceanic distance, in the world-reverberating jungle roar of India's wisdom. . . .

[3.] In the Orient, philosophic wisdom does not come under the head of general information. It is a specialized learning directed to the attainment of a higher state of being. The philosopher is one whose nature has been transformed, re-formed to a pattern of really superhuman stature, as a result of being pervaded by the magic power of truth. That is why the prospective pupil must be carefully tested. The word *adhikārin* means, literally, as adjective, "entitled to, having a right to, possessed of authority, possessed of power, qualified, authorized, fit for"; also, "belonging to, owned by"; and as noun, "an officer, a functionary, head, director, rightful claimant, master, owner, a personage qualified to perform some sacrifice or holy work."

Philosophy is but one of many kinds of wisdom or knowledge (*vidyā*), each leading to some practical end. As the other vidyās lead to such attainments as belong to the special masterships of the craftsman, priest, magician, poet, or dancer, so philosophy ends in the attainment of a divine state both here and hereafter. Every kind of wisdom brings to its possessor its specific power, and this comes inevitably in consequence of the mastery of the respective materials. The doctor is the master of diseases and drugs, the carpenter the master of wood and other building materials, the priest of demons and even of gods by virtue of his charms, incantations, and rituals of offering and propitiation. Correspondingly, the yogī-philosopher is the master of his own mind and body, his passions, his reactions, and his meditations. He is one who has transcended the illusions of wishful thinking and of all other kinds of normal human thought. He feels no challenge or defeat in misfortune. He is absolutely beyond the touch of destiny.

Wisdom, in the Orient, no matter what its kind, is to be guarded jealously and communicated sparingly, and then only to one capable of becoming its perfect receptacle; for besides representing a certain skill, every department of learning carries with it a power that can amount almost to magic, a power to bring to pass what without it would seem a miracle. Teaching not intended to communicate such a power is simply of no consequence, and the communication to one unfit to wield the power properly would be disastrous. Furthermore, the possession of the wisdom and its special potencies was in ancient times regarded as one of the most valuable portions of the family heritage. Like a treasure, it was handed down with all care, according to the patrilineal order of descent. Charms, spells, the techniques of the various crafts and professions, and, finally, philosophy itself originally were communicated only in this way. Son followed father. For the growing generation there was little leniency of choice. This is how the instruments of family prestige were kept from slipping away.

In the West, on the other hand, the pride of philosophy is that it is open to the understanding and criticism of all. Our thought is exoteric, and that is regarded as one of the signs and proofs of its universal validity. Western philosophy has no secret doctrine, but challenges all to scrutinize her arguments, demanding no more than intelligence and an open-minded fairness in discussion. By this general appeal she has won her ascendency over the wisdom and teaching of the Church—which required that certain things should be taken for granted as once and for all established by divine revelation, and unquestionably settled by the interpretations of the inspired fathers, popes, and councils. Our popular modern philosophy, sailing in the broad wake of the natural sciences, recognizes no other authority than proof by experiment and pretends to rest upon no other assumptions than those rationally drawn as the logical theoretical result of critically and methodically digested data derived through sense-experience, registered and controlled by the mind and the faultless apparatus of the laboratories.

I wonder to what extent we feel in our civilization that the man who takes up the profession of the philosopher becomes mysteriously powerful. The business people controlling our economics, social life, internal politics, and foreign affairs generally feel suspicious of philosophers. Absorbed with lofty notions not easily applicable to current emergencies, the "professors" tend only to complicate issues with their abstract approach—and besides, they are not conspicuously fortunate themselves as bread-winners or practical managers. . . .

India, dreamy India, philosophical, unpractical, and hopelessly unsuccessful in the maintenance of her political freedom, has always stood for the idea that wisdom can be power if (and this is an "if" that must be kept in mind) the wisdom permeates, transforms, controls, and molds the whole of the personality. The sage is not to be a library of philosophy stalking about on two legs, an encyclopedia with a human voice. Thought itself is to be converted in him into life, into flesh, into being, into a skill in act. And then the higher his realization, the greater will be his power. The magic of Mahātma Gandhi is to be understood, for example, in this way. The force of his model presence on the Hindu masses derives from the fact that in him is expressed an identity of ascetic wisdom (as a style of existence) with politics (as an effective attitude toward worldly issues, whether of daily life or of national policy). His spiritual stature is expressed and honored in the title bestowed upon him: Mahātma: "whose essence of being is great," "he in whom the supra-personal, supra-individual, divine essence, which pervades the whole universe and dwells within the microcosm of the human heart as the animating grace of God (ātman), has grown to such magnitude as to have become utterly predominant (mahat)." The Spiritual Person has swallowed and dissolved in him all traces of ego, all the limitations proper to personal individuation, all those limiting, fettering qualities and propensities that belong to the normal human state, and even every trace remaining from ego-motivated deeds (karma), whether good or evil, whether derived from this life or from deeds in former births. Such traces of personality bias and distort a man's outlook on worldly affairs and prevent his approach to divine truth. But the Mahātma is the man who has become transformed in his being through wisdom; and the power of such a presence to work magic we may yet live to see.

Campbell
THE DIALOGUE IN MYTH OF EAST AND WEST*

[I]   The myth of eternal return, which is still basic to Oriental life, displays an order of fixed forms that appear and reappear through all time. The daily round of the sun, the waning and waxing moon, the cycle of the year, and the rhythm of organic birth, death, and new birth, represent a miracle of continuous arising that is fundamental to the nature of the universe. We all know the archaic myth of the four ages of gold, sliver, bronze, and iron, where the world is shown declining, growing ever worse. It will disintegrate presently in chaos, only to burst forth again, fresh as a flower, to recommence spontaneously the inevitable course. There never was a time when time was not. Nor will there be a time when this kaleidoscopic play of eternity in time will have ceased.

There is therefore nothing to be gained, either for the universe or for man, through individual originality and effort. Those who have identified themselves with the mortal body and its affections will necessarily find that all is painful, since everything—for them—must end. But for those who have found the still point of eternity, around which all—including themselves—revolves, everything is acceptable as it is; indeed, can even be

* Joseph Campbell (1904–   ): American mythologist (see footnote on P. 141). The selection is from *The Masks of God: Oriental Mythology*, constituting part of Chapter 1. *Oriental Mythology* is an examination of Eastern mythology as it has developed in the religions of India, China, and Japan. From *The Masks of God: Oriental Mythology* by Joseph Campbell. Copyright © 1962 by Joseph Campbell. All Rights Reserved. Reprinted by permission of The Viking Press, Inc., N.Y. and Martin Secker & Warburg Limited, London.

experienced as glorious and wonderful. The first duty of the individual, consequently, is simply to play his given role—as do the sun and moon, the various animal and plant species, the waters, the rocks, and the stars— without resistance, without fault; and then, if possible, so to order his mind as to identify its consciousness with the inhabiting principle of the whole.

The dreamlike spell of this contemplative, metaphysically oriented tradition, where light and darkness dance together in a world-creating cosmic shadow play, carries into modern times an image that is of incalculable age. In its primitive form it is widely known among the jungle villages of the broad equatorial zone that extends from Africa eastward, through India, Southeast Asia, and Oceania, to Brazil, where the basic myth is of a dreamlike age of the beginning, when there was neither death nor birth, which, however, terminated when a murder was committed. The body of the victim was cut up and buried. And not only did the food plants on which the community lives arise from those buried parts, but on all who ate of their fruit the organs of reproduction appeared; so that death, which had come into the world through a killing, was countered by its opposite, generation, and the self-consuming thing that is life, which lives on life, began its interminable course.

Throughout the dark green jungles of the world there abound not only dreadful animal scenes of tooth and claw, but also terrible human rites of cannibal communion, dramatically representing—with the force of an initiatory shock—the murder scene, sexual act, and festival meal of the beginning, when life and death became two, which had been one, and the sexes became two, which also had been one. Creatures come into being, live on the death of others, die, and become the food of others, continuing, thus, into and through the transformations of time, the timeless archetype of the mythological beginning; and the individual matters no more than a fallen leaf. Psychologically, the effect of the enactment of such a rite is to shift the focus of the mind from the individual (who perishes) to the everlasting group. Magically, it is to reinforce the ever-living life in all lives, which appears to be many but is really one; so that the growth is stimulated of the yams, coconuts, pigs, moon, and breadfruits, and of the human community as well. . . .

For the West, however, the possibility of such an egoless return to a state of soul antecedent to the birth of individuality has long since passed away; and the first important stage in the branching off can be seen to have occurred in that very part of the nuclear Near East where the earliest god-kings and their courts have been for centuries ritually entombed: namely Sumer, where a new sense of the separation of the spheres of god and man began to be represented in myth and ritual about 2350 B.C. The king, then, was no longer a god, but a servant of the god, his Tenant Farmer, supervisor of the race of human slaves created to serve the gods with unremitting toil. And no longer identity, but relationship, was the paramount concern. Man had been made not to *be* God but to know, honor, and serve him; so that even the king, who, according to the earlier mythological view, had been the chief embodiment of divinity on earth, was now but a priest offering sacrifice in tendance to One above—not a god returning himself in sacrifice to Himself.

In the course of the following centuries, the new sense of separation led to a counter-yearning for return—not to identity, for such was no longer possible of conception (creator and creature were not the same), but to the presence and vision of the forfeited god. Hence the new mythology brought forth, in due time, a development away from the earlier static view of returning cycles. A progressive, temporally oriented mythology arose, of a creation, once and for all, at the beginning of time, a subsequent fall, and a work of restoration, still in progress. The world no longer was to be known as a mere showing in time of the paradigms of eternity, but as a field of unprecedented cosmic conflict between two powers, one light and one dark.

The earliest prophet of this mythology of cosmic restoration was, apparently, the Persian Zoroaster, whose dates, however, have not been securely established. They have been variously placed between c. 1200 and c. 550 B.C., so that, like Homer (of about the same span of years), he should perhaps be regarded rather as symbolic of a tradition than as specifically, or solely, one man. The system associated with his name is based on the idea of a conflict between the wise lord, Ahura Mazda, "first father of the Righteous Order, who gave to the sun and stars their path," and an independent evil principle, Angra Mainyu, the Deceiver, principle of the lie, who, when all had been excellently made, entered into it in every particle. The world, consequently, is a compound wherein good and evil, light and dark, wisdom and violence, are contending for a victory. And the privilege and duty of each man—who, himself, as a part of creation, is a compound of good and evil—is to elect, voluntarily, to engage in the battle in the interest of the light. It is supposed that with the birth of Zoroaster, twelve thousand years following the creation of the world, a decisive turn was given the conflict in favor of the good, and that when he returns, after another twelve millennia, in the person of the messiah Saoshyant, there will take place a final battle and cosmic conflagration, through which the principle of darkness and the lie will be undone. Whereafter, all will be light, there will be no further history, and the Kingdom of God (Ahura Mazda) will have been established in its pristine form forever.

It is obvious that a potent mythical formula for the reorientation of the human spirit is here supplied—pitching it forward along the way of time, summoning man to an assumption of autonomous responsibility for the renovation of the universe in God's name, and thus fostering a new, potentially political (not finally contemplative) philosophy of holy war. "May we be such," runs a Persian prayer, "as those who bring on this renovation and make this world progressive, till its perfection shall have been achieved."

The first historic manifestation of the force of this new mythic view was in the Achaemenian empire of Cyrus the Great (died 529 B.C.) and Darius I (reigned c. 521–486 B.C.), which in a few decades extended its domain from

India to Greece, and under the protection of which the post-exilic Hebrews both rebuilt their temple (Ezra 1:1–11) and reconstructed their traditional inheritance. The second historic manifestation was in the Hebrew application of its universal message to themselves; the next was in the world mission of Christianity; and the fourth, in that of Islam.

"Enlarge the place of your tent, and let the curtains of your habitations be stretched out; hold not back, lengthen your cords and strengthen your stakes. For you will spread abroad to the right and to the left, and your descendants will possess the nations and will people the desolate cities" (Isaiah 54:2–3; c. 546–536 B.C.).

"And this gospel of the kingdom will be preached throughout the whole world as a testimony to all nations; and then the end will come" (Matthew 24:14; c. 90 A.D.).

"And slay them wherever you catch them, and turn them out from where they have turned you out; for tumult and oppression are worse than slaughter. . . . And fight them on until there is no more tumult or oppression and there prevail justice and faith in Allah; but if they cease, let there be no hostility except to those who practice oppression" (Koran 2:191, 193; c. 632 A.D.).

Two completely opposed mythologies of the destiny and virtue of man, therefore, have come together in the modern world. And they are contributing in discord to whatever new society may be in the process of formation. For, of the tree that grows in the garden where God walks in the cool of the day, the wise men westward of Iran have partaken of the fruit of the knowledge of good and evil, whereas those on the other side of that cultural divide, in India and the Far East, have relished only the fruit of eternal life. However, the two limbs, we are informed, come together in the center of the garden, where they form a single tree at the base, branching out when they reach a certain height. Likewise, the two mythologies spring from one base in the Near East. And if man should taste of both fruits he would become, we have been told, as God himself (Genesis 3:22)—which is the boon that the meeting of East and West today is offering to us all.

[II]   The extent to which the mythologies—and therewith psychologies—of the Orient and Occident diverged in the course of the period between the dawn of civilization in the Near East and the present age of mutual rediscovery appears in their opposed versions of the shared mythological image of the first being, who was originally one but became two.

"In the beginning," states an Indian example of c. 700 B.C., preserved in the Brihadaranyaka Upanishad,

this universe was nothing but the Self in the form of a man. It looked around and saw that there was nothing but itself, whereupon its first shout was, "It is I!"; whence the concept "I" arose. (And that is why, even now, when addressed, one answers first, "It is I!" only then giving the other name that one bears.)

Then he was afraid. (That is why anyone alone is afraid.) But he considered: "Since there is no one here but myself, what is there to fear?" Whereupon the fear departed. (For what should have been feared? It is only to a second that fear refers.)

However, he still lacked delight (therefore, we lack delight when alone) and desired a second. He was exactly as large as a man and woman embracing. This Self then divided itself in two parts; and with that, there were a master and a mistress. (Therefore this body, by itself, as the sage Yajnavalkya declares, is like half of a split pea. And that is why, indeed, this space is filled by a woman.)

The male embraced the female, and from that the human race arose. She, however, reflected: "How can he unite with me, who am produced from himself? Well then, let me hide!" She became a cow, he a bull and united with her; and from that cattle arose. She became a mare, he a stallion; she an ass, he a donkey and united with her; and from that solid-hoofed animals arose. She became a goat, he a buck; she a sheep, he a ram and united with her; and from that goats and sheep arose. Thus he poured forth all pairing things, down to the ants. Then he realized: "I, actually, am creation; for I have poured forth all this." Whence arose the concept "Creation" [Sanskrit sṛṣṭiḥ: "what is poured forth"].

Anyone understanding this becomes, truly, himself a creator in this creation.

The best-known Occidental example of this image of the first being, split in two, which seem to be two but are actually one, is, of course, that of the Book of Genesis, second chapter, where it is turned, however, to a different sense. For the couple is separated here by a superior being, who, as we are told, caused a deep sleep to fall upon the man and, while he slept, took one of his ribs. In the Indian version it is the god himself that divides and becomes not man alone but all creation; so that everything is a manifestation of that single inhabiting divine substance: there is no other; whereas in the Bible, God and man, from the beginning, are distinct. Man is made in the image of God, indeed, and the breath of God has been breathed into his nostrils; yet his being, his self, is not that of God, nor is it one with the universe. The fashioning of the world, of the animals, and of Adam (who then became Adam and Eve) was accomplished not within the sphere of divinity but outside of it. There is, consequently, an *intrinsic*, not merely *formal*, separation. And the goal of knowledge cannot be to *see* God here and now in all things; for God is not in things. God is transcendent. God is beheld only by the dead. The goal of knowledge has to be, rather, to know the *relationship* of God to his creation, or, more specifically, to man, and through such knowledge, by God's grace, to link one's own will back to that of the Creator.

Moreover, according to the biblical version of this myth, it was only after creation that man fell, whereas in the Indian example creation itself was a fall—the fragmentation of a god. And the god is not condemned. Rather, his creation, his "pouring forth" (sṛṣṭiḥ), is described as an act of voluntary, dynamic will-to-be-more, which anteceded creation and has, therefore, a metaphysical, symbolical, not literal, historical meaning. The fall of Adam and Eve was an event within the already created frame of time and space, an accident that should not have taken place. The myth of the Self in the form of a man, on the other hand, who looked around and saw nothing but himself, said "I," felt fear, and then desired to be two, tells of an intrinsic, not errant, factor in the manifold of being, the correction or undoing of which would not improve, but dissolve, creation. The Indian point of view is metaphysical, poetical; the biblical, ethical and historical.

Adam's fall and exile from the garden was thus in no sense a metaphysical departure of divine substance from itself, but an event only in the history, or pre-history, of man. And this event in the created world has been followed throughout the remainder of the book by the record of man's linkage and failures of linkage back to God—again, historically conceived. For, as we next hear, God himself, at a certain point in the course of time, out of his own volition, moved toward man, instituting a new law in the form of a covenant with a certain people. And these became, therewith, a priestly race, unique in the world. God's reconciliation with man, of whose creation he had repented (Genesis 6:6), was to be achieved only by virtue of this particular community—in time: for in time there should take place the realization of the Lord God's kingdom on earth, when the heathen monarchies would crumble and Israel be saved, when men would "cast forth their idols of silver and their idols of gold, which they made to themselves to worship, to the moles and to the bats."

> Be broken, you peoples, and be dismayed;
>   give ear, all you far countries;
> gird yourselves and be dismayed;
>   gird yourselves and be dismayed.
> Take counsel together, but it will come to nought;
>   speak a word, but it will not stand,
>   for God is with us.

In the Indian view, on the contrary, what is divine here is divine there also; nor has anyone to wait—or even to hope—for a "day of the Lord." For what has been lost is in each his very self (*ātman*), here and now, requiring only to be sought. Or, as they say: "Only when men shall roll up space like a piece of leather will there be an end of sorrow apart from knowing God."

The question arises (again historical) in the world dominated by the Bible, as to the identity of the favored community, and three are well known to have developed claims: the Jewish, the Christian, and the Moslem, each supposing itself to have been authorized by a particular revelation. God, that is to say, though conceived as outside of history and not himself its substance (transcendent: not immanent), is supposed to have engaged himself miraculously in the enterprise of restoring fallen man through a covenant, sacrament, or revealed book, with a view to a general, communal experience of fulfillment yet to come. The world is corrupt and man a sinner; the individual, however, through engagement along with God in the destiny of the only authorized community participates in the coming glory of the kingdom of righteousness, when "the glory of the Lord shall be revealed, and all flesh shall see it together."

In the experience and vision of India, on the other hand, although the holy mystery and power have been understood to be indeed transcendent ("other than the known; moreover, above the unknown"), they are also, at the same time, immanent ("like a razor in a razorcase, like fire in tinder"). It is not that the divine is every*where*: it is that the divine is every*thing*. So that one does not require any outside reference, revelation, sacrament, or authorized community to return to it. One has but to alter one's psychological orientation and recognize (re-cognize) what is within. Deprived of this recognition, we are removed from our own reality by a cerebral shortsightedness which is called in Sanskrit *māyā*, "delusion" (from the verbal root *mā*, "to measure, measure out, to form, to build," denoting, in the first place, the power of a god or demon to produce illusory effects, to change form, and to appear under deceiving masks; in the second place, "magic," the production of illusions and, in warfare, camouflage, deceptive tactics; and finally, in philosophical discourse, the illusion superimposed upon reality as an effect of ignorance). Instead of the biblical exile from a geographically, historically conceived garden wherein God walked in the cool of the day, we have in India, therefore, already c. 700 B.C. (some three hundred years before the putting together of the Pentateuch), a *psychological* reading of the great theme.

The shared myth of the primal androgyne is applied in the two traditions to the same task—the exposition of man's distance, in his normal secular life, from the divine Alpha and Omega. Yet the arguments radically differ, and therefore support two radically different civilizations. For, if man has been removed from the divine through a historical event, it will be a historical event that leads him back, whereas if it has been by some sort of psychological displacement that he has been blocked, psychology will be his vehicle of return. And so it is that in India the final focus of concern is not the community (though, as we shall see, the idea of the holy community plays a formidable role as a disciplinary force), but yoga.

[III] The Indian term *yoga* is derived from the Sanskrit verbal root *yuj*, "to link, join, or unite," which is related etymologically to "yoke," a yoke of oxen, and is in sense analogous to the word "religion" (Latin *re-ligio*), "to link back, or bind." Man, the creature, is by religion bound back to God. However, religion, *religio*, refers to a linking historically conditioned by way of a covenant, sacrament, or Koran, whereas yoga is the psychological linking of the mind to that superordinated principle "by which the mind knows." Furthermore, in yoga what is linked is finally the self to itself, consciousness to consciousness; for what had seemed, through *māyā*, to be two are in reality not so; whereas in religion what are linked are God and man, which are not the same.

It is of course true that in the popular religions of the Orient the gods are worshiped as though external to their devotees, and all the rules and rites of a covenanted relationship are observed. Nevertheless, the ultimate realization, which the sages have celebrated, is that the god worshiped as though without is in reality a reflex of the same mystery as oneself. As long as an illusion of ego remains, the commensurate illusion of a separate deity also will be there; and vice versa, as long as the idea of a separate deity is cherished, an illusion of ego, related to it in love, fear, worship, exile, or atonement, will also be there. But precisely that illusion of duality is the trick of *māyā*. "Thou art that" (*tat tvam asi*) is the proper thought for the first step to wisdom.

In the beginning, as we have read, there was only the Self; but it said "I" (Sanskrit, *aham*) and immediately felt fear, after which, desire.

It is to be remarked that in this view of the instant of creation (presented from within the sphere of the psyche of the creative being itself) the same two basic motivations are identified as the leading modern schools of depth analysis have indicated for the *human* psyche: aggression and desire. Carl G. Jung, in his early paper on *The Unconscious in Normal and Pathological Psychology* (1916), wrote of two psychological types: the introvert, harried by fear, and the extrovert, driven by desire. Sigmund Freud also, in his *Beyond the Pleasure Principle* (1920), wrote of "the death wish" and "the life wish": on the one hand, the will to violence and the fear of it (*thanatos, destrudo*), and, on the other hand, the need and desire to love and be loved (*eros, libido*). Both spring spontaneously from the deep dark source of the energies of the psyche, the *id*, and are governed, therefore, by the self-centered "pleasure principle": *I want: I am afraid.* Comparably, in the Indian myth, as soon as the self said "I" (*aham*), it knew first fear, and then desire.

But now—and here, I believe, is a point of fundamental importance for our reading of the basic difference between the Oriental and Occidental approaches to the cultivation of the soul—in the Indian myth the principle of ego, "I" (*aham*), is identified completely with the pleasure principle, whereas in the psychologies of both Freud and Jung its proper function is to know and relate to external reality (Freud's "reality principle"): not the reality of the metaphysical but that of the physical, empirical sphere of time and space. In other words, spiritual maturity, as understood in the modern Occident, requires a differentiation of *ego* from *id*, whereas in the Orient, throughout the history at least of every teaching that has stemmed from India, ego (*aham-kāra*: "the making of the sound 'I' ") is impugned as the principle of libidinous delusion, to be dissolved. . . .

In the classic Indian doctrine of the four ends for which men are supposed to live and strive, love and pleasure (*kāma*), power and success (*artha*), lawful order and moral virtue (*dharma*), and, finally, release from delusion (*mokṣa*)—we note that the first two are manifestations of what Freud has termed "the pleasure principle," primary urges of the natural man, epitomized in the formula "I want." In the adult, according to the Oriental view, these are to be quelled and checked by the principles of *dharma*, which, in the classic Indian system, are impressed upon the individual by the training of his caste. The infantile "I want" is to be subdued by a "thou shalt," socially applied (not individually determined), which is supposed to be as much a part of the immutable cosmic order as the course of the sun itself.

Now it is to be observed that in the version . . . of the temptation of the Buddha, the Antagonist respresents all three of the first triad of ends . . . for in his character as the Lord Desire he personifies the first; as the Lord Death, the aggressive force of the second; while in his summons to the meditating sage to arise and return to the duties of his station in society, he promotes the third. And, indeed, as a manifestation of that Self which not only poured forth but permanently supports the universe, he is the proper incarnation of these ends. For they do, in fact, support the world. And in most of the rites of all religions, this triune god, we may say, in one aspect or another, is the one and only god adored.

However, in the name and achievement of the Buddha, the "Illuminated One," the fourth end is announced: release from delusion. And to the attainment of this, the others are impediments, difficult to remove, yet, for one of purpose, not invincible. Sitting at the world navel, pressing back through the welling creative force that was surging into and through his own being, the Buddha actually broke back into the void beyond, and—ironically—the universe immediately burst into bloom. Such an act of self-noughting is one of individual effort. There can be no question about that. However, an Occidental eye cannot but observe that there is no requirement or expectation anywhere in this Indian system of four ends—neither in the primary two of the natural organism and the impressed third of society, nor in the exalted fourth of release—for a maturation of the personality through intelligent, fresh, individual adjustment to the time-space world round about, creative experimentation with unexplored possibilities, and the assumption of personal responsibility for unprecedented acts performed within the context of the social order. In the Indian tradition all has been perfectly arranged from all eternity. There can be nothing new, nothing to be learned but what the sages have taught from of yore. And fnally, when the boredom of this nursery horizon of "I want" against "thou shalt" has become insufferable, the fourth and final aim is all that is offered—of an extinction of the infantile ego altogether: disengagement or release (mokṣa) from both "I" and "thou."

In the European West, on the other hand, where the fundamental doctrine of the freedom of the will essentially dissociates each individual from every other, as well as from both the will in nature and the will of God, there is placed upon each the responsibility of coming intelligently, out of his own experience and volition, to some sort of relationship with—not identity with or extinction in—the all, the void, the suchness, the absolute, or whatever the proper term may be for that which is beyond terms. And, in the secular sphere likewise, it is normally expected that an educated ego should have developed away from the simple infantile polarity of the pleasure and obedience principles toward a personal, uncompulsive, sensitive relationship to empirical reality, a certain adventurous attitude toward the unpredictable, and a sense of personal responsibility for decisions. Not life as a good soldier, but life as a developed, unique individual, is the ideal. And we shall search the Orient in vain for anything quite comparable. There the ideal, on the contrary, is the quenching, not development, of ego. That is the formula turned this way and that, up and down the line, throughout the literature: a systematic, steady, continually drumming devaluation of the "I" principle, the reality function––which has remained, consequently, undeveloped, and so, wide open to the seizures of completely uncritical mythic identifications. . . .

Chapter 9

Salvation and reconciliation

Almost every religious perspective, whether it is primitive or modern, Eastern or Western, testifies to the fact that human existence is "broken": it stands in desperate need of reunion with the divine ground of existence. The crisis of the human predicament is that man existing in fundamental or radical finitude, anxiety, and suffering, cannot find or create a meaningful center for his life apart from a proper relationship to or realization of true spirituality. Religious ideas, in providing an interpretation of man's condition, represent human life as estranged, in some manner, from its distinct spiritual origin or destiny. Rituals, ceremonies, covenants, and moral codes are forms of religious living which can materially effect the spiritual destiny of a man who observes them or governs his life according to them. Such practical forms of the religious life are not always means of re-establishing or realizing spiritual health. Frequently, they are celebrations of that accomplished realization or reunion. The symbols of the Fall of Man in the Judeo-Christian tradition and of the Bondage of Illusion in the Hindu and Buddhist traditions, refer to the crisis of human existence and its broken nature. The symbols of the Covenant of Law, the Grace of Christ and the Attainment of Enlightenment refer to the spiritual destiny of existing men in whom existential estrangement, suffering, anxiety, and even death may be overcome. In almost every religion, the symbols of the broken character of human life exist in relation to the symbols of redemption and reconciliation. And no account of the forms of religious life is complete without some consideration of the religious ideas pertaining to salvation and reconciliaton.

We consider here four different models of reconciliation or redemption: Hindu realization of Brahman, Buddhist enlightenment, Christian atonement, and humanistic love. The correlation between concepts relating to man's predicament and concepts representing the ways in which this predicament is resolved or overcome becomes evident upon careful study of these models. It should not surprise us, however, to find that a religious *diagnosis* of man's spiritual malaise is implied in the *prognosis* regarding both the means to, and the nature of, spiritual health.

"That thou art." This simple formula which a Hindu father explains to his son is the dominant teaching of the Upanishads and expresses the deepest truth of Hinduism. Although the world presents to us a multiplicity of individual entities, differentiated by words and forms, the task of the Hindu in quest of spiritual illumination is to penetrate this veil of ignorance and so come to the realization that all is Brahman. Despite all appearances to the contrary, ultimate truth is found only in the nondualistic principle of the Self, which is one, though showing itself through the diversity of individuals and objects of the world. All natural and living things are proclaimed to be Brahman, one Self, undergoing multiple transformations.

According to the Hindu tradition, we are blinded by our ignorance, prone to distinguishing objects from each other and reifying our distinctions. Hence, selves are believed to be separate, unique identities and are thought to constitute entirely different kinds of beings than the entities of nature. However, this world of variety, of multiple names and forms, must become transparent in its spiritual unity so that we can realize the essence that we really are and always have been. The vast illusions (maya) of the world process which hold us enthralled must be abolished so that we can stand in the pure light of Brahman. This highest reality is portrayed as invisible, like the void in the fig seed, yet curiously omnipresent, like the salt which suffuses the water. Only by breaking through to this realization can man end his bondage to the sorrowful round of births and the pervasive ignorance that hides from him his true spiritual identity.

According to the Buddhist appraisal of the human predicament, as outlined in Zimmer's essay, the ground of man's bondage to endless suffering, birth, and death is his enslavement to the demonic forces of the cosmic illusion. Man, through ignorance of his real spiritual destiny, is caught in the thralldom of desire and pleasure, and, as a consequence, suffers pain, death and rebirth. Every attachment to his individual selfhood and to the cosmos yields, by an inexorable law, a chain of consequences which bind a man ever more firmly to natural existence, to the wheel of birth, suffering, death and rebirth. Yet the tighter the chains of illusion become, the more they evoke, in a dialetical fashion, the urge to escape, to be liberated from the ceaseless, meaningless round of pain and birth.

Desiring absolute emancipation, a man seeks to realize another dimension of existence which is not subject to the relentless rush of time and universal becoming. The human spirit seeks a realm of freedom that is non-temporal and which entirely transcends the human condition. In short a man seeks the death of temporality and rebirth in a mode of being unconditioned by time and change. Such a realm of absolute freedom is symbolized in the concept of Nirvana, the shore completely beyond the chains of temporal illusion. The path taken to reach unconditional liberation, the Eightfold path of the Buddha, leads one progressively away from involvement in one's self, the world, and their incessant becoming. By the discipline of the Buddha's path, a man nurtures within himself a new thirst, a desire for a transtemporal mode of being which entails a depreciation of, and detachment from, the world and the narrow confines of individuality.

The aim of the Buddhist discipline is not simply to comprehend the plight of man's bondage to illusion, but also to overcome that enslavement by the nullification of the factors which cause the bondage, e.g., desire, pleasure, pain, birth, and death. Complete emancipation from the broken character of human life is the great promise and affirmation of Buddhist doctrine.

In direct contrast stands the Christian concept of man's "fallen" nature and its doctrine of atonement. D. M. Baillie's essay on the Christian doctrine of atonement shows that the divine act of reconciliation, which has its origin in God's love and mercy, is required because of man's alienation from God as a result of man's sin. According to the Christian interpretation of the human predicament, man's spirit is bound to the fallen world in such a manner that man lives in radical estrangement from the divine source of his being. Human bondage to time and history and to the radically contingent character of human existence bespeaks the "fallen" nature and broken existence of man. Sin is the symbol of man's improper relationship with God and is innate to the human condition.

The great affirmation of the Christian religion relates to the overcoming of sin and alienation by God's atoning act, in history, through Christ. The love and mercy of God are concretely expressed in the life, death, and resurrection of Christ, who stands as the great symbol of redemption in Christian faith. Baillie understands the atonement as an "objective process . . . that goes on in the very life of God." Redemption is an act of God which breaks down man's bondage to sin and restores his essential goodness. The broken relationship between man and God, manifested by the crisis of man's existential condition, is made whole and is healed, through God's initiative. The paradox of Grace is that what is unacceptable, man's sin and rebellion, is made acceptable through God's love and mercy without being changed in character. Emancipation from sin into a new relationship with God is made possible by human participation in the redemptive work of God through faith.

The contrast between the Christian doctrine of atonement and the Buddhist conception of enlightenment or Nirvana is striking. The Christian views man's fallen condition as a form of bondage to the destructive consequences of sin, such as anxiety, guilt, pride, self-centeredness and evil. This is a deplorable condition to be in; it is nevertheless a *real* condition. Man's sin has an ontological character. On the other hand, the Buddhist does not look upon man's enslavement to the cosmic illusion—to individuality, desire, pleasure, pain, birth, and rebirth—as a *real* condition at all. It is a consequence of the magic play of *maya* or illusion which is principally the result of man's ignorance. The world of passing forms, so subject to the disintegrating effects of time, does not really participate in Being. The world and human life exhibit ceaseless becoming and change, and these have no real or ontological status. Thus, for the Buddhist, man's condition, insofar as it seems to participate in time, change, birth, desire, and suffering has no real being; it is, literally, non-being. The urge to emancipation in Buddhism is a striving for realization of a mode of living that does not share in the cosmic illusion; the Buddhist seeks a mode of eternal being far beyond the shores of this familiar existence and world. In contrast, the Christian views the overcoming of sin as a renewal and transformation of the "old" man such that a proper relationship is re-established with God. Separation is overcome not by realization of one's identity with divine reality but rather by God's creation of the possibility of a new mode of relationship between Himself and mankind.

Erich Fromm's essay on "Mature Love" may be viewed as providing a third possibility for understanding how the crisis in the human situation can be met. The categories used in the analysis of mankind's predicament by Fromm are almost entirely 'naturalistic': they are restricted to an environmental and psychological analysis of the structures of human life and have no recourse to supernatural or spiritualistic metaphysics. The human feeling of aloneness, separation, anxiety, and guilt are the consequence of human transcendence, through self-awareness, of the purely natural foundations of life. The awareness of separation gives rise to a yearning for reunion, a desire to break out of the solitude and fragmentary quality characteristic of life.

Fromm recognizes that there are a variety of ways in which men attempt to overcome the alienation and fragmentation of existence, in work, in routine everyday life, in conformity. His central thesis is that the most profound and satisfactory method of achieving "at-one-ment" is through an interpersonal fusion in the form of "mature love." Such love breaks down human separation and its destructive consequences while preserving the integrity, freedom, and responsibility of the participating persons.

Our examination of the modes of religious life began with a consideration of the divergent patterns of thought and dispositional structures in the Eastern and Western traditions. We have seen how this divergence is concretely manifested in the types of resolutions proposed for the dilemmas of human life. The variety of proposed resolutions is made the more striking by what *appears* to be a common assessment of the human predicament in the Buddhist, Hindu, Christian, and humanistic frameworks. The suspicion arises that the four perspectives are not "talking" about the same thing. Can all four be literally true? Perhaps they are all "talking" about the same thing and only their language differs. But what is the function of language in religious discourse? We must turn further on to the problems of the meaning and function of religious language and to the question of the cognitive value of religious statements.

Upanishads
HINDU REALIZATION OF BRAHMAN*

Section One

1. There lived once Svetaketu Aruneya (the grandson of Aruna). To him his father (Uddalaka, the son of Aruna) said: "Svetaketu, go to school; for there is none belonging to our race, darling, who, not having studied (the Veda), is, as it were, a Brahmana by birth only."

2. Having begun his apprenticeship (with a guru) when he was twelve years of age, Svetaketu returned to his father; when he was twenty-four, having then studied all the Vedas,—conceited, considering himself well-read, and stern.

3. His father said to him: "Svetaketu, as you are so conceited, considering yourself so well-read, and so stern, my dear, have you ever asked for that instruction by which we hear what cannot be heard, by which we perceive what cannot be perceived, by which we know what cannot be known?"

4. "What is that instruction, Sir?" he asked. The father replied: "My dear, as by one clod of clay all that is made of clay is known, the difference being only a name, arising from speech, but the truth being that all is clay;

5. "And as, my dear, by one nugget of gold all that is made of gold is known, the difference being only a name, arising from speech, but the truth being that all is gold;

6. "And as by one pair of nail-scissors all that is made of iron is known, the difference being only a name, arising from speech, but the truth being that all is iron,—thus, my dear, is that instruction."

7. The son said: "Surely, those venerable men (my teachers) did not know that. For if they had known it, why should they not have told it to me? Do you, Sir, therefore tell me that." "Be it so," said the father.

Section Two

1. "In the beginning there was that only which is, one only, without a second. Others say, in the beginning there was that only which is not, one only, without a second; and from that which is not, that which is was born.

2. "But how could it be thus?" the father continued. "How could that which is, be born of that which is not? No, only that which is, was in the beginning, one only, without a second.

* All of the major systems of Hindu religious philosophy derive from the Upanishads, and all claim the Upanishads as their primal authority. Originally, the Upanishads were the secret instructions given to aspiring religious novitiates who sat at the feet of the great teachers of the Hindu tradition. This selection is taken from the *Chandogya-Upanishad* (composed sometime between the ninth and fourth centuries B.C.). Reprinted from F. Max Müller, trans., *The Sacred Books of the East*, Vol. 1 (1879), Modified.

3. "It thought, may I be many, may I grow forth. It sent forth fire. That fire thought, may I be many, may I grow forth. It sent forth water. And therefore whenever anybody anywhere is hot and perspires, water is produced on him from fire alone.

4. "Water thought, may I be many, may I grow forth. It sent forth earth (food). Therefore whenever it rains anywhere, most food is then produced. From water alone is eatable food produced.

Section Three

1. "Of all living things there are indeed three origins only, that which springs from an egg, that which springs from a living being, and that which springs from a germ.

2. "That Being (i.e., the producer of fire, water, and earth) thought, let me now enter those three beings (fire, water, earth) with this living Self, and let me then reveal (develop) names and forms.

3. "Then that Being having said, Let me make each of these three tripartite (so that fire, water, and earth should each have itself for its principal ingredient, besides an admixture of the other two) entered into those three beings with this living self only, and developed names and forms.

4. "He made each of these tripartite; and how these three beings become each of them tripartite, that learn from me, my son."...

Section Eight

1. Uddalaka said to his son Svetaketu: "Learn from me the true nature of sleep. When a man sleeps here, then he becomes united with the True, he is gone to his own (Self). Therefore they say he sleeps, because he is gone to his own.

2. "As a bird when tied by a string flies first in every direction, and finding no rest anywhere, settles down at last on the very place where it is fastened, exactly in the same manner, my son, that mind (the jiva, or living Self in the mind), after flying in every direction, and finding no rest anywhere, settles down on breath; for indeed, my son, mind is fastened to breath.

3. "Learn from me, my son, what are hunger and thirst. When a man is thus said to be hungry, water is carrying away (digests) what has been eaten by him. Therefore as they speak of a cow-leader, a horse-leader, a man-leader, so they call water (which digests food and causes hunger) food-leader. Thus (by food digested, etc.) know this offshoot (the body) to be brought forth, for this body could not be without a root (cause).

4. "And where could its cause be except in food (earth)? And in the same manner, my son, as food too is an offshoot, seek after its root, viz. water. And as water too is an offshoot, seek after its root, viz, fire. And as fire too

is an offshoot, seek after its root, viz. the True. Yes, all these creatures have their root in the True, they dwell in the True, they rest in the True.

5. "When a man is thus said to be thirsty, fire carries away what has been drunk by him. Therefore as they speak of a cow-leader, of a horse-leader, of a man-leader, so they call fire a water-leader. Thus (by water digested, etc.) know this offshoot (the body) to be brought forth: this body could not be without a root (cause).

6. "And where could its root be except in water? As water is an offshoot, seek after its root, viz. fire. As fire is an offshoot, seek after its root, viz. the True. Yes, all these creatures have their root in the True, they dwell in the True, they rest in the True. And how these three things, fire, water, earth, when they reach man become each of them tripartite, has been said before. When a man departs from hence, his speech is merged in his mind, his mind in his breath, his breath in heat, heat in the Highest Being.

7. "Now that which is that subtle essence (the root of all), in it all that exists has its self. It is the True. It is the Self, and That Thou Art, Svetaketu." "Please inform me still more," said the son. "So be it," said the father.

Section Nine

1. "As the bees make honey by collecting the juices of distant trees, and reduce the juice into one form,

2. "And as these juices have no discrimination, so that they might say, I am the juice of this tree or that, in the same manner, my son, all these creatures, when they have become merged in the True (either in deep sleep or in death), know not that they are merged in the True.

3. "Whatever these creatures are here, whether a lion, or a wolf, or a boar, or a worm, or a midge, or a gnat, or a mosquito, that they become again and again.

4. "Now that which is that subtle essence, in it all that exists has its self. It is the True, It is the Self, and That Thou Art, O Svetaketu."

Section Ten

1. "These rivers run, the eastern towards the east, the western towards the west. They go from sea to sea. They become indeed sea. And as those rivers, when they are in the sea, do not know, I am this or that river,

2. "In the same manner, my son, all these creatures, when they have come back from the True, know not that they have come back from the True. Whatever these creatures are here, whether a lion, or a wolf, or a boar, or a worm, or a midge, or a gnat, or a mosquito, that they become again and again.

3. "That which is that subtle essence, in it all that exists has its self. It is the True. It is the Self, and That Thou Art, O Svetaketu.

Section Eleven

1. "If someone were to strike at the root of this large tree here, it would bleed, but live. If he were to strike at its stem, it would bleed, but live. If he were to strike at its top, it would bleed, but live. Pervaded by the living Self that tree stands firm, drinking in its nourishment and rejoicing;

2. "But if the life (the living Self) leaves one of its branches, that branch withers; if it leaves a second, that branch withers; if it leaves a third, that branch withers. If it leaves the whole tree, the whole tree withers. In exactly the same manner, my son, know this.

3. "This body indeed withers and dies when the living Self has left it; the living Self dies not. That which is that subtle essence, in it all that exists has its self. It is the True. It is the Self, and That Thou Art, O Svetaketu.

Section Twelve

1. "Fetch me from thence a fruit of the Nyagrodha tree."
   "Here is one, Sir."
   "Break it."
   "It is broken, Sir."
   "What do you see there?"
   "These seeds, almost infinitesimal."
   "Break one of them."
   "It is broken, Sir."
   "What do you see there?"
   "Nothing, Sir."

2. The father said: "My son, that subtle essence which you do not perceive there, of that very essence this great Nyagrodha tree exists.

3. "Believe it, my son. That which is the subtle essence, in it all that exists has its self. It is the True. It is the Self, and That Thou Art, O Svetaketu.

Section Thirteen

1. "Place this salt in water, and then wait on me in the morning." The son did as commanded. The father said, "Bring me the salt, which you placed in the water last night." The son looked for it but found it not for it had melted.

2. The father said, "Taste it from the surface of the water. How is it?" The son replied, "It is salt." "Taste it from the middle. How is it?" The son replied, "It is salt." "Taste it from the bottom. How is it?" The son replied, "It is salt." The father said, "Throw it away and then wait for me." He did so; but salt exists for ever. Then the father said: "Here also, in this body, forsooth, you do not perceive the True, my son; but indeed it is there.

3. "That which is the subtle essence, in it all that exists has its self. It is the True. It is the Self, and That Thou Art.

Section Fourteen

1. "As one might lead a person with his eyes covered away from the Gandharas, and leave him in a place where there are no human beings; and as that person would turn towards the east, north, or the west and shout, 'I have been brought here with my eyes covered, I have been left here with my eyes covered.'

2. "And as thereupon some one might loose his bandage and say to him, 'Go in that direction, it is Gandhara, go in that direction'; and as thereupon, having been informed and being able to judge for himself, he would by asking his way from village to village arrive as last at Gandhara,—in exactly the same manner does a man, who meets with a teacher to inform him, obtain the true knowledge. For him there is only delay so long as he is not delivered (from the body); then he will be perfect.

3. "That which is the subtle essence, in it all that exists has its self. It is the True. It is the Self, and That Thou Art, O Svetaketu.

Section Fifteen

1. "If a man is ill, his relatives assemble around him and ask: 'Dost thou know me? Dost thou know me?' Now as long as his speech is not merged in his mind, his mind in his breath, breath in heat, heat in the Highest Being, he knows them.

2. "But when his speech is merged in his mind, his mind in breath, breath in heat, heat in the Highest Being, then he knows them not. That which is the subtle essence, in it all have their selves. It is the True. It is the Self, and That Thou Art, O Svetaketu.

Section Sixteen

1. "They bring a man hither whom they have taken by the hand and they say: 'He has taken something, he has committed a theft.' (When he denies it, they say), 'Heat the hatchet for him.' If he committed the theft, then he makes himself to be what he is not. Then the false-minded, having covered his true Self by a falsehood, grasps the heated hatchet—he is burnt, and he is killed.

2. "But if he did not commit the theft, then he makes himself to be what he is. Then the true-minded, having covered his true Self by truth, grasps the heated hatchet—he is not burnt, and he is delivered. As that truthful man is not burnt, thus has all that exists its self in That. It is the True. It is the Self, and That Thou Art."

Zimmer

BUDDHIST NIRVANA*

The Buddha's doctrine is called *yāna*. The word means "a vehicle," or, more to the point, "a ferryboat." The "ferryboat" is the principal image employed in Buddhism to render the sense and function of the doctrine. The idea persists through all the differing and variously conflicting teachings of the numerous Buddhist sects that have evolved in many lands, during the long course of the magnificent history of the widely disseminated doctrine. Each sect describes the vehicle in its own way, but no matter how described, it remains always the ferry.

To appreciate the full force of this image, and to understand the reason for its persistence, one must begin by realizing that in everyday Hindu life the ferryboat plays an extremely prominent role. It is an indispensable means of transportation in a continent traversed by many mighty rivers and where bridges are practically nonexistent. To reach the goal of almost any journey one will require a ferry, time and time again, the only possible crossing of the broad and rapid streams being by boat or by a ford. The Jainas called their way of salvation the ford (*tīrtha*), and the supreme Jaina teachers were, as we have seen, Tīrthaṅkaras, "those making, or providing, a ford." In the same sense, Buddhism, by its doctrine, provides a ferryboat across the rushing river of saṁsāra to the distant bank of liberation. Through enlightenment (*bodhi*) the individual is transported.

The gist of Buddhism can be grasped more readily and adequately by fathoming the main metaphors through which it appeals to our intuition than by a systematic study of the complicated superstructure, and the fine details of the developed teaching. For example, one need only think for a moment about the actual, everyday experience of the process of crossing a river in a ferryboat, to come to the simple idea that inspires and underlies all of the various rationalized systematizations of the doctrine. To enter the Buddhist vehicle—the boat of the discipline—means to begin to cross the river of life, from the shore of the common-sense experience of non-enlightenment, the shore of spiritual ignorance (*avidyā*), desire (*kāma*), and death (*māra*), to the yonder bank of transcendental wisdom (*vidyā*), which is liberation (*mokṣa*) from this general bondage. Let us consider, briefly, the actual stages involved in any crossing of a river by ferry, and see if we can

* Heinrich Zimmer (1890–1943): German Indologist (see footnote on P. 177). The selection is taken from Part I of Zimmer's *Philosophies of India*. In these chapters, Zimmer introduces his survey of the history of Indian religious thought with an examination of the contrast between East and West. From *Philosophies of India* by Heinrich Zimmer, edited by Joseph Campbell. Bollingen Series XXVI. Copyright 1951 by Bollingen Foundation, New York. Distributed by Pantheon Books. Pp. 474–487. Reprinted by permission of the Bollingen Foundation, N.Y. and Routledge & Kegan Paul Ltd., London.

experience the passage as a kind of initiation-by-analogy into the purport of the stages of the Buddhist pilgrim's progress to his goal.

Standing on the nearer bank, this side the stream, waiting for the boat to put in, one is a part of its life, sharing in its dangers and opportunities and in whatever may come to pass on it. One feels the warmth or coolness of its breezes, hears the rustle of its trees, experiences the character of its people. and knows that its earth is underfoot. Meanwhile the other bank, the far bank, is beyond reach—a mere optical image across the broad, flowing waters that divide us from its unknown world of forms. We have really no idea what it will be like to stand in that distant land. How this same scenery of the river and its two shorelines will appear from the other side we cannot imagine. How much of these houses will be visible among the trees? What prospects up and down the river will unfold? Everything over here, so tangible and real to us at present—these real, solid objects, these tangible forms—will be no more than remote, visual patches, inconsequential optical effects, without power to touch us, either to help or to harm. This solid earth itself will be a visual, horizontal line beheld from afar, one detail of an extensive scenic view, beyond our experience, and of no more force for us than a mirage.

The ferryboat arrives; and as it comes to the landing we regard it with a feeling of interest. It brings with it something of the air of that yonder land which will soon be our destination. Yet when we are entering it we still feel like members of the world from which we are departing, and there is still that feeling of unreality about our destination. When we lift our eyes from the boat and boatman, the far bank is still only a remote image, no more substantial than it was before.

Softly the ferryboat pushes off and begins to glide across the moving waters. Presently one realizes that an invisible line has been recently imperceptibly passed, beyond which the bank left behind is assuming gradually the unsubstantiality of a mere visual impression, a kind of mirage, while the farther bank, drawing slowly nearer, is beginning to turn into something real. The former dim remoteness is becoming the new reality and soon is solid ground, creaking under keel—real earth—the sand and stone on which we tread in disembarking; whereas the world left behind, recently so tangible, has been transmuted into an optical reflex devoid of substance, out of reach and meaningless, and has forfeited the spell that it laid upon us formerly—with all its features, all its people and events—when we walked upon it and ourselves were a portion of its life. Moreover, the new reality, which now possesses us, provides an utterly new view of the river, the valley, and the two shores, a view very different from the other, and completely unanticipated.

Now while we were in the process of crossing the river in the boat, with the shore left behind becoming gradually vaguer and more meaningless— the streets and homes, the dangers and pleasures, drawing steadily away— there was a period when the shoreline ahead was still rather far off too; and during that time the only tangible reality around us was the boat, contending stoutly with the current and precariously floating on the rapid waters. The only details of life that then seemed quite substantial and that greatly concerned us were the various elements and implements of the ferryboat itself: the contours of the hull and gunwales, the rudder and the sail, the various ropes, and perhaps a smell of tar. The rest of existence, whether out ahead or left behind, signified no more than a hopeful prospect and a fading recollection—two poles of unrealistic sentimental association affiliated with certain clusters of optical effects far out-of-hand.

In the Buddhist texts this situation of the people in a ferryboat is compared to that of the good folk who have taken passage in the vehicle of the doctrine. The boat is the teaching of the Buddha, and the implements of the ferry are the various details of Buddhist discipline: meditation, yoga-exercises, the rules of ascetic life, and the practice of self-abnegation. These are the only things that disciples in the vehicle can regard with deep conviction; such people are engrossed in a fervent belief in the Buddha as the ferryman and the Order as their bounding gunwale (framing, protecting, and defining their perfect ascetic life) and in the guiding power of the doctrine. The shoreline of the world has been left behind but the distant one of release not yet attained. The people in the boat, meanwhile, are involved in a peculiar sort of middle prospect which is all their own.

Among the conversations of the Buddha known as the "Medium-length Dialogues," there appears a discourse on the value of the vehicle of the doctrine. First the Buddha describes a man who, like himself or any of his followers, becomes filled with a loathing of the perils and delights of secular existence. That man decides to quit the world and cross the stream of life to the far land of spiritual safety. Collecting wood and reeds, he builds a raft, and by this means succeeds in attaining the other shore. The Buddha confronts his monks, then, with the question.

"What would be your opinion of this man," asks the Buddha, "would he be a clever man, if, out of gratitude for the raft that has carried him across the stream to safety, he, having reached the other shore, should cling to it, take it on his back, and walk about with the weight of it?"

The monks reply. "No, certainly the man who would do that would not be a clever man."

The Buddha goes on. "Would not the clever man be the one who left the raft (of no use to him any longer) to the current of the stream, and walked ahead without turning back to look at it? Is it not simply a tool to be cast away and forsaken once it has served the purpose for which it was made?"

The disciples agree that this is the proper attitude to take toward the vehicle, once it has served its purpose.

The Buddha then concludes. "In the same way the vehicle of the doctrine is to be cast away and forsaken, once the other shore of Enlightenment (nirvāna) has been attained."

The rules of the doctrine are intended for beginners and advanced pupils, but become meaningless for the perfect. They can be of no service to the truly enlightened, unless to serve him, in his role of teacher, as a convenient medium by which to communicate some suggestion of the truth to which he has attained. It was by means of the doctrine that the Buddha sought to express what he had realized beneath the tree as inexpressible. He could communicate with the world through his doctrine and thus help his unprepared disciples when they were at the start, or somewhere in the middle, of the way. Talking down to the level of relative or total ignorance, the doctrine can move the still imperfect yet ardent mind; but it can say nothing any more, nothing ultimately real, to the mind that has cast away darkness. Like the raft, it must be left behind, therefore, once the goal has been attained; for it can thenceforth be no more than an inappropriate burden.

Moreover, not the raft only, but the stream too, becomes void of reality for the one who has attained the other shore. When such a one turns around to look again at the land left behind, what does he see? What *can* one see who has crossed the horizon beyond which there is no duality? He looks— and there *is* no "other shore"; there is no torrential separating river; there is no raft; there is no ferryman; there can have been no crossing of the nonexistent stream. The whole scene of the two banks and the river between is simply gone. There can be no such thing for the enlightened eye and mind, because to see or think of anything as something "other" (a distant reality, different from one's own being) would mean that full Enlightenment had not yet been attained. There can be an "other shore" only for people still in the spheres of dualistic perception; those this side the stream or still inside the boat and heading for the "other shore"; those who have not yet disembarked and thrown away the raft. Illumination means that the delusory distinction between the two shores of a worldly and a transcendental existence no longer holds. There *is* no stream of rebirths flowing between two separated shores: no saṁsāra and no nirvāṇa.

Thus the long pilgrimage to perfection through innumerable existences, motivated by the virtues of self-surrender and accomplished at the cost of tremendous sacrifices of ego, disappears like a landscape of dreams when one awakes. The long-continued story of the heroic career, the many lives of increasing self-purfication, the picture-book legend of detachment won through the long passion, the saintly epic of the way to become a savior— enlightened and enlightening—vanishes like a rainbow. All becomes void; whereas once, when the dream was coming to pass step by step, with ever-recurrent crises and decisions, the unending series of dramatic sacrifices held the soul completely under its spell. The secret meaning of Enlightenment is that this titan-effort of pure soul-force, this ardent struggle to reach the goal by acts, ever-renewed, of beautiful self-surrender, this supreme, long strife through ages of incarnations to attain release from the universal law of moral causation (*karma*)—is without reality. At the threshold of its own realization it dissolves, together with its background of self-entangled life, like a nightmare at the dawn of day.

For the Buddha, therefore, even the notion of nirvāṇa is without meaning. It is bound to the pairs-of-opposites and can be employed only in opposition to saṁsāra—the vortex where the life-force is spellbound in ignorance by its own polarized passions of fear and desire.

The Buddhist way of ascetic training is designed to conduce to the understanding that there is no substantial ego—nor any object anywhere—that lasts, but only spiritual processes, welling and subsiding: sensations, feelings, visions. These can be suppressed or set in motion and watched at will. The idea of the extinction of the fire of lust, ill will, and ignorance becomes devoid of meaning when this psychological power and point of view has been attained; for the process of life is no longer experienced as a burning fire. To speak seriously, therefore, of nirvāṇa as a goal to be attained is simply to betray the attitude of one still remembering or experiencing the process as the burning of the fire. The Buddha himself adopts such an attitude only for the teaching of those still suffering, who feel that they would like to make the flames extinct. His famous Fire Sermon is an accommodation, not by any means the final word of the sage whose final word is silence. From the perspective of the Awake, the Illumined One, such opposed verbalizations as nirvāṇa and saṁsāra, enlightenment and ignorance, freedom and bondage, are without reference, void of content. That is why the Buddha refused to discuss nirvāṇa. The pointlessness of the connotations that would inevitably seem to be intended by his words would confuse those trying to follow his mysterious way. They being still in the ferryboat framed of these conceptions and requiring them as devices of transport to the shore of understanding, their teacher would not deny before them the practical function of such convenient terms; and yet would not give the terms weight, either, by discussion. Words like "enlightenment," "ignorance," "freedom," and "entanglement" are preliminary helps, referring to no ultimate reality, mere hints or signposts for the traveler, which serve to point him to the goal of an attitude beyond their own suggestions of a contrariety. The raft being finally left behind, and the vision lost of the two banks and the separating river, then there is in truth neither the realm of life and death nor that of release. Moreover, there is no Buddhism—no boat, since there are neither shores nor waters between. There is no boat, and there is no boatman—no Buddha.

The great paradox of Buddhism, therefore, is that no Buddha has ever come into existence to enlighten the world with Buddhist teachings. The life and mission of Gautama Śākyamuni is only a general misunderstanding by the unenlightened world, helpful and necessary to guide the mind toward illumination, but to be discarded when—and if—enlightenment is to be attained. Any monk failing to get rid of such ideas clings (by clinging to them) to the general mundane delusion which he imagines himself to be striving to leave behind. For, briefly, so long as nirvāṇa is looked upon as something different from saṁsāra, the most elementary error about existence still has to be overcome. These two ideas mirror contrary attitudes of the semiconscious individual toward himself and the outer sphere in which he lives; but beyond this subjective range they have no substantiation.

Buddhism—this popular creed which has won the reverence of all Eastern Asia—contains this boldest paradox at its very root; the most startling reading of reality ever whispered into human ear. All good Buddhists tend to avoid, therefore, statements about existence and non-existence. Their "Middle Path" goes between by simply pointing out that the validity of a conception is always relative to one's position along the road of progress from Ignorance to Buddhahood. Attitudes of assertion and negation belong to worldly beings on the hither bank of ignorance, and to pious people making headway in the crowded ferryboat of the doctrine. Such a conception as Voidness (śūnyatā) can have meaning only for an ego clinging to the reality of things; one who has lost the feeling that things are real can make no sense of such a word. And yet words of this kind remain in all the texts and teachings. Indeed, the great *practical* miracle of Buddhism is that terms of this kind, used successfully as steppingstones, do not become rocks on which to found and build a creed.

The greater portion of the Buddhist literature that has become available and familiar to us in translation is adjusted in this way, pedagogically, to the general human attitude of partial ignorance. It is intended for the teaching and guidance of disciples. It outlines and points the way along the path of the Buddhas (*buddha-mārga*), depicting the career of the hero "going to enlightenment" (*bodhicarya*). Its position, therefore, is comparable to that of the ferryman inviting people on our hither bank to enter his boat and cross the waters, or guiding his crew in their handling of the craft during the passage. The yonder bank is represented only in a preliminary, very sketchy way; only hinted at and attractively suggested, for the captivation and continued inspiration of those still spellbound by the notions of this dualistic shore—men and women trying to make up their minds to leave, or else in the toilsome stages of crossing to an absolutely contrary point of view, which they will perceive presently to be utterly inconsistent with their expectation.

This pedagogical interest of Buddhism entails, unavoidably, a screening of the ultimate essence of the doctrine. The introductory statements, graded as they are, lead right up to the goal—but then have to be put behind, or the goal itself will never be attained. Anyone wishing to gain some inkling of the transformation of perspective intended will have to turn from the great volumes of initiatory conversations, questions, analyses, and codifications to a somewhat less conspicuous, curious, special branch of Buddhist writings, in which an attempt is made actually to state something of the supreme experience.

One may well marvel at the bold experiment—an effort to represent the ultimate essence of an incommunicable intuition through words and conceptions familiar to the usual philosophical and pious understanding. But, wonderful to relate, a vivid sense of the ineffable reality known in "extinction" (nirvāṇa) is actually conveyed in this unexampled body of strange, esoteric texts. They are named Prajñā-pāramitā: "The Accomplishment of Transcendental Wisdom," or "The Wisdom (prajñā) Gone to the Other

Shore (*pāram-itā*)." And they are a series of the most curious dialogues, conducted in a sort of conversation-circle of Buddhas and Bodhisattvas—mostly legendary beings, superhuman saviors, without a single merely human, still half-bewildered aspirant-to-enlightenment among them.

The Illumined Ones behave in a way that should be rather shocking and confusing to any sound thinker, who, from habit and firm determination, is resolved to keep his feet on the ground. In a sort of mocking conversation, these Buddhas and Bodhisattvas entertain themselves with enigmatical statements of the unstatable truth. They delight in declaring, time and again, that there is no such thing as Buddhism, no such thing as Enlightenment, nothing remotely resembling the extinction of nirvāṇa, setting traps for each other and trying to trick each other into assertions that might imply —even remotely—the reality of such conceptions. Then, most artfully, they always elude the cleverly placed hazards and hidden pitfalls—and all engage in a glorious, transoiympian laugh; for the merest hint of a notion of nirvāṇa would have betrayed a trace of the vestige of the opposite attitude, saṁsāra, and the clinging to individual existence.

For example, in one of the texts the Buddha makes the following declaration to his pupil Subhūti. "Whosoever stands in the ferryboat of the saviors-who-lead-to-the-far-bank shall bear in mind the rescue of all living beings, conducting them to release-and-extinction in the pure and perfect nirvāṇa. And when, by virtue of this attitude, he has rescued all living beings, no being whatsoever has been made to reach nirvāṇa."

Following this paradoxical remark, the Buddha supplies his explanation. "Why, O Subhūti, is this so? Because, if this savior had the notion of the actual existence of any being, he could not be called a perfect Enlightened One. If there could occur to him the conception of a living being donning the garb of various bodies and migrating through numerous existences, or the idea of an individual personality, then he could not be called a Bodhisattva, 'a being whose essence is Enlightenment.' And why is this so? Because there is no such thing as anything or anybody standing in the vehicle of the Enlightened Ones."

Another text states that on a certain day, when myriads of gods had flocked together to celebrate with a great feast the solemn occasion of the Buddha's preaching of a sermon, they were all saying joyfully: "Forsooth, this is the second time that the wheel of the true law has been set in motion on Indian soil, let us go and watch!" But the Buddha, turning stealthily to Subhūti, whispered something that he would not tell the gods; for it was beyond their power of understanding. "This is not the second time that the wheel of the true law has been set in motion; there is no setting in motion of anything, nor any stopping of the motion of anything. Knowing just that, is the perfection of wisdom (*prajñā-pāramitā*), which is characteristic of the beings whose essence is enlightenment."

These bewildering texts, with their explicit teaching of the Wisdom of the Far Bank (*prajñā-pāramitā*), belong to a later period of the Buddhist tradition, the stage of the so-called "Great Ferryboat," or Mahāyāna, which teaches that the secret meaning and goal of the doctrine is the universal Buddhahood of *all* beings. This is in contrast to the earlier doctrine of the so-called "Little Ferryboat," the Hīnayāna, where, though an effective way to *individual release* is disclosed, the accomplishment of *Buddhahood* is regarded as a goal attained only by very few throughout the cycling ages. The *Prajñā-pāramitā* texts of the Mahāyānā were intended to counteract what their authors regarded as a basic misunderstanding, in the Hīnayāna, of the very essence of the wisdom of the Buddha, a misunderstanding caused by thinking that the preliminary teaching was an expression of the Buddha's transcendental realization. The emphasis on the means, the path, the rules of the order, and the ethical disciplines of the ferry-ride was stifling the essence of the tradition within the very fold of Buddhism itself. The Mahāyāna way, on the other hand, was to reassert this essence by means of a bold and stunning paradox.

"The Enlightened One," we read, "sets forth in the Great Ferryboat; but there is nothing from which he sets forth. He starts from the universe; but in truth he starts from nowhere. His boat is manned with all the perfections; and is manned by no one. It will find its support on nothing whatsoever and will find its support on the state of all-knowing, which will serve it as a non-support. Moreover, no one has ever set forth in the Great Ferryboat; no one will ever set forth in it, and no one is setting forth in it now. And why is this? Because neither the one setting forth nor the goal for which he sets forth is to be found: therefore, who should be setting forth, and whither?"

The conceptions that go to make up the communicated doctrine are, from the point of view of the Enlightened One, without corresponding ultimate realities. They are part of a raft, which is good and helpful for the crossing of a stream of ignorance and indispensable for disciples on the way, but they are devoid of meaning for the finished master whose crossing is accomplished. They mirror shapes of the transitory processes of life, and so have no lasting substance. They lead to enlightenment, and yet are fallacious, broken reflections of its truth. Indeed, they are different from what is known to the enlightened; just as the boat, or raft, is different from the farther shore. Such helpful concepts emerge, together with all the rest of these visible and thinkable things round about us, from an infinitely pure reality, which is beyond conceptions, void of limiting qualities, undifferentiated, and untouched by the dialectic of the pairs-of-opposites, of which it is the ground—just as the heavens and the atmosphere, which are visible stand as apparitions on the fundamentally pure void of ether.

"Just as, in the vast ethereal sphere, stars and darkness, light and mirage, dew, foam, lightning and clouds emerge, become visible, and vanish again, like the features of a dream—so everything endowed with an individual shape is to be regarded." Thus we read in one of the most celebrated of these Mahāyāna texts of meditation. From the intangible matter that pervades the universe, tangible shapes emerge as its ephemeral transformations. But their breaking into existence and their vanishing away does not affect the limpid, profound serenity of the basic element, the space of which they fill for their short spell of being. Comparably, the Enlightened Ones, with unruffled self-composure, watch their own sensations, feelings, and other experiences of the outer world and their inner life, remaining untouched by them, beyond the changes continually coming to pass in them, like the reposeful ether beyond the changes of the forms within its infinite space.

So far as the Awakened One is concerned, the notion of Awakening is at bottom as devoid of meaning as the notion that there is a dreamlike state that precedes it (the state of ordinary life—our own attitude and atmosphere). It is unreal. It does not exist. It is the sail of the nonexistent raft. The Buddhist yogī is taught, by means of the disciplines, to realize, within, such a peace as one perceives looking outward into the vast ethereal realm with its sublime display of transient forms. He is taught to experience, gazing inward, through successive stages of self-control and meditation, an ethereal essence of his own—sheer voidness, unsullied by any process of the mind and not changed by any effect of the senses in their contact with the outer world. By imbuing himself completely with an utter aloofness comparable to that of the celestial atmosphere in relation to the various luminous and darkening phenomena that pass through it, he realizes the real meaning of the Buddhist transcendental wisdom, the nature of the view from the yonder shore. He comes to know that fundamentally nothing whatsoever is happening to the true essence of his nature, nothing to give cause for either distress or joy. . . .

Baillie
CHRISTIAN ATONEMENT*

St. Anselm[†] has sometimes been accused of beginning at the wrong end in his study of the Atonement, because he began by exhibiting in an abstract way the exigency of the situation which called for such a divine atonement before proceeding very belatedly to contemplate the actual provision made by God in Jesus Christ. I may be accused of making the same mistake. But

* D. M. Baillie (1887–1954): Scottish Theologian. The selection from God Was In Christ is Chapter 8 of that volume entitled, "The Lamb of God." It is Baillie's interpretation of the meaning of Christ's death and of Christian atonement. The whole book is an essay on the meaning of incarnation and atonement. "The Lamb of God" is reprinted with the permission of Charles Scribner's Sons from GOD WAS IN CHRIST, pp. 180–202, by D. M. Baillie. Copyright 1948, Charles Scribner's Sons. Used by permission, also, from Faber & Faber Ltd., London.
† [cf. Selection 20. Ed.]

though I should then be in very good company, I think it would be truer to say that I have tried to exhibit the Christian experience of reconciliation in order to work back from it to a consideration of that which made it possible, the Cross and Passion of Christ.

I: Why did Jesus Die?

If we are to understand the relation between divine Atonement and the Cross of Christ, we must surely begin by turning to the Gospel story and to the Jesus of history. The men who shaped the tradition and wrote the story down in the four Gospels devoted an altogether disproportionate amount of their space to the passion and death of their Master, because to them and their fellow-Christians this was of supreme importance. But they also took a great deal of trouble to prepare for that climax by giving vivid and elaborate reminiscences of the words and deeds of Jesus throughout His public career, as these had been preserved in the tradition, because the meaning of the Cross could not be understood without some knowledge and understanding of the person who died on it. And if we say, with the voice of the Christian ages, that Jesus died for sinners, it will be well for us to realize at the outset that this is profoundly true, not merely as a matter of theological interpretation, concerning the overruling purpose of God, but also in a purely historical sense, in respect of Jesus' personal relations with the sinners in ancient Galilee.

It has often been remarked that the question, *Why did Jesus die?* embraces several distinct questions.[1] It may mean: Why was He condemned to death by the Roman Procurator? or: Why did the Jewish authorities contrive to get Him condemned? It may also mean the theological question: What was the ultimate purpose of the death of Jesus in the divine economy, the providence of God? Or again it may mean: In what sense and for what reason did Jesus Himself 'lay down His life' on the Cross? All of these questions, though not unconnected, can be distinguished from each other, and it is especially important to see that the last two are two different questions. It is true, I believe, that Jesus accepted the Cross as from the will and purpose of God. But it was by human faith that He did it, not by the superhuman knowledge which can 'declare the end from the beginning'. And as it would be artificial to think of Him as setting forth from the beginning with the clear consciousness He had come into the world to die a violent death for human salvation, it would be equally artificial to think of Him as forming the *intention*, at any point in His career, of being condemned to death.[2] The evidence of the Gospels leaves no room for such an

---

[1] This is worked out in detail in Dr. A. B. Macaulay's penetrating volume of Cunningham Lectures, *The Death of Christ* (1938).

[2] Cf. A. B. Macaulay: 'The voluntariness of His death is totally misconceived if He be represented as inviting it.' Op. cit., p. 114.

idea of Jesus' plans, though it has sometimes been entertained by modern writers. The Gospels were written at a time when Christians could look back and glory in the Cross as ordained by the purpose of God; but they do not conceal the fact that to Jesus Himself, when He looked forward and saw that it was likely, and even when He embraced it by faith, it appeared as an unspeakable tragedy, and that up to the last night He hoped and prayed that it might not come.

At the same time, it is important to realize, Jesus did not die as a helpless victim: He could have escaped, and He went on with His eyes open. Not only in the Galilee days, but even in Jerusalem almost up to the last, He could have steered clear of the trouble and danger by changing His course. If He had been content to give up His troublesome activities and retire into private life, the authorities would doubtless have been glad to let Him do it: indeed that was precisely what, by opposition and intimidation of various kinds, they tried to make Him do. It would have saved them a great deal of trouble. And He would have saved His life. That was the choice He had to face. But though even His own disciples would have liked Him to take a safe course—which added greatly to the stress of the choice[3]—He could not hesitate. 'He that saveth his life shall lose it': so He had taught. He *could* have saved His own life, but it would have meant the loss of all that He had lived for. So He would not turn aside from the path that was leading Him to suffering, shame and death.

What then was the path that He would not give up though He should have to die for it? What did He die for? What brought Him to such an end? In a word, it was, more than anything else, His attitude to 'sinners'.

In the preceding chapter I spoke of Paul's discovery that God loves sinners, not waiting for them to earn His love or become worthy of it, but loving them while they are still sinners. Where did that revolutionary discovery come from? What was its ultimate source? Whatever may have been the process by which it came home to Paul in his conversation, it seems indubitable that the discovery came in the first instance from the plain story of how Jesus, as He moved about Galilee, had taken people's breath away by showing Himself a 'friend of sinners'. There is nothing more unmistakable or better authenticated in the Gospel records than this: that the Rabbi from Nazareth astonished and alienated people by His habit of intercourse with men and women of doubtful character and by His attitude to them. He was friendly towards them, would go to their houses and talk familiarly with them. He appeared to be more interested in these people than in anybody else, and He practically said that God was too. He said that His own mission was not to the 'righteous' people but to 'sinners'; and the supreme examples in the world's literature of the experience of the divine forgiveness are to be found in the stories of how Jesus said to such men and women individually: 'Thy sins are forgiven: go and sin no more.' Not that He regarded the 'righteous' people, the Scribes and Pharisees, as being without

[3] See Mark viii, 31–5.

sin. They might be even worse in God's eyes than the 'publicans and sinners'. They also were sinners and needed to repent. And when He spoke such scarifying words to them about their sins, was it not, in the last analysis, because He loved them too and would fain bring them to repentance? But they could not tolerate His words and His ways—His words to themselves and His ways with the 'publicans and sinners'. (Neither could Paul the Pharisee when he first heard of these things: this was doubtless partly why he hated the new 'Way', though he afterwards came to class himself among the 'sinners'). Jesus seemed to be subverting all rules by lumping together the good and the bad that they might all depend on God's mercy; and this was at least one of the main things that got Him into trouble with the leaders of His people. But He would not be turned aside by their opposition, for what they so disliked was of the very essence of what He knew He had to do. So He went straight on as the 'friend of sinners', and got deeper and deeper into trouble, until in the end He was condemned to death.

We can hardly do more than reverently conjecture as to how far it was given Him by faith to grasp the divine purpose that would use His death for the salvation of sinners, though there are various indications in the Gospels that He applied to Himself the Deutero-Isaianic prophecy of the Suffering Servant. But quite apart from that, and from all subsequent theological interpretations, it is true in the plainest historical sense that He died for sinners: it was His love for them that brought Him to the Cross.[4] Moreover when we speak of the 'passion' of Jesus, we are not speaking merely of His dying, but of the whole course of suffering of which that was the climax, and not only physical suffering, but also and indeed chiefly the spiritual agony of the entire situation. He wept not for Himself but for the sons and daughters of Jerusalem who were rejecting Him. It was the contemplation of that immense moral and spiritual tragedy that made the situation almost unbearably terrible to Jesus. In that most literal and immediate sense His love was bearing their sins at infinite cost as He approached the Cross. That was the passion of Christ: and all this is even more important than the question as to how far He interpreted His coming death. For it is entirely congruous with the whole meaning and method of the Incarnation that He who, on the ultimate interpretation, died 'for the sins of the whole world' should in His own consciousness be mainly concerned with those sinners who were His immediate environment, the 'lost sheep of the house of Israel' in His own time.

II: The Cross and the Love of God

The crucifixion of Jesus set men thinking more than anything else that has ever happened in the life of the human race. And the most remarkable

---

[4] This whole thesis is developed impressively in the first chapter of Dr. D. M. Ross's *The Cross of Christ* (1928), a book that deserves to be much better known than it is.

fact in the whole history of religious thought is this: that when the early Christians looked back and pondered on the dreadful thing that had happened, it made them think of the redeeming love of God.

Not simply of the love of Jesus, but of the love of God.

One 'might have expected them rather to lose all faith in the love of God, for the crucifixion might well seem to be the final *reductio ad absurdum* of the belief that the world is governed by a gracious providence. If in the religious history of Israel we find men continually being staggered by the spectacle of the sufferings of the good and the triumph of the forces of evil, if we find a psalmist confessing that he almost lost his foothold altogether when he saw things happening so, we should have expected to find all this doubt and rebellion increased a hundredfold in the minds of the followers of Jesus when they contemplated the unspeakably dreadful thing that had been done to their Lord and Master. If God was good, how could He allow such a thing to happen? There could be no doubt about the goodness of Jesus, or of His love for men: that had been made plainer than ever. But how could they believe any longer in the love of God? Would they not renounce God, and take Jesus as their Prometheus, who had brought warmth and light into their lives and then suffered crucifixion for what He had done, under the sky of a remote and angry God?

If the followers of Jesus did not feel like that, was it because the tragedy of the crucifixion was soon followed by the experiences of Easter morning? That was certainly all-important, determining the whole substance and tone of the early Christian message. But even then we might have expected something very different from what we find, and something very much less. We should have expected to find the resurrection regarded as reversing a tragic defeat, righting a dreadful wrong, by snatching Jesus back from the powers of evil which had had their way and worked their will upon Him. That was indeed one way of regarding it: the crucifixion *was* a dreadful wrong, and it had been brought about not merely by wicked men, but by demonic forces of evil, the 'rulers of this Age' who had 'crucified the Lord of Glory'. Yet the followers of Jesus had more than that to say about the crucifixion. Apparently from the very earliest days of the Church they maintained that somehow it had also been brought about by the purpose of God, and, moreover, by His merciful purpose of sending forgiveness to sinners—a forgiveness which could even embrace the men who had crucified Jesus.[5] We cannot trace the steps of the process by which this conviction was reached. The whole teaching of Jesus Himself must have contributed largely, though it is difficult to say how far He had prepared the way by speaking specifically of the significance of His death. As I have said, there is good reason for holding that as He saw His death approaching He applied to Himself

---

[5] The evidence for this may be found in Acts ii, 23, 38f.; iii, 17–19, 26; iv, 27f, and in I Cor. xv, 3, where we have St. Paul's evidence as to what was passed on to him by those who were Christians before him.

the words of Deutero-Isaiah about the death of the Servant of the Lord, which do not seem ever to have been applied to the Messiah before.[6] Certainly the primitive Christian community began at a very early date to use that passage in its thinking and preaching about Jesus, and it may have played an important part in the development of a theology of the Atonement. But however that development may have come about, there is no doubt that when we come to the main types of New Testament teaching, the Pauline and the Johannine, we find the death of Jesus not only connected with a divine purpose, but quite expressly and even confidently traced to the working of the love of God. Moreover, this is conceived as a sacrificial love. It is not a case merely of a gracious action or a gracious gift; it is something infinitely costly, a giving up by God of His only Son in the process of dealing with our sins, so great is His love towards us. In one place St. Paul speaks of how rare a thing it is for anyone to be ready to lay down his life even for a good man who deserved it: and then when he goes on to speak of Christ laying down His life for sinners, we should have expected him to take this as proving signally the love of *Christ*. But instead of that we find him, without any explanation, taking it as a signal proof of the love of *God*. 'God commendeth *his own* love towards us, in that, while we were yet sinners, Christ died for us.'[7] He 'did not spare his own Son, but gave him up for us all'.[8] And in Johannine language: 'God so loved the world that he gave his only begotten Son',[9] and 'herein is love, not that we loved God, but that he loved us, and sent his Son to be the propitiation for our sins'.[10]

Throughout the whole of this New Testament material there is no trace of any contrast between the wrath of God and the love of Christ, or of the idea that God's attitude to sinners had to be changed by the sacrifice of Christ from wrath and justice to love and mercy. There is ample use of the terminology of the Jewish sacrificial system, but it is highly doubtful whether even in the Old Testament period the purpose of the sin-offerings was to change God's attitude in that sense. A great deal of confusion has been caused by the fact that the English word 'atonement' has moved away from the sense it had when the Bible was translated, viz., reconciliation. The Hebrew word which lies behind it originally meant 'covering' or 'wiping out', and it may have included the idea of an 'expiation' that had to be made before the sinner could be acquitted, but it certainly did not imply anything like propitiation of an angry God. For, as scholars have pointed out,[11] it is always God Himself who is regarded, in the Old Testament, as having appointed the ritual of sin-offering, in His desire for reconciliation.

[6] Isa. liii.
[7] Rom. v, 8.
[8] Rom. viii, 32.
[9] I John iii, 16.
[10] I John iv, 10.
[11] See e.g. A. C. Welch, *Prophet and Priest in Old Israel*, p. 139.

That is highly important. Man has, of course, to provide the offering (the victim or other material) and to carry out the ritual, but it is God that has provided this means of reconciliation, taking this merciful initiative because He does not desire the death of a sinner but his restoration.

But when we come to the New Testament, we can go much farther than this. For the Greek word used (καταλλαγή) to correspond with the Old Testament 'atonement', means simply 'reconciliation'.[12] Moreover, the New Testament does not speak of God being reconciled to man, but of man being reconciled to God, and of God as the Reconciler, taking the initiative in Christ to that end.[13] There are indeed three passages, one Pauline and two Johannine, where we find another word in the English Bible: 'propitiation'. As regards the Johannine passages, it is clear that the word (ἱλασμός) does not mean anything like the appeasing of an angry God, for the *love* of God is the starting-point. 'Herein is love, not that we loved God but that he loved us and sent his Son to be the propitiation for our sins.'[14] The Pauline passage has been much discussed by commentators. 'Being justified freely by his grace, through the redemption that is in Christ Jesus, whom God hath set forth as a propitiation (ἱλαστήριον) through faith, by his blood. . . .'[15] Professor C. H. Dodd, who has made a careful study of the word, assures us that the rendering 'propitiation' is misleading, being in accord with pagan usage but foreign to Biblical usage, and that the real meaning of the passage is that God has set forth Christ as 'a means by which guilt is annulled' or even 'a means by which sin is forgiven'.[16] It is just possible that the Greek word ought here to be given the meaning that it regularly bears in the Septuagint (and which also appears in Heb. ix, 5), and that we should translate it simply as 'mercy-seat' or 'place of forgiveness'.

But however we translate those terms borrowed from the Jewish sacrificial system, it is quite plain that in the New Testament they undergo a transformation of meaning because of the really extraordinary setting which is now given to them. We saw that even in the Old Testament usage the pagan meanings had been left behind because it was God Himself who was regarded as having mercifully appointed the ritual of expiation, though man had of course to supply the victim. But this is the amazing new fact that emerges when we come to the New Testament: that God even provides the victim that is offered, and the victim is His own Son, the Only-begotten. In short, 'it is *all* of God': the desire to forgive and reconcile, the appointing of means, the provision of the victim as it were from His own bosom at infinite cost. It all takes place within the very life of God Himself: for if we

---

[12] In the A.V. it is only once translated 'atonement', in Rom. v, 11, and even there it becomes 'reconciliation', in line with all the rest of the passage, in the R.V.

[13] See especially 2 Cor. v, 18f.

[14] I John iv, 10. The other passage is ii, 2.

[15] Rom. iii, 24f.

[16] See C. H. Dodd's *Romans* (Moffatt Commentary) in loc. What Professor Dodd says is based on a careful study of the background of the term.

take the Christology of the New Testament at its highest we can only say
that 'God was in Christ' in that great atoning sacrifice, and even that the
Priest and the Victim both were none other than God. There is in the New
Testament no uniformity of conception as the *how* this sacrifice brings
about the reconciliation, and indeed some of its interpretations of the
meaning of the Cross are in terms drawn from quite other realms than that
of the sacrificial system. But in whatever way the process of salvation
through the Cross is conceived, God's merciful attitude towards sinners is
never regarded as the *result* of the process, but as its cause and source.[17] It
all took place because God so loved the world. Its background is the eternal
love of God. This does not mean that there is no place for the idea of the
'wrath' of God, or that 'the Wrath' from which we are saved is something
impersonal and apart from God in New Testament thought, as Professor
Dodd suggests.[18] But His wrath must not be regarded as something which
has to be 'propitiated' and so changed into love and mercy, but rather as
being identical with the consuming fire of inexorable divine love in relation
to our sins. 'The wrath of God', writes Brunner, 'is not the ultimate reality;
it is the divine reality which corresponds to sin. But it is not the essential
reality of God. In Himself God is love.' And the revelation in Christ is
'the place where the love of God breaks through the wrath of God. This
revelation of the divine mystery of love in the midst of the reality of wrath
is the "propitiation" (ἱλασμός).[19] Moreover there is in the New Testament a
remarkable identification of the love of Christ which led Him to the Cross
and the love of God which sent or gave Him. The identification is the more
striking because it is made so tacitly. It does not appear as a theological
consequence of an actual identification of Christ with God, for St. Paul's
Christology had hardly got so far as that in express formulation. But when
he is speaking of the great reconciliation, he runs ahead of his Christology
and speaks of the love of Christ and the love of God almost interchangeably.
'Who shall separate us from the love of Christ?' he asks, in one great
passage; and then in his eloquent answer he speaks of 'the love of God
which was in Christ Jesus our Lord'.[20] There was no distinction: the two were
one and the same thing. In discoursing of the love that was shown in the
Cross of Christ the New Testament is never able to stop short of tracing it
up-stream to the eternal love of God dealing sacrificially with the sins of
the world.

[17] In Rom. iii, 24ff., there does seem to be a suggestion that God's attitude to human
sin was different after the Cross from what it had been before. But if the suggestion is
there, what is suggested is not that there was a change from wrath to mercy, but rather,
as Dr. Vincent Taylor points out, that there was a change from forbearance to righteousness, from mere 'passing over' to 'justifying'. What Dr. Taylor says further on this point
is well worth reading. See *The Atonement in New Testament Thought*, pp. 133f.
[18] C. H. Dodd, op. cit., pp. 20ff.
[19] Emil Brunner, *The Mediator*, pp. 519ff.
[20] Rom. viii, 35ff.

III: Historical and Eternal Atonement

In the preceding chapter we reached the conclusion that the whole Christian life rests upon a doctrine of the forgiveness of sins which implies a redemptive sin-bearing, a costly atonement, in the heart of God. But of course it was not by any mere 'implication' that such a divine sin-bearing was conceived: the idea arose out of the historical event that we have been considering in this chapter, the death of Jesus Christ, in which the New Testament found the redeeming love of God. What are we now to say about the relation between this historical atonement and the eternal sin-bearing of the divine Love? To reduce the importance of the historical event would be contrary to every instinct of Christian faith; and yet it seems impossible to say that the divine sin-bearing was confined to that moment of time, or is anything less than eternal.

Here we are confronted with a problem with which theology is continually beset, that of the relation between time and eternity. We are accustomed to say that while we finite creatures are subject to temporality in our experience, living always in a present moment which is between the remembered past and the unlived future, God 'inhabits eternity', living in an eternal present, in which past, present and future are all one. But we must be careful. There is a danger that we should come to think of the life of God as simply *timeless*, out of all relation to time, as an abstraction is timeless, or in a sense which would imply that time is a mere illusion from which God is free. If we think of the eternity of God in such ways, then to speak of an eternal atonement in the heart of God for human sin will be likely to mean something like the resolution of all contradictions in a timeless Absolute, in a sense that would obscure the reality of evil, and that would reduce the historical episode of the Cross to a merely accidental symbol of a timeless truth. But when we say that God lives in eternity, not in time, we ought to mean something different. We ought to mean, not that God has no relation to time and no experience of it (which would imply *either* that time is a sheer illusion *or* that God's experience falls short of that aspect of reality!) but that, while embracing time in His experience, while knowing past, present and future, God is not confined, as we are, within the limits of temporality and successiveness, but transcends these limits, so that He can experience past, present and future all in one. If He is 'a God who *does* things', a living God, we must think of Him as having the positive kind of eternity which has a direct 'vertical' relation to each moment of our temporal experience; and when we speak of His activity we are bound to use temporal expressions, verbs with past, present and future tenses, though we know that they are inadequate, because the eternal reality is beyond anything that we can imagine or express.

And thus when we speak of divine Atonement we will not hesitate to say that God was uniquely present in the passion and death of Jesus, making Atonement, 'reconciling the world unto Himself'. As God was incarnate in Jesus, so we may say that the divine Atonement was incarnate in the passion of Jesus. And if we then go on to speak of an eternal Atonement in the very being and life of God, it is not by way of reducing the significance of the historical moment of the Incarnation, but by way of realizing the relation of the living God to every other historical moment. God's reconciling work cannot be confined to any one moment of history. We cannot say that God was unforgiving until Christ came and died on Calvary; nor can we forget that God's work of reconciliation still goes on in every age in the lives of sinful men, whose sins He still bears. 'The Atonement', says Brunner, 'is not history. The Atonement, the expiation of human guilt, the covering of sin through His sacrifice is not anything which can be conceived from the point of view of history. This event does not belong to the historical plane. It is super-history, it lies in the dimension which no historian knows in so far as he is a mere historian.'[21] Brunner does not mean that the historical episode of the passion of Christ is of limited importance, but that the mystery of divine Atonement involved in it is not one of those empirical factors with which historical science can reckon. It is not that the historical episode is a mere symbol of something 'timeless': it is actually a part (the incarnate part) of the eternal divine sin-bearing. But it would be quite false to think of *any* moment of human history as having no direct relation to this divine sin-bearing, which transcends the temporality of past, present and future, without destroying it. There has never been an age when it would have been true to say that God was not carrying the load of the sins of His people and thus making atonement and offering forgiveness. 'In his love and in his pity he redeemed them, and he bare them and carried them all the days of old,' even when they 'grieved his holy Spirit'.[22] That is the truth of the picture of 'the Lamb slain from the foundation of the world'.[23] And beside it we may place Pascal's complementary picture: 'Jesus will be in agony until the end of the world.'[24] These pictures give us one side of the truth. And if this eternal aspect has not had a large place in traditional doctrine, it is doubtless partly because of the danger of reducing the importance of the historical episode, but also partly because false ideas of propitiation obscured the truth that the Atonement is something within the life of God, wrought by God Himself, and applied by Him to men in every age.

It is deeply interesting to note that there was a genuine recognition of this in the old Protestant tradition. It was an old theological problem whether and how the believing souls in Israel before the coming of Christ

[21] Brunner, op. cit., p. 504.

[22] Isa. lxiii, 9, 10.

[23] Rev. xiii, 8. I am, of course, aware that a comparison of this verse with Rev. xvii, 8, makes it highly doubtful whether the usual translation, which I have used, is correct. I do not base any argument on it, but I quote it partly because its traditional use in this connection comes up a page or two later.

[24] Pascal, *Pensées* (ed. Brunschvicg), 553.

actually had their sins forgiven and received the benefits of the Atonement which was prefigured by the types and sacrifices of the old dispensation. The medieval teaching was that those ordinances did not actually *communicate* to believers in Israel the benefits which they foreshadowed. The benefits of the Atonement were not yet available because the sacrifice on Calvary had not yet been made. Therefore the Old Testament believers could not pass into the bliss of heaven when they died, but had to remain in the *limbus patrum* until Christ, after His atoning death, descended to release them and take them to heaven. But Reformed theology rejected all that, and taught that Old Testament believers had no such waiting. Though Christ had not yet come and suffered and died, they could already by faith have the full benefits of His Atonement: they not only looked forward to it, but actually received, as truly as we do, the forgiveness and salvation which it brought.[25] The old Reformed divines doubtless conceived this as a *proleptic* appropriation of the benefits, through a faith that looked forward to Christ. Yet what could this mean except that the divine work of reconciliation was already present, that in some sense God was already making atonement, and the same atonement which was afterwards to appear on the plane of history in the Cross of Christ? There is more than a hint of this in the Westminster Confession of 1647. 'Although the work of redemption was not actually wrought by Christ till after his incarnation, yet the virtue, efficacy and benefits thereof were communicated unto the elect in all ages successively from the beginning of the world, in and by those promises, types, and sacrifices, wherein he was revealed and signified to be the Seed of the woman, which should bruise the serpent's head, and *the Lamb slain from the beginning of the world, being yesterday and to-day the same, and for ever.*'[26] I need not discuss whether the one side or the other was right in that controversy, as we should hardly formulate the question in the same way. But surely the Protestant answer reveals a sound theological judgment, even in its somewhat unexpected use of the notion of the Lamb eternally slain. For we must believe that the faithful in Israel did, in their measure and according to their lights, receive the divine reconciliation; and whether or not they should be conceived as looking *forward* in this matter, it would obviously be absurd to say that *God* had to look

---

[25] St. Augustine had said: 'The sacraments of the New Testament give salvation: the sacraments of the Old Testament promised a Saviour.' Calvin maintains that the scholastics misinterpreted this, and he writes: 'The scholastic dogma . . . by which the difference between the sacraments of the old and the new dispensation is made so great, that the former did nothing but shadow forth the grace of God, while the latter actually confer it, must be altogether exploded'. (*Inst.* IV, xiv, 23.) The Old Testament believers 'both had and knew Christ the Mediator, by whom they were united to God, and made capable of receiving his promises'. 'Who will presume to represent the Jews as destitute of Christ, when we know that they were parties to the Gospel covenant, which has its only foundation in Christ?' (Ibid., II, x, 4.)

[26] *Westminster Confession of Faith*, chap. viii, § 6 (my italics). Cf. chap. vii § 5; chap. xi, § 6; chap. xxvii, § 5.

forward to the historical Atonement in order to be able to forgive and save! The work of atonement is His own work, incarnate in the Passion of Jesus Christ because it is 'eternal in the heavens' in the very life of God— love of God bearing the sin of the world.[27] 'There was a cross in the heart of God', wrote Charles Allen Dinsmore, 'before there was one planted on the green hill outside Jerusalem.'[28]

As regards the idea that the divine sin-bearing, the atoning work, which appeared in history once for all on Calvary, goes on *ever since* in the heavenly sphere, there are hints of this in the Christian tradition from the beginning. When Paul at his conversion hears the voice of Christ saying: 'I am Jesus whom thou persecutest', and when the Epistle to the Hebrews speaks of apostates as 'crucifying the Son of God afresh for themselves and putting him to open shame',[29] there is the idea that Christ still suffers at the hands of men though His historical Passion is past and over. Deissmann pointed out that when St. Paul speaks of 'Christ crucified', the participle he uses is not in the aorist but in the perfect tense (not $\sigma\tau\alpha\nu\rho\omega\theta\epsilon\iota\varsigma$ but $\dot{\epsilon}\sigma\tau\alpha\nu\rho\omega\mu\dot{\epsilon}\nu\alpha\varsigma$) which means not 'Christ who was once crucified' but 'Christ who is crucified' or 'Christ who has been crucified and bears the marks upon Him still' (perhaps we might even say, 'Christ on the Cross'). Dr. H. G. Wood, who refers to this, quotes also from the Fourth Gospel: 'He showed them his hands and his side', which gives the idea of Christ's risen body as still bearing the marks of the wounds.[30] But far more important is the idea worked out in the Epistle to the Hebrews and carried further in the catholic tradition, that the atoning work of Christ, as Priest and Victim in one, is not confined to His Passion on earth and did not end with His death on the Cross. That work on Calvary was indeed a finished work, a perfect sacrifice made once for all on earth. Yet it was the beginning of a priesthood which goes on for ever in the unseen realm, in heaven, in the Holy Place beyond the Veil, into which our High Priest entered through death, and where he 'ever liveth to make intercession for us', being continually

[27] Canon J. K. Mozley (*Doctrine of the Atonement*, p. 90 and note) says that Dean Inge, who advocated a doctrine of eternal atonement, and Dr. Denney, who criticized him, both seem to confuse two meanings of that phrase (a) 'eternal atonement viewed as an eternal truth', and (b) 'eternal atonement as implying something which has been part of God's eternal purpose'. Dr. Mozley himself holds, I understand, that the second is the only sound meaning. He says: 'Atonement is no afterthought, since God knows that it will be required. No questions as to the relation of the historical to the eternal, of temporal fact and supratemporal reality, need be raised.' But this seems to me to simplify the matter unduly. 'God knows that it will be required': required by whom, or by what? It is not anything outside God's own nature that requires it, and it is only God that can accomplish it. Surely, then, it must in the last analysis be an eternal work of atonement, supratemporal as the life of God is, but not 'timeless' as an abstraction is; appearing incarnate once, but touching every point of history, and going on as long as sins continue to be committed and there are sinners to be reconciled.

[28] C. A. Dinsmore, *Atonement in Literature and Life*, p. 232.

[29] Heb. vi, 6.

[30] H. G. Wood, *Christianity and History*, p. 212.

'touched with the feeling of our infirmities'. I do not think this Epistle contains the idea of the atoning *sacrifice* of Christ being repeated or continued by Him in the heavenly realm, but it certainly is full of the idea that His work as High Priest goes on for ever in heaven and that He can still enter into our trials and temptations because He passed through such experiences Himself.

But all of this has received a further interpretation in the theology of the catholic tradition, particularly in the doctrine of the eucharistic sacrifice, which has often been perverted into something sub-Christian, but which at its best has certainly not minimized the 'once-for-all-ness' of the 'finished work of Christ' on Calvary, but rather made it fundamental. There has been a considerable development of this kind within recent years in Anglican circles, with a new emphasis on the idea of the continued exercise by Christ of His priestly office in heaven, and its representation on earth in the Eucharist. As long ago as 1901 Bishop Gore wrote: 'In the Epistle to the Hebrews all that goes before the ascension is the preparation of Christ for His priestly work. His work as the great high priest, and His entrance into at least the effectiveness of His office, begins with His entrance into the true holy of holies, in the power of His own blood once for all surrendered in death. . . . It is at the entrance into heaven, and not upon the cross, that He accomplishes His atonement for us, according to the Epistle to the Hebrews, and His work as high priest, which begins with His entrance into heaven, is perpetual. His propitiation and His intercession are identical: and both consist in His "appearing" or presenting Himself for us.' And Gore finds the Church of the early centuries teaching that in the eucharistic sacrifice 'God has united the offerings of the church to the everliving sacrifice of the great High Priest in the heavenly sanctuary'.[31] 'We offer on the earthly altar', wrote Canon Holmes, 'the same sacrifice that is being perpetually offered on the Heavenly Altar.'[32] 'The Eucharist', wrote Canon Quick, '. . . is the perpetual externalization in human ritual of the self-offering of Christ, which was once for all in fact externalized on Calvary, but is ever real in the inward and heavenly sphere.' 'In the Eucharist . . . we make before God an offering which is one with Christ's present and eternal offering of Himself.'[33] A similar line of thought was pursued by Bishop Hicks, with special emphasis on the thesis that in the Old Testament sacrifices it was not the *death* of the victim in itself that was supposed to be effectual, but rather the *life*, set free by the act of sacrifice upon the altar and thus offered to God. 'The death is vital to the sacrifice, because it sets free the blood, which is the life. But the victim is, in a true sense, operative, not as dead, but as alive "as it had been slain":

[31] Charles Gore, *The Body of Christ*, pp. 212, 252f.
[32] E. E. Holmes, *The Church, Her Books and Her Sacraments*, p. 87 (quoted by Arseniev).
[33] O. C. Quick, *The Christian Sacraments*, pp. 198, 200.

not as νεκρόν but ὡς ἐσφαγμένον.[34] And so the sacrificial death of Christ on the Cross is not the end of His atoning work, but makes possible His entry into the heavenly sphere where His self-offering goes on for ever.

Very similar is the following from Professor Arseniev of the Eastern Orthodox Church. In the Eucharist 'we are raised above our human, earthly plane to contemplate the perpetual self-offering of the Lamb of God before the face of the Father. He suffered once on earth and He offers continually His death to the Father on the heavenly altar. . . . Our Eucharist is the true representation of His true and continuous sacrifice, once for all time offered on the earth—on Golgotha, and perpetually presented to the Father on our behalf in Eternity.'[35] It is deeply interesting, in this connection, to learn that in modern Orthodox theology, especially among the Russians, there has developed the idea that the divine kenosis, self-emptying or humiliation was not confined to the historical Passion or even to the Incarnation, but is something eternal in the life of God. It was apparently from the Kenotic school in Protestantism that Russian Orthodox thinkers first borrowed kenosis as an important theological concept. While criticizing the Protestant use of the idea,[36] they have used it in their own way, maintaining that divine kenosis is involved in the whole divine conflict with evil, in the very act of creation, and even in the life of the Trinity. But here is what concerns our present argument: 'The kenosis of Christ is still going on. As far as is evil in the world, the Lamb is still slain. Christ is still humbling Himself and waiting for the decision of man's freedom.'[37]

I have brought together these various statements from such diverse quarters, not to endorse all that they say, but to illustrate the widespread sense, among those who make the historical Cross quite central, that the divine Atonement cannot be confined within any one moment of time, but, so far as it can be described in temporal terms at all, is as old and as endless as the sin with which it deals. 'The Lamb slain from the foundation of the world.' 'Jesus will be in agony until the end of the world.' 'Behold the Lamb of God which taketh away the sin of the world.'

IV: Objective and Subjective Atonement

What, then, is the divine Atonement, which is thus both historical and eternal? Is it an 'objective' reality, something done by Christ, something ordained and accepted by God, in 'expiation' of human sin, quite apart

[34] F. C. N. Hicks, The Fullness of Sacrifice, p. 18.
[35] Nicholas Arseniev in The Ministry and Sacraments (edited by Headlam and Dunkerley), p. 86.
[36] See above.
[37] Gorodetzky, The Humiliated Christ in Modern Russian Thought, p. 171. This book gives an account of the whole movement, mentioning as its main representatives Vladimir Soloviev, M. M. Tareev and Sergius Bulgakov.

from our knowledge of it and its effect upon us? Or is it a 'subjective' process, a reconciling of us to God through a persuasion in our hearts that there is no obstacle, a realizing of His eternal love? Surely these two aspects cannot be separated at all, though the attempt has often been made to classify atonement-theories in that way. In theological argument on this subject we are apt to forget that we are dealing with a realm of personal relationships and nothing else. If we use the terminology of an ancient sacrificial system, we should remember that in the last analysis the only offering we can make to God is the offering of ourselves in faith and love. What Jesus offered to God was Himself. But to offer oneself thus to God means at the same time to love men without limit, and so to carry the load of their sins. That is what Jesus did, in a passion which included physical suffering, social persecution and obloquy, even to the point of a shameful death, and above all the spiritual agony of seeing other lives go wrong. But if, on the deepest interpretation, this was not only an offering made by a man to God, but also a sacrifice made by God Himself, then it is part of the sacrifice that God is continually making, because He is infinite Love confronted with human sin. And it is an *expiatory* sacrifice, because sin is a dreadfully real thing which love cannot tolerate or lightly pass over, and it is only out of the suffering of such inexorable love that true forgiveness, as distinct from an indulgent amnesty, could ever come. That is the objective process of atonement that goes on in the very life of God.

All this may seem to conflict with the traditional doctrine of the divine impassibility, and perhaps the prevalence of that doctrine, which excludes all suffering from the divine nature, is one of the factors that have hindered the acceptance of such ideas as I have been developing. But it is hard to see how a rigid acceptance of the doctrine can leave room for any belief in costly divine sin-bearing at all, even in the incarnate life. There is little help in the traditional solution, that while the impassible God bore suffering in His incarnate life, it was not God the Father but God the Son that suffered, and He suffered not in His divine but in His human nature; for that leaves us asking whether it was really *God* that suffered, and if not, how can we say that God bore our sins. I cannot but think (in spite of Baron von Hügel's impressive protest[38]) that there is some truth in the widespread modern tendency to modify the impassibility doctrine. Perhaps we can observe both sides of the truth by saying, paradoxically, that while there is suffering (for human sin) in the life of God, it is eternally swallowed up in victory and blessedness, and that is how God 'expiates' our sins, as only God could do.

In this connection it is not irrelevant to remember that St. Paul connects the atoning work of Christ very closely not only with His Cross and passion, but also with His Resurrection, His victory, His risen life. If, as we saw,

---

[38] See his essay on 'Suffering and God', in the Second Series of his *Essays and Addresses*.

the important points for the author of *Hebrews* are the death and the ascension, the vital points for St. Paul in this connection are the death and the resurrection, and very closely joined together. Christ 'was delivered up for our offences and raised again for our justification'.[39] 'Who shall lay anything to the charge of God's elect? It is God that justifieth. Who is he that shall condemn? It is Christ Jesus that died, yea, rather, that was raised from the dead. . . .'[40] 'Not having a righteousness of my own, even that which is of the law, but that which is through faith in Christ, the righteousness which is of God by faith; that I may know him, and the power of his resurrection and the fellowship of his sufferings, being conformed unto his death, if by any means I might attain unto the resurrection of the dead.'[41] When we contemplate the story of Jesus we are bound to speak of the suffering and the victory as successive phases; and so does St. Paul: 'Christ being raised from the dead dieth no more; death no more hath dominion over him. For the death that he died, he died unto sin once; but the life that he liveth, he liveth unto God,'[42] But the same chapters gives us Paul's mystical doctrine of the union of the believer with the dying and rising Christ; with the implication that in some sense the passion and the resurrection are not simply episodes in the past, but are, both together, a present reality, an eternal conflict with evil which is also an eternal victory.

This brings us very close to the 'Christus Victor' conception of the Atonement which is advocated by Bishop Aulén as being the truly classic Christian view, and as holding the hope of the future, though at some periods it has been obscured.[43] According to this view, the Atonement is essentially, from start to finish, the costly but victorious conflict of God Himself, in Christ, with the forces of evil. This is a cosmic warfare against a very real enemy, and it involves divine self-sacrifice, but it is thereby triumphant over evil, with an eternal victory which is ever-present as well as past. Bishop Aulén is well aware that this 'classic' view has usually been expressed in highly dramatic and pictorial terms which cannot remain stereotyped for the future, but he is also sure that in this realm the truth can never be forced into a purely rational scheme or get rid of its tremendous paradoxes. It is plain that the New Testament, in dealing with this whole matter, while freely using figures drawn from the ancient system of sacrifices, does not confine itself to such imagery, but uses many other figures too. It is doubtless impossible

[39] Rom. iv, 25.
[40] Rom. viii, 33f.
[41] Phil. iii, 9–11.
[42] Rom. vi, 9f.
[43] Bishop Aulén's book in its English translation is entitled *Christus Victor* (1931). It will occur to readers of his book that the 'classic' view, as expounded by Aulén, stresses the 'cosmic' aspect of the Atonement more than I have done. 'The classic type regards sin as an objective power standing behind men, and the Atonement as the triumph of God over sin, death and the devil.' But Aulén also emphasizes that the 'classic' view gives the most *personal* conception of sin, and that it is the 'Latin' type of theory that really tends to obscure the personal relationship between God and the sinner.

to speak of such things without using symbolic language. But it is good to let one figure of speech correct and supplement another, and to remind ourselves that all of these are but attempts to exhibit the love of God dealing with the sin of the world and overcoming it as only love can do. That is the 'objective' work of atonement.

But since it is neither a 'material' nor a 'legal' victory, neither a battle conducted outside human life altogether nor a transaction completed as it were behind our backs or before we were born, but a spiritual process in the realm of personal relationships, the objective work cannot be separated from its subjective aspect by which it becomes a reality in the hearts and lives of men. And this happens above all through the story of the Cross of Christ, the point in human history where we find the actual outcropping of the divine Atonement. That is what brings us individually back to God. 'God was in Christ, reconciling the world unto himself; . . . we beseech you on behalf of Christ, be ye reconciled to God.'[11]

That is the only kind of answer that can be given to the questions with which we began our seventh chapter, as to why God became man, and what difference the Incarnation makes. We cannot answer speculative questions as to what might have been, what God might or might not have done; and we certainly dare not say that God *could* not have been merciful but for the Cross of Christ. But we can now say about the Incarnation not only that it gives us the Christian view of God, but also that it gives us that outcropping of divine atonement in human history which makes His mercy effectual for our salvation. The Christian message tells us that God was incarnate in Jesus, and that His sin-bearing was incarnate in the Passion of Jesus. His love is inexorable towards our sins, just because it is infinite love and sin is its opposite (self-centredness, lovelessness); and for the same reason it persists indefatigably through all our sinning. That is how He bears our sin. And that is how He overcomes them. That is the costly 'expiation' out of which forgiveness comes. And the story of that, as it was incarnate in Jesus, is what gives us the liberation which leads to a new life. For that story, with the Christian interpretation of it, makes us willing to bring our sins to God, to see them in His light, and to accept from Him the forgiveness which we could never earn. That brings release and a new beginning. And that leads to a new kind of goodness, not the 'Pharisaic' kind, which grows in those who try to save themselves and take credit to themselves for having (as they may think) achieved it; but the Christian kind, which is never conscious of its own merit but only of God's mercy. That is the very secret of the Christian character.

In an earlier chapter I spoke at some length of how the religion of the Incarnation has given rise to a new and highly paradoxical consciousness in the religious experience of mankind, which is expressed in the typical Christian confession: Not I, but the grace of God. But we can now see that

[11] 2 Cor. v, 19f.

more than the Incarnation was needed to awaken in us sinful men and women the sense of that paradox of grace. It is because the religion of the Incarnation became also the religion of Atonement that it has been able to do this. It is because 'God was in Christ, reconciling the world unto himself, *not reckoning unto them their trespasses'*. When we receive that message, and accept the forgiveness of our sins, then we begin to be set free from ourselves. Because God does not reckon unto us our trespasses, we will not reckon unto us our virtues. Our confession will be: Not I, but the grace of God.

Fromm
MATURE LOVE*

Any theory of love must begin with a theory of man, of human existence. While we find love, or rather, the equivalent of love, in animals, their attachments are mainly a part of their instinctual equipment; only remnants of this instinctual equipment can be seen operating in man. What is essential in the existence of man is the fact that he has emerged from the animal kingdom, from instinctive adaptation, that he has transcended nature—although he never leaves it; he is a part of it—and yet once torn away from nature, he cannot return to it; once thrown out of paradise—a state of original oneness with nature—cherubim with flaming swords block his way, if he should try to return. Man can only go forward by developing his reason, by finding a new harmony, a human one, instead of the prehuman harmony which is irretrievably lost.

When man is born, the human race as well as the individual, he is thrown out of a situation which was definite, as definite as the instincts, into a situation which is indefinite, uncertain and open. There is certainty only about the past—and about the future only as far as that it is death.

Man is gifted with reason; he is *life being aware of itself*; he has awareness of himself, of his fellow man, of his past, and of the possibilities of his future. This awareness of himself as a separate entity, the awareness of his own short life span, of the fact that without his will he is born and against his will he dies, that he will die before those whom he loves, or they

* Erich Fromm (1900–   ): American psychiatrist and social analyst. *The Art of Loving* is an analysis of 20th century culture and the possibilities of mature love in that context. This selection, Part 1 of Chapter II, is Fromm's exposition of the theory of love in relation to the problem of existence. From Pp. 7–33, THE ART OF LOVING by Erich Fromm, edited by Ruth Nanda Anshen. Copyright © 1956 by Erich Fromm. Reprinted by permission of Harper & Row, Publishers, New York and George Allen & Unwin Ltd., London.

before him, the awareness of his aloneness and separateness, of his help-lessness before the forces of nature and of society, all this makes his separate, disunited existence an unbearable prison. He would become insane could he not liberate himself from this prison and reach out, unite himself in some form or other with men, with the world outside.

The experience of separateness arouses anxiety; it is, indeed, the source of all anxiety. Being separate means being cut off, without any capacity to use my human powers. Hence to be separate means to be helpless, unable to grasp the world—things and people—actively; it means that the world can invade me without my ability to react. Thus, separateness is the source of intense anxiety. Beyond that, it arouses shame and the feeling of guilt. This experience of guilt and shame in separateness is expressed in the Biblical story of Adam and Eve. After Adam and Eve have eaten of the "tree of knowledge of good and evil," after they have disobeyed (there is no good and evil unless there is freedom to disobey), after they have become human by having emancipated themselves from the original harmony with nature, i.e., after their birth as human beings—they saw "that they were naked—and they were ashamed." Should we assume that a myth as old and ele-mentary as this has the prudish morals of the nineteenth-century outlook, and that the important point the story wants to convey to us is the em-barrassment that their genitals were visible? This can hardly be so, and by understanding the story in a Victorian spirit, we miss the main point, which seems to be the following: after man and woman have become aware of themselves and of each other, they are aware of their separateness, and of their difference, inasmuch as they belong to different sexes. But while recognizing their separateness they remain strangers, because they have not yet learned to love each other (as is also made very clear by the fact that Adam defends himself by blaming Eve, rather than by trying to defend her). *The awareness of human separation, without reunion by love—is the source of shame. It is at the same time the source of guilt and anxiety.*

The deepest need of man, then, is the need to overcome his separateness, to leave the prison of his aloneness. The *absolute* failure to achieve this aim means insanity, because the panic of complete isolation can be overcome only by such a radical withdrawal from the world outside that the feeling of separation disappears—because the world outside, from which one is separated, has disappeared.

Man—of all ages and cultures—is confronted with the solution of one and the same question: the question of how to overcome separateness, how to achieve union, how to transcend one's own individual life and find atonement. The question is the same for primitive man living in caves, for nomadic man taking care of his flocks, for the peasant in Egypt, the Phoenician trader, the Roman soldier, the medieval monk, the Japanese samurai, the modern clerk and factory hand. The question is the same, for it springs from the same ground: the human situation, the conditions of human existence. The answer varies. The question can be answered by animal worship, by human sacrifice or military conquest, by indulgence in luxury, by ascetic renunciation, by obsessional work, by artistic creation, by the love of God, and by the love of Man. While there are many answers —the record of which is human history—they are nevertheless not innumerable. On the contrary, as soon as one ignores smaller differences which belong more to the periphery than to the center, one discovers that there is only a limited number of answers which have been given, and only could have been given by man in the various cultures in which he has lived. The history of religion and philosophy is the history of these answers, of their diversity, as well as of their limitation in number.

The answers depend, to some extent, on the degree of individuation which an individual has reached. In the infant I-ness has developed but little yet; he still feels one with mother, has no feeling of separateness as long as mother is present. Its sense of aloneness is cured by the physical presence of the mother, her breasts, her skin. Only to the degree that the child develops his sense of separateness and individuality is the physical presence of the mother not sufficient any more, and does the need to overcome separateness in other ways arise.

Similarly, the human race in its infancy still feels one with nature. The soil, the animals, the plants are still man's world. He identifies himself with animals, and this is expressed by the wearing of animal masks, by the worshipping of a totem animal or animal gods. But the more the human race emerges from these primary bonds, the more it separates itself from the natural world, the more intense becomes the need to find new ways of escaping separateness.

One way of achieving this aim lies in all kinds of *orgiastic states*. These may have the form of an auto-induced trance, sometimes with the help of drugs. Many rituals of primitive tribes offer a vivid picture of this type of solution. In a transitory state of exaltation the world outside disappears, and with it the feeling of separateness from it. Inasmuch as these rituals are practiced in common, an experience of fusion with the group is added which makes this solution all the more effective. Closely related to, and often blended with this orgiastic solution, is the sexual experience. The sexual orgasm can produce a state similar to the one produced by a trance, or to the effects of certain drugs. Rites of communal sexual orgies were a part of many primitive rituals. It seems that after the orgiastic experience, man can go on for a time without suffering too much from his separateness. Slowly the tension of anxiety mounts, and then is reduced again by the repeated performance of the ritual.

As long as these orgiastic states are a matter of common practice in a tribe, they do not produce anxiety or guilt. To act in this way is right, and even virtuous, because it is a way shared by all, approved and demanded by the medicine men or priests; hence there is no reason to feel guilty or ashamed. It is quite different when the same solution is chosen by an individual in a culture which has left behind these common practices. Alcoholism and drug addiction are the forms which the individual chooses in a non-orgiastic culture. In contrast to those participating in the socially patterned solution, such individuals suffer from guilt feelings and remorse. While they try to escape from separateness by taking refuge in alcohol or drugs, they feel all the more separate after the orgiastic experience is over, and thus are driven to take recourse to it with increasing frequency and intensity. Slightly different from this is the recourse to a sexual orgiastic solution. To some extent it is a natural and normal form of overcoming separateness, and a partial answer to the problem of isolation. But in many individuals in whom separateness is not relieved in other ways, the search for the sexual orgasm assumes a function which makes it not very different from alcoholism and drug addiction. It becomes a desperate attempt to escape the anxiety engendered by separateness, and it results in an ever-increasing sense of separateness, since the sexual act without love never bridges the gap between two human beings, except momentarily.

All forms of orgiastic union have three characteristics: they are intense, even violent; they occur in the total personality, mind *and* body; they are transitory and periodical. Exactly the opposite holds true for that form of union which is by far the most frequent solution chosen by man in the past and in the present: the union based on *conformity* with the group, its customs, practices and beliefs. Here again we find a considerable development.

In a primitive society the group is small; it consists of those with whom one shares blood and soil. With the growing development of culture, the group enlarges; it becomes the citizenry of a *polis*, the citizenry of a large state, the members of a church. Even the poor Roman felt pride because he could say *"civis romanus sum"*; Rome and the Empire were his family, his home, his world. Also in contemporary Western society the union with the group is the prevalent way of overcoming separateness. It is a union in which the individual self disappears to a large extent, and where the aim is to belong to the herd. If I am like everybody else, if I have no feelings or thoughts which make me different, if I conform in custom, dress, ideas, to the pattern of the group, I am saved; saved from the frightening experience of aloneness. The dictatorial systems use threats and terror to induce this conformity; the democratic countries, suggestion and propaganda. There is, indeed, one great difference between the two systems. In the democracies non-conformity is possible and, in fact, by no means entirely absent; in the totalitarian systems, only a few unusual heroes and martyrs can be expected to refuse obedience. But in spite of this difference the democratic societies show an overwhelming degree of conformity. The reason lies in the fact that there *has* to be an answer to the quest for union, and if there is no other or better way, then the union of herd conformity becomes the predominant one. One can only understand the power of the fear to be different, the fear to be only a few steps away from the herd, if one understands the depths of the need not to be separated. Sometimes this fear of non-conformity is rationalized as fear of practical dangers which could threaten the non-conformist. But actually, people *want* to conform to a much higher degree than they are *forced* to conform, at least in the Western democracies.

Most people are not even aware of their need to conform. They live under the illusion that they follow their own ideas and inclinations, that they are individualists, that they have arrived at their opinions as the result of their own thinking—and that it just happens that their ideas are the same as those of the majority. The consensus of all serves as a proof for the correctness of "their" ideas. Since there is still a need to feel some individuality, such need is satisfied with regard to minor differences; the initials on the handbag or the sweater, the name plate of the bank teller, the belonging to the Democratic as against the Republican party, to the Elks instead of to the Shriners become the expression of individual differences. The advertising slogan of "it is different" shows up this pathetic need for difference, when in reality there is hardly any left.

This increasing tendency for the elimination of differences is closely related to the concept and the experience of equality, as it is developing in the most advanced industrial societies. Equality had meant, in a religious context, that we are all God's children, that we all share in the same human-divine substance, that we are all one. It meant also that the very differences between individuals must be respected, that while it is true that we are all one, it is also true that each one of us is a unique entity, is a cosmos by itself. Such conviction of the uniqueness of the individual is expressed for instance in the Talmudic statement: "Whosoever saves a single life is as if he had saved the whole world; whosoever destroys a single life is as if he had destroyed the whole world." Equality as a condition for the development of individuality was also the meaning of the concept in the philosophy of the Western Enlightenment. It meant (most clearly formulated by Kant) that no man must be the means for the ends of another man. That all men are equal inasmuch as they are ends, and only ends, and never means to each other. Following the ideas of the Enlightenment, Socialist thinkers of various schools defined equality as abolition of exploitation, of the use of man by man, regardless of whether this use were cruel or "human."

In contemporary capitalistic society the meaning of equality has been transformed. By equality one refers to the equality of automatons; of men who have lost their individuality. *Equality today means "sameness," rather than "oneness."* It is the sameness of abstractions, of the men who work in the same jobs, who have the same amusements, who read the same newspapers, who have the same feelings and the same ideas. In this respect one must also look with some skepticism at some achievements which are usually praised as signs of our progress, such as the equality of women. Needless to say I am not speaking against the equality of women; but the positive aspects of this tendency for equality must not deceive one. It is part of the trend toward the elimination of differences. Equality is bought at this very price: women are equal because they are not different any more. The proposition of Enlightenment philosophy, *l'âme n'a pas de sexe*, the soul has no sex, has become the general practice. The polarity of the sexes is disappearing, and with it erotic love, which is based on this polarity. Men and women become the *same*, not *equals* as opposite poles. Contemporary society preaches this ideal of unindividualized equality because it needs human atoms, each one the same, to make them function in a mass aggregation, smoothly, without friction; all obeying the same commands, yet everybody being convinced that he is following his own desires. Just as modern mass production requires the standardization of commodities, so the social process requires standardization of man, and this standardization is called "equality."

Union by conformity is not intense and violent; it is calm, dictated by routine, and for this very reason often is insufficient to pacify the anxiety of separateness. The incidence of alcoholism, drug addiction, compulsive sexualism, and suicide in contemporary Western society are symptoms of this relative failure of herd conformity. Furthermore, this solution concerns mainly the mind and not the body, and for this reason too is lacking in comparison with the orgiastic solutions. Herd conformity has only one advantage: it is permanent, and not spasmodic. The individual is introduced into the conformity pattern at the age of three or four, and subsequently never loses his contact with the herd. Even his funeral, which he anticipates as his last great social affair, is in strict conformance with the pattern.

In addition to conformity as a way to relieve the anxiety springing from separateness, another factor of contemporary life must be considered: the role of the work routine and of the pleasure routine. Man becomes a "nine to fiver," he is part of the labor force, or the bureaucratic force of clerks and managers. He has little initiative, his tasks are prescribed by the organization of the work; there is even little difference between those high up on the ladder and those on the bottom. They all perform tasks prescribed by the whole structure of the organization, at a prescribed speed, and in a prescribed manner. Even the feelings are prescribed: cheerfulness, tolerance, reliability, ambition, and an ability to get along with everybody without friction. Fun is routinized in similar, although not quite as drastic ways. Books are selected by the book clubs, movies by the film and theater owners and the advertising slogans paid for by them; the rest is also uniform: the Sunday ride in the car, the television session, the card game, the social parties. From birth to death, from Monday to Monday, from morning to evening—all activities are routinized, and prefabricated. How should a man caught in this net of routine not forget that he is a man, a unique individual, one who is given only this one chance of living, with hopes and disappointments, with sorrow and fear, with the longing for love and the dread of the nothing and of separateness?

A third way of attaining union lies in *creative activity*, be it that of the artist, or of the artisan. In any kind of creative work the creating person unites himself with his material, which represents the world outside of himself. Whether a carpenter makes a table, or a goldsmith a piece of jewelry, whether the peasant grows his corn or the painter paints a picture, in all types of creative work the worker and his object become one, man unites himself with the world in the process of creation. This, however, holds true only for productive work, for work in which *I* plan, produce, see the result of my work. In the modern work process of a clerk, the worker on the endless belt, little is left of this uniting quality of work. The worker becomes an appendix to the machine or to the bureaucratic organization. He has ceased to be he—hence no union takes place beyond that of conformity.

The unity achieved in productive work is not interpersonal; the unity achieved in orgiastic fusion is transitory; the unity achieved by conformity is only pseudo-unity. Hence, they are only partial answers to the problem of existence. The full answer lies in the achievement of interpersonal union, of fusion with another person, in *love*.

This desire for interpersonal fusion is the most powerful striving in man. It is the most fundamental passion, it is the force which keeps the human race together, the clan, the family, society. The failure to achieve it means insanity or destruction—self-destruction or destruction of others. Without love, humanity could not exist for a day. Yet, if we call the achievement of interpersonal union "love," we find ourselves in a serious difficulty. Fusion can be achieved in different ways—and the differences are not less significant than what is common to the various forms of love. Should they all be called love? Or should we reserve the word "love" only for a specific kind of union, one which has been the ideal virtue in all great humanistic religions and philosophical systems of the last four thousand years of Western and Eastern history?

As with all semantic difficulties, the answer can only be arbitrary. What matters is that we know what kind of union we are talking about when we speak of love. Do we refer to love as the mature answer to the problem of existence, or do we speak of those immature forms of love which may be called *symbiotic union*? In the following pages I shall call love only the former. I shall begin the discussion of "love" with the latter.

Symbiotic union has its biological pattern in the relationship between the pregnant mother and the foetus. They are two, and yet one. They live "together," (*sym-biosis*), they need each other. The foetus is a part of the mother, it receives everything it needs from her; mother is its world, as it were; she feeds it, she protects it, but also her own life is enhanced by it. In the *psychic* symbiotic union, the two bodies are independent, but the same kind of attachment exists psychologically.

The *passive* form of the symbiotic union is that of submission, or if we use a clinical term, of *masochism*. The masochistic person escapes from the unbearable feeling of isolation and separateness by making himself part and parcel of another person who directs him, guides him, protects him; who is his life and his oxygen, as it were. The power of the one to whom one submits is inflated, may he be a person or a god; he is everything, I am nothing, except inasmuch as I am part of him. As a part, I am part of greatness, of power, of certainty. The masochistic person does not have to make decisions, does not have to take any risks; he is never alone—but he is not independent; he has no integrity; he is not yet fully born. In a religious context the object of worship is called an idol; in a secular context of a masochistic love relationship the essential mechanism, that of idolatry, is the same. The masochistic relationship can be blended with physical, sexual desire; in this case it is not only a submission in which one's mind participates, but also one's whole body. There can be masochistic submission to fate, to sickness, to rhythmic music, to the orgiastic state produced by drugs or under hypnotic trance—in all these instances the person renounces his integrity, makes himself the instrument of somebody or something outside of himself; he need not solve the problem of living by productive activity.

The *active* form of symbiotic fusion is domination or, to use the psychological term corresponding to masochism, *sadism*. The sadistic person wants to escape from his aloneness and his sense of imprisonment by making another person part and parcel of himself. He inflates and enhances himself by incorporating another person, who worships him.

The sadistic person is as dependent on the submissive person as the latter is on the former; neither can live without the other. The difference is only that the sadistic person commands, exploits, hurts, humiliates, and that the masochistic person is commanded, exploited, hurt, humiliated. This is a considerable difference in a realistic sense; in a deeper emotional sense, the difference is not so great as that which they both have in common: fusion without integrity. If one understands this, it is also not surprising to find that usually a person reacts in both the sadistic and the masochistic manner, usually toward different objects. Hitler reacted primarily in a sadistic fashion toward people, but masochistically toward fate, history, the "higher power" of nature. His end—suicide among general destruction—is as characteristic as was his dream of success—total domination.[1]

In contrast to symbiotic union, mature *love* is *union under the condition of preserving one's integrity*, one's individuality. *Love is an active power in man*; a power which breaks through the walls which separate man from his fellow men, which unites him with others; love makes him overcome the sense of isolation and separateness, yet it permits him to be himself, to retain his integrity. In love the paradox occurs that two beings become one and yet remain two.

If we say love is an activity, we face a difficulty which lies in the ambiguous meaning of the word "activity." By "activity," in the modern usage of the word, is usually meant an action which brings about a change in an existing situation by means of an expenditure of energy. Thus a man is considered active if he does business, studies medicine, works on an endless

---

[1] Cf. a more detailed study of sadism and masochism in E. Fromm, *Escape from Freedom*, Rinehart & Company, New York, 1941.

belt, builds a table, or is engaged in sports. Common to all these activities is that they are directed toward an outside goal to be achieved. What is *not* taken into account is the *motivation* of activity. Take for instance a man driven to incessant work by a sense of deep insecurity and loneliness; or another one driven by ambition, or greed for money. In all these cases the person is the slave of a passion, and his activity is in reality a "passivity" because he is driven; he is the sufferer, not the "actor." On the other hand, a man sitting quiet and contemplating, with no purpose or aim except that of experiencing himself and his oneness with the world, is considered to be "passive," because he is not "doing" anything. In reality, this attitude of concentrated meditation is the highest activity there is, an activity of the soul, which is possible only under the condition of inner freedom and independence. One concept of activity, the modern one, refers to the use of energy for the achievement of external aims; the other concept of activity refers to the use of man's inherent powers, regardless of whether any external change is brought about. The latter concept of activity has been formulated most clearly by Spinoza. He differentiates among the affects between active and passive affects, "actions" and "passions." In the exercise of an active affect, man is free, he is the master of his affect; in the exercise of a passive affect, man is driven, the object of motivations of which he himself is not aware. Thus Spinoza arrives at the statement that virtue and power are one and the same.[2] Envy, jealousy, ambition, any kind of greed are passions; love is an action, the practice of a human power, which can be practiced only in freedom and never as the result of a compulsion.

Love is an activity, not a passive affect; it is a "standing in," not a "falling for." In the most general way, the active character of love can be described by stating that love is primarily *giving*, not receiving.

What is giving? Simple as the answer to this question seems to be, it is actually full of ambiguities and complexities. The most widespread misunderstanding is that which assumes that giving is "giving up" something, being deprived of, sacrificing. The person whose character has not developed beyond the stage of the receptive, exploitative, or hoarding orientation, experiences the act of giving in this way. The marketing character is willing to give, but only in exchange for receiving; giving without receiving for him is being cheated.[3] People whose main orientation is a non-productive one feel giving as an impoverishment. Most individuals of this type therefore refuse to give. Some make a virtue out of giving in the sense of a sacrifice. They feel that just because it is painful to give, one *should* give; the virtue of giving to them lies in the very act of acceptance of the sacrifice. For them, the norm that it is better to give than to receive means that it is better to suffer deprivation than to experience joy.

---

[2] Spinoza, *Ethics* IV, Def. 8.
[3] Cf. a detailed discussion of these character orientations in E. Fromm, *Man for Himself*, Rinehart & Company, New York, 1947, Chap. III, pp. 54–117.

For the productive character, giving has an entirely different meaning. Giving is the highest expression of potency. In the very act of giving, I experience my strength, my wealth, my power. This experience of heightened vitality and potency fills me with joy. I experience myself as overflowing, spending, alive, hence as joyous.[1] Giving is more joyous than receiving, not because it is a deprivation, but because in the act of giving lies the expression of my aliveness.

It is not difficult to recognize the validity of this principle by applying it to various specific phenomena. The most elementary example lies in the sphere of sex. The culmination of the male sexual function lies in the act of giving; the man gives himself, his sexual organ, to the woman. At the moment of orgasm he gives his semen to her. He cannot help giving it if he is potent. If he cannot give, he is impotent. For the woman the process is not different, although somewhat more complex. She gives herself too; she opens the gates to her feminine center; in the act of receiving, she gives. If she is incapable of this act of giving, if she can only receive, she is frigid. With her the act of giving occurs again, not in her function as a lover, but in that as a mother. She gives of herself to the growing child within her, she gives her milk to the infant, she gives her bodily warmth. Not to give would be painful.

In the sphere of material things giving means being rich. Not he who *has* much is rich, but he who *gives* much. The hoarder who is anxiously worried about losing something is, psychologically speaking, the poor, impoverished man, regardless of how much he has. Whoever is capable of giving of himself is rich. He experiences himself as one who can confer of himself to others. Only one who is deprived of all that goes beyond the barest necessities for subsistence would be incapable of enjoying the act of giving material things. But daily experience shows that what a person considers the minimal necessities depends as much on his character as it depends on his actual possessions. It is well known that the poor are more willing to give than the rich. Nevertheless, poverty beyond a certain point may make it impossible to give, and is so degrading, not only because of the suffering it causes directly, but because of the fact that it deprives the poor of the joy of giving.

The most important sphere of giving, however, is not that of material things, but lies in the specifically human realm. What does one person give to another? He gives of himself, of the most precious he has, he gives of his life. This does not necessarily mean that he sacrifices his life for the other—but that he gives him of that which is alive in him; he gives him of his joy, of his interest, of his understanding, of his knowledge, of his humor, of his sadness—of all expressions and manifestations of that which is alive in him. In thus giving of his life, he enriches the other person, he enhances the other's sense of aliveness by enhancing his own sense of alive-

---

[1] Compare the definition of joy given by Spinoza.

ness. He does not give in order to receive; giving is in itself exquisite joy. But in giving he cannot help bringing something to life in the other person, and this which is brought to life reflects back to him; in truly giving, he cannot help receiving that which is given back to him. Giving implies to make the other person a giver also and they both share in the joy of what they have brought to life. In the act of giving something is born, and both persons involved are grateful for the life that is born for both of them. Specifically with regard to love this means: love is a power which produces love; impotence is the inability to produce love. This thought has been beautifully expressed by Marx: "Assume," he says, "*man as man*, and his relation to the world as a human one, and you can exchange love only for love, confidence for confidence, etc. If you wish to enjoy art, you must be an artistically trained person; if you wish to have influence on other people, you must be a person who has a really stimulating and furthering influence on other people. Every one of your relationships to man and to nature must be a definite expression of your *real, individual* life corresponding to the object of your will. If you love without calling forth love, that is, if your love as such does not produce love, if by means of an *expression of life* as a loving person you do not make of yourself· a *loved person*, then your love is impotent, a misfortune."[5] But not only in love does giving mean receiving. The teacher is taught by his students, the actor is stimulated by his audience, the psychoanalyst is cured by his patient––provided they do not treat each other as objects, but are related to each other genuinely and productively.

It is hardly necessary to stress the fact that the ability to love as an act of giving depends on the character development of the person. It presupposes the attainment of a predominantly productive orientation; in this orientation the person has overcome dependency, narcissistic omnipotence, the wish to exploit others, or to hoard, and has acquired faith in his own human powers, courage to rely on his powers in the attainment of his goals. To the degree that these qualities are lacking, he is afraid of giving himself ––hence of loving.

Beyond the element of giving, the active character of love becomes evident in the fact that it always implies certain basic elements, common to all forms of love. These are *care, responsibility, respect* and *knowledge*.

That love implies *care* is most evident in a mother's love for her child. No assurance of her love would strike us as sincere if we saw her lacking in care for the infant, if she neglected to feed it, to bathe it, to give it physical comfort; and we are impressed by her love if we see her caring for the child. It is not different even with the love for animals or flowers. If a woman told us that she loved flowers, and we saw that she forgot to water them, we would not believe in her "love" for flowers. *Love is the active*

---

[5] "Nationalökonomie und Philosophie," 1844, published in Karl Marx' *Die Frühschriften*, Alfred Kröner Verlag, Stuttgart, 1953, pp. 300, 301. (My translation, E. F.)

concern for the life and the growth of that which we love. Where this active concern is lacking, there is no love. This element of love has been beautifully described in the book of Jonah. God has told Jonah to go to Nineveh to warn its inhabitants that they will be punished unless they mend their evil ways. Jonah runs away from his mission because he is afraid that the people of Nineveh will repent and that God will forgive them. He is a man with a strong sense of order and law, but without love. However, in his attempt to escape, he finds himself in the belly of a whale, symbolizing the state of isolation and imprisonment which his lack of love and solidarity has brought upon him. God saves him, and Jonah goes to Nineveh. He preaches to the inhabitants as God had told him, and the very thing he was afraid of happens. The men of Nineveh repent their sins, mend their ways, and God forgives them and decides not to destroy the city. Jonah is intensely angry and disappointed; he wanted "justice" to be done, not mercy. At last he finds some comfort in the shade of a tree which God had·made to grow for him to protect him from the sun. But when God makes the tree wilt, Jonah is depressed and angrily complains to God. God answers: "Thou hast had pity on the gourd for the which thou hast not labored neither madest it grow; which came up in a night, and perished in a night. And should I not spare Nineveh, that great city, wherein are more than sixscore thousand people that cannot discern between their right hand and their left hand; and also much cattle?" God's answer to Jonah is to be understood symbolically. God explains to Jonah that the essence of love is to "labor" for something and "to make something grow," that love and labor are inseparable. One loves that for which one labors, and one labors for that which ones loves.

Care and concern imply another aspect of love; that of *responsibility.* Today responsibility is often meant to denote duty, something imposed upon one from the outside. But responsibility, in its true sense, is an entirely voluntary act; it is my response to the needs, expressed or unexpressed, of another human being. To be "responsible" means to be able and ready to "respond." Jonah did not feel responsible to the inhabitants of Nineveh. He, like Cain, could ask: "Am I my brother's keeper?" The loving person responds. The life of his brother is not his brother's business alone, but his own. He feels responsible for his fellow men, as he feels responsible for himself. This responsibility, in the case of the mother and her infant, refers mainly to the care for physical needs. In the love between adults it refers mainly to the psychic needs of the other person.

Responsibility could easily deteriorate into domination and possessiveness, were it not for a third component of love, *respect.* Respect is not fear and awe; it denotes, in accordance with the root of the word (*respicere* = to look at), the ability to see a person as he is, to be aware of his unique individuality. Respect means the concern that the other person should grow and unfold as he is. Respect, thus, implies the absence of exploitation. I want the loved person to grow and unfold for his own sake, and in his own ways, and not for the purpose of serving me. If I love the other person, I feel one with him or her, but with him *as he is,* not as I need him to be as an object for my use. It is clear that respect is possible only if *I* have achieved independence; if I stand and walk without needing crutches, without having to dominate and exploit anyone else. Respect exists only on the basis of freedom: "l'amour est l'enfant de la liberté" as an old French song says; love is the child of freedom, never that of domination.

To respect a person is not possible without *knowing* him; care and responsibility would be blind if they were not guided by knowledge. Knowledge would be empty if it were not motivated by concern. There are many layers of knowledge; the knowledge which is an aspect of love is one which does not stay at the periphery, but penetrates to the core. It is possible only when I can transcend the concern for myself and see the other person in his own terms. I may know, for instance, that a person is angry, even if he does not show it overtly; but I may know him more deeply than that; then I know that he is anxious, and worried; that he feels lonely, that he feels guilty. Then I know that his anger is only the manifestation of something deeper, and I see him as anxious and embarrassed, that is, as the suffering person, rather than as the angry one.

Knowledge has one more, and a more fundamental, relation to the problem of love. The basic need to fuse with another person so as to transcend the prison of one's separateness is closely related to another specifically human desire, that to know the "secret of man." While life in its merely biological aspects is a miracle and a secret, man in his human aspects is an unfathomable secret to himself—and to his fellow man. We know ourselves, and yet even with all the efforts we may make, we do not know ourselves. We know our fellow man, and yet we do not know him, because we are not a thing, and our fellow man is not a thing. The further we reach into the depth of our being, or someone else's being, the more the goal of knowledge eludes us. Yet we cannot help desiring to penetrate into the secret of man's soul, into the innermost nucleus which is "he."

There is one way, a desperate one, to know the secret: it is that of complete power over another person; the power which makes him do what we want, feel what we want, think what we want; which transforms him into a thing, our thing, our possession. The ultimate degree of this attempt to know lies in the extremes of sadism, the desire and ability to make a human being suffer; to torture him, to force him to betray his secret in his suffering. In this craving for penetrating man's secret, his and hence our own, lies an essential motivation for the depth and intensity of cruelty and destructiveness. In a very succinct way this idea has been expressed by Isaac Babel. He quotes a fellow officer in the Russian civil war, who has just stamped his former master to death, as saying: "With shooting—I'll put it this way —with shooting you only get rid of a chap. . . . With shooting you'll never get at the soul, to where it is in a fellow and how it shows itself. But I don't spare myself, and I've more than once trampled an enemy for over an hour.

You see, I want to get to know what life really is, what life's like down our way."[6]

In children we often see this path of knowledge quite overtly. The child takes something apart, breaks it up in order to know it; or it takes an animal apart; cruelly tears off the wings of a butterfly in order to know it, to force its secret. The cruelty itself is motivated by something deeper: the wish to know the secret of things and of life.

The other path to knowing "the secret" is love. Love in active penetration of the other person, in which my desire to know is stilled by union. In the act of fusion I know you, I know myself, I know everybody—and I "know" nothing. I know in the only way knowledge of that which is alive is possible for man—by experience of union—not by any knowledge our thought can give. Sadism is motivated by the wish to know the secret, yet I remain as ignorant as I was before. I have torn the other being apart limb from limb, yet all I have done is to destroy him. Love is the only way of knowledge, which in the act of union answers my quest. In the act of loving, of giving myself, in the act of penetrating the other person, I find myself, I discover myself, I discover us both, I discover man.

The longing to know ourselves and to know our fellow man has been expressed in the Delphic motto "Know thyself." It is the mainspring of all psychology. But inasmuch as the desire is to know all of man, his innermost secret, the desire can never be fulfilled in knowledge of the ordinary kind, in knowledge only by thought. Even if we knew a thousand times more of ourselves, we would never reach bottom. We would still remain an enigma to ourselves, as our fellow man would remain an enigma to us. The only way of full knowledge lies in the *act* of love: this act transcends thought, it transcends words. It is the daring plunge into the experience of union. However, knowledge in thought, that is psychological knowledge, is a necessary condition for full knowledge in the act of love. I have to know the other person and myself objectively, in order to be able to see his reality, or rather, to overcome the illusions, the irrationally distorted picture I have of him. Only if I know a human being objectively, can I know him in his ultimate essence, in the act of love.[7]

The problem of knowing man is parallel to the religious problem of knowing God. In conventional Western theology the attempt is made to know God by thought, to make statements *about* God. It is assumed that I can know God in my thought. In mysticism, which is the consequent outcome of monotheism (as I shall try to show later on), the attempt is given up to know God by thought, and it is replaced by the experience of union

---

[6] I. Babel, *The Collected Stories*, Criterion Book, New York, 1955.

[7] The above statement has an important implication for the role of psychology in contemporary Western culture. While the great popularity of psychology certainly indicates an interest in the knowledge of man, it also betrays the fundamental lack of love in human relations today. Psychological knowledge thus becomes a substitute for full knowledge in the act of love, instead of being a step toward it.

with God in which there is no more room—and no need—for knowledge *about* God.

The experience of union, with man, or religiously speaking, with God, is by no means irrational. On the contrary, it is as Albert Schweitzer has pointed out, the consequence of rationalism, its most daring and radical consequence. It is based on our knowledge of the fundamental, and not accidental, limitations of our knowledge. It is the knowledge that we shall never "grasp" the secret of man and of the universe, but that we can know, nevertheless, in the act of love. Psychology as a science has its limitations, and, as the logical consequence of theology is mysticism, so the ultimate consequence of psychology is love.

Care, responsibility, respect and knowledge are mutually interdependent. They are a syndrome of attitudes which are to be found in the mature person; that is, in the person who develops his own powers productively, who only wants to have that which he has worked for, who has given up narcissistic dreams of omniscience and omnipotence, who has acquired humility based on the inner strength which only genuine productive activity can give.

Thus far I have spoken of love as the overcoming of human separateness, as the fulfillment of the longing for union. But above the universal, existential need for union rises a more specific, biological one: the desire for union between the masculine and feminine poles. The idea of this polarization is most strikingly expressed in the myth that originally man and woman were one, that they were cut in half, and from then on each male has been seeking for the lost female part of himself in order to unite again with her. (The same idea of the original unity of the sexes is also contained in the Biblical story of Eve being made from Adam's rib, even though in this story, in the spirit of patriarchalism, woman is considered secondary to man.) The meaning of the myth is clear enough. Sexual polarization leads man to seek union in a specific way, that of union with the other sex. The polarity between the male and female principles exists also *within* each man and each woman. Just as physiologically man and woman each have hormones of the opposite sex, they are bisexual also in the psychological sense. They carry in themselves the principle of receiving and of penetrating, of matter and of spirit. Man—and woman—finds union within himself only in the union of his female and his male polarity. This polarity is the basis for all creativity. . . .

Chapter 10

Religious symbols and language

Religious symbolism, whether expressed in art, act, or language, has its origin in mythic consciousness and belief. The myth is the source, form and primal expression for symbols and is probably the most primitive form of man's imaginative response to life. Primitive religious belief and ritual probably did not exist beyond the circumference of their mythic contexts, so that all symbolic forms made uniform and unambiguous reference to different aspects of the reality revealed through the dominant myth.

In the pre-scientific and pre-philosophical orientation of primitive peoples the vast range of symbolism to which they responded was inextricably tied to the basic myths that governed their views of the totality of existence. It was only gradually that the objects of mythical experience became also objects of scientific and philosophical inquiry. Language, as a form of symbolic response and expression only gradually detached itself from the mythical framework and acquired its independent status and function. As man's scientific and philosophical efforts matured, men became progressively aware of the diversity and relative autonomy of self-created symbols. The objects of mythical awareness were increasingly transformed into objects for empirical examination. Thus, for example, the crow, which might have served for a primitive people as a potent symbol of a divine power, with the advent of a scientific approach could be studied as an object of empirical interest and classified with other empirical objects of a similar nature. The word 'crow' which previously might have evoked a sense of awe and reverence, might, in a scientific context, function merely as a verbal sign, and hence, lose its special religious status.

Thus we can see that language can operate in a variety of ways: as descriptive of empirical phenomena or as a non-literal expression of mythic reality. The claim frequently made for the language of myth is that it provides an access to truth quite distinct from other forms of language use—specifically the form used by empirical science. At the very least, one must admit that the language of myth is frequently quite distinct in its intention from the language of the empirical sciences. Parable, metaphor, and paradox illustrate the difference.

Whereas language may be a principal means of conveying religious symbols, it is clear that symbols are not restricted to verbal expression. But, then, what defines the nature of a symbol and what distinguishes a religious symbol from all other symbolic forms? Do religious symbols and the human grasp of them involve a kind of knowledge which differs sharply from the cognitive claims of linguistic propositions in religion? What is the relation between cognitive claims made in the empirical sciences and cognitive claims in religion? What does it mean to say that metaphorical and paradoxical statements of the kind found in religious language are true? Is there any telling objection to the representation of religious dimensions of reality metaphorically or symbolically when such realities cannot be expressed through conventional imagery and linguistic forms? The selections by Hesse, Tillich, and Wilson are addressed to some of these questions.

The basic issue raised by the short excerpt from Hesse's novel *Siddhartha* concerns the problem of capturing and communicating religious truth in discursive language. Both of the characters participating in the dialogue, Govinda and Siddhartha, have traveled their separate paths in search of spiritual fulfilment. In this final interview, Siddhartha explains to Govinda that he cannot communicate his discoveries because he has found that language fails to convey the deepest religious truth. Siddhartha affirms that there is religious knowledge but that words, even thoughts, cannot encompass that knowledge. Without providing an argument supporting this conclusion, he does outline some of the reasons why he believes language is inadequate as a means for communication of religious cognitions; for example, words are one-sided, words are abstract, words tend to fragment the unity of things and to separate arbitrarily. But if words are inadequate, as Siddhartha claims, by what means can religious comprehension be communicated?

One of the most significant and meaningful contributions that Tillich made to religious thought was his analysis of religious symbols. The importance of Tillich's discussion lies in his claims regarding the relationship between religious symbols and that which they symbolize. He speaks of the innate power of the symbol to point beyond itself to a reality not accessible to rational and empirical inquiry. While the relationship of sign to what is signified is entirely contingent, that between symbol and symbolized is necessary. What precisely is the character of this "necessity"? Is it essential to the cognition of the religious reality symbolized or is it merely a psychological necessity?

Religious symbols, for Tillich, are expressions of man's ultimate concern, i.e. his faith. The only legitimate question to ask concerning such symbols, says Tillich, is whether the symbols expressing the faith are the most adequate for symbolizing the ultimate. The literal acceptance of either religious symbols or myths constitutes idolatry. Hence, religious symbols, in linguistic form, cannot be evaluated or criticized according to the norms of empirical science or rational philosophy. The linguistic form of the symbolic response of faith should not mislead us into thinking that religious propositions are intended, in the usual sense, as true or false. The truths expressed in religious language are not validated by the principles of verification and logic applicable to assertions in the natural and social sciences or in philosophy. Hence, religious language, like scientific language, has its own principles of validation and these are relative to the context in which such language appropriately may be used.

John Wilson's essay expresses a fundamental concern with the precise meaning and informative value of religious language. According to Wilson, the problem of the cognitive meaning of religious statements is necessarily related to the question of whether verification procedures can be established for religious assertions. His thesis is that the informative value of religious discourse depends upon whether religious statements which intend to convey knowledge are susceptible of being disproved.

Wilson insists that the religious believer who desires some measure of philosophical respectability must give serious attention to the problem of whether informative religious discourse can be assured of meaningfulness through the discovery of definite verification procedures. This is not a matter of arbitrarily deciding what might count as evidence for or against religious assertions because any discussion of religious discourse should attend to the manner in which religious ideas arise from, and find their meaning in, religious experience. Perhaps religious thinkers have too long evaded or ignored the question of the correlation between cognitive meaningfulness in religious discourse and the problem of verification procedures. After all, it makes little sense to set about the task of compiling evidence for a religious hypothesis before the logically prior question of deciding what may count as evidence has even been considered, much less settled! Wilson is convinced that failure to clarify the precise meaning of religious ideas (which results from failing to consider what could count as evidence for verification or falsification purposes) has led religious thinkers into indefensible positions regarding the informative value of their statements.

There is, in Tillich's examination of the symbolic character of religious language, the presumption that all language is inadequate, hence "broken", in its capacity to inform us about the divine reality. Wilson, however, makes the provocative suggestion that even metaphorical religious discourse has meanings that are capable of empirical analysis and, perhaps, verification. The impassible gulf between the symbol and the symbolized in Tillich's view is only bridged by the courage and risk of faith; Wilson suggests that another bridge might be found between religious metaphor and the objects of experience to which the metaphor refers.

Hesse

*THE ADEQUACY OF RELIGIOUS LANGUAGE**

Govinda said: "It seems to me, Siddhartha, that you still like to jest a little. I believe you and know that you have not followed any teacher, but have you not yourself, if not a doctrine, certain thoughts? Have you not discovered certain knowledge yourself that has helped you to live? It would give me great pleasure if you would tell me something about this."

Siddhartha said: "Yes, I have had thoughts and knowledge here and there. Sometimes, for an hour or for a day, I have become aware of knowledge, just as one feels life in one's heart. I have had many thoughts, but it would be difficult for me to tell you about them. But this is one thought that has impressed me, Govinda. Wisdom is not communicable. The wisdom which a wise man tries to communicate always sounds foolish."

"Are you jesting?" asked Govinda.

"No, I am telling you what I have discovered. Knowledge can be communicated, but not wisdom. One can find it, live it, be fortified by it, do wonders through it, but one cannot communicate and teach it. I suspected this when I was still a youth and it was this that drove me away from teachers. There is one thought I have had, Govinda, which you will again think is a jest or folly: that is, in every truth the opposite is equally true. For example, a truth can only be expressed and enveloped in words if it is one-sided. Everything that is thought and expressed in words is one-sided, only half the truth; it all lacks totality, completeness, unity. When the Illustrious Buddha taught about the world, he had to divide it into Sansara and Nirvana, into illusion and truth, into suffering and salvation. One cannot do otherwise, there is no other method for those who teach. But the world itself, being in and around us, is never one-sided. Never is a man or a deed wholly Sansara or wholly Nirvana; never is a man wholly a saint or a sinner. This only seems so because we suffer the illusion that time is something real. Time is not real, Govinda. I have realized this repeatedly. And if time is not real, then the dividing line that seems to lie between this world and eternity, between suffering and bliss, between good and evil, is also an illusion."

"How is that?" asked Govinda, puzzled.

"Listen, my friend! I am a sinner and you are a sinner, but someday the sinner will be Brahma again, will someday attain Nirvana, will someday be-

---

* Hermann Hesse (1877–1962): Swiss novelist. This selection is an excerpt from Hesse's novel *Siddhartha*, which traces the quest of an Indian Brahmin for spiritual enlightenment. Nearly all of Hesse's novels center on the motifs of the journey of the spirit toward truth and self-identity. From Hermann Hesse, *Siddhartha*, translated by Hilda Rosner, pp. 143–148. Copyright 1951 by New Directions Publishing Corporation.

come a Buddha. Now this 'someday' is illusion; it is only a comparison. The sinner is not on the way to a Buddha-like state; he is not evolving, although our thinking cannot conceive things otherwise. No, the potential Buddha already exists in the sinner; his future is already there. The potential hidden Buddha must be recognized in him, in you, in everybody. The world, Govinda, is not imperfect or slowly evolving along a long path to perfection. No, it is perfect at every moment; every sin already carries grace within it, all small children are potential old men, all sucklings have death within them, all dying people—eternal life. It is not possible for one person to see how far another is on the way; the Buddha exists in the robber and dice player; the robber exists in the Brahmin. During deep meditation it is possible to dispel time, to see simultaneously all the past, present and future, and then everything is good, everything is perfect, everything is Brahmin. Therefore, it seems to me that everything that exists is good—death as well as life, sin as well as holiness, wisdom as well as folly. Everything is necessary, everything needs only my agreement, by assent, my loving understanding; then all is well with me and nothing can harm me. I learned through my body and soul that it was necessary for me to sin, that I needed lust, that I had to strive for property and experience nausea and the depths of despair in order to learn not to resist them, in order to learn to love the world, and no longer compare it with some kind of desired imaginary world, some imaginary vision of perfection, but to leave it as it is, to love it and be glad to belong to it. These, Govinda, are some of the thoughts that are in my mind."

Siddhartha bent down, lifted a stone from the ground and held it in his hand.

"This," he said, handling it, "is a stone, and within a certain length of time it will perhaps be soil and from the soil it will become plant, animal or man. Previously I should have said: This stone is just a stone; it has no value, it belongs to the world of Maya, but perhaps because within the cycle of change it can also become man and spirit, it is also of importance. That is what I should have thought. But now I think: This stone is stone; it is also animal, God and Buddha. I do not respect and love it because it was one thing and will become something else, but because it has already long been everything and always is everything. I love it just because it is a stone, because today and now it appears to me a stone. I see value and meaning in each one of its fine markings and cavities, in the yellow, in the grey, in the hardness and the sound of it when I knock it, in the dryness or dampness of its surface. There are stones that feel like oil or soap, that look like leaves or sand, and each one is different and worships Om in its own way; each one is Brahman. At the same time it is very much stone, oily or soapy, and that is just what pleases me and seems wonderful and worthy of worship. But I will say no more about it. Words do not express thoughts very well. They always become a little different immediately they are expressed, a little distorted, a little foolish. And yet it also pleases me and seems right that what is of value and wisdom to one man seems nonsense to another."

Govinda had listened in silence.

"Why did you tell me about the stone?" he asked hesitatingly after a pause.

"I did so unintentionally. But perhaps it illustrates that I just love the stone and the river and all these things that we see and from which we can learn. I can love a stone, Govinda, and a tree or a piece of bark. These are things and one can love things. But one cannot love words. Therefore teachings are of no use to me; they have no hardness, no softness, no colors, no corners, no smell, no taste—they have nothing but words. Perhaps that is what prevents you from finding peace, perhaps there are too many words, for even salvation and virtue. Sansara and Nirvana are only words, Govinda. Nirvana is not a thing; there is only the word Nirvana."

Govinda said: "Nirvana is not only a word, my friend; it is a thought."

Siddhartha continued: "It may be a thought, but I must confess, my friend, that I do not differentiate very much between thoughts and words. Quite frankly, I do not attach great importance to thoughts either. I attach more importance to things. For example, there was a man at this ferry who was my predecessor and teacher. He was a holy man who for many years believed only in the river and nothing else. He noticed that the river's voice spoke to him. The river seemed like a god to him and for many years he did not know that every wind, every cloud, every bird, every beetle is equally divine and knows and can teach just as well as the esteemed river. But when this holy man went off into the woods, he knew everything; he knew more than you and I, without teachers, without books, just because he believed in the river."

Tillich

RELIGIOUS SYMBOLS*

1. The Meaning of Symbol

Man's ultimate concern must be expressed symbolically, because symbolic language alone is able to express the ultimate. This statement demands explanation in several respects. In spite of the manifold research about the meaning and function of symbols which is going on in contemporary phi-

* Paul Tillich (1886–1965): America's foremost contemporary theologian. This selection is Chapter III entitled, "Symbols of Faith," in *Dynamics of Faith*. In this book, Tillich analyzes diverse interpretations of the meaning of faith and presents his own constructive alternative. He takes up such questions as the truth of faith, the life of faith, types of faith and so on. From Pp. 41–54, "Symbols of Faith" in *Dynamics of Faith* by Paul Tillich. Copyright © 1957 by Paul Tillich. Reprinted by permission of Harper & Row, New York and George Allen & Unwin Ltd., London.

losophy, every writer who uses the term "symbol" must explain his understanding of it.

Symbols have one characteristic in common with signs; they point beyond themselves to something else. The red sign at the street corner points to the order to stop the movement of cars at certain intervals. A red light and the stopping of cars have essentially no relation to each other, but conventionally they are united as long as the convention lasts. The same is true of letters and numbers and partly even words. They point beyond themselves to sounds and meanings. They are given this special function by convention within a nation or by international conventions, as the mathematical signs. Sometimes such signs are called symbols; but this is unfortunate because it makes the distinction between signs and symbols more difficult. Decisive is the fact that signs do not participate in the reality of that to which they point, while symbols do. Therefore, signs can be replaced for reasons of expediency or convention, while symbols cannot.

This leads to the second characteristic of the symbol: It participates in that to which it points: the flag participates in the power and dignity of the nation for which it stands. Therefore, it cannot be replaced except after an historic catastrophe that changes the reality of the nation which it symbolizes. An attack on the flag is felt as an attack on the majesty of the group in which it is acknowledged. Such an attack is considered blasphemy.

The third characteristic of a symbol is that it opens up levels of reality which otherwise are closed for us. All arts create symbols for a level of reality which cannot be reached in any other way. A picture and a poem reveal elements of reality which cannot be approached scientifically. In the creative work of art we encounter reality in a dimension which is closed for us without such works. The symbol's fourth characteristic not only opens up dimensions and elements of reality which otherwise would remain unapproachable but also unlocks dimensions and elements of our soul which correspond to the dimensions and elements of reality. A great play gives us not only a new vision of the human scene, but it opens up hidden depths of our own being. Thus we are able to receive what the play reveals to us in reality. There are within us dimensions of which we cannot become aware except through symbols, as melodies and rhythms in music.

Symbols cannot be produced intentionally—this is the fifth characteristic. They grow out of the individual or collective unconscious and cannot function without being accepted by the unconscious dimension of our being. Symbols which have an especially social function, as political and religious symbols, are created or at least accepted by the collective unconscious of the group in which they appear.

The sixth and last characteristic of the symbol is a consequence of the fact that symbols cannot be invented. Like living beings, they grow and they die. They grow when the situation is ripe for them, and they die when the situation changes. The symbol of the "king" grew in a special period of history, and it died in most parts of the world in our period. Symbols do not grow because people are longing for them, and they do not die because of scientific or practical criticism. They die because they can no longer produce response in the group where they originally found expression.

These are the main characteristics of every symbol. Genuine symbols are created in several spheres of man's cultural creativity. We have mentioned already the political and the artistic realm. We could add history and, above all, religion, whose symbols will be our particular concern.

2. Religious Symbols

We have discussed the meaning of symbols generally because, as we said, man's ultimate concern must be expressed symbolically! One may ask: Why can it not be expressed directly and properly? If money, success or the nation is someone's ultimate concern, can this not be said in a direct way without symbolic language? Is it not only in those cases in which the content of the ultimate concern is called "God" that we are in the realm of symbols? The answer is that everything which is a matter of unconditional concern is made into a god. If the nation is someone's ultimate concern, the name of the nation becomes a sacred name and the nation receives divine qualities which far surpass the reality of the being and functioning of the nation. The nation then stands for and symbolizes the true ultimate, but in an idolatrous way. Success as ultimate concern is not the natural desire of actualizing potentialities, but is readiness to sacrifice all other values of life for the sake of a position of power and social predominance. The anxiety about not being a success is an idolatrous form of the anxiety about divine condemnation. Success is grace; lack of success, ultimate judgment. In this way concepts designating ordinary realities become idolatrous symbols of ultimate concern.

The reason for this transformation of concepts into symbols is the character of ultimacy and the nature of faith. That which is the true ultimate transcends the realm of finite reality infinitely. Therefore, no finite reality can express it directly and properly. Religiously speaking, God transcends his own name. This is why the use of his name easily becomes an abuse or a blasphemy. Whatever we say about that which concerns us ultimately, whether or not we call it God, has a symbolic meaning. It points beyond itself while participating in that to which it points. In no other way can faith express itself adequately. The language of faith is the language of symbols. If faith were what we have shown that it is not, such an assertion could not be made. But faith, understood as the state of being ultimately concerned, has no language other than symbols. When saying this I always expect the question: Only a symbol? He who asks this question shows that he has not understood the difference between signs and symbols nor the power of symbolic language, which surpasses in quality and strength the power of any nonsymbolic language. One should never say "only a symbol," but one should say "not less than a symbol." With this in mind we can now describe the different kinds of symbols of faith.

The fundamental symbol of our ultimate concern is God. It is always present in any act of faith, even if the act of faith includes the denial of God. Where there is ultimate concern, God can be denied only in the name of God. One God can deny the other one. Ultimate concern cannot deny its own character as ultimate. Therefore, it affirms what is meant by the word "God." Atheism, consequently, can only mean the attempt to remove any ultimate concern—to remain unconcerned about the meaning of one's existence. Indifference toward the ultimate question is the only imaginable form of atheism. Whether it is possible is a problem which must remain unsolved at this point. In any case, he who denies God as a matter of ultimate concern affirms God, because he affirms ultimacy in his concern. God is the fundamental symbol for what concerns us ultimately. Again it would be completely wrong to ask: So God is nothing but a symbol? Because the next question has to be: A symbol for what? And then the answer would be: For God! God is symbol for God. This means that in the notion of God we must distinguish two elements: the element of ultimacy, which is a matter of immediate experience and not symbolic in itself, and the element of concreteness, which is taken from our ordinary experience and symbolically applied to God. The man whose ultimate concern is a sacred tree has both the ultimacy of concern and the concreteness of the tree which symbolizes his relation to the ultimate. The man who adores Apollo is ultimately concerned, but not in an abstract way. His ultimate concern is symbolized in the divine figure of Apollo. The man who glorifies Jahweh, the God of the Old Testament, has both an ultimate concern and a concrete image of what concerns him ultimately. This is the meaning of the seemingly cryptic statement that God is the symbol of God. In this qualified sense God is the fundamental and universal content of faith.

It is obvious that such an understanding of the meaning of God makes the discussions about the existence or non-existence of God meaningless. It is meaningless to question the ultimacy of an ultimate concern. This element in the idea of God is in itself certain. The symbolic expression of this element varies endlessly through the whole history of mankind. Here again it would be meaningless to ask whether one or another of the figures in which an ultimate concern is symbolized does "exist." If "existence" refers to something which can be found within the whole of reality, no divine being exists. The question is not this, but: which of the innumerable symbols of faith is most adequate to the meaning of faith? In other words, which symbol of ultimacy expresses the ultimate without idolatrous elements? This is the problem, and not the so-called "existence of God"— which is in itself an impossible combination of words. God as the ultimate in man's ultimate concern is more certain than any other certainty, even that of oneself. God as symbolized in a divine figure is a matter of daring faith, of courage and risk.

God is the basic symbol of faith, but not the only one. All the qualities we attribute to him, power, love, justice, are taken from finite experiences and applied symbolically to that which is beyond finitude and infinity. If faith calls God "almighty," it uses the human experience of power in order to symbolize the content of its infinite concern, but it does not describe a highest being who can do as he pleases. So it is with all the other qualities and with all the actions, past, present and future, which men attribute to God. They are symbols taken from our daily experience, and not information about what God did once upon a time or will do sometime in the future. Faith is not the belief in such stories, but it is the acceptance of symbols that express our ultimate concern in terms of divine actions.

Another group of symbols of faith are manifestations of the divine in things and events, in persons and communities, in words and documents. This whole realm of sacred objects is a treasure of symbols. Holy things are not holy in themselves, but they point beyond themselves to the source of all holiness, that which is of ultimate concern.

3. Symbols and Myths

The symbols of faith do not appear in isolation. They are united in "stories of the gods," which is the meaning of the Greek word "mythos"— myth. The gods are individualized figures, analogous to human personalities, sexually differentiated, descending from each other, related to each other in love and struggle, producing world and man, acting in time and space. They participate in human greatness and misery, in creative and destructive works. They give to man cultural and religious traditions, and defend these sacred rites. They help and threaten the human race, especially some families, tribes or nations. They appear in epiphanies and incarnations, establish sacred places, rites and persons, and thus create a cult. But they themselves are under the command and threat of a fate which is beyond everything that is. This is mythology as developed most impressively in ancient Greece. But many of these characteristics can be found in every mythology. Usually the mythological gods are not equals. There is a hierarchy, at the top of which is a ruling god, as in Greece; or a trinity of them, as in India; or a duality of them, as in Persia. There are savior-gods who mediate between the highest gods and man, sometimes sharing the suffering and death of man in spite of their essential immortality. This is the world of the myth, great and strange, always changing but fundamentally the same: man's ultimate concern symbolized in divine figures and actions. Myths are symbols of faith combined in stories about divine-human encounters.

Myths are always present in every act of faith, because the language of faith is the symbol. They are also attacked, criticized, and transcended in each of the great religions of mankind. The reason for this criticism is the very nature of the myth. It uses material from our ordinary experience. It puts the stories of the gods into the framework of time and space although it belongs to the nature of the ultimate to be beyond time and space. Above all, it divides the divine into several figures, removing ultimacy from each of them without removing their claim to ultimacy. This inescapably leads to conflicts of ultimate claims, able to destroy life, society, and consciousness.

The criticism of the myth first rejects the division of the divine and goes beyond it to one God, although in different ways according to the different types of religion. Even one God is an object of mythological language, and if spoken about is drawn into the framework of time and space. Even he loses his ultimacy if made to be the content of concrete concern. Consequently, the criticism of the myth does not end with rejection of the polytheistic mythology.

Monotheism also falls under the criticism of the myth. It needs, as one says today, "demythologization." This word has been used in connection with the elaboration of the mythical elements in stories and symbols of the Bible, both of the Old and the New Testaments—stories like those of the Paradise, of the fall of Adam, of the great Flood, of the Exodus from Egypt, of the virgin birth of the Messiah, of many of his miracles, of his resurrection and ascension, of his expected return as the judge of the universe. In short, all the stories in which divine-human interactions are told are considered as mythological in character, and objects of demythologization. What does this negative and artificial term mean? It must be accepted and supported if it points to the necessity of recognizing a symbol as a symbol and a myth as a myth. It must be attacked and rejected if it means the removal of symbols and myths together. Such an attempt is the third step in the criticism of the myth. It is an attempt which never can be successful, because symbol and myth are forms of the human consciousness which are always present. One can replace one myth by another, but one cannot remove the myth from man's spiritual life. For the myth is the combination of symbols of our ultimate concern.

A myth which is understood as a myth, but not removed or replaced, can be called a "broken myth." Christianity denies by its very nature any unbroken myth, because its presupposition is the first commandment: the affirmation of the ultimate as ultimate and the rejection of any kind of idolatry. All mythological elements in the Bible, and doctrine and liturgy should be recognized as mythological, but they should be maintained in their symbolic form and not be replaced by scientific substitutes. For there is no substitute for the use of symbols and myths: they are the language of faith.

The radical criticism of the myth is due to the fact that the primitive mythological consciousness resists the attempt to interpret the myth of myth. It is afraid of every act of demythologization. It believes that the broken myth is deprived of its truth and of its convincing power. Those who live in an unbroken mythological world feel safe and certain. They resist, often fanatically, any attempt to introduce an element of uncertainty by "breaking the myth," namely, by making conscious its symbolic character. Such resistance is supported by authoritarian systems, religious or political, in order to give security to the people under their control and unchallenged power to those who exercise the control. The resistance against demythologization expresses itself in "literalism." The symbols and myths are understood in their immediate meaning. The material, taken from nature and history, is used in its proper sense. The character of the symbol to point beyond itself to something else is disregarded. Creation is taken as a magic act which happened once upon a time. The fall of Adam is localized on a special geographical point and attributed to a human individual. The virgin birth of the Messiah is understood in biological terms, resurrection and ascension as physical events, the second coming of Christ as a telluric, or cosmic, catastrophe. The presupposition of such literalism is that God is a being, acting in time and space, dwelling in a special place, affecting the course of events and being affected by them like any other being in the universe. Literalism deprives God of his ultimacy and, religiously speaking, of his majesty. It draws him down to the level of that which is not ultimate, the finite and conditional. In the last analysis it is not rational criticism of the myth which is decisive but the inner religious criticism. Faith, if it takes its symbols literally, becomes idolatrous! It calls something ultimate which is less than ultimate. Faith, conscious of the symbolic character of its symbols, gives God the honor which is due him.

One should distinguish two stages of literalism, the natural and the reactive. The natural stage of literalism is that in which the mythical and the literal are indistinguishable. The primitive period of individuals and groups consists in the inability to separate the creations of symbolic imagination from the facts which can be verified through observation and experiment. This stage has a full right of its own and should not be disturbed, either in individuals or in groups, up to the moment when man's questioning mind breaks the natural acceptance of the mythological visions as literal. If, however, this moment has come, two ways are possible. The one is to replace the unbroken by the broken myth. It is the objectively demanded way, although it is impossible for many people who prefer the repression of their questions to the uncertainty which appears with the breaking of the myth. They are forced into the second stage of literalism, the conscious one, which is aware of the questions but represses them, half consciously, half unconsciously. The tool of repression is usually an acknowledged authority with sacred qualities like the Church or the Bible, to which one owes unconditional surrender. This stage is still justifiable, if the questioning power is very weak and can easily be answered. It is unjustifiable if a mature mind is broken in its personal center by political or psychological methods, split in his unity, and hurt in his integrity. The enemy of a critical theology is not natural literalism but conscious literalism with repression of and aggression toward autonomous thought.

Symbols of faith cannot be replaced by other symbols, such as artistic ones, and they cannot be removed by scientific criticism. They have a genuine standing in the human mind, just as science and art have. Their symbolic character is their truth and their power. Nothing less than symbols and myths can express our ultimate concern.

One more question arises, namely, whether myths are able to express every kind of ultimate concern. For example, Christian theologians argue that the word "myth" should be reserved for natural myths in which repetitive natural processes, such as the seasons, are understood in their ultimate meaning. They believe that if the world is seen as a historical process with beginning, end and center, as in Christianity and Judaism, the term "myth" should not be used. This would radically reduce the realm in which the term would be applicable. Myth could not be understood as the language of our ultimate concern, but only as a discarded idiom of this language. Yet history proves that there are not only natural myths but also historical myths. If the earth is seen as the battleground of two divine powers, as in ancient Persia, this is an historical myth. If the God of creation selects and guides a nation through history toward an end which transcends all history, this is an historical myth. If the Christ—a transcendent, divine being—appears in the fullness of time, lives, dies and is resurrected, this is an historical myth. Christianity is superior to those religions which are bound to a natural myth. But Christianity speaks the mythological language like every other religion. It is a broken myth, but it is a myth: otherwise Christianity would not be an expression of ultimate concern.

Wilson

*VERIFICATION AND RELIGIOUS LANGUAGE**

Let us begin by taking a superficial glance at the language of religion. In religious works of literature, creeds, ritual, and so on we come across different types of sentences which have (or appear to have) different uses. On this superficial level, we can list these without difficulty:

1. Sentences expressing commands, injunctions, exhortations, wishes, etc., such as "Thou shalt love the Lord thy God," "Let us love one another," and so on.

2. Sentences expressing moral views, such as "Brethren, these things ought not so to be," "It is not good for man to be alone," etc.

3. Sentences expressing factual truths, often historical, such as "Christ was born in Bethlehem," "Mary was a virgin," etc.

4. Sentences giving information about the meanings of words, expressing analytic truths. A statement like "A sacrament is an outward and visible sign of an inward and spiritual grace" is analytic, and should be taken as informing the hearer about the meaning of "sacrament."

5. Sentences which appear to be informative, but informative about the supernatural or metaphysical rather than the natural or physical world. For instance, "God exists," "Christ is the Son of God," and so on.

* John Wilson (1928–   ): English philosopher. The selection is from Chapter I of Wilson's *Language and Christian Belief*. In this book, Wilson explores the insights gained into Christian doctrine by the application of the methodology of linguistic analysis. From *Language and Christian Belief* by John Wilson. Copyright © 1958 by St. Martin's Press, Inc. Reprinted by permission of St. Martin's Press, Inc., New York and Macmillan & Co., Ltd., London.

So far the philosopher has not yet got to work. But when he does, it is likely that he will be tempted to make two changes in our scheme above. The first does not concern us here: it involves merging what I have called "moral views" with "commands, injunctions, etc.," at least to some extent. The second is to attempt to distribute sentences in (5), metaphysical sentences, among the other classes, in such a way that the possibility of supernaturally informative sentences is excluded. He could say, for instance, that some of these sentences are really analytic, and others really commands: this is one of the commonest ways in which this particular move is made.

Let us look, for example, at one of the ablest attempts to make this kind of move which has recently appeared. It has been made by Professor Braithwaite. He regards religious belief as primarily the intention or resolution to adopt a certain way of life, this intention being supported by what he calls "stories": that is, what appear to be empirical statements of fact, statements about the world, which are however not verifiable in the way that ordinary empirical statements are verifiable. (Presumably the only sense in which they could be said to be verifiable at all is the sense in which we say that a statement in a story or work of fiction is verifiable, i.e. within the context of the work as a whole.) These statements are believed because the religious believer finds them psychologically helpful, inasmuch as they bolster up his intention to adopt the way of life which he has chosen. But they are not central to religious belief; and we should verify whether a man is to be regarded as adhering to or following a certain religion, not by seeing how many "stories" or how much of any "story" he accepts as true, but by seeing how far he genuinely tries to carry out his intention to adopt a religious way of life. This intention, according to Braithwaite, has a great deal in common with what is expressed in ethical statements. Religion, in fact, is an ethical outlook bolstered up with "stories."

I have chosen to mention this particular attempt to deal with religious statements because it is typical as well as skilful. Its typicality consists in trying to show that metaphysical statements, statements about the supernatural are other than they appear: in particular, that they cannot be regarded as genuinely informative. This in itself is not a misconceived attempt: plenty of statements are not what they appear. But it is necessary to be very careful in assigning statements to classes in this way; and I do not think that writers of this kind have always kept a firm grasp of certain necessary points in connection with the use of language.

The most important of these is the point that it is primarily people who mean, and not statements. Language does not exist in the abstract, but is used by people with certain intentions, who desire to communicate. The appropriate question, therefore, is really not "What does such-and-such a statement mean?" but "What does so-and-so mean by this statement?" The same point applies to verification: we should ask not "How is this statement verified?" but "How do people who make this statement verify it?" This point may seem trivial. But to appreciate it entails appreciating that we may get different answers to our questions. It is easy to assume that statements have single meanings and single methods of verification; and though this may be generally true of other informative statements, it may not be true of metaphysical statements. Indeed, the answers which are given to a question about the meaning of a religious belief show a remarkable variety of opinion, even amongst those who share a common religion.

It would be erroneous to suppose, therefore, that because there is no standard meaning or verification for religious statements they are meaningless and unverifiable. Nearly all philosophers today admit that they are meaningful; indeed, it was never possible to hold that they were meaningless without adopting a monopolistic and unfairly restricted sense of "meaning." But it is an equal mistake to suppose that because all religious believers are not agreed upon what is to count as evidence for the truth of their statements, therefore nothing counts or could ever count. It may not be at all clear how these statements are to be verified or falsified, but this does not entail that they are not verifiable or falsifiable in principle. Neither does it entail that they are not informative.

In other words, the religious believer may meet the cross-questioning of the philosopher with a straight *nolle prosequi*. He may say simply, "This statement is intended by me as informative." The philosopher cannot sensibly reply, "No, it's not." He may point to a lack of agreed meaning and verification, show that most if not all other informative statements have agreed meaning and verification, and so on, but he cannot deny the speaker's intention: and he cannot show that the intention cannot in principle be fulfilled. For it may be possible to provide meaning and verification for the statement, or to agree on them. What the philosopher can try to do, however, is to show that whatever the intentions of the speaker, the statement is not actually informative. He will try to do this by showing that being informative, in the case of all statements, depends on the existence of agreed verification.

The religious believer is here faced with two alternatives. He can either say that his statements are not, after all, informative, thereby evading the attack altogether: or say that established meaning and verification is not in fact necessary for informative statements, thereby standing up to it. This is the crux of the matter, the rock which all metaphysics and religious belief must either escape or be wrecked on. And it seems to me tragic that religious believers do not realise that neither of the two alternatives I have mentioned are at all satisfactory.

First, the attempt to evade the attack. The attempt must fail, because it is these allegedly informative assertions which give to any religion its importance and distinctive character. Statements which lay down language-rules ("A sacrament is an outward and visible sign of an inward and spiritual grace"), historical statements ("The man Jesus Christ was crucified in Palestine during the reign of Tiberius"), exhortations ("Brethren, let us love one another"), and moral injunctions ("Judge not"), all have obvious uses; but they would, none of them, have any peculiarly religious interest unless backed by a number of assertions about the supernatural. Thus, we are only interested in defining "sacrament" clearly because it is held that the Son of God instituted certain sacraments: historical statements about Jesus concern us only because we believe certain metaphysical statements about Him: and exhortations and injunctions have religious force only because they derive from supernatural fact—hence we see arguments like: "Let us love one another, for love is of God." Most Christians, except under philosophical cross-examination, would surely regard the "good news" of the Gospel as factually informative. To say "There is a God" is to state a fact: God is real in the same *sense*, though not in the same way, as physical objects are real:[1] and the information which religious beliefs contain is not only supposed to be genuine, but of the utmost importance in the conduct of our lives.

The second alternative, that of claiming that statements can be informative without being verifiable in the sense required by philosophers, is more difficult to prove unsatisfactory. To begin with, many believers would hold that there was evidence for their beliefs. For some Christians, for instance, the supposed majesty and order of the natural universe is a proof of God's existence: to others, the life and personality of Christ is verification for His divinity: and so on. They might also admit that certain things counted against their beliefs: that the existence of pain and evil, for instance, counted against their belief in a loving and omnipotent God. Why is it, then, that philosophers still wish to insist that religious statements may not be verifiable? What precisely is this test of verification which they claim that all informative statements must pass?

The philosopher's point may be better made (as one or two philosophers have themselves suggested) in terms of falsification rather than verification; and the principle may be stated thus: "If a statement is not decisively falsifiable, in principle as well as in practice, then the statement is not informative." Of course this statement is itself somewhat vague: we may wonder what the phrase "in principle" means, for instance. But the reasons for making it are tolerably clear. If you are trying to tell somebody that something is the case, this logically excludes certain other things being the case. For example, suppose I say, "There is a tiger in the room." Asked what evidence there was for this statement, or how it could be verified, I should mention pieces of evidence like there being a growling noise, a large striped animal with teeth and four legs, and so on. To say "there is a tiger" entails there being a large striped animal, etc., because they are part of the meaning of the statement. The statement is vacuous without them. "There is a tiger" is only informative if there is actually a large striped animal. Consequently, it must be decisively falsifiable: falsifiable, that is, if the pieces of evidence could not be found. Of course, the absence of only some of the evidence would not falsify it decisively: the growl might be absent, for instance, and there might still be a tiger. But there comes a time when the absence of

[1] This point is of central importance to my thesis: I have tried to expand and elucidate it on pp. 13–14.

evidence is overwhelming. An animal with three legs and no growl might still be a tiger; but an animal with no legs at all and a trunk could not be.

Moreover, statements are informative to the same degree as they are falsifiable or vulnerable. For the more precise information they give, the easier it is to upset them. "There is something in the room" is very uninformative and not very vulnerable: "there is an animal in the room" slightly more informative, but *ipso facto* more vulnerable: because more criteria have to be satisfied for "animal" than for "something"—the statement has to pass more verification-tests. "There is a six-foot tiger exactly in the middle of the room, possessing only four teeth and pointing its tail consistently at an angle of seventy-eight degrees" is very precise, and very vulnerable. To put this more generally, any informative statement specifies that a part of reality is such-and-such; and the more precise the specification—the more the specification specifies, so to speak—then the more things there might be wrong with it.

If, then, a statement's truth is consistent with any evidence that might be forthcoming, it cannot be at all informative. Making a statement of this kind would be like saying: "There is a tiger in the room, and nothing could count as evidence which decisively falsifies this truth." Of course if there actually is a tiger, then the statement cannot actually be decisively falsified: for it is true. But it is still decisively falsifiable as a statement: for there is no logical compulsion about its being true. To say "nothing could count as evidence against the existence of God" might mean "since God exists, there can be no decisive evidence against it": but it might also mean that the statement "God exists" is logically exempt from decisive evidence against it. And if this is true, then it cannot be informative. For saying "God exists" is a particular instance of saying "Such-and-such is the case"; and it is always logically possible that such-and-such is not the case. Whether it is or not precisely constitutes the test which any informative statement must pass.

Since therefore neither of these two alternatives is satisfactory, religious believers have to face up to the problem of providing their religious statements with established meaning and verification. In view of the points mentioned, they should be anxious rather than unwilling to make it clear what would decisively falsify the statements, since their informativeness corresponds to their falsifiability. Just how this process of giving verification to religious statements is to be gone through, I shall endeavour to explain in the next essay. So far as we are here concerned, the point I wish to establish is that our fifth class of statements—those apparently informative about the supernatural world—must be claimed as genuinely informative, with all that this implies. If they are to be merged with any other class, it must be with the third: those expressing factual truths, or what are generally known as empirical statements.

Providing statements with verification, however, is not an arbitrary process; and there is one further point which must be allowed to the philosopher. Informative statements inform us about something in our experience, and must therefore be verifiable ultimately by our experience. I do not mean, of course, that they are about something which we are actually touching, seeing, feeling, etc., or which we have touched, seen, felt, etc. "There is a tiger in the room" is informative even though we may never have seen a tiger. But they must be about something of which we could in principle have experience: for if they were not, they would not inform us about anything at all which had any connection with our lives and interests. To say "There is a tiger in the room" would be senseless, and certainly not informative, if I added "but nobody could ever have any experience of such a thing." The whole interest of making such a statement is that, if we enter the room, we can expect to experience certain things—growls, stripes, being eaten, and so on. Statements which are of public interest and are informative, like this one, are based on the experiences of some people, and on the possibility that other people may also have similar experiences. This is the purpose of informative communication.

Past writers have attempted to discover many loopholes which might enable them to avoid this point also; and it is impossible to demonstrate that all of them are culs-de-sac. A typical loophole is to say that God "transcends" human experience, and that therefore we cannot expect to verify statements about God by human experience; though of course the first of these two statements need not be understood in such a way that the second follows from it. But the same dilemma presents itself. Either "God" stands for something at least partly within our experience, so that statements with the word "God" in them are to that extent experimentally verifiable: or else "God" does not stand for something within our actual or potential experience, in which case (to put it bluntly) statements about God can have no possible interest for us, and may well be meaningless. Of course this dilemma could be put more forcibly. We could say that if a descriptive word is supposed to refer to something which could not be experienced, then it seems doubtful whether it describes anything at all: since to be a thing involves the capability of being experienced, and can only be known through experience.

Nor need the Christian attempt to take evasive action over the issue of verification in any other way. Philosophers have been concerned to clarify the logical characteristics of informative assertions by various observations. They have said that they must be meaningful and verifiable: that we must know what would count as evidence for or against them: that their verification must ultimately be conducted by somebody's experience: that unless these conditions were satisfied they could not qualify for truth or falsehood, and so on. All this can be accepted; and there seems little use in trying to break out of the circle of these observations at any point, e.g. by saying that Christian assertions are "true" in the sense of "illuminating," or can be "verified" "by the Christian way of life itself." For though the points being made here may be valid and important, they are insufficient; because Christian assertions are also supposed, by Christians themselves, to be true and verifiable in the (possibly more usual) sense in which philosophers have used these words.

This attempt to put religious assertions in the same logical boat, as it were, with straightforward empirical statements looks naïve and old-fashioned, because it suggests a naïve and old-fashioned view of religious language. We are accustomed to regard religious language as inadequate for its purposes; in particular, it is said to be "metaphor" or "analogy." When challenged at every point, the metaphor becomes "eroded" or "evaporates," until nothing may be left. Hence the Christian and the philosopher seem both driven to the view that the metaphorical assertions cannot be informative, and must be in a different logical category from empirical statements, with a different sort of meaning and verification, if indeed they have any verification at all. But this is deceptive; because a metaphor may assert something quite as precise and informative as any other assertion. A word used metaphorically or analogically may lose something of its straightforward meaning; but it may gain some other significance. For example, "sugar is sweet" may be a straightforward empirical assertion, and "Mary is sweet" a metaphor; but it would be wrong to suppose that what we are saying about Mary is less definite or meaningful than what we are saying about sugar. The word "sweet" simply means different things, and has a different method of verification, in either case. This might well be true of religious assertions. They are expressed in language borrowed from non-religious contexts, just as "Mary is sweet" uses a word borrowed from taste-experience; but this language may well have a new and precise significance, though of course the fact that the same word is used suggests that there are points of contact between the two uses—points which might help to make the new use more comprehensible to someone who did not understand the metaphorical meaning.

One essential task which religious believers have to perform, therefore, is to give the individual words in religious language a clear and unambiguous descriptive meaning where such meaning is required. This applies both to what we might call technical religious words—words like "God," "soul," "grace," and so on—and also to words used metaphorically—"love," "father," "kingdom," etc. Hitherto many believers have clung desperately to these words, but have been more able to say what they do not mean than what they do. Yet if religious language is ever to be genuinely and importantly informative, it is important that the criteria for the use of these words should be clear. If this task is not achieved, we shall be reduced to saying, as the Vedantist says when asked to describe his deity, "Not this, not this."

To many people this might seem to imply that God is an object, much like a table or an elephant, Who can be immediately and wholly comprehended by experience: the only slight difference being that a different kind of experience is required. Yet this is plainly absurd; and a God of this kind is not the sort of God in which anybody believes. But we must be careful to understand the point. I have said earlier in this chapter that God is real in the same sense, though not in the same way, that physical objects are real. He must be real in the same sense: for the word "real" has, in fact, only one sense—either something is real and exists, or it is unreal and does not exist. "Real" and "exists" are definitely not ambiguous words. But He is not (putting it roughly) real in the same *way*, because He is not the same sort of thing as a table or an elephant: indeed, we might say that He is not a *thing* at all, and certainly that He is not an object. Briefly, then, my contention is that if God is real and exists, the unambiguous logic and language of statements about existence, and the verification needed for these statements, must apply to God as much as to anything else, for these are part and parcel of what we mean by words like "exist" and "real;" but this is not to deny that much of His nature may be mysterious and uncomprehended by men. In much the same way, we might hold that love, or Martians, or the fourth dimension exist and are real: we might be able to give these words and phrases clear and unambiguous descriptive meanings and verification-methods: but they might still be very different from other things, highly mysterious, and largely uncomprehended.

Instead of the Vedantist's "Not this, not this", Christians must be able to say, "At least this, and at least this." They must be able to assert definitely about God, whilst admitting that there is far more to be known about Him than we can perhaps ever hope to know. Moreover, as we come to learn more about God, there is nothing in logic to prevent our expanding the meaning of the word "God". In just such a way the word "desire" has, since Freudian psychology, become expanded to include the concept of unconscious desires. In the light of new experience, words change their meaning in order to incorporate and communicate the experience. A due observance of logic, therefore, does nothing to remove the mystery of God on which Christians rightly insist; but it does serve the useful purpose of reminding us that if we are to talk meaningfully about God at any particular time, we must know what the word "God" is agreed to mean at that time, and that we can ultimately know this only by reference to experience.

Another and equally important task for believers is to adopt a firm and unambiguous classification of the statements and sentences in their religion. Much that is spoken and written about religion is vitiated by the absence of such a classification; and it is particularly difficult for non-believers to achieve a firm grasp of the logical structure of religious doctrine. It is annoying, for instance, to argue at length about whether the soul is immortal, only to find after a time that the word "soul" is being used to mean "the immortal part of man". This of course makes the statement "The soul is immortal" analytic or tautologous, and therefore not empirically informative. In trying to assess the truth of a complex metaphysical system, such as the doctrines of the Roman church, it is essential to be clear about which statements are supposed to be informative and verifiable, and which are supposed to follow by deductive arguments from other statements. For example, if we were intended to accept a number of statements on the authority of Christ, the Bible, the Church or some other source, we should be particularly interested in verifying the statements which were relevant to showing that source to be reliable, and not waste time in examining the statements deduced from its reliability.

This task of establishing meaning and verification, and classifying statements in religious belief according to their logic, has hardly been started. Hitherto Christian apologists have been chiefly interested in trying to collect and assess evidence for their beliefs, not realising the importance of the (logically prior) question of what is to count as evidence. Until this question is settled, it is unlikely that many people will be convinced by this collected "evidence": for it may not be evidence to them at all. One cannot tell whether something is evidence for a statement or not unless one first knows what sort of statement it is supposed to be, and what sorts of things count as evidence for it. And it is this lack of clarity, if I may be permitted to conclude with a sociological sidelight, which has engendered a situation in which many intelligent people are now neither convinced of, nor hostile to, Christian belief, but merely uninterested in it.

Chapter 11

Religious knowledge

The transition from an interest in the nature and function of religious discourse to the question of religious knowledge is natural. While religious language obviously serves many purposes, among which are the hortatory and confessional, one of its principal functions is to convey knowledge about religious realities, whether those realities be historical events, acts of divine beings, or descriptions of the nature of deity. Is the mode of religious cognition, in principle, radically different from other ways in which man knows?

What, then, is religious knowledge? What is its origin and how is it to be distinguished from mere belief? Can we have, through religious consciousness or faith, a revelation of an objective religious reality just as verifiable as the knowledge we have of physical objects through perception? Certainly with regard to our perceptual experience, we can, ordinarily, reach some public consensus concerning the particular perceptual characteristics of the object confronting us. However, even casual examination of the knowledge claims made for religious objects reveals that no such consensus exists with respect to their nature or existence. Nevertheless, at the core of the religious life is the belief that religious objects are known, in some manner and to some degree, and that such knowledge as men have of divine reality can perhaps be meaningfully stated and communicated.

It is through the "knowledge claims" of religious persons that the worldviews of religion are articulated and made accessible to rational investigation. Attempts to insulate these claims from the icy blasts of reflective doubt and criticism are questionable undertakings. Because a religion purports to answer questions relating to the total meaning of human life and experience, it is essential that we face the question: "Is this religion true?" If the claims of a religious belief are true, then what evidence substantiates religious knowledge? In considering this question, the more general question, "what constitutes knowledge and warrants the assertion of its presence?," cannot be avoided.

St. Thomas Aquinas regarded the roles of reason and faith in the attainment of religious knowledge as sharply distinct. Philosophy and the natural sciences depend solely upon the natural function of reason, but theology receives its basic principles from divine revelation which is apprehended only through faith. A theologian may use the power of reason and its forms in an attempt to explain and clarify revealed truths, but the use of reason in the service of faith is restricted to an explanatory role. No application of reason to religious truths revealed by faith can result in an extension of our knowledge of divine reality. The fundamental truths of religion are not arrived at by a process of human reasoning; they are never conclusions to rational argument. Truths revealed to faith are apprehended by man in the form appropriate to his understanding, namely in the form of propositions. Faith, therefore, involves the assent of the intellect to that which is believed, even though the assent of the intellect in this case does not result from its adherence to the rules of logic. Belief is the acceptance of truths on authority by faith, whereas knowing is always the result of rational demonstration. The origin of knowledge by faith is Divine revelation wherein God moves men "inwardly by grace."

The discussion in the symposium entitled, "Theology and Falsification," is focused upon the nature of religious assertions and the problem of their cognitive import. In that symposium, Antony Flew is sceptical about the meaningfulness of religious statements on the grounds that religious statements do not seem to deny any assertion regarding observable matters of fact. His general point is that if religious assertions affirm that some definite state of affairs is true, then, in principle, assertions about matters of fact contrary to the religious assertions would qualify as denials of the religious assertions. Flew suspects, however, that, for the theologian, nothing empirical is denied by religious statements. Hence, religious assertions really don't affirm anything at all about matters of fact; they thus have no cognitive meaning.

Flew sets the basic problem with which the symposium deals. R. M. Hare contributes his conception of "bliks" (fundamental convictions) as an alternative way of understanding the nature of religious doctrines. Hare does not take religious propositions to be explanations or hypotheses in the scientific sense. Basil Mitchell argues that religious beliefs are intended as assertions about matters of fact, and, in opposition to Flew, insists that theologians do recognize that certain empirical evidence counts against their beliefs. However, because the religious person makes his assertion from within the circle of faith, he will not accept the notion that anything counts decisively against his beliefs. Mitchell argues that religious beliefs do make a difference in a man's experience and behavior, and that his experience, in turn, effects his religion.

Crombie's essay is an excellent summary of the nature of the problem discussed by Flew, Hare, and Mitchell, as well as an attempt to criticize the positions they develop while advancing his own view of the function and cognitive import of religious statements. Crombie does not think that religious assertions are literally descriptive of objective matters of fact, but rather that they function like parables which operate as meaningful pointers to a divine reality beyond the scope of our experience and comprehension. The religious person knows the meaning of the statements from within the context of the parable and is convinced that they have cognitive meaning within that framework. If pressed for justification for his faith, the religious man, says Crombie, falls back upon some authority, such as revelation, which guarantees that his parables do somehow apply to divine reality.

Suppose, however, that the question of religious truth is not a matter for objective determination at all, but rather, as Kierkegaard claims, a process of utmost inwardness and passion. Under those circumstances, the search for objective proofs of religious knowledge is both futile and misguided. Indeed, Kierkegaard seems to put greater emphasis upon the *how* of religious faith, what he terms the "approximation" process, than upon the object that faith has in view. In such a view, truth becomes a function of the internal character of a person's life rather than a quality of a judgment or proposition. Thus, Kierkegaard challenges the traditional assumption that the question of truth centers in the relationship between propositions and the objects to which they refer. The center of focus in Kierkegaard shifts to the mode of the relationship that the existing person has to the object of his concern, that is, to the nature of his subjectivity. Truth becomes, thereby, an intensely personal and individual matter with the corresponding loss of its traditional universal and communal elements.

Aquinas
FAITH AND REASON*

[Q. 1] Second Article
Whether the Object of Faith Is Something Complex, Such as a Proposition?

We proceed thus to the Second Article:—

Objection 1. It would seem that the object of faith is not something complex such as a proposition. For the object of faith is the First Truth, as was stated above. Now the First Truth is something simple. Therefore the object of faith is not something complex.

Obj. 2. Further, The exposition of faith is contained in the symbol. Now the symbol does not contain propositions, but things; for it is not stated therein that God is almighty, but: *I believe in God . . . almighty.* Therefore the object of faith is not a proposition but a thing.

Obj. 3. Further, Faith is succeeded by vision, according to *1 Cor.* xiii. 12: *We see now through a glass in a dark manner, but then face to face. Now I know in part, but then I shall know even as I am known.* But the object of

---

* St. Thomas Aquinas (1224–1274): Dominican friar and medieval philosopher and theologian. These selections, taken from Aquinas' greatest work, *Summa Theologica,* II–II, Questions 1, 2, 4 and 6, are concerned fundamentally with the relations of faith to knowledge. *Summa Theologica* is Aquinas' systematic treatment of all theological questions from the point of view of his interpretation of Christian truth. From BASIC WRITINGS OF SAINT THOMAS AQUINAS, Volumes I and II, edited by Anton C. Pegis. Copyright 1945 by Random House, Inc. Reprinted by permission of Random House, Inc., New York and Burns & Oates Ltd., London.

the heavenly vision is something simple, for it is the divine essence. Therefore the faith of the wayfarer is also.

On the contrary, Faith is a mean between science and opinion. Now the mean is in the same genus as the extremes. Since, then, science and opinion are about propositions, it seems that faith is likewise about propositions; so that its object is something complex.

I answer that, The thing known is in the knower according to the mode of the knower. Now the mode proper to the human intellect is to know the truth by composition and division, as was stated in the First Part. Hence things that are simple in themselves are known by the intellect with a certain complexity, just as on the other hand the divine intellect knows, without any complexity, things that are complex in themselves.

Accordingly, the object of faith may be considered in two ways. First, as regards the thing itself which is believed, and thus the object of faith is something simple, namely, the thing itself about which we have faith; secondly, on the part of the believer, and in this respect the object of faith is something complex, such as a proposition.

Hence in the past both opinions have been held with a certain amount of truth.

Reply Obj. 1. This argument considers the object of faith on the part of the thing believed.

Reply Obj. 2. The symbol mentions the things about which faith is, in so far as the act of the believer is terminated in them, as is evident from the manner of speaking about them. Now the act of the believer does not terminate in a proposition, but in a thing. For we do not form propositions, except in order to have knowledge about things through their means; and this is true of faith as well as of science.

Reply Obj. 3. The object of the heavenly vision will be the First Truth seen in itself, according to *1 John* iii. 2: *We know that when He shall appear, we shall be like to Him: because we shall see Him as He is.* Hence that vision will not be by way of a proposition, but by way of simple understanding. On the other hand, by faith, we do not apprehend the First Truth as it is in itself. Hence the comparison fails.

[Q. 1] Fourth Article
Whether the Object of Faith
Can Be Something Seen?

We proceed thus to the Fourth Article:—

Objection 1. It would seem that the object of faith is something seen. For our Lord said to Thomas (*Jo.* xx. 29): *Because thou hast seen Me, Thomas, thou hast believed.* Therefore vision and faith regard the same object.

Obj. 2. Further, The Apostle, while speaking of the knowledge of faith, says (*1 Cor.* xiii. 12): *We see now through a glass in a dark manner.* Therefore what is believed is seen.

Obj. 3. Further, Faith is a spiritual light. Now something is seen under every light. Therefore faith is about things seen.

Obj. 4. Further, *Every sense is a kind of sight*, as Augustine states. But faith is of things heard, according to *Rom.* x. 17: *Faith . . . cometh by hearing.* Therefore faith is about things seen.

On the contrary, The Apostle says (*Heb.* xi. 1) that *faith is the evidence of things that appear not.*

I answer that, Faith signifies the assent of the intellect to that which is believed. Now the intellect assents to a thing in two ways. First, through being moved to assent by its very object, which is known either by itself (as in the case of first principles, which are held by the habit of understanding), or through something else already known (as in the case of conclusions which are held by the habit of science). Secondly, the intellect assents to something, not through being sufficiently moved to this assent by its proper object, but through an act of choice, whereby it turns voluntarily to one side rather than to the other. Now if this be accompanied by doubt and fear of the opposite side, there will be opinion; while, if there be certainty and no fear of the other side, there will be faith.

Now those things are said to be seen which, of themselves, move the intellect or the senses to knowledge of them. Therefore it is evident that neither faith nor opinion can be of things seen either by the senses or by the intellect.

Reply Obj. 1. Thomas *saw one thing, and believed another*. He saw the Man and, believing Him to be God, he made profession of his faith, saying: *My Lord and my God.*

Reply Obj. 2. Those things which come under faith can be considered in two ways. First, in particular, and in this way they cannot be seen and believed at the same time, as was shown above. Secondly, in general, that is, under the common aspect of credibility; and in this way they are seen by the believer. For he would not believe unless, on the evidence of signs, or of something similar, he saw that they ought to be believed.

Reply Obj. 3. The light of faith makes us see what we believe. For just as, by the habits of the other virtues, man sees what is becoming to him in respect of that habit, so, by the habit of faith, the human mind is inclined to assent to such things as are becoming to a right faith, and not to assent to others.

Reply Obj. 4. Hearing is of words signifying what is of faith, but not of the things themselves that are believed. Hence it does not follow that these things are seen.

[Q. 1] Fifth Article
Whether Those Things That Are of Faith Can Be an Object of Science?

We proceed thus to the Fifth Article:—

Objection 1. It would seem that those things that are of faith can be an object of science. For where science is lacking there is ignorance, since ignorance is the opposite of science. Now we are not in ignorance of those things we have to believe, since ignorance of such things belongs to unbelief, according to 1 *Tim.* i. 13: *I did it ignorantly in unbelief.* Therefore things that are of faith can be an object of science.

Obj. 2. Further, Science is acquired by arguments. Now sacred writers employ arguments to inculcate things that are of faith. Therefore such things can be an object of science.

Obj. 3. Further, Things which are demonstrated are an object of science, since a *demonstration is a syllogism that produces science.* Now certain matters of faith have been demonstrated by the philosophers, such as the existence and unity of God, and so forth. Therefore things that are of faith can be an object of science.

Obj. 4. Further, Opinion is further from science than faith is, since faith is said to stand between opinion and science. Now opinion and science can, in a way, be about the same object, as is stated in *Posterior Analytics* i. Therefore faith and science can be about the same object also.

On the contrary, Gregory says that *when a thing is manifest, it is the object, not of faith, but of perception.* Therefore things that are of faith are not the object of perception, whereas what is an object of science is the object of perception. Therefore there can be no faith about things which are an object of science.

I answer that, All science is derived from self-evident and therefore seen principles; and so all objects of science must needs be, in a fashion, seen.

Now, as was stated above, it is impossible that one and the same thing should be believed and seen by the same person. Hence it is equally impossible for one and the same thing to be an object of science and of belief for the same person. It may happen, however, that a thing which is an object of vision or science for one, is believed by another; for we hope to see some day what we now believe about the Trinity, according to 1 *Cor.* xiii. 12: *We see now through a glass in a dark manner; but then face to face.* And this vision the angels possess already, so that what we believe, they see. In like manner, it may also happen that what is an object of vision or scientific knowledge for one man, even in the state of a wayfarer, is, for another man, an object of faith, because he does not know it by demonstration.

Nevertheless, that which is proposed to be believed equally by all is equally unknown by all as an object of science. Such are the things which are of faith absolutely. Consequently, faith and science are not about the same things.

Reply Obj. 1. Unbelievers are in ignorance of things that are of faith, for neither do they see or know them in themselves, nor do they know them to be credible. The faithful, on the other hand, know them, not as by demonstration, but by the light of faith which makes them see that they ought to believe them, as was stated above.

Reply Obj. 2. The arguments employed by holy men to prove things that are of faith are not demonstrations; they are either persuasive arguments showing that what is proposed to our faith is not impossible, or else they are proofs drawn from the principles of faith, i.e., from the authority of Holy Scripture, as Dionysius declares. Whatever is based on these principles is as well proved in the eyes of the faithful as a conclusion drawn from self-evident principles is in the eyes of all. Hence, again, theology is a science, as we stated at the outset of this work.

Reply Obj. 3. Things which can be proved by demonstration are reckoned among what is of faith, not because they are believed absolutely by all, but because they are a necessary presupposition to matters of faith; so that those who do not know them by demonstration must possess them at least by faith.

Reply Obj 4. As the Philosopher says, *science and opinion about the same object can certainly be in different men,* as we have stated above about science and faith; yet it is possible for one and the same man to have science and faith about the same thing relatively, *i.e.* in relation to the object, but not in the same respect. For it is possible for the same person, about one and the same object, to know one thing and to have an opinion about another; and, in like manner, one may know by demonstration the unity of God, and believe that there are three Persons in God. On the other hand, in one and the same man, about the same object, and in the same respect, science is incompatible with either opinion or faith, but for different reasons. For science is incompatible with opinion about the same object absolutely, for the reason that science demands that its object should be deemed impossible to be otherwise, whereas it is essential to opinion that its object should be deemed possible to be otherwise. But that which is the object of faith, because of the certainty of faith, is also deemed impossible to be otherwise; and the reason why science and faith cannot be about the same object, and in the same respect, is because the object of science is something seen, whereas the object of faith is the unseen, as was stated above.

[Q. 2] First Article
Whether to Believe Is to Think with Assent?

We proceed thus to the First Article:—

Objection 1. It would seem that to believe is not to think with assent. Because the Latin word *cogitatio* [*thought*] implies an inquiry, for *cogitare* [*to think*] seems to be equivalent to *coagitare,* i.e., *to discuss together.* Now Damascene says that faith is *an assent without inquiry.* Therefore thinking has no place in the act of faith.

Obj. 2. Further, Faith resides in the reason, as we shall show further on. Now to think is an act of the cogitative power, which belongs to the sensitive part, as was stated in the First Part. Therefore thought has nothing to do with faith.

Obj. 3. Further, To believe is an act of the intellect, since its object is truth. But assent seems to be an act, not of the intellect, but of the will, even as consent is, as was stated above. Therefore to believe is not to think with assent.

On the contrary, This is how *to believe* is defined by Augustine.

I answer that, To think can be taken in three ways. First, in a general way for any kind of actual consideration of the intellect, as Augustine observes: *By understanding I mean now the power whereby we understand when thinking.* Secondly, *to think* is more strictly taken for that consideration of the intellect which is accompanied by some kind of inquiry, and with the certitude of vision. In this sense Augustine says that *the Son of God is not called the Thought, but the Word of God. When our thought realizes what we know and takes form therefrom, it becomes our word. Hence the Word of God must be understood without any thinking on the part of God, for there is nothing there that can take form, or be uniformed.* In this way thought is, properly speaking, the movement of the soul while yet deliberating, and not yet perfected by the clear vision of truth. Since, however, such a movement of the soul may be one of deliberation either about universal intentions, which belongs to the intellectual part, or about particular intentions, which belongs to the sensitive part, hence it is that *to think* is taken secondly for an act of the deliberating intellect, and thirdly for an act of the cogitative power.

Accordingly, if *to think* be understood broadly according to the first sense, then *to think with assent* does not express completely what is meant by *to believe*; for, in this way, a man thinks with assent even when he considers what he knows by science or what he understands. If, on the other hand, *to think* be understood in the second way, then this expresses completely the nature of the act of believing. For among the acts belonging to the intellect, some have a firm assent without any such kind of thinking, as when a man considers the things that he knows by science or what he understands, for this consideration is already formed. But some acts of the intellect have unformed thought devoid of a firm assent, whether they incline to neither side, as in one who *doubts*; or incline to one side rather than the other, but because of some slight motive, as in one who *suspects*; or incline to one side, yet with fear of the other, as in one who *opines*. But this act, *to believe*, cleaves firmly to one side, in which respect belief has something in common with science and understanding; yet its knowledge does not attain the perfection of clear vision, wherein it agrees with doubt, suspicion and opinion. Hence it is proper to the believer to think with assent; so that the act of believing is distinguished from all the other acts of the intellect which are about the true or the false.

Reply Obj. 1. Faith has not that inquiry of natural reason which demonstrates what is believed, but an inquiry into those things whereby a man is induced to believe, for instance, that such things have been uttered by God and confirmed by miracles.

Reply Obj. 2. *To think* is not taken here for the act of the cogitative power, but for an act of the intellect, as was explained above.

Reply Obj. 3. The intellect of the believer is determined to one object, not by the reason, but by the will, and so assent is taken here for an act of the intellect as determined to one object by the will.

[Q. 2] Fourth Article
Whether It Is Necessary to Believe Those Things Which Can Be Proved by Natural Reason?

We proceed thus to the Fourth Article:—

Objection 1. It would seem unnecessary to believe those things which can be proved by natural reason. For nothing is superfluous in God's works, much less even than in the works of nature. Now it is superfluous to employ other means, where one already suffices. Therefore it would be superfluous to receive by faith things that can be known by natural reason.

Obj. 2. Further, Those things must be believed which are the object of faith. Now science and faith are not about the same object, as was stated above. Since, therefore, all things that can be known by natural reason are an object of science, it seems that there is no need to believe what can be proved by natural reason.

Obj. 3. Further, All things knowable by science would seem to have one nature; so that if some of them are proposed to man as objects of faith, in like manner the others should also be believed. But this is not true. Therefore it is not necessary to believe those things which can be proved by natural reason.

On the contrary, It is necessary to believe that God is one and incorporeal; which things philosophers prove by natural reason.

I answer that, It is necessary for man to receive by faith not only things which are above reason, but also those which can be known by reason; and this for three motives. First, in order that man may arrive more quickly at the knowledge of divine truth. For the science to whose province it belongs to prove the existence of God and many other such truths is the last of all to offer itself to human inquiry, since it presupposes many other sciences; so that it would be far along in life that man would arrive at the knowledge of God. The second reason is, in order that the knowledge of God may be more widespread. For many are unable to make progress in the study of science, either through dullness of ability, or through having a number of occupations and temporal needs, or even through laziness in learning; and all these persons would be altogether deprived of the knowledge of God, unless divine things were brought to their knowledge by way of faith. The third reason is for the sake of certitude. For human reason is very deficient in things concerning God. A sign of this is that philosophers, in their inquiry into human affairs by natural investigation, have fallen into many errors, and have disagreed among themselves. And consequently, in order that men might have knowledge of God, free of doubt and uncertainty, it was necessary for divine truths to be delivered to them by way of faith, being told to them, as it were, by God Himself Who cannot lie.

Reply Obj. 1. The inquiry of natural reason does not suffice mankind for the knowledge of divine truths, even of those that can be proved by reason; and so it is not superfluous if these be believed.

Reply Obj. 2. Science and faith cannot be in the same subject and about the same object; but what is an object of science for one can be an object of faith for another, as was stated above.

Reply Obj. 3. Although all things that can be known by science have the notion of science in common, they do not all alike lead man to beatitude; and hence they are not all equally proposed to our belief.

[Q. 2] Tenth Article
Whether Reasons in Support of What We Believe Lessen the Merit of Faith?

We proceed thus to the Tenth Article:—

Objection 1. It would seem that reasons in support of what we believe lessen the merit of faith. For Gregory says that *there is no merit in believing what is shown by reason.* If, therefore, human reason provides sufficient proof, the merit of faith is altogether taken away. Therefore it seems that any kind of human reasoning in support of matters of faith diminishes the merit of believing.

Obj. 2. Further, Whatever lessens the measure of virtue, lessens the amount of merit, since *happiness is the reward of virtue,* as the Philosopher states. Now human reasoning seems to diminish the measure of the virtue of faith, since it is essential to faith to be about the unseen, as was stated above. Now the more a thing is supported by reasons, the less it is unseen. Therefore human reasons in support of matters of faith diminish the merit of faith.

Obj. 3. Further, Contrary things have contrary causes. Now an inducement in opposition to faith increases the merit of faith, whether it consist in persecution inflicted by one who endeavors to force a man to renounce his faith, or in an argument persuading him to do so. Therefore reasons in support of faith diminish the merit of faith.

On the contrary, It is written (*1 Pet.* iii. 15): *Being ready always to satisfy every one that asketh you a reason of that faith and hope which is in you.* Now the Apostle would not give this advice, if it would imply a diminution in the merit of faith. Therefore reason does not diminish the merit of faith.

I answer that, As we have stated above, the act of faith can be meritorious in so far as it is subject to the will, not only as to the use, but also as to the assent. Now human reasoning in support of what we believe may stand in a twofold relation to the will of the believer.—First, as preceding the act of the will, as, for instance, when a man either has not the will, or not a prompt will, to believe, unless he be moved by human reasons; and in this way human reasoning diminishes the merit of faith. In this sense it has been said above that, in moral virtues, a passion which precedes choice makes the virtuous act less praiseworthy. For just as a man ought to perform acts of moral virtue because of the judgment of his reason, and not because of a passion, so he ought to believe matters of faith, not because of human reasoning, but because of the divine authority.—Secondly, human reasons may be consequent to the will of the believer. For when a man has a will ready to believe, he loves the truth he believes, he thinks out and takes to heart whatever reasons he can find in support thereof; and in this way, human reasoning does not exclude the merit of faith, but is a sign of greater merit. Thus, again, in moral virtues, a consequent passion is the sign of a more prompt will, as was stated above. We have an indication of this in the words of the Samaritans to the woman, who is a type of human reason: *We now believe, not for thy saying* (Jo. iv. 42).

Reply Obj. 1. Gregory is referring to the case of a man who has no will to believe what is of faith, unless he be induced by reasons. But when a man has the will to believe what is of faith, on the authority of God alone, although he may have reasons in demonstration of some of them, *e.g.*, of the existence of God, the merit of his faith is not, for that reason, lost or diminished.

Reply Obj. 2. The reasons which are brought forward in support of the authority of faith are not demonstrations which can bring intellectual vision to the human intellect; and so the unseen is not removed. But they remove obstacles to faith, by showing that what faith proposes is not impossible; and hence such reasons do not diminish the merit or the measure of faith. On the other hand, though demonstrative reasons in support of the preambles of faith, but not of the articles of faith, diminish the measure of faith, since they make the thing believed to be seen; yet they do not diminish the measure of charity, which makes the will ready to believe them, even if they were unseen. And so the measure of merit is not diminished.

Reply Obj. 3. Whatever is in opposition to faith, whether it consist in a man's thoughts, or in outward persecution, increases the merit of faith in so far as the will is shown to be more prompt and firm in believing. Hence the martyrs had more merit of faith, through not renouncing faith because of persecution; and even the wise have greater merit of faith, through not renouncing their faith because of the reasons brought forward by philosophers or heretics in opposition to faith. On the other hand, things that are favorable to faith do not always diminish the promptness of the will to believe, and therefore they do not always diminish the merit of faith.

[Q. 4] First Article
Whether This Is a Fitting Definition of Faith: Faith
Is the Substance of Things to Be Hoped for, the
Evidence of Things That Appear Not?

We proceed thus to the First Article:—

Objection 1. It would seem that the Apostle gives an unfitting definition of faith when he says (*Heb.* xi. 1): *Faith is the substance of things to be hoped for, the evidence of things that appear not.* For no quality is a substance, whereas faith is a quality, since it is a theological virtue, as was stated above. Therefore it is not a substance.

Obj. 2. Further, Different virtues have different objects. Now things to be hoped for are the object of hope. Therefore they should not be included in a definition of faith, as though they were its object.

Obj. 3. Further, Faith is perfected by charity rather than by hope, since charity is the form of faith, as we shall state further on. Therefore the definition of faith should have included the thing to be loved rather than the thing to be hoped for.

Obj. 4. Further, The same thing should not be placed in different genera. Now *substance* and *evidence* are different genera, and neither is subalternate to the other. Therefore it is unfitting to state that faith is both *substance* and *evidence*. Therefore faith is unfittingly defined.

Obj. 5. Further, Evidence manifests the truth of the matter for which it is adduced. Now a thing is said to be apparent when its truth is made manifest. Therefore it seems to imply a contradiction to speak of the *evidence of things that appear not,* for an argument makes a previously obscure thing to be apparent. And so faith is unfittingly defined.

On the contrary, The authority to the Apostle suffices.

I answer that, Though some say that the above words of the Apostle are not a definition of faith, because the definition reveals the quiddity and essence of a thing, as it is said in *Metaph.* vii., yet if we consider the matter rightly, this definition overlooks none of the points in reference to which faith can be defined, although the words themselves are not arranged in the form of a definition, just as the philosophers touch on the principles of the syllogism without employing the syllogistic form.

In order to make this clear, we must observe that since habits are known by their acts, and acts by their objects, faith, being a habit, should be defined by its proper act in relation to its proper object. Now the act of faith is to believe, as was stated above, which is an act of the intellect determined to one object by the will's command. Hence an act of faith is related both to the object of the will, *i.e.,* to the good and the end, and to the object of the intellect, *i.e.,* to the true. And since faith, through being a theological virtue, as was stated above, has one and the same thing for object and end, its object and end must, of necessity, be in proportion to one another. Now it has been already stated that the object of faith is the First Truth, as unseen, and whatever we hold because of it; so that it must needs be under the aspect of something unseen that the First Truth is the end of the act of faith, which aspect is that of a thing hoped for, according to the Apostle (*Rom.* viii. 25): *We hope for that which we see not.* For to see the truth is to possess it, and no one hopes for what one has already, but for what one has not, as was stated above.

Accordingly, the relation of the act of faith to its end, which is the object of the will, is indicated by the words: *Faith is the substance of things to be hoped for.* For we are wont to call by the name of substance the first beginning of a thing, especially when the whole subsequent thing is virtually contained in the first beginning. For instance, we might say that the first self-evident principles are the substance of science, because, namely, these principles are in us the first beginnings of science, the whole of which is itself contained in them virtually. In this way, then, faith is said to be the *substance of things to be hoped for,* for the reason that in us the first beginning of things to be hoped for is brought about by the assent of faith, which contains virtually all things to be hoped for. For we hope to be made happy through seeing the unveiled truth to which our faith cleaves, as was made evident when we were speaking of happiness.

The relationship of the act of faith to the object of the intellect, considered as the object of faith, is indicated by the words, *evidence of things that appear not,* where *evidence* is taken for the result of evidence. For evidence induces the intellect to adhere to a truth, and so the firm adhesion of the intellect to the non-apparent truth of faith is called *evidence* here. Hence another reading has *conviction,* because, namely, the intellect of the believer is convinced by divine authority, so as to assent to what it sees not.

Accordingly, if anyone would reduce the foregoing words to the form of a definition, he may say that *faith is a habit of the mind, whereby eternal life is begun in us, making the intellect assent to what is non-apparent.* In this way faith is distinguished from all other things pertaining to the intellect. For when we describe it as *evidence,* we distinguish it from opinion, suspicion and doubt, which do not make the intellect adhere to anything firmly; when we go on to say, *of things that appear not,* we distinguish it from science and understanding, the object of which is something apparent; and when we say that it is *the substance of things to be hoped for,* we distinguish the virtue of faith from faith commonly so called, which has no reference to the beatitude we hope for.

Whatever other definitions are given of faith are explanations of this one given by the Apostle. For when Augustine says that *faith is a virtue whereby we believe what we do not see,* and when Damascene says that *faith is an assent without inquiry,* and when others say that *faith is that certainty of the mind about absent things which surpasses opinion but falls short of science,* these all amount to the same as the Apostle's words:

Evidence of things that appear not; and when Dionysius says that *faith is the solid foundation of the believer, establishing him in the truth, and showing forth the truth in him,* this comes to the same as *substance of things to be hoped for.*

Reply Obj. 1. *Substance,* here, does not stand for the supreme genus co-divided against the other genera, but for that likeness to substance which is found in each genus, namely, inasmuch as the first thing in a genus contains the others virtually and is said to be substance thereof.

Reply Obj. 2. Since faith pertains to the intellect as commanded by the will, it must needs be directed, as to its end, to the objects of those virtues which perfect the will, among which is hope, as we shall prove further on. For this reason the definition of faith includes the object of hope.

Reply Obj. 3. Love may be of the seen and of the unseen, of the present and of the absent. Consequently a thing to be loved is not so adapted to faith, as a thing to be hoped for, since hope is always of the absent and the unseen.

Reply Obj. 4. *Substance* and *evidence,* as included in the definition of faith, do not denote various genera of faith, nor different acts, but different relationships of one act to different objects, as is clear from what has been said.

Reply Obj. 5. Evidence taken from the proper principles of a thing makes it apparent, whereas evidence taken from divine authority does not make a thing apparent in itself; and such is the evidence referred to in the definition of faith.

[Q. 6] First Article
Whether Faith Is Infused into Man by God?

We proceed thus to the First Article:—

Objection 1. It would seem that faith is not infused into man by God. For Augustine says that *science begets faith in us, and nourishes, defends and strengthens it.* Now those things which science begets in us seem to be acquired rather than infused. Therefore faith does not seem to be in us by divine infusion.

Obj. 2. Further, That to which man attains by hearing and seeing seems to be acquired by him. Now man attains to belief both by seeing miracles and by hearing the teachings of faith; for it is written (*Jo.* iv. 53): *The father . . . knew that it was at the same hour, that Jesus said to him, Thy son liveth; and himself believed, and his whole house;* and (*Rom.* x. 17) it is said that *faith is through hearing.* Therefore man attains to faith by acquiring it.

Obj. 3. Further, That which depends on a man's will can be acquired by him. But *faith depends on the believer's will,* according to Augustine. Therefore faith can be acquired by man.

On the contrary, It is written (*Ephes.* ii, 8, 9): *By grace you are saved through faith, and that not of yourselves . . . that no man may glory . . . for it is the gift of God.*

I answer that, Two things are requisite for faith. First, that the things which are of faith should be proposed to man; and this is necessary in order that man believe something explicitly. The second thing requisite for faith is the assent of the believer to the things which are proposed to him. Accordingly, as regards the first of these, faith must needs be from God. For the things which are of faith surpass human reason, and hence they do not come to man's knowledge, unless God reveal them. To some, indeed, they are revealed by God immediately, as those things which were revealed to the Apostles and prophets, while to some they are proposed by God in sending preachers of the faith, according to *Rom.* x. 15: *How shall they preach, unless they be sent?*

As regards the second, viz., man's assent to the things which are of faith, we may observe a twofold cause, one of external inducement, such as seeing a miracle, or being persuaded by someone to embrace the faith; neither of which is a sufficient cause, since of those who see the same miracle, or who hear the same sermon, some believe, and some do not. Hence we must assert another and internal cause, which moves man inwardly to assent to what belongs to faith.

The Pelagians held that this cause was nothing else than man's free choice, and consequently they said that the beginning of faith is from ourselves, inasmuch as, namely, it is in our power to be ready to assent to the things which are of faith, but that the consummation of faith is from God, Who proposes to us the things we have to believe. But this is false, for since, by assenting to what belongs to faith, man is raised above his nature, this must needs come to him from some supernatural principle moving him inwardly; and this is God. Therefore faith, as regards the assent which is the chief act of faith, is from God moving man inwardly by grace.

Reply Obj. 1. Science begets and nourishes faith by way of external persuasion afforded by some science; but the chief and proper cause of faith is that which moves man inwardly to assent.

Reply Obj. 2. This argument likewise refers to the cause that proposes outwardly the things that are of faith, or persuades man to believe by words or deeds.

Reply Obj. 3. To believe does indeed depend on the will of the believer; but man's will needs to be prepared by God with grace, in order that he may be raised to things which are above his nature, as was stated above.

Flew and Others
THEOLOGY AND FALSIFICATION*

Antony Flew

Let us begin with a parable. It is a parable developed from a tale told by
John Wisdom in his haunting and revelatory article "Gods." Once upon a
time two explorers came upon a clearing in the jungle. In the clearing were
growing many flowers and many weeds. One explorer says, "Some gardener
must tend this plot." The other disagrees, "There is no gardener." So they
pitch their tents and set a watch. No gardener is ever seen. "But perhaps he
is an invisible gardener." So they set up a barbed-wire fence. They electrify
it. They patrol with bloodhounds. (For they remember how H. G. Wells's
The Invisible Man could be both smelt and touched though he could not be
seen.) But no shrieks ever suggest that some intruder has received a shock.
No movements of the wire ever betray an invisible climber. The bloodhounds never give cry. Yet still the Believer is not convinced. "But there
is a gardener, invisible, intangible, insensible to electric shocks, a gardener
who has no scent and makes no sound, a gardener who comes secretly to
look after the garden which he loves." At last the Skeptic despairs, "But
what remains of your original assertion? Just how does what you call an
invisible, intangible, eternally elusive gardener differ from an imaginary
gardener or even from no gardener at all?"

In this parable we can see how what starts as an assertion, that' something exists or that there is some analogy between certain complexes of
phenomena, may be reduced step by step to an altogether different status,
to an expression perhaps of a "picture preference."[1] The Skeptic says there
is no gardener. The Believer says there is a gardener (but invisible, etc.).
One man talks about sexual behaviour. Another man prefers to talk of
Aphrodite (but knows that there is not really a superhuman person additional to, and somehow responsible for, all sexual phenomena). The
process of qualification may be checked at any point before the original
assertion is completely withdrawn and something of that first assertion will
remain (tautology). Mr. Wells's invisible man could not, admittedly, be
seen, but in all other respects he was a man like the rest of us. But though
the process of qualification may be, and of course usually is, checked in

---

* This symposium, portions of which were originally carried on BBC, is part of a
collection of essays entitled, *New Essays in Philosophical Theology*. The contributors
to the symposium, all prominent contemporary English philosophers, are Antony Flew,
R. M. Hare, Basil Mitchell, and I. M. Crombie. From NEW ESSAYS IN PHILOSOPHI-
CAL THEOLOGY by Antony Flew and Alasdair MacIntyre. Reprinted with permission
of The Macmillan Company. First published in 1955.

[1] Cf. J. Wisdom, "Other Minds," *Mind* (1940), reprinted in his *Other Minds* (Oxford:
Basil Blackwell, 1952).

time, it is not always judiciously so halted. Someone may dissipate his assertion completely without noticing that he has done so. A fine brash hypothesis may thus be killed by inches, the death by a thousand qualifications.

And in this, it seems to me, lies the peculiar danger, the endemic evil, of theological utterance. Take such utterances as "God has a plan," "God created the world," "God loves us as a father loves his children." They look at first sight very much like assertions, vast cosmological assertions. Of course, this is no sure sign that they either are, or are intended to be, assertions. But let us confine ourselves to the cases where those who utter such sentences intend them to express assertions. (Merely remarking parenthetically that those who intend or interpret such utterances as crypto-commands, expressions of wishes, disguised ejaculations, concealed ethics, or as anything else but assertions are unlikely to succeed in making them either properly orthodox or practically effective.)

Now to assert that such and such is the case is necessarily equivalent to denying that such and such is not the case. Suppose then that we are in doubt as to what someone who gives vent to an utterance is asserting, or suppose that, more radically, we are skeptical as to whether he is really asserting anything at all, one way of trying to understand (or perhaps it will be to expose) his utterance is to attempt to find what he would regard as counting against, or as being incompatible with, its truth. For if the utterance is indeed an assertion, it will necessarily be equivalent to a denial of the negation of that assertion. And anything which would count against the assertion, or which would induce the speaker to withdraw it and to admit that it had been mistaken, must be part of (or the whole of) the meaning of the negation of that assertion. And to know the meaning of the negation of an assertion is as near as makes no matter to know the meaning of that assertion. And if there is nothing which a putative assertion denies then there is nothing which it asserts either: and so it is not really an assertion. When the Skeptic in the parable asked the Believer, "Just how does what you call an invisible, intangible, eternally elusive gardener differ from an imaginary gardener or even from no gardener at all?" he was suggesting that the Believer's earlier statement had been so eroded by qualification that it was no longer an assertion at all.

Now it often seems to people who are not religious as if there was no conceivable event or series of events the occurrence of which would be admitted by sophisticated religious people to be a sufficient reason for conceding "There wasn't a God after all" or "God does not really love us then." Someone tells us that God loves us as a father loves his children. We are reassured. But then we see a child dying of inoperable cancer of the throat. His earthly father is driven frantic in his efforts to help, but his Heavenly Father reveals no obvious sign of concern. Some qualification is made— God's love is "not a merely human love" or it is "an inscrutable love," perhaps—and we realize that such sufferings are quite compatible with the truth of the assertion that "God loves us as a father (but, of course, . . .)." We are reassured again. But then perhaps we ask: what is this assurance of God's (appropriately qualified) love worth, what is this apparent guarantee really a guarantee against? Just what would have to happen not merely (morally and wrongly) to tempt but also (logically and rightly) to entitle us to say "God does not love us" or even "God does not exist"? I therefore put to the succeeding symposiasts the simple central questions, "What would have to occur or to have occurred to constitute for you a disproof of the love of, or of the existence of, God?"

R. M. Hare

I wish to make it clear that I shall not try to defend Christianity in particular, but religion in general—not because I do not believe in Christianity, but because you cannot understand what Christianity is, until you have understood what religion is.

I must begin by confessing that, on the ground marked out by Flew, he seems to me to be completely victorious. I therefore shift my ground by re lating another parable. A certain lunatic is convinced that all dons want to murder him. His friends introduce him to all the mildest and most respectable dons that they can find, and after each of them has retired, they say, "You see, he doesn't really want to murder you; he spoke to you in a most cordial manner; surely you are convinced now?" But the lunatic replies "Yes, but that was only his diabolical cunning; he's really plotting against me the whole time, like the rest of them; I know it I tell you." However many kindly dons are produced, the reaction is still the same.

Now we say that such a person is deluded. But what is he deluded about? About the truth or falsity of an assertion? Let us apply Flew's test to him. There is no behaviour of dons that can be enacted which he will accept as counting against his theory; and therefore his theory, on this test, asserts nothing. But it does not follow that there is no difference between what he thinks about dons and what most of us think about them—otherwise we should not call him a lunatic and ourselves sane, and dons would have no reason to feel uneasy about his presence in Oxford.

Let us call that in which we differ from this lunatic, our respective *bliks*. He has an insane *blik* about dons; we have a sane one. It is important to realize that we have a sane one, not no *blik* at all; for there must be two sides to any argument—if he has a wrong *blik*, then those who are right about dons must have a right one. Flew has shown that a *blik* does not consist in an assertion or system of them; but nevertheless it is very important to have the right *blik*.

Let us try to imagine what it would be like to have different *bliks* about other things than dons. When I am driving my car, it sometimes occurs to me to wonder whether my movements of the steering-wheel will always continue to be followed by corresponding alternations in the direction of the car. I have never had a steering failure, though I have had skids, which must be similar. Moreover, I know enough about how the steering of my car is made to know the sort of thing that would have to go wrong for the steering to fail—steel joints would have to part, or steel rods break, or something—but how do I know that this won't happen? The truth is, I don't know; I just have a *blik* about steel and its properties, so that normally I trust the steering of my car; but I find it not at all difficult to imagine what it would be like to lose this *blik* and acquire the opposite one. People would say I was silly about steel; but there would be no mistaking the reality of the difference between our respective *bliks*—for example, I should never go in a motor-car. Yet I should hesitate to say that the difference between us was the difference between contradictory assertions. No amount of safe arrivals or bench-tests will remove my *blik* and restore the normal one; for my *blik* is compatible with any finite number of such tests.

It was Hume who taught us that our whole commerce with the world depends upon our *blik* about the world; and that differences between *bliks* about the world cannot be settled by observation of what happens in the world. That was why, having performed the interesting experiment of doubting the ordinary man's *blik* about the world, and showing that no proof could be given to make us adopt one *blik* rather than another, he turned to back-gammon to take his mind off the problem. It seems, indeed, to be impossible even to formulate as an assertion the normal *blik* about the world which makes me put my confidence in the future reliability of steel joints, in the continued ability of the road to support my car, and not gape beneath it revealing nothing below; in the general non-homicidal tendencies of dons; in my own continued well-being (in some sense of that word that I may not now fully understand) if I continue to do what is right according to my lights; in the general likelihood of people like Hitler coming to a bad end. But perhaps a formulation less inadequate than most is to be found in the Psalms: "The earth is weak and all the inhabiters thereof: I bear up the pillars of it."

The mistake of the position which Flew selects for attack is to regard this kind of talk as some sort of *explanation*, as scientists are accustomed to use the word. As such, it would obviously be ludicrous. We no longer believe in God as an Atlas—*nous n'avons pas besoin de cette hypothèse*. But it is nevertheless true to say that, as Hume saw, without a *blik* there can be no explanation; for it is by our *bliks* that we decide what is and what is not an explanation. Suppose we believed that everything that happened, happened by pure chance. This would not of course be an assertion; for it is compatible with anything happening or not happening, and so, incidentally, is its contradictory. But if we had this belief, we should not be able to explain or predict or plan anything. Thus, although we should not be *asserting* anything different from those of a more normal belief, there would be a great difference between us; and this is the sort of difference that there is between those who really believe in God and those who really disbelieve in him.

The word "really" is important, and may excite suspicion. I put it in. because when people have had a good Christian upbringing, as have most of those who now profess not to believe in any sort of religion, it is very hard to discover what they really believe. The reason why they find it so easy to think that they are not religious is that they have never got into the frame of mind of one who suffers from the doubts to which religion is the answer. Not for them the terrors of the primitive jungle. Having abandoned some of the more picturesque fringes of religion, they think that they have abandoned the whole thing—whereas in fact they still have got, and could not live without, a religion of a comfortably substantial, albeit highly sophisticated, kind, which differs from that of many "religious people" in little more than this, that "religious people" like to sing Psalms about theirs —a very natural and proper thing to do. But nevertheless there may be a big difference lying behind—the difference between two people who, though side by side, are walking in different directions. I do not know in what direction Flew is walking; perhaps he does not know either. But we have had some examples recently of various ways in which one can walk away from Christianity, and there are any number of possibilities. After all, man has not changed biologically since primitive times; it is his religion that has changed, and it can easily change again. And if you do not think that such changes make a difference, get acquainted with some Sikhs and some Mussulmans of the same Punjabi stock; you will find them quite different sorts of people.

There is an important difference between Flew's parable and my own which we have not yet noticed. The explorers do not *mind* about their garden; they discuss it with interest, but not with concern. But my lunatic, poor fellow, minds about dons; and I mind about the steering of my car; it often has people in it that I care for. It is because I mind very much about what goes on in the garden in which I find myself, that I am unable to share the explorers' detachment.

Basil Mitchell

Flew's article is searching and perceptive, but there is, I think, something odd about his conduct of the theologian's case. The theologian surely would not deny that the fact of pain counts against the assertion that God loves men. This very incompatibility generates the most intractable of theological problems—the problem of evil. So the theologian *does* recognize the fact of pain as counting against Christian doctrine. But it is true that he will not allow it—or anything—to count decisively against it; for he is committed by his faith to trust in God. His attitude is not that of the detached observer, but of the believer.

Perhaps this can be brought out by yet another parable. In time of war in an occupied country, a member of the resistance meets one night a stranger who deeply impresses him. They spend that night together in conversation. The Stranger tells the partisan that he himself is on the side of the resistance—indeed that he is in command of it, and urges the partisan to have faith in him no matter what happens. The partisan is utterly convinced at that meeting of the Stranger's sincerity and constancy and undertakes to trust him.

They never meet in conditions of intimacy again. But sometimes the Stranger is seen helping members of the resistance, and the partisan is grateful and says to his friends, "He is on our side."

Sometimes he is seen in the uniform of the police handing over patriots to the occupying power. On these occasions his friends murmur against him: but the partisan still says, "He is on our side." He still believes that, in spite of appearances, the Stranger did not deceive him. Sometimes he asks the Stranger for help and receives it. He is then thankful. Sometimes he asks and does not receive it. Then he says, "The Stranger knows best." Sometimes his friends, in exasperation, say "Well, what *would* he have to do for you to admit that you were wrong and that he is not on our side?" But the partisan refuses to answer. He will not consent to put the Stranger to the test. And sometimes his friends complain, "Well, if *that's* what you mean by his being on our side, the sooner he goes over to the other side the better."

The partisan of the parable does not allow anything to count decisively against the proposition "The Stranger is on our side." This is because he has committed himself to trust the Stranger. But he of course recognizes that the Stranger's ambiguous behaviour *does* count against what he believes about him. It is precisely this situation which constitutes the trial of his faith.

When the partisan asks for help and doesn't get it, what can he do? He can (a) conclude that the stranger is not on our side; or (b) maintain that he is on our side, but that he has reasons for withholding help.

The first he will refuse to do. How long can he uphold the second position without its becoming just silly?

I don't think one can say in advance. It will depend on the nature of the impression created by the Stranger in the first place. It will depend, too, on the manner in which he takes the Stranger's behaviour. If he blandly dismisses it as of no consequence, as having no bearing upon his belief, it will be assumed that he is thoughtless or insane. And it quite obviously won't do for him to say easily, "Oh, when used of the Stranger the phrase 'is on our side' *means* ambiguous behaviour of this sort." In that case he would be like the religious man who says blandly of a terrible disaster "It is God's will." No, he will only be regarded as sane and reasonable in his belief, if he experiences in himself the full force of the conflict.

It is here that my parable differs from Hare's. The partisan admits that many things may and do count against his belief: whereas Hare's lunatic who has a *blik* about dons doesn't admit that anything counts against his *blik*. Nothing *can* count against *bliks*. Also the partisan has a reason for having in the first instance committed himself, viz., the character of the Stranger whereas the lunatic has no reason for his *blik* about dons—because, of course, you can't have reasons for *bliks*.

This means that I agree with Flew that theological utterances must be assertions. The partisan is making an assertion when he says, "The Stranger is on our side."

Do I want to say that the partisan's belief about the Stranger is, in any sense, an explanation? I think I do. It explains and makes sense of the Stranger's behaviour: it helps to explain also the resistance movement in the context of which he appears. In each case it differs from the interpretation which the others put upon the same facts.

"God loves men" resembles "the Stranger is on our side" (and many other significant statements, e.g., historical ones) in not being conclusively falsifiable. They can both be treated in at least three different ways: (1) as provisional hypotheses to be discarded if experience tells against them (2) as significant articles of faith, (3) a vacuous formulae (expressing, perhaps, a desire for reassurance) to which experience makes no difference and which make no difference to life.

The Christian, once he has committed himself, is precluded by his faith from taking up the first attitude: "Thou shalt not tempt the Lord thy God." He is in constant danger, as Flew has observed, of slipping into the third. But he need not; and, if he does, it is a failure in faith as well as in logic.

Antony Flew

It has been a good discussion; and I am glad to have helped to provoke it. But now . . . it must come to an end: and [I shall] make some concluding remarks. Since it is impossible to deal with all the issues raised or to comment separately upon each contribution, I will concentrate on Mitchell and Hare, as representative of two very different kinds of response to [my] challenge. . . .

The challenge, it will be remembered, ran like this. Some theological utterances seem to, and are intended to, provide explanations or express assertions. Now an assertion, to be an assertion at all, must claim that things stand thus and thus; *and not otherwise.* Similarly an explanation, to be an explanation at all, must explain why this particular thing occurs; *and not something else.* Those last clauses are crucial. And yet sophisticated religious people—or so it seemed to me—are apt to overlook this, and tend to refuse to allow, not merely that anything actually does occur, but that anything conceivably could occur, which would count against their theological assertions and explanations. But insofar as they do this their supposed explanations are actually bogus, and their seeming assertions are really vacuous.

Mitchell's response to this challenge is admirably direct, straightforward, and understanding. He agrees "that theological utterances must be assertions." He agrees that if they are to be assertions, there must be something that would count against their truth. He agrees, too, that believers are in constant danger of transforming their would-be assertions into "vacuous formulae." But he takes me to task for an oddity in my "conduct of the theologian's case. The theologian surely would not deny that the fact of pain counts against the assertion that God loves men. This very incompatibility generates the most intractable of theological problems, the problem of evil." I think he is right. I should have made a distinction between two very different ways of dealing with what looks like evidence against the love of God; the way I stressed was the expedient of qualifying the original assertion; the way the theologian usually takes, at first, is to admit that it looks bad but to insist that there is—there must be—some explanation which will show that, in spite of appearances, there really is a God who loves us. His difficulty, it seems to me, is that he has given God attributes which rule out all possible saving explanations. In Mitchell's parable of the Stranger it is easy for the Believer to find plausible excuses for ambiguous behaviour; for the Stranger is a man. But suppose the Stranger is God. We cannot say that he would like to help but cannot; God is omnipotent. We cannot say that he would help if he only knew; God is omniscient. We cannot say that he is not responsible for the wickedness of others; God creates those others. Indeed an omnipotent, omniscient God must be an accessory before (and during) the fact to every human misdeed; as well as being responsible for every non-moral defect in the universe. So, though I entirely concede that Mitchell was absolutely right to insist against me that the theologian's first move is to look for an *explanation*, I still think that in the end, if relentlessly pursued, he will have to resort to the avoiding action of *qualification*. And there lies the danger of that death by a thousand qualifications, which would, I agree, constitute "a failure in faith as well as in logic."

Hare's approach is fresh and bold. He confesses that "on the ground marked out by Flew, he seems to me to be completely victorious." He therefor introduces the concept of *blik*. But while I think that there is room for some such concept in philosophy, and that philosophers should be grateful to Hare for his invention, I nevertheless want to insist that any attempt to analyze Christian religious utterance as expressions or affirmations of a *blik* rather than as (at least would-be) assertions about the cosmos is fundamentally misguided. First, because thus interpreted they would be entirely unorthodox. If Hare's religion really is a *blik*, involving no cosmological assertions about the nature and activities of a supposed personal creator, then surely he is not a Christian at all? Second, because thus interpreted, they could scarcely do the job they do. If they were not even intended as assertions, then many religious activities would become fraudulent, or merely silly. If "You ought *because* it is God's will" asserts no more than "You ought," then the person who prefers the former phraseology is not really given a reason, but a fraudulent substitute for one, a dialectical dud check. If "My soul must be immortal *because* God loves his children, etc." asserts no more than "My soul must be immortal," then the man who reassures himself with theological arguments for immortality is being as silly as the man who tries to clear his overdraft by writing his bank a check on the same account. (Of course neither of these utterances would be distinctively Christian; but this discussion never pretended to be so confined.) Religious utterances may indeed express false or even bogus assertions: but I simply do not believe that they are not both intended and interpreted to be or at any rate to presuppose assertions, at least in the context of religious practice, whatever shifts may be demanded, in another context, by the exigencies of theological apologetic.

One final suggestion. The philosophers of religion might well draw upon George Orwell's last appalling nightmare, *1984*, for the concept of *doublethink*. "*Doublethink* means the power of holding two contradictory beliefs simultaneously, and accepting both of them. The party intellectual knows that he is playing tricks with reality, but by the exercise of *doublethink* he also satisfies himself that reality is not violated." Perhaps religious intellectuals too are sometimes driven to doublethink in order to retain their faith in a loving God in face of the reality of a heartless and indifferent world. But of this more another time, perhaps.

I. M. Crombie[2]

There are some who hold that religious statements cannot be fully meaningful, on the ground that those who use them allow nothing to count decisively against them, treat them, that is, as incapable of falsification. This paper is an attempted answer to this view; and in composing it I have had particularly in mind [the above] article by Antony Flew. I shall offer only a very short, and doubtless tendentious, summary of my opponents' views.

Briefly, then, it is contended that there are utterances made from time to time by Christians and others, which are said by those who make them to be statements, but which are thought by our opponents to lack some of the properties which anything must have before it deserves to be called a statement. "There is a God," "God loves us as a father loves his children," "He shall come again with glory . . ." are examples of such utterances. *Prima facie* such utterances are neither exhortations, nor questions, nor expressions of wishes; *prima facie* they appear to assert the actuality of some state of

---

[2] This paper was composed to be read to a non-philosophical audience. In composing it I have also filched shamelessly (and shamefully no doubt distorted) some unpublished utterances of Dr. A. M. Farrer's.

affairs; and yet (and this is the objection) they are allowed to be compatible with any and every state of affairs. If they are compatible with any and every state of affairs, they cannot mark out some one state of affairs (or group of states of affairs); and if they do not mark out some one state of affairs, how can they be statements? In the case of any ordinary statement, such as "It is raining," there is at least one situation (the absence of falling water) which is held to be incompatible with the statement, and it is the incompatibility of the situation with the statement which gives the statement its meaning. If, then, religious "statements" are compatible with anything and everything, how can they be statements? How can the honest inquirer find out what they mean, if nobody will tell him what they are incompatible with? Are they not much more like such exhortations as "Keep smiling," whose confessed purpose is to go on being in point whatever occurs? Furthermore, is it not true that they only appear to be statements to those of us who use them, because we deceive ourselves by a sort of conjuring trick, oscillating backwards and forwards between a literal interpretation of what we say when we say it, and a scornful rejection of such anthropomorphism when anybody challenges us? When we *say:* "He shall come again with glory . . . ," do we not picture real angels sitting on real clouds; when asked whether we really mean the clouds, we hedge; offer perhaps another picture, which again we refuse to take literally; and so on indefinitely. Whatever symbolism we offer, we always insist that only a crude man would take it literally, and yet we never offer him anything but symbolism; deceived by our imagery into supposing that we have something in mind, in fact there is nothing on which we are prepared to take our stand.

This is the position I am to try to criticize. It is, I think, less novel than its clothes; but nonetheless it is important. I turn to criticism.

Let me begin by dismissing from our inquiry the troublesome statement "There is a God" or "God exists." As every student of logic knows, all statements asserting the existence of something offer difficulties of their own, with which we need not complicate our embarrassment.

That being dismissed, I shall want to say of statements about God that they consist of two parts. Call them, if you like, subject and predicate. Whatever you call them, there is that which is said, and that which it is said about—namely God. It is important to make this distinction, for different problems arise about the different parts. As a first approximation towards isolating the difference, we may notice that the predicate is normally composed of ordinary words, put to unordinary uses, whereas the subject-word is "God," which has no other use. In the expression "God loves us," the word "God" is playing, so to speak, on its home ground, the phrase "loves us" is playing away. Now there is one set of questions which deal with the problem of why we say, and what we mean by saying, that God loves us, rather than hates us, and there is another set of questions concerned with the problem of what it is that this statement is being made about.

To approach the matter from an angle which seems to me to afford a good view of it, I shall make a few observations about the epistemological nature of religious belief. Let me caution the reader that, in doing so, I am not attempting to describe how religious belief in fact arises.

Theoretically, then, not in how it arises, but in its logical structure, religious belief has two parents; and it also has a nurse. Its logical mother is what one might call *undifferentiated theism*, its logical father is particular events or occasions interpreted as theophanic, and the extra-parental nurture is provided by religious activity.

A word, first, about the logical mother. It is in fact the case that there are elements in our experience which lead people to a certain sort of belief, which we call a belief in God. (We could, if we wished, call it rather an attitude than a belief, so long as we were careful not to call it an attitude to life; for it is of the essence of the attitude to hold that nothing whatever in life may be identified with that towards which it is taken up.) Among the elements in experience which provoke this belief or attitude, perhaps the most powerful is what I shall call a sense of contingency. Others are moral experience, and the beauty and order of nature. Others may be actual abnormal experience of the type called religious or mystical. There are those to whom conscience appears in the form of an unconditional demand; to whom the obligation to one's neighbor seems to be something imposed on him and on me by a third party who is set over us both. There are those to whom the beauty and order of nature appears as the intrusion into nature of a realm of beauty and order beyond it. There are those who believe themselves or others to be enriched by moments of direct access to the divine. Now there are two things that must be said about these various theistic interpretations of our experience. The first is that those who so interpret need not be so inexpert in logic as to suppose that there is anything of the nature of a deductive or inductive argument which leads from a premise asserting the existence of the area of experience in question to a conclusion expressing belief in God. Nobody who takes seriously the so-called moral argument need suppose that the *prima facie* authority of conscience cannot be naturalistically explained. He can quite well acknowledge that the imperativeness which so impresses him could be a mere reflection of his jealousy of his father, or a vestigial survival of tribal taboo. The mystic can quite well acknowledge that there is nothing which logically forbids the interpretation of the experience which he enjoys in terms of the condition of his liver or the rate of his respiration. If, being acquainted with the alternative explanations, he persists in rejecting them, it need not be, though of course it sometimes is, because he is seized with a fallacious refutation of their validity. All that is necessary is that he should be honestly convinced that, in interpreting them, as he does, theistically, he is in some sense facing them more honestly, bringing out more of what they contain or involve than could be done by interpreting them in any other way. The one interpretation is preferred to the other, not because the latter is thought to be refutable on paper, but because it is judged to be unconvincing in the light of familiarity with the facts. There is a partial parallel to this in historical judgment. Where you and I differ in our interpretation of a series of events, there is nothing outside the events in question which can overrule either of us, so that each man must accept the interpretation which seems, on fair and critical scrutiny, the most convincing to him. The parallel is only partial, however, for in historical (and literary) interpretation there is something which to some extent controls one's interpretation, and that is one's general knowledge of human nature; and in metaphysical interpretation there is nothing analogous to this. That, then, is my first comment on theistic interpretations; for all that these journeys of the mind are often recorded in quasi-argumentative form, they are not in any ordinary sense arguments, and their validity cannot be assessed by asking whether they conform to the laws either of logic or of scientific method. My second comment upon them is that, in stating them, we find ourselves saying things which we cannot literally mean. Thus the man of conscience uses some such concept as the juridical concept of authority, and locates his authority outside nature; the man of beauty and order speaks of an intrusion from another realm; the mystic speaks of experiencing God. In every case such language lays the user open to devastating criticism, to which he can only retort by pleading that such language, while it is not to be taken strictly, seems to him to be the natural language to use.

To bring these points into a somewhat stronger light, let me say something about the sense of contingency, the conviction which people have, it may be in blinding moments, or it may be in a permanent disposition of a man's mind, that we, and the whole world in which we live, derive our being from something outside us. The first thing I want to say about this is that such a conviction is to no extent like the conclusion of an argument; the sense of dependence feels not at all like being persuaded by arguments, but like seeing, as it were, through a gap in the rolling mists of argument, which alone, one feels, could conceal the obvious truth. One is not *persuaded* to believe that one is contingent; rather one feels that one is contingent; rather one feels that it is only by persuasion that one could ever believe anything else. The second thing I want to say about this conviction of contingency is that in expressing it, as Quinton has admirably shown, we turn the word "contingent" to work which is not its normal employment, and which it cannot properly do.

For the distinction between necessity and contingency is not a distinction between different sorts of entities, but between different sorts of statement. A necessary statement is one whose denial involves a breach of the laws of logic, and a contingent statement is one in which this is not the case. (I do not, of course, assert that this is the only way in which these terms have been used in the history of philosophy; but I do assert that this is the only use of them which does not give rise to impossible difficulties. I have no space to demonstrate this here; and indeed I do not think that it is any longer in need of demonstration.) But in this, the only coherent, sense of "contingent," the existence of the world may be contingent fact, but so unfortunately is that of God. For *all* existential statements are contingent; that is to say, it is never true that we can involve ourselves in a breach of the laws of logic by merely denying of something that it exists. We cannot therefore in this sense contrast the contingent existence of the world with the necessary existence of God.

It follows that if a man persists in speaking of the contingency of the world, he must be using the term in a new or transferred sense. It must be that he is borrowing[3] a word from the logician and putting it to work which it cannot properly do. Why does he do this, and how can he make clear what precisely this new use is? For it is no good saying that when we are talking about God we do not use words in their ordinary senses unless we are prepared to say in what senses it is that we do use them. And yet how can we explain to the honest inquirer what is the new sense in which the word "contingent" is being used when we use it of the world? For if it is proper to use it, in this sense, of everything with which we are acquainted, and improper to use it only of God, with whom we are not acquainted, how can the new use be learnt? For we normally learn the correct use of a word by noticing the differences between the situations in which it may be applied and those in which it may not; but the word "contingent" is applicable in all the situations in which we ever find ourselves. If I said that everything but God was flexible, not of course in the ordinary sense, but in some other, how could you discover what the new sense was?

The answer must be that when we speak of the world as contingent, dependent, an effect or product, and so contrast it with a necessary, self-existent being, a first cause or a creator, we say something which on analysis will not do at all (for devastating criticisms can be brought against all these formulations), but which seems to us to be the fittest sort of language for our purpose. Why we find such language appropriate, and how, therefore, it is to be interpreted, is not at all an easy question; that it does in some way, it may be in some logically anomalous way, convey the meaning of those who use it, seems however to be an evident fact. How it is that the trick is worked, how it is that this sort of distortion of language enables believers to give expression to their beliefs, this it is the true business of the natural theologian to discuss. Farrer, for example, in *Finite and Infinite*, has done much to elucidate what it is that one is striving to express when one speaks of the contingency of the world, and so to enlighten the honest inquirer who wishes to know how the word "contingent" is here being used.

What I have said about contingency and necessity applies also to obligation and its transcendent ground (or goodness and its transcendent goal), to design and its transcendent designer, to religious experience and its tran-

---

[3] It might be argued that, historically, the borrowing was the other way round. To decide that we should have to decide where the frontier between logic and metaphysics really comes in the work of those whose doctrine on the relationship between these disciplines is unsatisfactory.

scendent object. In all these cases we use language which on analysis will not do, but which seems to us to be appropriate for the expression of our beliefs; and in all these cases the question can be, and is, discussed, why such language is chosen, and how it is to be understood.

That then is the logical mother of religious belief; call her natural theism, or what you will, she is a response, not precisely logical, and yet in no sense emotional or evaluative, to certain elements in our experience, whose characteristic is that they induce us, not to make straightforward statements about the world, but to strain and distort our media of communication in order to express what we make of them. In herself she is an honest woman; and if she is sometimes bedizened in logical trappings, and put out on the streets as an inductive argument, the fault is hardly hers. Her function is not to prove to us that God exists, but to provide us with a "meaning" for the word "God." Without her we should not know whither statements concerning the word were to be referred; the subject in theological utterances would be unattached. All that we should know of them is that they were not to be referred to anything with which we are or could hope to be acquainted; that, and also that they were to be understood in terms of whatever it is that people suppose themselves to be doing when they build churches and kneel down in them. And that is not entirely satisfactory; for while there is much to be said in practice for advising the honest inquirer into the reference of the word "God" to pursue his inquiry by familiarizing himself with the concrete activity of religion, it remains true that the range and variety of possible delusions which could induce such behaviour is theoretically boundless, and, as visitors to the Pacific coast of the United States can testify, in practice very large.

The logical father of religious belief, that which might bring us on from the condition of merely possessing the category of the divine, into the condition of active belief in God, this consists, in Christianity (and if there is nothing analogous in other religions, so much the worse for them), in the interpretation of certain objects or events as a manifestation of the divine. It is, in other words, because we find that, in thinking of certain events in terms of the category of the divine, we can give what seems to us the most convincing account of them, that we can assure ourselves that the notion of God is not just an empty aspiration. Without the notion of God we could interpret nothing as divine, and without concrete events which we felt impelled to interpret as divine we could not know that the notion of divinity had any application to reality. Why it is that as Christians we find ourselves impelled to interpret the history of Israel, the life and death of Christ, and the experience of his Church as revelatory of God, I shall not here attempt to say; it is an oft-told tale, and I shall content myself with saying that we can hardly expect to feel such an impulse so long as our knowledge of these matters is superficial and altogether from without. Whyever we feel such an impulse, it is not, of course, a logical impulse; that is, we may resist it (or fail to feel it) without thereby contravening the laws of logic, or the rules of any pragmatically accredited inductive procedure. On the anthropological level the history of Israel, Old and New, is certainly the history of a religious development from its tribal origins. We may decide, or we may not, that it is something more, something beyond the wit of man to invent, something which seems to us to be a real coherent communication from a real coherent, though superhuman, mind. We may decide, or we may not; neither decision breaks the rules, for in such a unique matter there are no rules to conform to or to break. The judgment is our own; and in the language of the New Testament it judges us; that is, it reveals what, up to the moment of our decision, the Spirit of God has done in us—but that, of course, is to argue in a circle.

Belief, thus begotten, is nurtured by the practice of the Christian life—by the conviction so aroused (or, of course, not aroused; but then it is starvation and not nurture) that the Christian warfare is a real warfare. Something will have to be said about this later on, but for the moment I propose to dismiss it, and to return to the consideration of the significance of religious utterances in the light of the dual parentage of religious belief.

I have argued that unless certain things seem to us to be signs of divine activity, then we may hope that there is a God, but we cannot properly believe that there is. It follows from this that religious belief must properly involve treating something as revelatory of God; and that is to say that it must involve an element of authority (for to treat something as divine revelation is to invest it with authority). That what we say about God is said on authority (and, in particular, on the authority of Christ) is of the first importance in considering the significance of these statements. In what way this is so, I shall hope to make clear as we go along.

If we remember that our statements about God rest on the authority of Christ, whom we call His Word, we can see what seems to me the essential clue to the interpretation of the logical nature of such utterances, and that is, in a word, the notion of parable. To elucidate what I mean by "parable" (for I am using the word in an extended sense) let us consider Christ's action on Palm Sunday, when he rode into Jerusalem on an ass. This action was an act of teaching. For it had been said to Jerusalem that her king would come to her riding upon an ass. Whoever, therefore, deliberately chose this method of entry, was saying in effect: "What you are about to witness (namely my Passion, Death and Resurrection) is the coming of the Messianic King to claim his kingdom." The prophecy of Messiah's kingdom was to be interpreted, not in the ordinary sense, but in the sense of the royal kingship of the Crucified. To interpret in this way is to teach by violent paradox, indeed, but nonetheless it is to teach. Part of the lesson is that it is only the kings of the Gentiles that lord it over their subjects; if any man will be a king in Israel (God's chosen people), he must humble himself as a servant; part of it is that the Crucifixion is to be seen as Messianic, that is as God's salvation of His chosen people. Now the logical structure which is involved here is something like this: You are told a story

(Behold, thy king cometh, meek and lowly, and riding upon an ass). You will not know just what the reality to which the story refers will be like until it happens. If you take the story at its face value (an ordinary, though humble, king, bringing an ordinary political salvation), you will get it all wrong. If you bring to bear upon its interpretation all that the Law and the Prophets have taught you about God's purposes for His people, though you will still not know just what it will be like until it happens, nonetheless you will not go wrong by believing it; for then you will know that Christ ought to have suffered these things, and to enter into his glory, and so you will learn what the story has to tell you of God's purposes for man, and something therefore, indirectly, of God. If you remember what Isaiah says about humility and sacrifice, you will see that what is being forecast is that God's purposes will be accomplished by a man who fulfills the Law and the Prophets in humble obedience.

This story is . . . one that can be fairly fully interpreted. There are others that cannot. There is, for example, Hosea's parable in which he likens himself to God, and Israel to his unfaithful wife, and expresses his grief at his wife's unfaithfulness. If, now, you ask for this to be fully interpreted, if you ask Hosea to tell you what he supposes it is like for the Holy One of Israel, of whom no similitude may be made, to be grieved, demanding to know, not what would happen in such a case to the unfaithful sinner who had provoked the divine wrath, but what was the condition of the divine mind in itself, then no doubt he would have regarded the very question as blasphemous. As an inspired prophet, he felt himself entitled to say that God was grieved, without presuming to imagine what such a situation was like, other than in its effects. What he said was said on authority; it was not his own invention, and therefore he could rely on its truth, without supposing himself to understand its full meaning. Insofar as Hosea's parable is "interpreted," the interpretation is confined to identifying the *dramatis personae* (Hosea = God, his wife = Israel). It is noteworthy that the interpretation which is sometimes given to the parables of the New Testament is usually of the same sketchy kind (the reapers are the angels). In Plato's famous parable of prisoners in a cave, it is quite possible to describe the situation which the parable seeks to illuminate. One can describe how a man can begin by being content to establish rough laws concerning what follows what in nature, how he may proceed from such a condition to desire explanations of the regularities which are forced on his attention, rising thus to more abstract and mathematical generalizations, and then, through the study of mathematics, to completely abstract speculation. One cannot similarly describe the situation which the parable of the Prodigal Son is intended to illustrate (or rather one can only describe the human end of it); and no attempt is ever made to do so.

I make no apology for these paragraphs about the Bible; after all the Bible is the source of Christian belief, and it cannot but illuminate the logical nature of the latter to consider the communicational methods of the former. But we must turn back to more general considerations. It is, then, characteristic of a parable that the words which are used in it are used in their ordinary senses. Elsewhere this is not always so. If you speak of the virtues of a certain sort of car, the word "virtue," being applied to a car, comes to mean something different from what it means in application to human beings. If you speak of hot temper, the word "hot" does not mean what it means in the ordinary way. Now many people suppose that something of the latter is happening in religious utterances. When God is said to be jealous, or active in history, it is felt that the word "jealous" or "active" must be being used here in a transferred sense. But if it is being used in a transferred sense, some means or other must be supplied whereby the new sense can be taken. The activity of God is presumably not like the activity of men (it does not make Him hot or tired); to say then that God is active must involve modifying the meaning of the word. But, if the word is undergoing modification, it is essential that we should know in what direction. In the case of ordinary transfers, how do we know what sort of modification is involved? This is a large question, but roughly, I think, the answer is in two ways. Firstly there is normally a certain appropriateness, like the appropriateness of "hot" in "hot temper"; and secondly we can notice the circumstances in which the word gets used and withheld in its transferred sense. If I hear the phrase "Baroque music," the meaning of the word "Baroque" in its normal architectural employment may set me looking in a certain direction; and I can clinch the matter by asking for examples, "Bach? Buxtehude? Beethoven?" But for either of these ways to be of any use to me, I must know something about *both* ends of the transfer. I must know something about Baroque architecture, *and* I must be able to run through musical styles in my head, to look for the musical analogue of Baroque features. If I cannot stumble on your meaning without assistance, I can still do so by eliciting from you that Bach and Buxtehude are, Handel and Mozart are not, examples of the sort of music you have in mind. This is informative to me if and only if I know something of Buxtehude and Bach, Handel and Mozart.

Now we all know what it is like for a man to be active. We can quote examples, decide correctly, and so forth. But what about divine activity? Surely we cannot have it both ways. Either God can be moderately like a man, so that the word "active," used of Him, can set us looking in the right direction; or He can be quite unlike a man, in which case it cannot. Nor can we be helped by the giving of examples, unless it is legitimate to point to examples of divine activity—to say, "Now here God is being active, but not there." This constitutes the force of Flew's demand that we should tell him how statements about God can be falsified. In essence Flew is saying: "When you speak about God, the words which occur in the predicate part of your statements are not being used in the ordinary sense; you make so great a difference between God and man that I cannot even find that the words you use set me looking in anything that might perhaps be the right direction. You speak of God as being outside time; and when I think what I mean by 'activity,' I find that that word, as used about a timeless being, suggests to me nothing whatsoever. There is only one resort left; give me examples of when one of your statements is, and is not, applicable. If, as no doubt you will say, that is an unfair demand, since they are always applicable (e.g., God is always active, so that there are no cases of His inactivity to be pointed to), I will not insist on actual examples; make them up if you like. But do not point to *everything* and say, '*That* is what I mean'; for *everything* is not *that*, but this and this and this and many other mutual incompatibles; and black and white and red and green and kind and cruel and coal and ink and everything else together cannot possibly elucidate to me the meaning of a word."

As I have said, the answer must be that when we speak about God, the words we use are intended in their ordinary sense (for we cannot make a transfer, failing familiarity with both ends of it), although we do not suppose that in their ordinary interpretation they can be strictly true of Him. We do not even know how much of them applies. To some extent it may be possible to take a word like "activity" and whittle away that in it which most obviously does not apply. It is, however, an exaggeration, at the least, to suppose that this process of whittling away leaves us in the end with a kernel about which we can say that we know that it does apply. A traditional procedure is to compose a scale on which inanimate matter is at the bottom, the characteristically human activities, such as thinking and personal relationship, at the top, and to suppose that the scale is pointing towards God; and so on this assumption the first thing to do is to pare away from the notion of human activity whatever in it is common to what stands below it on the scale—for example actual physical moving about. Taking the human residue, we try to decide what in it is positive, and what is negative, mere limitation. The tenuous ghost of a concept remaining we suppose to be the essential structure of activity (that structure which is common to running and thinking) and so to be realized also in divine activity. Perhaps this is how we imagine our language to be related to the divine realities about which we use it; but such ghostly and evacuated concepts are clearly too tenuous and elusive to be called the meanings of the words we use. To think of God thus is to think of Him not in our own image, but in the rarefied ghost of our own image; and so we think of Him in our own image, but do not suppose that in so thinking of Him we begin to do Him justice. What we do, then, is in essence to think of God in parables. The things we say about God are said on the authority of the words and acts of Christ, who spoke in human language, using parable; and so we too speak of God in parable— authoritative parable, authorized parable; knowing that the truth is not literally that which our parables represent, knowing therefore that now we see in a glass darkly, but trusting, because we trust the source of the parables, that in believing them and interpreting them in the light of each other, we shall not be misled, that we shall have such knowledge as we need to possess for the foundation of the religious life.

So far so good. But it is only the predicates of theological utterances which are parabolic; it is only in what is *said about* God that words are put to other than customary employment. When we say "God is merciful," it is "merciful" that is in strange company—deprived of its usual escort of human sentiments. But the word "God" only occurs in statements about God. Our grasp of this word, therefore, cannot be derived from our grasp of it in ordinary human contexts, for it is not used in such contexts. How then is our grasp of it to be accounted for? In other words, if I have given some account of how, and in what sense, we understand the meaning of the things we say about God, I have still to give some account of how, and in what sense, we know what it is we are saying them about.

In thus turning back from the predicate to the subject of religious utterances, we are turning from revealed theology to natural theology, from the logical father to the logical mother of religious belief. And the answer to the question: "What grasp have we of the meaning of the word 'God'?" must be dealt with along the following lines. Revelation is important to the believer not for what it is in itself (the biography of a Jew, and the history of his forerunners and followers), nor because it is revelation of nothing in particular, but because it is revelation of God. In treating it as something important, something commanding our allegiance, we are bringing to bear upon it the category of the transcendent, of the divine. Of the nature of that category I have already spoken. In other words, there must exist within a man's mind the contrast between the contingent and the necessary, the derivative and the underivative, the finite and the infinite, the perfect and the imperfect, if anything is to be for him a revelation of God. Given that contrast, we are given also that to which the parables or stories are referred. What is thus given is certainly not knowledge of the object to which they apply; it is something much more like a direction. We do not, that is, know to what to refer our parables; we know merely that we are to refer them out of experience, and out of it in which direction. The expression "God" is to refer to that object, whatever it is, and if there be one, which is such that the knowledge of it would be to us knowledge of the unfamiliar term in the contrast between finite and infinite.

Statements about God, then, are in effect parables, which are referred, by means of the proper name "God," out of our experience in a certain direction. We may, if we like, by the process of whittling away, which I have mentioned, try to tell ourselves what part of the meaning of our statements applies reasonably well, what part outrageously badly; but the fact remains that, in one important sense, when we speak about God, we do not know what we mean (that is, we do not know what that which we are talking about is like), and do not need to know, because we accept the images, which we employ, on authority. Because our concern with God is religious and not speculative (it is contemplative in part, but that is another matter), because our need is not to know what God is like, but to enter into relation with him, the authorized images serve our purpose. They belong to a type of discourse —parable—with which we are familiar, and therefore they have communication value, although in a sense they lack descriptive value.

If this is so, how do we stand with regard to verification and falsification?

Must we, to preserve our claim to be making assertions, be prepared to say what would count against them? Let us see how far we can do so. Does anything count against the assertion that God is merciful? Yes, suffering. Does anything count decisively against it? No, we reply, because it is true. Could anything count decisively against it? Yes, suffering which was utterly, eternally, and irredeemably pointless. Can we then design a crucial experiment? No, because we can never see all of the picture. Two things at least are hidden from us; what goes on in the recesses of the personality of the sufferer, and what shall happen hereafter.

Well, then, the statement that God is merciful is not testable; it is compatible with any and every tract of experience which we are in fact capable of witnessing. It cannot be verified; does this matter?

To answer this, we must make up our minds why the demand for verification or falsification is legitimate. On this large matter I shall be summary and dogmatic, as follows. (1) The demand that a statement of fact should be verifiable is a conflation of two demands. (2) The *first* point is that all statements of fact must be verifiable in the sense that there must not exist a *rule of language* which precludes testing the statement. That is to say, the way the statement is to be taken must not be such that to try to test it is to show that you do not understand it. If I say that it is wrong to kill, and you challenge my statement and adduce as evidence against it that thugs and headhunters do so out of religious duty, then you have not understood my statement. My statement was not a statement of fact, but a moral judgment, and your statement that it should be tested by anthropological investigations shows that you did not understand it. But so long as there exists no *logical* (or we might say *interpretational*) ban on looking around for verification, the existence of a *factual* ban on verification does not matter. "Caesar had mutton before he crossed the Rubicon" cannot in fact be tested, but by trying to devise ways of testing it you do not show that you have not understood it; you are merely wasting your time. (3) The *second* point is that, *for me fully* to understand a statement, *I* must know what a test of it would be like. If I have no idea how to test whether somebody had mutton, then I do not know what "having mutton" means. This stipulation is concerned not with the logical nature of the expression, but with its communication value for me. (4) There are then two stipulations, and they are different. The first is a logical stipulation, and it is to the effect that nothing can be a statement of fact if it is untestable in the sense that the notion of testing it is precluded by correctly interpreting it. The second is a communicational stipulation, and it is to the effect that nobody can fully understand a statement, unless he has a fair idea how a situation about which it was true would differ from a situation about which it was false.

Now with regard to these two stipulations, how do religious utterances fare? With regard to the first, there is no language rule implicit in a correct understanding of them which precludes putting them to the test (there may be a rule of faith, but that is another matter). If a man says, "How can God be loving, and allow pain?" he does *not* show that he has misunderstood the statement that God is loving. There *is a prima facie* incompatibility between the love of God, and pain and suffering. The Christian maintains that it is *prima facie* only; others maintain that it is not. They may argue about it, and the issue cannot be decided; but it cannot be decided, not because (as in the case of, e.g., moral or mathematical judgments) the appeal to facts is *logically* the wrong way of trying to decide the issue, and shows that you have not understood the judgment; *but* because, since our experience is limited in the way it is, we cannot get into position to decide it, any more than we can get into position to decide what Julius Caesar had for breakfast before he crossed the Rubicon. For the Christian the operation of getting into position to decide it is called dying; and, though we can all do that, we cannot return to report what we find. By this test, then, religious utterances can be called statements of fact; that is their *logical* classification.

With regard to the second stipulation, the case is a little complicated, for here we are concerned with communication value, and there are the two levels, the one on which we remain within the parable, and the other on which we try to step outside it. Now, on the first level we know well enough how to test a statement like "God loves us"; it is, for example, like testing "My father loves me." In fact, of course, since with parents and schoolmasters severity is notoriously a way of displaying affection, the decisive testing of such a statement is not easy; but there is a point beyond which it is foolish to continue to have doubts. Now, within the parable, we are supposing "God loves us" to be a statement like "My father loves me," "God" to be a subject similar to "My father," "God loves us" being thus related to "My father loves me" as the latter is related to "Aristotle's father loved him." We do not suppose that we can actually test "God loves us," for reasons already given (any more than we can test the one about Aristotle); but the communication value of the statement whose subject is "God" is derived from the communication value of the same statement with a different proper name as subject. If we try to step outside the parable, then we must admit that we do not know what the situation about which our parable is being told is like; we should only know if we could know God, and know even as also we have been known; see, that is, the unfolding of the divine purposes in their entirety. Such ignorance is what we ought to expect. We do not know how what we call the divine wrath differs from the divine mercy (because we do not know how they respectively resemble human wrath and mercy); but we do know how what *we mean* when we talk about the wrath of God differs from what *we mean* when we talk about His mercy, because then we are within the parable, talking within the framework of admitted ignorance, in language which we accept because we trust its source. We know what is meant *in* the parable, when the father of the Prodigal sees him coming a great way off and runs to meet him, and we can therefore think in terms of this image. We know that we are here promised that whenever we come to ourselves and return to God, He will come to meet us. This is enough to encourage us to return, and to make us alert to catch the signs of the divine response; but it does not lead us to presume to an understanding of the mind and heart of God. In talking we remain within the parable, and so our statements communicate; we do not know how the parable applies, but we believe that it does apply, and that we shall one day see how. (Some even believe, perhaps rightly, that in our earthly condition we may by direct illumination of our minds be enabled to know progressively more about the realities to which our parables apply, and in consequence about the manner of their application.)

Much of what I have said agrees very closely with what the atheist says about religious belief, except that I have tried to make it sound better. The atheist alleges that the religious man supposes himself to know what he means by his statements only because, until challenged, he interprets them anthropomorphically; when challenged, however, he retreats rapidly backwards towards complete agnosticism. I agree with this, with two provisos. The first is that the religious man does not suppose himself to know what he means by his statements (for what religious man supposes himself to be the Holy Ghost?); he knows what his statements mean within the parable, and believes that they are the right statements to use. (Theology is not a science; it is a sort of art of enlightened ignorance.) The second proviso is that the agnosticism is not complete; for the Christian, under attack, falls back not in any direction, but in one direction; he falls back upon the person of Christ, and the concrete realities of the Christian life.

Let us consider this for a moment with regard to the divine love. I could be attacked in this sort of way: "You have contended," my opponent might argue, "that when we say that God loves us the communication value of the statement is determined by the communication value of a similar statement about a human subject; and that we know the statement to be the right statement, but cannot know *how* it is the right statement, that is, what the divine love is like. But this will not do. Loving is an activity with two poles, the lover and the loved. We may not know the lover, in the case of God, but we *are*, and therefore *must know*, the loved. Now, to say that the image or parable of human love is the right image to use about God must imply that there is some similarity or analogy between human and divine love. Father's love may be superficially very unlike mother's, but, unless there is some similarity of structure between them, we cannot use the same word of both. But we cannot believe that there is any similarity between the love of God and human love, unless we can detect some similarity between being loved by God and being loved by man. But if being loved by God is what we experience all the time, then it is not like being loved by man; it is like being let down right and left. And in the face of so great a discrepancy, we cannot believe that God loves us, if that is supposed to be in any sense a statement of sober fact."

I cannot attempt to answer this objection; it involves the whole problem of religion. But there is something I want to say about it, which is that the Christian does not attempt to evade it either by helter-skelter flight, or by impudent bluff. He has his prepared positions onto which he retreats; and he knows that if these positions are taken, then he must surrender. He does not believe that they can be taken, but that is another matter. There are three main fortresses behind which he goes. For, first, he looks for the resurrection of the dead, and the life of the world to come; he believes, that is, that we do not see all of the picture, and that the parts which we do not see are precisely the parts which determine the design of the whole. He admits that if this hope be vain then we are of all men the most miserable. Second, he claims that he sees in Christ the verification, and to some extent also the specification, of the divine love. That is to say, he finds in Christ not only convincing evidence of God's concern for us, but also what sort of love the divine love is, what sort of benefits God is concerned to give us. He sees that, on the New Testament scale of values, it is better for a man to lose the whole world if he can thereby save his soul (which means his relationship to God); and that for that hope it is reasonable to sacrifice all that he has, and to undergo the death of the body and the mortification of the spirit. Third, he claims that in the religious life, of others, if not as yet in his own, the divine love may be encountered, that the promise "I will not fail thee nor forsake thee" is, if rightly understood, confirmed there. If, of course, this promise is interpreted as involving immunity from bodily suffering, it will be refuted; but no reader of the New Testament has any right so to interpret it. It is less glaringly, but as decisively, wrong to interpret it as involving immunity from spiritual suffering; for the New Testament only the undergoing of death (which means the abdication of control over one's destiny) can be the beginning of life. What then does it promise? It promises that to the man who begins on the way of the Christian life, on the way that is of seeking life through death, of seeking relationship with God through the abdication of the self-sovereignty claimed by Adam, that to him the fight will be hard but not impossible, progress often indiscernible, but real, progress which is towards the paring away of self-hood, and which is therefore often given through defeat and humiliation, but a defeat and humiliation which are not final, which leave it possible to continue. This is the extra-parental nurture of religious belief of which I spoke earlier, and it is the third of the prepared positions onto which the Christian retreats, claiming that the image and reflection of the love of God may be seen not only hereafter, not only in Christ, but also, if dimly, in the concrete process of living the Christian life.

One final word. Religion has indeed its problems; but it is useless to consider them outside their religious context. Seen as a whole religion makes rough sense, though it does not make limpidity.

Kierkegaard
TRUTH AND SUBJECTIVITY*

When the question of truth is raised in an objective manner, reflection is directed objectively to the truth, as an object to which the knower is related. Reflection is not focused upon the relationship, however, but upon the question of whether it is the truth to which the knower is related. If only the object to which he is related is the truth, the subject is accounted to be in the truth. When the question of the truth is raised subjectively, reflection is directed subjectively to the nature of the individual's relationship; if only the mode of this relationship is in the truth, the individual is in the truth even if he should happen to be thus related to what is not true. Let us take as an example the knowledge of God. Objectively, reflection is directed to the problem of whether this object is the true God; subjectively, reflection is directed to the question whether the individual is related to a something *in such a manner* that his relationship is in truth a God-relationship. On which side is the truth now to be found? Ah, may we not here resort to a mediation, and say: It is on neither side, but in the mediation of both? Excellently well said, provided we might have it explained how an existing individual manages to be in a state of mediation. For to be in a state of mediation is to be finished, while to exist is to become. Nor can an existing individual be in two places at the same time—he cannot be an identity of subject and object. When he is nearest to being in two places at the same time he is in passion; but passion is momentary, and passion is also the highest expression of subjectivity. . . .

When subjectivity is the truth, the conceptual determination of the truth must include an expression for the antithesis to objectivity, a memento of the fork in the road where the way swings off; this expression will at the same time serve as an indication of the tension of the subjective inwardness. Here is such a definition of truth: *An objective uncertainty held fast in an appropriation-process of the most passionate inwardness is the truth*, the highest truth attainable for an *existing* individual. At the point where the way swings off (and where this is cannot be specified objectively, since it is a matter of subjectivity), there objective knowledge is placed in abeyance. Thus the subject merely has, objectively, the uncertainty; but it is this which precisely increases the tension of that infinite passion which constitutes

* Søren Kierkegaard (1813–1855): Danish theologian and philosopher. This selection is from Kierkegaard's work *Concluding Unscientific Postscript* in which he attempts to define the task of becoming a Christian. From Søren Kierkegaard, *Concluding Unscientific Postscript*, tr. by D. F. Swenson and W. Lowrie (copyright 1941 © 1969 by Princeton University Press; Princeton Paperback, 1968) pp. 178, 182–188, 196–197, 200–201. Omission of footnotes on pp. 184–185. Reprinted by permission of Princeton University Press and the American Scandinavian Foundation.

his inwardness. The truth is precisely the venture which chooses an objective uncertainty with the passion of the infinite. I contemplate the order of nature in the hope of finding God, and I see omnipotence and wisdom; but I also see much else that disturbs my mind and excites anxiety. The sum of all this is an objective uncertainty. But it is for this very reason that the inwardness becomes as intense as it is, for it embraces this objective uncertainty with the entire passion of the infinite. In the case of a mathematical proposition the objectivity is given, but for this reason the truth of such a proposition is also an indifferent truth.

But the above definition of truth is an equivalent expression for faith. Without risk there is no faith. Faith is precisely the contradiction between the infinite passion of the individual's inwardness and the objective uncertainty. If I am capable of grasping God objectively, I do not believe, but precisely because I cannot do this I must believe. If I wish to preserve myself in faith I must constantly be intent upon holding fast the objective uncertainty, so as to remain out upon the deep, over seventy thousand fathoms of water, still preserving my faith.

In the principle that subjectivity, inwardness, is the truth, there is comprehended the Socratic wisdom, whose everlasting merit it was to have become aware of the essential significance of existence, of the fact that the knower is an existing individual. For this reason Socrates was in the truth by virtue of his ignorance, in the highest sense in which this was possible within paganism. To attain to an understanding of this, to comprehend that the misfortune of speculative philosophy is again and again to have forgotten that the knower is an existing individual, is in our objective age difficult enough. . . .

When subjectivity, inwardness, is the truth, the truth becomes objectively a paradox; and the fact that the truth is objectively a paradox shows in its turn that subjectivity is the truth. For the objective situation is repellent; and the expression for the objective repulsion constitutes the tension and the measure of the corresponding inwardness. The paradoxical character of the truth is its objective uncertainty; this uncertainty is an expression for the passionate inwardness, and this passion is precisely the truth. So far the Socratic principle. The eternal and essential truth, the truth which has an essential relationship to an existing individual because it pertains essentially to existence (all other knowledge being from the Socratic point of view accidental, its scope and degree a matter of indifference), is a paradox. But the eternal essential truth is by no means in itself a paradox; but it becomes paradoxical by virtue of its relationship to an existing individual. The Socratic ignorance gives expression to the objective uncertainty attaching to the truth, while his inwardness in existing is the truth. To anticipate here what will be developed later, let me make the following remark. The Socratic ignorance is an analogue to the category of the absurd, only that there is still less of objective certainty in the absurd, and in the repellent effect that the absurd exercises. It is certain only that it is absurd, and precisely on that account it incites to an infinitely greater tension in the corresponding inwardness. The Socratic inwardness in existing is an analogue to faith; only that the inwardness of faith, corresponding as it does, not to the repulsion of the Socratic ignorance, but to the repulsion exerted by the absurd, is infinitely more profound.

Socratically the eternal essential truth is by no means in its own nature paradoxical, but only in its relationship to an existing individual. This finds expression in another Socratic proposition, namely, that all knowledge is recollection. This proposition is not for Socrates a cue to the speculative enterprise, and hence he does not follow it up; essentially it becomes a Platonic principle. Here the way swings off; Socrates concentrates essentially upon accentuating existence, while Plato forgets this and loses himself in speculation. Socrates' infinite merit is to have been an *existing* thinker, not a speculative philosopher who forgets what it means to exist. For Socrates therefore the principle that all knowledge is recollection has at the moment of his leave-taking and as the constantly rejected possibility of engaging in speculation, the following two-fold significance: (1) that the knower is essentially *integer*, and that with respect to the knowledge of the eternal truth he is confronted with no other difficulty than the circumstance that he exists; which difficulty, however, is so essential and decisive for him that it means that existing, the process of transformation to inwardness in and by existing, is the truth; (2) that existence in time does not have any decisive significance, because the possibility of taking oneself back into eternity through recollection is always there, though this possibility is constantly nullified by utilizing the time, not for speculation, but for the transformation to inwardness in existing.

The infinite merit of the Socratic position was precisely to accentuate the fact that the knower is an existing individual, and that the task of existing is his essential task. Making an advance upon Socrates by failing to understand this, is quite a mediocre achievement. This Socratic principle we must therefore bear in mind, and then inquire whether the formula may not be so altered as really to make an advance beyond the Socratic position.

Subjectivity, inwardness, has been posited as the truth; can any expression for the truth be found which has a still higher degree of inwardness? Aye, there is such an expression, provided the principle that subjectivity or inwardness is the truth begins by positing the opposite principle: that subjectivity is untruth. Let us not at this point succumb to such haste as to fail in making the necessary distinctions. Speculative philosophy also says that subjectivity is untruth, but says it in order to stimulate a movement in precisely the opposite direction, namely, in the direction of the principle that objectivity is the truth. Speculative philosophy determines subjectivity negatively as tending toward objectivity. This second determination of ours, however, places a hindrance in its own way while proposing to begin, which has the effect of making the inwardness far more intensive. Socratically speaking, subjectivity is untruth if it refuses to understand that subjectivity is truth, but, for example, desires to become objective. Here, on the other hand, subjectivity in beginning upon the task of becoming the truth through a subjectifying process, is in the difficulty that it is already untruth. Thus, the labor of the task is thrust backward, backward, that is, in inwardness. So far is it from being the case that the way tends in the direction of objectivity, that the beginning merely lies still deeper in subjectivity.

But the subject cannot be untruth eternally, or eternally be presupposed as having been untruth; it must have been brought to this condition in time, or here become untruth in time. The Socratic paradox consisted in the fact that the eternal was related to an existing individual, but now existence has stamped itself upon the existing individual a second time. There has taken place so essential an alteration in him that he cannot now possibly take himself back into the eternal by way of recollection. To do this is to speculate; to be able to do this, but to reject the possibility by apprehending the task of life as a realization of inwardness in existing, is the Socratic position. But now the difficulty is that what followed Socrates on his way as a rejected possibility, has become an impossibility. If engaging in speculation was a dubious merit even from the point of view of the Socratic, it is now neither more nor less than confusion.

The paradox emerges when the eternal truth and existence are placed in juxtaposition with one another; each time the stamp of existence is brought to bear, the paradox becomes more clearly evident. Viewed Socratically the knower was simply an existing individual, but now the existing individual bears the stamp of having been essentially altered by existence.

Let us now call the untruth of the individual *Sin*. Viewed eternally he cannot be sin, nor can he be eternally presupposed as having been in sin. By coming into existence therefore (for the beginning was that subjectivity is untruth), he becomes a sinner. He is not born as a sinner in the sense that he is presupposed as being a sinner before he is born, but he is born in sin and as a sinner. This we might call *Original Sin*. But if existence has in this manner acquired a power over him, he is prevented from taking himself back into the eternal by way of recollection. If it was paradoxical to posit the eternal truth in relationship to an existing individual, it is now absolutely paradoxical to posit it in relationship to such an individual as we have here defined. But the more difficult it is made for him to take himself out of existence by way of recollection, the more profound is the inwardness that his existence may have in existence; and when it is made impossible for him, when he is held so fast in existence that the back door of recollection is forever closed to him, then his inwardness will be the most profound possible. But let us never forget that the Socratic merit was to stress the fact that the knower is an existing individual; for the more difficult the matter becomes, the greater the temptation to hasten along the easy road of speculation, away from fearful dangers and crucial decisions, to the winning of renown and honors and property, and so forth. If even Socrates understood the dubiety of taking himself speculatively out of existence back into the eternal, although no other difficulty confronted the existing individual except that he existed, and that existing was his essential task, now it is impossible. Forward he must, backward he cannot go.

Subjectivity is the truth. By virtue of the relationship subsisting between the eternal truth and the existing individual, the paradox came into being. Let us now go further, let us suppose that the eternal essential truth is itself a paradox. How does the paradox come into being? By putting the eternal essential truth into juxtaposition with existence. Hence when we posit such a conjunction within the truth itself, the truth becomes a paradox. The eternal truth has come into being in time: this is the paradox. If in accordance with the determinations just posited, the subject is prevented by sin from taking himself back into the eternal, now he need not trouble himself about this; for now the eternal essential truth is not behind him but in front of him, through its being in existence or having existed, so that if the individual does not existentially and in existence lay hold of the truth, he will never lay hold of it.

Existence can never be more sharply accentuated than by means of these determinations. The evasion by which speculative philosophy attempts to recollect itself out of existence has been made impossible. With reference to this, there is nothing for speculation to do except to arrive at an understanding of this impossibility; every speculative attempt which insists on being speculative shows *eo ipso* that it has not understood it. The individual may thrust all this away from him, and take refuge in speculation; but it is impossible first to accept it, and then to revoke it by means of speculation, since it is definitely calculated to prevent speculation.

When the eternal truth is related to an existing individual it becomes a paradox. The paradox repels in the inwardness of the existing individual, through the objective uncertainty and the corresponding Socratic ignorance. But since the paradox is not in the first instance itself paradoxical (but only in its relationship to the existing individual), it does not repel with a sufficient intensive inwardness. For without risk there is not faith, and the greater the risk the greater the faith; the more objective security the less inwardness (for inwardness is precisely subjectivity), and the less objective security the more profound the possible inwardness. When the paradox is paradoxical in itself, it repels the individual by virtue of its absurdity, and the corresponding passion of inwardness is faith. But subjectivity, inwardness, is the truth; for otherwise we have forgotten what the merit of the Socratic position is. But there can be no stronger expression for inwardness than when the retreat out of existence into the eternal by way of recollection is impossible; and when, with truth confronting the individual as a paradox, gripped in the anguish and pain of sin, facing the tremendous risk of the objective insecurity, the individual believes. But without risk no faith, not even the Socratic form of faith, much less the form of which we here speak.

When Socrates believed that there was a God, he held fast to the objective uncertainty with the whole passion of his inwardness, and it is precisely in this contradiction and in this risk, that faith is rooted. Now it is otherwise. Instead of the objective uncertainty, there is here a certainty, namely, that objectively it is absurd, and this absurdity, held fast in the passion of inwardness, is faith. The Socratic ignorance is as a witty jest in comparison with the earnestness of facing the absurd; and the Socratic existential inwardness is as Greek light-mindedness in comparison with the grave strenuosity of faith.

What now is the absurd? The absurd is—that the eternal truth has come into being in time, that God has come into being, has been born, has grown up, and so forth, precisely like any other individual human being, quite indistinguishable from other individuals. For every assumption of immediate recognizability is pre-Socratic paganism, and from the Jewish point of view, idolatry; and every determination of what really makes an advance beyond the Socratic must essentially bear the stamp of having a relationship to God's having come into being; for faith *sensu strictissimo*, as was developed in the *Fragments*, refers to becoming. . . .

What does it mean in general to explain anything? Does it consist in showing that the obscure something in question is not this but something else? This would be a strange sort of an explanation; I thought it was the function of an explanation to render it evident that the something in question was this definite thing, so that the explanation took the obscurity away but not the object. Otherwise the explanation would not be an explanation, but something quite different, namely, a correction. An explanation of the paradox makes it clear what the paradox is, removing any obscurity remaining; a correction takes the paradox away, and makes it clear that there is no paradox. But if the paradox arises from putting the eternal and an existing particular human being into relation with one another, when the speculative explanation takes the paradox away, does the explanation also take existence away from the existing individual? And when an existing individual, with or without assistance from another, has arrived at or been brought to the point where it seems to him as nearly as possible that he does not exist, what is he then? Why, then he is absent-minded. So that the explanation of the absolute paradox which concludes that there is no paradox except to a certain degree, which means that there are only relative paradoxes, is an explanation not for existing individuals, but for absent-minded persons. Thus everything is in order. The explanation is that the paradox is the paradox only to a certain degree, and it is quite in order that such an explanation should be valid for an existing individual who is an existing individual only to a certain degree, since he forgets it every other moment. Such an existing individual is precisely a person who suffers from absent-mindedness.

When one ventures to speak of the absolute paradox, characterizing it as a stumblingblock to the Jews, foolishness to the Greeks, and an absurdity to the understanding, and in this connection addresses himself to speculative philosophy, philosophy is not so impolite as to tell him directly that he is a fool. But it offers him an explanation which contains a correction, thus indirectly giving him to understand that he is in error; so a humane and superior mind always deals with an individual of more limited intelligence. The procedure is strictly Socratic; the only thing that might be un-Socratic in this connection would be if the speaker were after all much nearer the truth than the speculative explanation, in which case the difference would be that while Socrates politely and indirectly took away an error from the learner and gave him the truth, speculative philosophy takes the truth away politely and indirectly, and presents the learner with an error. But the politeness remains as the common feature. And when Christianity itself declares that it is a paradox, the speculative explanation is not an explanation but a correction, a polite and indirect correction to be sure, as befits a superior intelligence over against a more limited understanding.

To *explain* the paradox: is that tantamount to reducing the term paradox to a *rhetorical expression*, to something which the worshipful speculative philosopher asserts to have indeed a certain validity—but then again also not to have validity? In that case it remains true after all *summa summarum* that there is no paradox. All honor to the Herr Professor! It is not to take his honor away from him that I say this, as if I, too, could revoke the paradox—by no means. But when the professor has abrogated the paradox it is of course abrogated, and so I may venture to say that it is abrogated—unless the abrogation concerned the professor more than the paradox, so that he, instead of abrogating the paradox, himself became a sort of dubious fantastic abrogation. In other cases it is assumed that explaining something means to make it clear in its signficance, that it is this and not something else. To explain the paradox would then mean to understand more and more profoundly what a paradox is, and that the paradox is the paradox. . . .

Speculative philosophy does not by any means say that Christianity is false; on the contrary, it says that speculative philosophy grasps the truth of Christianity. Surely one could not demand anything more; has Christianity ever claimed to be more than the truth? And when speculative philosophy apprehends its truth, everything is in order. And yet, no, it is not so; in relation to Christianity, systematic philosophy is merely skilled in the use of all sorts of diplomatic phraseology, which deceives the unsuspicious. Christianity as understood by the speculative philosopher is something different from Christianity as expounded for the simple. For them it is a paradox; but the speculative philosopher knows how to abrogate the paradox. So that it is not Christianity which is and was and remains the truth, and what the speculative philosopher understands is not that Christianity is the truth; no, it is the philosopher's understanding of Christianity that constitutes the truth of Christianity. The understanding is thus to be distinguished from the truth it understands; here it is not the case that only when the understanding has understood everything contained in the truth, is the truth understood. Here rather it is the case that when the potential truth has been understood as the philosopher understands it, then—aye, then it is not the case that speculative philosophy has arrived at a true understanding, but that the truth which it understands has come into being.

The truth is not first given, and the understanding of it awaited afterwards, but we look for the completion of the speculative understanding as that which alone can bring the truth into being. The knowledge that speculative philosophy represents is thus different from knowledge generally, where the knowledge as such is assumed to be indifferent to the object known, so that the latter is not altered by being known, but remains the same. No, the knowledge of speculative philosophy is itself the object known, and the latter is no longer the same as it was before becoming known; it has come into being at the same time with speculative philosophy and its truth.

Whether speculative philosophy is right is another question. Here we merely inquire how its explanation of Christianity is related to the Christianity which it purports to explain. And what would this relation be, in accordance with what one might naturally expect? Speculative philosophy is objective, and objectively there is no truth for existing individuals, but only approximations; for the existing individual is precluded from becoming altogether objective by the fact that he exists. Christianity on the contrary is subjective; the inwardness of faith in the believer constitutes the truth's eternal decision. And objectively there is no truth; for an objective knowledge of the truth of Christianity, or of its truths, is precisely untruth. To know a confession of faith by rote is paganism, because Christianity is inwardness.

SUGGESTIONS FOR FURTHER READING

Baillie, John, *Our Knowledge of God*. (New York: Scribner's, 1939). *Defends the thesis that religious experience is a pervasive part of human experience.*

Blackstone, William, *The Problems of Religious Language*. (Englewood Cliffs, N.J.: Prentice-Hall, 1963). *Competent survey of the contemporary debate concerning the function and cognitive import of religious language.*

Eliade, Mircea, *Patterns in Comparative Religion*. (New York: Sheed & Ward, 1958). *A study of mythological and conceptual frameworks in diverse religious traditions.*

Flew, Antony, and MacIntyre, Alasdair, eds., *New Essays in Philosophical Theology*. (New York: Macmillan, 1955). *A volume comprised of discussion of a wide range of religious problems. The point of view of analytic and linguistic philosophy is well represented.*

Hick, John, *Faith and Knowledge*, 2nd edition, revised. (Ithaca, N.Y.: Cornell University Press, 1966). *Introduction to the problems of religious knowledge. Hick advances his view of faith as an interpretative element within experience. See particularly Part II.*

Martin, C. B., *Religious Belief*. (Ithaca, N.Y.: Cornell University Press, 1959). *Chapter 5 contains a searching criticism of the philosophical use of religious experience.*

Moore, Charles A., ed., *Philosophy—East and West.* (Princeton, N.J.: Princeton University Press, 1944). *Essays contrasting and comparing Eastern and Western philosophical perspectives.*

Northrop, F. S. C., *The Meeting of East and West.* (New York: Macmillan, 1946). *Systematic investigation of the fundamental presuppositions of Eastern and Western cultures as they are reflected in thought and action. Not elementary.*

Temple, William, *Nature, Man and God.* (London: Macmillan Co. Ltd., 1934). *Lecture XII contains Temple's theory of divine revelation.*

Vahanian, Gabriel, *The Death of God: The Culture of Our Post-Christian Era.* (New York: George Braziller, 1957). *An examination of the meaning for culture of the premise of the death of God.*

PART 4

THE DOCTRINE OF GOD

Debates concerning the idea of God have played a central role in Western religious thought, and a cluster of problems issue from the widely divergent opinions advanced with respect to conceptions of God. Is it possible for rational or empirical arguments to remove unnecessary obstacles to belief in God? May we discover a God worthy of worship by means of proofs for God's existence? What is the relationship between our faith, our religious experience, and our conception of the nature of God? Is the search for an adequate idea of God merely the quest for a rational clarification of a belief already manifested in worship and religious commitment?

Questions such as these receive their impetus from the facts of religion: (1) Religious life is usually expressed in the form given to worship while the aspirations of religion are most apparent in the religious conception of God. (2) The doctrine of God, while shaped by the religious experiences of men, in turn supports the value orientations manifested in the conduct of such religious persons. The fact that concepts of God vary markedly in different religions, while sharing a fundamental focus of religious concern, provides an unusual challenge to critical thought about the origin and justification of this vital conception and its practical consequences.

One approach to the problems involved in formulating an adequate and defensible idea of God might focus upon the contrast between theism and atheism. Theism is a name used to designate a "family" of western religious traditions which have exercised an important influence in the development of our civilization. Most theistic religions view God as the creative source of the universe and the ground of ultimate value. For most theistic religions, God has unconditioned reality, is the creator and sustainer of the universe, and is completely good and perfect in knowledge.

Atheism, on the other hand, usually denies belief in God. Frequently, however, what the atheist has in mind when he denies belief in God is some specific concept of God. Some forms of atheism turn out, upon careful inspection, to be "religious" in character. A "religious" atheism often is produced by a quarrel in the religious "family" regarding the proper understanding of that reality to which man's religious experience and worship points. Irreligious atheism, however, bespeaks a radical doubt about all doctrines of such religious reality and all notions of a ground of value transcending man. This distinction between an irreligious atheism and a "religious" atheism is made apparent in the concluding sections of this part.

Chapter **12**

The defense of theism

For most religious perspectives in the West the doctrine of God is central. In the history of Western religious philosophy considerable attention has been given to the question of whether man can provide a rational basis for belief in God's existence.

In the eleventh century, St. Anselm advanced his ontological proof for the existence of God. Anselm's proof was an argument from God's Essence, from the *idea* of a perfect Being, which he believed necessarily involved the *existence* of that Being. If we have the idea of a perfect Being, says Anselm, then we immediately recognize that the idea of a perfect Being entails the *idea* of the *existence* of that Being. Furthermore, the idea of a perfect Being entails the concrete, real existence of God, for a Being who exists in fact is more perfect than a Being who exists merely as idea. Anselm also insisted that the relation that a perfect Being has to existence is a necessary one.

Much discussion has taken place over the validity of Anselm's "proof." The usual response to Anselm's argument is that sensible men know that we cannot discover what exists merely by analyzing our ideas. The most serious attack was made by Kant, who maintained that existence is not a real predicate; in other words, according to Kant, Anselm treated existence as though it were just another property of a thing, like weight is a property of a rock, or yellow of a sunset. Kant thought that Anselm's argument treated existence as a legitimate predicate which, as a positive characteristic, perfection must have in order to be perfection. Kant's objection rests upon his insistence that existence is not a property and, hence, adds nothing to the idea of the subject. To use Kant's own example, the idea of 'one hundred dollars' is the same regardless of whether I have one hundred dollars or only hope to.

Two centuries following Anselm, Thomas Aquinas, in the thirteenth century, presented five ways in which he thought that God's existence could be proved. According to Aquinas, there are basically two ways in which something can be known, *by itself* or *by us*. God knows his own Being through His unlimited powers of knowing. Our knowledge of God, however, is not God's knowledge of himself. As a consequence, Aquinas argued that we cannot know God through His Essence (as He knows Himself), but rather, we know of His existence only through inference from what is, from God's creation. Since the creation does not exhaust

God's Essence or Being, knowing God by inference from the creation is not equivalent to knowing God from His Essence.

Each of Aquinas' five arguments proceeds from an observable characteristic of the world to the conclusion that the only explanation of that particular character of the world is God as its cause. All of the proofs make use of the category of causality and involve a causal inference. Structurally the arguments are identical, and Aquinas believed that any one of them would be conclusive in demonstrating God's existence.

Aquinas' proofs are forms of the cosmological argument for God's existence. As such, they assume the universal applicability of the principle of causality. Our knowledge of the causal principle is derived from experience, and in its bearing on empirical phenomena we know something of its usefulness and limitations. Can we, however, infer that the causal principle is applicable outside of the empirical world, which is precisely what is presumed by Aquinas' arguments? Is it legitimate to reason from one particular series of cause and effect (a limited and conditioned series), to another kind of cause which is universal, unlimited and unconditioned.

The basic features of the moral argument for God's existence are to be found in Kant's moral philosophy. Kant did not intend to set forth a demonstrative proof of God's existence which would be satisfactory to theoretical reason; rather, he attempted to establish grounds for assurance in the reality of God as the presupposition for the moral life. According to Kant, man's consciousness of moral imperatives leads by itself to faith in God and also determines the conception of God as Author of the moral law. Human reason in its pure or theoretical application cannot comprehend the nature of God. However, the practical function of reason in relation to moral situations reveals a conception of God as a precondition for moral consciousness. Faith is concerned with rational willing in conformity with moral principles. Action based upon moral principles brings an individual into unity with other free agents and with a transcendent power which can be called God. Thus, human commitment to moral action (to rational willing) is a commitment to something which, while within us, transcends our individuality.

As Kant views it, natural religion involves the recognition that our moral consciousness (our recognition of imperatives of duty) puts us in touch with the highest good to which we can aspire. There ought to be a connection between the highest good (virtue), discovered in moral conscience and pursued in practical life, and the realization of happiness in life. Isn't it reasonable to assume that the pursuit of virtue will lead to happiness? Kant insists that only the postulate of God as moral law-giver and Creator of the universe can assure such harmony between the pursuit of virtue and the realization of happiness. The recognition of God as the foundation of the moral life leads to our viewing all duties as divine commands.

Kierkegaard's sermon on the unchangeableness of God requires little commentary. Delivered in the form of an exhortation, it brings the immutability and implacability of God into juxtaposition with the inconstancy and radical limitations of human life. Kierkegaard's great talents of intellectual analysis and aesthetic construction are united in this address, producing a powerful statement of the classical theistic position. Implicit in Kierkegaard's statements are all of the attributes generally assigned to God in traditional theistic philosophy, e.g. omniscience, omnipotence, immutability, impassivity, eternality. This address is not an argument for God's existence but rather a theistic confession of faith. The correlation between the human predicament and the doctrine of God is clearly exhibited in Kierkegaard's conclusions concerning the importance of the God of theism for human life.

The approach to the nature of God taken in Martin Buber's *I and Thou* differs sharply from the traditional theological endeavor to define God in terms of his attributes and also from the philosophic concern for finding a reasoned proof for God's existence. Buber asserts that God cannot be encountered by making his existence an object of reflection. God is met and known only in the relationship he calls *I-Thou*.

There are two primary attitudes that a person might take: *I-Thou* and *I-It*. Fundamental differences between these two elemental postures derive not from the objects to which the *I* relates, but rather from the mode of relating itself. Subject-object interchanges in which the *I* attempts to control, use, or manipulate the other are typical forms of the *I-It* relation. In such relations, the person assumes a kind of identity that is determined entirely by the way he relates to the other. To take up the hammer as an instrument to pound the nail establishes a relation between the subject and the object that is definitive for both. By contrast, the *I-Thou* relation entails openness, mutuality, and a freeing of the other fully to be itself in its uniqueness.

God, the eternal *Thou*, is somehow present whenever persons relate to each other in this latter way. As Buber put it: "The extended lines of relations meet in the eternal *Thou*." Thus, we find in Buber no characterization of a God in terms of images that can be pictured or seen; rather, he speaks of a God who can be listened to, heard.

Anselm

THE ONTOLOGICAL ARGUMENT*

[I]   For I do not seek to understand that I may believe, but I believe in order to understand. For this also I believe,—that unless I believed, I should not understand.

* St. Anselm (1033–1109): Archbishop of Canterbury and medieval philosopher and theologian. The selection is from the *Proslogium*, Chapters 2–4. The whole of the *Proslogium* is devoted to the proof of God's existence and an explanation of the nature of God. From *Proslogium* by St. Anselm, translated by Sidney Deane (Chicago: Open Court Publishing Co., 1903).

Truly there is a God, although the fool hath said in his heart, There is no God.

[II]   AND SO, Lord, do thou, who dost give understanding to faith, give me, so far as thou knowest it to be profitable, to understand that thou art as we believe; and that thou art that which we believe. And, indeed, we believe that thou art a being than which nothing greater can be conceived. Or is there no such nature, since the fool hath said in his heart, there is no God? (Psalms xiv. 1). But, at any rate, this very fool, when he hears of this being of which I speak—a being than which nothing greater can be conceived— understands what he hears, and what he understands is in his understanding; although he does not understand it to exist.

For, it is one thing for an object to be in the understanding, and another to understand that the object exists. When a painter first conceives of what he will afterwards perform, he has it in his understanding, but he does not yet understand it to be, because he has not yet performed it. But after he has made the painting, he both has it in his understanding, and he understands that it exists, because he has made it.

Hence, even the fool is convinced that something exists in the understanding, at least, than which nothing greater can be conceived. For, when he hears of this, he understands it. And whatever is understood, exists in the understanding. And assuredly that, than which nothing greater can be conceived, cannot exist in the understanding alone. For, suppose it exists in the understanding alone: then it can be conceived to exist in reality; which is greater.

Therefore, if that, than which nothing greater can be conceived, exists in the understanding alone, the very being, than which nothing greater can be conceived, is one, than which a greater can be conceived. But obviously this is impossible. Hence, there is no doubt that there exists a being, than which nothing greater can be conceived, and it exists both in the understanding and in reality.

God cannot be conceived not to exist.—God is that, than which nothing greater can be conceived.—That which can be conceived not to exist is not God.

[III]   AND it assuredly exists so truly, that it cannot be conceived not to exist. For, it is possible to conceive of a being which cannot be conceived not to exist; and this is greater than one which can be conceived not to exist. Hence, if that, than which nothing greater can be conceived, can be conceived not to exist, it is not that, than which nothing greater can be conceived. But this is an irreconcilable contradiction. There is, then, so truly a being than which nothing greater can be conceived to exist, that it cannot even be conceived not to exist; and this being thou art, O Lord, our God.

So truly, therefore, dost thou exist, O Lord, my God, that thou canst not be conceived not to exist; and rightly. For, if a mind could conceive of a being better than thee, the creature would rise above the Creator; and this is most absurd. And, indeed, whatever else there is, except thee alone, can be conceived not to exist. To thee alone, therefore, it belongs to exist more truly than all other beings, and hence in a higher degree than all others. For, whatever else exists does not exist so truly, and hence in a less degree it belongs to it to exist. Why, then, has the fool said in his heart, there is no God (Psalms xiv. 1), since it is so evident, to a rational mind, that thou dost exist in the highest degree of all? Why, except that he is dull and a fool?

How the fool has said in his heart what cannot be conceived.—A thing may be conceived in two ways: (1) when the word signifying it is conceived; (2) when the thing itself is understood. As far as the word goes, God can be conceived not to exist; in reality he cannot.

[IV] BUT how has the fool said in his heart what he could not conceive; or how is it that he could not conceive what he said in his heart? since it is the same to say in the heart, and to conceive.

But, if really, nay, since really, he both conceived, because he said in his heart; and did not say in his heart, because he could not conceive; there is more than one way in which a thing is said in the heart or conceived. For, in one sense, an object is conceived, when the word signifying it is conceived; and in another, when the very entity, which the object is, is understood.

In the former sense, then, God can be conceived not to exist; but in the latter, not at all. For no one who understands what fire and water are can conceive fire to be water, in accordance with the nature of the facts themselves, although this is possible according to the words. So, then, no one who understands what God is can conceive that God does not exist; although he says these words in his heart, either without any, or with some foreign, signification. For, God is that than which a greater cannot be conceived. And he who thoroughly understands this, assuredly understands that this being so truly exists, that not even in concept can it be non-existent. Therefore, he who understands that God so exists, cannot conceive that he does not exist.

I thank thee, gracious Lord, I thank thee; because what I formerly believed by thy bounty, I now so understand by thine illumination, that if I were unwilling to believe that thou dost exist, I should not be able not to understand this to be true.

Aquinas
THE FIVE WAYS*

[Q. 2] Third Article
Whether God Exists?

We proceed thus to the Third Article:—
Objection 1. It seems that God does not exist; because if one of two contraries be infinite, the other would be altogether destroyed. But the name *God* means that He is infinite goodness. If therefore, God existed, there would be no evil discoverable; but there is evil in the world. Therefore God does not exist.

Obj. 2. Further, it is superfluous to suppose that what can be accounted for by a few principles has been produced by many. But it seems that everything we see in the world can be accounted for by other principles, supposing God did not exist. For all natural things can be reduced to one principle, which is nature; and all voluntary things can be reduced to one principle, which is human reason, or will. Therefore there is no need to suppose God's existence.

On the contrary, It is said in the person of God: *I am Who am (Exod.* iii. 14).

I answer that, The existence of God can be proved in five ways.

The first and more manifest way is the argument from motion. It is certain, and evident to our senses, that in the world some things are in motion. Now whatever is moved is moved by another, for nothing can be moved except it is in potentiality to that towards which it is moved; whereas a thing moves inasmuch as it is in act. For motion is nothing else than the reduction of something from potentiality to actuality. But nothing can be reduced from potentiality to actuality, except by something in a state of actuality. Thus that which is actually hot, as fire, makes wood, which is potentially hot, to be actually hot, and thereby moves and changes it. Now it is not possible that the same thing should be at once in actuality and potentiality in the same respect, but only in different respects. For what is actually hot cannot simultaneously be potentially hot; but it is simultaneously potentially cold. It is therefore impossible that in the same respect and in the same way a thing should be both mover and moved, *i.e.,* that it should move

* St. Thomas Aquinas (1224–1274): Medieval philosopher and theologian (see footnote on P. 258). This selection is taken from *Summa Theologica,* I, Question 2, Article 3. In Part I of the *Summa Theologica,* Aquinas devotes himself systematically to problems relating to God's existence, nature, etc. From BASIC WRITINGS OF SAINT THOMAS AQUINAS, Volumes I and II, edited by Anton C. Pegis. Copyright 1945 by Random House, Inc., New York and Burns & Oates Ltd., London.

itself. Therefore, whatever is moved must be moved by another. If that by which it is moved be itself moved, then this also must needs be moved by another, and that by another again. But this cannot go on to infinity, because then there would be no first mover, and, consequently, no other mover, seeing that subsequent movers move only inasmuch as they are moved by the first mover; as the staff moves only because it is moved by the hand. Therefore it is necessary to arrive at a first mover, moved by no other; and this everyone understands to be God.

The second way is from the nature of efficient cause. In the world of sensible things we find there is an order of efficient causes. There is no case known (neither is it, indeed, possible) in which a thing is found to be the efficient cause of itself; for so it would be prior to itself which is impossible. Now in efficient causes it is not possible to go on to infinity, because in all efficient causes following in order, the first is the cause of the intermediate cause, and the intermediate is the cause of the ultimate cause, whether the intermediate cause be several, or one only. Now to take away the cause is to take away the effect. Therefore, if there be no first cause among efficient causes, there will be no ultimate, nor any intermediate, cause. But if in efficient causes it is possible to go on to infinity, there will be no first efficient cause, neither will there be an ultimate effect, nor any intermediate efficient causes; all of which is plainly false. Therefore it is necessary to admit a first efficient cause, to which everyone gives the name of God.

The third way is taken from possibility and necessity, and runs thus. We find in nature things that are possible to be and not to be, since they are found to be generated, and to be corrupted, and consequently, it is possible for them to be and not to be. But it is impossible for these always to exist, for that which can not-be at some time is not. Therefore, if everything can not-be, then at one time there was nothing in existence. Now if this were true, even now there would be nothing in existence, because that which does not exist begins to exist only through something already existing. Therefore, if at one time nothing was in existence, it would have been impossible for anything to have begun to exist; and thus even now nothing would be in existence—which is absurd. Therefore, not all beings are merely possible, but there must exist something the existence of which is necessary. But every necessary thing either has its necessity caused by another, or not. Now it is impossible to go on to infinity in necessary things which have their necessity caused by another, as has been already proved in regard to efficient causes. Therefore we cannot but admit the existence of some being having of itself its own necessity, and not receiving it from another, but rather causing in others their necessity. This all men speak of as God.

The fourth way is taken from the gradation to be found in things. Among beings there are some more and some less good, true, noble, and the like. But *more* and *less* are predicated of different things according as they resemble in their different ways something which is the maximum, as a thing is said to be hotter according as it more nearly resembles that which is hottest;

so that there is something which is truest, something best, something noblest, and, consequently, something which is most being, for those things that are greatest in truth are greatest in being, as it is written in *Metaph*. ii.[1] Now the maximum in any genus is the cause of all in that genus, as fire, which is the maximum of heat, is the cause of all hot things, as is said in the same book.[2] Therefore there must also be something which is to all beings the cause of their being, goodness, and every other perfection; and this we call God.

The fifth way is taken from the governance of the world. We see that things which lack knowledge, such as natural bodies, act for an end, and this is evident from their acting always, or nearly always, in the same way, so as to obtain the best result. Hence it is plain that they achieve their end, not fortuitously, but designedly. Now whatever lacks knowledge cannot move towards an end, unless it be directed by some being endowed with knowledge and intelligence; as the arrow is directed by the archer. Therefore some intelligent being exists by whom all natural things are directed to their end; and this being we call God.

Reply Obj. 1. As Augustine says: *Since God is the highest good, He would not allow any evil to exist in His works, unless His omnipotence and goodness were such as to bring good even out of evil.*[3] This is part of the infinite goodness of God, that He should allow evil to exist, and out of it produce good.

Reply Obj. 2. Since nature works for a determinate end under the direction of a higher agent, whatever is done by nature must be traced back to God as to its first cause. So likewise whatever is done voluntarily must be traced back to some higher cause other than human reason and will, since these can change and fail; for all things that are changeable and capable of defect must be traced back to an immovable and self-necessary first principle, as has been shown.

[1] *Metaph*. Ia, 1 (993b 30).
[2] *Ibid*. (993b 25).
[3] *Enchir*., XI (PL 40, 236).

Kant

THE MORAL ARGUMENT*

So far as morality is based upon the conception of man as a free agent who, just because he is free, binds himself through his reason to unconditioned laws, it stands in need neither of the idea of another Being over him, for him to apprehend his duty, nor of an incentive other than the law itself, for him to do his duty. At least it is man's own fault if he is subject to such a need; and if he is, this need can be relieved through nothing outside himself; for whatever does not originate in himself and his own freedom in no way compensates for the deficiency of his morality. Hence for its own sake morality does not need religion at all (whether objectively, as regards willing, or subjectively, as regards ability [to act]); by virtue of pure practical reason it is self-sufficient. For since its laws are binding, as the highest condition (itself unconditioned) of all ends, through the bare form of universal legality of the maxims, which must be chosen accordingly, morality requires absolutely no material determining ground of free choice,[1] that is, no end, in order either to know what duty is or to impel the performance of duty. On the contrary, when it is a question of duty, morality is perfectly able to ignore all ends, and it ought to do so. Thus, for example, in order to know whether I should (or indeed can) be truthful in my testimony before a court, or whether I should be faithful in accounting for another man's property entrusted to me, it is not at all necessary for me to

---

* Immanuel Kant (1724–1804): German philosopher. This selection is taken from part of the Preface, part of the conclusion of Book III and portions of the first part of Book IV of Kant's *Religion Within the Bounds of Reason Alone*. In this book, Kant treats all of the major problems of religious philosophy, including problems of truth and falsity of religious ideas, the nature of religion, and interpretation of Christianity. From *Religion Within the Bounds of Reason Alone* by Immanuel Kant, translated by Theodore M. Greene and Hoyt H. Hudson. Copyright 1934 by Open Court Publishing Co. Reprinted by permission of The Open Court Publishing Company, La Salle, Illinois.

[1] Those who, in the conception of duty, are not satisfied with the merely formal determining ground as such (conformity to law) as the basis of determination, do indeed admit that such a basis cannot be discovered in *self-love* directed to one's own *comfort*. Hence there remain but two determining grounds: one, which is rational, namely, one's own *perfection*, and another, which is empirical, the *happiness* of others. Now if they do not conceive of the first of these as the moral determining ground (a will, namely, unconditionally obedient to the law) which is necessarily unique—and if they so interpreted it they would be expounding in a circle—they would have to have in mind man's natural perfection, so far as it is capable of enhancement, and this can be of many kinds, such as skill in the arts and sciences, taste, bodily adroitness, etc. But these are always good only on the condition that their use does not conflict with the moral law (which alone commands unconditionally); set up as an end, therefore, perfection cannot be the principle of concepts of duty. The same holds for the end which aims at the happiness of other men. For an act must, first of all, itself be weighed according to the moral law before it is directed to the happiness of others. The requirement laid down by this end, therefore, is a duty only conditionally and cannot serve as the supreme principle of moral maxims.

search for an end which I might perhaps propose to achieve with my declaration, since it matters not at all what sort of end this is; indeed, the man who finds it needful, when his avowal is lawfully demanded, to look about him for some kind of [ulterior] end, is, by this very fact, already contemptible.

But although for its own sake morality needs no representation of an end which must precede the determining of the will, it is quite possible that it is necessarily related to such an end, taken not as the ground but as the [sum of] inevitable consequences of maxims adopted as conformable to that end. For in the absence of all reference to an end no determination of the will can take place in man, since such determination cannot be followed by no effect whatever; and the representation of the effect must be capable of being accepted, not, indeed, as the basis for the determination of the will and as an end antecedently aimed at, but yet as an end conceived of as the result ensuing from the will's determination through the law (*finis in consequentiam veniens*). Without an end of this sort a will, envisaging to itself no definite goal for a contemplated act, either objective or subjective (which it has, or ought to have, in view), is indeed informed as to *how* it ought to act, but not *whither*, and so can achieve no satisfaction. It is true, therefore, that morality requires no end for right conduct; the law, which contains the formal condition of the use of freedom in general, suffices. Yet an end does arise out of morality; for how the question, *What is to result from this right conduct of ours?* is to be answered, and towards what, as an end—even granted it may not be wholly subject to our control—we might direct our actions and abstentions so as at least to be in harmony with that end: these cannot possibly be matters of indifference to reason. Hence the end is no more than an idea of an object which takes the formal condition of all such ends as we *ought* to have (duty) and combines it with whatever is conditioned, and in harmony with duty, in all the ends which we *do* have (happiness proportioned to obedience to duty)—that is to say, the idea of a highest good in the world for whose possibility we must postulate a higher, moral, most holy, and omnipotent Being which alone can unite the two elements of this highest good. Yet (viewed practically) this idea is not an empty one, for it does meet our natural need to conceive of some sort of final end for all our actions and abstentions, taken as a whole, an end which can be justified by reason and the absence of which would be a hindrance to moral decision. Most important of all, however, this idea arises out of morality and is not its basis; it is an end the adoption of which as one's own presupposes basic ethical principles. Therefore it cannot be a matter of unconcern to morality as to whether or not it forms for itself the concept of a final end of all things (harmony with which, while not multiplying men's duties, yet provides them with a special point of focus for the unification of all ends); for only thereby can objective, practical reality be given to the union of the purposiveness arising from freedom with the purposiveness of nature, a union with which we cannot possibly dispense. Take a man who, honoring the moral law, allows the thought to occur to him (he can scarcely avoid doing so) of what sort of world he would create, under the guidance of practical reason, were such a thing in his power, a world into which, moreover, he would place himself as a member. He would not merely make the very choice which is determined by that moral idea of the highest good, were he vouchsafed solely the right to choose; he would also will that [such] a world should by all means come into existence (because the moral law demands that the highest good possible through our agency should be realized) and he would so will even though, in accordance with this idea, he saw himself in danger of paying in his own person a heavy price in happiness—it being possible that he might not be adequate to the [moral] demands of the idea, demands which reason lays down as conditioning happiness. Accordingly he would feel compelled by reason to avow this judgment with complete impartiality, as though it were rendered by another and yet, at the same time, as his own; whereby man gives evidence of the need, morally effected in him, of also conceiving a final end for his duties, as their consequence.

Morality thus leads ineluctably to religion, through which it extends itself* to the idea of a powerful moral Lawgiver, outside of mankind, for Whose will that is the final end (of creation) which at the same time can and ought to be man's final end.

* If the proposition, There is a God, hence there is a highest good in the world, is to arise (as a dogma) from morality alone, It is a synthetic *a priori* proposition: for even though accepted only for practical reference, it does yet pass beyond the concept of duty which morality contains (and which presupposes merely the formal laws, and not the matter, of choice), and hence cannot analytically be evolved out of morality. *But how is such a proposition* a priori *possible?* Agreement with the bare idea of a moral Lawgiver for all men is, indeed, identical with the general moral concept of duty, and so far the proposition commanding this agreement would be analytic. But the acknowledgment of His existence asserts more than the bare possibility of such a thing. The key to the solution of this problem, so far as I believe myself to understand it, I can only indicate here and not develop.

An *end* is always the object of an *inclination*, that is, of an immediate craving for possession of a thing through one's action, just as the *law* (which commands practically) is an object of *respect*. An objective end (*i.e.*, the end which we ought to have) is that which is proposed to us as such by reason alone. The end which embraces the unavoidable and at the same time sufficient condition of all other ends is the *final end*. The subjective final end of rational worldly beings is their own happiness (each of them *has* this end by virtue of having a nature dependent upon sensuous objects, and hence it would be absurd to say that anyone *ought* to have it) and all practical propositions which are based on this final end are synthetic, and at the same time empirical. But that everyone ought to make the highest *good* possible in the world a *final end* is a synthetic practical proposition *a priori* (and indeed objectively practical) given by pure reason; for it is a proposition which goes beyond the concept of duties in this world and adds a consequence (an effect) thereof which is not contained in the moral laws and therefore cannot be evolved out of them analytically. For these laws command absolutely, be the consequence what it will; indeed, they even require that the consideration of such consequence be completely waived when a particular act is concerned; and thereby they make duty an object of highest respect without offering or proposing to us an end (or a final end) such as would have to constitute duty's recommendation and the incentive to the fulfillment of our duty. All men could have sufficient incentive if (as they should) they adhered solely to the dictation of pure reason in the law. What need have they to know the outcome of their moral actions and abstentions, an outcome which the world's

Book III

Investigation into the inner nature of all kinds of faith which concern religion invaribly encounters a *mystery*, i.e., something *holy* which may indeed be *known* by each single individual but cannot be *made known* publicly, that is, shared universally. Being something *holy*, it must be moral, and so an object of reason, and it must be capable of being known from within adequately for practical use, and yet, as something *mysterious*, not for theoretical use, since in this case it would have to be capable of being shared with everyone and made known publicly.

Belief in what we are yet to regard as a holy mystery can be looked upon as *divinely prompted* or as *a pure rational faith*. Unless we are impelled by the greatest need to adopt the first of these views, we shall make it our maxim to abide by the second. Feelings are not knowledge and so do not indicate [the presence of] a mystery; and since the latter is related to reason, yet cannot be shared universally, each individual will have to search for it (if ever there is such a thing) solely in his own reason.

It is impossible to settle, a priori and objectively, whether there are such mysteries or not. We must therefore search directly in the inner, the subjective, part of our moral predisposition to see whether any such thing is to be found in us. Yet we shall not be entitled to number among the holy mysteries the *grounds* of morality, which are inscrutable to us; for we can thus classify only that which we can know but which is incapable of being communicated publicly, whereas, though morality can indeed be communi-

---

course will bring about? It suffices for them that they do their duty; even though all things end with earthly life and though, in this life, happiness and desert may never meet. And yet it is one of the inescapable limitations of man and of his faculty of practical reason (a limitation, perhaps, of all other worldly beings as well) to have regard, in every action, to the consequence thereof, in order to discover therein what could serve him as an end and also prove the purity of his intention—which consequence, though last in practice (nexu effectivo) is yet first in representation and intention (nexu finali). In this end, if directly presented to him by reason alone, man seeks something that he can *love*; therefore the law, which merely arouses his *respect*, even though it does not acknowledge this object of love as a necessity does yet extend itself on its behalf by including the moral goal of reason among its determining grounds. That is, the proposition: Make the highest good possible in the world your own final end! is a synthetic proposition a priori, which is introduced by the moral law itself; although practical reason does, indeed, extend itself therein beyond the law. This extension is possible because of the moral law's being taken in relation to the natural characteristic of man, that for all his actions he must conceive of an end over and above the law (a characteristic which makes man an object of experience). And further, this extension (as with theoretical propositions a priori which are synthetic) is possible only because this end embraces the a priori principle of the knowledge of the determining grounds in experience of a free will, so far as this experience, by exhibiting the effects of morality in its ends, gives objective though merely practical reality to the concept or morality as causal in the world. But if, now, the strictest obedience to moral laws is to be considered the cause of the ushering in of the highest good (as end), then, since human capacity does not suffice for bringing about happiness in the world proportionate to worthiness to be happy, an omnipotent moral Being must be postulated as ruler of the world, under whose care this [balance] occurs. That is, morality leads inevitably to religion.

cated publicly, its cause remains unknown to us. Thus freedom, an attribute of which man becomes aware through the determinability of his will by the unconditioned moral law, is no mystery, because the knowledge of it can be *shared* with everyone; but the ground, inscrutable to us, of this attribute is a mystery because this ground is *not given* us as an object of knowledge. Yet it is this very freedom which, when applied to the final object of practical reason (the realization of the idea of the moral end), alone leads us inevitably to holy mysteries.[3]

The idea of the highest good, inseparably bound up with the purely moral disposition, cannot be realized by man himself (not only in the matter of the happiness pertaining thereto, but also in the matter of the union of men necessary for the end in its entirety); yet he discovers within himself the duty to work for this end. Hence he finds himself impelled to believe in the cooperation or management of a moral Ruler of the world, by means of which alone this goal can be reached. And now there opens up before him the abyss of a mystery regarding what God may do [toward the realization of this end], whether indeed *anything* in general, and if so, *what* in particular should be ascribed to God. Meanwhile man knows concerning each duty nothing but what he must himself do in order to be worthy of that supplement, unknown, or at least incomprehensible, to him.

This idea of a moral Governor of the world is a task presented to our practical reason. It concerns us not so much to know what God is in Himself (His nature) as what He is for us as moral beings; although in order to know the latter we must conceive and comprehend all the attributes of the divine nature (for instance, the unchangeableness, omniscience, omnipotence, etc. of such a Being) which, in their totality, are requisite to the carrying out of the divine will in this regard. Apart from this context we can know nothing about Him.

---

[3] Similarly, the *cause* of the universal gravity of all matter in the world is unknown to us, so much so, indeed, that we can even see that we shall never know it: for the very concept of gravity presupposes a primary motive force unconditionally inhering in it. Yet gravity is no mystery but can be made public to all, for its *law* is adequately known. When Newton represents it as similar to divine omnipresence in the [world of] appearance (*omnipræsentia phænomenon*), this is not an attempt to explain it (for the existence of God in space involves a contradiction), but a sublime analogy which has regard solely to the union of corporeal beings with a world-whole, an incorporeal cause being here attributed to this union. The same result would follow upon an attempt to comprehend the self-sufficing principle of the union of rational beings in the world into an ethical state, and to explain this in terms of that principle. All we know is the duty which draws us toward such a union; the possibility of the achievement held in view when we obey that duty lies wholly beyond the limits of our insight.

There are mysteries which are hidden things in nature (*arcana*), and there can be mysteries (secrecies, *secreta*) in politics which *ought* not to be known publicly; but both *can*, after all, become known to us, inasmuch as they rest on empirical causes. There can be no mystery with respect to what all men are in duty bound to know (*i.e.*, what is moral); only with respect to that which God alone can do and the performance of which exceeds our capacity, and therefore our duty, can there be a genuine, that is, a holy mystery (*mysterium*) of religion; and it may be expedient for us merely to know and understand that there is such a mystery, not to comprehend it.

Now the universal true religious belief conformable to this requirement of practical reason is belief in God (1) as the omnipotent Creator of heaven and earth, *i.e.*, morally as *holy* Legislator, (2) as Preserver of the human race, its *benevolent* Ruler and moral Guardian, (3) as Administrator of His own holy laws, *i.e.*, as *righteous* Judge. . . .

Book IV

Religion is (subjectively regarded) the recognition of all duties as divine commands.[4] That religion in which I must know in advance that something is a divine command in order to recognize it as my duty, is the *revealed* religion (or the one standing in need of a revelation); in contrast, that religion in which I must first know that something is my duty before I can accept it as a divine injunction is the *natural* religion. He who interprets the natural religion alone as morally necessary, *i.e.*, as duty, can be called the *rationalist* (in matters of belief); if he denies the reality of all supernatural divine revelation he is called a *naturalist*; if he recognizes revelation, but asserts that to know and accept it as real is not a necessary requisite to religion, he could be named a *pure rationalist*; but if he holds that belief in

[4] By means of this definition many an erroneous interpretation of the concept of a religion in general is obviated. *First*, in religion, as regards the theoretical apprehension and avowal of belief, no assertorial knowledge is required (even of God's existence), since, with our lack of insight into supersensible objects, such avowal might well be dissembled; rather is it merely a *problematical* assumption (hypothesis) regarding the highest cause of things that is presupposed speculatively, yet with an eye to the object toward which our morally legislative reason bids us strive—an *assertorial* faith, practical and therefore free, and giving promise of the realization of this its ultimate aim. This faith needs merely *the idea of God*, to which all morally earnest (and therefore confident) endeavor for the good must inevitably lead; it need not presume that it can certify the objective reality of this idea through theoretical apprehension. Indeed, the *minimum* of knowledge (it is possible that there may be a God) must suffice, subjectively, for whatever can be made the duty of every man. *Secondly*, this definition of a religion in general obviates the erroneous representation of religion as an aggregate of *special* duties having reference directly to God; thus it prevents our taking on (as men are otherwise very much inclined to do) *courtly obligations* over and above the ethico-civil duties of humanity (of man to man) and our seeking, perchance, even to make good the deficiency of the latter by means of the former. There are no special duties to God in a universal religion, for God can receive nothing from us; we cannot act for Him, nor yet upon Him. To wish to transform a guilty awe of Him into a duty of the sort described is to forget that awe is not a special act of religion but rather the religious temper in all our actions done in conformity with duty. And when it is said: "We ought to obey God rather than men," [Cf. Acts V, 29] this means only that when statutory commands, regarding which men can be legislators and judges, come into conflict with duties which reason prescribes unconditionally, concerning whose observance or transgression God alone can be the judge, the former must yield precedence to the latter. But were we willing to regard the statutory commands, which are given out by a church as coming from God, as constituting that wherein God must be obeyed more than man, such a principle might easily become the war-cry, often heard, of hypocritical and ambitious clerics in revolt against their civil superiors. For that which is permissible, *i.e.*, which the civil authorities command, is *certainly* duty; but whether something which is indeed permissible in itself, but cognizable by us only through divine revelation, is really commanded by God—that is (at least for the most part) highly uncertain.

it is necessary to universal religion, he could be named the pure *super-naturalist* in matters of faith.

The rationalist, by virtue of his very title, must of his own accord restrict himself within the limits of human insight. Hence he will never, as a naturalist, dogmatize, and will never contest either the inner possibility of revelation in general or the necessity of a revelation as a divine means for the introduction of true religion; for these matters no man can determine through reason. Hence the question at issue can concern only the reciprocal claims of the pure rationalist and the supernaturalist in matters of faith, namely, what the one or the other holds as necessary and sufficient, or as merely incidental, to the unique true religion.

When religion is classified not with reference to its first origin and its inner possibility (here it is divided into natural and revealed religion) but with respect to its characteristics which make it *capable of being shared widely with others*, it can be of two kinds: either the *natural* religion, of which (once it has arisen) everyone can be convinced through his own reason, or a *learned* religion, of which one can convince others only through the agency of learning (in and through which they must be guided). This distinction is very important: for no inference regarding a religion's qualification or disqualification to be the universal religion of mankind can be drawn merely from its origin, whereas such an inference is possible from its capacity or incapacity for general dissemination, and it is this capacity which constitutes the essential character of that religion which ought to be binding upon every man.

Such a religion, accordingly, can be *natural*, and at the same time *revealed*, when it is so constituted that men *could and ought to have discovered it* of themselves merely through the use of their reason, although they *would* not have come upon it so early, or over so wide an area, as is required. Hence a revelation theory at a given time and in a given place might well be wise and very advantageous to the human race, in that, when once the religion thus introduced is here, and has been made known publicly, everyone can henceforth by himself and with his own reason convince himself of its truth. In this event the religion is *objectively* a natural religion, though *subjectively* one that has been revealed; hence it is really entitled to the former name. For, indeed, the occurrence of such a supernatural revelation might subsequently be entirely forgotten without the slightest loss to that religion either of comprehensibility, or of certainty, or of power over human hearts. It is different with that religion which, on account of its inner nature, can be regarded only as revealed. Were it not preserved in a completely secure tradition or in holy books, as records, it would disappear from the world, and there must needs transpire a supernatural revelation, either publicly repeated from time to time or else enduring continuously within each individual, for without it the spread and propagation of such a faith would be impossible.

Yet in part at least every religion, even if revealed, must contain certain principles of the natural religion. For only through reason can thought add revelation to the concept of a *religion*, since this very concept, as though deduced from an obligation to the will of a *moral* legislator, is a pure concept of reason. Therefore we shall be able to look upon even a revealed religion on the one hand as a *natural*, on the other as a *learned* religion, and thus to test it and decide what and how much has come to it from one or the other source.

If we intend to talk about a revealed religion (at least one so regarded) we cannot do so without selecting some specimen or other from history, for we must devise instances as examples in order to be intelligible, and unless we take these from history their possibility might be disputed. We cannot do better than to adopt, as the medium for the elucidation of our idea of revealed religion in general, some book or other which contains such examples, especially one which is closely interwoven with doctrines that are ethical and consequently related to reason. We can then examine it, as one of a variety of books which deal with religion and virtue on the credit of a revelation, thus exemplifying the procedure, useful in itself, of searching out whatever in it may be for us a pure and therefore a universal religion of reason. Yet we do not wish thereby to encroach upon the business of those to whom is entrusted the exegesis of this book, regarded as the summary of positive doctrines of revelation, or to contest their interpretation based upon scholarship. Rather is it advantageous to scholarship, since scholars and philosophers aim at one and the same goal, to wit, the morally good, to bring scholarship, through its own rational principles, to the very point which it already expects to reach by another road. Here the New Testament, considered as the source of the Christian doctrine, can be the book chosen. In accordance with our intention we shall now offer our demonstration in two sections, first, the Christian religion as a natural religion, and, second, as a learned religion, with reference to its content and to the principles which are found in it.

Natural religion, as morality (in its relation to the freedom of the agent) united with the concept of that which can make actual its final end (with the conception of *God* as moral Creator of the world), and referred to a continuance of man which is suited to this end in its completeness (to immortality), is a pure practical idea of reason which, despite its inexhaustible fruitfulness, presupposes so very little capacity for theoretical reason that one can convince every man of it sufficiently for practical purposes and can at least require of all men as a duty that which is its effect. This religion possesses the prime essential of the true church, namely, the qualification for universality, so far as one understands by that a validity for everyone (*universitas vel omnitudo distributiva*), i.e., universal unanimity. To spread it, in this sense, as a world religion, and to maintain it, there is needed, no doubt, a body of servants (*ministerium*) of the invisible church, but not officials (*officiales*), in other words, teachers but not dignitaries, because in the rational religion of every individual there does not yet exist a church as a universal *union* (*omnitudo collectiva*), nor is this really contemplated in the above idea.

Yet such unanimity could not be maintained of itself and hence could not, unless it became a visible church, be propagated in its universality; rather is this possible only when a collective unanimity, in other words a union of believers in a (visible) church under the principles of a pure religion of reason, is added; though this church does not automatically arise out of that unanimity nor, indeed, were it already established, would it be brought by its free adherents (as was shown above) to a permanent status as a *community* of the faithful (because in such a religion none of those who has seen the light believes himself to require, for his religious sentiments, fellowship with others). Therefore it follows that unless there are added to the natural laws, apprehensible through unassisted reason, certain statutory ordinances attended by legislative prestige (authority), that will still be lacking which constitutes a special duty of men, and a means to their highest end, namely, their enduring union into a universal visible church; and the authority mentioned above, in order to be a founder of such a church, presupposes a realm of fact and not merely the pure concepts of reason.

Let us suppose there was a teacher of whom an historical record (or, at least, a widespread belief which is not basically disputable) reports that he was the first to expound publicly a pure and searching religion, comprehensible to the whole world (and thus natural). His teachings, as preserved to us, we can in this case test for ourselves. Suppose that all he did was done even in the face of a dominant ecclesiastical faith which was onerous and not conducive to moral ends (a faith whose perfunctory worship can serve as a type of all the other faiths, at bottom merely statutory, which were current in the world at the time). Suppose, further, we find that he had made this universal religion of reason the highest and indispensable condition of every religious faith whatsoever, and then had added to it certain statutes which provided forms and observances designed to serve as means of bringing into existence a church founded upon those principles. Now, in spite of the adventitiousness of his ordinances directed to this end, and the elements of arbitrariness in them, and though we can deny the name of true universal church to these, we cannot deny to him himself the prestige due the one who called men to union in this church; and this without further adding to this faith burdensome new ordinances or wishing to transform acts which he had initiated into peculiar holy practices, required in themselves as being constituent elements of religion.

After this description one will not fail to recognize the person who can be reverenced, not indeed as the *founder* of the *religion* which, free from every dogma, is engraved in all men's hearts (for it does not have its origin in an arbitrary will), but as the founder of the first true *church*. For attestation of his dignity as of divine mission we shall adduce several of his teachings as indubitable evidence of religion in general, let historical records be what they may (since in the idea itself is present adequate ground for its acceptance), these teachings, to be sure, can be no other than those of pure reason, for such alone carry their own proof, and hence upon them must chiefly depend the attestation of the others.

First, he claims that not the observance of outer civil or statutory churchly duties but the pure moral disposition of the heart alone can make man well-pleasing to God (Matthew V, 20–48); that sins in thought are regarded, in the eyes of God, as tantamount to action (V, 28) and that, in general, holiness is the goal toward which man should strive (V, 48); that, for example, to hate in one's heart is equivalent to killing (V, 22); that injury done one's neighbor can be repaired only through satisfaction rendered to the neighbor himself, not through acts of divine worship (V, 24), and that, on the point of truthfulness, the civil device for extorting it, by oath,[5] does violence to respect for truth itself (V, 34–37); that the natural but evil propensity of the human heart is to be completely reversed, that the sweet sense of revenge must be transformed into tolerance (V, 39, 40) and the hatred of one's enemies into charity (V, 44). Thus, he says, does he intend to do full justice to the Jewish law (V, 17); whence it is obvious that not scriptural scholarship but the pure religion of reason must be the law's interpreter, for taken according to the letter, it allowed the very opposite of all this. Furthermore, he does not leave unnoticed, in his designations of the strait gate and the narrow way the misconstruction of the law which men allow themselves in order to evade their true moral duty and, holding themselves immune through having fulfilled their churchly duty (VII, 13).[6] He further requires of these pure dispositions that they manifest themselves also in *works* (VII, 16) and, on the other hand, denies the insidious hope of those who imagine that, through invocation and praise of the Supreme Lawgiver in the person

[5] It is hard to understand why this clear prohibition against the method of forcing confession before a civil tribunal of religious teachers—a method based upon mere superstition, not upon conscientiousness—is held as so unimportant. For that it is superstition whose efficacy is here most relied on is evident from the fact that the man whom one does not trust to tell the truth in a solemn statement, on the truthfulness of which depends a decision concerning the rights of a human being (the holiest of beings in this world) is yet expected to be persuaded to speak truly, by the use of a formula through which, over and above that statement, he simply calls down upon himself divine punishment (which in any event, with such a lie, he cannot escape), just as though it rested with him whether or not to render account to this supreme tribunal. In the passage of Scripture cited above, the mode of confirmation by oath is represented as an *absurd* presumption, the attempt to make actual, as though with magical words, what is really not in our power. But it is clearly evident that the wise Teacher who here says that whatever goes beyond Yea, Yea, and Nay, Nay, in the asseveration of truth comes of evil, had in view the bad effect which oaths bring in their train—namely, that the greater importance attached to them almost sanctions the common lie.

[6] The *strait gate* and the narrow way, which leads to life, is that of good life-conduct; the *wide gate* and the broad way, found by many, is the *church*. Not that the church and its doctrines are responsible for men being lost, but that the *entrance* into it and the knowledge of its statutes or celebration of its rites are regarded as the manner in which God really wishes to be served.

of His envoy, they will make up for their lack of good works and ingratiate themselves into favor (VII, 21). Regarding these works he declares that they ought to be performed publicly, as an example for imitation (V, 16), and in a cheerful mood, not as actions extorted from slaves (VI, 16); and that thus, from a small beginning in the sharing and spreading of such dispositions, religion, like a grain of seed in good soil, or a ferment of goodness, would gradually, through its inner power, grow into a kingdom of God (XIII, 31–33). Finally, he combines all duties (1) in one *universal* rule (which includes within itself both the inner and the outer moral relations of men), namely: Perform your duty for no motive other than unconditioned esteem for duty itself, *i.e.*, love God (the Legislator of all duties) above all else; and (2) in a *particular* rule, that, namely, which concerns man's external relation to other men as universal duty: Love every one as yourself, *i.e.*, further his welfare from good-will that is immediate and not derived from motives of self-advantage. These commands are not mere laws of virtue but precepts of *holiness* which we ought to pursue, and the very pursuit of them is called *virtue*.

Accordingly he destroys the hope of all who intend to wait upon this moral goodness quite passively, with their hands in their laps, as though it were a heavenly gift which descends from on high. He who leaves unused the natural predisposition to goodness which lies in human nature (like a talent entrusted to him) in lazy confidence that a higher moral influence will no doubt supply the moral character and completeness which he lacks, is confronted with the threat that even the good which, by virtue of his natural predisposition, he may have done, will not be allowed to stand him in stead because of this neglect (XXV, 29).

As regards men's very natural expectation of an allotment of happiness proportional to a man's moral conduct, especially in view of the many sacrifices of the former which must be undergone for the sake of the latter, he promises (V, 11, 12) a reward for these sacrifices in a future world, but one in accordance with the differences of disposition in this conduct between those who did their duty *for the sake of the reward* (or for release from deserved punishment) and the better men who performed it merely for its own sake; the latter will be dealt with in a different manner. When the man governed by self-interest, the god of this world, does not renounce it but merely refines it by the use of reason and extends it beyond the constricting boundary of the present, he is represented (Luke XVI, 3–9) as one who, in his very person [as servant], defrauds his master [self-interested] and wins from him sacrifices in behalf of "duty." For when he comes to realize that sometime, perhaps soon, the world must be forsaken, and that he can take along into the other world nothing of what he here possessed, he may well resolve to strike off from the account what he or his master, self-interest, has a legal right to exact from the indigent, and, as it were, thereby to acquire for himself bills of exchange, payable in another world. Herein he acts, no doubt, *cleverly* rather than *morally*, as regards the motives of such charitable actions, and yet in conformity with the moral law, at least according to the letter of that law; and he can hope that for this too he may not stand unrequited in the future.[7] Compare with this what is said of charity toward the needy from sheer motives of duty (Matthew XXV, 35–40), where those, who gave succor to the needy without the idea even entering their minds that such action was worthy of a reward or that they thereby obligated heaven, as it were, to recompense them, are, for this very reason because they acted thus without attention to reward, declared by the Judge of the world to be those really chosen for His kingdom, and it becomes evident that when the Teacher of the Gospel spoke of rewards in the world to come he wished to make them thereby not an incentive to action but merely (as a soul-elevating representation of the consummation of the divine benevolence and wisdom in the guidance of the human race) an object of the purest respect and of the greatest moral approval when reason reviews human destiny in its entirety.

Here then is a complete religion, which can be presented to all men comprehensibly and convincingly through their own reason; while the possibility and even the necessity of its being an archetype for us to imitate (so far as men are capable of that imitation) have, be it noted, been made evident by means of an example without either the truth of those teachings nor the authority and the worth of the Teacher requiring any external certification (for which scholarship or miracles, which are not matters for everyone, would be required). When appeals are here made to older (Mosaic) legislation and prefiguration, as though these were to serve the Teacher as means of confirmation, they are presented not in support of the truth of his teachings but merely for the introduction of these among people who clung wholly, and blindly, to the old. This introduction, among men whose heads, filled with statutory dogmas, have been almost entirely unfitted for the religion of reason, must always be more difficult than when this religion is to be brought to the reason of people uninstructed but also unspoiled. For this reason no one should be astonished to find an exposition, that adapted itself to the prejudices of those times, now puzzling and in need of painstaking exegesis; though indeed it everywhere permits a religious doctrine to shine forth and, in addition, frequently points explicitly to that which must be comprehensible and, without any expenditure of learning, convincing to all men.

---

[7] We know nothing of the future, and we ought not to seek to know more than what is rationally bound up with the incentives of morality and their end. Here belongs the belief that there are no good actions which will not, in the next world, have good consequences for him who performs them; that, therefore, however reprehensible a man may find himself at the end of his life, he must not on that account refrain from doing at least *one* more good deed which is in his power, and that, in so doing, he has reason to hope that, in proportion as he possesses in this action a purely good intent, the act will be of greater worth than those actionless absolutions which are supposed to compensate for the deficiency of good deeds without providing anything for the lessening of the guilt.

Kierkegaard
THE UNCHANGEABLENESS OF GOD*

Prayer

O THOU who art unchangeable, whom nothing changes! Thou who are unchangeable in love, precisely for our welfare not submitting to any change: may we too will our welfare, submitting ourselves to the discipline of Thy unchangeableness, so that we may, in unconditional obedience, find our rest and remain at rest in Thy unchangeableness. Not art Thou like a man; if he is to preserve only some degree of constancy he must not permit himself too much to be moved, nor by too many things. Thou on the contrary art moved, and moved in infinite love, by all things. Even that which we human beings call an insignificant trifle, and pass by unmoved, the need of a sparrow, even this moves Thee; and what we so often scarcely notice, a human sigh, this moves Thee, O Infinite Love! But nothing changes Thee, O Thou who art unchangeable! O Thou who in infinite love dost submit to be moved, may this our prayer also move Thee to add Thy blessing, in order that there may be wrought such a change in him who prays as to bring him into conformity with Thy unchangeable will, Thou who art unchangeable!

Text: The Epistle of James 1:17–21

EVERY good gift and every perfect gift is from above, coming down from the Father of lights, with whom can be no variation; neither shadow that is cast by turning. Of His own will He brought us forth by the word of truth, that we should be a kind of first-fruits of His creatures. Ye know this, my beloved brethren. But let every man be swift to hear, slow to speak, slow to wrath: for the wrath of man worketh not the righteousness of God. Wherefore putting away all filthiness and overflowing of wickedness, receive with meekness the implanted word, which is able to save your souls.

My hearer, you have listened to the reading of the text. How near at hand does it seem now to turn our thoughts in the opposite direction, to the mutability of temporal and earthly things, to the changeableness of men. How depressing and wearisome to the spirit that all things are corruptible,

---

* Søren Kierkegaard (1813–1855): Danish theologian and philosopher. This selection is the final essay in Kierkegaard's work *For Self-Examination and Judge for Yourselves!* In this work, Kierkegaard defends the thesis that the substance of religion is the imitation of the lowly life of Christ. A central aim of the book is to bring into violent juxtaposition the life of faith and the way of the world. From *For Self-Examination and Judge for Yourselves!* by Søren Kierkegaard, translated by Walter Lowrie (1944), pp. 470–482. Reprinted by permission of Princeton University Press.

that men are changeable, you, my hearer, and I! How sad that the change is so often for the worse! Poor human consolation, but yet a consolation, that there is still another change to which the changeable is subject, namely that it has an end!

And yet, if we were to speak in this manner, especially in this spirit of dejection, and hence not in the spirit of an earnest consideration of corruptibility, of human inconstancy, then we would not only fail to keep close to the text, but would depart from it, aye, even alter it. For the text speaks of the opposite, of the unchangeableness of God. The spirit of the text is unmixed joy and gladness. The words of the Apostle, coming as it were from the lofty silences of the highest mountain peaks, are uplifted above the mutabilities of the earthly life; he speaks of the unchangeableness of God, and of nothing else. He speaks of a "father of light," who dwells above, with whom there is no variableness, not even the shadow of any change. He speaks of "good and perfect gifts" that come to us from above, from this father, who as the father of "lights" or light is infinitely well equipped to make sure that what comes from Him really is a good and perfect gift; and as a father He has no other ambition, nor any other thought, than invariably to send good and perfect gifts. And therefore, my beloved brethren, let every man be "swift to hear"; not swift to listen to all sorts of loose talk, but swift to direct his attention upward, from whence comes invariably only good news. Let him be "slow to speak"; for our ordinary human talk, especially in relation to these things, and especially that which comes first over our lips, serves most frequently only to make the good and perfect gifts less good and perfect. Let him be "slow to wrath"; lest when the gifts do not seem to us good and perfect we become angry, and thus cause that which was good and perfect and intended for our welfare to become by our own fault ruinous to us—this is what the wrath of man is able to accomplish, and the "wrath of man worketh not the righteousness of God." "Wherefore put aside all filthiness and overflowing of wickedness"—as when we cleanse and decorate the house and bedeck our persons, festively awaiting the visit, that we may worthily receive the good and perfect gifts. "And receive with meekness the implanted word, which is able to save your souls."

With meekness! In truth, were it not the Apostle speaking, and did we not immediately obey the injunction to be "slow to speak, slow to wrath," we might well be tempted to say: This is a very strange mode of speech; are we then altogether fools, that we need an admonition to be meek in relation to one who desires only our welfare?—it is as if it were meant to mock us, in this context to make use of the word "meekness." For suppose someone were about to strike me unjustly, and another stood by, and said admonishingly: "Try to endure this treatment with meekness"—that would be straightforward speech. But imagine the friendliest of beings, one who is love itself: he has selected a gift for me, and the gift is good and perfect, as love itself; he comes to me and proposes to bestow this gift upon me—and then another man stands by and says admonishingly: "See that you accept this treatment meekly!" And yet, so it is with us human beings. A pagan, and only a human being, the simple sage of antiquity,[1] complains that whenever he proposed to take away from a man some folly or other, and so help him to a better insight, thus bestowing a benefit upon him, he had often experienced that the other became so angry that he even wished to bite him, as the simple sage said jestingly in earnest. Ah, and what has God not had to endure these six thousand years, what does He not endure from morning until night from each of mankind's many millions—for we are sometimes most wroth when He most intends our welfare. Indeed, if we men truly understood what conduces to our welfare, and in the deepest sense truly willed our own welfare, then there would be no need to admonish us to be meek in this connection. But we human beings (and who has not verified this in his own experience) are in our relationship to God as children. And hence there is need of an admonition to be meek in connection with our reception of the good and perfect—so thoroughly is the Apostle convinced that all good and perfect gifts come from Him who is eternally unchangeable.

Different viewpoints! The merely human tendency (as paganism indeed gives evidence) is to speak less about God, and to speak almost exclusively and with sadness about the mutability of human affairs. The Apostle, on the other hand, desires only and alone to speak of God's unchangeableness. Thus so far as the Apostle is concerned. For him the thought of God's unchangeableness is one of pure and unmixed comfort, peace, joy, happiness. And this is indeed eternally true. But let us not forget that the Apostle's joy has its explanation in the fact that the Apostle is the Apostle, that he has already long since wholly yielded himself in unconditional obedience to God's unchangeableness. He does not stand at the beginning, but rather at the end of the way, the narrow but good way which he had chosen in renunciation of everything pursuing it invariably and without a backward look, hasting toward eternity with stronger and ever stronger strides. But we on the contrary, who are still beginners, and subject to discipline, for us the unchangeableness of God must have also another aspect; and if we forget this, we readily run in danger of taking the lofty serenity of the Apostle in vain.

LET US THEN SPEAK, IF POSSIBLE TO THE PROMOTION BOTH OF A WHOLESOME FEAR AND OF A GENUINE PEACE, OF THEE, WHO ART UNCHANGEABLE, OR ABOUT THY UNCHANGEABLENESS.

God is unchangeable. In His omnipotence He created this visible world— and made Himself invisible. He clothed Himself in the visible world as in a garment; He changes it as one who shifts a garment—Himself unchanged. Thus in the world of sensible things. In the world of events He is present everywhere in every moment; in a truer sense than we can say of the most

[1] Socrates.

watchful human justice that it is present everywhere, God is omnipresent, though never seen by any mortal; present everywhere, in the least event as well as in the greatest, in that which can scarcely be called an event and in that which is the only event, in the death of a sparrow and in the birth of the Saviour of mankind. In each moment every actuality is a possibility in His almighty hand; He holds all in readiness, in every instant prepared to change everything: the opinions of men, their judgments, human greatness and human abasement; He changes all, Himself unchanged. When everything seems stable (for it is only in appearance that the external world is for a time unchanged, in reality it is always in flux) and in the overturn of all things, He remains equally unchanged; no change touches Him, not even the shadow of a change; in unaltered clearness He, the father of lights, remains eternally unchanged. In unaltered clearness—aye, this is precisely why He is unchanged, because He is pure clearness, a clarity which betrays no trace of dimness, and which no dimness can come near. With us men it is not so. We are not in this manner clear, and precisely for this reason we are subject to change: now something becomes clearer in us, now something is dimmed, and we are changed; now changes take place about us, and the shadow of these changes glides over us to alter us; now there falls upon us from the surroundings an altering light, while under all this we are again changed within ourselves.

This thought *is terrifying, all fear and trembling*. This aspect of it is in general perhaps less often emphasized: we complain of men and their mutability, and of the mutability of all temporal things; but God is unchangeable, this is our consolation, an entirely comforting thought—so speaks even frivolity. Aye, God is in very truth unchangeable.

But first and foremost, do you also have an understanding with God? Do you earnestly consider and sincerely strive to understand—and this is God's eternally unchangeable will for you as for every human being, that you should sincerely strive to attain this understanding—what God's will for you may be? Or do you live your life in such a fashion that this thought has never so much as entered your mind? How terrifying then that He is eternally unchangeable! For with this immutable will you must nevertheless some time, sooner or later, come into collision—this immutable will, which desired that you should consider this because it desired your welfare; this immutable will, which cannot but crush you if you come into hostile collision with it.

In the second place, you who have some degree of understanding with God, do you also have a good understanding with Him? Is your will unconditionally His will, your wishes, each one of them, His commandments, your thoughts, first and last, His thoughts? If not, how terrifying that God is unchangeable, everlastingly, eternally, unchangeable! Consider but in this connection what it means to be at odds merely with a human being. But perhaps you are the stronger, and console yourself with the thought that the other will doubtless be compelled to change his attitude. But now if he happens to be the stronger—well, perhaps you think to have more endurance. But suppose it is an entire contemporary generation with which you are at odds; and yet, in that case you will perhaps say to yourself: seventy years is not eternity. But when the will is that of one eternally unchangeable—if you are at odds with this will it means an eternity: how terrifying!

Imagine a wayfarer. He has been brought to a standstill at the foot of a mountain, tremendous, impassable. It is this mountain—no, it is not his destiny to cross it, but he has set his heart upon the crossing; for his wishes, his longings, his desires, his very soul, which has an easier mode of conveyance, are already on the other side; it only remains for him to follow. Imagine him coming to be seventy years old; but the mountain still stands there, unchanged, impassable. Let him become twice seventy years; but the mountain stands there unalterably blocking his way, unchanged, impassable. Under all this he undergoes changes, perhaps; he dies away from his longings, his wishes, his desires; he now scarcely recognizes himself. And so a new generation finds him, altered, sitting at the foot of the mountain, which still stands there, unchanged, impassable. Suppose it to have happened a thousand years ago: the altered wayfarer is long since dead, and only a legend keeps his memory alive; it is the only thing that remains—aye, and also the mountain, unchanged, impassable. And now think of Him who is eternally unchangeable, for whom a thousand years are but as one day— ah, even this is too much to say, they are for Him as an instant, as if they did not even exist—consider then, if you have in the most distant manner a will to walk a different path than that which He wills for you: .how terrifying!

True enough, if your will, if my will, if the will of all these many thousands happens to be not so entirely in harmony with God's will: things nevertheless take their course as best they may in the hurlyburly of the so-called actual world; it is as if God did not pay any attention. It is rather as if a just man—if there were such a man!—contemplating this world, a world which, as the Scriptures say, is dominated by evil, must needs feel disheartened because God does not seem to make Himself felt. But do you believe on that account that God has undergone any change? Or is the fact that God does not seem to make Himself felt any the less a terrifying fact, as long as it is nevertheless certain that He is eternally unchangeable? To me it does not seem so. Consider the matter, and then tell me which is the more terrible to contemplate: the picture of one who is infinitely the stronger, who grows tired of letting himself be mocked, and rises in his might to crush the refractory spirits—a sight terrible indeed, and so represented when we say that God is not mocked, pointing to the times when His annihilating punishments were visited upon the human race—but is this really the most terrifying sight? Is not this other sight still more terrifying: one infinitely powerful, who—eternally unchanged!—sits quite still and sees everything, without altering a feature, almost as if He did not exist; while all the time, as the just man must needs complain, lies achieve success and win to power, violence and wrong gain the victory, to such an extent as even to tempt a better man to think that if he hopes to accomplish anything for the good he must in part use the same means; so that it is as if God were being mocked, God the infinitely powerful, the eternally unchangeable, who none the less is neither mocked nor changed—is not this the most terrifying sight? For why, do you think, is He so quiet? Because He knows with Himself that He is eternally unchangeable. Anyone not eternally sure of Himself could not keep so still, but would rise in His strength. Only one who is eternally immutable can be in this manner so still.

He gives men time, and He can afford to give them time, since He has eternity and is eternally unchangeable. He gives time, and that with premeditation. And then there comes an accounting in eternity, where nothing is forgotten, not even a single one of the improper words that were spoken; and He is eternally unchanged. And yet, it may be also an expression for His mercy that men are thus afforded time, time for conversion and betterment. But how fearful if the time is not used for this purpose! For in that case the folly and frivolity in us would rather have Him straightway ready with His punishment, instead of thus giving men time, seeming to take no cognizance of the wrong, and yet remaining eternally unchanged.

Ask one experienced in bringing up children—and in relation to God we are all more or less as children; ask one who has had to do with transgressors—and each one of us has at least once in his life gone astray, and goes astray for a longer or a shorter time, at longer or shorter intervals: you will find him ready to confirm the observation that for the frivolous it is a great help, or rather, that it is a preventive of frivolity (and who dares wholly acquit himself of frivolity!) when the punishment follows if possible instantly upon the transgression, so that the memory of the frivolous may acquire the habit of associating the punishment immediately with the guilt. Indeed, if transgression and punishment were so bound up with one another that, as in a double-barrelled shooting weapon, the pressure on a spring caused the punishment to follow instantly upon the seizure of the forbidden fruit, or immediately upon the commitment of the transgression—then I think that frivolity might take heed. But the longer the interval between guilt and punishment (which when truly understood is an expression for the gravity of the case), the greater the temptation to frivolity; as if the whole might perhaps be forgotten, or as if justice itself might alter and acquire different ideas with the passage of time, or as if at least it would be so long since the wrong was committed that it will become impossible to make an unaltered presentation of it before the bar of justice. Thus frivolity changes, and by no means for the better. It comes to feel itself secure; and when it has become secure it becomes more daring; and so the years pass, punishment is withheld, forgetfulness intervenes, and again the punishment is withheld, but new transgressions do not fail, and the old evil becomes still more malignant. And then finally all is over; death rolls down the curtain—and to all this (it was only frivolity!) there was an eternally unchangeable witness: is this also frivolity? One eternally unchangeable, and it is with this witness that you must make your reckoning. In the instant that the minute-hand of time showed seventy years, and the man died, during all that time the clock of eternity has scarcely moved perceptibly: to such a degree is everything present for the eternal, and for Him who is unchangeable.

And therefore, whoever you may be, take time to consider what I say to myself, that for God there is nothing significant and nothing insignificant, that in a certain sense the significant is for Him insignificant, and in another sense even the least significant is for Him infinitely significant. If then your will is not in harmony with His will, consider that you will never be able to evade Him. Be grateful to Him if through the use of mildness or of severity He teaches you to bring your will into agreement with His—how fearful if He makes no move to arrest your course, how fearful if in the case of any human being it comes to pass that he almost defiantly relies either upon the notion that God does not exist, or upon His having been changed, or even upon His being too great to take note of what we call trifles! For the truth is that God both exists and is eternally unchangeable; and His infinite greatness consists precisely in seeing even the least thing, and remembering even the least thing. Aye, and if you do not will as He wills, that He remembers it unchanged for an eternity!

There is thus sheer fear and trembling, for us frivolous and inconstant human beings, in this thought of God's unchangeableness. Oh, consider it well! Whether God makes Himself immediately felt or not, He is eternally unchangeable. He is eternally unchangeable, consider this, if we say you have any matter outstanding with Him: He is unchangeable. You have perhaps promised Him something, obligated yourself in a sacred pledge—but in the course of time you have undergone a change, and now you rarely think of God—now that you have grown older, have you perhaps found more important things to think about? Or perhaps you now have different notions about God, and think that He does not concern Himself with the trifles of your life, regarding such beliefs as childishness. In any case you have just about forgotten what you promised Him; and thereupon you have proceeded to forget that you promised Him anything; and finally, you have forgotten, forgotten—aye, forgotten that He forgets nothing, since He is eternally unchangeable, forgotten that it is precisely the inverted childishness of mature years to imagine that anything is insignificant for God, or that God forgets anything, He who is eternally unchangeable!

In human relationships we so often complain of inconstancy, one party accuses the other of having changed. But even in the relationship between man and man, it is sometimes the case that the constancy of one party may come to seem like a tormenting affliction for the other. A man may, for example, have talked to another person about himself. What he said may have been merely a little childish, pardonably so. But perhaps, too, the matter was more serious than this: the poor foolish vain heart was tempted to speak in lofty tones of its enthusiasm, of the constancy of its feelings, and of its purposes in this world. The other man listened calmly; he did not even smile, or interrupt the speech; he let him speak on to the end, listened and kept silence; only he promised, as he was asked to do, not to forget what had been said. Then some time elapsed, and the first man had long since forgotten all this; only the other had not forgotten. Aye, let us suppose something still stranger: he had permitted himself to be moved inwardly by the thoughts that the first man had expressed under the influence of his mood, when he poured out, so to speak, his momentary feeling; he had in sincere endeavor shaped his life in accordance with these ideas. What torment in this unchanged remembrance by one who showed only too clearly that he had retained in his memory every last detail of what had been said in that moment!

And now consider Him, who is eternally unchangeable—and this human heart! O this human heart, what is not hidden in your secret recesses, unknown to others—and that is the least of it—but sometimes almost unknown to the individual himself! When a man has lived a few years it is almost as if it were a burial-plot, this human heart! There they lie buried in forgetfulness: promises, intentions, resolutions, entire plans and fragments of plans, and God knows what—aye, so say we men, for we rarely think about what we say; we say: there lies God knows what. And this we say half in a spirit of frivolity, and half weary of life—and it is so fearfully true that God does know what to the last detail, knows what you have forgotten, knows what for your recollection has suffered alteration, knows it all unchanged. He does not remember it merely as having happened some time ago, nay, He remembers it as if it were today. He knows whether, in connection with any of these wishes, intentions, resolutions, something so to speak was said to Him about it—and He is eternally unchanged and eternally unchangeable. Oh, if the remembrance that another human being carries about with him may seem as it were a burden to you—well, this remembrance is after all not always so entirely trustworthy, and in any case it cannot endure for an eternity: sometime I may expect to be freed from this other man and his remembrance. But an omniscient witness and an eternally unchangeable remembrance, one from which you can never free yourself, least of all in eternity: how fearful!

No, in a manner eternally unchanged, everything is for God eternally present, always equally before Him. No shadow of variation, neither that of morning nor of evening, neither that of youth or of old age, neither that of forgetfulness nor of excuse, changes Him; for Him there is no shadow. If we human beings are mere shadows, as is sometimes said, He is eternal clearness in eternal unchangeableness. If we are shadows that glide away—my soul, look well to thyself; for whether you will it or not, you go to meet eternity, to meet Him, and He is eternal clearness. Hence it is not so much that He keeps a reckoning, as that He is Himself the reckoning. It is said that we must render up an account, as if we perhaps had a long time to prepare for it, and also perhaps as if it were likely to be cluttered up with such an enormous mass of detail as to make it impossible to get the reckoning finished: O my soul, the account is every moment complete! For the unchangeable clearness of God is the reckoning, complete to the last detail, preserved by Him who is eternally unchangeable, and who has forgotten nothing of the things that I have forgotten, and who does not, as I do, remember some things otherwise than they really were.

There is thus sheer fear and trembling in this thought of the unchangeableness of God, almost as if it were far, far beyond the power of any human being to sustain a relationship to such an unchangeable power; aye, as if this thought must drive a man to such unrest and anxiety of mind as to bring him to the verge of despair.

But then it is also true that *there is rest and happiness in this thought.* It is really true that when, wearied with all this human inconstancy, this temporal and earthly mutability, and wearied also of your own inconstancy, you might wish to find a place where rest may be found for your weary head, your weary thoughts, your weary spirit, so that you might rest and find complete repose: Oh, in the unchangeableness of God there is rest! When you therefore permit this unchangeableness to serve you according to His will, for your own welfare, your eternal welfare; when you submit yourself to discipline, so that your selfish will (and it is from this that the change chiefly comes, more than from the outside) dies away, the sooner the better—and there is no help for it, you must whether willing or resisting, for think how vain it is for your will to be at odds with an eternal immutability; be therefore as the child when it profoundly feels that it has over against itself a will in relation to which nothing avails except obedience —when you submit to be disciplined by His unchangeable will, so as to renounce inconstancy and changeableness and caprice and self-will: then you will steadily rest more and more securely, and more and more blessedly, in the unchangeableness of God.

For that the thought of God's unchangeableness is a blessed thought —who can doubt it? But take heed that you become of such a mind that you can rest happily in this immutability! Oh, as one is wont to speak who has a happy home, so speaks such an individual. He says: my home is eternally secure, I rest in the unchangeableness of God. This is a rest that no one can disturb for you except yourself; if you could become completely obedient in invariable obedience, you would each and every moment, with the same necessity as that by which a heavy body sinks to the earth or a light body moves upward, freely rest in God.

And as for the rest, let all things change as they do. If the scene of your activity is on a larger stage, you will experience the mutability of all things in greater measure; but even on a lesser stage, or on the smallest stage of all, you will still experience the same, perhaps quite as painfully. You will learn how men change, how you yourself change; sometimes it will even seem to you as if God Himself changed, all of which belongs to the upbringing. On this subject of the mutability of all things one older than I would be able to speak in better fashion, while perhaps what I could say might seem to someone very young as if it were new. But this we shall not further expound, leaving it rather for the manifold experiences of life to unfold for each one in particular, in a manner intended especially for him, that which all other men have experienced before him. Sometimes the changes will be such as to call to mind the saying that variety is a pleasure —an indescribable pleasure! There will also come times when you will have occasion to discover for yourself a saying which the language has suppressed, and you will say to yourself: "Change is not pleasant—how could I ever have said that variety is a pleasure!" When this experience comes to you, you will have especial occasion (though you will surely not forget this in the first case either) to seek Him who is unchangeable.

My hearer, this hour is now soon past, and the discourse. Unless you yourself will it otherwise, this hour and its discourse will soon be forgotten. And unless you yourself will it otherwise, the thought of God's unchangeableness will also soon be forgotten in the midst of life's changes. But for this He will surely not be responsible, He who is unchangeable! But if you do not make yourself guilty of forgetfulness with respect to it, you will in this thought have found a sufficiency for your entire life, aye, for eternity.

Imagine a solitary wayfarer, a desert wanderer. Almost burned by the heat of the sun, languishing with thirst, he finds a spring. O refreshing coolness! Now God be praised, he says—and yet it was merely a spring he found; what then must not he say who found God! and yet he too must say: "God be praised, I have found God—now I am well provided for. Your faithful coolness, O beloved well-spring, is not subject to any change. In the cold of winter, if winter visited this place, you would not become colder, but would preserve the same coolness unchanged, for the waters of the spring do not freeze! In the midday heat of the summer sun you preserve precisely the same coolness, for the waters of the spring do not become lukewarm!" There is nothing untrue in what he says, no false exaggeration in his eulogy. (And he who chooses a spring as subject for his eulogy chooses in my opinion no ungrateful theme, as anyone may better understand the more he knows what the desert signifies, and solitude.) However, the life of our wanderer took a turn otherwise than he had thought; he lost touch with the spring, and went astray in the wide world. Many years later he returned to the same place. His first thought was of the spring—but it was not, it had run dry. For a moment he stood silent in grief. Then he gathered himself together and said: "No, I will not retract a single word of all that I said in your praise; it was all true. And if I praised your refreshing coolness while you were still in being, O beloved well-spring, let me now also praise it when you have vanished, in order that there may be some proof of unchangeableness in a human breast. Nor can I say that you deceived me; had I found you, I am convinced that your coolness would have been quite unchanged—and more you had not promised."

But Thou O God, who are unchangeable, Thou art always and invariably to be found, and always to be found unchanged. Whether in life or in death, no one journeys so far afield that Thou art not to be found by him, that Thou art not there, Thou who art everywhere. It is not so with the well-springs of earth, for they are to be found only in special places. And besides—overwhelming security!—Thou dost not remain, like the spring, in a single place, but Thou dost follow the traveller on his way. Ah, and no one ever wanders so far astray that he cannot find the way back to Thee, Thou who art not merely as a spring that may be found—how poor and inadequate a description of what Thou art!—but rather as a spring that itself seeks out the thirsty traveller, the errant wanderer: who has ever heard the like of any spring! Thus Thou art unchangeably always and everywhere to be found. And whenever any human being comes to Thee, of whatever age, at whatever time of day, in whatever state: if he comes in sincerity he always finds Thy love equally warm, like the spring's unchanged coolness, O Thou who art unchangeable! Amen!

Buber

THE I-THOU RELATION"

To man the world is twofold, in accordance with his twofold attitude.

The attitude of man is twofold, in accordance with the twofold nature of the primary words which he speaks.

The primary words are not isolated words, but combined words.

The one primary word is the combination I-Thou.

The other primary word is the combination I-It; wherein, without a change in the primary word, one of the words He and She can replace It.

Hence the I of man is also twofold.

For the I of the primary word I-Thou is a different I from that of the primary word I-It.

Primary words do not signify things, but they intimate relations.

Primary words do not describe something that might exist independently of them, but being spoken they bring about existence.

Primary words are spoken from the being.

* Martin Buber (1878–1965): Austrian-Jewish existentialist theologian. The inspirational source of Buber's religious thought is Hasidism, a mystical movement which flourished in Eastern European Jewish communities in the eighteenth and nineteenth centuries. This selection is from Buber's seminal work, I And Thou, and contains some of the basic principles of his dialogical philosophy. Reprinted by permission of Charles Scribner's Sons from I and Thou by Martin Buber, translated by Walter Kaufmann, pp. 3–4, 7–9, 11, 75–76, 78–79, 112, 134–137. Copyright © 1970 Charles Scribner's Sons. Reprinted also by permission of T. & T. Clark Ltd.

If *Thou* is said, the *I* of the combination *I-Thou* is said along with it.
If *It* is said, the *I* of the combination *I-It* is said along with it.
The primary word *I-Thou* can only be spoken with the whole being.
The primary word *I-It* can never be spoken with the whole being.

There is no *I* taken in itself, but only the *I* of the primary word *I-Thou* and the *I* of the primary word *I-It*.

When a man says *I* he refers to one or other of these. The *I* to which he refers is present when he says *I*. Further, when he says *Thou* or *It*, the *I* of one of the two primary words is present.

The existence of *I* and the speaking of *I* are one and the same thing.

When a primary word is spoken the speaker enters the word and takes his stand in it. . . .

I consider a tree.

I can look on it as a picture: stiff column in a shock of light, or splash of green shot with the delicate blue and silver of the background.

I can perceive it as movement: flowing veins on clinging, pressing pith, suck of the roots, breathing of the leaves, ceaseless commerce with earth and air—and the obscure growth itself.

I can classify it in a species and study it as a type in its structure and mode of life.

I can subdue its actual presence and form so sternly that I recognize it only as an expression of law—of the laws in accordance with which a constant opposition of forces is continually adjusted, or of those in accordance with which the component substances mingle and separate.

I can dissipate it and perpetuate it in number, in pure numerical relation.

In all this the tree remains my object, occupies space and time, and has its nature and constitution.

It can, however, also come about, if I have both will and grace, that in considering the tree I become bound up in relation to it. The tree is now no longer *It*. I have been seized by the power of exclusiveness.

To effect this it is not necessary for me to give up any of the ways in which I consider the tree. There is nothing from which I would have to turn my eyes away in order to see, and no knowledge that I would have to forget. Rather is everything, picture and movement, species and type, law and number, indivisibly united in this event.

Everything belonging to the tree is in this: its form and structure, its colours and chemical composition, its intercourse with the elements and with the stars, are all present in a single whole.

The tree is no impression, no play of my imagination, no value depending on my mood; but it is bodied over against me and has to do with me, as I with it—only in a different way.

Let no attempt be made to sap the strength from the meaning of the relation: relation is mutual.

The tree will have a consciousness, then, similar to our own? Of that I have no experience. But do you wish, through seeming to succeed in it with yourself, once again to disintegrate that which cannot be disintegrated? I encounter no soul or dryad of the tree, but the tree itself.

If I face a human being as my *Thou*, and say the primary word *I-Thou* to him, he is not a thing among things, and does not consist of things.

Thus human being is not *He* or *She*, bounded from every other *He* and *She*, a specific point in space and time within the net of the world; nor is he a nature able to be experienced and described, a loose bundle of named qualities. But with no neighbour, and whole in himself, he is *Thou* and fills the heavens. This does not mean that nothing exists except himself. But all else lives in *his* light.

Just as the melody is not made up of notes nor the verse of words nor the statue of lines, but they must be tugged and dragged till their unity has been scattered into these many pieces, so with the man to whom I say *Thou*. I can take out from him the colour of his hair, or of his speech, or of his goodness. I must continually do this. But each time I do it he ceases to be *Thou*.

And just as prayer is not in time but time in prayer, sacrifice not in space but space in sacrifice, and to reverse the relation is to abolish the reality, so with the man to whom I say *Thou*. I do not meet with him at some time and place or other. I can set him in a particular time and place; I must continually do it: but I set only a *He* or a *She*, that is an *It*, no longer my *Thou*.

So long as the heaven of *Thou* is spread out over me the winds of causality cower at my heels, and the whirlpool of fate stays its course.

I do not experience the man to whom I say *Thou*. But I take my stand in relation to him, in the sanctity of the primary word. Only when I step out of it do I experience him once more. In the act of experience *Thou* is far away.

Even if the man to whom I say *Thou* is not aware of it in the midst of his experience, yet relation may exist. For *Thou* is more that *It* realises. No deception penetrates here; here is the cradle of the Real Life. . . .

The *Thou* meets me through grace—it is not found by seeking. But my speaking of the primary word to it is an act of my being, is indeed *the* act of my being.

The *Thou* meets me. But I step into direct relation with it. Hence the relation means being chosen and choosing, suffering and action in one; just as any action of the whole being, which means the suspension of all partial actions and consequently of all sensations of actions grounded only in their particular limitation, is bound to resemble suffering.

The primary word *I-Thou* can be spoken only with the whole being. Concentration and fusion into the whole being can never take place through my agency, nor can it ever take place without me. I become through my relation to the *Thou;* as I become *I,* I say *Thou.*

All real living is meeting. . . .

The extended lines of relations meet in the eternal *Thou.*

Every particular *Thou* is a glimpse through to the eternal *Thou;* by means of every particular *Thou* the primary word addresses the eternal *Thou.* Through this mediation of the *Thou* of all beings fulfilment, and non-fulfilment, of relations comes to them: the inborn *Thou* is realised in each relation and consummated in none. It is consummated only in the direct relation with the *Thou* that by its nature cannot become *It.*

Men have addressed their eternal *Thou* with many names. In singing of Him who was thus named they always had the *Thou* in mind: the first myths were hymns of praise. Then the names took refuge in the language of *It;* men were more and more strongly moved to think of and to address their eternal *Thou* as an *It.* But all God's names are hallowed, for in them He is not merely spoken about, but also spoken to.

Many men wish to reject the word God as a legitimate usage, because it is so misused. It is indeed the most heavily laden of all the words used by men. For that very reason it is the most imperishable and most indispensable. What does all mistaken talk about God's being and works (though there has been, and can be, no other talk about these) matter in comparison with the one truth that all men who have addressed God had God Himself in mind? For he who speaks the word God and really has *Thou* in mind (whatever the illusion by which he is held), addresses the true *Thou* of his life, which cannot be limited by another *Thou,* and to which he stands in a relation that gathers up and includes all others.

But when he, too, who abhors the name, and believes himself to be godless, gives his whole being to addressing the *Thou* of his life, as a *Thou* that cannot be limited by another, he addresses God. . . .

Every real relation with a being or life in the world is exclusive. Its *Thou* is freed, steps forth, is single, and confronts you. It fills the heavens. This does not mean that nothing else exists; but all else lives in *its* light. As long as the presence of the relation continues, this its cosmic range is inviolable. But as soon as a *Thou* becomes *It,* the cosmic range of the relation appears as an offence to the world, its exclusiveness as an exclusion of the universe.

In the relation with God unconditional exclusiveness and unconditional inclusiveness are one. He who enters on the absolute relation is concerned with nothing isolated any more, neither things nor beings, neither earth nor heaven; but everything is gathered up in the relation. For to step into pure relation is not to disregard everything but to see everything in the *Thou,* not to renounce the world but to establish it on its true basis. To look away from the world, or to stare at it, does not help a man to reach God; but he who sees the world in Him stands in His presence. "Here world, there God" is the language of *It*; "God in the world" is another language of *It*; but to eliminate or leave behind nothing at all, to include the whole world in the *Thou*, to give the world its due and its truth, to include nothing beside God but everything in him—this is full and complete relation.

Men do not find God if they stay in the world. They do not find Him if they leave the world. He who goes out with his whole being to meet his *Thou* and carries to it all being that is in the world, finds Him who cannot be sought.

Of course God is the "wholly Other"; but He is also the wholly Same, the wholly Present. Of course He is the *Mysterium Tremendum* that appears and overthrows; but He is also the mystery of the self-evident, nearer to me than my *I*.

If you explore the life of things and of conditional being you come to the unfathomable, if you deny the life of things and of conditioned being you stand before nothingness, if you hallow this life you meet the living God. . . .

The eternal *Thou* can by its nature not become *It*; for by its nature it cannot be established in measure and bounds, not even in the measure of the immeasurable, or the bounds of boundless being; for by its nature it cannot be understood as a sum of qualities, not even as an infinite sum of qualities raised to a transcendental level; for it can be found neither in nor out of the world; for it cannot be experienced, or thought; for we miss Him, Him who is, if we say "I believe that He is"—"He" is also a metaphor, but "Thou" is not.

And yet in accordance with our nature we are continually making the eternal *Thou* into *It*, into some thing—making God into a thing. Not indeed out of arbitrary self-will; God's history as a thing, the passage of God as a Thing through religion and through the products on its brink, through its bright ways and its gloom, its enhancement and its destruction of life, the passage away from the living God and back again to Him, the changes from the present to establishment of form, of objects, and of ideas, dissolution and renewal—all are one way, are *the* way. . . .

The question is, how can the eternal *Thou* in the relation be at once exclusive and inclusive? How can the *Thou*-relationship of man to God, which is conditioned by an unconditioned turning to him, diverted by nothing, nevertheless include all other *I-Thou* relations of this man, and bring them as it were to God?

Note that the question is not about God, but about our relation to him. And yet in order to be able to answer I must speak of him. For our relation to him is as above contradictions as it is, because he is as above contradictions as he is.

Of course we speak only of what God is in his relation to a man. And even that is only to be expressed in paradox; more precisely, by the paradoxical use of a concept; more precisely still, by the paradoxical combination of a substantive concept with an adjective which contradicts its normal content. The assertion of this contradiction must yield to the insight that the indispensable description of the object by this concept can be justified only in this way. The content of the concept is revolutionised, transformed, and extended—but this is indeed what we experience with every concept which we take out of immanence—compelled by the reality of faith—and use with reference to the working of transcendence.

The description of God as a Person is indispensable for everyone who like myself means by "God" not a principle (although mystics like Eckhart sometimes identify him with "Being") and like myself means by "God" not an idea (although philosophers like Plato at times could hold that he was this): but who rather means by "God," as I do, him who—whatever else he may be—enters into a direct relation with us men in creative, revealing and redeeming acts, and thus makes it possible for us to enter into a direct relation with him. This ground and meaning of our existence constitutes a mutuality, arising again and again, such as can subsist only between persons. The concept of personal being is indeed completely incapable of declaring what God's essential being is, but it is both permitted and necessary to say that God is *also* a Person. If as an exception I wished to translate what is meant by this into philosophical language, that of Spinoza, I should have to say that of God's infinitely many attributes we men do not know two, as Spinoza thinks, but three: to spiritual being (in which is to be found the source of what we call spirit) and to natural being (which presents itself in what is known to us as nature) would be added the attribute of personal being. From this attribute would stem my and all men's being as person, as from those other attributes would stem my and all men's being as spirit and being as nature. And only this third attribute of personal being would be given to us to be known direct in its quality as an attribute.

But now the contradiction appears in the appeal to the familiar content of the concept person. This says that it is indeed the property of a person that its independence should consist in itself, but that it is limited in its total being by the plurality of other independent entities; and this can of course not be true of God. This contradiction is countered by the paradoxical description of God as the absolute Person, i.e. the Person who cannot be limited. It is as the absolute Person that God enters into direct relation with us. The contradiction yields to deeper insight.

As a Person God gives personal life, he makes us as persons become capable of meeting with him and with one another. But no limitation can come upon him as the absolute Person, either from us or from our relations with one another; in fact we can dedicate to him not merely our persons but also our relations to one another. The man who turns to him therefore need not turn away from any other *I-Thou* relation; but he properly brings them to him, and lets them be fulfilled "in the face of God."

One must, however, take care not to understand this conversation with God—the conversation of which I have to speak in this book and in almost all the works which followed—as something happening solely alongside or above the everyday. God's speech to men penetrates what happens in the life of each one of us, and all that happens in the world around us, biographical and historical, and makes it for you and me into instruction, message, demand. Happening upon happening, situation upon situation, are enabled and empowered by the personal speech of God to demand of the human person that he take his stand and make his decision. Often enough we think there is nothing to hear, but long before we have ourselves put wax in our ears.

The existence of mutuality between God and man cannot be proved, just as God's existence cannot be proved. Yet he who dares to speak of it, bears witness, and calls to witness him to whom he speaks—whether that witness is now or in the future.

Chapter 13

Atheism

While the interest in providing arguments for the existence of God and explanations of his nature has occupied a central place in Western thought, it has not obscured other questions of equal importance. Both Oman's and Kierkegaard's essays attempt to show concretely what it means to respond to experience, life, and the world in a theistic fashion. Of equal interest, however, are the implications of a denial of God's existence. For what reasons might a person reject belief in God, and what view of human existence might be taken as a consequence of that denial?

Two forms of atheism are presented in the essays by Max Otto and Jean-Paul Sartre. Both forms are built upon humanistic foundations, although the particular humanism which underlies each is different. The position from which Otto speaks might be called 'scientific humanism', while that of Sartre is more appropriately called 'existential humanism'. It should not surprise us to find, in the light of this fact, that Otto and Sartre advance different reasons for their atheistic affirmations and envision different consequences for human life and experience as a result of their perspectives.

According to Otto, a sharp distinction should be drawn between a positive belief in the nonexistence of God (atheism) and the absence of any opinion, one way or the other, on the question (agnosticism). These two postures are dissimilar in their effects upon other beliefs, attitudes, and patterns of conduct. Implicit in Otto's whole argument is the contention that human reliance upon divine initiative and providence with respect to everyday problems has the effect of inhibiting the full development of human resources and powers. As a problem-solver, man has demonstrated, in his mastery over the powers of nature and the harnessing of natural forces, that he does not require the belief in divine assistance. In fact, when man does not believe in God's existence, he is forced to assume, in a complete and total fashion, the responsibility for shaping his fate on earth by the full employment of his own talents.

Sartre, in contrast to Otto, presents himself as a spokesman for "atheistic existentialism." In his thought we find the synthesis of the atheistic hypothesis, the nonexistence of God, and the existential hypothesis, 'existence precedes essence'. If we operate on the hypothesis that God created the universe and man, then we are committed, says Sartre, to the notion that man has a universal nature, an essence. In this view, human existence is fully determined by the particular nature which man shares in common with all men. When, however, we deny God's existence, then an altogether new formula becames appropriate for understanding human reality, namely, 'existence precedes essence'. A man exists before he begins to define himself through his will and projects. A man is an activity of freedom and this means that each man is entirely responsible not only for his own life but for all human life.

Since there is no divinely created moral order, each human action constitutes a free creation of value and is a "commitment on the behalf of all mankind." In fashioning his own existence, an individual man shapes the being of humanity as a whole. No appeal can be made outside of the range of human freedom for decisions and actions; consequently nothing justifies or can justify any human choice. The choosing supplies its own justification by the sheer fact of human willing. Sartre would object violently to the humanistic form of atheism expressed by Otto, for he would see in it a complete failure of nerve, an evasion of the radical implications involved when God is absent. Otto's form of enlightened atheism manages to delete the hypothesis of God while retaining a value orientation which is quite unchanged by the fact of God's non-existence. Sartre speaks of the "embarrassment" of the absence of God, meaning that man's existence now becomes rootless and groundless, and his value commitments and decisions are without objective foundation. Man is forfeit to an unjustified existence which is identified with radical freedom and responsibility. As Sartre puts it, "man is condemned to be free."

The sharp contrast between Sartre's and Otto's visions of the implications of atheism for human experience should be carefully studied. For example, Otto finds the fact that man is an aspiring being to be a source of hope and confidence mitigating against the necessity for a divine prop for moral action. Sartre, however, cannot view man's will to surpass himself with quite the same aplomb as Otto; although such pursuit of transcendent goals is constitutive of human life, it has no objective ground or justification outside man's will. In other words, while it is true that man aspires beyond himself and seeks to transcend present conditions, the aspiring occurs out of a groundless, rootless condition and is a source of anxiety and guilt. From Sartre's perspective, what Otto misses in this aspiring leap of faith or will is that man acts totally without hope. Otto seems to ignore the fact, which Sartre takes to be evident, that a necessary consequence of God's nonexisence is that now "everything is permitted" and "man is without excuse" and justification. The anguish of total responsibility and complete freedom is not recognized by Otto in his appraisal of the consequences of the absence of God for human beings.

M. Otto

THE NONEXISTENCE OF GOD*

What has been the effect of turning away from hoped-for divine aid, and relying instead upon human initiative and effort?

Well, what is the answer? That in proportion as men have ceased to lean on God, they have not only learned to bend mechanical forces to good use and to control the physical conditions of human well-being, but they have opened up undreamed-of resources for the satisfaction of the noblest desires of which they are capable. In the securing of food, clothing, and shelter it has proved to be better to proceed as if the existence of God were irrelevant. The advance of medical science in safeguarding life, caring for bodily and mental health, and putting up a winning fight against diseases that had decimated mankind for centuries, is perhaps the most conspicuous example. It is not theism to which we must ascribe the development of medicine. Medical progress has had to fight against theistic prejudice. It was likewise theistic prejudice that stood in the way of a hopeful treatment of psychic disorders, of sex and population problems, of antisocial propensities, and similar difficulties.

Whenever men and women have been able to act as if there were no divinity to shape human ends, and have themselves assumed responsibility, they have discovered how to turn their abilities to good account. Is it likely that this process will be reversed in the future? I am convinced that we are nearer the beginning than the end of it, as helpless to change this general direction as we are to prevent ourselves from getting older. What we *can* do is to try to go forward intelligently, as in growing older we may try to grow wiser.

Not believing in God has worked well. It has worked better than believing did. It is responsible for a realistic acquaintance with our world and a better understanding of human nature. This would seem to furnish evidence, of a kind usually considered good, that there is no superhuman being who cares what becomes of mankind. And the vast majority of people have apparently been convinced. They show it by the way they live day in and day out. They go about their business from morning to night taking no counsel of God. True enough, they would not dream of admitting it and they are offended if anyone else does, but such paradoxical behavior is not unusual. Their refusal

* Max Otto (1876–   ): American philosopher. The selection is part of Chapter 11 entitled, "The Existence of God," from Otto's *The Human Enterprise*. In this work, Otto attempts to analyze human existence on earth in light of the scientific revolution. The whole work is designed as an apology for humanism. From THE HUMAN ENTERPRISE by Max Otto. Copyright 1940 by Crofts & Company, Inc. Reprinted by permission of Appleton-Century-Crofts, New York.

to be called unbelievers, like their continued attendance upon church services, though they do not subscribe to the church creed, merely shows that something holds them back from openly admitting what they take for granted six days of the week and most of the seventh. What is it that holds them back?

One thing that holds them back is human mortality. Much of the persisting theism is crisis theism. Many people, even of those who ordinarily give no thought to God, and who never lift a finger on behalf of the values of life most intimately associated with his name, are transformed into theists when confronted by the fact or thought of death. They cannot admit that death is the ruin of life, and since the existence of God is required to save it from being just that, a sufficient belief to meet the emergency lingers, though inert, in the background of their minds. I admit that it is a shallow belief, one that does not pervade their lives but comes forward only to attend funerals, weddings, and like occasions, yet it may be singularly genuine while it lasts. It lifts the believer for the moment, however temporary his belief, above the struggle for material advantage. He is made tender toward failure. A mood of reverence is awakened and a sense of the mystery of life. In a word, he lives for the time being in his better impulses. And when the theistic mood has retired again to the outermost fringe of interest, which it often does with shocking suddenness, the good words that were spoken for God in the interim echo and re echo in memory. It is these echoes which hold many people back from accepting an explanation of the world which leaves out God, and makes them feel that anyone who faces death in the same nontheistic spirit as he faces life must be exceptionally hardhearted, if not downright vicious.

No one would claim, I trust, that belief in God is a necessity for creatures who know that they must die. For one thing, few people are called upon to undergo the ordeal of their own death. As a rule they are planning to be alive when unconsciousness overtakes them, and when they die they know nothing about it. Since men have foresight and imagination, however, it is not enough for them to know that they will not experience dying, if they also know that the time will come when they will be dead. It is usually taken for granted that unless they are supported by the hope of immortality it is a kindness not to allude to their last hours.

Statistical evidence is not available one way or the other. If it were, we could show, I believe, that a certain personal quality, more than any belief a man holds for or against theism, determines his behavior in the expectation of death. I wonder whether the commander of a regiment could tell by the behavior of soldiers under fire, who was a believer and who was not. I wonder whether a sea captain whose ship is sinking could divide his sailors into the two classes. I wonder whether the confirmed criminal who walks with a firm step to his execution is sustained by theistic faith or by the same psychic hardness, reckless nerve, and need for display which made a life of crime attractive. And as for bravely bearing the death of others, I have never witnessed greater fortitude than that of devastated hearts for whom there was no balm in Gilead.

The crucial test of how a man will meet his own end is reserved for one who is snatched by the powerful arm of the law, and as he believes un-justly, out of active, sincere preoccupation with social reform and is con-demned to die at a stated hour. By that test Bartolomeo Vanzetti, who was not upheld by faith in God, but by the vision of a social ideal for which he felt he was giving his life, and by the loyalty of friends, will bear compari-son with Socrates. Since we are considering the possibility of meeting death without divine aid, it is well to recall the statement of Vanzetti when he was sentenced to die:

If it had not been for these thing, I might have die unmarked, unknown, a failure. Now we are not a failure. This is our career and our triumph. Never in our full life could we hope to do such work for tolerance, for justice, for man's under-standing of man as now we do by accident! Our words—our lives—our pains—nothing! The taking of our lives—lives of a good shoemaker and a poor fish-peddler—all! That last moment belongs to us—that agony is our triumph.

Another reason for the retention of theism is man's low opinion of him-self as a moral being. Thousands who leave God out when engaged in practical pursuits, or in following the promptings of desire, are careful to keep him on hand for the sake of ideals. They feel that God is needed to validate and enforce the moral life. This they believe is especially true of "the masses." Without God, man is a purely natural creature and must act, so they think, like any other animal, though he may express his animality with superior shrewdness. A naturalistic attitude may suffice, indeed must suffice, when the need is one of feeding and housing men, keeping their bodies clean and healthy, increasing their efficiency as producers of material wealth; it can do nothing to make men decent human beings, and it is worse than useless in the attainment of moral character. Generosity, ethical ideal-ism, civic-mindedness, interest in moral growth can be expected from none but those who are inspired by God.

To say it in another way, the higher life, however conceived, does not pay in its own terms, so that unless men believe in a God who makes good the losses incurred in living it, no one will find it attractive. A general acceptance of a nontheistic philosophy, so the argument runs, would "eat all nobility out of our conception of conduct and all worth out of their conception of life."

Here we have one of those persistent half-truths that manage to outlive repeated refutation. "But men are better," said Emerson, "than their theology. Their daily life gives it the lie. Every ingenuous and aspiring soul leaves the doctrine behind him in his own experience, and all men feel some-times the falsehood which they cannot demonstrate." *Aspiration is much older than man's acquaintance with the gods, and it does not die when faith in them is lost.* A natural discontent with objects less perfect than they can be imagined, and the pursuit of idealized objects that stir the feelings, are the vital forces at work in men's upward striving. The visible results at a given time may seem slight; they are not slight when estimated over years and generations and centuries.

Evidence is everywhere about us, in the community where we live, in the street that runs by our door, in our own hearts. Men are aroused to adore supremely, to triumph over the cold hard misery of life, to serve and die without reward. I remember Justice Holmes and the Law, Jane Addams and World Peace, La Follette and the People. I think of Flaubert and his worship of Beauty, of "The Worst Journey in the World," made by three heroes to fill a gap in the evidence for Evolution. I stand with Captain Ahab on the deck of the *Pequod*, scanning the horizon for Moby Dick. I follow a lantern through the darkness and the churchyard to the tomb of the Capulets with its testimony to the power of romantic love. So my mind wanders on—for there is no end to the number and variety of examples of supreme devotion —wanders on until lost in the thicket of life. There I find devotion, heroism, self-sacrifice, loyalty to causes. What is it but this original virtue in human beings that faith in God draws upon to give itself vitality?

No; the conclusion cannot be withstood that greatness, from every point of view, has been achieved by individuals and by whole peoples in the absence of faith in God. Men can and do develop great conceptions of conduct, can and do devote themselves to social causes with enthusiasm and self-sacrifice, without counting on help from higher powers. Co-operative faith in the intelligent use of natural and human resources has provided a sufficient incentive to high-minded conduct.

The number of those who have adopted this platform as a working hypothesis for themselves, and are solicitous that it be tried on the largest possible scale, is growing. Say against these men and women what we please, we cannot truthfully say that they are the riffraff of human nature. In my judgment theirs is the only dependable type of idealism left to man in the modern world.

Perhaps the most plausible argument to be made against the foregoing considerations is that after all a study of the world in which we live discloses the slow working out of a great ethical purpose. And what can such a purpose be but the will of God? The evidence, however, does not, I think, support this interpretation.

In the first place, selection of the goal of natural events is premature. Suppose we were able to prove that a definite tendency is observable in the evolution of life on our globe, and suppose we could argue from tendency to *intendency*, neither of which we are in a position to do, we would still be unable to clinch the argument. We have not seen the drama to the end. Once it looked as if it were designed for fishes; then for reptiles, then for lower mammals. Now it may look as if designed for man. But the play is not over. The curtain has not dropped. How can we talk about the climax of a performance of which we have witnessed only the opening scenes?

What have we actually observed? Has everything moved in a steadily maintained direction toward man as the culminating goal? Evolution has been an incredible spendthrift of life. Highly organized creatures have been developed again and again only to be pushed up blind alleys and left there to die. If there is a God whose method has been Evolution, his slogan must have been, "We'll fight it out along this line if it takes a billennium!" But, unlike Grant, he has always surrendered.

In this maelstrom the human species, as Thomas Huxley said—and he knew something about the subject—"plashed and floundered amid the general stream of evolution, keeping its head above water as best it might, and thinking neither of whence or whither." If the great scene we look upon, with its waxing and waning of suns, its appearance and disappearance of plant worlds, its rise and fall of animal dynasties—if all this or any part of it is the working out of divine purpose, "friendly to man's intellectual, moral and religious education," this purpose is well hidden.

What if we disregard Evolution and examine human history? Do we then observe the unfolding of a divine plan? Do we find demonstrable proof of a Power not ourselves that sides with the ethical best? Does it thwart the wrongdoer and circumvent the morally indifferent? Do we, or do we not, see "the wicked in great power and spreading himself like a green bay tree"? What happened to Socrates? To Jesus? According to the best authorities, they gave their lives to God and in the hour of their need he deserted them. They are conspicuous examples, but the fact which they illustrate is a commonplace of experience.

So far as the course of human life testifies, there is no indication that anything or anyone superhuman is bent upon the triumph of humane or ethical principles. *It seems to be up to us and us alone.* And since on the appearance of things man is forced to make shift with such powers as he can discover in himself and in his social and natural environment, why not be open and above-board at least about the appearances? Why not admit that for the practical realization of the good life we are obliged to act as we do in tilling the ground or baking bread, that is, to rely upon experimental knowledge to find out what it is we want and how to get it?

This surely offers a sufficient program for the most aspiring soul to work at. It has the added advantage of providing an escape from the chief risk of the ethical life, the danger of being victimized by our ideals. And we are less easily deceived by the type of leadership that would beguile our eyes from what we want to "higher things," in order that someone else may help himself to what he wants of things high or low.

If it is impossible to demonstrate the working presence of a divine ethical purpose in the world, there are, in the second place, certain demonstrable facts which make the existence of any such purpose very doubtful. I avail myself of a statement made by Bishop Ernest William Barnes in one of the profoundest books I have read, *Scientific Theory and Religion.* I do this because Bishop Barnes cannot be suspected of twisting the facts against the theistic position and because his writings are sincere not only in the usual sense that he refuses to say what he does not believe to be true, but in the far more unusual sense of taking the trouble to assure himself that he is justified, in view of the evidence at hand, to say what he does. The statement is this:

> The whole process of creation now appears to be nonmoral. There is no evidence to lead us to infer that variations in the genes are directed towards ends which in our judgment are good. In such variations there seems, in fact, to be no ethical quality whatever. They have led to odious parasitism, to the carnage of the jungle, to the microbic diseases which cause such suffering to humanity, to those animal appetites which are useful in the struggle for survival and are the basis of sin in man. This, the immoral, brutal, lustful side of creation is as characteristic as the parental self-sacrifice, the adventurous curiosity, the instinct for truth, the enthusiasm for righteousness, the beauty of form and the physical well-being which equally result from the evolving process.

In such facts as these "we are confronted," Bishop Barnes points out, "by a dilemma from which there is, at present, no escape." And he makes this further remark, which, coming from him, should have a salutary effect: "Verbal dexterity and the skilful use of those evasive phrases which are too common in modern theology might seem to offer escape to some: but to the man of science evasion is high treason against truth." To which I add that unless theism can find a solution for just this dilemma, the best we can in truth say for the cosmos is that up to date it has not prevented the human experiment from being tried. Anything more is too much.

For the reasons adduced in this chapter, and such as these, I have for myself arrived at an affirmative faith in the nonexistence of God. The affirmation is important. One may be *without* a belief in the *existence* of God or *have* a belief in the *nonexistence* of God. The two are not identical. Each is associated with distinctive further beliefs and distinctive individual and social commitments. What I desire to make clear, without taking space to elaborate the point, is the tentative, undogmatic, yet outspoken character of the belief in question. It is essentially a kind of faith, but the kind of faith we act on in daily life when we call a doctor or drive an automobile, in fact when we take any step whatever, a faith that is rooted in tested experience. It is militant, though not belligerent; convinced, but aware of difficulties in holding the position; an aggressive belief that is tempered by appreciative understanding of the motives and claims on the other side.

Sartre
ATHEISTIC HUMANISM*

[T]here are two kinds of existentialists. There are, on the one hand, the Christians, amongst whom I shall name Jaspers and Gabriel Marcel, both professed Catholics; and on the other the existential atheists, amongst whom we must place Heidegger as well as the French existentialists and myself. What they have in common is simply the fact that they believe that *existence* comes before *essence*— or, if you will, that we must begin from the subjective. What exactly do we mean by that?

If one considers an article of manufacture—as, for example, a book or a paper-knife—one sees that it has been made by an artisan who had a conception of it; and he has paid attention, equally, to the conception of a paper-knife and to the pre-existent technique of production which is a part of that conception and is, at bottom, a formula. Thus the paper-knife is at the same time an article producible in a certain manner and one which, on the other hand, serves a definite purpose, for one cannot suppose that a man would produce a paper-knife without knowing what it was for. Let us say, then, of the paper-knife that its essence—that is to say the sum of the formulae and the qualities which made its production and its definition possible—precedes its existence. The presence of such-and-such a paper-knife or book is thus determined before my eyes. Here, then, we are viewing the world from a technical standpoint, and we can say that production precedes existence.

When we think of God as the creator, we are thinking of him, most of the time, as a supernal artisan. Whatever doctrine we may be considering, whether it be a doctrine like that of Descartes, or of Leibnitz himself, we always imply that the will follows, more or less, from the understanding or at least accompanies it, so that when God creates he knows precisely what he is creating. Thus, the conception of man in the mind of God is comparable to that of the paper-knife in the mind of the artisan: God makes man according to a procedure and a conception, exactly as the artisan manufactures a paper-knife, following a definition and a formula. Thus each individual man is the realisation of a certain conception which dwells in the divine understanding. In the philosophic atheism of the eighteenth century, the notion of God is suppressed, but not, for all

* Jean-Paul Sartre (1905–   ): French novelist, playwright and philosopher. This selection is from Sartre's short work, *Existentialism and Humanism*. The work is a short introduction to Sartre's existential philosophy, touching upon such themes as freedom, responsibility, guilt, despair, and the nature of existence. From EXISTENTIALISM AND HUMANISM by Jean-Paul Sartre, translated by Philip Mairet. Copyright 1948 by Methuen & Co., Ltd., London. Reprinted by permission of Associated Book Publishers Ltd., London.

that, the idea that essence is prior to existence; something of that idea we still find everywhere, in Diderot, in Voltaire and even in Kant. Man possesses a human nature; that "human nature," which is the conception of human being, is found in every man; which means that each man is a particular example of an universal conception, the conception of Man. In Kant, this universality goes so far that the wild man of the woods, man in the state of nature and the bourgeois are all contained in the same definition and have the same fundamental qualities. Here again, the essence of man precedes that historic existence which we confront in experience.

Atheistic existentialism, of which I am a representative, declares with greater consistency that if God does not exist there is at least one being whose existence comes before its essence, a being which exists before it can be defined by any conception of it. That being is man or, as Heidegger has it, the human reality. What do we mean by saying that existence precedes essence? We mean that man first of all exists, encounters himself, surges up in the world—and defines himself afterwards. If man as the existentialist sees he is not definable, it is because to begin with he is nothing. He will not be anything until later, and then he will be what he makes himself. Thus there is no human nature, because there is no God to have a conception of it; man simply is. Not that he is simply what he conceives himself to be, but he is what he wills, and as he conceives himself after already existing—as he wills to be after that leap towards existence; man is nothing else but that which he makes of himself. That is the first principle of existentialism. And this is what people call its "subjectivity," using the word as a reproach against us. But what do we mean to say by this, but that man is of a greater dignity than a stone or a table? For we mean to say that man primarily exists—that man is, before all else, something which propels itself towards a future and is aware that it is doing so. Man is, indeed, a project which possesses a subjective life, instead of being a kind of moss, or a fungus or a cauliflower. Before that projection of the self nothing exists; not even in the heaven of intelligence: man will only attain existence when he is what he purposes to be. Not, however, what he may wish to be. For what we usually understand by wishing or willing is a conscious decision taken—much more often than not—after we have made ourselves what we are. I may wish to join a party, to write a book or to marry—but in such a case what is usually called my will is probably a manifestation of a prior and more spontaneous decision. If, however, it is true that existence is prior to essence, man is responsible for what he is. Thus, the first effect of existentialism is that it puts every man in possession of himself as he is, and places the entire responsibility for his existence squarely upon his own shoulders. And, when we say that man is responsible for himself, we do not mean that he is responsible only for his own individuality, but that he is responsible for all men. The word "subjectivism" is to be understood in two senses, and our adversaries play upon only one of them. Subjectivism means, on the one hand, the freedom of the individual subject and, on the other, that man cannot pass beyond human subjectivity. It is the latter which is the deeper meaning of existentialism. When we say that man chooses himself, we do mean that every one of us must choose himself; but by that we also mean that in choosing for himself he chooses for all men. For in effect, of all the actions a man may take in order to create himself as he wills to be, there is not one which is not creative, at the same time, of an image of man such as he believes he ought to be. To choose between this or that is at the same time to affirm the value of that which is chosen; for we are unable ever to choose the worse. What we choose is always the better; and nothing can be better for us unless it is better for all. If, moreover, existence precedes essence and we will to exist at the same time as we fashion our image, that image is valid for all and for the entire epoch in which we find ourselves. Our responsibility is thus much greater than we had supposed, for it concerns mankind as a whole. If I am a worker, for instance, I may choose to join a Christian rather than a Communist trade union. And if, by that membership, I choose to signify that resignation is, after all, the attitude that best becomes a man, that man's kingdom is not upon this earth, I do not commit myself alone to that view. Resignation is my will for everyone, and my action is, in consequence, a commitment on behalf of all mankind. Or if, to take a more personal case, I decide to marry and to have children, even though this decision proceeds simply from my situation, from my passion or my desire, I am thereby committing not only myself, but humanity as a whole, to the practice of monogamy. I am thus responsible for myself and for all men, and I am creating a certain image of man as I would have him to be. In fashioning myself I fashion man.

This may enable us to understand what is meant by such terms—perhaps a little grandiloquent—as anguish, abandonment and despair. As you will soon see, it is very simple. First, what do we mean by anguish? The existentialist frankly states that man is in anguish. His meaning is as follows— When a man commits himself to anything, fully realising that he is not only choosing what he will be, but is thereby at the same time a legislator deciding for the whole of mankind—in such a moment a man cannot escape from the sense of complete and profound responsibility. There are many, indeed, who show no such anxiety. But we affirm that they are merely disguising their anguish or are in flight from it. Certainly, many people think that in what they are doing they commit no one but themselves to anything: and if you ask them, "What would happen if everyone did so?" they shrug their shoulders and reply, "Everyone does not do so." But in truth, one ought always to ask oneself what would happen if everyone did as one is doing; nor can one escape from that disturbing thought except by a kind of self-deception. The man who lies in self-excuse, be saying "Everyone will not do it" must be ill at ease in his conscience, for the act of lying implies the universal value which it denies. By its very disguise his anguish reveals itself. This is the anguish that Kierkegaard called "the anguish of Abraham." You know the story: An angel commanded Abraham to sacrifice his son: and obedience was obligatory, if it really was an angel who had appeared and said, "Thou, Abraham, shalt sacrifice thy son." But anyone in such a case would wonder, first, whether it was indeed an angel and secondly, whether I am really Abraham. Where are the proofs? A certain mad woman who suffered from hallucinations said that people were telephoning to her, and giving her orders. The doctor asked, "But who is it that speaks to you?" She replied: "He says it is God." And what, indeed, could prove to her that it was God? If an angel appears to me, what is the proof that it is an angel; or, if I hear voices, who can prove that they proceed from heaven and not from hell, or from my own subconsciousness or some pathological condition? Who can prove that they are really addressed to me?

Who, then, can prove that I am the proper person to impose, by my own choice, my conception of man upon mankind? I shall never find any proof whatever; there will be no sign to convince me of it. If a voice speaks to me, it is still I myself who must decide whether the voice is or is not that of an angel. If I regard a certain course of action as good, it is only I who choose to say that it is good and not bad. There is nothing to show that I am Abraham: nevertheless I also am obliged at every instant to perform actions which are examples. Everything happens to every man as though the whole human race had its eyes fixed upon what he is doing and regulated its conduct accordingly. So every man ought to say, "Am I really a man who has the right to act in such a manner that humanity regulates itself by what I do?" If a man does not say that, he is dissembling his anguish. Clearly, the anguish with which we are concerned here is not one that could lead to quietism or inaction. It is anguish pure and simple, of the kind well known to all those who have borne responsibilities. When, for instance, a military leader takes upon himself the responsibility for an attack and sends a number of men to their death, he chooses to do it and at bottom he alone chooses. No doubt he acts under a higher command, but its orders, which are more general, require interpretation by him and upon that interpretation depends the life of ten, fourteen or twenty men. In making the decision, he cannot but feel a certain anguish. All leaders know that anguish. It does not prevent their acting, on the contrary it is the very condition of their action, for the action presupposes that there is a plurality of possibilities, and in choosing one of these, they realise that it has value only because it is chosen. Now it is anguish of that kind which existentialism describes, and moreover, as we shall see, makes explicit through direct responsibility towards other men who are concerned. Far from being a screen which could separate us from action, it is a condition of action itself.

And when we speak of "abandonment"—a favourite word of Heidegger —we only mean to say that God does not exist, and that it is necessary to draw the consequences of his absence right to the end. The existentialist is strongly opposed to a certain type of secular moralism which seeks to suppress God at the least possible expense. Towards 1880, when the French professors endeavoured to formulate a secular morality, they said something like this:—God is a useless and costly hypothesis, so we will do without it. However, if we are to have morality, a society and a law-abiding world, it is essential that certain values should be taken seriously; they must have *à priori* existence ascribed to them. It must be considered obligatory *à priori* to be honest, not to lie, not to beat one's wife, to bring up children and so forth; so we are going to do a little work on this subject, which will enable us to show that these values exist all the same, inscribed in an intelligible heaven although, of course, there is no God. In other words—and this is, I believe, the purport of all that we in France call radicalism—nothing will be changed if God does not exist; we shall re-discover the same norms of honesty, progress and humanity, and we shall have disposed of God as an out-of-date hypothesis which will die away quietly of itself. The existentialist, on the contrary, finds it extremely embarrassing that God does not exist, for there disappears with Him all possibility of finding values in an intelligible heaven. There can no longer be any good *à priori*, since there is no infinite and perfect consciousness to think it. It is nowhere written that "the good" exists, that one must be honest or must not lie, since we are now upon the plane where there are only men. Dostoievsky once wrote "If God did not exist, everything would be permitted"; and that, for existentialism, is the starting point. Everything is indeed permitted if God does not exist, and man is in consequence forlorn, for he cannot find anything to depend upon either within or outside himself. He discovers forthwith, that he is without excuse. For if indeed existence precedes essence, one will never be able to explain one's action by reference to a given and specific human nature; in other words, there is no determinism—man is free, man *is* freedom. Nor, on the other hand, if God does not exist, are we provided with any values or commands that could legitimise our behaviour. Thus we have neither behind us, nor before us in a luminous realm of values, any means of justification or excuse. We are left alone, without excuse. That is what I mean when I say that man is condemned to be free. Condemned, because he did not create himself, yet is nevertheless at liberty, and from the moment that he is thrown into this world he is responsible for everything he does. The existentialist does not believe in the power of passion. He will never regard a grand passion as a destructive torrent upon which a man is swept into certain actions as by fate, and which, therefore, is an excuse for them. He thinks that man is responsible for his passion. Neither will an existentialist think that a man can find help through some sign being vouchsafed upon earth for his orientation: for he thinks that the man himself interprets the sign as he chooses. He thinks that every man, without any support or help whatever, is condemned at every instant to invent man. . . .

As for "despair," the meaning of this expression is extremely simple. It merely means that we limit ourselves to a reliance upon that which is within our wills, or within the sum of the probabilities which render our action feasible. Whenever one wills anything, there are always these elements of probability. If I am counting upon a visit from a friend, who may be coming by train or by tram, I presuppose that the train will arrive at the appointed time or that the tram will not be derailed. I remain in the realm of possibilities; but one does not rely upon any possibilities beyond those that are strictly concerned in one's action. Beyond the point at which the possibilities under consideration cease to affect my action, I ought to disinterest myself. For there is no God and no prevenient design, which can adapt the world and all its possibilities to my will. When Descartes said, "Conquer yourself rather than the world," what he meant was, at bottom, the same—that we should act without hope. . . .

What is at the very heart and center of existentialism, is the absolute character of the free commitment, by which every man realises himself in realising a type of humanity—a commitment always understandable, to no matter whom in no matter what epoch—and its bearing upon the relativity of the cultural pattern which may result from such absolute commitment. One must observe equally the relativity of Cartesianism and the absolute character of the Cartesian commitment. In this sense you may say, if you like, that every one of us makes the absolute by breathing, by eating, by sleeping of by behaving in any fashion whatsoever. There is no difference between free being—being as self-committal, as existence choosing its essence—and absolute being. And there is no difference whatever between being as an absolute, temporarily localised—that is, localised in history—and universally intelligible being. . . .

Man is all the time outside of himself: it is in projecting and losing himself beyond himself that he makes man to exist; and, on the other hand, it is by pursuing transcendent aims that he himself is able to exist. Since man is thus self-surpassing, and can grasp objects only in relation to his self-surpassing, he is himself the heart and centre of his transcendence. There is no other universe except the human universe, the universe of human subjectivity. This relation of transcendence as constitutive of man (not in the sense that God is transcendent, but in the sense of self-surpassing) with subjectivity (in such a sense that man is not shut up in himself but forever present in a human universe)—it is this that we call existential humanism. This is humanism, because we remind man that there is no legislator but himself; that he himself, thus abandoned, must decide for himself; also because we show that it is not by turning back upon himself, but always by seeking, beyond himself, an aim which is one of liberation or of some particular realisation, that man can realise himself as truly human.

You can see from these few reflections that nothing could be more unjust than the objections people raise against us. Existentialism is nothing else but an attempt to draw the full conclusions from a consistently atheistic position. Its intention is not in the least that of plunging men into despair.

And if by despair one means—as the Christians do—any attitude of unbelief, the despair of the existentialists is something different. Existentialism is not atheist in the sense that it would exhaust itself in demonstrations of the non-existence of God. It declares, rather, that even if God existed that would make no difference from its point of view. Not that we believe God does exist, but we think that the real problem is not that of His existence; what man needs is to find himself again and to understand that nothing can save him from himself, not even a valid proof of the existence of God. In this sense existentialism is optimistic, it is a doctrine of action, and it is only by self-deception, by confusing their own despair with ours that Christians can describe us as without hope.

Chapter 14

The death of god

Seldom do we find in Kafka's works explicit mention of God, and yet his parables, stories, and novels reflect the anguished consciousness of the absence of God. Kafka's characters live in and experience a world where the deafening silence of God evokes a somber tone in the human quest for meaning and purpose. The sacred dimension is pointedly missing in the imaginative landscapes of his fiction. While his stories seem filled with symbols pointing to a transcendent order (the Emperor, for example), the order is completely ambivalent in its relation to man or totally without efficacy in altering the predicament of human beings.

Paradox replaces order in the world Kafka created. Appearances always seem on the threshold of becoming reality, but reality threatens persistently to reveal itself as illusion. Innocence and reconciliation are never celebrated in his works. His characters know only alienation, frustration, and defeat. Yet somehow they continue to struggle to make sense of their situations, even in the total absence of any sign from above.

If Kafka's literary works reflect the consciousness of the human plight in the face of the absence of God, Nietzsche's philosophical works follow through the consequences of that absence. Nietzsche's proclamation of the death of God is not the straightforward assertion of atheism, the denial that God ever existed. That Nietzsche's announcement has a religious cast is evident from the fact that he makes a madman the spokesman of the vision; and from the anguished tone of the shocking revelation it is obvious that his madman is also a mourner. Nietzsche's madman is beside himself with dread in proclaiming that man "murdered" God, for he sees that the consequence of man's participation in God's death is nihilism.

For many centuries mankind in Europe had been organizing their pursuits and cultures from within the circles of Christian faith. Nietzsche's judgment is that Western man had progressively moved away from a transforming faith in the Christian God, to a more conventional, second-hand Christianity. While European man continued to express Christian sentiments, and even participate in Christian ceremonies, the actual principles by which life was lived had little to do with whether or not God existed. Thus, in proclaiming the death of God, Nietzsche was merely pointing to a cultural and historical fact.

Nietzsche believed that modern man lived in a post-Christian era but had no awareness of the vast implications of this fact. In order to understand the enormity of the consciousness of the death of God, one must comprehend how interwoven religious ideas and practices are with the everyday affairs of societies and individuals. In a Christian world, the values which societies and individuals seek are grounded in the Christian understanding of human life and its relation to God. God, as the author of human life and the cosmos, is the center of all valuations of man's existence on earth. But if God is no longer alive in the hearts and minds of men, then their value commitments, which are the products of their religious perspectives no longer have any foundation. The realization of the loss of the sense of deity means madness, an existence-shattering anxiety, but also, perhaps, the possibility of a new innocence, a fresh beginning. Nietzsche was appalled that the husks of Christendom remained intact when the content, the encounter with the living God, was no longer effective in human life. According to Nietzsche, the recognition of the death of God results in a rootless, groundless human existence. Yet, man must "become like God" in order to be worthy of this awesome event he has perpetrated. Only in the absence of God can man seek and create his own norms for existence. Only when God is banished can man become free, responsible, and creative without the weakening effects of guilt and remorse.

Kafka
THE IMPERIAL MESSAGE*

The Emperor, so it runs, has sent a message to you, the humble subject, the insignificant shadow cowering in the remotest distance before the imperial sun; the Emperor from his deathbed has sent a message to you alone. He has commanded the messenger to kneel down by the bed, and has whispered the message to him; so much store did he lay on it that he ordered the messenger to whisper it back into his ear again. Then by a nod of the head he has confirmed that it is right. Yes, before the assembled spectators of his death—all the obstructing walls have been broken down, and on the spacious and loftily-mounting open staircases stand in a ring the great princes of the Empire—before all these he has delivered his message. The messenger immediately sets out on his journey; a powerful, an indefatigable man; now pushing with his right arm, now with his left, he cleaves a way for himself through the throng; if he encounters resistance he

* Franz Kafka (1883–1924): Czechoslovakian novelist. All Kafka's works explore the landscape of the human soul, and they are usually characterized by bizarre settings and situations and enigmatic happenings. This selection is a parable from his short work *The Great Wall of China.* Reprinted by permission of Schocken Books Inc. from *The Great Wall of China* by Franz Kafka. Copyright © 1946 by Schocken Books Inc.

points to his breast, where the symbol of the sun glitters; the way, too, is made easier for him than it would be for any other man. But the multitudes are so vast; their numbers have no end. If he could reach the open fields how fast he would fly, and soon doubtless you would hear the welcome hammering of his fists on your door. But instead how vainly does he wear out his strength; still he is only making his way through the chambers of the innermost palace; never will he get to the end of them; and if he succeeded in that nothing would be gained; he must fight his way next down the stairs; and if he succeeded in that nothing would be gained; the courts would still have to be crossed; and after the courts the second outer palace; and once more stairs and courts; and once more another palace; and so on for thousands of years; and if at last he should burst through the outermost gate—but never, never can that happen—the imperial capital would lie before him, the center of the world, crammed to bursting with its own refuse. Nobody could fight his way through here, least of all one with a message from a dead man.—But you sit at your window when evening falls and dream it to yourself.

Nietzsche
*PROCLAMATION OF GOD'S DEATH**

[125]   *The Madman.* Have you not heard of that madman who lit a lantern in the bright morning hours, ran to the market place, and cried incessantly, "I seek God! I seek God!" As many of those who do not believe in God were standing around just then, he provoked much laughter. Why, did he get lost? said one. Did he lose his way like a child? said another. Or is he hiding? Is he afraid of us? Has he gone on a voyage? or emigrated? Thus they yelled and laughed. The madman jumped into their midst and pierced them with his glances.

"Whither is God" he cried. "I shall tell you. *We have killed him*—you and I. All of us are his murderers. But how have we done this? How were we able to drink up the sea? Who gave us the sponge to wipe away the entire horizon? What did we do when we unchained this earth from its sun? Whither is it moving now? Whither are we moving now? Away from all suns? Are we not plunging continually? Backward, sideward, forward, in

* Friedrich Nietzsche (1844–1900): German philosopher and poet (see footnote on P. 35). This selection is from *The Gay Science*, Book III, Aphorism 125. *The Gay Science* is a collection of Nietzsche's aphorisms, covering a wide range of subjects from love to the origin of religion. In it, we find in embryonic form some of the major concepts of his thought, such as the death of God, nihilism and eternal recurrence. From THE PORTABLE NIETZSCHE by Friedrich Nietzsche, edited and translated by Walter Kaufmann. Copyright 1954 by The Viking Press, Inc. Reprinted by permission of The Viking Press, Inc.

all directions? Is there any up or down left? Are we not straying as through an infinite nothing? Do we not feel the breath of empty space? Has it not become colder? Is not night and more night coming on all the while? Must not lanterns be lit in the morning? Do we not hear anything yet of the noise of the gravediggers who are burying God? Do we not smell anything yet of God's decomposition? Gods too decompose. God is dead. God remains dead. And we have killed him. How shall we, the murderers of all murderers, comfort ourselves? What was holiest and most powerful of all that the world has yet owned has bled to death under our knives. Who will wipe this blood off us? What water is there for us to clean ourselves? What festivals of atonement, what sacred games shall we have to invent? Is not the greatness of this deed too great for us? Must not we ourselves become gods simply to seem worthy of it? There has never been a greater deed; and whoever will be born after us—for the sake of this deed he will be part of a higher history than all history hitherto."

Here the madman fell silent and looked again at his listeners; and they too were silent and stared at him in astonishment. At last he threw his lantern on the ground, and it broke and went out. "I come too early," he said then; "my time has not come yet. This tremendous event is still on its way, still wandering—it has not yet reached the ears of man. Lightning and thunder require time, the light of the stars requires time, deeds require time even after they are done, before they can be seen and heard. This deed is still more distant from them than the most distant stars—*and yet they have done it themselves.*"

It has been related further that on that same day the madman entered divers churches and there sang his *requiem aeternam deo*. Led out and called to account, he is said to have replied each time, "What are these churches now if they are not the tombs and sepulchers of God?"

Chapter 15

Theology and the contemporary world

When Nietzsche announced the death of God in the latter part of the nineteenth century, he did not believe that modern man was prepared to enter into the full consciousness of that event. He has the madman announce that he has come too early and that "this tremendous event . . . has not yet reached the ears of men." In the mid-twentieth century, however, several young theologians have responded to the Nietzschean pronouncement, and the result has been a radical reinterpretation of the meaning of Christian theology. Two such respondents are Thomas J. J. Altizer and Harvey Cox.

The cornerstone of Altizer's constructive thought is the death of God and its implications for understanding the Christian confession of faith. When he speaks of the death of God reference is intended to an actual cosmic and historical event. God died in Christ in a redemptive and revelatory act of self-negation. While historical Christianity has accomplished a "religious reversal" of this divine act of self-annihilation, it cannot annul the real fact of God's forward movement into profane history through his death. Altizer draws a sharp distinction between "the original or primal death of God in Christ and the actualization or historical realization of his death throughout the whole gamut of human experience." No single idea, event, or objective expression can embody what Altizer calls the "incarnational process," the progressive and historical descent of spirit into flesh. Only the Christian who has opened himself to the actuality of God's death can attain freedom from an alien other. The radical Christian attains freedom only at the risk of an existence-shattering nihilism. He may rest secure in the established form of faith and the obligations of Christian morality, or he may live through the death of God in a radical faith that God's death in Christ sets in motion a continual redemptive act by which man can attain a new innocence and freedom.

Harvey Cox interprets the death-of-God theology in terms of the collapse of a system of religious symbols and language that was once appropriate in a pretechnological, preurban world setting, but that no longer has any real power to illuminate our contemporary world. His constructive proposal is that we move towards a secular theology, "a mode of thinking whose horizon is human history and whose idiom is 'political'. . . ."

One of the most provocative examples of what Cox means by "speaking of God politically" can be found in the essay by Rosemary Ruether. Ruether examines traditional theological concepts such as sin, resurrection, redemption, and church from the point of view of the experience of women, their oppression, and their hope for a new freedom and a more viable, open community. As current theologizing becomes more political (in the sense defined by Cox and manifested by Ruether), the question becomes whether the theology for the oppressed in a social system is fundamentally different from the theology articulated by the oppressors. What is the relationship between theological discourse and political power structures and how do they interact?

In recent years America and the Western world in general seem to have been witnessing a vibrant, new religious awakening. This revitalization of religion in the West occurs at a time when the death-of-God mood is having an important impact upon contemporary theologizing and when there is a movement towards secularity in theological ethics. Although direct involvement in institutional forms of religious life seems to have been declining during the past few years, noninstitutional interest in religion has mushroomed. Such growth is manifested by the fascination of young people with Eastern religions and many other modes of religious quest, including evangelical and pentecostal forms of Christianity.

Our final essay takes note of this religious renaissance by examining some aspects of the Jesus movement. The brief description presented here is intended to suggest certain general features of this movement and to pose some questions about it. To write of present history while it is "in the making" is somewhat risky, but the relevance of this resurgence of religious concern and the forms that it is taking to the range of issues we have examined in this text will be evident to the reader.

Altizer
"DEATH OF GOD" THEOLOGY*

IV: The Self-Annihilation of God

[I]   What can it mean to speak of the death of God? Indeed, how is it even possible to speak of the death of God, particularly at a time when the

* Thomas Altizer (1927–   ): American theologian. The selection is from his book, *The Gospel of Christian Atheism*. It comprises the first part of the fourth chapter entitled, "The Self-Annihilation of God," and part of the fifth chapter entitled, "A Wager." In his book, Altizer defends a "radical theology" whose first principle is "the death of God." Drawing upon the testimony of 19th century artists and philosophers, Altizer traces the origin of the idea of the death of God and explains its implications for the modern world. From THE GOSPEL OF CHRISTIAN ATHEISM by Thomas J. J. Altizer. The Westminster Press. Copyright © 1966, W. L. Jenkins. Used by permission of The Westminster Press, Philadelphia and Wm. Collins Sons & Co. Ltd., London.

name of God would seem to be unsayable? First, we must recognize that the proclamation of the death of God is a Christian confession of faith. For to know that God is dead is to know the God who died in Jesus Christ, the God who passed through what Blake symbolically named as "Self-Annihilation" or Hegel dialetically conceived as the negation of negation. Only the Christian can truly speak of the death of God, because the Christian alone knows the God who negates himself in his own revelatory and redemptive acts. Just as a purely religious apprehension of deity must know a God who is transcendent and beyond, so likewise a purely rational and nondialectical conception of deity must know a God who is impassive and unmoving, or self-enclosed in his own Being. Neither the religious believer nor the non-dialectical thinker can grasp the God whose actuality and movement derives from his own acts of self-negation. Thus it is only the radical, or the profane, or the nonreligious Christian who knows that God has ceased to be active and real in his preincarnate or primordial reality.

Nevertheless, it is essential that the radical Christian make clear what he means by his confession, eliminating so far as possible all that confusion and ambiguity arising from the language of the death of God, and clearly establishing both his Christian claim and his repudiation of all forms of religious Christianity. To confess the death of God is to speak of an actual and real event, not perhaps an event occurring in a single moment of time or history, but notwithstanding this reservation an event that has actually happened both in a cosmic and in a historical sense. There should be no confusion deriving from the mistaken assumption that such a confession refers to an eclipse of God or a withdrawal of God from either history or the creation. Rather, an authentic language speaking about the death of God must inevitably be speaking about the death of God himself. The radical Christian proclaims that God has actually died in Christ, that this death is both a historical and a cosmic event, and, as such, it is a final and irrevocable event, which cannot be reversed by a subsequent religious or cosmic movement. True, a religious reversal of the death of God has indeed occurred in history, is present in the religious expressions of Christianity, and is now receding into the mist of an archaic, if not soon to be forgotten, past. But such a religious reversal cannot annul the event of the death of God; it cannot recover the living God of the old covenant, nor can it reverse or bring to an end the progressive descent of Spirit into flesh. Religious Christians may know a resurrected Lord of the Ascension, just as they may be bound to an almighty and distant Creator and Judge. Yet such a flight from the finality of the Incarnation cannot dissolve the event of the Incarnation itself even if it must finally impel the Christian to seek the presence and the reality of Christ in a world that is totally estranged from Christianity's established vision of the sacred.

Once again we must attempt to draw a distinction between the original or primal death of God in Christ and the actualization or historical realization of his death throughout the whole gamut of human experience. Remembering the radical Christian affirmation that God has fully and totally become incarnate in Christ, we must note that neither the Incarnation nor the Crucifixion can here be understood as isolated and once-and-for-all events; rather, they must be conceived as primary expressions of a forward-moving and eschatological process of redemption, a process embodying a progressive movement of Spirit into flesh. At no point in this process does the incarnate Word or Spirit assume a final and definitive form, just as God himself can never be wholly or simply identified with any given revelatory event or epiphany, if only because the divine process undergoes a continual metamorphosis, ever moving more deeply and more fully toward an eschatological consummation. While the Oriental mystic knows an incarnational process whereby the sacred totally annihilates or transfigures the profane, a process providing us with our clearest image of the primordial reality of the sacred, it is Christianity alone which witnesses to a concrete and actual descent of the sacred into the profane, a movement wherein the sacred progressively abandons or negates its particular and given expressions, thereby emptying them of their original power and actuality. Radical Christianity knows this divine or incarnational process as a forward-moving Totality. Neither a primordial God nor an original garden of innocence remains immune to this process of descent: here all things whatsoever are drawn into and transfigured by this cosmic or total process of metamorphosis. This movement from "Innocence" to "Experience" is potentially or partially present at every point of time and space, and in every epiphany of the divine process: thus we could even say that God dies in some sense wherever he is present or actual in the world, for God actualizes himself by negating his original or given expressions. Yet we truly know this divine process of negativity only by knowing God's death in Christ.

Estranged as we are from our Christian heritage, and distant as we most certainly are from the actual faith of the earliest disciples, what can the contemporary Christian know of the original epiphany of God in Christ? Initiated as we are, moreover, into a historical consciousness that has unveiled a whole new world of New Testament thought and imagery, a world that is subject neither to theological systemization nor to translation into modern thought and experience, how can we hope to ascertain the fundamental meaning for us of the original Christian faith? Let us openly confess that there is no possibility of our returning to a primitive Christian faith, and that the Christ who can become contemporary to us is neither the original historical Jesus nor the Lord of the Church's earliest proclamation. Given our historical situation in the twilight of Christendom, we have long since died to the possibility of a classical or orthodox Christian belief, and must look upon both the New Testament and early Christianity as exotic and alien forms of religion. Nevertheless, and here we continue to have much to learn from the radical Christian, we cannot neglect the possibility that it is precisely our alienation from the religious world of primitive Christianity which can make possible our realization of the fundamental if underlying meaning of the earliest expressions of the Christian faith. For if a religious movement necessarily embodies a backward movement of involution and return, then the very fact that we have died to the religious form of early Christianity can make possible our passage through a reversal of religious Christianity, a reversal that can open to us a new and fuller participation in the forward movement of the Incarnation.

We know that the proclamation of both Jesus and the earliest Palestinian churches revolved about the announcement of the glad tidings or the gospel of the dawning of the Kingdom of God. But thus far neither the theologian nor the Biblical scholar has been able to appropriate the eschatological symbol of the Kingdom of God in such a manner as to make it meaningful to the modern consciousness without thereby sacrificing its original historical meaning. It is scarcely questionable, however, that this symbol originally pointed to the final consummation of a dynamic process of the transcendent's becoming immanent: of a distant, a majestic, and a sovereign Lord breaking into time and space in such a way as to transfigure and renew all things whatsoever, thereby abolishing the old cosmos of the original creation, and likewise bringing to an end all that law and religion which had thus far been established in history. The very form of Christianity's original apocalyptic proclamation rests upon an expectation that the actualization of the Kingdom of God will make present not the almighty Creator, Lawgiver, and Judge, but rather a wholly new epiphany of the deity, an epiphany annihilating all that distance separating the creature from the Creator. Despite Paul's conviction that the victory which Christ won over the powers of sin and darkness had annulled the old Israel and initiated the annihilation of the old creation, to say nothing of his assurance that God will be all in all, both Paul and the early Church were unable fully or decisively to negate the religious forms of the old history, or to surmount their bondage to the transcendent and primordial epiphany of God. Consequently, early Christianity was unable either to negate religion or to absorb and fully assimilate an apocalyptic faith, with the result that it progressively became estranged from its own initial proclamation.

Already we have seen that the modern radical Christian has evolved an apocalyptic and dialectical mode of vision or understanding revolving about an apprehension of the death of God in Christ, and it is just this self-negation or self-annihilation of the primordial reality of God which actualizes the metamorphosis of an all-embracing Totality. Can we not make the judgment that it is precisely this vision of the death of God in Christ that can make possible for us a realization of the deeper meaning of the Christian and eschatological symbol of the dawning of the Kingdom of God? Thereby we could know that the victory of the Kingdom of God in Christ is the fruit of the final movement of God into the world, of Spirit into flesh, and that the Christian meaning of the Kingdom of God is inseparable from an abolition or reversal of all those preincarnate forms or epiphanies of Spirit. By so conceiving the underlying meaning of the original Christian proclamation, we can also see that it is the religious vision of early Christianity which reverses the Christian reality of the Kingdom of God. Inevitably, the orthodox expressions of Christianity abandoned an eschatological ground, and no doubt the radical Christian's recovery of an apocalyptic faith and vision was in part occasioned by his own estrangement from the dominant and established forms of the Christian tradition. Such a contemporary appropriation of the symbol of the Kingdom of God can also make possible our realization of the gospel, or the "good news," of the death of God: for the death of God does not propel man into an empty darkness, it liberates him from every alien and opposing other, and makes possible his transition into what Blake hailed as "The Great Humanity Divine," or the final coming together of God and man.

Whether or not we choose to so understand the original Christian gospel of the dawning of the Kingdom of God, it is clear that the radical Christian affirms that God has died in Christ, and that the death of God is a final and irrevocable event. All too obviously, however, we cannot discover a clear and decisive witness to the meaning of this event in either the Bible or the orthodox teachings and visions of Christianity. But the radical Christian envisions a gradual and progressive metamorphosis of Spirit into flesh, a divine process continually negating or annihilating itself, as it ever moves forward to an eschatological goal. While the Christian proclaims that this process is triumphant in Christ, or that it is inaugurated in its final form by the events of the Incarnation and the Crucifixion, it does not follow that the process itself ceases to move forward in all that history following the death of Christ. Simply by noting the overwhelming power and the comprehensive expression of the modern Christian experience of the death of God, we can sense the effect of the ever fuller movement of the Word or Spirit into history, a movement whose full meaning only dawns with the collapse of Christendom, and in the wake of the historical realization of the death of God in our history as the historical realization of the dawning of death of God. A contemporary faith that opens itself to the actuality of the the Kingdom of God can know the spiritual emptiness of our time as the consequence in human experience of God's self-annihilation in Christ, even while recovering in a new and universal form the apocalyptic faith of the primitive Christian. Insofar as the kenotic or negative movement of the divine process is a movement into the actuality of human experience, it can neither be isolated in a given time and place nor be understood as wholly occurring within a given moment. On the contrary, the actualization of the metamorphosis of the Word into flesh is a continual and forward-moving process, a process initially occurring in God's death in Christ, yes, but a process that is only gradual and progressively realized in history, as God's original self-negation eventually becomes actualized throughout the total range of human experience.

Once again we have detected a Christian religious reversal of God's act in Christ: for a faith that isolates the sacred events of Christ's passion from the profane actuality of human experience must inevitably enclose Christ within a distant and alien form and refuse his presence in the immediacy of our existence. Every Christian attempt to create an unbridgeable chasm between sacred history and human history gives witness to a refusal of the Incarnation and a betrayal of the forward-moving process of salvation. We can discover a reversal of the kenotic movement of the Word in the very insistence of the religious Christian that faith has for once and for all been given, that it is fully and finally present in the Scriptures, the liturgies, the creeds, and the dogmas of the past, and can in no sense undergo a development or transformation that moves beyond its original expression to new and more universal forms. All such religious claims not only attempt to solidify and freeze the life and movement of the divine process, but they foreclose the possibility of the enlargement and evolution of faith, and ruthlessly set the believer against the presence of Christ in an increasingly profane history, thereby alienating the Christian from the actuality of his own time. The radical Christian calls upon his hearer to open himself to the fullness of our history, not with the illusory belief that our history is identical with the history that Jesus lived, but rather with the conviction that the death of God which has dawned so fully in our history is a movement into the total body of humanity of God's original death in Christ. Once we grasp the radical Christian truth that a radically profane history is the inevitable consummation of an actual movement of the sacred into the profane, then we can be liberated from every preincarnate form of Spirit, and accept our destiny as an occasion for the realization in the immediacy of experience of the self-emptying or self-annihilation of the transcendent and primordial God in the passion and death of Christ.

From this perspective it would even be possible to understand Christendom's religious reversal of the movement of Spirit into flesh as a necessary consequence of the Incarnation, preparing the way for a more comprehensive historical realization of the death of God by its progressive banishment of the dead body of God to an ever more transcendent and inaccessible realm. If we conceive of the Word or Spirit as moving more and more fully into the body of the profane in response to the self-negation of God in Christ, then we can understand how the Christian God gradually becomes more alien and beyond, receding into a lifeless and oppressive form, until it finally appears as an empty and vacuous nothingness. The God who is progressively manifest in human experience as an empty and alien other is the inevitable consequence of the Spirit who descends ever more deeply into flesh. Not only does the distant and alien God witness to the historical actualization of the Word in the flesh, but his epiphany as a vacuous and empty formlessness dissolves the possibility of a living and actual faith in God, thus impelling the Christian to seek a new epiphany of Christ in the world. Let the contemporary Christian rejoice that Christianity has evolved the most alien, the most distant, and the most oppressive deity in history: it is precisely the self-alienation of God from his original redemptive form that has liberated humanity from the transcendent realm, and made possible the total descent of the Word into the fullness of human experience. The God who died in Christ is the God who thereby gradually ceases to be present in a living form, emptying himself of his original life and power, and thereafter receding into an alien and lifeless nothingness.

The death of God in Christ is an inevitable consequence of the movement of God into the world, of Spirit into flesh, and the actualization of the death of God in the totality of experience is a decisive sign of the continuing and forward movement of the divine process, as it continues to negate its particular and given expressions, by moving ever more fully into the depths of the profane. A faith that knows this process as a self-negating and kenotic movement, as both embodied and symbolically enacted in the passion of Christ, knows that it becomes manifest in the suffering and the darkness of a naked human experience, an experience banished from the garden of innocence, and emptied of the sustaining power of a transcendent ground or source. So far from regarding the vacuous and rootless existence of modern man as the product of an abandonment of faith, the radical Christian recognizes the spiritual emptiness of our time as the historical actualization of the self-annihilation of God, and despite the horror and anguish embedded in such a condition of humanity, the radical Christian can greet even this darkness as a yet more comprehensive embodiment and fulfillment of the original passion of Christ. Hence a radical faith claims our contemporary condition as an unfolding of the body of Christ, an extension into the fullness of history of the self-emptying of God. No evasion of an autonomous human condition is possible for the Christian who confesses his participation in a Word that has negated its primordial and transcendent ground: the Christian who lives in a fully incarnate Christ is forbidden either to cling to an original innocence or to yearn nostalgically for a preincarnate Spirit. Indeed, it is precisely the Christian's life in the kenotic Word which impels him to accept and affirm a world in which God is dead as the realization in history of God's self-annihilation in Christ.

Once the Christian has been liberated from all attachment to celestial and transcendent Lord, and has died in Christ to the primordial reality of God, then he can say triumphantly: God is dead! Only the Christian can speak the liberating word of the death of God because only the Christian has died in Christ to the transcendent realm of the sacred and can realize in his own participation in the forward-moving body of Christ the victory of the self-negation of Spirit. Just as the primitive Christian could call upon his hearer to rejoice in the Crucifixion because it effected the advent of the Kingdom of God, the contemporary Christian can announce the glad tidings of the death of God, and speak with joy of the final consummation of the self-annihilation of God. True, every man today who is open to experience knows that God is absent, but only the Christian knows that God is dead, that the death of God is a final and irrevocable event, and that God's death has actualized in our history a new and liberated humanity. How does the Christian know that God is dead? Because the Christian lives in the fully incarnate body of Christ, he acknowledges the totality of our experience as the consummation of the kenotic passion of the Word, and by giving himself to the Christ who is present to us he is liberated from the alien power of an emptied and darkened transcendence. Rather than being mute and numb in response to the advent of a world in which the original name of God is no longer sayable, the Christian can live and speak by pronouncing the word of God's death, by joyously announcing the "good news" of the death of God, and by greeting the naked reality of our experience as the triumphant realization of the self-negation of God. What can the Christian fear of the power of darkness when he can name our darkness as the fulfillment of the self-emptying of God in Christ?

V: A Wager

Once again we are called upon to make a wager. Dare we bet that the Christian God is dead, that the ultimate ground of guilt and resentment is broken, and that our guilty condition is created by our clinging to the wholly alien power of a now emptied transcendent realm? If we can truly know that God is dead, and can fully actualize the death of God in our own experience, then we can be liberated from the threat of condemnation, and freed from every terror of a transcendent beyond. Even though we may be mute and speechless in confronting the terror of our time, we cannot evade its pervasive presence, and to relapse into immobility and silence is to foreclose the possibility of being freed from its life-negating power.

Yet the "good news" of the death of God can liberate us from our dread of an alien beyond, releasing us from all attachment to an opposing other, and freeing us for a total participation in the actuality of the immediate moment. By wagering that God is dead, we bet that the awesome and alien power of an infinitely distant and wholly other is finally created by our own guilt and resentment, by our refusal of the life and energy about and within us. Of course, every man who negates and opposes life becomes bound to an alien power. But the Christian knows that Christ is the source of energy and life: hence the Christian must identify all No-saying as a refusal and resistance of Christ. When the Christian bets that God is dead, he is betting upon the real and actual presence of the fully incarnate Christ. Thus a Christian wager upon the death of God is a wager upon the presence of the living Christ, a bet that Christ is now at least potentially present in a new and total form. No, we are not guilty, says the Christian who bets that God is dead. His very bet denies the alien authority of the imperative, and refuses all that guilt arising from a submission to repression. He bets that he is even now forgiven, that he has been delivered from all bondage to the law, and that guilt is finally a refusal of the gift of life and freedom in Christ.

Needless to say, such a wager entails a risk, and an ultimate risk at that. For the Christian who bets that God is dead risks both moral chaos and his own damnation. While the religious or the ecclesiastical Christian has increasingly become incapable of speaking about damnation, the radical Christian, who has been willing to confront the totally alien form of God which has been manifest in our time, has known the horror of Satan and Hell, and can all too readily speak the language of guilt and damnation. He knows that either God is dead or that humanity is now enslaved to an infinitely distant, absolutely alien, and wholly other epiphany of God. To refuse a deity who is a sovereign and alien other, or to will the death of the transcendent Lord, is certainly to risk an ultimate wrath and judgment, a judgment which Christianity has long proclaimed to be damnation. Nor can we pretend that it is no longer possible to envision damnation; the modern artist has surpassed even Dante in envisioning the tortures of the damned. So likewise modern man has known a moral chaos, a vacuous nihilism dissolving every ground of moral judgment, which is unequaled in history. The contemporary Christian who bets that God is dead must do so with a full realization that he may very well be embracing a life-destroying nihilism; or, worse yet, he may simply be submitting to the darker currents of our history, passively allowing himself to be the victim of an all too human horror. No honest contemporary seeker can ever lose sight of the very real possibility that the willing of the death of God is the way to madness, dehumanization, and even to the most totalitarian form of society yet realized in history. Who can doubt that a real passage through the death of God must issue in either an abolition of man or in the birth of a new and transfigured humanity?

The Christian, however, cannot escape the fact that he must make a choice. He must either choose the God who is actually manifest and real in the established form of faith, or he must confess the death of God and give himself to a quest for a whole new form of faith. If he follows the latter course, he will sacrifice an established Christian meaning and morality, abandoning all those moral laws which the Christian Church has sanctioned, and perhaps even negating the possibility of an explicitly Christian moral judgment. Certainly he will be forced to renounce every moral imperative with a transcendent ground, and this means that he must forswear the possibility of an absolute moral law, and at best look upon all forms of moral judgment as penultimate ways which must inevitably act as barriers to the full realization of energy and life. Indeed, the Christian who bets that God is dead must recognize that he himself has not yet passed through the death of God at whatever point he clings to moral law and judgment. True, he can look forward to the promise of total forgiveness, but the forgiveness which he chooses can only be realized here and now; it must evaporate and lose all meaning to the extent that it is sought in a distant future or a transcendent beyond. Yet the Christian who wagers upon the death of God can be freed from the alien power of all moral law, just as he can be liberated from the threat of an external moral judgment, and released from the burden of a transcendent source of guilt. Knowing that his sin is forgiven, such a Christian can cast aside the crutches of guilt and resentment. Only then can he rise and walk.

Cox
THEOLOGY IN A SECULAR WORLD*

Part 1

In one sense there is no future for theology in an age of the "death of God," but in another sense we cannot be certain of this until we know what the phrase means and what the function of theology is. For "death of God" is sometimes used to mean different things, even by the same writer in a single paragraph. My own investigation has isolated three distinct meanings.

The first is nontheistic or atheistic. As Paul Van Buren has said, "Christianity is about man and not about God." For Van Buren it is futile to say anything at all about "God," since the word has no viable empirical referent. We must therefore construct some form of theology in which we stop talking about God. Religious devotion and even religious language may remain, but the referents are entirely changed.

Van Buren's methodology is borrowed from the rigorous techniques of British and American philosophical analysis. A very different viewpoint is that of Thomas Altizer, who seems to be informed by certain Buddhist and Hegelian themes that have led him to assert that there once was a transcendent, real God, but that this God became immanent in Jesus and finally died in his crucifixion. In contrast to Van Buren, Altizer insists that we must not only use the word "God," but we must make the announcement of his death central to our proclamation today. He is not puzzled by the word; he not only knows what it means but is willing to say more about the history of God than most Christian theologies have said in the past. Furthermore, Altizer insists that "only the Christian can experience the death of God." Experiencing the death of God is, for Altizer, close to what has traditionally been associated with conversion.

The second sense in which the phrase "death of God" is used occurs in the context of cultural analysis. For Gabriel Vahanian and sometimes William Hamilton, it simply means that the culturally conditioned ways in which people have experienced the holy have become eroded. Religious ex-

* Harvey Cox (1929–   ): American theologian. This selection comes from two works by Cox. The first part is taken from an essay written by Cox in response to the death-of-God theology and suggests the direction he thinks contemporary theology must go as a consequence of that movement. The second part of our selection is from his major work, *The Secular City*, in which he examines the rise of urban civilization in the light of Christian theology. Part one is from *The New Christianity*, edited by William R. Miller (1967). Reprinted by permission of Harvey Cox. Part two of the selection is reprinted with permission of Macmillan Publishing Co., Inc. from *The Secular City* by Harvey Cox. Copyright © Harvey Cox 1965, 1966, pp. 255–257.

perience is learned in any culture just as other experience is learned, in the unspoken assumptions and attitudes which children absorb from their parents and from their closest environment. Our forebears learned from their forebears to expect the experience of the holy in socially defined ways, whether in the sunset, in a camp-meeting conversion or in holy communion. This experience was structured by a culture of residual Christendom, still bearing traces of what Paul Tillich calls "theonomy." But the coming of modern technology and massive urbanization shook the structures of traditional society and thereby dissipated the cultural ethos within which the holy had been experienced. Hence the "God" of Christendom is "dead." For most modern writers the phrase is metaphorical, but in a culture strongly influenced by pietism, where the reality of God is identified with the experience of God, the phrase may be taken literally as a somber and threatening event.

The third sense in which "God" is "dead" is one that I discussed in the last chapter of my book *The Secular City*, and it is in some respects similar both to Vahanian's and Van Buren's viewpoints. For me, the idea of the "death of God" represents a crisis in our religious language and symbol structure, which makes the word "God" ambiguous. It is not that the word means nothing to "modern man" as Van Buren contends, but that it means so many things to different people that it blurs communication rather than facilitating it.

For years the doctrine of God has been in trouble. Paul Tillich, who assailed the very idea that God "is" (in his *Systematic Theology*), would never have settled for an undialectical non-theism, although his attempts to move "beyond theism" (in *The Courage to Be*) probably contributed to the present situation in theology. Karl Barth's christological positivism may also have prepared the way. The "death of God" movement is an inheritance from them, dramatizing the bankruptcy of the categories we have been trying to use. It is more the symptom of a serious failure in theology than a contribution to the next phase.

Modes of religious experience are, as we have noted, shaped by cultural patterns. When social change jars the patterns, conventional ways of experiencing the holy disappear. When the thickly clotted symbol system of a pre-urban society is replaced by a highly differentiated and individuated urban culture, modalities of religious experience shift. When this happens gradually, over a long span of time, the religious symbols have a chance to become adapted to the new cultural patterns. The experience of the death of the gods, or of God, is a consequence of an abrupt transition which causes the traditional symbols to collapse, since they no longer illuminate the shifting social reality.

The "death of God" syndrome can only occur where the controlling symbols of the culture have been more or less uncritically fused with the transcendent God. When a civilization collapses and its gods topple, theological speculation can move either toward a God whose being lies beyond culture (Augustine, Barth), toward some form of millenarianism or toward a religious crisis that takes the form of the "death of God."

In our own period, which is marked by man's historical consciousness reaching out and encompassing everything in sight, the nooks and crannies formerly reserved for the transcendent have all been exposed. Pluralism and radical historicism have become our permanent companions. We know that all doctrines, ideals, institutions and formulations, whether religious or secular, arise within history and must be understood in terms of their historical milieu. How then do we speak of a God who is somehow present in history, yet whose being is not exhausted by the limits of history? How, in short, do we maintain an affirmation of transcendence within the context of a culture whose mood is relentlessly immanentist? Perhaps a rediscovery of the millenarian tradition, a reappropriation of eschatology tradition, is the way we must go.

The crisis in our doctrine of God is a serious one. This cannot be denied. Nevertheless, our continued and correct insistence on the need to encounter God in *all* of life and not just in a "religious" or cultic precinct fails to express anything that really transcends "history," the source of our experiential reference for what we usually talk about. Some theologians, like Schubert M. Ogden, have responded to the present impasse by going back to the only significant constructive work that has been done in recent decades in American theology—the thought of Charles Hartshorne and Henry Nelson Wieman—and to the philosophy of Alfred North Whitehead. This tactic may eventually produce results, but so far it has not really resolved any of the radical criticisms raised by the "death-of-God" writers.

My own response to the dead-end signaled by the "death of God" mood is to continue to move away from any spatial symbolization of God and from all forms of metaphysical dualism. I am trying to edge cautiously toward a secular theology, a mode of thinking whose horizon is human history and whose idiom is "political" in the widest Aristotelian sense of that term, i.e. the context in which man becomes fully man. . . .

Part 2

But are we using the word *politics* too loosely? The word itself, as Paul Lehmann reminds us, was given its classic meaning by Aristotle. For Aristotle, politics was "the science of the polis," the activity which used all the other sciences to secure not only the good for man but the good for the whole city-state, since that is naturally higher than the good of any one man. Lehmann suggests that what God is doing in the world is politics, which means making and keeping life human. Politics also describes man's role in response to God. It is "activity, and reflection on activity, which aims at and analyzes what it takes to make and keep human life human in the world." Theology today must be that reflection-in-action by which the church finds out what this politician-God is up to and moves in to work along with him. In the epoch of the secular city, politics replaces metaphysics as the language of theology.

We speak of God politically whenever we give occasion to our neighbor to become the responsible, adult agent, the fully post-town and post-tribal man God expects him to be today. We speak to him of God whenever we cause him to realize consciously the web of interhuman reciprocity in which he is brought into being and sustained in it as a man. We speak to him of God whenever our words cause him to shed some of the blindness and prejudice of immaturity and to accept a larger and freer role in fashioning the instrumentalities of human justice and cultural vision. We do not speak to him of God by trying to make him religious but, on the contrary, by encouraging him to come fully of age, putting away childish things.

The Swiss theologian Gerhard Ebeling, though he does not use the term political, means something similar when he talks about the "nonreligious." He insists that secular speaking about God must always be concrete, clear, and active or productive (wirkendes). That is, it must not consist of generalities but must meet people at a point where they feel addressed. God comes to speech truly only as an event in which man and the world are seen for what they really are. In short, ". . . worldly talk of God is godly talk of the world."

The New Testament writers constantly exhorted their readers not to be anxious about what to say. They were repeatedly assured that if they were obedient, if they did what they were supposed to be doing, the right words would be supplied them when the moment came. Speaking about God in a secular fashion requires first of all that we place ourselves at those points where the restoring, reconciling activity of God is occurring, where the proper relationship between man and man is appearing. This means that evangelism, the speaking about God, is political, and Phillippe Maury is right when he says that "politics is the language of evangelism." We cannot know in advance what to say in this or that situation, what acts and words will reveal God's Word to men. Obedience and love precede the gift of tongues. The man who is doing what God intends him to do at the place He intends him to be will be supplied with the proper words. Christian evangelism, like Christian ethics, must be unreservedly contextual.

To say that speaking of God must be political means that it must engage people at particular points, not just "in general." It must be a word about their own lives—their children, their job, their hopes or disappointments. It must be a word to the bewildering crises within which our personal troubles arise—a word which builds peace in a nuclear world, which contributes to justice in an age stalked by hunger, which hastens the day of freedom in a society stifled by segregation. If the word is not a word which arises from a concrete involvement of the speaker in these realities, then it is not a Word of God at all but empty twaddle.

We speak of God to secular man by speaking about man, by talking about man as he is seen in the biblical perspective. Secular talk of God occurs only when we are away from the ghetto and out of costume, when we are participants in that political action by which He restores men to each other in mutual concern and responsibility. We speak of God in a secular fashion when we recognize man as His partner, as the one charged with the task of bestowing meaning and order in human history.

Speaking of God in a secular fashion is thus a political issue. It entails our discerning where God is working and then joining His work. Standing in a picket line is a way of speaking. By doing it a Christian speaks of God. He helps alter the word "God" by changing the society in which it has been trivialized, by moving away from the context where "God-talk" usually occurs, and by shedding the stereotyped roles in which God's name is usually intoned.

Ruether

SEXISM AND THE THEOLOGY OF LIBERATION*

"Women will be saved through bearing children" (I Tim. 2:15). In this crisp sentence, the author of the pastoral epistles sums up what has been a normative view of woman's way to salvation in Christian history. A different view is offered by the gnostic Gospel of the Egyptians (Clement of Alexandria; *Strom.* 111, 9, 63). There Jesus announces, "I have come to destroy the works of the female." What is meant by this statement is that Jesus has come to destroy the works of sexual feeling and maternity, to put an end to the making of babies. Only when the processes of becoming, represented by procreation, are brought to a halt can the cycle of entrapment in the fallen cosmos be overcome and the spirit return to its true home in heaven. Women then are saved by "becoming male"—by renouncing the maternal function and being translated into the realm of disincarnate spirituality (beyond sexuality).

"You are the Devil's gateway," cries Tertullian in a famous phrase from his *De Cultu Feminarum;* and he decrees for women a doubled repression —not only of their bodily feelings but of their feminine image as well—as the price of their presumed "original" culpability for causing the Fall.

These classical notions of the special burdens to be accepted by women must be analyzed by feminists as part of the problem, not of the solution. That is to say, the analysis of sin or the Fall according to such male ideologies must be recognized as being itself an expression of a fallen state of human relationships which finds its fundamental imagery in alienation from

* Rosemary Ruether (1930–   ): American theologian. Ruether examines traditional theological concepts from the point of view of the feminist movement. Dr. Ruether, a Catholic, teaches at Howard University in the school of religion. From "Sexism and the Theology of Liberation" by Rosemary Ruether. Copyright 1973 Christian Century Foundation. Reprinted by permission from the December 12, 1973 issue of *The Christian Century,* pp. 1224–1229.

the body and in sexual oppression. The scenarios of salvation dictated by this ideology are simply restatements or recapitulations of the problem.

Much the same inversion appears in Freudianism, indicating how largely psychoanalysis stands as the secular form of traditional religious sexism. Freud's analysis of woman's dilemma takes the classic form of dictating for her a way of salvation which is designed to re-create or reinforce the very neurosis by which her "nature" is defined; namely, as a "castrated" being, lacking by nature the "male" qualities of initiative and intellect. Hence women become neurotic or hysterical when they engage in a wrong-headed effort to possess the autonomy, will and intellect which their lack of a penis must ever debar them from attaining. This desire is woman's sin. Her salvation lies in giving up "penis-envy" and resigning herself to maternity and to that passive, dependent relation to men which is her anatomical destiny.

In effect Freud, like I Timothy, says that women shall be saved by bearing children. The road of autonomy and self-esteem which is regarded as mature and healthy for the male is for women the road to neurosis. Rarely do Freudians pause to wonder why 80 per cent of mental patients are women while 80 per cent of therapists are male. Even Freud at the end of his life exclaimed in puzzlement that he "didn't know what it was that women wanted." No wonder that women have become so alienated from the male healers, whether doctors or priests. Those healers have revealed themselves as sick-makers. Women must overthrow these sick-making prescriptions, must start believing in themselves and sinning bravely against the male formulas for salvation.

Sexism as Sin

We must begin by examining sexism. If the Fall consists in an alienation between humanity and God, which takes social form in the alienated, oppressive relationship between persons, then sexism must be seen as the original and primary model for analyzing the state of the Fall. Social alienation begins in self-alienation, experienced as an estrangement between the self and the body. The oppressive relationship of the man to the woman is essentially a social projection of the self-alienation which translates certain initial biological differences into a power relationship. This relationship in turn is totalized in social structures and cultural modes that eliminate woman's autonomous personhood to define her solely in terms of male needs and negations. In classical times, that totalization took the form of an identification of women with the "lower half" of self-alienated experience. Woman was stultifying matter over against male intellectuality. Woman was emotionality, sexuality, over against male spirituality. Woman was the power of the past, the immanent, the static, over against male mobility and transcendence. These images become self-fulfilling prophecies by being socially incarnated and culturally enforced through the exclusion of women from education and participation in public life and their immobilization in the home. To forbid woman enlarging cultural experiences is to internalize these self-images in her, to make her *be* what she symbolizes to self-alienated male perception. Women become the victims of the very process by which the male seeks to triumph over the conflict represented by these dualities; are limited and repressed into that same sphere of immanence and materiality which the male sought to escape, transcend and dominate.

Fear of sexuality is the primary way of experiencing the alienation of mind from body. Through this alienation woman is depersonalized and turned into a body-object to be used or abused sexually, but not really encountered—as a person—through sexuality. Male-female relations are envisioned as a kind of social extension of mind-body relations. This implies a subject-object or I-It relation between men and women sexually. The characteristic of the subject-object relation between persons is the negation of the other as a "thou" to be met in and through the bodily presence. This negation abolishes the possibility of bodily relations as the sacrament of mutuality and intersubjectivity. In classical Christian spirituality, the translation of male-female relations into an analogue of self-alienated body-mind dualism blotted out the possibility of bodily relations as a real meeting of persons and constricted sexual relations into the framework of "use" or "abuse." Woman was defined as a "sex object," either rightly "used" for procreation or wrongly abused for "carnal pleasure." In neither case does woman appear as a person.

The 'Puritan-Prurient' Syndrome

The ascetic and libertine ways of thus depersonalizing woman are the two sides of the same coin. We might call this the "Puritan-Prurient" syndrome. Sex is either repressed and/or functionalized, or else sought after, but in a way that regards woman as a tool of male gratification. Either must depersonalize her. The power relationship of supra- and sub-ordination between men and women is essential to this schism. Only by making one person in the relation inferior and dependent and objectified as "body" can a sexuality without the demands of interpersonalism be assured. In this respect, asceticism is one nadir of patriarchalism. It does not prevent the ascetic from having sexual experience. Rather, it assures that this experience will always be treated as "sin," as a debasing loss of control over the alien lower self, which fantasizes woman, whether capitulated to or repudiated, as the image of this debasing lower self.

To the married—those third-class citizens of the church—sex was permitted, but here too it was strictly functionalized within the ascetic definition of the "dirtiness" of sexual pleasure. The married were to have sexual intercourse only "for" procreation. But the erotic experience intrinsic to this act was regarded, especially in the Augustinian tradition, as in itself sinful and indeed the vehicle for the transmission of the "taint" of the Fall. The sin was forgiven the married if they despised the erotic experience and engaged in sex only for its "good end" in procreation, but sinfulness still adhered to the objective fact of orgasmic experience and was thereby passed on to the child in the form of the "taint" of original sin. This analysis of sex prevented the recognition that the real fall takes place in the dehumanization of woman. *There* is the essence of that original sin which is perpetuated, not through sex, biologically, but through *sexism*, morally and socially.

Today people are seeking to throw off the long heritage of sexual repression. But what the media call the "sexual revolution" often does little more than establish the prurient side of this puritan schism. The sexual revolution began with Freud as a revolt against that hypocrisy of the Victorian family which repressed and sublimated sex in the home and compensated for the repression by the proliferation of houses of prostitution. A similar split obtained in our southern society, with its repression and idealization of "virginal" white womanhood and its sexual exploitation of "carnal" black women.

The sexual revolution prompted women to begin reclaiming their right to sexual experience. At first, this move was regarded as a profound threat to "home" and "family." But it soon became apparent that the sexualizing of middle-class women could tie them to traditional sexist relations as effectively as sexual repression had done. Indeed, this sexual revolution appeared at the very moment when the sexually repressive work culture of a capitalistic society was being transformed into the hedonistic culture of the consumer society. This latter enlisted the eroticization of the private sector of life as the prime advertising image to sell consumer products and also as the chief means of pacifying the work-alienation and political powerlessness of the male in the public sphere. The split between home and work becomes essential to the maintenance of the consumer society. The domesticated female becomes the prime buyer, and the home, which has lost all productive functions, the voracious mouth devouring consumer goods. And at the same time the domesticated woman's sexual image is used to whet the appetite for wasteful consumption.

But even the New Left—which is presumably in revolt against the "bourgeois family"— does not protest sexism. It has understood sexual liberation in male terms simply as freedom to use women outside the confining family structure. In the '60s radical women received a painful but galvanizing shock when Stokely Carmichael announced that the "only position for women in the Movement is prone." That remark made them realize that they had been betrayed into a male-oriented sexual libertinism which had nothing to do with recognizing women as persons but was only the repressed side of puritanism. In the popular culture, sexual frankness begins to look more and more like pornography and carries increasingly sadistic overtones. In patriarchal cultures, the two sides of the same psychosocial alienation are still manifest in the repression and exploitation of women as both the despised and the desired body-object. In all these contexts, it is not the liberation of women that surfaces but the prurient side of puritan repression.

The Resurrection of Woman

Sexual alienation and the depersonalizing of women define the Fall. But salvation cannot be found in these terms, since the solutions derived from them only recapitulate the problem. Salvation cannot appear save as the resurrection of woman; that is, in woman's self-definition as an autonomous person. Rather than being co-opted into male projections that make her the image of male ideals and phobias, she must establish herself as an autonomous person in any encounter. Her resurrection begins as an inner psychic revolution that gives her the transcending power to disaffiliate herself from male objectifications and to make her exodus from incorporations of her as an extension of male demands and alienation.

Oppression in society is never a matter of open force only. It always seeks to become socially incorporated and to operate through modes of cultural conditioning which make the subjects internalize the image projected upon them. Since, of all power relations, that between men and women is the most intimate, carefully hidden forms of persuasion are necessarily demanded in order to shape women to be what, according to male ideology, they are, and to lead them to internalize a self-image appropriate to this status. From their earliest years women are culturally conditioned to be willing cooperators in their enslavement and unconscious of their objective situation. Thus their liberation begins as a terrifying explosion of consciousness, a self- and world-transforming conversion experience.

Anger and Pride as Theological Virtues

The theological virtues which mediate this transformation of consciousness are *anger* and *pride*. Anger corresponds to the power to transcend false consciousness and break its chains. Pride corresponds to the exorcism of demeaning self-images and the re-establishment of authentic personhood as the ground of one's being. In Christianity, anger and pride have generally been regarded as sin, as the revolt of the creature against its Creator and "all lawful authority." But the prophetic God is also an angry God, a God who is angry against exploiters and who says "I am who I am" against all falsification. Anger and pride are sinful as the stance of oppressors who seek, through their pride and hate, to perpetuate false power systems. But anger in the service of love and justice places all oppressive systems under judgment. Self-esteem resurrects in the oppressed, from beneath the mire of denigration which had hitherto smothered it, the image of human nature as originally created—as good.

It is in this framework that anger and pride are theological virtues. Any who confuse the opposite kinds of anger and pride legitimatize evil power. The gospel becomes a gospel of acquiescence in a status quo that is antithetical to the liberation struggle. Passivity and meekness are taught those who are already humiliated. Servility is inculcated and false consciousness reinforced in them. Thus Christian love becomes a slave ethic rather than the ethic of the freed person.

To those who have internalized the psychology of denigration, the inbreaking of anger and pride comes as grace welling up from the ground of their being, yet from beyond their present condition, to spring the trap of their pacification. Anger and pride are the power for Exodus, for disaffiliation from the Egypt of male definition and use. This nay-saying is also a yea-saying. It is an ecstatic leap of consciousness transforming the basis of existence, an *élan* of liberated power to be. Woman is empowered to depart from and define herself over against that subjugation to immanence stemming from a male-centered transcendence that reduces the others to objects of domination. This exodus is a rebellion against the dead world of I-It relationships.

Debilitating Alternatives

But this revelation of a new self and a new world remains proleptic and unfulfilled. It gives a foretaste of what a transformed humanity might look like. But the power structures of the fallen world remain, though their mask of authority has been stripped off. Even when the legal subjugation which, only a century ago, still defined the condition of women has been largely repealed, economic and social ways of enforcing that subjugation remain. At every turn women still find themselves confronted by falsifying role definition, sexist power plays and agonizing choices between equally debilitating alternatives. These are the typical conditions of life offered women. Give up marriage and motherhood and we will let you compete, in an inferior and handicapped sort of way, with ourselves, the male world says to them. If you don't care to be a celibate, then be prepared to see the wasting of all your dreams for autonomous accomplishment. This last is an updating, in somewhat modified form, of the alternative of nun or wife traditionally offered by the church. A woman might rise to spirituality at the price of giving up marriage and sexuality; or else she might accept the status of the married woman: to have no "head of her own" but be under the dominion of the husband who is "her head."

Not only are these alternatives enforced by cultural conditioning; the ideology behind them itself expresses the power relationships between men and women that are systemic to existing social and economic relationships. Socially, women form a caste within every class. That is, they share a common oppression as women; but they find it hard to unite across class and racial lines because they are divided by the class and race oppression that the ruling class and race exercise over subjugated classes and races. As women, they are the domestic servants of society, bearing all the auxiliary and supportive chores and thus freeing the male for the monolithic work day. When let into the work world, they are generally structured into the same kind of domestic services and auxiliary support systems of male executive roles—as nurses, secretaries and the like. Economically, women provide the support system for male mobility and work. Domesticated in the private sector, they are also the child nurturers (for what has come to be an intensive and extended period of childhood) and, in addition, the providers of that sphere of rest, recreation and erotic life which moderates male work alienation. Thus the cult of True Womanhood, which idealizes the role of woman as a glorified servant, is an essential part of the ideology of modern industrial society. The very structuring of the urban-suburban ecology reflects this interdependence of male work and female domestication.

All this means that the woman who wishes both to be married and to have a career must try to do the two jobs at once. Since she has no wife to provide a support system for herself, and can hardly (1) do a job defined on the basis of having such a support system, (2) provide her own support system and (3) provide a support system for another person similarly employed—such being her case, we must conclude that under present male-defined work patterns it is almost impossible for a woman both to be married and to have a career. This combination is available only to the rich, to the manically energetic, or to those who manage to break out of the trap by juggling these relationships in some unorthodox way. Most women are beaten before they have even begun to fight. When the thought crosses their minds that their present lot is humanly unacceptable, the odds are already quite hopelessly against them.

A Communitarian Socialist Society

We must say then that the liberation of women as a caste is impossible within the present socioeconomic system. Only in a system totally restructured in all its basic interdependencies (especially in the relationship between work-time and -place and the domestic support system) can women emerge into the full range of human activities now available to men. This probably means a revolutionary reform of society along the lines of communitarian socialism. State socialist societies, such as Russia, have collectivized some of the work of the home and thus liberated women for the male work day; but they have left the psychology of sexism in the nuclear family unchanged, and they still place the fundamental burdens of housework and food procurement upon women. The communitarian socialist society, on the other hand, would communalize the home while keeping the basic decisions over daily life in a primary community, rather than relegating these to the state. Such a communitarian socialist society, where a large part of

the goods and tools of life would be produced in the workshop closely related to the primary community, is probably also the only type of society
that is compatible with the long-term survival of humanity on the planet;
for the present self-infinitizing industrial system is rapidly eating up the
organic foundations of earthly existence.

We must, however, also understand the tension that will necessarily exist
between the rise of women's consciousness and that future transformation
of the world which can incarnate social justice. This tension corresponds to
the tension between conversion and incorporation into the community of new
consciousness on the one hand, and the future New World that overthrows
the present structures of oppression and redeems the world. Some Nie-
buhrians will argue that even such a communitarian socialist society cannot
represent final redemption. Perhaps so, but the qualitative difference between
social justice and social injustice is not thereby reduced. The society of
social justice represents the available horizon of redemption of the world.
If it is dangerous to conflate the critical principle with a realized new society,
however improved, it is equally wrong not to interrelate the final or ultimate
horizon of redemption, which is beyond all imagining, with that available
horizon of social justice, peace and love toward which we can begin to
struggle here and now. It is by divorcing ultimate salvation from the available horizon of salvation, and insisting that human depravity makes all
social relations equally evil, that the revolutionary thrust of the gospel is
cut off and Christianity becomes an ideology of social conservatism.

Just as ultimate redemption cannot be divorced from historical redemption,
so conversion cannot be privatized and internalized as something that can
be completed merely by personal consciousness-raising and does not demand
a transformation of the world. Redemption is not redemption *from* the world
in a flight from outward society and nature, but redemption *of* the world—a
redemption which overthrows the false world of powers and principalities
that was created not by God but by man out of his self-alienation and
social exploitation. Conversion, therefore, cannot be fulfilled in a private,
inward way; it must move outward toward that transformation of reality
which redeems creation from bondage. This means that a tension between
conversion and redemption exists as the present state of the church; a
proleptic vision of a new world arises that sets us in tension also with the
unredeemed state of our actual lives. Here and now our new consciousness
stands as a principle of discernment and suffering conflict that struggles
against the power structures in the light of a vision of redeemed humanity
and a redeemed creation.

Sisterhood as Therapeutic Community

The church represents our present vantage point on this redeemed community. It is both a real foretaste of that community and the party of redemptive struggle against the power structures. But it is a foretaste of

redeemed humanity only in the sense of being a community of raised consciousness—not in the sense of being a community unaware of the many ways in which alienating power structures continue to exist and people's lives continue to be governed by them. From this vantage point, is it possible to speak of sisterhood as the church from the perspective of the women's movement? From the perspective of the struggle against the sexual power structure, sisterhood represents redemptive and revelatory co-humanity in many ways. It is a therapeutic community which enables women to articulate their repressed alienation, to arrive at the consciousness—which all the social conditioning forces of patriarchy contrive to repress—that their present portion is dehumanizing. Sisterhood affords women the basic support community which allows them to become conscious of oppression without being delivered over to loneliness and madness. Sisterhood is a healing community that makes weak women strong, able to confront the sources of their debilitation with confidence and to become whole people. Sisterhood is also redemptive co-humanity, which overcomes that internalization of self-hatred and of those demeaning self-images that the oppressed typically act out not by attacking the sources of their oppression but by attacking each other. Women in patriarchy are isolated from each other, made individually dependent on men; competitive with each other for men; prostitutes of their sexuality and domestic service for survival. Sisterhood breaks these bonds of alienation between women and restores women to redemptive co-humanity with each other.

But this development only provides a base of healed selfhood from which to grapple with the real sources of debilitation. Since the alienation between women is only a by-product of the fundamental alienation of sexism—namely, the alienation between men ond women—sisterhood is inadequate to represent the church. The church must be represented by a community of men and women of raised consciousness who discern how the full humanity of both men and women has been distorted by sexism. Let me explain why this is the case. I do not mean that co-humanity can be represented only by the heterosexual married couple, as in sexist doctrines of complementarity. The church is as much beyond heterosexist complementarity as it is beyond racism or class relationships. The church is neither male nor female, slave nor free, Jew nor Greek; it is not a complementarity of male and female, slave and free, Jew and Greek, in which each half of these alienated relationships represents a partial humanity. The church takes us beyond these stereotypes to the community which is possible only between whole persons.

Liberating Both Oppressor and Oppressed

What I mean, rather, is that the community of the oppressed against the oppressors, while it is a necessary part of the process of liberation, cannot represent the community of reconciliation. That can be represented only by a community which brings together oppressor and oppressed in a new relationship that liberates both from their previous pathologies in relation to each other. But we must be very clear about the uses of anger in liberation. Anger is necessary to explode the bonds of fear and self-denigration from power structures and for tearing off their masks of authority. Anger is necessary for the liberation struggle. But redeeming anger is at the service of love, not of hate. One struggles against the system of oppression; one does not hate the other person who acts as vehicle of oppression.

Not that the other person is merely a passive tool of alien powers. He is a concrete beneficiary of unjust power and to that extent is guilty, responsible, still in his sins so long as the system of oppression by which he benefits continues to exist. But the point is that we do not confuse nature with the Fall; we do not confuse white people with the white system or males with the system of male domination; and we do not confuse the demons we seek to exorcise with the human beings we seek to liberate from demonic possession. We seek to overthrow the master as a master, but in order to reclaim him as a friend. We seek to overthrow oppressive psychologies and structures in order to redeem a wholeness of personhood for those on each side of the alienated relationship and reveal the possibility of co-humanity for the first time.

The rise of women's consciousness must not translate the "other" into an object that makes him alien territory to be spurned or dominated. To do so simply reverses the oppressor-oppressed relationship and leaves its psychodynamics intact. Rather, women's consciousness, indeed the consciousness of all oppressed people, becomes redemptive when it reveals a co-humanity beneath the master-slave distortion as the authentic ground of our being, and fights its battle in a way that takes its stand upon this ground and constantly reaffirms it. Women's movements win little by simply winning new opportunities for power and practice in a world still structured by alienated consciousness. We must reach beyond this to the dissolution of both sides of every falsifying polarity and the redemption of the soul of humanity from its bondage to destruction.

Enroth, Ericson, Peters
THE JESUS MOVEMENT*

* * *

The Jesus People are overwhelmingly—one could almost say exclusively —experience-oriented. It is important to recognize that they were so even

* This selection is from a book entitled *The Jesus People*, a study of the contemporary ferment in Christianity and the revival of interest, particularly among young people, in evangelical forms of Christianity. The exerpts come from Chapter Eight, "The Simple Gospel," and Chapter Nine, "The Last Days." From *The Jesus People* by R. Enroth, E. Ericson, and C. Peters (1972), pp. 164–171, 179–180. Used by permission of William B. Eerdmans Publishing Company.

before they became the Jesus People. The word "trip," as used by the counter-culture and now by the Jesus People, is a synonym for experience; a "high" is an experience. To be high on drugs means to have a drug-induced experience. To be high on Jesus means to have a certain religious experience. When those in the counter-culture talk about being turned on to Jesus, they are referring to an emotional experience that, for them, has striking similarity to the emotional experience induced by drugs.

Reason has always been highly prized in Western civilization, the tradition formed by the fusion of the classical and Christian cultures. It is not by accident that reason has throughout the centuries been seen as harmonious with Christian faith. But the carefully worked out relationships between faith and reason that loom so large in the works of Augustine and Thomas Aquinas are totally foreign to the Jesus People—and for a good reason. These new converts have come out of a background in the counter-culture with its emphasis upon drugs and other experiences. What the counter-culture is attempting to counter is the Western tradition in which rationality plays so large a part. That is why so many counter-culture adherents have turned eagerly to Oriental mysticisms of one sort or another in order to find meaning in life. Timothy Leary in his prime argued that drugs were the way to discover authentic religious experiences. Religious yearnings are innate in all men, but the counter-culture has concluded that these yearnings must find satisfaction outside the Western tradition. And the component of the Western synthesis that is most adamantly opposed by the counter-culture is, precisely, reason.

One of the primary roles of reason in Christianity is apologetics, defense of the faith. Peter had this in mind when he exhorted his readers to "be ready always to give an answer to every man that asketh you a reason of the hope that is in you with meekness and fear" (I Peter 3:15). The lack of a carefully thought-out apologetic is one of the great weaknesses of the Jesus Movement in general, as the Children of God delight in pointing out about the other Jesus People. It is sad to stand on the sidewalk of Old Town in Chicago and listen to one of the Jesus People being soundly trounced in an argument by a well-read youthful unbeliever. In such a situation, the Jesus person is reduced to saying something like, "But I've had this experience, and I know it's true. I know I'm right." The Bible, however, exhorts its readers to test the spirits. Other persons have had other experiences, and for them these experiences have been most profound and earthshaking. According to what criterion can these competing experiences be judged? The criterion must lie outside the realm of experience itself. The following quotation from *Maranatha*, a Jesus Paper out of Vancouver, illustrates the dilemma of the Jesus People:

How do we know it works? We know by the only method you can really trust . . . by experience. . . . After everything . . . ideology and the rest . . . has been stripped away, there's only the down-to-earth "Heavenly" experience as evidence that it really works. . . . I can accept other people with different beliefs . . . I doubt if there are any two people on this earth who believe exactly the same way . . . but I'm not talking about beliefs. My beliefs merely left me with a messed up head and nothing inside. . . . Experience is what really counts. . . . I'm not gonna try to say that Buddhism is wrong. . . . I haven't tried it and neither do I plan to. I have found where peace, love, joy and the rest are available in abundance and, once I've found what I'd been crying out for inside for as long as I can remember. I'm not gonna walk away from it and try something else. . . .

That answer may be good enough for its author, but it won't do much to convince the Buddhist.

A similarly excessive reliance on feeling may be seen in the following words, which we heard from several Jesus People: "I haven't had a 'down' day since I found the Lord." What will happen to these converts when they finally do have a bad day? For surely the bad days will come. Scripture makes it quite clear that the servants of God are not exempt from "down days." Those who speak about being "high on the love of my Jesus" often add that that is a high that never stops.

In C. S. Lewis' *Screwtape Letters,* the devil Screwtape tells Wormwood about emotional troughs, which are a natural part of the psychological makeup of all men. There is a psychological principle of undulation. All men have their emotional ups and downs, and these are not always directly related to one's spiritual condition. Screwtape encourages Wormwood to capitalize on this situation by confusing the psychological with the spiritual.

But there is an even better way of exploiting the Trough; I mean through the patient's own thoughts about it. As always, the first step is to keep knowledge out of his mind. Do not let him suspect the law of undulation. Let him assume that the first ardours of his conversion might have been expected to last, and ought to have lasted, forever, and that his present dryness is an equally permanent condition (p. 42).

The other side of experience-oriented Christianity is the anti-intellectualism of the Jesus People. They delight in quoting out of context such Bible passages as "Hath not God made foolish the wisdom of this world?" and "But God hath chosen the foolish things of the world to confound the wise," and "Beware lest any man spoil you through philosophy and vain deceit." In keeping with the all-or-nothing mentality that prevails in our times, they do not understand these passages to be saying that, whatever the intrinsic value of the wisdom of the world, it is foolishness in comparison to the revelation of God. God does not place a premium upon ignorance, though some of the Jesus People literally and emphatically do. Many are shocked to learn that Paul himself, the author of these statements, quoted from pagan poets right in Holy Writ at least three times.

Many of the Jesus People claim to read only the Bible, though some will allow that there are certain devotional guides that may be profitable, such as the books by Watchman Nee. Susan Alamo says that at the Christian

Foundation the only person who reads anything other than the Bible is her husband, Tony, who reads the newspapers to see what prophecies, if any, have been fulfilled that day. The Jesus People feel no need to acquaint themselves with the issues of the day that should be met by an application of Scripture. A good witness must understand enough about his hearer's outlook to be able to apply the Scriptures to his particular needs. How can one who reads only the Bible ever know the specific issues to which its truth applies?

Although they read the Bible constantly, they tend to be proof-texters of the worst sort, taking verses out of context with abandon. (The Children of God even trot out a proof-text in favor of proof-texting—II Timothy 3:16.) This kind of Bible reading is designed to find some sort of scriptural support for previously decided positions. . . .

Just as the Jesus People are anti-intellectual, so they are anti-cultural. In terms of H. Richard Niebuhr's four approaches to the relationship between Christianity and human culture (elaborated in his *Christ and Culture*), the Jesus People are casebook examples of the Christ-against-culture approach. This places them at odds with Augustine, Aquinas, Luther, Calvin, and a host of other great Christian thinkers. Rather than seeing the Bible as the criterion by which to judge all human attempts to discover truth, the Jesus People see the Bible as exhaustive truth. But the Bible does not provide an exhaustive exposition of all truth· it gives no description of the physical universe in all its complexity; and it is obviously a logical impossibility that the Scriptures, revealed during a certain time span in history, could have an exhaustive account of history that followed the time of the writing of the Bible. Such examples could, of course, be multiplied almost endlessly, but the point is clear. The anti-intellectual, anti-cultural bias of the Jesus People can rest only on an obviously erroneous understanding of the Bible.

The root of the anti-cultural fundamentalism of the Jesus People is their inadequate understanding of the nature of man. On the basis of an extreme view of man's depravity, they see culture as something demonic, wholly bad, not as something human, therefore good and bad. Typical expression of this viewpoint is found in the books of Watchman Nee, one of the few extra-biblical sources that Jesus People are likely to read. In his book, *Love Not the World*, Nee asserts that "Christian civilization is the outcome of an attempt to reconcile the world and Christ" (p. 46). In his view,

Politics, education, literature, science, art, law, commerce, music—such are the things that constitute the *kosmos*, and these are things we meet daily. Subtract them and the world as a coherent system ceases to be. . . . In the book of Genesis we find in Eden no hint of technology, no mention of mechanical instruments. After the Fall, however, we read that among the sons of Cain there was a forger of cutting instruments of brass and iron. . . . The same thing applies to music and the arts. For the pipe and the harp seem also to have originated with the family of Cain, and today in unconsecrated hands their God-defying nature becomes increasingly clear. . . . As for commerce, its connections are perhaps even more suspect. Satan was the first merchant, trading ideas with Eve for his own advantage. . . . But what of education? Surely, we protest, that must be harmless. Anyway, our children have to be taught. But education, no less than commerce or technology, is one of the things of the world. It has its roots in the tree of knowledge (pp. 14–15).

Obviously it is not a long step from Watchman Nee to the Children of God. Many Jesus People are susceptible to the radical teachings of the Children, for they share the common ground of being anti-cultural. Culture is not human, but Satanic:

Do we acknowledge that Satan is today the prince of education and science and culture and the arts, and that they, with him, are doomed? . . . Test yourself. If you venture into one of these approved fields, and then someone exclaims to you: "You have touched the world there," will you be moved? Probably not at all. It takes someone whom you really respect to say to you very straightly and earnestly: "Brother, you have become involved with Satan there!" before you will as much as hesitate. Is that not so? How would you feel if anyone said to you: "You have touched education there," or "You have touched medical science," or "You have touched commerce"? Would you react with the same degree of caution as you would if he had said, "You have touched the Devil there"? If we truly believed that whenever we touch any of these things that constitute the world we touch the prince of this world, then the awful seriousness of being in any wise involved in worldly things could not fail to strike home to us . . . (pp. 17–18).

Or suppose you are in engineering, or farming, or publishing. Take heed, for these too are things of the world, just as much as running a place of entertainment or a haunt of vice. Unless you tread softly you will be caught up somewhere in Satan's snares and will lose the liberty that is yours as a child of God (p. 24).

These anti-cultural assertions of Watchman Nee represent the kind of thinking that permeates the Jesus People. This outlook propounds a radical separation of Christianity from culture and blithely assumes that this is the only possible outlook that is genuinely scriptural. It is based upon the acceptance of the absolute worthlessness of the natural man. It is based, that is to say, on a view of man that is deficient and subscriptural. The Bible does say, "There is none that doeth good, no, not one." But the context of this passage refers to a man's inability to be justified by his own efforts. The emphasis is that man comes short of God's standard of perfection. The Bible also speaks of man's being created in the image of God, and one must be very careful about calling the pinnacle of God's creation bad. Francis Schaeffer reminds us that the Bible does not allow us to call man "junk." It is true that man fell and that the fall *marred* the image of God bestowed on man at creation, but that image was not *erased*. Even fallen men are still in the image of God. They have such characteristics of God as rationality, aesthetic sensibility, personality, ability to communicate, ability to have personal relationships.

Total depravity does not mean that every time man has a choice, he makes the very worst possible one. Common sense and observation are enough to show that some unregenerate men are on occasion good neighbors and capable of performing good deeds. But God's standard for a personal relationship with him is perfection, and no man is capable of this. Total depravity means that man's sinfulness cuts across every area of his life—spiritual, emotional, physical, moral, and others.

The doctrine of creation balances the doctrine of man's sinfulness. Created in the image of God, man—even though fallen—is to subdue the earth and have dominion over it. This is what makes cultural enterprises—education, art, science, human government, technology, and the like—legitimate. On the other side the doctrine of sin shows that man will never be able to operate in these spheres with perfection and that he must not therefore hope for a solution to the human condition in human achievements.

Christian literature demonstrates over and over again that man is both great and miserable, but he is never viewed as worthless, as a piece of junk. It is only since the Christian synthesis of the Middle Ages and the Renaissance has broken down and man has come to consider himself as a god that the view of man has taken a turn for the worse. In general, modern literature does not show man as great; it shows him only as miserable. It has reduced man's status to that of the animal or the machine. If a Christian thinks that secular society views man as good and not in need of help from an outside source, he is only showing his ignorance of the society in which he lives. Inadvertently, he demonstrates the need for education that will give him the knowledge of the culture in which he lives, even if for no other reason than to be an effective witness in it. The pacesetters of our culture today see man not as great but as miserable. It is the greatness which has been lost and which the Christian must be at pains to assert in order to recall the biblical image of man. . . .

Next to the simple gospel, perhaps the most prominent idea of the Jesus People is that we are living in the last days. Without exception, the Jesus People with whom we talked believe that these are the last days and that Christ will return in their lifetimes. They cannot imagine themselves growing old and dying a natural death. Many believe that they will not die at all. Others believe that they will die as martyrs for Christ.

Everything in the Jesus Movement is colored by this apocalyptic mentality. Bumper stickers flaunt it; songs repeat it; witnessing returns to it over and over again; sermons and personal conversations are obsessed by it. Typical is Larry Norman's song, "I Wish We'd All Been Ready," which envisions a married couple being separated by the rapture, since one member is saved and one is not. The standard handbill passed out on Hollywood Boulevard by the Christian Foundation teams reads, "Repent now. Jesus is coming soon." Chuck Smith, Pastor of Calvary Chapel, says,

The last days are upon us, and the Spirit of God is being poured out upon us. And it's just God's plan. It's just coming to completion. The Bible is full of prophetic utterances which described the last times, and we can see that the world's really living in a whole lot of chaotic, bad ways. You want to call it sin. That's what the Bible would call it. It's prophesied in the Bible that the Lord will pour the Spirit down upon all men, and I believe that is happening. And I believe that it won't be long until we see the Second Coming of the Lord.

David Hoyt has written,

We look forward to the end harvest and the coming of our Lord. He is coming soon for a living bride, full of Grace and Truth and eagerly waiting his return. Our wonderful Lord deserves much more than a barren old maid of stale religion based on carnal division and the doctrines of men.

Linda Meissner concurs:

As the final stages of fulfillment are upon us of Jesus' immortal words 'Go ye into all the world, and preach the gospel to every creature,' God is raising up a great last day army. It is becoming a reality through the method of reproducing re-producers.

To our question about whether we are living in the last days, she replied:

Absolutely. We believe this is the last generation. And what are the signs? They're all over the place. . . . I believe the return of Christ is very, very close. We also believe that . . . there's a heavy storm coming. . . . No one can say the day and the hour. If you would ask the people in the Jesus People Movement, they would say three to twenty years. That's not very long, when you think that it's our job to fulfil the Great Commission in this generation. And it's storm conditions in which we're going to have to do it.

Similar sentiments abound in the Jesus underground papers.

SUGGESTIONS FOR FURTHER READING

Collins, James, *The Existentialists: A Critical Study.* (Chicago: Henry Regnery Co., 1952). *An exposition and critical examination of the Existentialist movement. Particularly interesting analysis of Sartre's "postulatory atheism." See Part II.*

Copleston, F. C., *Aquinas.* (London: Penguin Books, 1955). *Excellent commentary upon Aquinas' Five Ways.*

D'Arcy, Martin C., *No Absent God* (New York: Harper & Row, 1962). *Defends the thesis that man loses his sense of identity when he loses contact with God.*

Hartshorne, Charles, *The Logic of Perfection and Other Essays in Neoclassical Metaphysics*. (La Salle, Ill.: Open Court Publishing Co., 1962). *Thorough examination and evaluation of the ontological argument. Consideration is given to the argument's historical critics and defenders. Decidedly not elementary.*

Hick, John and McGill, Arthur, eds., *A Proof of God's Existence: Recent Essays on the Ontological Argument*. (New York: Macmillan, 1965). *Collection of essays which either defend or criticize the ontological argument.*

Hume, David, *Dialogue Concerning Natural Religion*. Ed. by H. D. Aiken. (New York: Hafner, 1948). *Hume's superb critique of the proofs of God's existence. Also an excellent introduction to the problems of religious knowledge.*

Kierkegaard, Søren, *Fear and Trembling*. Tr. by Walter Lowrie. (Garden City, N.Y.: Doubleday and Co., 1954). *Interesting presentation of the types of existence available to man. The contrast between the life of faith and the moral life is developed in a striking manner.*

Lubac, Henri De, *The Drama of Atheist Humanism*. Tr. by Edith Riley. (New York: Meridian Books, 1950). *Survey of the history of atheistic humanism. Consideration is given to Nietzsche, Feuerbach, Marx, Kierkegaard and others.*

Sorley, W. R., *Moral Values and the Idea of God*. (New York: Cambridge University Press, 1919). *A modern defence of the moral argument for God's existence.*

Webb, C. C. J., *Kant's Philosophy of Religion*. Oxford: The Clarendon Press, 1926). *Lucid explanation and evaluation of Kant's moral argument for God.*

EDITOR'S POSTSCRIPT

The meaning of Nietzsche's proclamation of the death of God lies in the complementary injunction to man to "become like God" in order to be worthy of the event that man has perpetrated. Nietzsche viewed the absence of God as an accomplished fact in the nineteenth century and as an event forming itself in the womb of the future, awaiting the maturation of the human spirit before it would dawn upon the consciousness of Western man. In the mid-twentieth century the first rays of that consciousness are appearing on man's horizon, and the dawn, as always, has the gray somber countenance of twilight. For twilight is that time of day when there is insufficient light to provide reassuring illumination, and the residual darkness, while heralding the approach of a new day, still retains the threatening portents of the deepest night.

Every new dawn, every fresh awakening repeats the enigma of birth in death and death in birth. Whether it be the rude expulsion of the infant from the idyllic comfort and security of the womb through the violence of labor, or the bewildering onslaught of a new cosmic dream wrapped in the decay and passage of an aging, majestic vision, the story is always the same. The birth of the new amid the death throes of the old is accompanied in human experience with a curious mixture of suffering, misgivings, dread, and childlike anticipation. Death comes hard to a religious myth that has used the spirit of Western man as creatively as has the transcendental, other-worldly vision of Christianity. The Christian myth has "played on" the talents of persons in Western culture with amazing results. For over nineteen centuries, this spiritual home (Christendom) has been our abiding place. It has inspired many of our greatest artists, fashioned men of genius among us, and given us a measure of order and coherence in our communal lives. To fold our tents in this land that has served us so well, to seek a new horizon wherein to fulfill our longings and to realize our dreams fills us with dread, with foreboding, and with morbid anticipation.

There can be no demonstration of the necessity for this new adventure of the human soul, just as there can be no formal demonstration of the necessity for the child giving up childish things to become a man. Decay, change, and passage without explicit direction or goal seems often to be our destiny. The relentless movement of time consumes all creatures under its sway. But the heroic genius of humanity has been its willingness to accept its temporal fate and to give shape to its future in accordance with its needs and aspirations. Only thus has humanity survived the death of those images and myths which have given form and meaning to its historical life. In accepting his destiny as a temporal creature, man yields up his life to the inexorable rush of time, giving himself over to decay and change, to birth and death, and to time's eternal control.

The "new" death-of-God theology seen on the broader scale of history is as old as the ages of man, for man is the creature who makes and responds to myths. Gods have been dying since the evolutionary emergence of man, and their deaths have always been greeted with traumatic misgivings and anxiety. My purpose in pointing out this obvious fact in the history of religion is not to provide solace in what some take to be our own deathwatch, but rather to suggest what we might learn both about human nature and the myth-making function. Just as it is no comfort to the dying man to provide him with mortality tables for past ages, neither is it a comfort to a civilization, just becoming dimly aware of the decay of its most formative myth, to reassure it on the basis of past history that this, too, can be endured.

What is more to the point is the organization of our intellectual and imaginative energies to the creative task that confronts us, namely that of uncovering and shaping the new myth that is to determine our destiny in the centuries to come. For if we have learned anything from the history of religion, it is that in regard to the heroes and holy powers, to the gods of our religious and mythical dreams, we are both their slaves *and* their masters. The gods use us in wonderful and terrible ways, bewitching our world and our experience with a transforming power. The sudden appearance of new deities in human history has always been accompanied by mighty works of creative imagination, evidenced by the marvelous variety of the forms of cultures in words, stone, music, dance, and color. These epiphanies strike such an awe in man that he finds he must offer himself up as the most appropriate form in which the holy presence might be revealed.

The advent of a new holy image evokes an ecstasy that is both destructive and creative. There is dread and destruction precisely because a new power is working its magic upon the energies and imagination of humanity. A kind of "madness" is generated by the appearance of a new mythic image which challenges and disrupts the placid serenity of conventional life. Caught up in the creative turbulence of a new holy presence, communicants are thought mad by nonbelievers. It is inevitable that advocates of the new faith will be thought beside themselves from the perspective of conventional existence.

The older religious forms already have been integrated into the pattern of everyday communal life and therefore have undergone a rather rich secularization. The appearance of a novel mythic image with its nascent urge to creativity involves such a drastic reforming of the concept of man and community that from the static, conventional standpoint, the new religious urge is viewed as inspiring man to subhuman modes of thought and action—that is, as dehumanizing. In some such manner, the Romans must have viewed the early Christians as mad and as threatening the very base of community life. Yet from the wider perspective of historical understanding, what was originally seen as destructive and dehumanizing can be seen as recreative of human culture. Expressed in another fashion, this "madness" is the clearest witness to and manifestation of man's incipient aspiration to be transformed into god. The epiphany of a new holy power is often first revealed in men becoming living monuments to this new presence through their "madness" and creativity.

Our age has witnessed and is living through violent revolutions of many sorts: socioeconomic, political, and technological. Now there is added a revolution that threatens to undo the religious and mythic tradition which has structured life in the West for twenty centuries. The dawning consciousness of the death of God is not, however, the result of the appearance of a new religious image. That event lies on the horizon of the future and constitutes the foremost task for the imagination and decision of contemporary man. The fading of the altar lights of Christianity heralds a new dawn, but the sun still lies beyond the horizon. The rhythm of birth and death in the ever-renewing cycle of life should teach us that out of the ashes of the old faith, the phoenixlike spirit of man will emerge touched by some new magic and imbued with a fruitful, creative greatness. Does this new creative myth already lie latent in the great poetry, philosophy, art, and music of our age, awaiting that moment of human recognition that will unfold its genius in an amazing fruition of life and culture?

Gods die and are born; such is a fact of our historical existence. The notion of god's eternal return is grounded in man's undying aspiration to surpass himself, to grow larger than this life he leads, larger than the incessant movement of life and time itself. In our immediate past lie two world wars, Stalin's purges, Buchenwald and Hiroshima, Vietnam; what new, creative myth can lift the human spirit beyond that inhumanity to a more mature realization of its latent urge to be godlike?

Index

Altizer, Thomas, "Death of God" Theology 400
Anselm, St., The Ontological Argument 345
Aquinas, St. Thomas, Faith and Reason 296; The Five Ways 348

Baillie, D. M., Christian Atonement 241
Buber, Martin, The I-Thou Relation 373
Buddhism, Thirst and Its Consequences 32
Bultmann, Rudolf, The Task of Demythologizing 169

Campbell, Joseph, The Dialogue in Myth of East and West 214; The Masks of God 161
Cox, Harvey, Theology in a Secular World 409
Crombie, I. M., see Flew

Dostoevsky, Fyodor, Underground Man 9
Durkheim, Emile, Religion's Origin in Society 133

Enroth, R., and others, The Jesus Movement 422
Ericson, E., see Enroth

Feuerbach, Ludwig, Religion as Projection of Human Nature 115
Flew, Anthony, and others, Theology and Falsification 309
Freud, Sigmund, Religion as Wish Fulfillment 107
Fromm, Erich, Mature Love 258

Goethe, Johann Wolfgang, Faust's Wager 44

Hare, R. M., see Flew
Hesse, Hermann, The Adequacy of Religious Language 276

Kafka, Franz, The Imperial Message 396
Kant, Immanuel, The Moral Argument 351
Kierkegaard, Søren, Truth and Subjectivity 332; The Unchangeableness of God 363

Malinowski, Bronislaw, Religion and Primitive Man 149
Marx, Karl, On the Future of Religion 129
Mitchell, Basil, see Flew

Nietzsche, Friedrich, The Overcoming of Man 37; Proclamation of God's Death 397

Otto, Max, The Nonexistence of God 382
Otto, Rudolf, The Idea of the Holy 179

Peters, C., see Enroth

Rilke, Rainer Maria, Chamberlain Brigge's Death 95
Ruether, Rosemary, Sexism and the Theology of Liberation 413

Sartre, Jean-Paul, Atheistic Humanism 388
Suzuki, D. T., The Nature of Zen 189

Tillich, Paul, Religious Symbols 278
Tolstoy, Leo, The Death of Iván Ilích 51

Upanishads, Hindu Realization of Brahman 228

Wilson, John, Verification and Religious Language 285

Zimmer, Heinrich, Buddhist Nirvana 233; The Meeting of East and West 206